LEGAL METHOD
AND WRITING

LEGAL METHOD
AND WRITING

FOURTH EDITION

CHARLES R. CALLEROS

PROFESSOR OF LAW
ARIZONA STATE UNIVERSITY

ASPEN LAW & BUSINESS
A Division of Aspen Publishers, Inc.
New York   Gaithersburg

> Permissions
> Aspen Law & Business
> 1185 Avenue of the Americas
> New York, NY 10036

Printed in the United States of America

1 2 3 4 5 6 7 8 9 0

ISBN 1-7355-2421-1

Library of Congress Cataloging-in-Publication Data

Calleros, Charles R.
   Legal method and writing / Charles R. Calleros.—4th ed.
      p. cm.
   Includes index.
   ISBN 0-7355-2421-1 (alk. paper)
   1. Legal composition. 2. Law—United States—Methodology. I. Title.
KF250.C345 2002
808′.06634—dc21   2001056585

About Aspen Law & Business
Legal Education Division

With a dedication to preserving and strengthening the long-standing tradition of publishing excellence in legal education, Aspen Law & Business continues to provide the highest quality teaching and learning resources for today's law school community. Careful development, meticulous editing, and an unmatched responsiveness to the evolving needs of today's discerning educators combine in the creation of our outstanding casebooks, coursebooks, texbooks, and study aids.

ASPEN LAW & BUSINESS
A Division of Aspen Publishers, Inc.
A Wolters Kluwer Company
www.aspenpublishers.com

About Aspen Law & Business
Legal Education Division

With a dedication to preserving and strengthening the long-standing tradition of publishing excellence in legal education, Aspen Law & Business continues to provide the highest quality teaching and learning resources for today's law school community. Careful development, meticulous editing, and an unmatched responsiveness to the evolving needs of today's discerning educators combine in the creation of our outstanding casebooks, coursebooks, texbooks, and study aids.

ASPEN LAW & BUSINESS
A Division of Aspen Publishers, Inc.
A Wolters Kluwer Company
www.aspenpublishers.com

To Dad, Charles (age 81), and Mom, Emily (age 79),
with love and appreciation

SUMMARY OF CONTENTS

CONTENTS

TABLE OF CHARTS AND SAMPLE DOCUMENTS

PREFACE

The activities of practicing attorneys speak volumes about the importance of legal writing classes in law school. Although analytic skills and a general knowledge of legal principles will form the intellectual foundation of your practice of law, legal analysis is only as effective as the quality with which it is expressed. In your practice, you undoubtedly will devote a substantial proportion of your time and effort to drafting legal documents such as office memoranda, letters, pleadings, motions, briefs, contracts, and wills. Moreover, techniques of expression are closely linked to the underlying substantive analysis; indeed, problems in writing style often betray confusion in the analysis.

Unfortunately, as a first-semester law student, you may have difficulty seeing the relationship between your efforts in legal writing classes and your short-term objectives for success in law school. With this book, I hope to reassure you that your work in your first-year legal writing courses will directly contribute to your success with law school exams as well as with legal documents that you draft in a summer clerking position or in post-graduate employment. I attempt to achieve that objective in two ways. First, I hope to eliminate any mystery in the study of law by comprehensively examining the three critical components for success in law school: (1) briefing and synthesizing cases, (2) reorganizing and summarizing course materials in course outlines, and (3) analyzing and answering essay examinations. Second, I demonstrate in Parts I through V that the skills you develop in analyzing a client's legal problem and drafting an office memorandum are directly transferable to your task of analyzing an essay exam and writing the exam answer.

Additionally, this book examines techniques of advocacy and client representation that should appeal to a broad spectrum of readers: participants in a first-year moot-court program, students in an advanced writing seminar, student law clerks, and practicing attorneys. For example, Parts VI through VIII examine written advocacy in the context of pleadings, pretrial motions, and appellate briefs. Moreover, they thoroughly examine principles of writing and persuasion that apply generally to any litigation document. Part IX provides a step-by-step approach to drafting simple contracts, advice letters, and demand letters. Finally, the extensive citations in footnotes, most of which first-year law students can pass over, will provide attorneys with a valuable source of authorities.

Chapters 1, 12 through 14, and 17 of this book address matters of style. They use problems and examples to outline a general approach to style that focuses on the policies underlying conventions of composition. In these chapters, I encourage you to adopt the following philosophy: We should not memorize and mechanically apply rules of composition any more than we would mechanically apply "black letter" rules of law. Instead, we must understand the goals and purposes of the conventions of legal writing, and we should apply them flexibly to satisfy those goals and purposes.

Of course, this book reflects my own style quirks and biases: I freely split infinitives but always use the serial comma, and I dislike sexism in language. While writing this book, I encountered the problem of sexism in language most often in the form of personal pronouns in the third person. If I constantly resorted to an ostensibly generic pronoun normally associated with the male gender, such as "his" or "him," I would offend those readers who do not view the pronoun as gender generic and who believe that the increasing number of female attorneys and judges deserves specific recognition. On the other hand, multiple pronouns such as "his or her" often needlessly clutter already complex sentences, and plural pronouns such as "they" are not always consistent with content. As a provocative response to the problem, I have alternated between male and female pronouns, for example, by referring to an associate in a law firm with the pronoun "he" and to his supervising attorney with the pronoun "she." This approach may distract readers at one time or another, perhaps because it catches readers assuming that a judge or a senior partner is male. If so, perhaps the distraction is constructive: It may help us to envision a profession so well integrated that feminine pronouns and ethnic names will sound natural and commonplace.

The text is heavily footnoted with source material and with acknowledgments to others whose ideas inspired the text. Readers may find some of the additional information in the footnotes to be illuminating or to be helpful in practice as a starting point for research. Otherwise, however, busy students can focus on the text and skip the footnotes without missing any significant points.

Charles R. Calleros

February 2002

ACKNOWLEDGMENTS

My interest and enthusiasm for legal writing stem largely from the inspiration and training that I received as a court law clerk at the Office of Central Staff Attorneys for the United States Court of Appeals for the Ninth Circuit. In particular, I am grateful to my primary supervisors, Peter Shaw and Gregory Hughes, now practicing in California law firms. I am equally grateful to United States Court of Appeals Judge Procter Hug, Jr., who sowed the seeds of my current views on flexible, policy-oriented approaches to legal writing.

Other attorneys, judges, and colleagues contributed to my first edition with their comments on early drafts. In particular, I thank Thomas Gordon, who is a staff attorney for the Arizona Court of Appeals, fellow legal writing instructor, and former classmate at the University of California at Davis School of Law. Mr. Gordon's keen analytic insights into the art of legal writing have contributed greatly to this book. Other important contributors include the rigorous reviewers who strongly influenced the organization and content of the book, and Janet Wagner, an attorney who skillfully and artfully critiqued my writing style. Several colleagues contributed to selected portions of the book. They include Fred Cole, Amy Gittler, Mark Hielman, Susan E. Klemmer, Christopher Mason, William Monahan, Roger Perry, Frank Placenti, Thomas Quarelli, Jeffrey P. Travers, Paul Ulrich, Sherin Vitro, Judge Noel Fidel, and Professors Jane Aiken, Rebecca Berch, Paul Brand, Betsy Grey, Mark Hall, David Kader, Robert Misner, Cathy O'Grady, Mary Richards, Judy Stinson, Bonnie Tucker, James Weinstein, and Larry Winer.

The truly indispensable contributors to this book, however, are the students and attorneys who accepted my instruction and used the early versions of the teaching materials from which this book is derived. I especially acknowledge the Phoenix law firm of Streich, Lang, Weeks & Cardon, now merged with Quarles & Brady, for its dedication to continuing education in legal writing. I also thank the hardworking student writing instructors who helped me direct an experimental first-year writing program at the College of Law in the 1985-1986 academic year. The continuing success of that program is a tribute to their early efforts.

I must also thank staff and student research assistants for their contributions to the four editions, in the order of their participation over the years: Donna Blair, Gail Geer, Kay Winn, and Vera Hamer-Sonn provided word-processing assistance; Janice Fuller, Mark Burgoz, Michael Rutledge, Virginia Vasquez, Toby Schmich, Victoria Stevens, Jane Proctor, Lizzette M. Alameda, and Brian M. Louisell provided student research, cite-checking, and proofreading assistance. I am also especially grateful to the law library staff at A.S.U., and particularly to Reference Librarian Alison Ewing, who provided research services for the third and fourth editions and also educated me about processes of research. Finally, I am indebted to Arizona State University College of Law, and especially to Deans Paul Bender, Richard Morgan, and Patricia White, who fully supported my efforts to produce the four editions of this text.

Finally, I thank my mother, Emily, for her early guidance in grammar and for creating the drawings (one for the first three editions, and a new one in its place for the fourth edition) illustrating the discussion of restrictive and nonrestrictive clauses in Chapter 13.

LEGAL METHOD
AND WRITING

Part I

Law School—

Getting Started

Welcome to law school! For many of you, law school will present at least two new educational challenges. First, the instructor in your legal writing course may encourage you to adopt a legal writing style that differs from the writing styles you displayed in undergraduate courses. Second, the instructors of your other law school courses typically will help you develop skills of legal analysis through the "case method," a teaching and study technique that complements your work in your legal writing course but that differs markedly from the simple lecture format used in many undergraduate courses.

Chapters 1 and 2 facilitate your orientation to law school by introducing you to some fundamental principles of legal writing style and of the case method of study. Later, after you have a few weeks of legal education under your belt, you can examine legal writing style and the case method in much greater detail in Chapters 7 and 13.

To get started, turn the page, and have a fruitful journey.

Chapter 1

Introduction to Writing Style:
Policy, Purpose, and Audience

I. GENERAL APPROACH

The two most important characteristics of good legal writing style are clarity and conciseness. The importance of clarity in legal writing should be obvious: Your legal memorandum will not enlighten, nor will your brief persuade, unless the reader of each can understand it. To appreciate the significance of conciseness, you need only consider the time pressures that a supervising attorney or a judge faces; neither has time to glean from 20 pages ideas that you could have clearly expressed in 10.[1]

The dual goals of clarity and conciseness are often compatible: Making a draft more concise by omitting surplus words and by organizing your

---

1. *See, e.g.*, Westinghouse Elec. Corp. v. NLRB, 809 F.2d 419, 424-25 (7th Cir. 1987) (imposing $1,000 penalty on counsel for evading federal rule limiting the number of pages of its opening brief); Morgan v. South Bend Cmty. Sch. Corp., 797 F.2d 471, 480 (7th Cir. 1986) ("A [page] limitation induces the advocate to write tight prose, which helps his client's cause."); Reliance Ins. Co. v. Sweeney Corp., Md., 792 F.2d 1137, 1139 (D.C. Cir. 1986) ("this court encourages short, tightly argued briefs in all cases, regardless of their complexity").

points more efficiently likely will enhance clarity as well. At the margin, however, further conciseness may come only at the expense of clarity; in those circumstances, you must give priority to clarity.

II. THE PERSPECTIVE OF THE LEGAL WRITER

Law students often complain that the emphasis on clarity and conciseness in legal writing courses compels them to abandon the literary eloquence that they strove so hard to develop in college and to replace it with a dry, uniform style. They may overstate their complaints; effective legal writing reflects application of principles of good writing generally. Nonetheless, as an inevitable consequence of the substance and purpose of legal documents, the substance and style of legal writing do indeed differ from other kinds of writing.

For example, consider how different writers might treat the subject of a male supervisor's sexual harassment of a female subordinate in the workplace. A poet might create an image of the pain and frustration of the victim of the harassment, so vivid an image that readers who had never experienced sexual harassment could appreciate the victim's plight.[2] A writer for a political journal might describe the specific incident as a symptom of more general oppression within a sexist society. A novelist might describe the harassment in particularly dramatic prose, perhaps as a vehicle of character development or perhaps purely to engage or shock the reader.

On the other hand, an associate for the law firm representing the victim of the harassment is understandably preoccupied with the legal significance of the supervisor's actions. In preparing an office memorandum, the associate will analyze whether the harassment constituted "extreme and outrageous conduct," thus satisfying an element of a claim under the tort of intentional infliction of emotional distress. The extent of the injury suffered by the victim will interest the associate at least partly as an indication of the damages that the victim can recover. Moreover, the associate may discuss events or circumstances that other writers would ignore completely. For example, the associate may confirm the status of the harassing employee as an office supervisor, so that the institutional employer could more easily be held liable for the supervisor's harassment under Title VII of the Civil Rights Act of 1964.[3]

The different perspectives of these writers necessarily influence their writing styles. The poet's meaning may be obscured in the interest of "avoiding dull exposition" and of gaining dramatic effect through rhythm

---

2. *Cf.* Elisabeth W. Schneider, POEMS AND POETRY 3 (1964) (discussing the difficulty of transferring an "experience whole and alive into the mind, emotions, and sensations of another person").

3. *See* Faragher v. City of Boca Raton, 524 U.S. 775, 802-09 (1998) (subject to some limitations and defenses, an employer is liable for supervisor's sexually harassing conduct under Title VII, 42 U.S.C. § 2000e-2(a)(1)(1994)).

and metaphor.[4] Similarly, the novelist may seek to entertain or stimulate the reader by resorting to elegant variation or other deliberate ambiguity.[5] But the legal writer can seldom afford to entertain at the expense of communicating clearly. On occasion, legal writers may have legitimate reasons for ambiguity, but deliberate ambiguity should be the exception, not the rule. A supervising attorney is not interested in dwelling on each sentence of an office memorandum to divine its meaning as he might dwell on each line of a poem. Similarly, a judge is not likely to be persuaded by a brief that she doesn't fully comprehend, even though it entertains her.

This does not mean that lawyers must always write from a legal perspective. If you desire to retain or develop literary eloquence, you may write poetry by night and easily adapt your writing style to the requirements of the law office by day. Nor does it mean that legal writing must be dull and dry. Clear, concrete, concise writing can and should be active, vivid, and engaging. Indeed, the persuasive effect of a brief may be enhanced with a telling metaphor or an unusually dramatic phrase.

Moreover, the legal perspective does not doom legal writers to absolute uniformity of style. The goals of clear communication or persuasion leave room for individuality. Indeed, you should approach rules of writing style in much the same way that you approach legal rules: You should extend the application of the rules no further than necessary to serve the policies that support the rules. Even seemingly inflexible conventions of punctuation or sentence structure may simply reflect a desire for clarity or proper emphasis, leaving room for writers' discretion in how best to achieve those objectives.

III. A POLICY-ORIENTED APPROACH

Many rules of composition are nothing more than conventions that reflect generalities about the best way to achieve clear, concise writing with effective emphasis and flow. Even the traditional rule against splitting infinitives appears to have given way to a more flexible discretionary approach: "Some infinitives seem to improve on being split, just as a stick of round stove wood does."[6] You will do well to familiarize yourself with rules of composition, including the recommendations summarized in Chapter 13, as general guides

---

4. Schneider, *supra* note 2, at 25-26.

5. *See* William Strunk, Jr. & E. B. White, THE ELEMENTS OF STYLE 79 (4th ed. 2000) ("There are occasions when obscurity serves a literary yearning, if not a literary purpose. . . .").

6. *Id.* at 78; *see also id.* at 58 (arguing against routine adherence to the traditional rule against splitting infinitives). A contemporary dictionary argues that the traditional rule against splitting infinitives was never well founded:

> Writers who insisted that English could be modeled on Latin long ago created a "rule" that the English infinitive must not be split: *to clearly state* was wrong; one must say *to state clearly.* But the Latin infinitive is one word, and cannot be split, so the "rule" is not firmly grounded, and treating two English words as one can lead to awkward, stilted sentences.

THE OXFORD AMERICAN DESK DICTIONARY 303 (American ed. 1998).

to achieving the objectives of clarity and conciseness rather than as ends in themselves.

For example, many writers believe that they may never start a sentence with "However," because teachers or editors told them of a rule against such placement. But it is difficult to justify an inflexible rule to that effect; instead, the placement of transitional words such as "however" likely is influenced by considerations of emphasis and flow in the sentence. Those considerations often call for placement of "however" at a natural breaking point in midsentence, because it subordinates "however" as a parenthetic transition guide and permits more substantive parts of the sentence to enjoy the prominence of the position at the beginning of the sentence:

The statute of frauds does not apply, however, because Vasquez could have performed the contract within one year.

However, if you wish to draw immediate attention to the change of direction signaled by the transition word or phrase, placement at the beginning of the sentence, as in this one, is perfectly appropriate.

The history of the debate about the "serial" comma rule further illustrates the benefits of understanding the justifications for rules or conventions of composition. According to the traditional rule, you should use a comma to separate each element of a series of three or more things, as in "meat, vegetables, and dairy products." During the "new English" and "new math" movements of the 1960s, elementary school teachers began teaching a discretionary trend to omit the last comma of the series on the ground that the conjunction "and" or "or" adequately separates the last two elements of the series. The trend never fully displaced the traditional rule: Strunk and White have never wavered in their support for the final comma,[7] and many elementary schools have now returned to the traditional teachings. Unfortunately, many students in the meantime had adopted an inflexible practice of always omitting the final comma.

In fact, omitting the final comma may hamper clarity in a series in which some elements have multiple subelements, such as "fish, fruits or grains and dairy products." Depending on the location of a final comma, this could mean either:

1. [fish], [fruits or grains], and [dairy products], or
2. [fish], [fruits], or [grains and dairy products].

Subtle, temporary ambiguities in structure sometimes arise even if the series uses only the coordinating conjunction "and" and not the disjunctive conjunction "or."[8]

Armed with these insights, you can choose either of two approaches to the comma controversy, depending on the emphasis that you place on differ-

---

7. Strunk & White, *supra* note 5, at 1-2 (1st ed. 1959); *id.* at 2 (2d ed. 1972); *id.* at 2 (3d ed. 1979); *id.* at 2 (4th ed. 2000).

8. *See, e.g.,* Bryan A. Garner, THE ELEMENTS OF LEGAL STYLE 18 (1991) (providing illustrations).

ent policies of composition. If you value consistency as well as clarity, you could reasonably adopt the traditional convention of always using the final comma, because you know that it will sometimes be necessary for clarity and will never cause confusion.[9] Alternatively, if you prefer to restrict punctuation to the necessary minimum, you could exercise stylistic discretion to insert the final comma when it is necessary for clarity and to omit it otherwise.

IV. PURPOSE AND AUDIENCE

In every legal document, you should adapt your writing style to achieve the purpose of the document and to suit the needs of your intended audience. Many of the chapters in this book thoroughly examine this feature of writing style in the context of essay examinations, office memoranda, briefs, and letters. An overview here will serve to introduce some fundamental principles.

A. Purpose

Many legal documents can be classified as having either of two essential purposes: (1) to communicate a balanced analysis or (2) to persuade. With few exceptions, essay examination answers, office memoranda, and advice letters to clients fall into the first category. Ordinarily, the purpose of each is to help your reader understand the strengths and the weaknesses of a legal claim or defense. Briefs to a court and demand letters to an opposing party, on the other hand, fall into the second category. The purpose of a brief is to persuade a judge or panel of judges to make a ruling that favors your client. The purpose of a demand letter is to persuade another party to take some practical action, such as pay a debt, drop a claim, or cease some activity that is causing injury to your client.

You should adapt the content and style of the writing in each of your documents to suit these distinct purposes. For example, in an office memorandum and an advice letter, you must communicate to your supervising attorney and to your client the strengths as well as the weaknesses of your client's claims or defenses. Thus, if your client seeks to prove that her employer breached an employment contract by discharging her without good cause, you should candidly reveal to her and to your supervisor that the contract language is ambiguous on that point:

> Each of the five grounds for discharge specifically listed in section IX of the employment contract describes some kind of misconduct or unsatisfactory performance by the employee. However, the prefatory phrase "such as" suggests that the list is not exhaustive, but illustrative. If so, the employer may argue that he retained the right to fire an employee for any reason and that he listed only the most obvious reasons in the contract.

9. Strunk & White, *supra* note 5, at 2 ("Always Use the Serial Comma"). This author adopts this approach.

> To establish that the contract requires just cause for dismissal, we should . . .

In contrast, in your brief to a court, you will attempt to persuade a judge or panel of judges to interpret the contract language in a way that limits grounds for discharge. Accordingly, you should adopt a writing style that reflects confidence in your client's position:

> Section IX of the contract limits grounds for discharge to employee misconduct or poor performance. Even if the five grounds listed in section IX are illustrative rather than exhaustive, as argued by the defendant, they all illustrate cases in which the employer has good cause for terminating the employment contract. Thus, section IX describes a limited category of grounds for discharge, one that does not justify the arbitrary discharge in this case. . . .

B. Audience

Even when you seek to achieve similar purposes with different documents, you may need to adapt your writing style to the needs of each audience. For example, in both an office memorandum and an advice letter, your purpose is to present a balanced analysis of your client's claims and defenses. The readers of these documents, however, may vary greatly in legal sophistication. The experienced attorney who reads your office memorandum will appreciate your use of fundamental legal terminology and legal authority, as in this excerpt from an analysis of a client's defense in a civil rights action:

> If the district court denies Officer Tippett's motion for summary judgment on a question of law, Officer Tippett can file an interlocutory appeal on the issue of qualified immunity. *See Mitchell v. Forsyth*, 472 U.S. 511, 524-30 (1985).

On the other hand, your client, Police Officer Tippett, presumably has little or no legal training in pretrial and appellate civil procedure. Accordingly, in an advice letter to Officer Tippett on the same issue, you should explain your analysis in nonlegal terms:

> Even if the trial court denies your request to dismiss the action against you before trial, you need not face a trial immediately. In many cases, you can immediately appeal the trial court's rejection of your immunity defense. In the meantime, the trial will be delayed while the appellate court determines whether your conduct was indeed sufficiently reasonable to warrant granting you immunity from liability for damages.

In some cases, your task is complicated by the presence of multiple purposes and audiences. You can best explore these matters further in later chapters, in the context of particular documents.

V. OVERVIEW OF THE PROCESS OF LEGAL WRITING

Chapter by chapter, this book introduces you to various steps in the process of analyzing a legal problem and expressing your analysis effectively in a legal document. The following overview provides a road map to what lies ahead.

A. Developing Skills of Legal Method and Analysis

First and foremost, you must have something to say. You cannot expect to communicate clearly or persuasively unless you have a clear understanding of the points that you wish to express. Much of Parts I-IV of this book provides you with the tools that you need to spot legal issues, analyze the issues, and develop legal arguments. Specifically, after the next chapter introduces you to the case method of study, Chapters 3 and 4 in Part II explore the roles of common law and legislation in our legal system. In Part III, Chapters 5 and 6 introduce you to important legal concepts and tools of analysis: the practice of following prior case law and the application of deductive reasoning to legal problems. In Part IV, Chapters 7-9 build on the foundation laid in earlier chapters, using law school study and examination techniques as a bridge from the legal methods discussed in Parts I-IV to the expression of analysis in an office memorandum. Part IV also examines the application of inductive reasoning to legal problems, including the processes of analogy and distinction.

B. Researching the Law

Once you understand how the law operates, how to spot legal issues, and how to analyze a legal problem, you must find the legal authorities that state the applicable law. Unless your instructor or supervising attorney provides you with a file of legal authority, you must research the law in the library or at your computer terminal, a process described in Part V, Chapter 10.

C. Prewriting

As you draft a legal document, you will find that the process of putting your thoughts in writing will sharpen and deepen your understanding of the analysis, enabling you to improve your analysis throughout the drafting process. Nonetheless, you will produce a better final product, and will do so more efficiently, if you carefully plan your writing strategy before you begin to write.

In its earliest and most tentative stages, this process of "prewriting" may take the form of expressing and refining the issues that you intend to research, taking your research notes in an organized manner, and developing your analysis of the law as your research proceeds. The most important stage of prewriting, however, is the process of organizing the points that you wish to express after you have completed your research. If you take this step seriously, you can develop an outline as a means of clarifying your analysis, allowing you to focus more of your attention on matters of composition when you begin writing.

To effectively organize your thoughts, you must have a general idea of the format of your document. Thus, Chapter 11 of Part V introduces the elements of an office memorandum of law, just as later chapters examine the formats of various kinds of briefs submitted to courts. The process of organizing your analysis, however, is introduced in Chapter 8 in the context of student course outlines and is discussed further in Chapter 10, Section V, in the context of organizing library notes, and in Chapter 12 in the context of organizing the discussion section of an office memorandum.

D. Writing

If you have conscientiously researched and analyzed your problem and have carefully organized your thoughts in outline form, you will be better prepared to focus your attention on the process of writing your document in full, with effective citation to authority. The process of writing an objective analysis is examined thoroughly in Chapters 13 and 14 of Part V, with further discussion of persuasive writing style appearing in later chapters.

An important thread, introduced in this chapter, runs through the discussion of writing style in Chapter 13: Good writers do not mechanically apply inflexible rules of composition, nor do they unconsciously react without attention to goals or guiding principles. Instead, good writers consciously choose among alternatives, and they flexibly adapt conventions of composition to the needs of their audience and to the purpose of their document, all with the aim of achieving clearly identified goals, such as clarity, conciseness, or persuasiveness.

E. Revising Your Writing

The extent to which your document requires revision will depend partly on the care with which you engaged in the prewriting and writing processes. Nonetheless, regardless of how carefully you wrote and revised your document, you can nearly always improve it with additional revision. Strategies for revising your writing, as well as economic limitations on multiple revisions, are discussed in Section III of Chapter 13.

VI. SUMMARY

Effective legal writing requires careful attention to the purpose of a document and to the needs of the intended audience. Rather than memorize and dogmatically apply rules of composition, legal writers should flexibly adapt their writing to achieve their goals of communicating or advocating clearly and concisely.

This chapter and Chapters 12-16 develop and describe a method of approaching and resolving problems of composition, much as Chapters 3-6 describe a method of approaching legal problems.

Chapters 12-16 thoroughly examine problems of organization and writing style in the context of office memoranda and briefs. You may benefit by glancing at selected topics in those chapters as you work through Parts II-IV of this book. However, because problems in writing style are often closely linked with problems in legal method and analysis, you can profitably delay close examination of Chapters 12-16 until you have studied legal method and analysis in Parts II-IV.

Exercise 1-1

Examine your previous education and experiences relating to writing. Consider whether the special characteristics of legal writing require you to depart from writing styles that you have successfully used in other contexts. Use this self-examination to prepare you for constructive criticism from your writing instructors.

To begin a dialogue with your writing instructor, write an essay in response to one or more of the questions posed at the end of the following problem, and discuss your response with your instructor. Do not feel compelled to identify a "correct answer" or to couch your response in any special legal format or style. Instead, simply develop an honest response based on your personal values and opinions, and express your response freely in a style that comes to you naturally and comfortably. Ask your writing instructor to assess the extent to which your natural writing style is consistent with or deviates from your instructor's view of effective legal writing.

SURVIVAL OF THE FITTEST AND THE COMMON LAW

Imagine that you are deciding cases in the nineteenth century as the chief justice of a state's highest appellate court. Your state has no criminal statutes; instead, the criminal law of the state is exclusively common law, a law fashioned by judges and based on custom, common sense, and community values.

Before you is an appeal from a murder conviction in the case of *State v. Blight*. After a full trial, the jury found that Fletcher Blight, the defendant and appellant, had killed Davie Jones by pushing him off a life raft and into the ocean.

The trial record shows that both men boarded the life raft after their sailing vessel had sunk on the high seas. After days of drifting, and with no ship or land on the horizon, it became apparent that the water rations would not sustain both men until a rescue ship arrived. Blight, the stronger of the two, decided to (1) save the remaining water supply for himself; (2) stop administering water to Jones, who was too weak to move; and (3) allow Jones to die. Jones suffered great pain as he slowly died of dehydration. To end Jones's misery and to spare himself the pain of watching Jones suffer, Blight tearfully pushed the helpless Jones into the sea, where Jones quickly died. When Blight was rescued by a passing ship a few days later, he was near death himself. Physicians testified at trial that both men undoubtedly would have died before the rescue ship arrived if Blight had continued sharing the water rations with Jones until the water was exhausted.

1. Do you think Blight's actions were morally justified? Why or why not?
2. In your state, the courts have defined the common law crime of murder as the "unlawful killing of a human being without justification." At the time of Blight's appeal, your court has recognized only one justification for killing another person: self-defense in the face of a potentially deadly attack from the other person. On appeal, Blight asks your court to expand the common law justifications to cover the circumstances of his case.
   a. Precisely what new common law rule or rules would justify Blight's deeds? Draft Blight's proposed rule or rules in the form of proposed trial court instructions to the jury: "You must acquit the defendant of the charge of murder if he was justified in killing Jones. In this case, the defendant was justified in killing Jones if you find that. . . ."
   b. As the chief justice of the appellate court, would you recognize the proposed rule? What reasons would you give for supporting or opposing an extension of the common law doctrine of justification that would result in Blight's acquittal?
   c. Would you support a new common law rule that would improve the law but would not necessarily result in acquittal for Blight? If so, describe the rule and explain your reasons for proposing it.

Chapter 2

Overview of the

Case Method of Study

In your first-year contracts course, you probably will study the case of *Hadley and Another v. Baxendale and Others*.[1] By examining the history of this case now, you can become acquainted with the methods by which you will study law in most of your classes.

The dispute between the Hadleys and Baxendale began as a business transaction during an economic boom in the midst of England's industrial revolution. Operators of a flour mill in Gloucester entered into a contract with a carrier for the transportation of a broken engine shaft to a manufacturer in Greenwich, on the other side of England.

The operators of the mill, the Hadleys, were anxious to transport the broken shaft to the manufacturer as quickly as possible; the failure of the shaft had halted the milling of corn, and the broken shaft would serve as a model for the manufacture of a new shaft. An employee of the carrier, Pickford and Co., promised that the shaft would be delivered to the manufacturer within two days after the date that the carrier took possession of the shaft. For this, the mill operators paid £2 4s. The carrier could have trans-

---

1. 9 Ex. 341, 156 Eng. Rep. 145 (1854).

ported the shaft as promptly as promised had it immediately used available means of land transportation. Presumably to reduce costs, however, it held the shaft for several days in London before loading it onto a canal barge along with a shipment of iron that was bound for the same manufacturer. As a consequence, the carrier delivered the shaft to the manufacturer on the seventh day after the carrier received it, resulting in an additional delay of five days during which the mill was stopped.

The mill operators demanded that the carrier compensate for an estimated £300 in lost profits that the mill suffered because of the additional delay. The carrier refused, and the mill operators sued the carrier's managing director, Baxendale, in a trial court in Gloucester, claiming approximately £200 in damages. Although the carrier offered to settle the dispute for £25, the mill operators rejected the offer, and the case went to trial before a jury. The mill operators presented witnesses who testified to £120 in damages, and the jury awarded the mill operators £50 in a compromise verdict that became the judgment of the trial court.

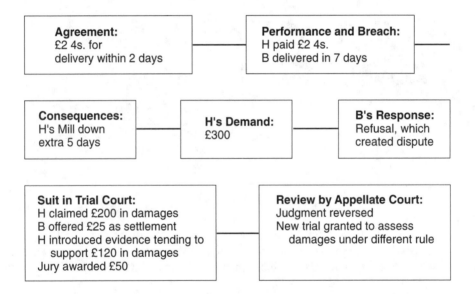

The carrier appealed to the Court of Exchequer. The carrier ultimately persuaded a panel of three judges on this appellate court to reverse the judgment of the trial court and to grant a new trial on the ground that the trial judge had given the jury excessive latitude in awarding damages for lost profits.

In the appellate court's written opinion, the authoring judge explained that a jury may award only those damages that would flow naturally from the breach of such a contract or that would be reasonably within the contemplation of the parties because of special circumstances communicated at the time of contracting. The appellate judges assumed that the mill would ordinarily have spare shafts with which to keep running; consequently, they concluded that lost profits stemming from an idle mill would not be the natural consequence of the breach of the contract for prompt carriage.

Whether the possibility of lost profits would nonetheless have been in the contemplation of the parties would depend on whether, at the time of contracting, the mill operators had communicated to the carrier the special circumstances that the broken shaft was the mill's only shaft and that the mill would be idle in its absence.

The appellate court concluded that the mill operators had informed the carrier only that they operated a mill and that the article to be transported was the broken shaft of a mill.[2] On this premise, the appellate court held that the trial judge should not have allowed the jury to consider any lost profits in its calculation of damages.

The case of *Hadley v. Baxendale* illustrates both how a case makes its way through the legal system and how you typically encounter the case only at the final destination in its legal journey. Reacting to a pressing commercial need, the mill operators entered into an agreement with the carrier to exchange money for certain services. Disappointed with the services rendered, the mill operators demanded compensation. Failing to secure the compensation through less formal means, they filed an action in a trial court to obtain a judgment compelling the carrier to pay compensation.

At trial, each party discovered that his claims or defenses were limited by his ability to present credible supporting evidence to the jury, to whom the court had delegated the task of finding facts. Hence, the mill operator's original demand dropped first from £300 to £200, and then to the £120 of losses for which it could produce evidence. Relying on centuries of development of law and custom, the court recognized the contractual relationship as one deserving of the protection of the Queen's courts, and it permitted the jury to award damages for the carrier's breach of the contract. The jury awarded less in damages than the trial court's instructions and the evidence would have allowed, but more than the carrier thought the law should permit. Accordingly, the carrier took the dispute before a court of higher authority, which ordered a new trial that would exclude lost profits from any recovery. The higher court explained its decision in a written judicial opinion.

In only a tiny percentage of disputes do the parties complete this process of full trial followed by review of the trial court's judgment in one or more appellate courts. Countless people become entangled in disputes that could give rise to legal claims, yet they seldom take the formal step of filing lawsuits to test their claims. In even fewer cases do they fully try their disputes in the trial court. In most lawsuits, the parties manage to settle their disputes before trial by agreeing to a compromise, thus avoiding the expense and risks of full trial. In many others, a full trial of the facts is unnecessary to resolve the dispute, and the trial court grants judgment for one of the parties before trial.

In cases that result in judgment after a full trial, only a small percentage of losing parties seek review of the adverse judgment in an appellate court.

---

2. Interestingly, this represents a departure from the summary of the trial proceedings prepared by the court reporter, who had reported at the beginning of the appellate opinion that the mill operators had informed the carrier that the mill was stopped. Richard Danzig, THE CAPABILITY PROBLEM IN CONTRACT LAW 80 (1978) (characterizing the finding of the Court of Exchequer as "remarkable").

Still fewer seek further review in a higher appellate court when one is available. Thus, the proportions of disputes that proceed to various levels of dispute resolution roughly describe a pyramid:

It is primarily to the decisions of the appellate courts that law school courses direct your attention. In nearly all first-year courses in law school, students encounter the law in casebooks, each of which presents judicial opinions on various topics that relate to a general field of law such as property, contracts, crimes, procedure, or torts.

The cases in a casebook are the disputes that parties bring to courts for resolution. Most of the judicial opinions that analyze the cases are the opinions of appellate courts. The edited appellate opinions published in casebooks often summarize the facts of the dispute and the proceedings in lower courts in the most economical way possible,[3] sometimes providing no more than a bare outline of the human drama that has preceded the appellate litigation. Most appellate opinions focus instead on using the cases before them as vehicles for developing and articulating general legal rules or principles. These rules not only resolve the dispute before the court; they also provide guidance to courts and litigants in future disputes of a similar nature, as well as to persons who desire to conform their actions to the law so as to avoid disputes.

Judicial opinions may mystify you in your first weeks at law school. They are peppered with legal terminology that will incrementally become part of your working vocabulary only after weeks and months of study. Even worse, some of the judicial language, particularly in the older cases, will be antiquated or overly formal and will have no place in your own writing; yet you must immerse yourself in the language to understand the opinions.

Moreover, the opinions assume a knowledge of the legal system and of the legal method that courts use when working within that system. For example, you might wonder how an early English decision such as *Hadley v. Baxendale* is relevant to your study of law in the United States. Also confusing to some new law students is the relationship between "common

3. Indeed, many of the details of *Hadley v. Baxendale* described in this book do not appear in the report of the Court of the Exchequer, much less in a casebook's edited version of that report. The source of this book's more detailed recounting of the case is Danzig, *supra* note 2, at 68-105.

law" and "statutory law," both of which may be addressed in the same judicial opinion.

Parts II and III of this book answer these and many other questions by introducing you to our legal system and to fundamental principles of legal method. This foundation should better prepare you to develop skills in studying law in first-year courses, in analyzing legal problems in a law office or judge's chambers, and in advocating a client's position to a court, all of which are discussed in Parts IV-VIII. Part II begins building the foundation with an introduction to the United States legal system.

You undoubtedly must prepare case briefs for class discussion beginning with the first day of class. Accordingly, before your first week of classes, you may wish to glance through Chapter 7, which examines the process of briefing cases for class discussion. You will learn that your instructors will discuss appellate opinions in a manner that suits their individual pedagogic preferences. Until you learn more about those preferences, or those of your legal writing instructor, you may start with the following format in briefing cases:

1. Identification of the Case (state the case name and authoring court)
2. Issue(s) and Holding(s) (state the questions addressed by the court, followed by the court's conclusion on each question)
3. Facts (summarize the facts that led to the legal dispute)
4. Procedural History (summarize the judicial proceedings preceding this court's opinion)
5. Reasoning (explain the court's reasons for its conclusions)
6. Evaluation (explain your agreement or disagreement with the court's conclusions and reasoning)
7. Synthesis (explain how this opinion compares to others that address the same issue)

After you later complete Parts II and III, you can study Chapters 7-9 more thoroughly to develop a comprehensive, three-point plan for success in your substantive courses: (1) briefing and synthesizing cases, (2) outlining course materials, and (3) applying effective examination techniques.

Part II

Introduction to the

Legal System

Chapter 3

Common Law

I. OVERVIEW—SOURCES OF LAWMAKING POWERS

The United States Constitution allocates powers between the state and national governments and thus establishes the framework for our federal system of government. In turn, each state's constitution establishes the framework for that state's government. A fundamental tenet of these state and federal constitutions is the separation of powers between the legislative, judicial, and executive branches of government. Although lawmaking functions rest primarily with the legislative branch, all three branches exercise some form of lawmaking power.

A. Legislative and Executive Branches

The state and federal legislatures create law by enacting statutes within the authority granted to them by the state and federal constitutions. Although the primary function of the executive branch is enforcement of laws, the executive branch may lead in policy development by proposing legislation

21

to a legislature. Moreover, a legislature may delegate some of its lawmaking power to the executive branch by statutorily authorizing an executive agency to issue rules and regulations designed to help implement a statutory scheme.

For example, in the exercise of its federal constitutional authority to regulate commerce, the United States Congress has enacted comprehensive labor relations statutes, such as the National Labor Relations Act.[1] It has also created the National Labor Relations Board (NLRB), an agency of the United States, and has authorized the board to issue administrative rules and regulations necessary to help the board enforce the labor relations statutes.[2]

Legislatures cannot amend a constitution in the same way that they enact statutes. For example, Article V of the United States Constitution authorizes Congress to propose constitutional amendments, but such proposals do not become effective until ratified by the legislatures or constitutional conventions of three-fourths of the states. For convenience, this book sometimes uses the terms "enacted law," "legislation," and "statutory law" to refer to both statutes and constitutions.

B. Judicial Branch

The judicial branch of government develops law in two ways, both of them in the context of particular disputes. First, state and federal courts contribute to the development of constitutional and statutory law by interpreting the necessarily general terms of such law and applying those terms to the facts of disputes. Second, as offspring of the English judicial system, courts in the United States have adopted and continue to develop a substantial body of common law—judge-made law that applies to issues that constitutional or statutory law does not address. State courts are the primary source of common law, because federal courts no longer create and develop "federal general common law."[3] Nonetheless, the federal courts retain the power in a few restricted fields, such as admiralty law, to develop "specialized federal common law."[4]

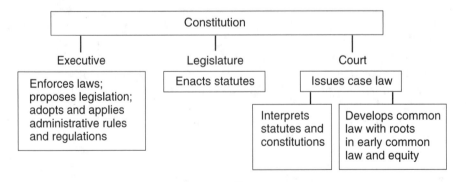

1. 49 Stat. 449 (1935).
2. 29 U.S.C. §§ 153, 156 (1994); American Hosp. Ass'n v. NLRB, 499 U.S. 606, 609 (1991).
3. Erie R.R. v. Tompkins, 304 U.S. 64, 78 (1938).
4. Henry J. Friendly, *In Praise of* Erie—*And of the New Federal Common Law*, 39 N.Y.U. L. Rev. 383, 405 (1964).

C. Common Law as a Backdrop for Legislation

An example of the interplay between statutory law and common law is provided in your first-year contracts course. Many principles of contract law, such as consideration, offer and acceptance, performance and breach, and remedies, find their source in a substantial body of common law, developed by judges, first in England and later in the United States.

The common law of contracts forms a backdrop against which state legislatures have enacted statutes, which supersede some of the common law rules. In the resulting hybrid system, the statutes provide the rule of law on issues to which they apply, while common law applies to gaps within and between statutes.

D. Other Systems of Government

These fundamental principles of state and federal lawmaking apply only in limited fashion to two other kinds of governments in the United States: (1) local governments of political subdivisions of the states, such as cities and counties, and (2) American Indian tribal governments.

Local governments come in a variety of models. Although many of them exercise legislative, executive, and judicial powers, they do not always practice the same degree of separation of these powers as do state and federal governments. A state's constitution and statutes may partially define the legal structure that a local government in the state can adopt and the powers that it can exercise. Some cities further define their structure with a city charter that operates within limits set by state law.

More nearly autonomous are American Indian tribes. Although their powers may be limited by federal law, they are otherwise sovereign governments with inherent powers to exercise tribal authority. Not all of the tribes have chosen to adopt every fundamental tenet of the state and federal governments. For example, the Navajo Nation of the southwestern United States has no constitution, and it has not always recognized complete separation of legislative, judicial, and executive powers. Nonetheless, its legal system is similar to the Anglo-American system in several important respects. Constituents elect the members of the Navajo Tribal Council, which enacts statutory law in the form of codes. The executive power rests primarily in the President, an elected official. Finally, the Navajo trial courts and the Navajo Supreme Court apply federal law and tribal codes, and they develop and apply a common law based on Navajo custom and cultural values or compatible state laws.

This book primarily addresses state and federal common law and statutes. The remainder of this chapter explores common law analysis. Chapter 4 examines statutory analysis before further addressing the relationship between legislation and the common law.

II. COMMON LAW

A. Historical Roots

The common law that courts in the United States develop and apply has its roots in the English common law, which was dispensed in the courts of the English king. This English law came to be known as the "common law" because it applied generally throughout medieval England. It thus largely replaced a less uniform system of customary law dispensed in local courts and in the private courts of feudal lords. The English Court of Chancery supplemented the remedies of the early common law courts by developing and applying a form of "equity" that provided relief when common law remedies were inadequate.

Distinctions between common law and equitable claims, defenses, and remedies continue to have significance for some purposes, such as determining the right to a jury trial in some circumstances.[5] Most United States jurisdictions, however, have eliminated the dual court system and have largely merged law and equity procedure.[6] Accordingly, this book uses the term "common law" to refer generally to laws created and developed by the courts, regardless of whether the principles have their roots in early common law or equity law.

Oliver Wendell Holmes traced the origins of some English and United States common law to early Germanic and Roman law.[7] Other common law principles simply reflect judicial recognition of community needs, habits, or customs, and are "accounted for by their manifest good sense."[8] More generally, common law is "the embodiment of broad and comprehensive unwritten principles . . . inspired by natural reason and an innate sense of justice."[9]

The term "common" may be misleading when applied to common law in the United States: The courts in each state are free to develop the common

---

5. *See, e.g.*, City of Monterey v. Del Monte Dunes at Monterey, 526 U.S. 687, 708-09 (1999) (discussing whether federal statutory claim was "legal" rather than "equitable," for purposes of applying the Seventh Amendment's guarantee of a jury trial to common law actions); Hutchinson v. Spanierman, 190 F.3d 815, 823 (7th Cir. 1999) (applying Indiana law and finding that stale claim was barred by the equitable doctrine of laches even though the legal statute of limitations had not expired); 1 Dan B. Dobbs, DOBBS LAW OF REMEDIES § 2.6(1), at 150-53 (2d ed. 1993) (discussing continuing limitations on equitable remedies, such as injunctive relief, that do not apply to legal remedy of money damages); *cf.* 5A Arthur L. Corbin, CORBIN ON CONTRACTS § 1136 (1964) (procedural merger of law and equity has resulted in partial substantive merger of legal and equitable principles of remedies).

6. *See, e.g.*, FED. R. CIV. P. 2 ("There shall be one form of action to be known as 'civil action.'"); Ross v. Bernhard, 396 U.S. 531, 539-40 (1970) (discussing the procedural joinder of legal and equitable claims and remedies under rules of procedure for federal courts); Dobbs, *supra* note 5, at 149 ("In most states and in the federal system, there are no longer separate equity rules of procedure.").

7. Oliver Wendell Holmes, Jr., THE COMMON LAW 2, 18, 34, 340-44, 360 (1923).

8. *Id.* at 2, 337-39.

9. Stanley Mosk, *The Common Law and the Judicial Decision-Making Process*, 11 Harv. J.L. & Pub. Pol'y 35 (1988) (citing Rodriguez v. Bethlehem Steel Co., 525 P.2d 669, 682-83 (Cal. 1974)). Indeed, some scholars believe that humans have a biological predisposition to prefer some forms of legal order. *See generally, e.g.*, Richard D. Alexander, THE BIOLOGY OF MORAL SYSTEMS (1987).

law of that state in a manner that reflects local policies; therefore, variations in common law among the states are inevitable. Nonetheless, to a surprising degree, courts in different states share common views on general principles of law. For example, a federal appellate court has noted that "the principles of contract law do not differ greatly from one jurisdiction to another."[10] Perhaps more important for law students and practitioners, the method employed by courts in deciding disputes and developing common law does not vary substantially among the states.

B. Examples: Common Law Burglary and Murder

The early common law crime of burglary, which was punishable by death, illustrates the judicial development of common law rules to serve particular needs of the community. In imposing capital punishment for this crime, the common law courts sought to deter a serious invasion of the home during hours of darkness, when the inhabitants were most vulnerable to attack and the invader most likely to escape recognition. Efforts by the common law courts to narrowly address that evil are reflected in the general definition of common law burglary, which separates the crime into distinct elements: (1) the breaking and (2) entering (3) of the dwelling house (4) of another (5) in the night (6) with the intent to commit a felony.

In defining and applying these elements of common law burglary in the context of successive cases, the courts were reluctant to extend the crime beyond the minimum reach necessary to achieve the underlying purposes of the crime, probably because of the severity of punishment. For example, the courts viewed an intruder as less culpable if the occupant of a dwelling encouraged the intrusion by failing to properly secure the dwelling. Accordingly, many courts held that a trespasser who gained entry by further opening a partially open door or window had not committed the "breaking" necessary for a burglary.[11]

The history of another common law crime, murder, illustrates the manner in which courts gradually developed common law doctrine "over several centuries of time as a parade of cases, involving different fact situations, came before the judges for decision."[12] The common law decisions generally defined murder as the unlawful killing of another human being with malice aforethought. Early decisions defined "malice aforethought" narrowly by requiring proof of a premeditated intent to kill. Subsequent cases, however, presented unpremeditated or even unintentional killings that reflected sufficient culpability to warrant classification as murder. In those cases, courts effectively expanded the definition of "malice aforethought" by recognizing other circumstances that would justify conviction for murder: intentional but unpremeditated killing without sufficient provocation; unintentional killing during the commission of another felony; unintentional killing through conduct that reflects a reckless disregard for the lives of others; and

10. *E.g.*, In re Cochise College Park, Inc., 703 F.2d 1339, 1348 n.4 (9th Cir. 1983).
11. Wayne R. LaFave, CRIMINAL LAW § 8.13, at 883-84 (3d ed. 2000).
12. *Id.* § 7.1, at 653.

killing while engaged in conduct with the intent to do serious bodily harm short of death.[13]

C. Common Law in Constant Change

This process of incremental development of the common law does not always proceed in an unbroken line. Courts sometimes abandon previously adopted lines of authority to chart new courses that better reflect current social, economic, and technological realities:

> The inherent capacity of the common law for growth and change is its most significant feature. It is constantly expanding and developing to keep up with the advancement of civilization and the new conditions and progress of society, and adapting itself to the gradual changes in trade, commerce, arts, inventions, and the needs of the country. . . . The vitality of the common law can flourish if the courts remain alert to their obligation and have the opportunity to change it when reason and equity so demand. The common law requires that each time a rule of law is applied, it must be carefully scrutinized to make sure that the conditions and needs of the times have not so changed as to make further application of the rule an instrument of injustice. Although the legislature may speak to the subject, in the common law system the primary instruments of legal evolution are the courts.[14]

A change in conditions is not the only possible inspiration for abandonment of existing common law. A court will occasionally conclude that a previous decision was flawed from its inception. Hindsight may show that the previous court premised its decision on erroneous factual assumptions about conditions existing at that time. Alternatively, the current court, which itself may have changed in political or intellectual composition, may simply reject the reasoning of the previous decision.[15] This process of evolution, however, is restricted by the doctrine of stare decisis, explored in Chapter 5.

III. SUMMARY

Legislatures enact statutes within the authority granted to them by state and federal constitutions. Courts create case law in the context of individual disputes by (1) interpreting and applying the provisions of constitutions and statutes and (2) developing and applying a separate body of judge-made common law. The common law continually grows as new cases present the courts with opportunities to keep the common law current with social, economic, and technological developments.

13. *Id.* at 653-55.
14. Mosk, *supra* note 9, at 36.
15. *See generally* Geoffrey R. Stone, *Precedent, the Amendment Process, and Evolution in Constitutional Doctrine*, 11 Harv. J.L. & Pub. Pol'y 67, 71 (1988).

Exercise 3-1

WRONGFUL CONCEPTION, WRONGFUL LIFE

In general, the common law of torts imposes civil liability on a physician who breaches a duty of care to a patient. By applying this general common law rule to new medical procedures, courts and juries necessarily refine the content of the rule. In the following problem, assume that the common law of the jurisdiction has not previously addressed the issues that are raised by the facts. You must decide how you would fashion the common law that applies to the issues if you were a judge approving instructions to a jury on the applicable legal rules. Specifically, you must decide to what extent you think the common law should impose liability on a physician for negligently permitting a child to be conceived.

Problem

When Sonia and her husband, Eddie, had their third child, they agreed that they desired no further children and that Eddie should undergo sterilization. They consulted Dr. Leonard, who performed a vasectomy. Although Dr. Leonard pronounced the operation a success, he in fact performed the vasectomy carelessly and neglected to order routine follow-up tests. Eddie impregnated Sonia within six months after the failed sterilization procedure.

a. In the process of developing the state's common law of torts, should a state court permit Sonia and Eddie to sue Dr. Leonard on a negligence theory of "wrongful conception"? If so, should the damages include only the medical expenses and other costs associated with the childbirth, or should they more broadly include the costs of raising the fourth child?

b. Suppose that the fourth child was born with severe mental retardation, but that the failed sterilization procedure did not contribute to the retardation. Should these facts affect the court's evaluation of the parents' claims based on wrongful conception? Should the court recognize a cause of action on the behalf of the fourth child for "wrongful life," permitting the child herself to collect damages on the theory that she would have been better off had she not been conceived?

c. Should the analysis of any of these questions be affected by the fact that Sonia could have legally aborted her fetus soon after discovering her pregnancy?

Chapter 4

Legislation

I. ROLES OF CONSTITUTIONAL AND STATUTORY LAW

"The Constitution states the framework for all our law. Legislation is one great tool of legal change and readaptation."[1] As expressed by a state supreme court, constitutional and statutory law reflect collective expressions of public policy: "As the expressions of our founders and those we have elected to our legislature, our state's constitution and statutes embody the public conscience of the people of this state."[2]

Of the three branches of government, the legislature is the paramount policymaking body. Consistent with that role, a legislature often enacts statutes to address problems that it concludes are not adequately addressed by the common law.

---

1. Karl N. Llewellyn, THE BRAMBLE BUSH 10 (10th prtg. 1996).
2. Wagenseller v. Scottsdale Mem'l Hosp., 710 P.2d 1025, 1033 (Ariz. 1985).

A. Example: Embezzlement

For example, the early common law crime of theft was defined as a trespassory taking and carrying away of personal property of another with intent to steal.[3] The requirement of a trespassory taking excluded the conduct of one who took possession of another's property lawfully, but who subsequently converted the property to his own use with the intent to permanently deprive the owner of it.

Legislators in England and the United States were aware that the common law did not impose criminal liability for the latter misappropriation, and they were determined to criminalize such conduct. Consequently, they created the statutory crime of embezzlement, generally defined as the fraudulent conversion of another's property by one who is already in lawful possession of it.[4] Had the legislatures not acted, the courts might have eventually achieved the same result through further development of the common law, but legislative action sometimes provides a quicker and more certain change of course.

B. Example: Bait-and-Switch Legislation

A more contemporary example deals with the process of reaching a legally binding agreement through the process of offer and acceptance. Under the common law of contracts, a department store's newspaper advertisement typically amounts to an invitation to negotiate rather than an offer to enter into a binding contract; in most cases, a customer makes the first offer by entering the store and requesting to purchase the advertised goods. Under common law, the store owner is free to reject the customer's offer without incurring any contractual liability.[5]

Unfortunately, this allocation of legal rights and obligations has encouraged some sellers to use bait-and-switch tactics: They lure customers into their stores with the "bait" of goods advertised at spectacularly reduced prices; then they "switch" goods by resisting the customer's desire to purchase the advertised goods and by persuading the customer to purchase a more expensive item. In response, state legislatures have promoted public policy favoring consumer protection by enacting legislation that restricts or prohibits such bait-and-switch tactics.[6] These statutes have altered rights and obligations as they were defined under the common law of contracts.

Common Law of Contracts: If store's ad is not an offer, Customer makes first offer. Store can reject that offer and can "switch" Customer to more expensive item.	**Consumer-Protection Legislation:** Legislature concludes that common law is deficient and enacts protective legislation to address the "bait-and-switch" problem.

---

3. Wayne R. LaFave, CRIMINAL LAW § 8.2, at 795 (3d ed. 2000).
4. *Id.* § 8.6.
5. *See* 1 Arthur L. Corbin, CORBIN ON CONTRACTS § 25 (1963); John D. Calamari & Joseph M. Perillo, CONTRACTS § 2.6(e), at 36 (4th ed. 1998).
6. *See, e.g.,* Note, *State Control of Bait Advertising*, 69 Yale L.J. 830 (1960).

C. Increasing Significance of Legislation

Prior to the twentieth century, legislatures in England and the United States tended not to replace common law wholesale with a comprehensive system of statutes. Instead, they typically enacted statutes to correct specific defects or fill gaps in a well-developed body of common law.

Statutory law thus assumed a role of secondary importance in the United States, inspiring one scholar to characterize them as "warts on the body of the common law."[7]

State and federal legislation, however, has so proliferated in recent history that "most American jurisdictions now are Code states."[8] This new prominence of statutory law in the United States warrants an examination of methods of statutory analysis.

II. JUDICIAL INTERPRETATION AND APPLICATION OF STATUTES

A federal statute imposes liability on certain employers for discrimination against any individual in the "terms" or "conditions" of employment "because of such individual's . . . sex." Would the statute impose liability on an employer who fired your clients, male and female homosexuals, because of their sexual orientation? Would it impose liability on an employer who made sexual advances toward only female employees, thus adversely affecting their working environment, but who did not withhold tangible job benefits in retaliation for the subordinate rejecting his advances? The answers to these questions depend on the intended meaning of the statutory language "because of . . . sex" and "terms" or "conditions" of employment.

A. Vagueness and Ambiguity

Questions such as these arise because statutory language sometimes is vague or ambiguous. An ambiguous term has multiple meanings, although each of the meanings may be precise and all of the meanings may be easily identified. A vague term is uncertain in its meaning and indefinite in its scope, making it difficult to identify the meaning or meanings that it encompasses.[9]

As discussed more fully below, some statutes are necessarily vague because the legislature deliberately used general language, and some statutes are ambiguous because the legislature unintentionally used less precise language than it should have. Consequently, parties to a dispute frequently may reasonably disagree about the way in which statutory language applies to the facts

7. Llewellyn, *supra* note 1, at 89; *see also* Roscoe Pound, *Common Law and Legislation*, 21 Harv. L. Rev. 383 (1908).

8. Stanley Mosk, *The Common Law and the Judicial Decision-Making Process*, 11 Harv. J.L. & Pub. Pol'y 35 (1988). "Codes" are collections of legislative enactments, organized by subject matter.

9. *See generally* William Van Orman Quine, WORD AND OBJECT 85, 129 (1960).

of their dispute. Courts give greater specificity and precision to the vague or ambiguous statutory language by interpreting and applying the statute in the context of the dispute.

According to one judge, legislatures should not be faulted for keeping judges so busy with cases requiring statutory interpretation,

> because however careful, wise and farseeing the Legislature, the abstract words of a statute often require fitting and tailoring when applied to real-life cases, which may be more bizarre than anyone could possibly have imagined. Fitting and tailoring are what judges do, and what they are supposed to do—they make judgments.[10]

On the other hand, a court does not engage in a wholly creative process when it interprets a vague or ambiguous statute. Rather, it seeks to determine and to give effect to the intent of the enacting legislature by analyzing the statutory language, the stated or apparent purpose of the statute, and the legislative activities related to enactment of the bill.[11]

This search for the intended meaning of a statute is governed by a separate layer of judicially developed rules of interpretation and construction. Although the terms "interpretation" and "construction" are often used interchangeably, this book recognizes the following distinction: "Interpretation" refers to the process of determining legislative intent; "construction" refers to the process of giving the statutory language a meaning that is consistent with general legislative and public policies, in the absence of conclusive evidence of legislative intent.

B. Intrinsic and Extrinsic Evidence of Legislative Intent

Evidence of legislative intent may be intrinsic to the statute, extrinsic to it, or both. Intrinsic evidence of legislative intent is the statutory text itself. This includes the statutory language in question and other portions of the statute that state or imply the statutory purpose or otherwise provide a context within which to interpret the language in question. Some statutes even include a section of defined terms, which may provide partial guidance even when it does not conclusively resolve a dispute over the proper interpretation of the language in question.

Extrinsic evidence of legislative intent includes other information about the social or legal context of the legislation in question. For example, contemporaneous case law or companion legislation may provide insights into the nature of the social problem that the statutory language in question was meant to address. When federal legislation applies to the dispute, however, the primary source of extrinsic evidence of legislative intent is the legislative history of the statute in question. This includes the text of congressional debates, preliminary drafts of the legislation, and hearings or reports of congressional committees assigned to study the proposed legislation. Unfor-

---

10. Judith S. Kaye, *Things Judges Do: State Statutory Interpretation*, 13 Touro L. Rev. 595, 608 (1997).
11. *See, e.g.*, Jackson Transit Auth. v. Local Div. 1285, Amalgamated Transit Union, 457 U.S. 15, 22-29 (1982); Mohasco Corp. v. Silver, 447 U.S. 807, 815 (1980).

tunately, the history of state legislation in many states is too sparse or inaccessible to be of much help to judges.[12]

Under the "plain meaning" rule of interpretation, if the statutory language in question has a plain meaning on its face, a court will be reluctant to consider legislative history supporting a less obvious interpretation.[13] However, many judges and scholars argue that the court is not precluded from doing so,[14] as when a federal court of appeals engaged in an exhaustive analysis of legislative history and statutory policy to interpret the statutory term "or" to mean the conjunction "and," rather than the disjunctive "either/or."[15]

Unfortunately, misuse of legislative history may mislead more than enlighten. The search for legislative intent is an attempt to reconstruct the collective intent of numerous legislators whose views on the wisdom or scope of the statute may conflict. Opposing advocates often can draw on different portions of legislative history to support conflicting views about the proper interpretation of a statute: They simply invoke isolated statements of legislators taken out of the context of the complete debate on a bill. Indeed, a court may then justify the result that it wants to reach by selectively drawing on portions of legislative history that support that result. These and other pitfalls have led one United States Supreme Court Justice to decry the "level of unreality that our unrestrained use of legislative history has attained."[16]

C. Statutory Construction When Interpretation Fails

If a court cannot obtain clear evidence of legislative intent through intrinsic or extrinsic evidence, it may use other means to resolve vagueness or ambiguity in statutory language. For example, if an administrative agency has developed expertise in administering the statute, the court may simply defer to that agency's interpretation of the statutory language.[17]

12. Kaye, *supra* note 10, at 600.
13. *See, e.g.*, Connecticut Nat'l Bank v. Germain, 503 U.S. 249, 253-54 (1992) (giving priority to the plain language of the statute over legislative history and canons of construction); Note, *Looking It Up: Dictionaries and Statutory Interpretation*, 107 Harv. L. Rev. 1437, 1440-44 (1994) (tracing increasing use of the plain language rule, supported by dictionary definitions, in the United States Supreme Court).
14. *E.g.*, Maine v. Thiboutot, 448 U.S. 1, 13-14 (1980) (Powell, J., dissenting); Kent Greenawalt, LEGISLATION: STATUTORY INTERPRETATION: 20 QUESTIONS 57 (1999) (concluding that judges may have reason to depart from the "evident meaning" of statutory text in the case of an obvious "slip" in drafting and, "[s]omewhat more controversially," when "a straightforward reading of the text . . . is clearly at odds with underlying statutory purpose, is manifestly absurd, or is undoubtedly unjust").
15. Unification Church v. INS, 762 F.2d 1077, 1083-90 (D.C. Cir. 1985); *see also* Tomka v. Seiler Corp., 66 F.3d 1295, 1313-17 (2d Cir. 1995) (plain meaning of statute is not controlling in rare cases in which the literal meaning of statutory language clearly conflicts with legislative intent).
16. Blanchard v. Bergeron, 489 U.S. 87, 98 (1989) (Scalia, J., concurring). Perhaps due to Justice Scalia's influence, the Supreme Court's reliance on legislative history has declined in the 1990s. Lori L. Outzs, *A Principled Use of Congressional Floor Speeches in Statutory Interpretation*, 28 Colum. J.L. & Soc. Probs. 297, 305-06 (1995).
17. *See, e.g.*, Young v. Community Nutrition Inst., 476 U.S. 974, 979-84 (1986); Chevron U.S.A., Inc. v. Natural Res. Def. Council, Inc., 467 U.S. 837, 843 (1984); *cf.* United States v. Mead Corp., 121 S.Ct. 2164 (2001) (describing circumstances in which an agency interpretation is entitled to deference only if it is affirmatively persuasive).

INTERPRETATION: EVIDENCE OF LEGISLATIVE INTENT

Intrinsic Evidence:

Start with Statutory Language

including the clause in question, defined terms, statements of purpose, related statutory provisions, and statute as a whole.

If the statutory language is ambiguous, or if extrinsic evidence would otherwise be helpful, consult extrinsic evidence of legislative intent:

Extrinsic Evidence:

Primarily, Legislative History

including preliminary drafts, committee hearings and reports, and legislative floor debates.

If legislative intent remains unclear, seek guidance from general rules of construction:

CONSTRUCTION: GENERALIZATIONS ABOUT PROBABLE LEGISLATIVE INTENT

Examples:

Construe criminal statutes narrowly, in favor of lenity.

Construe remedial statutes liberally to provide an adequate remedy for the full range of problems that inspired the legislation.

Avoid a construction that would render a statute invalid or a clause superfluous.

If a statute specifically lists some items for statutory treatment, the legislature likely intended to exclude other items that are not listed.

Otherwise, the court may resort to a judicial rule of construction, such as the general rule that ambiguities in criminal statutes "should be resolved in favor of lenity."[18] Such a rule may reflect general policies with which the legislature is likely to agree, but it does not necessarily reflect the legislative purpose of the particular statute in question.[19] Accordingly, a court will resort to a general rule of construction only if a "statute's language, structure, purpose, and legislative history leave its meaning genuinely in doubt."[20]

III. CASE STUDIES IN STATUTORY INTERPRETATION

In the following subsections, analyses of two kinds of uncertainty in statutory language provide vehicles for examining techniques that the courts use to clarify the scope and effect of statutes. First, an analysis of ambiguous statutory language illustrates general rules of statutory interpretation and construction. Second, an analysis of vague statutory language illustrates the manner in which courts gradually give concrete meaning to abstract statutory language by applying general terms to particular disputes.

A. Illustration: Imprecision Leading to Ambiguity

Ambiguity may result from imprecision in the words or phrases selected by the drafter. The question concerning sexual orientation raised at the beginning of Section II above addresses the proper interpretation of a federal statute popularly known as Title VII of the Civil Rights Act of 1964. Section 703(a) of the Act prohibits certain kinds of employment discrimination:

> It shall be an unlawful employment practice for an employer . . . to discriminate against any individual with respect to his compensation, terms, conditions, or privileges of employment, because of such individual's race, color, religion, sex, or national origin. . . .[21]

1. THE PROBLEM

It is unclear from the quoted language whether section 703(a) prohibits an employer from discriminating against gay and lesbian employees because of

18. Bell v. United States, 349 U.S. 81, 83 (1955); *accord*, State v. Tarango, 914 P.2d 1300, 1302 (Ariz. 1996); Johnson v. State, 602 So. 2d 1288, 1290 (Fla. 1992).
19. *See, e.g.*, Bell v. United States, 349 U.S. 81, 83-84 (1955).
20. United States v. Otherson, 637 F.2d 1276, 1285 (9th Cir. 1980). Some commentators are more critical of established canons of statutory construction and would replace them wholesale with other means of resolving legislative ambiguities. *See, e.g.*, Richard A. Posner, *Statutory Interpretation—In the Classroom and in the Courtroom*, 50 U. Chi. L. Rev. 800 (1983); *cf.* EEOC v. Arabian Am. Oil Co., 499 U.S. 244, 260-61 (1991) (Marshall, J., dissenting) (arguing that majority of the Court gave undue weight to a rule of construction disfavoring extraterritorial application of congressional legislation).
21. 42 U.S.C. § 2000e-2(a) (1994).

their sexual orientation. Perhaps Title VII's reference to "sex" as a protected classification would prohibit such an employment policy. It would most clearly do so if Congress used the term "sex" to refer broadly to any sexual characteristic, including an individual's sexual identity, activities, preferences, or orientation, rather than only to the characteristic of being male or female.

2. INTRINSIC EVIDENCE

Judicial interpretation of a statute should start with the most direct intrinsic evidence of legislative intent: the statutory language in question.[22] An analysis of the language of section 703(a), however, reveals no single, plain meaning of the statutory term "sex." Dictionaries and common usage define "sex" as, among other things, either (1) the division of species between male and female or (2) more general sexual behavior and characteristics:

> 1: either of two divisions of organisms distinguished respectively as male or female 2: the sum of the structural, functional, and behavioral peculiarities of living beings that subserve reproduction by two interacting parents and distinguish males and females 3a: sexually motivated phenomena or behavior b: sexual intercourse.[23]

Thus, the statutory term "sex" is truly ambiguous, and the process of judicial interpretation will require an inquiry that goes beyond searching for a plain meaning in the term itself.

Other provisions of Title VII may provide intrinsic evidence of the intended meaning of "sex" in section 703(a). In a different subsection of the same legislative act, section 703(h), Congress probably used the term in the narrow sense of the division of species between male and female.[24] There it used "sex" in a reference to the Equal Pay Act of 1963, which more clearly prohibits only certain kinds of discrimination based on the status of an employee as male or female.[25] If Congress consciously used "sex" in that sense in section 703(h), the obvious virtues of consistency in statutory drafting suggest the likelihood, though not the certainty, that

---

22. Laurence H. Tribe, *Judicial Interpretation of Statutes: Three Axioms*, 11 Harv. J.L. & Pub. Pol'y 51 (1988) ("Axiom one is: *Language first*."); Unification Church v. INS, 762 F.2d 1077, 1083 (D.C. Cir. 1985).

23. WEBSTER'S SEVENTH NEW COLLEGIATE DICTIONARY 347 (1970), *as quoted in* Holloway v. Arthur Andersen & Co., 566 F.2d 659, 662 n.4 (9th Cir. 1977).

24. Section 703(h) incorporates a limitation set forth in the Equal Pay Act:

> It shall not be . . . unlawful . . . to differentiate upon the basis of *sex* . . . if such differentiation is authorized by the provisions of [the Equal Pay Act].

42 U.S.C. § 2000e-2(h) (1994) (emphasis added).

25. The Equal Pay Act refers to members of the "opposite sex":

> No employer . . . shall discriminate . . . between employees on the basis of *sex* by paying wages to employees . . . at a rate less than the rate at which he pays wages to employees of the *opposite sex* . . . for equal work. . . .

29 U.S.C. § 206(d) (1994) (emphasis added). The phrase "opposite sex" is commonly used to refer only to distinctions between males and females. Therefore, the Equal Pay Act is nearly unambiguous in its classifying only on the basis of employees being male or female.

Congress ascribed the same meaning to "sex" when it used that term in section 703(a) of the same act.

3. EXTRINSIC EVIDENCE

Thus, intrinsic evidence of the intended meaning in section 703(a) of the word "sex" is helpful but inconclusive. Therefore, a court interpreting "sex" would likely seek guidance from extrinsic evidence, such as legislative history. The original House bill did not include "sex" as a prohibited basis of discrimination. Instead, Howard Smith, a southern Democrat and Chair of the House Rules Committee, proposed the addition of "sex" as a protected classification in a last-minute amendment on the House floor. He apparently hoped that the amendment would spark sufficient controversy to cause the defeat of the entire bill.[26]

Smith's unsuccessful strategy left the courts with "little legislative history to guide us in interpreting the Act's prohibition against discrimination based on 'sex.' "[27] However, the few statements made on the House floor about the proposed amendment, both by Smith and by representatives who more sincerely favored equality of the sexes, suggest that the speakers interpreted "sex" to refer narrowly to the characteristic of being male or female.[28] That interpretation is supported by postenactment evidence of congressional intent. First, the House report on the 1972 Amendments to Title VII clearly shows that Congress was primarily concerned with putting women on equal economic footing with men. Second, successive congressional rejections of several bills proposing to amend Title VII by adding "sexual preference" as a protected classification suggest that members of Congress probably had never collectively intended the statutory term "sex" to encompass sexual preference.[29]

Relying on this legislative history, courts have interpreted the word "sex" in section 703(a) to refer only to male or female status and not also to sexual orientation.[30] Interpreted in that way, Title VII does not clearly prohibit an employer from discriminating against employees because of their homosexuality, provided that the employer applies the same policy to gay males as it does to lesbians.[31]

Had the evidence of specific congressional intent been less convincing, the interpreting court might have applied the general rule of construction that "remedial" statutes should be liberally construed. Title VII is remedial in its purpose of redressing the pervasive social and economic problem of

---

26. Charles Whalen & Barbara Whalen, THE LONGEST DEBATE 84, 115-16 (1985).

27. Meritor Sav. Bank, FSB v. Vinson, 477 U.S. 57, 64 (1986).

28. *See* Whalen & Whalen, *supra* note 26, at 116-17.

29. Holloway v. Arthur Andersen & Co., 566 F.2d 659, 662 (9th Cir. 1977).

30. *E.g., id.* at 662-63; Spearman v. Ford Motor Co., 231 F.3d 1080, 1084-85 (7th Cir. 2000).

31. *See, e.g.*, De Santis v. Pacific Tel. & Tel. Co., 608 F.2d 327 (9th Cir. 1979); Bibby v. Philadelphia Coca-Cola Bottling Co., 260 F.3d 257, 261-64 (3d Cir. 2001) (distinguishing between sexual orientation discrimination, which is not prohibited by Title VII, from same-sex gender discrimination, which is). *But cf.* Gay Law Students Ass'n v. Pacific Tel. & Tel. Co., 595 P.2d 592 (Cal. 1979) (different result under California constitutional and statutory law); Sam Marcosson, *Harassment on the Basis of Sexual Orientation: A Claim of Sex Discrimination Under Title VII*, 81 Geo. L.J. 1, 3-10 (1992) (critiquing *De Santis*).

employment discrimination.[32] Therefore, the rule of construction would favor a liberal construction of the term "sex," which might encompass sexual orientation. However, this general rule of construction is subordinate to evidence of more specific congressional intent relating to the statute in question.[33]

B. Illustration: Generality Resulting in Vagueness

Even if the legislature chooses its words carefully, most statutory language is necessarily general, because almost all legislation addresses broad categories of activities or disputes rather than particular cases. Legislators simply do not possess the stamina and prescience required to consider every potential dispute within the scope of legislation and to provide a specific resolution for each. Instead, courts put the flesh on the bones of legislation by applying the general terms of the statute to the facts of particular disputes, thus adding precision to statutory language in much the same way that they develop common law—incrementally and in the context of successive disputes.

For example, section 703(a) of Title VII of the Civil Rights Act of 1964 prohibits discrimination only with respect to an individual's "compensation, terms, conditions, or privileges of employment."[34] That statutory phrase is necessarily general, because Congress could not practicably describe in more specific terms all of the possible kinds of discrimination that have a sufficient relationship to employment to trigger congressional concern about equal opportunity in the workplace. That generality results in a vagueness that promotes disputes over the interpretation and application of the statute in particular cases.

For instance, parties have reasonably disputed whether sexual advances made by an employer's agent to an employee affect the employee's "terms, conditions, or privileges of employment" if the agent does not withhold tangible benefits of employment in retaliation for rejection of these advances.[35] Courts have given more specific meaning to the statutory phrase by adopting a more specific legal standard for determining the circumstances in which the statute is satisfied: To give effect to Title VII's remedial purpose, courts have decided that sexual advances by an employer's agent may affect "terms, conditions, or privileges of employment" if they create "a substantially discriminatory work environment, regardless of whether the complaining employees lost any tangible job benefits as a result of the discrimination."[36]

---

32. Bell v. Brown, 557 F.2d 849, 853 (D.C. Cir. 1977).

33. *See* Mohasco Corp. v. Silver, 447 U.S. 807, 818-19 (1980) (Title VII is remedial legislation, but also is the product of legislative compromise).

34. 42 U.S.C. § 2000e-2(a) (1994).

35. Such conduct constitutes sex discrimination if the harasser would not have engaged in the conduct but for the employee's gender; that requirement normally is satisfied in the case of a heterosexual or homosexual harasser, but not necessarily in the case of a bisexual harasser. *See* Barnes v. Costle, 561 F.2d 983, 990 n.55 (D.C. Cir. 1977). That analysis, however, does not answer the question whether the discrimination alters conditions of employment, as required by Title VII.

36. Bundy v. Jackson, 641 F.2d 934, 943-44 (D.C. Cir. 1981).

Although the "discriminatory work environment" standard adds a judicial gloss to the statutory language by identifying a specific subset of employment relations within the scope of the statute, the judicial standard is itself abstract and suffers from its own problems of vagueness. True, the United States Supreme Court provided a small measure of guidance by approving liability only if the harassment is "sufficiently severe or pervasive 'to alter the conditions of . . . employment and create an abusive working environment.' "[37] Additionally, the Supreme Court later provided more detailed guidance by listing a number of factors that courts should consider in determining whether a working environment has become abusive.[38] Nonetheless, the precise parameters of the judicial standard, and thus of the statutory language that it seeks to effectuate, will take form only when courts repeatedly apply the standard to the facts of different disputes.

In one case, for example, a federal trial court found that an employer's chief executive created a discriminatory work environment for an employee by giving her a pornographic magazine, leaving an article on her desk about extramarital affairs, and subjecting her to unwelcome sexual advances on at least seven occasions.[39] In contrast, in another case, a federal trial court found that a supervisor did not create a discriminatory work environment by displaying a condescending and impatient attitude toward an employee and by teasing her about her personal relationship with a coworker.[40] If you examine those and other decisions addressing the same issue in different factual contexts, you can gain a better understanding of the intended reach of the statute than is provided by the general statutory language, "terms, conditions, or privileges of employment," or even the more specific judicial interpretation, "discriminatory work environment."

Unfortunately, you should be prepared to encounter cases at the margin that add to your confusion rather than your understanding. For example, a federal appellate court has held in two cases that supervisors and coworkers did not create a discriminatory work environment by subjecting employees to conduct and lewd comments that were relatively "isolated," even though the conduct included physical contact, such as a hand on an employee's shoulder or a slap on an employee's buttocks.[41] A federal trial court in a different geographic jurisdiction, however, found that a supervisor created a discriminatory work environment by subjecting an employee to a single slap on her buttocks and by threatening to repeat that conduct.[42] You could

---

37. Meritor Sav. Bank, FSB v. Vinson, 477 U.S. 57, 67 (1986) (*quoting* Henson v. Dundee, 682 F.2d 897, 904 (11th Cir. 1982)).

38. Harris v. Forklift Sys., 510 U.S. 17, 23 (1993). More recently, the Supreme Court emphasized the value of employing "[c]ommon sense and an appropriate sensitivity to social context" in distinguishing "ordinary socializing in the workplace" from unlawful harassment. Oncale v. Sundowner Offshore Serv., Inc., 523 U.S. 75, 81-82 (1998).

39. Ross v. Twenty-Four Collection, Inc., 681 F. Supp. 1547, 1551 (S.D. Fla. 1988), *aff'd*, 875 F.2d 873 (11th Cir. 1989).

40. Saxton v. American Tel. & Tel. Co., 785 F. Supp. 760, 765 (N.D. Ill. 1992).

41. Weiss v. Coca-Cola Bottling Co., 990 F.2d 333, 337 (7th Cir. 1993); Scott v. Sears, Roebuck & Co., 798 F.2d 210, 211-14 (7th Cir. 1986).

42. Campbell v. Kansas State Univ., 780 F. Supp. 755, 761-62 (D. Kan. 1991). This decision gains some support from the Supreme Court's subsequent dictum illustrating the importance of context, in Oncale v. Sundowner Offshore Serv., Inc., 523 U.S. 75, 81 (1998) (a coach may be acting abusively when smacking his secretary on the buttocks in the office, though not when smacking a football player on the buttocks as he heads out to the field).

reasonably interpret such cases as reflecting disagreement among the courts about the proper interpretation and application of the legal standard, a phenomenon addressed in succeeding chapters in this book, particularly Chapter 7, Section II.B.7.

Exercise 4-1

1. JUDICIAL INTERPRETATION OF LEGISLATION

A statute of State Y provides without qualification that "any landlord of a residential unit may prohibit tenants from keeping pets in their units and may evict any tenant who violates such a prohibition and fails to cure the violation within one week of receiving notice of the violation." Does this statute permit a landlord of residential apartments in State Y to evict a tenant who refuses to get rid of a single goldfish that the tenant keeps in a two-gallon fish bowl in her apartment? You may assume that State Y has no helpful legislative history relating to this statute. Can opposing attorneys reasonably argue for and against application of the statute? Can different judges reasonably reach opposite conclusions on the proper interpretation and application of the statute in this case?[43]

2. STATUTORY POLICY AND CLASSIFICATION

The Highway Patrol of State X informed legislators of State X that motorists were causing accidents by consuming soft drinks while driving. The Highway Patrol was not overly concerned that drivers could keep only one hand on the wheel while consuming soft drinks. Instead, they were concerned that drivers often obstructed their own vision, and thus lost partial control of their automobiles, when they tilted their heads back and tipped their soft drink containers upward to consume the last of their soft drinks. In response, state legislators amended the State X Vehicle Code to make it a misdemeanor "to operate a motor vehicle while consuming any beverage from a can or bottle." If the concerns that motivated this bill are recorded in legislative history, should the new law apply to:

a. a driver who tilts her head back to drink water from a paper cup?
b. a driver who keeps his head level while he sips a soft drink through a straw from a bottle?
c. a driver who eats a submarine sandwich in a way that distracts her and obstructs her vision? In addressing these cases, ask yourself to what extent a court should adhere to the strict terms of the statute, even if such an interpretation in a specific case is not perfectly consistent

43. This problem is derived from a hypothetical case posed by Shirley Abrahamson, Chief Justice of the Wisconsin Supreme Court, and related by New York Court of Appeals Judge Judith S. Kaye in *Things Judges Do: State Statutory Interpretation*, 13 Touro L. Rev. 595, 606 (1997).

with the legislative purpose. To what extent should the court interpret the statutory language flexibly to more closely achieve the legislative purpose?

3. LEGISLATIVE HISTORY

The current codification of a Reconstruction era civil rights act prohibits certain kinds of discrimination:

> *All persons* within the jurisdiction of the United States shall have the same right in every State and Territory to make and enforce contracts . . . *as is enjoyed by white citizens.* . . .

42 U.S.C. § 1981(a) (1994) (emphasis added). The original predecessor to this statute contained similar language:

> [C]itizens of the United States . . . , of every race and color, without regard to any previous condition of slavery or involuntary servitude, . . . shall have the same right, in every State and Territory in the United States, to make and enforce contracts . . . *as is enjoyed by white citizens.* . . .

Civil Rights Act of 1866 § 1, 14 Stat. 27 (1866) (emphasis added); *see also* Civil Rights Act of 1870 §§ 16, 18, 16 Stat. 144 (1870) (reenacting and adding to 1866 Act). The "immediate impetus" for the original statute was "the necessity for further relief of the constitutionally emancipated former Negro slaves."[44] However, to allay fears among some legislators that the proposed bill would favor nonwhites, proponents of the bill defended it at several stages of the legislative process as one that would protect *all* citizens.[45] More than a century after the initial enactment, the United States Supreme Court applied the modern version of this statute to prohibit private, commercially operated, nonsectarian schools from discriminating against African Americans in admission to the schools.[46]

 a. Should a court apply the statute to protect nonwhites other than African Americans from race discrimination in contractual relations?

 b. Should a court apply the statute to protect white citizens from race discrimination? *See McDonald v. Santa Fe Trail Transp. Co.,* 427 U.S. 273 (1976).

 c. If the statute applies to protect racial groups other than African Americans, how does one define "race" for purposes of finding prohibited discrimination? Would the statute apply to prohibit discrimination against a person because he is Arab rather than Anglo-American? *See St. Francis College v. Al-Khazraji,* 481 U.S. 604 (1987) (looking to racial classifications recognized at time of enactment of predecessors to 42 U.S.C. § 1981). Would it apply to discrimination because one is Jewish? *See Shaare Tefila*

---

44. McDonald v. Santa Fe Trail Transp. Co., 427 U.S. 273, 289 (1976).
45. *Id.* at 289-95.
46. Runyon v. McCrary, 427 U.S. 160 (1976), *reaff'd in part,* Patterson v. McLean Credit Union, 491 U.S. 164 (1989).

Congregation v. Cobb, 481 U.S. 615 (1987) (same analysis under companion statute, 42 U.S.C. § 1982).

IV. LEGISLATIVE ENACTMENT AND CHANGE

As a serious student of the law, you should not be content to simply interpret statutory law. You should also evaluate the political merits of current or proposed legislation.

When you encounter a social problem that you believe is not adequately addressed by current constitutional or common law, consider whether you would propose legislation to address the problem. In light of questions of statutory interpretation explored in the previous sections, consider how you would draft legislation so that it achieves your statutory purpose with a minimum of ambiguity.

Of course, a legislature that has the power to enact legislation also has the power to repeal or amend it. A constant critique of current legislation helps to fuel the dynamic process of the growth and development of statutory law.

For example, the discussion in the previous section shows that Congress probably intended Title VII's prohibition of sex discrimination to apply to discrimination on the basis of gender but not on the basis of sexual orientation. In reaching that conclusion, however, some courts have suggested that sexual orientation discrimination, such as harassment on the basis of sexual orientation, warrants a remedy, though Title VII does not currently afford one:

> [H]arassment because of sexual orientation . . . is a noxious practice, deserving of censure and opprobrium. But we are called upon here to construe a statute . . . and we regard it as settled law that, as drafted and authoritatively construed, Title VII does not proscribe harassment simply because of sexual orientation.[47]

The first exercise below asks you to consider whether the policies underlying Title VII's current prohibitions apply as well to discrimination because of sexual orientation, and whether Congress should amend Title VII to prohibit such discrimination.

Exercise 4-2

1. LEGISLATIVE AMENDMENT: INVIDIOUS DISCRIMINATION

Thirty years after the 1963 civil rights march in Washington, D.C., for racial equality, hundreds of thousands of lesbians and gays rallied in the nation's

---

47. Higgins v. New Balance Athletic Shoe, Inc., 194 F.3d 252, 259 (1st Cir. 1999), *quoted in* Rene v. MGM Grand Hotel, Inc., 243 F.2d 1206, 1209 (9th Cir. 2001).

capital to demand freedom from discrimination.[48] President Clinton later equated "the gay rights movement with the struggle for racial equality."[49]

Consider the bases of discrimination covered by Title VII of the Civil Rights Act of 1964: race, color, religion, sex, and national origin. Other federal statutes prohibit discrimination based on age or disability. Why are these classes entitled to special protection? Should Congress amend Title VII to include sexual orientation as a protected characteristic? Of what significance are debates about the extent to which sexual orientation is determined by biology, culture, or choice?[50]

In formulating your support or opposition to such an amendment, how do you define your role as legislator? Should you vote according to your best personal judgment on the ground that your constituents expressed confidence in your judgment and values by electing you to office? Or should you vote in a manner consistent with the latest opinion poll in your district, even if that differs from your personal convictions?

2. ENACTING MANDATORY SAFETY RULES

Do you support state legislation requiring a person to wear a protective helmet while driving or riding as a passenger on a motorcycle on a public street or highway? What policy arguments support or oppose such legislation?

3. ENACTING LEGISLATION PERMITTING PHYSICIAN-ASSISTED SUICIDE

In 1997, the United States Supreme Court refused to recognize a constitutional right to physician-assisted suicide, and it left the matter of prohibition, regulation, or permission of physician-assisted suicide to be resolved in other legal arenas, such as state criminal legislation.[51] As a state legislator, what position would you take on this issue? Would you vote for a bill making it a crime for a physician to actively promote the death of any patient, regardless of the circumstances? Conversely, would you legislatively grant immunity to a physician who hastened the death of any patient who requested such

48. Jeffrey Schmalz, *Gay Americans Throng Capital in Appeal for Rights*, N.Y. Times, Apr. 26, 1993, at A1.

49. Peter Baker, *Clinton Equates Gay Rights, Civil Rights*, Wash. Post, Nov. 9, 1997, at A18 (reporting on "the first speech by a sitting President to a gay rights organization"). In 2000, a second rally in Washington, D.C., again drew hundreds of thousands. Robin Toner, *A Gay Rights Rally Over Gains and Goals*, N.Y. Times, May 1, 2000, at A14. A little more than one year later, the United States Department of Agriculture began recruiting for "a 'gay and lesbian program specialist' who would help improve working conditions for the agency's gay employees." Eric Schmitt, *U.S. Agency Plans to Hire a Specialist on Gay Issues*, N.Y. Times, June 20, 2001, at A15.

50. *Compare* E. Gary Spitko, *A Biologic Argument for Gay Essentialism-Determinism: Implications for Equal Protection and Substantive Due Process*, 18 U. Haw. L. Rev. 571, 576-84 (1996) (reviewing studies tending to show a physiological or genetic basis for gay male sexual orientation), *with* Janet E. Haley, *Sexual Orientation and the Politics of Biology: A Critique of the Argument from Immutability*, 46 Stanf. L. Rev. 503 (1994) (arguing that immutability argument is divisive and is not necessary for advancing gay rights). *Compare* Natalie Angier, *Study Suggests Strong Genetic Role in Lesbianism*, N.Y. Times, Mar. 12, 1993, at A8, *with* Erica Goode, *Scientist Says Study Shows Gay Change Is Possible*, N.Y. Times, May 9, 2001, at A15 (reporting on unpublished study).

51. Washington v. Glucksberg, 521 U.S. 702 (1997); Vacco v. Quill, 521 U.S. 793 (1997).

assistance? Would you permit physician-assisted suicide, but regulate it by restricting it to certain circumstances? How would you draft your legislation?

4. OVERRULING COMMON LAW

In August 1997, a North Carolina jury awarded $1 million to a jilted wife who sued her husband's secretary for committing adultery with her husband and breaking up their marriage. The award was based partly on the common law tort of alienation of affection, defined as wrongful conduct that deprives a married person of the love and companionship of his or her spouse in what was a harmonious marriage. Most states have legislatively abolished this and related torts, partly because the torts invite abusive legal tactics and are based on outdated notions about the nature of intimate relationships.[52] Indeed, the North Carolina Court of Appeals had judicially abandoned the common law tort of alienation of affection in 1984, but the North Carolina Supreme Court reversed on the ground that it had recognized the tort of alienation of affection in its own case law, which the court of appeals was not free to ignore.[53]

Do you believe such torts should be retained or abandoned? As a member of the state's highest court, would you abolish the tort of alienation of affection in the course of developing the state's common law, or would you view such a major policy change as one best left to the state legislature? As a state legislator, would you support or oppose a bill to abolish the common law tort of alienation of affection?

V. INTERPLAY BETWEEN LEGISLATION AND COMMON LAW

A. Relationship Between Legislation and Common Law

1. LEGISLATIVE PRIMACY

Although the legislature and the judiciary both exercise lawmaking powers, the legislature is the paramount lawmaking authority, and legislative enactments supersede inconsistent common law. The Supreme Court's following statement about the federal system applies as well to the state governments:

> [W]e consistently have emphasized that the federal lawmaking power is vested in the legislative, not the judicial, branch of government; therefore, federal common law is "subject to the paramount authority of Congress."[54]

52. *See* Foon Rhee, *Jury Award Turns Attention to "Homewrecker" Law*, Wash. Post, Aug. 10, 1997, at A25.
53. Cannon v. Miller, 322 S.E.2d 780 (N.C. Ct. App. 1984), *vacated*, 327 S.E.2d 888 (N.C. 1985).
54. Northwest Airlines, Inc. v. Transport Workers Union, 451 U.S. 77, 95 (1981) (quoting New Jersey v. New York, 283 U.S. 336, 348 (1931)).

Accordingly, the legislature may enact statutes that modify, overrule, or codify existing common law.

2. LEGISLATION AS GUIDANCE FOR COMMON LAW

Even if no statute currently applies to a dispute, a court may decline to extend common law principles to the area if it concludes that the matter is better left to legislative action.[55] Moreover, if the court decides to develop and apply the common law, it nonetheless may look to statutory law for expressions of public policy that help the court formulate the common law rule.

In one case, for example, a court addressed the question whether, under the common law of torts, retailers should assume liability for injuries stemming from their sales of guns without regard to the care that they exercised in the sales. The court looked to the policy of federal and state gun control legislation to apply this common law doctrine of strict liability to the sale of some, but not all, kinds of guns.[56] Another court drew guidance from an enacted, but not yet effective, commercial code to develop a common law doctrine of unconscionability in sales contracts.[57]

3. COMMON LAW AS BACKGROUND FOR LEGISLATION

Although statutory law supersedes common law, the common law at the time of a statute's enactment may provide a helpful context for analyzing legislative intent.[58] If a statute overrules a common law rule or seeks to address a problem left untouched by the common law, a court can better understand the statute's intended scope if it appreciates the deficiencies of the common law to which the legislature responded.[59] Conversely, if a statute codifies existing common law, cases that developed the common law rule obviously will provide guidance in interpreting the statute.

Moreover, a statute often addresses only selected issues within the general subject matter touched by the statute, thereby creating gaps that common law may fill. In some cases, the statute itself provides for reference to common law, as in the Uniform Commercial Code:

> Unless displaced by the particular provisions of this Act, the principles of law and equity, including the law merchant and the law relative to capacity to contract, principal and agent, estoppel, fraud, misrepresentation, duress, coercion, mistake, . . . or other validating or invalidating cause shall supplement its provisions.[60]

55. *See, e.g.*, City & County of S. Fr. v. United Ass'n of Journeymen etc. of U.S. & Can., 726 P.2d 538 (Cal. 1986).
56. Kelley v. R.G. Indus., 497 A.2d 1143 (Md. 1985).
57. Williams v. Walker-Thomas Furniture Co., 350 F.2d 445 (D.C. Cir. 1965).
58. 2B Norman J. Singer, SUTHERLAND STATUTORY CONSTRUCTION § 50.01 (6th ed. 2000); *see* Wayne R. LaFave, CRIMINAL LAW § 2.2, at 85 (3d ed. 2000) (discussing interpretation of criminal statutes in light of common law); City of Okla. City v. Tuttle, 471 U.S. 808, 835-38 (1985) (Stevens, J., dissenting).
59. *See, e.g.*, Heydon's Case, 76 Eng. Rep. 637, 638 (1584), *quoted in* Singer, *supra* note 58, § 45-05, at 25-26.
60. U.C.C. § 1-103 (2000).

In other cases, statutes only implicitly incorporate common law principles. For example, a federal civil rights statute imposes liability for certain conduct without any express qualifications or limitations. Yet, courts have assumed that Congress intended the statute to implicitly incorporate common law defenses of immunity from liability for money damages:

> It is by now well settled that the tort liability created by [42 U.S.C.] § 1983 cannot be understood in a historical vacuum. In the Civil Rights Act of 1871, Congress created a federal remedy against a person who, acting under color of state law, deprives another of constitutional rights. . . . One important assumption underlying the Court's decisions in this area is that members of the 42d Congress were familiar with common-law principles, including defenses previously recognized in ordinary tort litigation, and that they likely intended these common-law principles to obtain, absent specific provisions to the contrary.[61]

B. Judicial Power and Limitations Regarding Legislation

Although legislatures can modify or overrule common law principles developed by courts, the courts retain an important role in the development of statutory law. Courts may review statutes for consistency with constitutional requirements and will refuse to enforce unconstitutional legislation.[62] Additionally, as discussed in Section III above, courts determine the scope and effect of legislation by interpreting statutes and applying them to particular disputes.

Nonetheless, courts have less flexibility in interpreting statutory law than in developing common law. True, if a court changes its previous analysis of legislative intent, it may overrule its earlier interpretation of a statute, just as it sometimes overrules its previous application of a principle of common law.[63] However, the court may not ignore a statute or modify its terms to reflect judicial views that are inconsistent with legislative intent. In contrast, a court may directly reject the substance and reasoning of a common law principle that it announced and applied in a prior decision: "[W]e have not hesitated to change the common law . . . where . . . such course was justified."[64]

Interestingly, some American Indian tribal court judges have boldly hinted that they may challenge the conventional hierarchy of laws in tribal governments. Under Anglo-American assumptions, tribal codes should have priority over tribal common law, because the tribal council has adopted the codes, just as a federal or state legislature enacts statutes. However, even though tribal codes are formally enacted by tribal councils, many were

---

61. City of Newport v. Fact Concerts, Inc., 453 U.S. 247, 258 (1981).
62. *See* Marbury v. Madison, 5 U.S. (1 Cranch) 137 (1803) (setting forth seminal dictum regarding judicial authority in the federal system); Dickerson v. United States, 530 U.S. 428 (2000) (striking down congressional attempt to legislatively overrule the celebrated *Miranda* decision, which protected constitutional rights).
63. *See, e.g.*, Monell v. Department of Soc. Servs. of N.Y., 436 U.S. 658 (1978) (overruling the Court's previous decision that the term "person" in 42 U.S.C. § 1983 does not include municipalities); Wayne R. LaFave, CRIMINAL LAW § 2.2, at 95-96 (3d ed. 2000).
64. Kelley v. R.G. Indus., 497 A.2d 1143, 1150-51 (Md. 1985).

conceived and drafted by Anglo-Americans and may reflect a poor under-standing of tribal culture. In contrast, some tribal courts more consciously seek to promote tribal culture and policies when they develop and apply tribal common law.

This phenomenon may justify a departure from Anglo-American legal method in tribal courts. For example, the Navajo Supreme Court has hinted that it may simply refuse to give effect to outdated tribal code sections that fail to promote Navajo values or are inconsistent with longstanding Navajo custom. In gestures acknowledging the role of the legislative branch of government, the Navajo Supreme Court has explicitly recommended in its opinions that the Navajo Tribal Council amend tribal codes that do not promote Navajo culture and policies.[65] This kind of communication between branches of government is not foreign to the Anglo-American legal system. However, not content to wait for action from its legislative branch, the Navajo Supreme Court has considered a more radical legal method. When necessary to preserve important values of tribal culture or sovereignty, the Navajo Supreme Court has hinted at its willingness to elevate Navajo com-mon law or custom above otherwise applicable tribal codes.[66]

One scholar supports similarly skeptical treatment of outdated state statutes.[67] Nonetheless, the more conventional hierarchy of laws in the Anglo-American legal system is firmly entrenched: A constitution defines the reach of statutory authority, and statutes can limit the application of common law.

VI. SUMMARY

A state or federal legislature is the primary policymaking body within a jurisdiction, and it can modify or overrule common law by enacting a super-seding statute. Nonetheless, courts review statutes for constitutionality, and they interpret and apply statutes in the context of particular disputes. In interpreting statutes, a court begins with the statutory language in question, viewed in the context of the statute as a whole. If that language is ambiguous, the court may look to other evidence of legislative intent, including legislative history. If evidence of legislative intent is inconclusive, the court may apply a rule of construction, which gives the statute a meaning that is consistent with general legislative and public policies.

For more problems and exercises related to Part II of this book, consult Appendix I, near the end of this book.

---

65. *E.g.*, *In re* Validation of Marriage of Francisco, 16 Indian L. Rep. 6113, 6115 (Navajo S. Ct. 1989).

66. *See id.* ("This court . . . does not rely on [the tribal code], but instead on Navajo custom.").

67. *See* Guido Calabresi, A COMMON LAW FOR THE AGE OF STATUTES 163-66 (1982) (recommending that Anglo-American courts refuse to enforce outdated statutes unless reaf-firmed by the legislature).

Part III

Legal Method

and Analysis

Chapter 5

The Role of Precedent:

The Court System and

Stare Decisis

I. INTRODUCTION TO STARE DECISIS

A. Efficiency, Predictability, and Fairness

In the United States, previous court decisions may influence, or even dictate, the result in a dispute currently before a court. The legal effect of the previous decisions is governed by a complex set of conventions for which the Latin phrase "stare decisis" is often used as convenient shorthand.

As defined in *Black's Law Dictionary*, "stare decisis" means "[t]o abide by, or adhere to, decided cases." Under the doctrine of stare decisis, a court endeavors to decide each case consistently with its own previous published decisions, which is called its "precedent." Moreover, the deciding court is strictly bound by the precedent of a higher court that reviews the decisions of the deciding court, if the precedent addressed essentially the same question currently before the deciding court.

51

Judicial adherence to the doctrine of stare decisis serves several significant goals:

- it promotes efficiency in judicial administration by relieving judges of the burden of revisiting settled legal questions in each case;
- it facilitates private and commercial transactions by ensuring a degree of certainty and predictability in the law that regulates such transactions; and
- it satisfies the common moral belief that persons in like circumstances should be treated alike.[1]

B. Illustration: Parental Decisionmaking

You can explore the third justification for stare decisis on a simple level by examining familiar decisions such as parents' reactions to the behavior of their children. Imagine that two parents, Carmen and Miguel, formulated rules for their two children, Mike and Monica, both of whom were excellent students. When the children entered their teen years, Carmen and Miguel required them to "use good sense" in restricting their hours away from home at night.

When Mike, the older child, entered his junior year of high school, he began to attend evening social and athletic events frequently. After he had stayed out past 11:00 P.M. three nights in a single week, his parents admonished him. In justifying their admonishment, Carmen and Miguel explained that Mike had not used the requisite good sense for a student of his age and responsibilities. The parents worried that excessively late hours would hamper their son's studies and even endanger his health. To avoid such evils, they announced a refinement of their previous "good sense" rule: Mike can stay out at night on nonfamily outings no more than twice in a week. Furthermore, despite Mike's arguments that midnight was a more reasonable curfew, Miguel and Carmen announced that Mike must come home by 11:00 P.M. on such occasions.

A year later, Monica entered her junior year of high school and also began to attend evening social and athletic events frequently. When Monica stayed out one night past 10:30 P.M., Carmen and Miguel admonished her about her hours. Both parents initially held the opinion that Monica should not stay out at night on nonfamily outings more than once in a week and that she must come home by 10:00 P.M. on such occasions. When Miguel and Carmen asked Monica for her reaction to these restrictions, Monica protested that the proposed rule would treat her unfairly: Although she and Mike were engaged in nearly identical activities, she would be subject to greater restrictions than would Mike.

On reflection, Carmen and Miguel realized that they had justified the proposed difference in treatment by distinguishing between their two children on the basis of gender: They had assumed that Monica needed extra protection because she is female. Monica persuaded them, however, that

---

1. *See* Edgar Bodenheimer, JURISPRUDENCE: THE PHILOSOPHY AND METHOD OF THE LAW 425-28 (rev. ed. 1974); Sol Wachtler, *Stare Decisis and a Changing New York Court of Appeals*, 59 St. John's L. Rev. 445, 447-52 (1985).

she and her brother were indeed similarly situated because of their activities and that gender was not relevant to the policies and purposes of the curfew rule. Accordingly, Carmen and Miguel applied the same restrictions to Monica that they had earlier devised for Mike.

Throughout months of applying their general curfew rule to Mike and Monica, Carmen and Miguel developed exceptions to meet special circumstances. For example, both Mike and Monica were members of high school basketball teams, both of which occasionally traveled by bus to night games at competing schools in a neighboring county. On such nights, the team bus often did not return the team members to school in time for Mike and Monica to return home before 11:00 P.M. Because they valued their children's participation in athletic events, Carmen and Miguel permitted late hours on such nights pursuant to one of a growing number of special exceptions to their general rule.

Midway through Mike's senior year at high school, Carmen and Miguel concluded that their general curfew rule was unworkable for two reasons. First, their rule had been excessively mechanical and inflexible from its inception: It required the formulation of numerous exceptions to meet special circumstances, and it completely failed to address questions about activities that should be prohibited rather than merely restricted in their hours and frequency. Second, circumstances had changed: Both Mike and Monica had increased their participation in worthy organizations and activities that occasionally required late hours or even overnight stays. The general rule now required so many exceptions to meet legitimate needs that it ceased to have significant meaning.

Carmen and Miguel were initially reluctant to abandon a rule that they had so thoughtfully developed and applied. After a year and a half, however, they abandoned their original curfew rule and substituted a new, more flexible one. They announced that they would evaluate any proposed activity primarily on the basis of the nature of the activity rather than solely on the frequency and degree to which it required late hours.

Thus, Carmen and Miguel strove for consistency in applying their rules to specific events, but they departed from past practice when new information or changes in circumstances suggested that their previous decisions no longer provided the best guide for satisfying their policy objectives. Specifically, they initially announced a general rule for Mike that satisfied general policy concerns about Mike's health and academic performance. They applied the same rule to Monica, rather than a more restrictive rule, because Monica persuaded them that her case was indistinguishable from that of Mike. Carmen and Miguel later developed special exceptions to their general rule to meet the needs of specific events. Eventually, they grew dissatisfied with their general rule, and they abandoned it. They replaced it with a new rule that used different criteria for evaluating their children's activities.

C. Judicial Acknowledgment of Stare Decisis

This parental decisionmaking illustrates some of the ways in which courts develop case law within the framework of stare decisis. However, most courts would not be quite as casual as were Carmen and Miguel in departing from precedent when they abandoned their original rules in favor of new ones.

Separate opinions by different Justices in a decision of the United States Supreme Court illustrate judicial concern for at least the appearance of adherence to the doctrine of stare decisis.[2] In that decision, the Supreme Court held that the Eleventh Amendment to the United States Constitution prohibits a federal trial court from exercising a certain kind of "jurisdiction," or judicial power. In reaching that result, a majority of the Court found a way to avoid the decisionmaking restrictions imposed by stare decisis, even though its prior decisions reached a contrary result regarding the exercise of jurisdiction. The Court concluded that the prior decisions had not specifically addressed the jurisdictional issue and therefore created no precedent on that issue:

> These cases thus did not directly confront the question before us. "[W]hen questions of jurisdiction have been passed on in prior decisions *sub silentio*,[3] this Court has never considered itself bound when a subsequent case finally brings the jurisdictional issue before us." [Citation omitted.] We therefore view the question as an open one.[4]

Other Justices on the Supreme Court complained in a separate dissenting opinion that the majority had mischaracterized the holdings of the prior decisions and thus had failed to accord them the deference demanded by stare decisis:

> None of these cases contain only "implicit" or *sub silentio* holdings; all of them explicitly consider and reject the claim that the Eleventh Amendment prohibits federal courts from issuing injunctive relief based on state law. There is therefore no basis for the majority's assertion that the issue presented by this case is an open one. . . .[5]

Indeed, the dissenters implicitly accused the majority of analyzing the prior decisions disingenuously:

> The majority incredibly claims that *Greene* contains only an implicit holding on the Eleventh Amendment question the Court decides today. . . . In plain words, the *Greene* Court held that the Eleventh Amendment did not bar consideration of the pendent state-law claims advanced in that case. The Court then considered and sustained those claims on their merits.[6]

Similarly sharp comments punctuated the 1987 hearings of the Senate Judiciary Committee on Judge Robert Bork's unsuccessful bid for confirmation to the United States Supreme Court. Judge Bork's nomination sparked heated debate about the extent to which he would follow the command of stare decisis and adhere to Supreme Court precedent if confirmed.[7]

Any governing principle that engenders such controversy is worth further exploration. The strength of an authority as precedent depends in part on

2. Pennhurst State Sch. & Hosp. v. Halderman, 465 U.S. 89 (1984).
3. "Sub silentio" is a Latin phrase meaning "[u]nder silence; without any notice being taken." BLACK'S LAW DICTIONARY 1442 (7th ed. 1999).
4. *Pennhurst*, 465 U.S. at 119.
5. *Id.* at 137 (Stevens, J., dissenting).
6. *Id.* at 137 n.14.
7. *Compare The White House Report: Information on Judge Bork's Qualifications, Judicial Record & Related Subjects* (July 31, 1987) (Statement on "General Judicial Philosophy" of Judge Bork), *reprinted in* 9 Cardozo L. Rev. 187, 191 (1987), *with The United States Senate Judiciary Committee Chairman's Consultants, Response Prepared to White House Analysis of Judge Bork's Record* § VI (Sept. 2, 1987), *reprinted in* 9 Cardozo L. Rev. 219, 287-96 (1987).

the relationship between the court that created the precedent and the court that may subsequently apply it. Therefore, our exploration should begin with an introduction to the court system.

II. THE COURT SYSTEM

A. Structure of State and Federal Courts

Most state court systems include courts of "limited jurisdiction," which hear disputes on limited matters such as domestic relations, traffic violations, and civil suits with small amounts in controversy. All other disputes are tried in branches of a trial court of "general jurisdiction," typically named "Superior Court," "Circuit Court," or "District Court."

In most states, final decisions of this trial court may be reviewed in appellate courts at two different levels: A disappointed litigant may appeal from a trial court judgment to an intermediate court of appeals; further appeals are taken to a court of last resort, most commonly known as the "Supreme Court" of the state. Some court systems have no intermediate appellate court. Instead, a single state court of last resort hears appeals directly from judgments of the trial courts of general jurisdiction.[8] Under either model, a disappointed litigant in state court may seek further review on questions of federal law in the United States Supreme Court.[9]

The state court system in California is representative of the four-tier model:

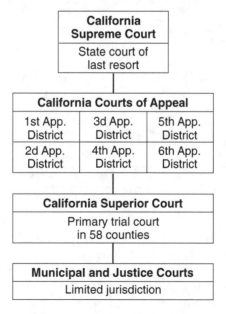

California Supreme Court		
State court of last resort		

California Courts of Appeal		
1st App. District	3d App. District	5th App. District
2d App. District	4th App. District	6th App. District

California Superior Court
Primary trial court in 58 counties

Municipal and Justice Courts
Limited jurisdiction

---

8. In 2001, those court systems included those of the District of Columbia and the following states: Delaware, Maine, Montana, Nevada, New Hampshire, Rhode Island, South Dakota, Vermont, West Virginia, and Wyoming. BNA's DIRECTORY OF STATE AND FEDERAL COURTS, JUDGES, AND CLERKS xi-xiv (2001) [hereinafter BNA's DIRECTORY OF COURTS].

9. 28 U.S.C. § 1257 (1994).

In California, two courts of limited jurisdiction, Justice Courts and Municipal Courts, hear restricted classes of cases. The trial court of general jurisdiction is the Superior Court, which serves each of 58 counties throughout the state. The Superior Court hears appeals from the courts of limited jurisdiction, and it entertains original actions in a wide variety of civil and criminal cases. Disappointed litigants in a criminal or civil case may appeal from a judgment of the Superior Court to the California Court of Appeal. This intermediate appellate body consists of six courts, each of which hears civil and criminal appeals from departments of the Superior Court in counties assigned to the appellate court's district. A disappointed litigant in the Court of Appeal may appeal to the California Supreme Court in certain kinds of cases and may petition for discretionary review in others.[10]

For example, California's Second Appellate District includes the counties of Los Angeles, San Luis Obispo, Santa Barbara, and Ventura. The California Court of Appeal for the Second Appellate District would hear appeals from the decisions of the California Superior Court in those counties. A litigant disappointed by a decision of the Court of Appeal for the Second Appellate District could appeal to the California Supreme Court or petition it for discretionary review.

The structure of the federal court system is similar to that of the California court system:

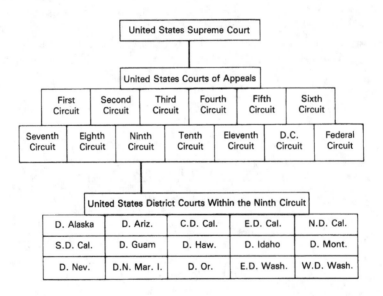

The primary federal trial courts are the United States District Courts. With few exceptions, disappointed litigants appeal from a judgment of a district court to the appropriate one of 13 "circuits" of the United States Courts of Appeals. Further appeals, most of them discretionary, are taken to the United States Supreme Court. The chart above shows the line of review from judgments of the United States District Courts that serve the geographical area within the jurisdiction of the United States Court of Appeals for the Ninth Circuit.

10. BNA's DIRECTORY OF COURTS, *supra* note 8, at 78.

The Ninth Circuit encompasses a large portion of the United States. Although Congress has repeatedly considered proposals to split this circuit into two circuits, as the Ninth Circuit entered the twenty-first century, it still included the states and territories of Alaska, Arizona, California, Guam, Hawaii, Idaho, Montana, Nevada, the Northern Mariana Islands, Oregon, and Washington. Each of those states and territories has at least one district court; California and Washington have more. For example, California is divided into four district courts: the United States District Courts for the Central, Eastern, Northern, and Southern Districts of California.

B. Court Structure and Stare Decisis

Precedent has only limited stare decisis effect on the decisionmaking of the court that created the precedent: Although a court will do so only in unusual circumstances, it can depart from its own prior rulings. For lower courts within the same court system, stare decisis is less flexible: Precedent on the same issue is binding on the lower courts for which the creating court acts as a court of review. As discussed further in Section III below, the lower court must either distinguish the reviewing court's precedent or apply it as controlling authority.

Stare decisis generally does not require a court to follow the precedent of coequal, autonomous courts, of lower courts within the same court system, or of any courts outside that system. For example, the Florida Supreme Court is not bound by the decisions of the other Florida courts or by those of the California Supreme Court. Similarly, the United States Court of Appeals for the First Circuit is not bound by the decisions of either the United States Court of Appeals for the Second Circuit or any United States District Court. Nonetheless, even if the precedent of another court is not binding on the deciding court, the deciding court is free to consider the nonbinding precedent as persuasive authority and to follow its reasoning as a matter of choice.

In some courts, a judicial unit of fewer than all members of the court may create precedent for the entire court. For example, the United States Court of Appeals for the Ninth Circuit has more than two dozen judges, but most appeals in the circuit are heard by panels of three judges each. Each three-judge panel creates precedent that must be followed by all other three-judge panels in the circuit. Within the circuit, a decision of a three-judge panel can be overruled only by a limited "en banc" panel of 11 members of the court.[11]

III. SCOPE AND APPLICATION OF STARE DECISIS

Some form of stare decisis is justified in any society that values efficiency, certainty, and at least those notions of fairness predicated on equal treatment

---

11. *See, e.g.*, United States v. McLennan, 563 F.2d 943, 948 (9th Cir. 1977); 9th Cir. R. 35-3 .

for similarly situated parties. On the other hand, unquestioning adherence to precedent may inappropriately extend the rule of previous decisions beyond the rationale and policy of the original decision, or it may retain outdated or otherwise unsound precedent.

Two limits to stare decisis help to strike the proper balance between consistency and rigidity in the law:

(1) A court may *distinguish* a prior decision if it concludes that the prior decision addressed a significantly different dispute from the one now before the court. If so, even if the prior decision was issued by the same court or by a higher court within the jurisdiction, the prior decision does not control the result in the case now before the court. Of course, if the prior decision was issued by a lower court or by a court from another jurisdiction, it would never be *binding* on the current court. Moreover, if such a prior decision is distinguishable from the current case, the prior decision may lose even the persuasive value that it might otherwise have had.

(2) Alternatively, a court's own precedent may be indistinguishable from the dispute currently before the court. If so, the court normally would be bound under the doctrine of stare decisis to follow the precedent. Nonetheless, in special circumstances the court may depart from the normal mandate of stare decisis and reject its own precedent as authority for the present dispute.

The following sections thoroughly examine each of these limits on stare decisis. Section A explores means of determining whether a prior decision is sufficiently analogous that it creates precedent on the issue now before the court, or whether the prior decision instead is distinguishable. Section B assumes that a court's own prior decision is not distinguishable and therefore creates precedent that normally would be controlling in the current dispute. It then discusses the special circumstances in which a court may depart from such precedent.

A. Analogizing and Distinguishing Precedent

1. AN INEXACT SCIENCE WITH AMPLE ROOM FOR ARGUMENT

Few disputes are so similar in their facts and legal issues that resolution of the first dispute provides a clear basis for resolving the second. In those relatively rare cases, the prior decision is clearly "controlling" precedent in the same court or a lower court within the jurisdiction. Such controlling precedent normally dictates the result of the subsequent case under stare decisis.[12]

More often, differences between two cases in the facts and in the nature of the legal claims and defenses raised by the litigants are sufficiently substantial that the prior decision does not clearly dictate the resolution of the second. Whether the differences meet this standard often is a question of degree on which reasonable lawyers may disagree.[13]

---

12. *See generally* Hutto v. Davis, 454 U.S. 370 (1982).
13. *Compare id.* at 372-75 (majority opinion), *and id.* at 375-81 (Powell, J., concurring), *with id.* at 381-88 (Brennan, J., dissenting).

Assuming that the precedent is not nearly identical to the current dispute and thus is not strictly controlling, it may still be sufficiently analogous to provide a strong basis for deciding the current dispute. Whether the prior decision is analogous or distinguishable is a matter of judgment and analysis, which provides opposing attorneys with plenty of room for argument.

In analyzing the precedential value of arguably distinguishable authority, you should pay attention to the rationale underlying the prior decision. Differences between the cases may be such that the reasons for the result in the prior decision do not apply to the current case. If so, the distinctions between the two cases justify a different result in the current case, or at least an analysis free of deference to the prior decision. Conversely, even though a prior decision does not provide a clear resolution of the current case because of differences between the two cases, many of the reasons for the legal result in the prior decision may apply equally to the current case. If so, the prior case—although not clearly controlling—is *analogous* to the current case in a way that may justify the same legal result in both.

Of course, this process of either restricting or extending the application of precedent in relation to a new dispute is far from an exact science. The determination whether a prior decision supports a proposed outcome in a new case may implicate the most deeply held values of those who must interpret and apply the precedent:

> Like the antebellum judges who denied relief to fugitive slaves . . . the Court today claims that its decision, however harsh, is compelled by existing legal doctrine. On the contrary, the question presented by this case is an open one, and our Fourteenth Amendment precedents may be read more broadly or narrowly depending upon how one chooses to read them. Faced with the choice, I would adopt a "sympathetic" reading, one which comports with dictates of fundamental justice and recognizes that compassion need not be exiled from the province of judging.[14]

Although uncertainty about the reasons for a prior decision often complicates the analysis, courts regularly engage in the processes of distinction and analogy to limit, extend, refine, and clarify the rules of prior decisions. Indeed, the precise parameters of the rule of a decision typically do not become clear until courts analyze the decision in subsequent decisions in the context of other disputes. This inquiry is largely one of defining, limiting, and extending the holdings of prior decisions; you will revisit it when you study techniques of briefing cases in Chapter 7.

2. EXAMPLE: WARRANTLESS SEARCHES OF CARS, HOUSES, AND MOBILE HOMES

Supreme Court decisions interpreting and applying the Fourth Amendment to the United States Constitution[15] illustrate the techniques of analogy and

14. DeShaney v. Winnebago County Dep't of Soc. Serv., 489 U.S. 189, 212-13 (1989) (Blackmun, J., dissenting).
15. The Fourth Amendment to the United States Constitution prohibits unreasonable searches and seizures by government officials:

> The right of the people to be secure in their persons, houses, papers, and effects, against unreasonable searches and seizures, shall not be violated, and no Warrants

distinction. In *Carroll v. United States*,[16] the Supreme Court held that the Fourth Amendment permitted federal officers to search an automobile without first obtaining a warrant. The Court reasoned that, although a suspect may have privacy interests in the contents of an automobile, the ready mobility of the automobile makes it impracticable for officers to obtain a warrant before searching.[17] Seven months later, in *Agnello v. United States*,[18] the Supreme Court held that the Fourth Amendment prohibited the warrantless search of the home of a suspect who had been arrested in another location.[19] In disapproving the warrantless search, the *Agnello* Court distinguished *Carroll* on the bases of the immobility of the house and the particularly great privacy interests the owner has in the contents of a house.[20]

Sixty years after *Carroll* and *Agnello*, in *California v. Carney*,[21] the Court considered whether the Fourth Amendment prohibited law enforcement officers from engaging in a warrantless search of a fully mobile motor home. Neither *Carroll* nor *Agnello* clearly controlled, because a motor home arguably combines the mobility of an automobile and the privacy interests associated with a house.[22] Consequently, the result in *Carney* under the doctrine of stare decisis depended on whether the Court found the facts of the case to be more nearly analogous to those of *Carroll* or to those of cases like *Agnello*.

The California Supreme Court had disapproved the search on two grounds. First, it had analogized *Carney* to cases like *Agnello*, reasoning that the nature of the contents of a motor home creates similarly high expectations of privacy in those contents as the privacy expectations that one has in the contents of a house. Second, it had distinguished *Carroll* on the basis of the comparatively low expectation of privacy that an owner has in the contents of an automobile.[23]

On review, the United States Supreme Court reversed the decision of the California Supreme Court. It analogized the case to *Carroll*, reasoning that an automobile and a motor home are not only similarly mobile but are similar in the reduced expectations of privacy in their contents. The expectations of privacy in a motor home are low partly because of the

---

shall issue, but upon probable cause, supported by Oath or affirmation, and particularly describing the place to be searched, and the persons or things to be seized.

16. 267 U.S. 132 (1925).

17. *Id.* at 153; California v. Carney, 471 U.S. 386, 390 (1985) (quoting and interpreting *Carroll*). Under *Carroll*, even if a warrant is not required, the searching officers must have probable cause to believe that the car contains contraband before they can search it. *Carroll*, 267 U.S. at 153-62. Discussion of the issue of probable cause, however, is not necessary to the analysis in the text above.

18. 269 U.S. 20 (1925), *overruled in part*, United States v. Havens, 446 U.S. 620 (1980).

19. Long before Carroll v. United States, the Supreme Court had assumed that police generally could not search a house without a warrant, unless the search was incidental to a lawful arrest in the house. *Agnello*, 269 U.S. at 32 (interpreting Boyd v. United States, 116 U.S. 616 (1886)). The Court did not directly decide that question, however, until *Agnello*, a few months after *Carroll*. *Agnello*, 269 U.S. at 32.

20. *Agnello*, 269 U.S. at 31-33; *see also* Payton v. New York, 445 U.S. 573, 585-90 (1980).

21. 471 U.S. 386 (1985).

22. *See id.* at 395 (Stevens, J., dissenting).

23. People v. Carney, 668 P.2d 807, 810-14 (Cal. 1983).

pervasive governmental regulation applicable to all licensed motor vehicles.[24] The state and federal Supreme Courts applied the precedent differently because they differed in their analyses, primarily factual, of the expectations of privacy that one has in the contents of a motor home.

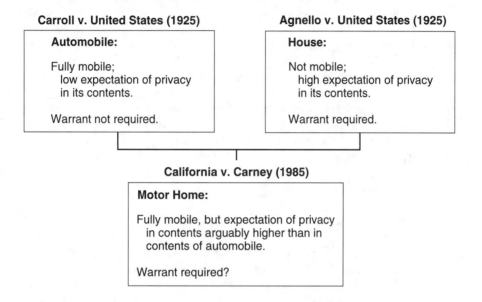

B. Overruling Precedent

1. STANDARDS FOR DEPARTING FROM NORMAL APPLICATION OF STARE DECISIS

A court's own precedent, or that of a higher court within the same jurisdiction, normally is controlling if it is materially indistinguishable from the dispute now before the court. In most court systems, a lower court is absolutely bound by the controlling precedent of the appellate courts that review its decisions.[25] However, the doctrine of stare decisis is more flexible in the courts that created the precedent.[26] In exceptional circumstances, a court may depart from a strict application of stare decisis and refuse to follow its own precedent that otherwise would be controlling. In so doing, it overrules the prior decision and substitutes new precedent in its place.

An early decision of the United States Supreme Court was surprisingly liberal in its approval of such departures from stare decisis:

> The rule of *stare decisis*, though one tending to consistency and uniformity of decision, is not inflexible. Whether it shall be followed or departed from

---

24. California v. Carney, 471 U.S. 386, 390-94 (1985); *see also* New York v. Class, 475 U.S. 106 (1986).
25. *See, e.g.*, Hutto v. Davis, 454 U.S. 370, 375 (1982).
26. *See, e.g.*, Jaffree v. Wallace, 705 F.2d 1526, 1532 (11th Cir. 1983), *aff'd*, 472 U.S. 38 (1985).

is a question entirely within the discretion of the court, which is again called upon to consider a question once decided.[27]

A more recent statement of the Supreme Court is more cautious: "[A]ny departure from the doctrine of stare decisis demands special justification."[28] More specifically, "informed by a series of prudential and pragmatic considerations," the Supreme Court may feel justified in overruling its prior decision in the following special circumstances:

1. "related principles of law have so far developed as to have left the old rule no more than a remnant of abandoned doctrine"; or
2. "facts have so changed or come to be seen so differently, as to have robbed the old rule of significant application or justification"; or
3. "a prior judicial ruling should come to be seen so clearly as error that its enforcement was for that very reason doomed"; or
4. "the rule has proved to be intolerable simply in defying practical workability."[29]

2. CHANGES IN SOCIAL AND LEGAL CONTEXT

In accordance with the first two justifications, a court may overrule a previous decision that was sensible in light of its original social, economic, technological, and legal context but that fails to serve important policies in current conditions. In one case, for example, a court overruled its own precedent to recognize a legal right on behalf of deceased fetus under wrongful death and survival statutes.[30] The court justified its departure from precedent partly on the basis of intervening advances in medical knowledge and on changes in the laws of other states.[31]

3. ABANDONMENT OF ERRONEOUS OR UNWORKABLE PRECEDENT

Even absent an intervening change in conditions, a court may overrule a prior decision simply because it thinks that the prior decision was poorly reasoned at the outset or has proved to be unworkable in light of experience.[32] In 1985, for example, the United States Supreme Court overruled a decision it had issued in 1976 on a question of state sovereignty under the Tenth Amendment,[33] even though that precedent had itself overruled another

---

27. Hertz v. Woodman, 218 U.S. 205, 212 (1910).
28. Arizona v. Rumsey, 467 U.S. 203, 212 (1984); *see also* Patterson v. McLean Credit Union, 491 U.S. 164, 172-73 (1989).
29. Planned Parenthood of S.E. Pa. v. Casey, 505 U.S. 833, 854-55 (1992).
30. Amadio v. Levin, 501 A.2d 1085 (Pa. 1985).
31. *Id.* at 1094-97.
32. *See* Geoffrey R. Stone, *Precedent, the Amendment Process, and Evolution in Constitutional Doctrine,* 11 Harv. J.L. & Pub. Pol'y 67, 71 (1988).
33. The Tenth Amendment to the United States Constitution reserves power to the states:

The powers not delegated to the United States by the Constitution, nor prohibited by it to the States, are reserved to the States respectively, or to the people.

decision that the Supreme Court had issued in 1968.[34] In the last of these three decisions the Court explained:

> We do not lightly overrule recent precedent. We have not hesitated, however, when it has become apparent that a prior decision has departed from a proper understanding of congressional power under the Commerce Clause.[35]

4. FLEXIBLE APPLICATION OF STARE DECISIS TO CONSTITUTIONAL ISSUES

The Supreme Court's double reverse on the proper interpretation of the Tenth Amendment in the space of 17 years may simply exemplify a more general relationship between the Supreme Court and the United States Constitution. Article V of the Constitution provides that an amendment to the Constitution is not effective unless approved by two-thirds of each house of Congress and ratified by three-fourths of the states. Thus, Congress cannot easily amend the Constitution to reflect changing social or economic conditions or to overrule judicial interpretations of the Constitution with which Congress disagrees. In recent history, for example, Congress marshaled sufficient votes to propose the Equal Rights Amendment and even to extend the time within which the states could ratify it, but fewer than the requisite number of states ratified.[36] Consequently, some scholars and judges believe that the Supreme Court should "keep [constitutional] law in accord with the dynamic flow of the social order," with less than the normal restraints of stare decisis.[37]

Nonetheless, countervailing considerations may justify adherence to stare decisis in some cases, even when fundamental constitutional rights are at issue. First, people may have so substantially relied on an established proposition of law that overruling the prior decision would result in "special hardship" and "inequity."[38] Second, an extraordinarily divisive issue may call for a ruling that is sufficiently durable to erase all doubts about its vulnerability to continuing political pressures. This consideration is present

---

34. Garcia v. San Antonio Metro. Transit Auth., 469 U.S. 528 (1985), *overruling* National League of Cities v. Usery, 426 U.S. 833, 854-55 (1976) (which itself had overruled Maryland v. Wirtz, 392 U.S. 183, 198 (1968), on the ground that *Wirtz* had relied on "simply wrong" dicta in United States v. California, 297 U.S. 175, 184-85 (1936)).

35. *Garcia*, 469 U.S. at 557.

36. *See* John E. Nowak, Ronald D. Rotunda & J. Nelson Young, CONSTITUTIONAL LAW 845 n.62 (6th ed. 2000). In an exceptional reaction to a particular ruling of the Supreme Court, Congress proposed, and the states ratified, the Eleventh Amendment as a way of overruling Chisholm v. Georgia, 2 U.S. (2 Dall.) 419 (1793). *See* Nowak, Rotunda & Young, at 47-48.

37. Edgar Bodenheimer, JURISPRUDENCE: THE PHILOSOPHY AND METHOD OF THE LAW 430 (rev. ed. 1974); *see also* Seminole Tribe of Fla. v. Florida, 517 U.S. 44, 63 (1996) (adopting flexible approach to stare decisis in abandoning Supreme Court precedent interpreting the Eleventh Amendment). *But cf.* Arizona v. Rumsey, 467 U.S. 203, 212 (1984) (even though stare decisis may be relaxed in constitutional cases, departure from precedent still "demands special justification").

38. Planned Parenthood of S.E. Pa. v. Casey, 505 U.S. 833, 854 (1992); *see also* Dickerson v. United States, 530 U.S. 428 (2000) (invoking stare decisis in declining to overrule Miranda v. Arizona, 384 U.S. 436 (1966), which spawned the *Miranda* warnings and which in turn "have become part of our national culture").

whenever the Court's interpretation of the Constitution calls the con-
tending sides of a national controversy to end their national division by
accepting a common mandate rooted in the Constitution.

The Court is not asked to do this very often. . . . But when the
Court does act in this way, its decision requires an equally rare precedential
force to counter the inevitable efforts to overturn it and to thwart its
implementation. . . . [O]nly the most convincing justification under accepted standards of precedent could suffice to demonstrate that a later
decision overruling the first was anything but a surrender to political
pressure. . . .[39]

In *Planned Parenthood of Southeastern Pennsylvania v. Casey*,[40] the Supreme
Court invoked both of these considerations in declining to abandon the
central rule of *Roe v. Wade*,[41] which established a woman's limited constitutional right to terminate a pregnancy.

The Court conceded that the reliance factor weighs most heavily in
commercial contexts, "where advance planning of great precision is most
obviously a necessity."[42] However, even in the noncommercial contexts of
reproduction and sexual equality, reliance could not be discounted:

> [F]or two decades of economic and social developments, people have orga-
> nized intimate relationships and made choices that define their views of
> themselves and their places in society, in reliance on the availability of
> abortion in the event that contraception should fail. The ability of women
> to participate equally in the economic and social life of the Nation has been
> facilitated by their ability to control their reproductive lives. . . . The
> Constitution serves human values, and while the effect of reliance on *Roe*
> cannot be exactly measured, neither can the certain cost of overruling *Roe*
> for people who have ordered their thinking and living around that case be
> dismissed.[43]

Moreover, in the context of extraordinary national division over abortion
rights, a dramatic change in the course of constitutional law might fan the
flames of controversy by suggesting that continued strife could inspire further
changes in course:

> The court's duty in the present case is clear. In 1973, it confronted
> the already-divisive issue of governmental power to limit personal choice
> to undergo abortion, for which it provided a new resolution based on the
> due process guaranteed by the Fourteenth Amendment. Whether or not
> a new social consensus is developing on that issue, its divisiveness is no less
> today than in 1973, and pressure to overrule the decision, like pressure to
> retain it, has grown only more intense. A decision to overrule *Roe*'s essential
> holding under the existing circumstances would address error, if error there

---

39. *Casey*, 505 U.S. at 867.
40. 505 U.S. 833 (1992).
41. 410 U.S. 113 (1973).
42. *Casey*, 505 U.S. at 855-56.
43. *Id.* at 856.

was, at the cost of both profound and unnecessary damage to the Court's legitimacy, and to the Nation's commitment to the rule of law.[44]

Moreover, the central rule of *Roe* had not proved unworkable and had not been eroded by changes in facts or in related principles of law. Accordingly, although the Court departed from *Roe* in other respects, it reaffirmed *Roe*'s "essential holding,"[45] staying substantially within the boundaries dictated by stare decisis.

IV. SUMMARY

Under the doctrine of stare decisis, a court endeavors to decide each case consistently with its prior decisions. This policy of consistency permits a court to depart from its prior decisions, or precedent, if those decisions are distinguishable from the current dispute. Even if a prior decision is not distinguishable, a court may depart from stare decisis and overrule its own precedent if a different rule of law would better respond to current social and economic conditions.

Stare decisis is less flexible with respect to the precedent of a higher court in the same jurisdiction: A trial court or intermediate court of appeals must distinguish or apply the precedent of a court that reviews its decisions. A court is never bound to apply the precedent of a lower court or any court in another jurisdiction, although it may treat such decisions as persuasive authority.

Exercise 5-1

Analyze the following problems based on decisions of the fictitious Calzona Supreme Court. For further practice in analyzing precedent, perform Problem 1 in Appendix II, near the end of this book.

PRECEDENT: *SMITH V. COLLIER*, 47 CALZ. 78 (1891)

On February 1, Smith and Collier agreed to marry before the end of the year. They later set a wedding date of December 1. In November, Smith complained about Collier's habit of playing poker on Saturday nights. In retaliation, Collier announced that Collier would not marry Smith. Smith sued Collier for breach of contract, requesting compensatory and punitive damages. Smith did not allege that Collier committed a tort.

---

44. *Id.* at 868-69.
45. *Id.* at 846.

The opinion of the Calzona Supreme Court includes the following excerpt:

> We affirm the trial court's factual findings that Collier breached the marriage contract with the malicious intent to cause Smith injury. Although the courts of this state recognize a general rule against punitive damages for breach of contract, the trial court correctly instructed the jury that it could award punitive damages as well as compensatory damages in this case.

1. DISTINGUISHING *SMITH V. COLLIER*

In the following cases, you represent the defendant. Identify the facts in *Smith v. Collier* that appear to have motivated the court to permit an award of punitive damages. Identify factual differences in your case that might motivate the Calzona Supreme Court to distinguish *Smith v. Collier* and to rule that punitive damages cannot be awarded against your client. Explain why those factual differences justify a different result from the ruling in *Smith v. Collier*. Identify any factual similarities between your case and *Smith v. Collier*. Explain why those similarities do not justify the same result as in *Smith v. Collier*. Which of the following cases is easiest to distinguish from *Smith v. Collier*?

a. *White v. Strunk*

White agreed to pay Strunk $100,000 for construction of a house on White's property. Strunk agreed to complete construction by August 1, regardless of weather or labor conditions. Unfortunately, abnormally frequent rainfall and faulty workmanship by subcontractors delayed Strunk's work. Despite Strunk's best efforts, he failed to complete construction by August 1, causing White to suffer economic losses.

b. *Roget v. Webster*

Roget agreed to pay Webster $100,000 in exchange for Webster's promise to construct a house on Roget's property. Before either Roget or Webster began performance, Ballentine offered to pay Webster $150,000 to build a similar house on Ballentine's property. Because he could not perform both jobs at once, and because a contract with Ballentine was more profitable, Webster repudiated his contract with Roget and accepted Ballentine's offer.

c. *White v. Benkowski*

White's property had no water supply. White agreed to pay Benkowski a monthly fee in exchange for fresh water supplied through pipes from Benkowski's well. After personal animosity developed between White and Benkowski, Benkowski maliciously shut off the water supply to White's property.

2. OVERRULING *SMITH V. COLLIER*

You represent the defendant in *Statler v. Corbin,* a contemporary case that is factually and procedurally indistinguishable from *Smith v. Collier.* Explain why the Calzona Supreme Court should overrule *Smith v. Collier* and disallow punitive damages for breach of a marriage agreement.

3. DISTINGUISHING *STATLER V. CORBIN*, 305 CALZ. 219 (2002)

In *Statler v. Corbin*, the Calzona Supreme Court overruled *Smith v. Collier* and held that punitive damages are not available to remedy even a malicious breach of a marriage contract. In the following case, *Jones v. Marsh*, you represent the plaintiff. Identify factual or procedural differences between *Statler v. Corbin* and your case and explain why those differences justify an award of punitive damages in your case.

    Jones v. Marsh—In July, Jones and Marsh agreed to marry on November 1. At a family reunion in August, Marsh broke off the engagement in a public statement in which he cruelly humiliated Jones. In addition to proving breach of contract, you have alleged and proved that Marsh intentionally inflicted emotional distress on Jones, conduct that is actionable as a tort in Calzona. In opposing Jones's request for punitive damages, Marsh relies on *Statler v. Corbin*.

Chapter 6

Deductive Reasoning and
IRAC—Introduction to Legal Analysis

I. OVERVIEW—SOLVING LEGAL PROBLEMS

Attorneys perform many tasks for clients that may not directly relate to litigation of legal disputes, including estate and tax planning, business counseling, and legislative lobbying. Even these tasks, however, may be inspired partly by the desire to avoid or influence future litigation. Moreover, many people consult an attorney only after they have become embroiled in a legal dispute in which litigation has commenced or is imminent. With a little luck and skill, the parties or their attorneys may still avoid formal litigation in court by using alternative dispute resolution (ADR) such as negotiation, mediation, or informal arbitration.[1] However, at least some of these methods of ADR require the parties to evaluate or present their cases within a general legal framework. Consequently, legal method relating to litigation of legal disputes is an important component of nearly every attorney's practice.

1. *See, e.g.,* Stephen G. Goldberg, Frank E. A. Sander & Nancy H. Rogers, Dispute Resolution (1992).

As explored in detail in Chapter 18, a lawsuit is formally commenced with the filing of "pleadings": The plaintiff brings suit by filing a "complaint" against the defendant, and the defendant responds by filing an "answer." If you represent a party in the early stages of such litigation, you must evaluate the strengths and weaknesses of your client's claims or defenses to help you prepare for various stages of advocacy, from the pleadings and settlement negotiations to trial and appeal. In a large or medium-sized law firm, you typically will communicate your evaluation to other members of the firm in an office memorandum of law, discussed in detail in Part V of this book. The principal means of persuading a judge or other adjudicatory body to accept your client's legal claims or defenses is a written brief, discussed in detail in Parts VI-VIII. To prepare either kind of document, you must apply fundamental skills of legal method and analysis that you develop in the first year of law school, as discussed in Parts II-IV.

This chapter examines methods of solving legal problems in the context of litigation of legal disputes. It builds on the groundwork laid in Chapters 3-5, and it provides an overview for more detailed discussions of legal method and analysis found throughout the remaining chapters.

II. OVERVIEW OF DEDUCTIVE REASONING AND IRAC

A. Deductive Reasoning in the Law—Uses and Limitations

1. The Legal Syllogism

Most essay examinations, office memoranda, and briefs require more than purely abstract legal analysis: They require you to apply legal standards to specific facts to reach a conclusion. In many cases, the analysis follows a pattern of deductive reasoning known as the "syllogism," which derives a conclusion from a major premise and a minor premise:

Major Premise:	All humans are mortal.
Minor Premise:	Socrates is human.
Conclusion:	Therefore, Socrates is mortal.[2]

In a legal argument, the major premise is a legal rule that helps resolve the issue raised by the parties to the dispute. It may represent the terms of a statute, the holding of a single judicial decision that acts as precedent, or a general principle derived from a series of previous decisions. The minor premise of a legal argument generally is a set of facts taken from the dispute that you are analyzing. The conclusion represents your resolution of the

---

2. *See* Irving M. Copi, Introduction to Logic § 1.6, at 24-27 (10th ed. 1998).

question whether the facts stated in the minor premise satisfy the legal standard stated in the major premise.

2. VALIDITY AND CORRECTNESS OF LEGAL SYLLOGISMS

A deductive argument is *valid* if its conclusion follows necessarily from its premises, but the *correctness* or *truth* of the conclusion of a valid argument depends on the truth of its premises.[3] For example, the Fourth Amendment to the United States Constitution ordinarily requires a police officer to obtain a search warrant from a judicial officer before searching an enclosed structure such as a house. Under the automobile exception, however, an officer may search an automobile without a warrant if she has probable cause to believe that it contains evidence of a crime. Suppose that a police officer searched Jack Greenberg's motor home without a warrant and found illegal drugs. In the state's criminal prosecution of Greenberg for possession of the illegal drugs, the state might advance the following valid deductive argument:

Major Premise:	The automobile exception to the Fourth Amendment's warrant requirement applies to all vehicles with mobility similar to that of an automobile on a street or highway.
Minor Premise:	Even while parked in Greenberg's backyard, Greenberg's motor home was a vehicle with mobility similar to that of an automobile on a street or highway.
Conclusion:	The automobile exception to the Fourth Amendment's warrant requirement applied to Greenberg's motor home while it was parked in Greenberg's backyard.

Although the conclusion of this valid argument follows necessarily from the premises, the conclusion is not true if either of the premises is untrue. The attorney for each party will attempt to persuade the judge to reach a certain conclusion by inviting the judge to accept particular formulations of the major and minor premises and by rejecting others. For example, Greenberg's attorney could raise the Fourth Amendment issue by asking the judge to exclude the evidence obtained in the warrantless search of Greenberg's motor home. In response, the state prosecutor would advance the deductive argument above to demonstrate that the Fourth Amendment did not require the police to obtain a warrant to search Greenberg's motor home. Greenberg's attorney could attack this argument either by arguing as a matter of law that the prosecutor's major premise exaggerates the scope of the automobile exception or by establishing as a matter of fact that the prosecutor's minor premise exaggerates the mobility of the motor home parked in Greenberg's backyard.

A deductive argument is not valid if its conclusion does not follow

3. *See id.* at 23.

necessarily from its premises. For example, if Greenberg's attorney proved that Greenberg's motor home was significantly less mobile than an automobile on the street or highway, the judge would undoubtedly replace the prosecutor's untrue minor premise with the minor premise established by Greenberg's attorney. As reconstructed, the deductive argument would no longer be valid, because the prosecutor's conclusion would not follow from the original major premise and the new minor premise.

3. LIMITATIONS OF THE LEGAL SYLLOGISM

Deductive reasoning provides at least a rough organizational framework for most legal analyses in office memoranda, answers to essay examinations, and briefs. The usefulness of the syllogism in legal reasoning, however, is limited by the flexibility and uncertainty inherent in legal analysis. For example, to establish the major premise of your argument, you may state your interpretation of the holding of a previous decision or your synthesis of the holdings of a series of decisions. Until a judge expresses his opinion on the matter, however, you cannot be certain whether he will agree with your interpretation of previous decisions and thus with your statement of the major premise.

Indeed, the dominant description of legal method since the twentieth century, known as "legal realism," rejects the notion that the law is external to the judges and other officials who apply and enforce it. Instead, the law is simply a prediction about what such officials will do in the face of a dispute. Moreover, their decisions will be based on a complex set of motivations, including personal values and prejudices not explicitly accounted for in the formal abstract rule of law. Thus, judges or juries can take advantage of uncertainty in law or facts by manipulating them to justify results that they reach on other than purely logical grounds.[4]

In short, legal disputes cannot be analyzed with mathematical certainty:

> The life of the law has not been logic: it has been experience. The felt necessities of the time, the prevalent moral and political theories, intuitions of public policy, avowed or unconscious, even the prejudices which judges share with their fellow-men, have had a good deal more to do than the syllogism in determining the rules by which men should be governed.[5]

4. *See* J. W. Harris, LEGAL PHILOSOPHIES 93-98 (1980). The more recent Critical Legal Studies movement goes beyond legal realism to broadly attack contemporary legal method, scholarship, and education as a system that legitimizes and perpetuates an oppressive socioeconomic order. *See generally* Roberto M. Unger, THE CRITICAL LEGAL STUDIES MOVEMENT (1986); Mark Kelman, A GUIDE TO CRITICAL LEGAL STUDIES (1987); *Critical Legal Studies Symposium*, 36 Stan. L. Rev. 1 (1984). Scholars of Critical Race Theory and Feminist Jurisprudence more specifically charge that traditional legal reasoning is grounded in and helps to perpetuate racist and sexist institutions and attitudes. *See generally* Frances Schmid Holland, FEMINIST JURISPRUDENCE (1996); Richard Delgado & Jean Stefancic, CRITICAL RACE THEORY: AN INTRODUCTION (2001). In recent years, Latino and Latina scholars have developed a new branch of Critical Race Theory, popularly known as "LatCrit" theory. *See, e.g.*, Jean Stefancic, *Latino and Latina Critical Theory: An Annotated Bibliography*, 85 Cal. L. Rev. 1509 (1997).

5. Oliver Wendell Holmes, Jr., THE COMMON LAW 1 (1923); *see also id.* at 312 ("The distinctions of the law are founded on experience, not on logic. It therefore does not make the dealings of men dependent on a mathematical accuracy."); Neil MacCormick, LEGAL REASONING AND LEGAL THEORY 65-72 (1978) (discussing "the limits of deductive justification").

Nonetheless, the syllogism provides a useful starting point for discussing general techniques of presenting legal analyses.

B. IRAC

Most law students use the acronym "IRAC" to help them remember the elements of deductive reasoning. IRAC stands for Issue, Rule, Application, and Conclusion. Thus,

1. after identifying an Issue, you should
2. state the legal Rule that will help resolve the issue,
3. Apply the rule to the relevant facts, and
4. reach a Conclusion on the question of whether the facts satisfy the legal rule.

For example, the following excerpt of an answer to an essay examination discusses the availability of punitive damages in a tort action. Although the examination answer itself should not explicitly refer to IRAC, the margin notes below represent the elements that a student should keep in mind when formulating a complete response. In this example, after raising an issue about punitive damages, the student has summarized general legal rules regarding the availability of punitive damages, has applied them to the facts of the examination, and has reached a conclusion.

Punitive Damages—In addition to demanding compensation for his actual losses, Ling may request punitive damages, designed to punish the tortfeasor and to deter others from engaging in similar wrongdoing.	**Issue**
A jury has the discretion to award punitive damages if the tortfeasor acted with the malicious intent to cause harm. In many jurisdictions, punitive damages are also permitted if the tortfeasor acted with reckless disregard for the risk of harm to others. Unless exceptional circumstances justify the risky conduct, a person acts recklessly if he consciously engages in conduct that he knows or should know poses a great risk of harm to others.	**Rules**
In this case, Con Motor Co. did not maliciously intend to cause injury when it designed its Backfire sports car. In fact, the discussion at the May meeting shows that the board of directors genuinely hoped that the risky design would not cause accidents. However, Con's chief engineer informed the board of directors of her opinion that placement of the gas tank near the rear exterior of the car would create a risk of deadly explosion in even minor rear-end collisions. Yet, the directors approved that de-	**Application to Facts**

Conclusion

sign solely because it would save production costs of $100 per car. In so doing, Con's directors knowingly created a great risk of death or terrible injury to consumers without any socially significant justification.

Con Motor Co. thus acted recklessly, permitting a jury in many jurisdictions to assess punitive damages against it. Indeed, in a jurisdiction that requires proof of malicious intent to injure, this case would be a good vehicle for arguing for a liberalization of the standards to include recklessness as a basis for an award of punitive damages.

To help you avoid the oversimplification that may result from an excessively mechanical application of IRAC, later chapters of this book explore some sophisticated techniques of analysis that build on the general framework of deductive reasoning. Chapter 8, Section II introduces two variations of inductive reasoning, and Chapter 12, Section III.D tackles problems of organization that arise when an issue or subissue presents different layers or levels of syllogisms.

In the meantime, the remainder of this chapter thoroughly examines each of the elements of IRAC. In the next four sections, you will learn more about identifying Issues, formulating Rules, Applying rules to facts, and reaching Conclusions.

III. *"I"*—IDENTIFYING ISSUES FOR ANALYSIS

A. Defining Issues

A legal issue is a question that a judge, jury, agency hearing officer, arbitrator, or other adjudicator must resolve to determine the outcome of a legal dispute. Whenever an event creates the conditions for a legal dispute, you can identify potential legal issues immediately after the event, even though no party has yet begun to litigate a claim or has even made any demands on another.

Constitutions, statutes, agency regulations, case law, and perhaps even the private law of an agreement between the parties impose duties on some parties and correlative rights on others in the context of the event. Armed with at least a general knowledge of the law and of the facts of the event, you can address the question whether any party is liable to another for breach of a legal duty. If the law and its application to the facts are clearly governed by settled law, the question of liability may be easily answered and is more likely to be addressed in a settlement between the parties than in litigation. In a surprising proportion of cases, however, uncertainty in the content of the law or in the application of the law to novel facts will block your efforts to supply a definite resolution to a legal dispute. In those cases, however, you can advance arguments in support of either a potentially wronged victim or a potentially liable party. If the arguments for both parties have potential merit, you have identified a legal issue.

1. ISSUES AND SUBISSUES

A general issue may encompass discrete subissues. For example, case law establishes that a defendant generally will be liable to the plaintiff for damages caused by breach of contract if (A) the parties formed an enforceable contract and (B) the defendant failed to perform his contractual promises, thus breaching the contract. At the broadest level, the facts of a dispute might raise the general issue of whether the defendant is liable for breach of contract. More specifically, the facts may raise separate subissues about (A) contract formation and (B) performance and breach.

You may want to further subdivide these subissues to recognize multiple legal elements associated with each. For example, case law establishes two primary requirements for contract formation: (1) an agreement reached through a process of offer and acceptance and (2) "consideration" in the form of a mutually induced exchange. These elements are distinct, because parties are capable of agreeing to a transaction that does not satisfy the consideration requirement. Thus, within the subissue of contract formation, the law and the facts may raise a second level of subissues regarding (1) offer and acceptance and (2) consideration. Similarly, within the subissue of performance and breach, the law and the facts may raise a second level of subissues regarding, for example, (1) interpretation of the defendant's contractual promises and (2) possible discharge of the defendant's obligations because unforeseen circumstances made his performance impossible.

2. CONTINUING DEVELOPMENT OF ISSUES

At the inception of a dispute, incomplete knowledge of the facts and vagueness or ambiguity in the arguably applicable legal rules make the eventual outcome of the dispute particularly uncertain. At that stage, you can identify the issues only tentatively. As the dispute proceeds through stages of litigation, the issues will become increasingly well defined.

For example, a demand letter or complaint may reveal which of numerous potential legal claims a claimant has decided to advance, thus raising some questions of liability and eliminating others. Under modern rules of civil procedure, each party to a civil lawsuit must disclose some kinds of information to the opposing party, and each party may use various "discovery" devices to obtain certain other kinds of information from witnesses and from the opposing party.[6] This court-supervised discovery and disclosure process or other investigation may reveal that some claims or defenses are meritless and may raise new questions about others. Moreover, as explored in Chapters 19 and 20, a litigant may request that the court help define the issues by

---

6. *See* Fed. R. Civ. P. 26-37; Roger W. Kaufman, *Amending the Disclosure Amendments,* Ariz. Att'y, Mar. 1997, at 16 (summarizing history of Arizona's ambitious disclosure rules and changes in the sanctions for violations of those rules).

ruling before trial that certain evidence will be excluded from trial or even
that the litigant is entitled to judgment without trial on one or more issues.
In turn, these pretrial motions may raise separate issues under applicable
rules of evidence or procedure concerning the admissibility of evidence or
the proper application of standards for summary disposition. Finally, if the
dispute goes to trial, the nature of the disposition in the trial court and the
factual record developed in the trial court will help determine which issues
the losing party might reasonably raise on appeal.

As illustrated by these examples, the parties help to define the issues by
making strategic decisions about what claims and defenses to assert and
about which procedural vehicles should be used to assert them. With few
exceptions, courts will decline to address questions that are not raised by
either party to a dispute.[7]

3. MATERIALITY

Not every potential disagreement about the facts or the law amounts to a
legal issue. Even a hotly disputed question of fact or law would not be "in
issue" if it were immaterial. A disputed point is immaterial if it could not
affect the outcome of the lawsuit in light of other facts and rules of law.

To take an obvious example, suppose that evidence shows that the
defendant drove her car through an intersection and struck the plaintiff in
a pedestrian crosswalk. The defendant's liability for negligence would not
be affected by even a heated disagreement over the color of the socks that
the defendant wore that day. Assuming that the identity of the driver of the
car is conclusively established through some means other than the color of
the socks she wore, the issues of law and fact would instead include such
material questions as the following:

1. Which party had the green light?
2. What injuries did the plaintiff sustain?
3. Does the law permit the jury to reduce the plaintiff's recovery if his
   own negligence combined with that of the defendant to cause his
   injuries?

Of course, many cases raise closer questions of materiality than that in
the example above. As discussed in the next section, some questions of

---

7. *See, e.g.*, Yee v. Escondido, 503 U.S. 519, 533 (1992) (Supreme Court "has, with
very rare exceptions, refused to consider petitioners' claims that were not raised or addressed
below."); Amcel Corp. v. International Exec. Sales, Inc., 170 F.3d 32 (1st Cir. 1999) (discussing
reasons for not addressing claims or legal theories that party neglected to raise in the trial
court); Hershinow v. Bonamarte, 735 F.2d 264, 266 (7th Cir. 1984) (waiver of claim presented
to appellate court in perfunctory manner); State v. Santana-Lopez, 613 N.W.2d 918, 921
n.3, 922 n.4 (Wis. App. 2000) (waiver of one argument not presented on appeal and of
another argument presented only in a footnote in an appellate brief). *But cf. Yee*, 503 U.S.
at 534-35 (if claim was properly presented below, appellate court will entertain a new *argument*
in support of that claim); Giannakos v. M/V Bravo Trader, 762 F.2d 1295, 1297 (5th Cir.
1985) (federal trial and appellate courts must address questions of federal subject-matter
jurisdiction on their own motions); *In re* Pizza of Haw. Inc., 761 F.2d 1374, 1377-78 (9th
Cir. 1985) (appellate court must determine appellate jurisdiction on its own motion); *In re*
Pacific Trencher & Equip., Inc., 735 F.2d 362, 364 (9th Cir. 1984) (discretionary appellate
consideration of pure question of law not raised in the trial court).

materiality may be a matter of degree requiring the exercise of judgment in selecting issues for discussion or argument in a legal document.

Exercise 6-1

Although United States jurisdictions have enacted criminal codes that largely supersede the early criminal common law, imagine a state that still applies the common law definition of the crime of burglary: the breaking and entering of a dwelling of another at night with the intent to commit a felony. As stated in Chapter 3, the law relating to this crime reflected a concern about a serious invasion of the right of habitation during hours of darkness, when the inhabitants were most vulnerable to attack and the invader most likely to escape recognition.

Armed only with this general knowledge of the law, identify the issues relating to the common law crime of burglary raised by the following facts:

> In June, Leova Rosales left her San Francisco apartment and drove her VW bus down the coast for a three-week vacation near Monterey Bay. Although she occasionally ate at restaurants or stayed with friends, she mostly slept in the back of the bus and prepared simple meals in the bus with groceries that she purchased at local stores.
>
> On the evening of June 20, Leova parked her bus in an overnight recreational-vehicle parking space at Seacliff State Beach. She prepared dinner from an ice chest in the back of the bus, leaving the driver's window in the cab completely open, with an expensive portable stereo radio and cassette player sitting on the driver's seat. She fell asleep in the back of her bus at 11:00 P.M. A curtain separated the sleeping area of the bus from the driver's cab; other curtains blocked light from the windows in the back of the van, enabling Leova to sleep late in the morning. At 5:15 A.M., just as the first hints of a sunrise glowed from the hilltops opposite the ocean, Robert Glass approached Leova's van. Through the open window next to the driver's seat, Robert spied the stereo equipment lying on the seat. Hoping to add it permanently to his own home system, Robert opened the closed but unlocked driver's door and placed his hand on the stereo equipment. At that moment, a patrolling police officer drove up to Leova's VW bus and arrested Robert for burglary and attempted larceny. Leova awoke only when the officer knocked on her bus after the arrest.

You may assume that theft of the stereo equipment would constitute felony larceny in the jurisdiction. In the prosecution of Robert Glass on the burglary charge, what elements of the common law crime of burglary would the prosecutor and defense attorney likely dispute? What elements of burglary are not reasonably in dispute? Would further facts help define or resolve the issues? Would case law that refines the law of burglary help define or resolve the issues? If you were assigned the task of preparing an office memorandum on this problem, what facts or law would you desire to investigate further?

B. Scope of Analysis

Any dispute of at least moderate complexity presents a range of potential legal theories and arguments that you might raise in litigation. At the near end of the spectrum are persuasive and conventional legal theories or arguments that a court would almost certainly address in analyzing the dispute. At the far end are legal theories or factual analogies of such doubtful merit or applicability that a court might view them as frivolous or immaterial to the outcome of the dispute.

The extent to which you discuss topics toward the far end of the spectrum is a question of "scope of analysis" and depends partly on the nature of your document. The scope of analysis typically is quite broad in a law school essay examination answer, somewhat narrower in an office memorandum addressed to a supervising attorney, and narrower still in a good brief addressed to a judge.

1. EXAMINATION ANSWERS

You will often touch on a broad range of issues in an examination answer because most law professors will specifically test your ability to spot issues. Indeed, on many examinations, you will earn a higher grade if you identify and briefly discuss all possible issues, including the less obvious and more exotic ones, than if you thoroughly analyze only the most obvious.

2. OFFICE MEMORANDA

In comparison, your supervising attorney may expect a slightly narrower scope of analysis in your office memorandum. She probably will want detailed discussion of significant issues and will generally encourage creative and aggressive analysis, but she may not have time to thoroughly examine more exotic theories or approaches if they are unlikely to have an effect on the outcome of the dispute. Unfortunately, you may be tempted to impress your supervisor with the long hours that you have spent in the library by describing in detail every legal theory or authority that made its way into your library notes. Your supervisor will not be impressed. She realizes that you will regularly investigate leads that bear no useful fruit, and she expects the final draft of your memorandum to shield her from the burden of retracing your steps down paths that led only to distracting tangents.

On the other hand, the materiality of a fact or theory may be difficult to assess in the early stages of litigation and fact investigation. Accordingly, if you draft an office memorandum at the early stages of a dispute, you should consider discussing close questions of scope of analysis with your supervising attorney before beginning to write. Absent specific direction from your supervisor, you probably should at least mention any argument of potential significance, even if only in a sentence or two. You can distinguish between a major theory and a less significant one in the depth of your analysis of each. Then, if later developments in the litigation establish the significance of an issue of previously questionable importance, you can analyze that issue in greater depth in a supplemental memorandum.

3. BRIEFS

When drafting a brief, you often must exercise even stricter control on the scope of analysis. Although creative and novel arguments often win appeals by inspiring changes in the law, some arguments are so clearly marginal that they may detract from the cumulative persuasiveness of the entire brief. If you add a nearly frivolous argument to one with greater merit, you reduce the number of pages within the maximum page limit that you can devote to the meritorious argument. Even worse, you may lose credibility on the whole brief.

This general advice about limiting the scope of briefs may apply with less force in criminal cases, in which a party's liberty, or even life, is at stake. In such cases, defense counsel may be reluctant to waive any argument that might possibly gain relief for her client, and she can realistically hope that some courts will carefully consider all plausible arguments.

IV. *"R"*—FORMULATING THE LEGAL RULE

A. Overview—Sources of Authority

Consistent with the general pattern of deductive reasoning, your first step in discussing a legal issue is to identify and analyze applicable legal rules. You will seldom find these rules clearly set forth in a single source of authority; the law that an adjudicator will apply to resolve a legal issue may be a combination of rules, any one of which may represent a synthesis of several sources of law. The relative importance of legal authorities to the analysis of the issue depends on such factors as

1. the primary or secondary nature of the authority;
2. the jurisdiction, in the sense of the political or geographical body, in which primary authority is controlling; and
3. if the primary authority is case law, the strength of the case law as precedent.

1. PRIMARY AND SECONDARY AUTHORITY

So far, this book has addressed only primary legal authority: direct statements of law issued by lawmaking bodies. Primary authority includes constitutions, statutes and local ordinances, administrative rules and regulations, and judicial opinions. Subject to limitations discussed in Sections 2 and 3 below, a primary authority or combination of primary authorities will supply the applicable rule in any legal dispute.

Secondary authorities, such as treatises, restatements of the law, and law review articles, do not directly supply the rule of law in a legal dispute. Instead, they express a commentator's explanation of the law or his opinions about what the law should be. A secondary authority has persuasive value only: It may influence a court or legislature to act in a particular way, but it has no mandatory or binding effect.

An example of a popular treatise is PROSSER AND KEETON ON TORTS. This secondary authority generally describes tort law in United States jurisdictions and examines the relevant policies supporting competing approaches in the tort law of different states.

Another frequently cited example of secondary authority is the collection of Restatements of Law issued by the American Law Institute (ALI). The ALI has drafted two restatements of contract law, the Restatement of Contracts (1932) and the Restatement (Second) of Contracts (1979). Each of these is divided into numerous sections and subsections, most of which attempt to summarize rules of the common law of contracts generally accepted when the restatement was drafted. A few sections, however, are meant to influence the law by promoting trends that had not yet been widely accepted at the time of drafting. Section 90 of the first restatement, for example, represented a relatively innovative view of a theory of recovery based on reliance, commonly known as "promissory estoppel." Although no court is required to follow the approach of either restatement, section 90 has influenced many courts. Beyond that, some courts have adopted the precise language of section 90 of the first or second restatement, thus incorporating it into their own case law and giving it the force of primary authority.[8] Beyond that, some courts have adopted a general policy of following the latest restatement rules on certain kinds of issues if no statute or case law addresses the point.[9]

Unless a court has adopted such a policy, however, or has already incorporated the content of a secondary authority into its primary authority, you should use secondary authority only as a starting point in your analysis. You may use secondary authorities to help you locate and understand primary authority or to help develop an argument not fully addressed or supported by primary authority. However, you should not base your legal analysis or argument on a secondary authority when helpful primary authority is available.

2. JURISDICTION IN WHICH PRIMARY AUTHORITY CONTROLS

Some federal constitutional, statutory, and special common laws apply broadly to all domestic jurisdictions. For example, the Thirteenth Amendment to the United States Constitution abolishes the institution of slavery

---

8. *See, e.g.*, Corbit v. J. I. Case Co., 424 P.2d 290, 300-01 (Wash. 1967) (en banc) (quoting § 90 as a "useful guideline").

9. *See, e.g.*, Smith v. Normart, 75 P.2d 38, 42 (Ariz. 1938) ("We have . . . announced that we would follow the Restatement of the Law where we are not bound by the previous decisions of this court or by legislative enactment. . . ."). *But cf.* Reed v. Real Detective Publ'g. Co., 162 P.2d 133, 138 (Ariz. 1945) ("We think it would be unwise to follow this rule blindly, particularly when to do so would result in the recognition of a new cause of action in this jurisdiction."); Ramirez v. Health Partners of So. Ariz., 972 P.2d 658, 665 (Ariz. Ct. App. 1999) ("Rather, we must consider whether the Restatement position, as applied to a particular claim, is logical, furthers the interests of justice, is consistent with Arizona law and policy, and has been generally acknowledged elsewhere.").

within the United States, whether practiced by a government or a private entity.

In contrast, the constitutional, statutory, and common laws of a state are mandatory, or must be applied, only within that state. For example, the Civil Code of California and the case law of the California courts interpreting that code do not have any binding effect on the law of torts, contracts, or property in New York. Similarly, the courts of one state are free to develop the common law of that state independently of the judicial development of common law in other states.

Even though the laws of one state do not directly apply to activities in another state, in some circumstances those laws may have at least persuasive influence in the other state. For example, in recognizing a common law tort of wrongful discharge of an employee, the Arizona Supreme Court drew guidance from the emerging common law of California and of other states.[10]

Indeed, even case law from one state interpreting a statute of that state could have a persuasive effect on the application of a statute of a different state, if the statutes in both states have similar or identical language and purposes. For example, the New York and New Hampshire legislatures have adopted identical versions of Uniform Commercial Code § 2-302, which authorizes a court to deny enforcement of a contract provision that is "unconscionable."[11] A New York trial court interpreting section 2-302 of New York's commercial code drew support from, though was not bound by, a decision of the New Hampshire Supreme Court interpreting the identical language in section 2-302 of New Hampshire's commercial code.[12]

3. STRENGTH OF CASE LAW AS PRECEDENT

As discussed in Chapter 5, the controlling or persuasive force of case law will depend on its strength as precedent under the doctrine of stare decisis. Section 2 above has further examined one aspect of this relationship: the relationship of the authority to the forum jurisdiction. The strength of case law as precedent also depends on

1. the relative levels of the court that created the precedent and the one applying it, and
2. the degree to which the precedent is directly controlling, rather than merely analogous, to the current dispute.

a. Level of Court

To summarize some of the lessons of Chapter 5, a trial court or intermediate court of appeals is strictly bound by squarely applicable precedent of a higher court within its court system. Moreover, although a court can overrule its

---

10. Wagenseller v. Scottsdale Mem'l Hosp., 710 P.2d 1025, 1030-31 (Ariz. 1985). This Arizona common law was later superseded by state legislation. ARIZ. REV. STAT. ANN. § 23-1501(3)(b) (West Supp. 1996).

11. N.H. Rev. Stat. Ann. § 382-A: 2-302 (1961); N.Y. U.C.C. LAW § 2-302 (McKinney 1964).

12. Jones v. Star Credit Corp., 59 Misc. 2d 189, 298 N.Y.S.2d 264 (N.Y. Sup. Ct. 1969) (citing American Home Improvement, Inc. v. MacIver, 201 A.2d 886 (N.H. 1964), for the proposition that § 2-302 applied to "price unconscionability").

own precedent, it will do so only in special circumstances warranting departure from the normal mandates of stare decisis. On the other hand, the court need not defer to the decisions of a lower court within the same system or decisions of courts from other systems; at most, those decisions would have persuasive effect.

Thus, whenever possible, you obviously should support your analyses or arguments with case law from an appellate court in your jurisdiction that is higher than the court in which your dispute is currently being adjudicated. The basis for a helpful illustration is provided by the description of the United States Courts of Appeals for the Ninth Circuit in Section II.A of Chapter 5. When writing a brief to that Court of Appeals, you should try to support your argument with United States Supreme Court precedent, which is binding on the Court of Appeals. If no Supreme Court authority applies, you can strongly support your argument with a previous decision of the Ninth Circuit Court of Appeals itself. Only a special 11-member panel of the Ninth Circuit can overrule such precedent. If no higher authority is available, you can derive some support for your argument from a published decision of the United States District Court for the Northern District of California, a federal trial court. However, because decisions of the District Court have only persuasive value in the Court of Appeals, you will then assume the burden of persuading the Court of Appeals that the District Court's decision represents the best legal approach, the approach that the Court of Appeals should adopt as its own. You might more strongly support your argument with a decision from the Court of Appeals for the Tenth Circuit, but that decision too would have only persuasive value.

b. Controlling, Analogous, and Distinguishable Authority

To once again summarize a portion of Chapter 5, the strength of case law as binding or persuasive authority also depends on the degree to which it squarely applies to the current dispute. Even precedent of a higher court within the same court system will not control the outcome of the dispute if it is distinguishable. The more significant are the distinctions between the precedent and the current dispute, the less nearly analogous is the precedent, thus decreasing the likelihood that the precedent from a higher court will control or even influence the outcome of the current dispute. Similarly, the persuasiveness of nonbinding authority from lower courts within the jurisdiction or from courts of other jurisdictions will depend in part on the degree of similarity between the precedent and the current dispute.

When evaluating the legally significant similarities or distinctions between precedent and the current dispute, you should resist the temptation to overemphasize superficial factual similarities that appear in legally distinct contexts. Consider, for example, a current dispute in which the plaintiff's new television set spontaneously generated an electrical fire, causing major damage to the plaintiff's home. In this dispute, the parties may raise the issue of whether the retailer is liable to the plaintiff on a claim of breach of the warranty of merchantability implied in the sales contract under the state's version of the Uniform Commercial Code (UCC).[13] Suppose further that

---

13. The UCC's warranty of merchantability implies a promise on the part of a merchant that goods are generally nondefective. U.C.C. § 2-314 (2000).

an appellate opinion in the state, issued in 1957, addresses another case in which a television set spontaneously burst into flames, setting fire to the plaintiff's home. The 1957 opinion, however, holds only that the plaintiff in that action, a consumer, failed to file his complaint within the time prescribed by the state's statute of limitations, which thus barred his action for negligent manufacture of the television set.

At first glance, the prior decision might appear significant because of the factual similarities of the events giving rise to the actions. In fact, however, the prior decision may be completely inapplicable. It does not interpret the UCC's warranty of merchantability in a contract for a sale of goods because it addresses a legally distinct cause of action in tort; indeed, the prior decision was issued before state enactment of the UCC and before the widespread adoption of more contemporary tort doctrines of products liability. Most important, the prior decision discusses only the bar of the statute of limitations; it does not directly address the elements of any claim for relief other than timely filing. More helpful to the current dispute would be analogous precedent that addresses the scope of the warranty of merchantability, even if in the context of different goods causing different kinds of accidents and injuries.

4. SUMMARY

Only primary authority within the forum jurisdiction is mandatory and potentially controlling. Primary authority from other jurisdictions and all secondary authority are persuasive only.

If the primary authority is case law within the forum jurisdiction, its strength as precedent will depend partly on the relative levels of the court that created the precedent and the court that will apply it. It will depend also on how closely analogous the precedent is to the current dispute.

Exercise 6-2

The Hazardous Materials Transportation Act (HMTA) of State X makes it a criminal offense to transport certain hazardous materials, such as toxic chemicals, except with statutorily specified safeguards. For example, the statute requires a transporter of regulated materials to first confine the materials in steel drums and then secure the drums within a cargo bay that is enclosed on the top and on all sides with material of specified strength. Leek Chemical Co. violated the HMTA by transporting highly toxic chemicals in steel drums secured to an open flatbed truck. The truck overturned on a slick highway, causing several of the barrels to roll across lanes of oncoming traffic. An automobile driven by Daniel Stein collided with one of the barrels, bursting the barrel and spreading the toxic chemical onto and into Stein's automobile. Stein was not seriously injured by the initial impact with the barrel; however, he was permanently injured by contact with the toxic chemical.

Stein sues Leek Chemical Co. in tort for damages, alleging both (1) strict liability for causing injury while engaged in an abnormally dangerous activity and (2) negligent transportation of the toxic chemicals. In State *X*, Leek Chemical Co. will be liable on the second claim for negligence if it engaged in a negligent act or omission through breach of a duty of care owed to Stein, causing Stein to suffer injury. Stein hopes to establish the element of negligent act through the doctrine of "negligence per se," which other states recognize but which the Supreme Court of State *X* has never squarely adopted. Under the strongest version of the doctrine of negligence per se, proof of Leek Chemical Co.'s violation of the HMTA, a safety statute, would conclusively establish the element of negligent act, without any further showing of a breach of a duty of care.

To help her evaluate proposed jury instructions at the close of the trial in Stein's lawsuit, the trial judge requests briefing and oral argument on the question of whether State *X* recognizes the doctrine of negligence per se. Stein has the following authority at his disposal:

1. abundant case law from other states recognizing the doctrine of negligence per se in a variety of contexts;
2. an opinion from the highest appellate court of neighboring State *Y* approving application of the doctrine of negligence per se to a violation of a similar hazardous materials transportation statute in State *Y*;
3. an opinion of the State *X* intermediate court of appeals holding that evidence of violation of the State *X* speed limit laws, proximately causing injury, supported a jury verdict of negligence, even in the absence of any other evidence of lack of due care;
4. an opinion of the Supreme Court of State *X* holding that a transporter of regulated hazardous materials may be criminally liable under the HMTA for intentional violations of that act's criminal provisions, even if the illegal transportation does not result in any accident or injury.

Discuss the relative strength of these authorities to Stein's position. How should Stein's attorney use each authority, if at all?

B. Analysis of Legal Standards

1. Depth of Analysis

In some legal disputes, formulation of the applicable legal rules is a simple task: The applicable laws are easily identified and their general content is clear, at least in the abstract. For example, a dispute over the jury's authority to grant punitive damages in a tort action may be governed by clearly defined rules in the forum state's case law. If so, you could summarize those rules directly and concisely in an office memorandum:

In this state, a jury may award punitive damages against a person who has committed a tort with either (1) intent to cause injury or (2) reckless disregard for the risk of harm to others. *Ray v. Bradbury.* . . . Unless exceptional circumstances justify the risky conduct, a person acts recklessly if he consciously engages in conduct that he knows poses a great risk of harm to others. *Id.* at 327.

In such a dispute, once the facts are found, any significant uncertainty about the outcome of the dispute typically derives from a mixed question of fact and law: Do the particular facts of the case satisfy the legal rule? Although analysis of such a mixed question necessarily involves refinement of the content of the legal rule, it also requires careful evaluation of the facts. Thus, assuming that *Ray v. Bradbury* reflects current policy in the jurisdiction, the alleged tortfeasor will not likely dispute the abstract rule governing the availability of punitive damages. More substantially in issue is a mixed question of fact and law: Do the facts of the case satisfy the legal rule by reflecting recklessness or an intent to injure?

In other disputes, however, the parties may raise substantial issues about the fundamental content of applicable legal rules, such as the issue discussed in Chapter 4 of whether the word "sex" in Title VII of the Civil Rights Act of 1964 refers narrowly to gender or more broadly to sexual identity, activities, and orientation. Compared to the dispute described in the preceding paragraph, resolution of this question requires less comprehensive fact analysis and more thorough analysis of the content of the rule at a fairly abstract level. An even more extreme example is provided by the question of whether a court should change the course of the common law by adopting a new theory of tort liability for wrongful discharge of an employee. Although such a question would arise in the context of the facts of a particular dispute, the question of whether to adopt a new common law theory of liability would be analyzed as a nearly pure question of law.

If an issue in a brief, office memorandum, or answer to a law school essay examination raises a question about the fundamental content of a legal rule at a general level, you should analyze the legal rule thoroughly, or in depth, before engaging in substantial fact analysis. The discussions of common law and statutory law in Chapters 3 and 4 provide a foundation for the development of techniques of legal analysis. Three techniques are particularly important

1. recognition of the hierarchical nature of authority,
2. consideration of policy concerns, and
3. synthesis of incremental authority.

2. HIERARCHY OF AUTHORITY

Constitutional, statutory, and common laws form a hierarchy in descending order of priority: Assuming that the applicable state or federal constitution authorizes the exercise of state or federal power, a legislature can overrule or modify the common law by enacting statutory law. Accordingly, rather than assume that an issue is governed by common law, you should first consider the possible applicability of constitutional or statutory law.

If a statute applies, you should begin your research and analysis with the relevant language of the statute, even though it may be insufficiently narrow to clearly resolve the issue by itself. Only after you have studied the letter of the statute and its context within an act or a code system can you fully appreciate interpretive case law on the matter. The following passage from an office memorandum illustrates the hierarchy of authority and the focus on statutory language.

Constitution

The Arizona Constitution grants municipalities the right to engage in industrial activities: "The State of Arizona and each municipal corporation within the State of Arizona shall have the right to engage in industrial pursuits." Ariz. Const. art. 2, § 24. The Arizona Public Utilities statute more specifically grants municipal corporations the power to acquire water utility corporations "within or without its corporate limits":

Statute

> [Municipal corporations may] engage in any business or enterprise which may be engaged in by persons by virtue of a franchise from the municipal corporation, and may construct, purchase, acquire, own and maintain within or without its corporate limits any such business or enterprise.

Ariz. Rev. Stat. Ann. § 9-511 (West 1996). The statutory reference to corporate limits appears without qualification to permit a municipal corporation to acquire utilities that provide service outside the municipality's corporate limits. Arizona case law, however, hints at a narrower interpretation of the statue that recognizes two limitations on the acquisition power.

Case Law

First, it is unclear whether a city may acquire a water company's property outside the city corporate limits unless the city has shown that it genuinely and reasonably anticipates future growth into that area. *See Sende Vista Water Co. v. City of Phoenix*, 617 P.2d 1158 (Ariz. Ct. App. 1980). In *Sende*, ...

In theory, the principle of analyzing statutory language before turning to interpretive case law also applies to constitutional provisions, as illustrated in the example above. As a practical matter, however, some constitutional provisions are so general that their actual language may provide quite limited guidance, and interpretive case law takes on special significance. For example, the reference to "equal protection" in the Fourteenth Amendment to the United States Constitution is purposefully vague; its generality invites the courts to shape its contours in a way that best satisfies its underlying policies. The mass of case law interpreting the Equal Protection Clause has embellished this simple clause with rich detail. Accordingly, when researching and analyzing an equal protection problem, you should not begin with a grammatical analysis of the words "equal protection." Instead, after identifying the Fourteenth Amendment as the source of the clause, you could appropriately turn immediately to interpretive case law.

3. POLICY ANALYSIS

Almost by definition, policy analysis lies at the heart of most lawmaking. A legislature pronounces public policy when it enacts public legislation within the framework of applicable constitutions. Any such enactment represents elected officials' choice among alternative means to address the socioeconomic needs of the jurisdiction. Not surprisingly, the search for legislative intent typically does not end with a conclusive grammatical analysis of language or with a reference to specific and definitive legislative history. Instead, statutory interpretation most often takes the form of a multifaceted analysis reconciling the statutory language, legislative history, and general rules of construction with the apparent policies or purposes on which the legislation is based. Constitutions are less specific than most statutes and are not so easily amended; consequently, analysis of policy and general purpose often is even more important in constitutional interpretation.

Similarly, because common law rules are largely a reflection of judicial recognition of community needs, habits, or customs, they constitute the judiciary's pronouncement of public policy within the framework of constitutional and statutory law. Any question about further development of the common law, such as adoption of a new theory of common law liability or elimination of a common law basis for damages, necessarily raises policy questions about the effect that the new rule will have on the community and about the relationship of the new rule to legislative policies.

The arguments and conclusions that you develop in response to a policy question depend in part on the values that you apply to the problem. A policy argument may be based on moral, economic, political, institutional, or other social values.[14] When developing or evaluating a legal argument, you should identify the values underlying the legislative purpose and judicial policy of applicable authorities, and you should determine which policy arguments would best advance your client's position.[15]

---

14. *See* P. S. Atiyah & Robert S. Summers, FORM AND SUBSTANCE IN ANGLO-AMERICAN LAW 5 (1987) (defining "substantive reasons" for legal decisions); *see also* Robert S. Summers, *Two Types of Substantive Reasons: The Core of a Theory of Common-Law Justification*, 63 Cornell L. Rev. 707 (1978).

15. *See generally* J. M. Balkin, *The Crystalline Structure of Legal Thought*, 39 Rutgers L. Rev. 1 (1986).

E x e r c i s e 6-3

POLICY ANALYSIS—SURROGATE MOTHERHOOD AND BABY SELLING

State *X* has a criminal "baby selling" statute making it a felony "to relinquish custody of one's child to another for payment, or to pay or offer to pay another to relinquish custody of the other's child." What is the likely policy behind this statute, and what kind of conduct should be its primary concern? In light of your understanding of the statutory policy, should a court interpret the statute to prohibit a surrogate mother from charging a fee for carrying the fertilized ovum of another couple to full term and surrendering custody of the child to the couple after birth? Does the analysis change if the one charging the fee agrees to artificial insemination of her own ovum, thus making her the biological mother? Should the state enact new legislation more specifically addressing surrogate mother contracts?

4. SYNTHESIS OF INCREMENTAL LAW

In few research problems is the legal standard set forth in a single, clearly controlling authority. More often, the legal rules that apply to a dispute are the products of a synthesis of multiple authorities. For example, a Reconstruction era civil rights statute imposes liability for racial discrimination in private contractual relations,[16] but its application is tempered by constitutional interests in privacy and free association.[17] Thus, the true reach of the statute is defined both by the language of the statute and by the First Amendment to the United States Constitution.

Synthesis of authority is particularly important in analysis of case law. Whether judicial opinions interpret statutory or constitutional law or develop common law, the resulting case law is inherently incremental. Courts express their legal analyses in the context of individual controversies, and an isolated holding in a judicial opinion is often too limited to support an accurate prediction about how the decision will influence subsequent cases. Instead, as discussed further in Chapters 7 and 8, a series of cases addressing the same topic in a variety of factual contexts will support a generalization about the case law. The generalization, or synthesis of the cases, can then be applied more broadly to a wide range of cases.

5. DEVELOPING ARGUMENTS FOR BOTH SIDES

With few exceptions, essay examinations and office memorandum assignments call on you to present a balanced discussion of legal issues. Although one party may be identified as your client, your professor or supervising

---

16. 42 U.S.C. § 1981 (1994).
17. *See generally* Runyon v. McCrary, 427 U.S. 160 (1976) (addressing, but rejecting, First Amendment challenges to application of § 1981 to racial discrimination in a private school).

attorney expects you to explore the weaknesses of the client's claims and defenses as well as the strengths.

When writing a brief, you should not take such a balanced approach; instead, you must advocate your client's position and discredit your opponent's arguments. Nonetheless, to maximize your own advocacy, you must anticipate and evaluate the arguments of your opponent. You might express that more balanced analysis in an office memorandum, or you might simply contemplate it as you outline the arguments for your brief.

Thus, to analyze a legal dispute effectively, you must develop arguments for both sides of the dispute. In synthesizing case law, you should consider alternative formulations of the general principles that emerge from a series of holdings. Similarly, in analyzing statutory language, you should consider intrinsic and extrinsic aids that support alternative interpretations.

For example, the common law of negligence imposes tort liability on a person who proximately causes injury to another by breaching a duty of care owed to the injured person. As a specific application of this tort law, physicians in most circumstances are liable for injuries caused by their failure to exercise reasonable skill and care in their practices. Suppose that the courts of State X have developed an additional common law doctrine of strict liability, which does not require proof of negligence, for injuries resulting from abnormally dangerous activities. The courts, however, have refused to apply this common law doctrine to medical practices, even risky or experimental ones. Against this background of common law, State X has enacted a statute that makes any "commercial enterprise strictly liable" for injuries caused by its use "of any toxic material."

Now suppose that a medical patient in State X died from a reaction to general anesthesia triggered by the patient's rare disorder of the nervous system. Much of the legal dispute in a malpractice action brought by the deceased patient's estate and surviving family members might center around the applicability of the statute. Assuming that anesthesiology is "a commercial enterprise," if the anesthetic is "a toxic material" within the meaning of the statute, the anesthesiologist or her employer would be statutorily liable without regard to the care that she exercised. In contrast, a companion claim based on common law negligence would require an inquiry into the duty of care that the anesthesiologist owed and the degree of care she actually exercised.

In preparing for advocacy, counsel for either side of this dispute would want to evaluate arguments for both sides on the question of the applicability of the statute. For example, without going beyond the face of the statute, counsel for the deceased patient's estate and survivors could argue that the statutory requirement of "toxic materials" is satisfied in this case because the ordinary meaning of "toxic" is "poisonous," and the anesthetic acted like a poison on the nervous system of the patient. Counsel for the estate and the survivors would also want to anticipate a strong counterargument: It is doubtful that the legislature intended to inhibit physicians' use of substances that produce medically beneficial results in almost all cases in which they are administered; rather, the statutory term "toxic materials" is likely intended to apply only to materials that are generally harmful to all persons, such as potent acids or pesticides. After formulating and evaluating the anesthesiologist's probable counterargument, counsel for the estate and the survivors should try to present their argument in a way that will reduce the impact of the counterargument.

Exercise 6-4

Review your responses to Exercise 6-3 above. Did you explore arguments for both sides on the question of interpretation? Summarize and list the opposing arguments on each issue. If you did not explore arguments on both sides of each of these issues, do so now.

V. "*A*"—APPLICATION OF LAW TO FACTS

A. Basic Patterns

At trial, the critical issues often are questions of purely historical fact. For example, the plaintiff in an employment discrimination suit might assume the burden of proving that an employer in fact exclaimed "Women can't perform this job!" when he rejected the plaintiff's application for employment.

As explored in later chapters, appellate courts will defer to some degree to the factual findings of a jury or trial judge; therefore, issues on appeal inevitably contain a more substantial element of law. However, even nearly pure questions of law are developed in the context of particular disputes and with an appreciation for the probable facts of future disputes. Moreover, most disputes present nontrivial questions about whether the facts satisfy the applicable legal standards, questions such as whether certain acts of preparation leading up to a murder satisfy the premeditation requirement of a first-degree murder statute.

A pattern should emerge from your treatment of facts in an office memorandum or brief. First, you will state all the important facts of the dispute at or near the beginning of the document. Second, you will separately analyze groups of facts as the minor premises of deductive arguments in the discussion section of a memorandum or the argument section of a brief. In that section, after discussing the legal rule applicable to a particular issue, you will discuss or argue whether the relevant facts satisfy the legal rule. You and your professor will follow a similar pattern in an essay examination: Your professor will state all the facts in the essay question, and you will analyze groups of facts as the minor premises of deductive arguments in your examination answer.

If your assignment does not call for great depth of analysis, you might directly explain why particular facts support or undermine the application of a legal rule. Suppose, for example, that you are writing an office memorandum analyzing the claims of a client seeking punitive damages, as introduced in a previous example in this chapter. After stating the legal rule that a malicious or reckless tortfeasor may be liable for punitive damages, you could identify the facts relevant to this issue and explain how each supports or defeats application of the legal rule:

Facts showing no intent	We have no evidence that Con Motor Co. maliciously intended to cause injury when it designed the Backfire sports car. In fact, our notes of the May meeting of the board of directors shows that the board members genuinely hoped that the risky design would not cause accidents.
Facts showing recklessness	However, we do have evidence of recklessness. Con's chief engineer informed the board of directors of her opinion that placement of the gas tank near the rear exterior of the car would create a risk of deadly explosion in even minor rear-end collisions. Yet, the directors approved that design solely because it would save production costs of $100 per car. In so doing, Con's directors knowingly created a great risk of death or terrible injury to consumers without any socially significant justification.

B. Developing Arguments for Both Sides

As with your analysis of more abstract legal rules, your fact analysis in an essay examination answer or office memorandum ought to explore arguments for both sides of the dispute. Similarly, when writing a brief, you should consider your opponent's factual arguments as you develop your own. In the typical dispute, some facts will support application of the legal rule and others will suggest that the legal rule is not satisfied. Still other facts may be used in different ways to support both positions. By balancing and weighing the facts, you can reach at least a qualified conclusion about whether the legal rule is satisfied.

This can be illustrated by extending one of the examples in the previous section on analysis of legal rules. If the parties dispute an anesthesiologist's liability on a claim of common law negligence, an office memorandum might call for analysis of the following facts:

1. The anesthesiologist informed a patient scheduled for heart surgery of the advantages and risks associated with the three most appropriate anesthetics. On the basis of relative costs, the patient rejected the safest anesthetic in favor of a generally safe and more widely used anesthetic.
2. The anesthesiologist administered general anesthesia without assistance, before the surgical team had arrived and while the circulating nurse was occupied with another patient.
3. While administering general anesthesia, the anesthesiologist concen-

trated intensely on gauges on her equipment that measured the patient's intake of the anesthetic.

4. The anesthesiologist did not maintain visual contact with the patient or with equipment monitoring the patient's vital signs; as a consequence, she failed to terminate the intake of anesthetic until 10 seconds after the first visible signs of an adverse reaction.
5. The patient suffered from a rare disorder of the nervous system that produced the fatal reaction to the anesthetic.
6. The patient died within a minute of the administration of general anesthesia.

The facts in the first paragraph suggest that the anesthesiologist followed a reasonable procedure in prescribing the anesthetic. Indeed, the facts in paragraph 5 suggest that the patient's unusual disorder, rather than the anesthesiologist's conduct, precipitated the fatal reaction. Moreover, the facts in paragraph 3 support an argument that the anesthesiologist used at least reasonable care in administering the anesthetic, because she concentrated intensely on an obviously important function.

In addition to providing some support for a finding of reasonable care, however, the facts of paragraph 5 emphasize the need for special care in administering the anesthetic. Moreover, the facts in paragraph 2 support an argument that the anesthesiologist breached a duty of care in administering the anesthetic without assistance. Although the facts in paragraph 3 reflect the anesthesiologist's genuine concern about the patient's potential sensitivity to anesthesia, they also raise a question about the appropriate focus of the anesthesiologist's attention. Finally, the facts in paragraph 4 support an argument that the anesthesiologist acted carelessly in focusing her attention so narrowly on the intake gauge.

To complete your deductive reasoning in an office memorandum, you must discuss whether the facts establish a breach of a physician's duty of care, thus satisfying the legal rule that defines an element of the cause of action. Because the facts in this case support opposing arguments, different legal analysts might reasonably reach different conclusions, depending on the significance the analysts assign to particular facts. Regardless of the author's conclusion, however, the office memorandum should present the best factual arguments for both sides of the dispute. Of course, an advocate writing a brief would emphasize the facts supporting her argument and would develop her argument in a way that lessened the impact of anticipated counterarguments.

Exercise 6-5

Review your response to Exercise 6-1 at the end of Section III.A of this chapter. For each issue that you identified in that exercise, discuss whether the relevant facts satisfy the applicable rule relating to the element of burglary that is in issue. Argue both sides of the facts whenever possible, but argue only the facts that help to resolve each issue.

For more practice in evaluating policy considerations and in applying law to facts, perform Problems 2 and 3 in Appendix II, near the end of this book.

VI. "C"—REACHING CONCLUSIONS

The final element of deductive reasoning is a conclusion derived from the law of your major premise and the facts of your minor premise. When writing a brief, you obviously must state a firm conclusion for each argument that you present. Your conclusions represent the critical points that the court must accept before granting your client relief.

You may hesitate to state conclusions in the more nearly neutral analysis of an office memorandum or essay examination answer, particularly if the dispute presents close questions. Nonetheless, most supervising attorneys and professors will want you to take a position and to reveal your best judgment about the probable outcome of each issue. If necessary, you may hedge your conclusions with qualifiers such as "probably," but you should remember to complete your deductive reasoning by stating a conclusion for each issue:

> On these facts, a jury likely will find that Con Motor Co. acted recklessly, permitting the jury to award punitive damages.

In some cases, you may find it appropriate to make your conclusion contingent on your ability to establish critical facts or law:

> Assuming that we can prove that most hospitals require a team of at least two personnel to administer anesthesia, a jury will almost certainly find that Humana Hospital was negligent in this case.

VII. SUMMARY

To analyze a legal problem, you should

1. identify the **issue,**
2. state the legal **rule** or rules that will help you resolve the issue,
3. **apply** the rule to the relevant **facts,** and

4. reach a **conclusion** on the question of whether the facts satisfy the legal rule.

A single dispute between two parties may present several issues. To achieve an appropriate scope of analysis, you must judge which issues and subissues are sufficiently significant and material to warrant discussion and which are sufficiently tangential to warrant exclusion or summary treatment.

Whenever the law or fact analysis is in doubt, you must evaluate arguments for both sides of the dispute. To evaluate arguments about the applicable legal rules, you should consider

1. the hierarchy of primary authority,
2. synthesis of authorities,
3. policy analysis, and
4. the relative strength of different kinds of case law as precedent.

Always state a conclusion for each issue, even in the analysis in an office memorandum or examination answer.

Exercise 6-6

Gaining Comfort and Experience with Uncertainty in the Law and with Making Arguments for Both Sides—The following exercise is set in a nonlegal context but effectively illustrates some fundamental features of common law analysis.[18]

A grocer explained to her employees that she places fresh produce either in the display case in the window or in the produce section in the middle of the store. As a general standard, she explains, she places produce in the window display case if it would have a tendency to draw impulse shoppers into the store. Employees have witnessed her apply this standard in two cases. In the first case, she arranged a crate of sweet, round, red apples in the window display case. In the second case, she placed a crate of unwashed, unpeeled carrots in the produce section in the interior of the store. On Monday morning, the grocer left to attend to family business for a day. She instructed employees to promptly display any goods that arrived in her absence. On Monday afternoon, a crate of round, red tomatoes arrived. Where should the employees place the tomatoes? In analyzing this problem, consider the following:

a. In the abstract, one may not be able to identify a single correct answer to this question. In practical terms, the "answer" is the location that will most please the grocer when she returns, but that is the "answer" only

18. This exercise is adapted and expanded from one developed by Professor Elisabeth Keller at Boston College Law School. *See* Jane Gionfriddo, *Using Fruit to Teach Analogy*, The Second Draft (newsletter of the Legal Writing Institute) 4 (Nov. 1997).

because the grocer is the boss and not because reasonable minds could reach only one conclusion on the best location for the tomatoes under the grocer's general standard. Moreover, in the meantime, employees must display the tomatoes in the grocer's absence and so must predict where she would place them.

b. To better predict where the grocer would place the tomatoes, employees might wish to explore the grocer's apparent reasoning in the previous two cases. They might ask two questions: (1) On what basis did the grocer conclude that the apples satisfied the grocer's general standard of placing produce in the window only if it would attract customers into the store? (2) Does that rationale also explain why the grocer concluded that the carrots did not satisfy that standard? If the employees can identify a rationale that explains both of the previous cases as a consistent application of the grocer's general standard, then perhaps the employees could apply the same rationale to the tomatoes. In that way, they might be able to better predict whether the grocer would conclude that the tomatoes satisfied her standard of attracting customers into the store. Assuming that the grocer did not explain her reasoning in the previous two cases to her employees, the employees may need to speculate on possible rationales.

c. Are the previous two cases potentially explainable on the basis of two or more equally plausible rationales? Do competing rationales sometimes point to different conclusions about where the employees should place the tomatoes? Does this explain why reasonable judges and attorneys can disagree about the application of a general rule to new facts and about the interpretation of previous judicial decisions? If so, maybe your professors are not playing "hide the ball" when they raise legal questions and state that they have no answers to the questions. Perhaps your task really is to identify issues, analyze the facts and the law, recognize arguments for both sides of the dispute, and either advocate for one party or make a prediction about the outcome, rather than look for a single, correct answer. After all, cases are litigated precisely because the outcome is uncertain and the parties cannot predict with certainty how a judge or jury will view the dispute. Perhaps an appellate court in the jurisdiction will eventually provide a definitive ruling in the dispute, providing its authoritative version of the answer. In the meantime, however, the dispute presents an opportunity for each party to work with law, facts, and policy in an effort to influence the judge, jury, or appellate panel in reaching a conclusion.

Part IV

Stepping Stones to Legal Memoranda—Case Briefs, Outlines, and Essay Exams

Chapter 7

I. STUDY OF CASES

When preparing for law school classes or researching an office memorandum, you must analyze cases: judicial decisions, mostly appellate, that resolve particular disputes. Although you will encounter case law differently in a law firm than in law school, you ultimately will perform similar analytic functions with it in either context.

In a law firm, your supervising attorney typically will request a memorandum that addresses the rights and liabilities of parties to an actual pending dispute, and you will research and analyze case law with that dispute in mind. The reported judicial decisions that you find in the library are unedited opinions that often address multiple issues, some of which may be irrelevant to the dispute that is the subject of your office memorandum.

In one way, your task in most classes in law school is simpler: Rather than search for unedited opinions in the library, you will read opinions that are grouped in some logical fashion in a casebook and are edited to isolate selected issues. Just as you typically will analyze case law in a law firm to determine its applicability to a new dispute presented by your client, you should analyze case law in law school with an eye to the next case that might arise. In other words, you should strive to appreciate the way in which the legal principles in an opinion might apply to facts other than those presented in the opinion itself. Professors will routinely test that facility with classroom hypotheticals and essay examinations.

II. PREPARING A CASE BRIEF

A. General Approach and Format

Both when researching a memorandum problem and when preparing for class, you should prepare "case briefs," written, analytic summaries of appellate opinions. Although you will eventually develop shorthand techniques for taking notes on cases that you find in the library or that are assigned in a casebook, you should prepare formal, thorough case briefs in the first semester to ensure that you develop skills of case analysis.

You should not be troubled if your instructors and textbooks recommend a variety of formats for case briefs. All the formats include essentially the same information; they vary chiefly in emphasis and organization. Below are outlines of two sample formats. If necessary, you can modify either one of them to suit the particular requirements of a classroom instructor who might ask students to recite parts of a case in a different order.

A	B
1. Identification	1. Identification
2. Issue(s) and Holding(s)	2. Facts
3. Facts	3. Procedural History
4. Procedural History	4. Issue(s) and Holding(s)
5. Reasoning	5. Reasoning
6. Evaluation	6. Evaluation
7. Synthesis	7. Synthesis

Although format B is probably the more conventional of the two, format A has the advantage of forcing you to frame the legal issue before stating the facts, thus ensuring that you state the facts with an appreciation for their legal significance. The issue and holding also provide an effective overview of the case brief.

Whichever format you select, your first step in briefing a case is to read it completely before beginning to write. To state some elements of a case brief, you must first understand other elements, and the organization of an appellate opinion may differ from that of either case brief format outlined above. Indeed, some elements of the case brief may not appear explicitly anywhere in the opinion. Instead, the precise issue and holding of a decision may be only implicit in the court's statement of the facts, legal reasoning, and disposition. Consequently, before beginning to brief a case, you should read the entire opinion as many times as is necessary to understand all the elements of the case.

B. Elements of a Case Brief

1. IDENTIFICATION OF THE CASE

In preparing a case for class, you should begin your case brief with

1. the name of the case, which is usually taken from the names of two adversary parties;[1]
2. the jurisdiction, in the sense of the geographical and political body, within which the court sits;
3. the level of the deciding court;
4. the date of decision; and
5. the page on which the case appears in the casebook ("CB"), to facilitate quick cross-reference between notes and casebook.

For example, the following notes identify a 1904 decision of the Supreme Court of Rhode Island, which appears in the student casebook at page 387:

Davis v. Smith, **Rhode Island Supreme Court (1904), CB 387**

Alternatively, to develop familiarity with citation form, you may also wish to record the full citation to the reporters in which the opinion appears in the library, if that citation is presented in your casebook. The following example includes such a full citation, along with an additional reference to the page on which the edited opinion begins in the student casebook:

Davis v. Smith, **26 R.I. 129, 58 A. 630 (1904), CB 387**

By citing to the official Rhode Island Reporter, "R.I.," without further identification of the court, you have referred to the Rhode Island Supreme Court under commonly accepted citation form. Consequently, both examples above identify the authoring court in *Davis v. Smith* as the court of last resort in Rhode Island. That information is significant: It shows that the court is not bound by lower court decisions within Rhode Island or by decisions in other states, although such decisions might provide persuasive authority.

The early date of the *Davis v. Smith* decision, 1904, helps identify the decision's place in Rhode Island law. As discussed in Chapter 5, any aging decision is vulnerable to changes in economic conditions, political and social

---

1. In some *in rem* actions, a named party may be an object, such as money, a plot of land, or a ship. *E.g.*, United States v. $129,374 in U.S. Currency, 769 F.2d 583 (9th Cir. 1985); Winooski Hydroelectric Co. v. Five Acres of Land, 769 F.2d 79 (2d Cir. 1985); Giannakos v. M/V Bravo Trader, 762 F.2d 1295 (5th Cir. 1985); *see* Oliver Wendell Holmes, Jr., THE COMMON LAW 28-30 (1923). In other cases, the case name will refer not to adversary parties but to events, relationships, or other subjects of proceedings. *E.g.*, *In re* Garland Corp., 6 Bankr. 456 (Bankr. 1st Cir. 1980) (bankruptcy proceeding); *In re* Validation of Marriage of Francisco, 16 Indian L. Rep. 6113 (Navajo S. Ct. 1989) (marriage validation proceeding).

attitudes, and the legal context over the years. In fact, such changes prompted the Rhode Island Supreme Court to overrule *Davis v. Smith* in 1967.[2]

The name of a case does not always clearly identify the original parties to the underlying dispute. A named party may be a representative of one of the original disputants or an assignee of its rights and obligations. For example, the dispute in *Hamer v. Sidway*[3] concerned the contract rights and obligations of William E. Story, Sr., and his nephew, William E. Story, II. The case name is taken from the parties to the lawsuit: (1) the executor of the senior Story's estate and (2) a person who acquired the nephew's contract rights through assignment.

Identifying the court may be problematic as well. *Hamer v. Sidway* is a decision of the Court of Appeals of New York, the court of last resort in New York. "Court of Appeals" is a label more commonly associated with an intermediate court of appeals, rather than the court of last resort. To add to the confusion, the decision in *Hamer v. Sidway* indicates that the Court of Appeals reviewed the judgment of the "general term" of the New York Supreme Court, which had reversed the judgment of the "special term" of the Supreme Court. "Supreme Court" is a name that in most states would signify the court of last resort. In fact, however, the opening paragraph of its opinion in *Hamer v. Sidway* reveals that the two different terms of the New York Supreme Court acted as the trial court and the intermediate appellate court.[4] Fortunately, most court systems use the more familiar labels "Court of Appeals" to refer to the intermediate appellate court and "Supreme Court" to refer to the court of last resort.

2. ISSUE AND HOLDING

a. Issue

An "issue" is a material question of fact or law that arises from the claims, defenses, and arguments of the parties. An issue may be a question of law, such as whether Congress intended the term "sex" in section 703(a) of Title VII of the Civil Rights Act of 1964 to encompass sexual orientation as well as gender. Except at the trial level, an issue rarely presents only a question of fact, such as whether the evidence shows that an employer exclaimed "Women can't perform this job!" when he rejected a woman's application for employment.

Most commonly, the issue before a trial or appellate court requires a combination of legal and factual analysis in the determination of whether the facts of a dispute satisfy a general legal rule. An example of such a question is whether certain conduct by an employer in fact created a discriminatory work environment, thus satisfying Title VII's rule regarding discrimination in "conditions . . . of employment." By applying the rule to the

---

2. Rampone v. Wanskuck Bldgs., Inc., 227 A.2d 586 (R.I. 1967).
3. 27 N.E. 256 (N.Y. 1891).
4. A recent guide identifies the current structure of the New York court system: The trial courts of general jurisdiction are the Supreme Court and the County Court. The intermediate appellate courts are the Appellate Divisions of Supreme Court and the Appellate Terms of Supreme Court. The Court of Appeals is the court of last resort. BNA's DIRECTORY OF STATE AND FEDERAL COURTS, JUDGES, AND CLERKS 281 (2001).

facts and reaching a conclusion, the court not only resolves the immediate dispute before it, it also refines the rule by adding more concrete substance to its abstract terms.

If you look for a concise statement of the issues in an appellate opinion, you may find only frustration. Courts do not always state the issues in simple terms before resolving them. When a court does formally state the issues, it may not state them with the narrowness and specificity to which you should aspire if you seek to maximize the development of your analytic skills. You may find clues to the precise question addressed by the court in the court's description of the trial court decision that it is reviewing, in its summary of the parties' arguments on appeal, in the emphasis it places on particular facts, and in its discussion of the law.

At a minimum, your statement of an issue should identify a substantive legal question that distinguishes the case from the bulk of case law in the casebook. In addition, you should specifically incorporate the facts of the case that are critical to the court's analysis and that therefore help to define the precedential effect of its decision.

For example, consider the following case summary, which is loosely based on the procedural history and appellate disposition of a tort claim in *Wagenseller v. Scottsdale Memorial Hospital.*[5]

> Catherine Wagenseller (the employee) worked for Scottsdale Memorial Hospital (the employer) as a staff nurse under an employment contract of indefinite term. She alleged that her supervisor discharged her partly because she refused to participate in a humorous skit in which the participants "mooned" fellow hospital employees. The trial court found that the parties did not dispute any material facts and that the employer was entitled to summary judgment, which is judgment before trial, because the indefinite term of the employment contract made it terminable at the will of either party. Such a contract is terminable at any time and for any reason, or for no reason at all. The intermediate court of appeals affirmed.
>
> The state supreme court reversed and remanded to the trial court, deciding that an employer is liable in tort to an employee if it discharges the employee for a reason that contravenes a clear mandate of public policy. The state supreme court found such a mandate in a state criminal statute that prohibited certain acts of "indecent exposure." In discussing the sources of public policy, the court compared criminal statutes to other sources, such as common law: "Although we do not limit our recognition of the public policy exception to cases involving a violation of a criminal statute, we do believe that our duty will seldom be clearer than when such a violation is involved."

The following statement of the issue in *Wagenseller* is obviously too general:

---

5. 710 P.2d 1025 (Ariz. 1985). Some of the pronouncements of common law in *Wagenseller* were later superseded by state legislation. ARIZ. REV. STAT. ANN. § 23-1501(3)(b) (West Supp. 1996). The discussion in the text, however, assumes that a student is briefing the case when it still presents applicable common law and that the student is interested in ways in which the authoring court will continue to develop the common law doctrine of *Wagenseller.*

Did the trial court correctly grant summary judgment for the defendant?

This issue statement describes the trial court's disposition and the stage of the proceedings at which it made the disposition, facts that are within the procedural history of the case. Unfortunately, if your statement of the issue does no more than identify elements of the procedural history, you will not distinguish the case from hundreds of others in first-year casebooks. The procedural facts will certainly help you understand the decision. Moreover, the standards for summary judgment may even be the central issue in a case raising a dispute about rules of civil procedure. However, this case presents substantive questions of tort and perhaps contract law, and the issue statement should identify them.

The following statement of the issue is an improvement, because it identifies a substantive legal dispute:

Is an employer liable in tort for discharging an at-will employee for a reason that violates public policy?

This statement of the issue identifies (1) a legally significant relationship between the parties (employer/employee), (2) the nature of the claim (tort), (3) the basis for the claim (public policy), and (4) the obstacle to relief on a contract claim (the at-will nature of the employment contract).

Though the second statement of the issue is much more informative, it still leaves room for improvement. Your issue statement will better define the effect of the decision as precedent if you more specifically refer to the critical facts of the case.

For example, the court discusses the sources of public policy. That discussion suggests that a subsequent case may raise the question of the legal significance of public policy that is expressed in a judicial opinion analyzing common law, rather than in a criminal statute. To help determine whether *Wagenseller* would be controlling on, distinguishable from, or persuasively analogous to the subsequent dispute, your statement of the issue in *Wagenseller* could incorporate material facts that provide a potential basis for analogy and distinction:

Is the employer liable in tort for discharging an at-will employee because of her refusal to participate in a public "mooning," a discharge that contravened the public policy against indecent exposure reflected in a criminal statute?

This statement of the issue identifies the source of public policy, and it gives sufficient factual details to permit an assessment of the importance of that policy.

The point at which the disadvantages of increased complexity begin to outweigh the benefits of enhanced specificity in the issue statement is a matter for your judgment and personal style. As discussed in Subsection b.

below, you can reduce the complexity of the issue statement by transferring some of the critical information to the statement of the holding.

Finally, although you should incorporate facts into your issue statement, you should not assume matters that are in dispute and that are thus themselves issues considered by the court. For example, the previous statement of the issue assumes that (1) the employment contract was terminable at will and (2) the criminal statute reflected a public policy against compelled "mooning" and therefore against an employer's discharging an at-will employee for refusing to engage in "mooning." The statement questions only whether state law recognizes a claim in tort for such retaliation against an at-will employee. Suppose instead that the employee had alleged breach of contract and had disputed that the employment contract was terminable at will. Suppose further that the employer had disputed that the criminal statute reflected a public policy against compelled "mooning." In those circumstances, you should add an issue relating to contract law and should divide the tort issue into two subissues:

1. Did the employee establish a genuine factual dispute on the question of whether the employer made a binding promise in its personnel manual to give the employee job security, thus entitling the employee to a trial on her contract claim?
2. Even if the employment contract was terminable at will, is the employer liable to the employee for discharging her for a reason that violates public policy?
   a. Should the court recognize a new exception to the at-will rule by imposing tort liability for such a discharge?
   b. Does a state criminal statute prohibiting public exposure of one's anus or genitalia reflect a public policy against compelled public exposure of bare buttocks?[6]

Issue #1 achieves specificity in procedural facts, as well as historical facts, by identifying the employee's burden on a motion for summary judgment.

b. Holding
The "holding" is simply the court's answer to the question presented in the issue. If you state the issue narrowly and specifically enough to provide a basis for evaluating the effect of the decision as precedent, you may state the holding with a simple "yes" or "no." Of course, if a professor asks you during class discussion for the holding of a case without first asking for the issue, she expects you to offer more than "yes" or "no." In those circumstances, you should transform the issue into a detailed holding in the form of a statement:

6. *See Wagenseller*, 710 P.2d at 1035 n.5 (admitting to "little expertise in the techniques of mooning").

The employee was entitled to a trial on her contract claim because she established a genuine factual dispute on the question of whether the employer made a binding promise in its personnel manual to give the employee job security.

Even when coupling the holding to a detailed statement of the issue, you may wish the holding to convey further information than "yes" or "no." For example, if a fully descriptive statement of the issue would be unwieldy, you can move some of the critical information to the holding:

Issue: Did the employer discharge the employee for a reason that violates public policy, thus rendering the employer liable in tort for wrongful discharge?
Holding: Yes. By discharging the employee because she refused to participate in public "mooning," the employer violated public policy reflected in a criminal statute prohibiting indecent exposure.

The holding and the issue obviously are simply the opposite sides of the same coin. Therefore, the following examination of the appropriate scope of statements of holding is simply a continuation and refinement of the preceding discussion of narrowness and specificity in issues.

Because narrowly drafted statements of the issue and holding represent an attempt to identify the effect of the decision under stare decisis, from a practical standpoint the precise contours of the issue and holding may not become clear until subsequent decisions interpret and apply them as precedent. Through that process of determining whether the prior decision is controlling, analogous, or distinguishable, subsequent decisions help explain, or perhaps redefine, the relative importance of various facts and policies to the prior decision. In turn, this process helps the court explain the relative importance of various facts and policies to the resolution of subsequent disputes.

For example, in *Monge v. Beebe Rubber Co.*[7] the New Hampshire Supreme Court held an employer liable for breach of contract for discharging a female employee in retaliation for her refusing his sexual advances. The court's own statement of its holding is reasonably consistent with a broad theory of liability that encompasses a wide range of employer actions:

We hold that a termination by the employer of a contract of employment at will which is motivated by bad faith or malice or based on retaliation is not in the best interest of the economic system or the public good and constitutes a breach of the employment contract.[8]

Six years later, in *Howard v. Dorr Woolen Co.*,[9] however, the same court adopted one of the narrowest of the possible interpretations of *Monge*'s

---

7. 114 N.H. 130, 316 A.2d 549 (1974).
8. *Id.* at 133, 316 A.2d at 551 (the unofficial reporter, "A.2d," omits the word "in" in the quoted passage).
9. 414 A.2d 1273 (N.H. 1980).

holding. The *Howard* court clearly required (1) a link to public policy beyond a general interest in good faith and fair play in a private employment relationship and (2) retaliation for a specific act or refusal to act on the part of the employee:

> We construe *Monge* to apply only to a situation where an employee is discharged because he performed an act that public policy would encourage, or refused to do that which public policy would condemn.[10]

The *Howard* court applied its view of the holding in *Monge* to refuse to impose liability for an employer discharging an employee because of the employee's sickness and age.[11]

This process of refining the holding of a prior decision may permit a court to interpret precedent in a way that was not intended by the court establishing that precedent. In most subsequent decisions, however, courts faithfully attempt to identify the considerations that were essential to the decision that acts as precedent and to evaluate the precedent's effect on the subsequent disputes.

If the holding of a decision is thus defined in terms of the way in which courts make use of the decision as precedent in subsequent cases, the issue and holding of the decision cannot be identified with perfect certainty when analyzing that decision in isolation. Rather, each decision presents a range of possible statements of the issue and holding.[12] When preparing for class, you should try to state an issue and holding that fall somewhere within a plausible range. Try also to appreciate how other statements nearer to either end of the plausible range would aid in the advocacy of either side of a subsequent dispute.

For example, if you had argued on behalf of one of the parties in the *Howard* case, you would have addressed the holding of *Monge,* a previous decision of the state court of last resort in the forum jurisdiction. If you had represented the plaintiff in *Howard,* you might have argued for the broadest plausible interpretation of the *Monge* precedent, so that it would strongly support recovery for your client. Specifically, you might have interpreted *Monge* to approve tort liability whenever an employer discharges an employee for a reason that would be viewed by the average person as unfair, because such a discharge would be both unfair to the discharged employee and harmful to the morale and productivity of all employees. Conversely, if you had represented the employer in *Howard,* you might have argued for a narrower interpretation of *Monge,* so that you could more easily distinguish it from the *Howard* case. Specifically, you might have interpreted *Monge* to impose liability only if an employer discharges an employee in retaliation for resisting a demand specifically prohibited by statute, a particularly strong source of public policy.

Finally, as a student analyzing *Monge* without the benefit of the appellate decision in *Howard,* you should formulate some reasonable statement of

10. *Id.* at 1274.
11. *Id., interpreted in* Wagenseller v. Scottsdale Mem'l Hosp., 710 P.2d 1025, 1032 n.3 (Ariz. 1985).
12. *See* Karl N. Llewellyn, THE BRAMBLE BUSH 75-76 (10th prtg. 1996).

the *Monge* holding within the range defined by plausible arguments of advocates. You should also be prepared to play the role of advocate and discuss the narrowest and broadest plausible interpretations of *Monge*. Of course, the *Howard* court in fact adopted a quite narrow interpretation of the holding in *Monge*. Such an interpretation was not inevitable, however, and you could reasonably have interpreted the holding of *Monge* more broadly until *Howard* came to your attention.

3. FACTS

a. Significance of Facts

Pressed for time, you may be tempted to skim over the facts of a case and rush to the middle of the opinion, searching for succinct statements of law that you can preserve in your notes. In the final analysis, however, legal rules are nothing more than statements of the legal consequences of particular facts:

> Wherever the law gives special rights to one, or imposes special burdens on another, it does so on the ground that certain special facts are true of those individuals. In all such cases, therefore, there is a twofold task. First, to determine what are the facts to which the special consequences are attached; second, to ascertain the consequences. The first is the main field of legal argument.[13]

Whether case law is based on statutory interpretation or common law, it generally develops gradually, with each new opinion adding refinements in the law through its application of legal standards to the facts of a new dispute. A court's statements about the law are fully meaningful only when read in light of the facts of the dispute that the court resolves. Consequently, you should master the facts of a case with the same intensity that you devote to appreciating the court's discussion of legal principles.

b. Selecting Facts for Your Fact Statement

Your statement of facts should include all "material" facts, facts that have legal significance and therefore directly influence the court's holding and reasoning. Identification of material facts is not an exact science; rather, it is a matter of judgment that requires an appreciation of the factors that the court considered in reaching its decision. In your statement of facts, you should also refer in general terms to any additional background facts that, although legally unimportant, are helpful to a full understanding of the dispute. At the least, your statement of facts should identify

1. the principal parties to the underlying dispute that gave rise to the legal proceedings,
2. the relationships among those parties, and
3. the events that led to the dispute.

13. Oliver Wendell Holmes, Jr., THE COMMON LAW 289 (1923).

You may wish to refer to such facts as "historical facts" to distinguish them from "procedural facts," which are discussed in Subsection 4 below.

For purposes of discussion, this book often uses the procedural term "plaintiff" to refer to the party who initiates a lawsuit and the term "defendant" to refer to the one against whom suit is brought. You can create a more concrete image of the underlying dispute, however, if you identify the parties with their more specific, formal names.

In addition, you should consider supplementing the formal names with labels that have substantive, rather than merely procedural, significance. Because statutes generally address broad categories of activities rather than individual cases, they often create rights and obligations in broad but carefully defined classifications of persons, such as "employers" and "employees" or "buyers" and "sellers."[14] Similarly, although courts interpret statutes and develop common law in the context of individual disputes, a series of judicial decisions on closely related points may create case law that allocates rights and obligations according to membership within general classes of persons, such as "landowners" and "trespassers."[15] Therefore, you can more clearly reveal the legal significance of material facts in your case brief if you identify the named parties or other important actors with labels that reflect undisputed and legally significant classifications, such as employer, buyer, seller, merchant, landlord, tenant, landowner, or invitee.

When you assign a label to a party or otherwise characterize a factual matter, do not prematurely state a conclusion on an issue that is disputed by the parties and that is later analyzed in the opinion. For example, your statement of facts should not refer to a seller as a "merchant" if the parties dispute whether the seller is a merchant for purposes of determining the seller's warranty obligations under the Uniform Commercial Code.[16] Similarly, your statement of facts should not state that the defendant in a criminal burglary prosecution "broke into" a "dwelling" if "breaking" and "dwelling" are elements of the charged offense and if the parties dispute those elements.[17]

Rather than state disputed legal conclusions in your statement of facts, summarize the subsidiary facts that the court analyzes in reaching its conclusion on the issue. For example, in the first case in the preceding paragraph, you might state that the seller of a computer system did not normally buy or sell goods, and that his sale of the computer system was an isolated transaction, but that the seller's occupation as a computer repair person led the buyer to believe that the seller had special knowledge of the performance capabilities of different computer systems. In other parts of your case brief, you can discuss whether those subsidiary facts satisfy the legal definition of "merchant."[18]

14. *See, e.g.*, Title VII of the Civil Rights Act of 1964, 42 U.S.C. §§ 2000e(b), 2000e-2(a) (1994) (defining and imposing obligations on "employers").

15. *See, e.g.*, W. Page Keeton et al., Prosser and Keeton on the Law of Torts § 58, at 393 (5th ed. 1984) (duties owed by landowner to trespassers, licensees, and invitees).

16. *See* U.C.C. § 2-314 (2000) (implying a warranty of merchantability in a contract for the sale of goods "if the seller is a merchant with respect to goods of that kind").

17. *See* Wayne R. LaFave, Criminal Law § 8.13 (3d ed. 2000).

18. The UCC definition focuses on regular practices and on representations of expertise:

Merchant means a person who deals in goods of the kind or otherwise by his

c. Mastering the Facts

In most cases, the appellate judge who wrote the opinion has already sifted and condensed the facts that were presented to the trial court. Nonetheless, you should try to be even more discriminating in your identification of material facts and helpful background facts, and you should try to summarize them further. You should also reorganize the opinion's facts if its organization is not satisfactory; chronological order is often the most logical.

To truly master the facts, however, you must go beyond simply summarizing or reorganizing the opinion's fact statement. Otherwise, you may find yourself simply transferring words and phrases from the casebook to your case brief without truly comprehending their meaning. Instead, seek a conceptual understanding of the facts, one that creates concrete images of the parties and transactions. If necessary to attain that goal, prepare charts, time lines, or other graphics that vividly represent the relationships between multiple parties and events.

To fully appreciate this point, return briefly to the discussion of *Hadley v. Baxendale* at the beginning of Chapter 2. Notice how the charts summarize the transactions and legal proceedings in a rough time line. Did those charts help you form a vivid image of the events? If so, imagine how your own charts or other graphics can help you visualize complex transactions or relationships among parties. As a practical matter, moreover, they will enhance your class performance in at least three ways. First, by preparing graphics, you will force yourself to thoroughly study and comprehend the facts, because you will not be able to represent the facts in a graphic form unless you truly understand what happened in the case. Second, by glancing at your graphic representation in class, you can quickly recall the facts. Third, by relying primarily on such a representation in your class recital of the facts, you will tend to describe the facts more naturally and spontaneously than if you mechanically read your summary of the facts verbatim from your notes.

4. PROCEDURAL HISTORY

a. Elements of Procedural History

In your statement of the procedural history of a case on appeal, you should identify

1. which party or parties originally brought legal action against which others,
2. the legal claims and defenses and the relief sought in that action,
3. the trial court's disposition along with the stage of the proceedings at which the trial court rendered its decision,
4. the dispositions of any intermediate courts below the authoring court, and
5. the authoring court's disposition.

occupation holds himself out as having knowledge or skill peculiar to the practices or goods involved in the transaction. . . .

U.C.C. § 2-104 (2000).

In some cases, it may also be helpful to summarize the arguments that the parties made to the trial or appellate courts.

The case name on appeal does not always reveal which party initiated the legal action in the trial court. Although the case name as it appears in the trial court begins with the plaintiff's name, the case name in the appellate courts of some jurisdictions begins with the name of the party who is dissatisfied with the trial court's decision and has thus appealed (the "appellant") or petitioned for review (the "petitioner").[19]

As with the statement of facts, you should not reach a premature conclusion in your statement of the procedural history regarding the nature of a legal claim if that is one of the issues disputed by the parties and analyzed by the court. For example, the parties may dispute whether a claim is properly classified as tort or contract, because that classification may determine the applicable statute of limitations or the availability of punitive damages.[20] In many cases, however, the nature of the legal claim will be undisputed and easily identifiable.

b. Significance of Procedural History

The nature of the plaintiff's legal claim and request for relief in the trial court may provide a key to the appellate court's analysis. For example, classification of a plaintiff's legal claim as one in tort rather than in contract may determine whether the claim is barred by a statute of limitations[21] or whether the plaintiff is entitled to punitive damages.[22] Similarly, whether a contract is sufficiently definite to enforce may depend on whether the plaintiff seeks enforcement through an award of damages or through injunctive relief granting specific enforcement.[23]

Moreover, by stating the dispositions of all the courts that rendered decisions in the case, you can identify precisely the ruling that the authoring court has reviewed. The "disposition" is the practical, procedural effect of the court's holding on the litigation. In an opinion of a trial court, it might be "action dismissed," "summary judgment for the plaintiff," or "judgment on the jury verdict for the defendant." In an opinion of an appellate court, it might be "affirmed," "reversed," or "reversed and remanded for further proceedings."

In stating the trial court's disposition, try to identify the stage of the

19. *See, e.g.*, Fiege v. Boehm, 123 A.2d 316 (Md. 1956) (Hilda Boehm had sued Louis Fiege in the trial court).
20. *See, e.g.*, Woodward v. Chirco Constr. Co., 687 P.2d 1275, 1278 (Ariz. Ct. App.), *approved as supplemented*, 687 P.2d 1269 (Ariz. 1984) (en banc) (implied warranty claim arose out of a written contract and therefore was governed by six-year limitations period rather than by shorter limitations period for tort claims); Gates v. Life of Mont. Ins. Co., 668 P.2d 213, 215 (Mont. 1983) (breach of implied duty of good faith and fair dealing in employment contract gives rise to a tort, thus permitting award of punitive damages).
21. *See, e.g.*, Salmon Rivers Sportsman Camps, Inc. v. Cessna Aircraft Co., 544 P.2d 306, 310 (Idaho 1975).
22. *See* John D. Calamari & Joseph M. Perillo, CONTRACTS § 14.3 (4th ed. 1998).
23. *See* E. Allan Farnsworth, CONTRACTS § 3.28 (3d ed. 1999); *cf.* 5A Arthur L. Corbin, CORBIN ON CONTRACTS § 1174, at 278-79 (1964) ("It is believed, however, that the required degree of definiteness and certainty [for specific enforcement] is seldom much greater than is required for enforcement by other remedies.").

proceedings at which the trial court rendered judgment. An appellate court gives varying degrees of deference to different kinds of trial court decisions. Therefore, the likelihood of reversal by an appellate court depends partly on the stage of the proceedings at which judgment is rendered and, in some cases, on the classification of critical issues as ones of fact or law.[24]

For example, although appellate courts review without restriction the legal rules formulated by trial courts, they restrict their review of the factual findings made by a trial judge or jury after a full trial, overturning such findings only in unusual circumstances.[25] On the other hand, a trial judge does not resolve disputes of fact when he uses summary judgment to dispose of claims before trial, and an appellate court will reverse summary judgment if it determines, without deference to the analysis of the trial court, that the parties genuinely dispute material facts.[26] Further, on a motion to dismiss an action for failure of the complaint to state a claim for relief, both the trial and appellate courts simply assume the truth of the allegations of fact in the complaint and analyze the legal significance of those allegations.[27]

5. REASONING

a. Rule and Rationale

In part, published appellate judicial decisions serve the function of ensuring the "correct" result in a particular case. However, their primary purpose is to serve the "institutional function" of "developing and declaring legal principles that will have application beyond the case that serves as the vehicle for expression of the principles."[28] The reasoning set forth in a judicial opinion should guide others in predicting how the court will apply its decision to subsequent, analogous cases. Because certainty in the law is not the only criterion for judicial rulemaking, courts should hesitate to extend a previous decision beyond the reasons that supported it.

By carefully studying the reasoning of opinions, you will gradually develop a feel for the way in which judges decide cases. With that acquired knowledge, you can develop the ability not only to analyze a problem and predict its likely outcome in court, but also to persuade a court to reach a conclusion favorable to your client.

Unfortunately, published opinions provide only an imperfect guide to the decisionmaking process. The reasons for an individual judge's vote on an appellate panel may be complex, and some of her reasons may be subcon-

---

24. *See infra* Chapter 21, Section II.

25. *See, e.g.,* Fed. R. Civ. P. 52(a) (federal appellate court may set aside trial judge's findings of fact only if the findings are "clearly erroneous"); Aetna Life Ins. Co. v. Kepler, 116 F.2d 1, 4 & n.1 (8th Cir. 1941) (reviewing court will overturn the fact findings of a jury only if they are not supported by substantial evidence).

26. *See* FED. R. CIV. P. 56 (summary judgment standards); Heiniger v. City of Phoenix, 625 F.2d 842, 843-44 (9th Cir. 1980) (standards for appellate review of summary judgment).

27. *See, e.g.,* Experimental Eng'g, Inc. v. United Techs. Corp., 614 F.2d 1244, 1246 (9th Cir. 1980) (dismissal is appropriate only if court is convinced that the plaintiff can prove no set of facts in support of a claim that would warrant relief).

28. Charles Richard Calleros, *Title VII and Rule 52(a): Standards of Appellate Review in Disparate Treatment Cases—Limiting the Reach of* Pullman-Standard v. Swint, 58 Tul. L. Rev. 403, 420-21 (1983).

scious.[29] Of the reasons on which the judge consciously relies, the judge may not express all of them to fellow panel members in panel discussions and memoranda. Finally, the published opinion of the panel may exclude some of the more pragmatic reasons privately expressed by panel members to one another and may focus instead on more conventional legal analysis. Because an opinion thus communicates a court's actual reasoning only imperfectly, do not hesitate to read between the lines and to identify facts or policy considerations that likely contributed to the court's decision, even though the court did not expressly identify them as critical factors.

On the most fundamental level, when stating a court's reasoning, note whether the court is interpreting and applying a constitution or statute or is developing common law. Many judicial opinions deal with a combination of different sources of law. Beyond that, you should summarize the court's reliance on precedent, its analysis of policy considerations, its explanation of the significance of critical facts, and its adoption or recognition of a legal rule of general application.

Some opinions do not formulate or restate a general legal rule that controls the analysis. Instead, they simply define a dispute on particular facts, reach a decision, and provide a justification that is fairly narrowly tailored to the dispute before the court. Such an opinion leaves you only with a "holding" in the narrowest sense. Using techniques described in the next chapter, however, you can synthesize several such cases addressing similar issues and derive your own rule of general application.

b. Holding and Dictum

One of your most challenging tasks is to distinguish the holding of a decision from dicta. Narrowly defined, a "holding" is the court's resolution of an issue before it, limited to the material facts of that dispute. It does not include statements in the opinion about the probable outcome of disputes not before the court.

"Dictum," on the other hand, is a statement in the opinion that helps explain the court's reasoning by addressing questions not squarely presented in the dispute before the court. Courts make and apply law in the context of individual disputes. As a natural consequence of the uniformity of treatment demanded by stare decisis, however, courts have developed general rules that apply to whole categories of disputes.[30] As a means of explaining the reasons supporting its holding, a court may in dicta compare its rule of decision with other rules that it does not apply to the dispute, or it may discuss in dicta how its rule of decision would apply to facts other than those presented in the dispute before it.

As illustrated by the following excerpt, the issue and holding of a previous decision limits its effect as precedent under stare decisis. Even a lower court that is absolutely bound by the holdings of the previous decision may choose not to follow the dicta of the decision. In this example from civil rights litigation, a United States Court of Appeals extended the same immunity defense to judges of limited jurisdiction state courts, such as traffic courts,

---

29. *See generally id.* at 424 & n.97.
30. *See generally* Karl N. Llewellyn, THE BRAMBLE BUSH 40-41 (10th prtg. 1996).

as had been applied to judges of general jurisdiction state courts, such as general trial courts. In doing so, it departed from United States Supreme Court dicta:

> The district court held that judges of courts of limited jurisdiction may be sued for judicial acts done merely in excess of jurisdiction. . . . Although the Supreme Court cases relied upon by the district court contain language supporting such a view, . . . we hold that judges of courts of limited jurisdiction are entitled to absolute immunity for their judicial acts unless they act in the clear absence of all jurisdiction.
>
> First, we emphasize that since the [Supreme Court] cases involved suits against judges of courts having general jurisdiction, any statements made by the Supreme Court about judges of courts having only limited or inferior jurisdiction were *dicta*.[31]

Dictum in an opinion is not meaningless; it may help you accurately predict the authoring court's action in a subsequent case that squarely presents the issue addressed in the dictum.[32] Nonetheless, because dictum does not have the force of precedent, you should take care to read all of the court's reasoning in light of its narrow, fact-specific holding. Do not confuse what a court says, or even what it says it is doing, with what it actually does in a case.

6. EVALUATION

You should resist any tendency to defer to the reasoning of a judicial decision as the expression of the single "correct" analysis of a dispute. Many disputes present close questions that are reasonably susceptible to alternative, inconsistent resolutions. You should read a decision critically to determine whether you agree with the result and the reasoning. Constant practice in critically examining judicial opinions will help you develop the ability later to persuade a court to adopt or reject the rule or reasoning of nonbinding authority.

On one level, you should examine an opinion for doctrinal integrity by asking questions such as these:

1. Does the court analogize or distinguish precedent in a convincing manner?
2. Does it apply the appropriate standard of review?
3. Does it analyze a statute under accepted principles of statutory interpretation and construction?
4. Does the court place excessive emphasis on certainty in a general rule at the expense of equitable considerations in the context of peculiar facts?

---

31. King v. Love, 766 F.2d 962, 966 (6th Cir. 1985).
32. *See* Robert E. Keeton, VENTURING TO DO JUSTICE 30-31 (1969).

On another, closely related level, you should examine the policy and practical implications of an opinion. For example, you might ask questions such as these:

1. Does a decision that promotes economic security for employees unwisely reduce economic efficiency at the expense of producers and consumers?
2. Does a court-developed tort standard allocate risks among parties in a way that encourages them to conduct themselves in a manner that avoids harm to others yet encourages socially productive ventures?

7. SYNTHESIS

a. A Bridge Between Case Briefs and Outlines

Perhaps the most important and the most challenging element of a case brief is the "synthesis," in which you explore the relationships between two or more cases that address the same issue or closely related ones. After comparing the critical elements of each in a series of cases, you can refine your view of the holding of each case in the series. With synthesis, you can either (1) formulate a general principle that explains all the decisions or (2) compare and evaluate the inconsistent approaches of different courts or of the same court over time. By synthesizing cases, you take a critical step in legal analysis that will have special significance when you look ahead to final examinations: Synthesis forms a bridge between daily briefing of isolated cases and periodic preparation of course outlines.

The process of synthesizing cases reveals that the study of case law is analogous in some ways to the study of a foreign language. After a brief introduction to the basic structure of a language and its rules of pronunciation, you typically proceed to study the language by gaining familiarity with a succession of words and phrases that gradually grow into a working vocabulary. The learning process is complicated by the relationship of parts to the whole: You cannot fully appreciate the nuances of meaning of a word or phrase without a working knowledge of its role in a larger body of the language; yet you cannot attain a working knowledge of the larger body of the language without first gaining at least a preliminary understanding of individual words and phrases. As you gradually add to your vocabulary and to your understanding of the relationship of words and phrases to one another, you continually refine your understanding of the individual words and phrases that you studied earlier, and you come closer to attaining fluency in the whole language.

Similarly, when studying law, you cannot fully appreciate the legal significance of a single judicial decision without examining its role within a larger body of case law; yet you cannot master the larger body of case law without first gaining at least an imperfect grasp of its parts, first one case in isolation and then a growing group of cases. As you brief a series of cases, you gain new insights by examining the cases' relationships to one another. Those insights may cause you to modify your early, less sophisticated understanding of a case standing alone or standing with fewer cases in the series. Additionally, they may enable you to identify a general legal principle, or at least a set of accepted criteria, that helps to explain the decisions.

b. Reconciling Disparate Results

The first step in synthesizing cases is to compare the cases' substantive results as conveyed by their holdings, regardless of the procedural dispositions of the appellate courts. For example, assume that two appellate decisions from different jurisdictions, States X and Y, have addressed the question of whether a particular newspaper advertisement amounts to an "offer," defined as an expression of willingness to enter into a contract that empowers the offeree to create a contract by accepting the offer. In Case A, an appellate court of State X affirmed a trial court judgment that a particular newspaper advertisement amounted to an offer to sell the advertised goods. In Case B, an appellate court of State Y affirmed a trial court judgment that another newspaper advertisement communicated only an invitation to negotiate rather than an offer to sell.[33] If you are not yet prepared to abandon hope of finding at least limited uniformity among the states in their application of common law, you should be curious about the reasons for the difference in results.

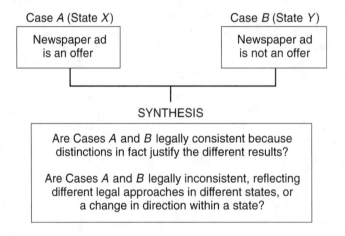

In the next step of the synthesis, you should determine whether Cases A and B are materially distinguishable and therefore warrant different results on application of the same legal principles, or whether they are legally inconsistent and simply represent different views of the law adopted by courts in different states. As a general approach, you should first attempt to reconcile the cases by searching for distinctions in facts, procedure, or both that support a conclusion that the cases are legally consistent. For example, unusually specific and detailed language of commitment in the advertisement in Case A might clearly communicate a willingness to conclude

---

33. *Compare* Lefkowitz v. Great Minneapolis Surplus Store, 86 N.W.2d 689 (Minn. 1957) (offer) *with* Craft v. Elder & Johnston Co., 38 N.E.2d 416 (Ohio Ct. App. 1941) (no offer).

a contract for sale on a customer's assent. In contrast, more general language in the advertisement in Case *B* might leave important terms of sale unaddressed, suggesting a need for further bargaining before the advertiser is willing to commit itself to a contract for sale.

In these circumstances, you could compose a single, narrow legal rule that is consistent with the reasoning of each case and that produces different results on application to the facts of both cases:

A newspaper advertisement is an offer only if it is so clear and definite that it leaves no important detail for future negotiation.

With such a synthesis, you will better understand the holdings of Cases *A* and *B,* more firmly grasp otherwise abstract legal principles, and improve your ability to predict the outcome of a new case that presents the same issue on novel facts.

If you fail to find material distinctions in facts or procedure between Cases *A* and *B,* you can safely conclude that the appellate decisions are legally inconsistent. In that event, you should analyze the reasons for the different views of the law. Perhaps States *X* and *Y* apply different legal approaches because they emphasize different policies. Such a synthesis helps you to put conflicting case law into perspective and to develop the ability to persuade a court in a future case to adopt one line of conflicting authority over another.

Different results in cases decided by the same court present particularly interesting questions of synthesis, because the court cannot depart from its prior decision without departing also from stare decisis and overruling the prior decision. If the cases are not obviously distinguishable but the court does not explicitly overrule the prior decision, you should search with particular care for possible distinguishing features before concluding that the court has implicitly overruled the prior decision. Of course, the proper synthesis may lie in middle ground: A decision may limit the range of possible interpretations of a prior holding without completely overruling it, as illustrated in the discussion of *Monge v. Beebe Rubber Co.* in Section II.B.2.b above.

c. Comparing Reasons for and Limits on Consistent Results

If two cases reach the same result, a synthesis should compare the facts and reasoning of the two cases to determine whether the courts were influenced by similar factors. For example, suppose that in Case *A* a court in State *X* held that a particular newspaper advertisement constituted an offer to sell the advertised goods. Suppose further that in Case *C* a court in State *Z* found a different newspaper advertisement to constitute an offer. Although both decisions find offers, a comparison of the facts may suggest that Case *C* represents a significant extension of the holding of Case *A.* Similarly, the reasoning of Case *A* might suggest that the court in State *X* would not have reached the same result if presented with the facts on which the court in State *Z* found an offer in Case *C.*

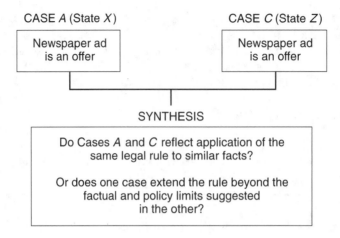

d. Limited Utility of a Case Viewed in Isolation

When you synthesize, you compare two or more cases, of course. Therefore, when you prepare a single case brief in isolation, you will not include a synthesis, except perhaps in the form of a prediction of the questions that may arise later from uncertainty in the breadth of the holding of the case. The late Professor Llewellyn may be forgiven for overstatement when he asserted that

> a case read by itself is meaningless, is nil, is blank, is blah. Briefing should begin *at the earliest* with the second case of an assignment. Only *after* you have read the second case have you any idea what to do with the first.[34]

Thus, in a perfect world, you could read all in a series of cases relating to a particular problem area before briefing any of them. You would then brief each case with an eye to the problems raised in the others, and finally prepare a single synthesis of the entire series of cases.

Unfortunately, class assignments and library research techniques seldom permit that luxury. As a more practical procedure, you should prepare a synthesis for each case in a series beginning with the second case. Each succeeding synthesis will reflect the addition of a case to the group of cases among which you can make comparisons, thus adding new insights to previous syntheses.

III. SUMMARY

In preparing a case brief, follow these steps:

1. Thoroughly read the entire case at least once.
2. Identify the case. Include details that help identify the case's place in the overall case law of the jurisdiction and the case's value as precedent.

34. Karl N. Llewellyn, THE BRAMBLE BUSH 55 (10th prtg. 1996).

3. State the issue and the holding as narrowly as possible without making your question cumbersome and unwieldy; tailor your statement of the issue to the facts.
4. Summarize the material facts and the helpful background facts.
5. Summarize the procedural history, including the dispositions in the trial court and on appeal.
6. Summarize the reasoning of the court. Distinguish holding from dictum. Identify general rules recognized by the court and pay particular attention to the authority, policy analysis, and logic on which the court relies.
7. Critically evaluate the court's holding and reasoning.
8. Synthesize the case with others that present the same or a similar issue. Attempt to explain apparently conflicting results among the cases.

Exercise 7-1

1. CASE BRIEF

Using the techniques described in this chapter, read the following excerpt of the appellate opinion in *White v. Benkowski* and prepare a case brief. The footnoted citations in this excerpt are taken from the opinion without revision and do not reflect current uniform citation style, so please do not emulate the opinion's citation form in your office memoranda. Additionally, do not be satisfied with the court's statement of the issue; try to improve it. Critically evaluate the court's holding and dicta regarding the availability of punitive damages; ask yourself whether you can defend the court's views on the grounds of economic efficiency, certainty in legal rules, equity in individual cases, the proper roles of compensation and deterrence, or any other policy considerations. You should not yet attempt to synthesize this case with any others, although you may comment on possible extensions of or limitations on its holding that subsequent cases could introduce. After completing your case brief, compare it with the sample set forth in Exercise 7-1(2) below.

WHITE v. BENKOWSKI
Supreme Court of Wisconsin
37 Wis. 2d 285, 155 N.W.2d 74 (1967)

This case involves a neighborhood squabble between two adjacent property owners.

Prior to November 28, 1962, Virgil and Gwynneth White, the plaintiffs, were desirous of purchasing a home in Oak Creek. Unfortunately, the particular home that the Whites were interested in was without a water supply. Despite this fact, the Whites purchased the home.

The adjacent home was owned and occupied by Paul and Ruth Benkowski, the defendants. The Benkowskis had a well in their yard which had piping that connected with the Whites' home.

On November 28, 1962, the Whites and Benkowskis entered into a written agreement wherein the Benkowskis promised to supply water to the Whites' home for 10 years or until an earlier date when either water was supplied by the municipality, the well became inadequate, or the Whites drilled their own well. The Whites promised to pay $3 a month for the water and one-half the cost of any future repairs or maintenance that the Benkowski well might require. As part of the transaction, but not included in the written agreement, the Whites gave the Benkowskis $400 which was used to purchase and install a new pump and an additional tank that would increase the capacity of the well.

Initially, the relationship between the new neighbors was friendly. With the passing of time, however, their friendship deteriorated and the neighbors actually became hostile. In 1964, the water supply, which was controlled by the Benkowskis, was intermittently shut off. Mrs. White kept a record of the dates and durations that her water supply was not operative. Her record showed that the water was shut off on the following occasions:

(1) March 5, 1964, from 7:10 P.M. to 7:25 P.M.
(2) March 9, 1964, from 3:40 P.M. to 4:00 P.M.
(3) March 11, 1964, from 6:00 P.M. to 6:15 P.M.
(4) June 10, 1964, from 6:20 P.M. to 7:03 P.M.

The record also discloses that the water was shut off completely or partially for varying lengths of time on July 1, 6, 7, and 17, 1964, and on November 25, 1964.

Mr. Benkowski claimed that the water was shut off either to allow accumulated sand in the pipes to settle or to remind the Whites that their use of the water was excessive. Mr. White claimed that the Benkowskis breached their contract by shutting off the water.

Following the date when the water was last shut off (November 25, 1964), the Whites commenced an action to recover compensatory and punitive damages for an alleged violation of the agreement to supply water. . . .

The jury returned a verdict which found that the Benkowskis maliciously shut off the Whites' water supply for harassment purposes. Compensatory damages were set at $10 and punitive damages at $2,000. On motions after verdict, the court reduced the compensatory award to $1 and granted defendants' motion to strike the punitive-damage question and answer.

Judgment for plaintiffs of $1 was entered and they appeal.

WILKIE, Justice.

Two issues are raised on this appeal. . . .

2. Are punitive damages available in actions for breach of contract? . . .

PUNITIVE DAMAGES

"If a man shall steal an ox, or a sheep, and kill it, or sell it; he shall restore five oxen for an ox, and four sheep for a sheep."[3]

3. Exodus 22:1.

Over one hundred years ago this court held that, under proper circumstances, a plaintiff was entitled to recover . . . punitive damages.[4]

Kink v. Combs [5] is the most recent case in this state which deals with the practice of permitting punitive damages. In *Kink* the court relied on *Fuchs v. Kupper* [6] and reaffirmed its adherence to the rule of punitive damages.

In Wisconsin compensatory damages are given to make whole the damage or injury suffered by the injured party.[7] On the other hand, punitive damages are given

> . . . on the basis of punishment to the injured party not because he has been injured, which injury has been compensated with compensatory damages, but to punish the wrongdoer for his malice and to deter others from like conduct.[8]

Thus we reach the question of whether the plaintiffs are entitled to punitive damages for a breach of the water agreement. The overwhelming weight of authority supports the proposition that punitive damages are not recoverable in actions for breach of contract.[9] In *Chitty on Contracts*, the author states that the right to receive punitive damages for breach of contract is now confined to the single case of damages for breach of a promise to marry.[10]

Simpson states:

> Although damages in excess of compensation for loss are in some instances permitted in tort actions by way of punishment . . . in contract actions the damages recoverable are limited to compensation for pecuniary loss sustained by the breach.[11]

Corbin states that as a general rule punitive damages are not recoverable for breach of contract.[12]

In Wisconsin, the early case of *Gordon v. Brewster* [13] involved the breach of an employment contract. The trial court instructed the jury that if the nonperformance of the contract was attributable to the defendant's wrongful act of discharging the plaintiff, then that would go to increase the damages sustained. On appeal, this court said that the instruction was unfortunate and might have led the jurors to suppose that they could give something more than actual compensation in a breach of contract case. We find no Wisconsin case in which breach of contract (other than breach of promise to marry)[14] has led to the award of punitive damages.

---

4. McWilliams v. Bragg (1854), 3 Wis. 377 (*424).
5. (1965), 28 Wis. 2d 65, 135 N.W.2d 789.
6. (1963), 22 Wis. 2d 107, 125 N.W.2d 360.
7. Malco, Inc. v. Midwest Aluminum Sales (1961), 14 Wis. 2d 57, 66, 109 N.W.2d 516, 521.
8. Id.
9. Annot. (1933), 84 A.L.R. 1345, 1346.
10. 1 Chitty, Contracts, (22d ed. 1961), p.1339.
11. Simpson, Contracts, (2d ed. hornbook series), p.394, sec. 195.
12. 5 Corbin, Contracts, p.438, sec. 1077.
13. (1858), 7 Wis. 309 (*355).
14. Simpson v. Black (1870), 27 Wis. 206.

Persuasive authority from other jurisdictions supports the proposition (without exception) that punitive damages are not available in breach of contract actions.[15] This is true even if the breach, as in the instant case, is willful.[16]

Although it is well recognized that breach of a contractual duty may be a tort,[17] in such situations the contract creates the relation out of which grows the duty to use care in the performance of a responsibility prescribed by the contract.[18] Not so here. No tort was pleaded or proved.

Reversed in part by reinstating the jury verdict relating to compensatory damages and otherwise affirmed.

2. SAMPLE CASE BRIEF

Compare the case brief that you prepared in Exercise 7-1(1) with the following sample. Remember that the sample is only an example of a reasonable reaction to the opinion; it is not necessarily the best interpretation and evaluation of the opinion, and it certainly is not the only reasonable one. In particular, the "evaluation" is a matter of individual opinion.

White v. Benkowski, 37 Wis. 2d 285, 155 N.W.2d 74 (1967), CB 12.

Issue and Holding: Is Buyer entitled to an award of punitive damages for Supplier's malicious breach of a contract to supply water, even though Buyer established no independent tort? No.

Facts: The Whites (Buyer) and Benkowskis (Supplier) are neighbors. By written agreement Supplier promised to supply Buyer's house with water from Supplier's well for 10 years, unless the well became inadequate or unnecessary. The relationship deteriorated, and Supplier maliciously shut off Buyer's water supply partially or completely on nine occasions for the purpose of harassing Buyer.

Procedural History: Buyer sued Supplier for compensatory and punitive damages, alleging only breach of contract. On a finding of malicious breach of contract, the jury awarded Buyer $10 in compensatory damages and $2,000 in punitive damages. On motions after verdict, the trial court disallowed punitive damages and reduced the compensatory damage award from $10 to $1. Buyer appealed. The appellate court reversed the trial court's reduction of the award for compensatory damages, but it affirmed the trial court's elimination of the award for punitive damages.

Reasoning: Prior Wisconsin case law, persuasive authority from other jurisdictions, and the views of three commentators support the following common law principle: Even an intentional and malicious breach of contract

15. White, Inc. v. Metropolitan Merchandise Mart (1954), 48 Del. 526, 9 Terry 526, 107 A.2d 892; Thompson v. Mutual Ben. Health & Acc. Ass'n of Omaha, Neb. (D.C. Iowa 1949), 83 F. Supp. 656; Cain v. Tuten (1950), 82 Ga. App. 102, 60 S.E.2d 485; Mabery v. Western Casualty & Surety Co. (1952), 173 Kan. 586, 250 P.2d 824; Bland v. Smith (1955), 197 Tenn. 683, 277 S.W.2d 377; 49 A.L.R.2d 1212.

16. McDonough v. Zamora (Tex. Civ. App. 1960), 338 S.W.2d 507; Holt v. Holt (Tex. Civ. App. 1954), 271 S.W.2d 477; Chelini v. Nieri (Cal. App. 1948), 188 P.2d 564.

17. Colton v. Foulkes (1951), 259 Wis. 142, 47 N.W.2d 901; Presser v. Siesel Construction Co. (1963), 19 Wis. 2d 54, 119 N.W.2d 405; Peterson v. Sinclair Refining Co. (1963), 20 Wis. 2d 576, 123 N.W.2d 479.

18. 38 Am. Jur., Negligence, p.661, sec. 20.

will not support an award of punitive damages. In dictum, the court suggests that punitive damages could be awarded if the breach of contract also constituted an independent tort; however, Buyer failed to plead and prove an independent tort. The court did not explicitly overrule a nineteenth-century decision in which it had approved punitive damages for breach of a marriage contract, thus leaving open the possibility of exceptions to the rule of the current case for breaches of extraordinary contracts.

Evaluation: In light of the maliciousness of Supplier's behavior, I think this decision is too restrictive. To deter such egregious conduct, I would allow punitive damages on a contract claim if the breaching party breached to maliciously injure the other party rather than to reallocate its resources to a more profitable and efficient use.

3. CASE BRIEFS WITH SYNTHESIS

Contracts are formed through a process of offer and acceptance. An offer is an expression of a willingness to enter into a contract. It gives to the party to whom it is addressed, the "offeree," the power to create the contract by assenting to the offer in a manner authorized by the offer. To constitute an offer, an expression must lead a reasonable person in the position of the offeree to understand that she has such power.

With that background, prepare a case brief for each of the following two cases. End the second case brief with a synthesis of the two cases. As with Exercise 7-1(1) above, do not assume that all the citations in these opinions are consistent with the current uniform citation style that you should use in your office memoranda.

For additional practice in synthesizing cases, perform Assignment 1 in Appendix III, near the end of this book.

CRAFT v. ELDER & JOHNSTON CO.
Ohio Court of Appeals
38 N.E.2d 416 (Ohio Ct. App. 1941)

BARNES, Judge. . . .

. . . On or about January 31, 1940, the defendant, the Elder & Johnston Company, carried an advertisement in the Dayton Shopping News, an offer for sale of a certain all electric sewing machine for the sum of $26 as a "Thursday Only Special." Plaintiff . . . alleges that the above publication is an advertising paper distributed in Montgomery County and throughout the city of Dayton; that on Thursday, February 1, 1940, she tendered to the defendant company $26 in payment for one of the machines offered in the advertisement, but that defendant refused to fulfill the offer and has continued to so refuse. The petition further alleges that the value of the machine offered was $175 and she asks damages in the sum of $149 plus interest from February 1, 1940. . . .

The trial court dismissed plaintiff's petition as evidenced by a journal entry, the pertinent portion of which reads as follows: "Upon consideration the court finds that said advertisement was not an offer which could be accepted by plaintiff to form a contract, and this case is therefore dismissed with prejudice to a new action, at costs of plaintiff." . . .

We will now briefly make reference to some of the authorities. "It is clear that in the absence of special circumstances an ordinary newspaper advertisement is not an offer, but is an offer to negotiate—an offer to receive offers—or, as it is sometimes called, an offer to chaffer." Restatement of the Law of Contracts, Par. 25, Page 31.

Under the above paragraph the following illustration is given, " 'A,' a clothing merchant, advertises overcoats of a certain kind for sale at $50. This is not an offer but an invitation to the public to come and purchase."

"Thus, if goods are advertised for sale at a certain price, it is not an offer and no contract is formed by the statement of an intending purchaser that he will take a specified quantity of the goods at that price. The construction is rather favored that such an advertisement is a mere invitation to enter into a bargain rather than an offer. So a published price list is not an offer to sell the goods listed at the published price." Williston on Contracts, Revised Edition, Vol. 1, Par. 27, Page 54.

"The commonest example of offers meant to open negotiations and to call forth offers in the technical sense are advertisements, circulars and trade letters sent out by business houses. While it is possible that the offers made by such means may be in such form as to become contracts, they are often merely expressions of a willingness to negotiate." Page on the Law of Contracts, 2d Ed., Vol. 1, Page 112, Par. 84. . . .

"But generally a newspaper advertisement or circular couched in general language and proper to be sent to all persons interested in a particular trade or business, or a prospectus of a general and descriptive nature, will be construed as an invitation to make an offer." 17 Corpus Juris Secundum, Contracts, Page 389, § 46, Column 2. . . .

We are constrained to the view that the trial court committed no prejudicial error in dismissing plaintiff's petition.

The judgment of the trial court will be affirmed and costs adjudged against the plaintiff-appellant.

Entry may be prepared in accordance with this opinion.

GEIGER, P.J., and HORNBECK, J., concur.

LEFKOWITZ v. GREAT MINNEAPOLIS SURPLUS STORE
Minnesota Supreme Court
251 Minn. 188, 86 N.W.2d 689 (1957)

MURPHY, Justice

This is an appeal from an order of the Municipal Court of Minneapolis. . . . The order for judgment awarded the plaintiff the sum of $138.50 as damages for breach of contract.

This case grows out of the alleged refusal of the defendant to sell to the plaintiff a certain fur piece which it had offered for sale in a newspaper advertisement. It appears from the record that . . . the defendant published the following advertisement in a Minneapolis newspaper:

. . . .

Saturday 9 A.M.

. . . .

> 1 Black Lapin Stole
> Beautiful,
> worth $139.50. . . . $1.00
> First Come
> First Served

The record supports the findings of the court that on . . . the Saturday[ ] following the publication of the above-described ad[ ] the plaintiff was the first to present himself at the appropriate counter in the defendant's store and . . . demanded the . . . stole so advertised and indicated his readiness to pay the sale price of $1. . . . [T]he defendant refused to sell the merchandise to the plaintiff. . . .

The defendant relies principally on *Craft v. Elder & Johnston Co.* . . . On the facts before us we are concerned with whether the advertisement constituted an offer, and, if so, whether the plaintiff's conduct constituted an acceptance.

There are numerous authorities which hold that a particular advertisement in a newspaper or circular letter relating to a sale of articles may be construed by the court as constituting an offer, acceptance of which would complete a contract. [citations omitted]. . . .

The authorities above cited emphasize that, where the offer is clear, definite, and explicit, and leaves nothing open for negotiation, it constitutes an offer, acceptance of which will complete the contract. The most recent case on the subject is *Johnson v. Capital City Ford Co.*, La. App., 85 So. 2d 75, in which the court pointed out that a newspaper advertisement relating to the purchase and sale of automobiles may constitute an offer, acceptance of which will consummate a contract and create an obligation in the offeror to perform according to the terms of the published offer.

Whether in any individual instance a newspaper advertisement is an offer rather than an invitation to make an offer depends on the legal intention of the parties and the surrounding circumstances. Annotation, 157 A.L.R. 744, 751; 77 C.J.S., Sales, § 25b; 17 C.J.S., Contracts, § 389. We are of the view on the facts before us that the offer by the defendant of the sale of the Lapin fur was clear, definite, and explicit, and left nothing open for negotiation. The plaintiff having successfully managed to be the first one to appear at the seller's place of business to be served, as requested by the advertisement, and having offered the stated purchase price of the article, he was entitled to performance on the part of the defendant. . . .

Affirmed.

Chapter 8

I. REORGANIZATION—MAPPING THE FOREST

When preparing for final examinations or preparing to write a legal memorandum, a law student or an attorney in a law firm must make a significant transition from analysis of individual cases to the final expression of a completed legal analysis of the assigned problem. In making that transition, the student or attorney begins by synthesizing the cases, as discussed in Chapter 7. She continues the transition by further analyzing and reorganizing the information in her library or class notes, eventually producing an outline that is organized around issues and legal principles rather than around individual cases.

An attorney or summer associate researching and analyzing a simple problem may not need to reorganize her modest library notes before expressing her analysis in a short memorandum. On the other hand, long hours of researching a complex, multiple-issue problem may produce a mass of

127

disorganized notes dealing with several issues and lines of authority. In those circumstances, the researching attorney may need to summarize and reorganize her notes in some manner before writing or even outlining the memorandum, and perhaps even before completely analyzing the problem.

Attorneys who take library notes by hand can facilitate this process of reorganization by using note cards and limiting the notes on each card to discussion of a single statute, case, or other authority. Indeed, if a single case separately discusses more than one issue relating to the assignment, the researching attorney should note the discussion of each issue on separate note cards:

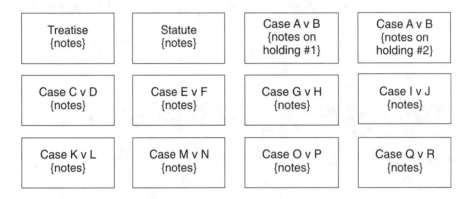

The associate can use these cards to help her prepare an outline of the fruits of her research. As an initial step, she can devise categories for the note cards that identify distinct legal issues and can assign each card to one of the groups:

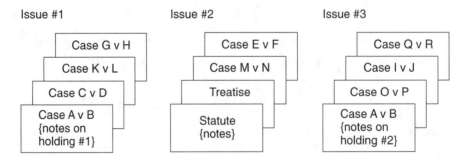

If the associate has used a note pad rather than note cards, she may wish to prepare an index of the cases, and perhaps even of distinct issues within a case, by assigning consecutive numbers to her case briefs:

1.	Treatise ———————	4.	Case C v D ———————	8.	Case K v L ———————
	{notes} ———————		{notes} ———————		{notes} ———————
2.	Statute ———————	5.	Case E v F ———————	9.	Case M v N ———————
	{notes} ———————		{notes} ———————		{notes} ———————
3.	Case A v B ———————	6.	Case G v H ———————	10.	Case O v P ———————
	{notes: ———————		{notes} ———————		{notes} ———————
	a. on holding #1	7.	Case I v J ———————	11.	Case Q v R ———————
	b. on holding #2}		{notes} ———————		{notes} ———————

When reorganizing the product of her research in an outline, she can refer to her notes on a case or other authority by its number on the note pad:

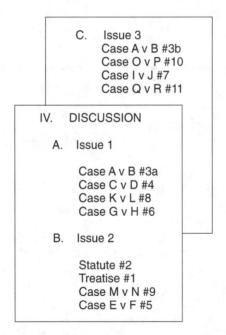

C.   Issue 3
     Case A v B #3b
     Case O v P #10
     Case I v J #7
     Case Q v R #11

IV.   DISCUSSION

A.   Issue 1

     Case A v B #3a
     Case C v D #4
     Case K v L #8
     Case G v H #6

B.   Issue 2

     Statute #2
     Treatise #1
     Case M v N #9
     Case E v F #5

With either technique, the associate can more easily analyze her notes because she has divided them into manageable portions, each of which relates to a distinct legal problem.

If the researching attorney takes her notes on a portable computer, as is increasingly common, she can reorganize the information even more easily, because she can copy or move passages in her notes so as to group together information according to the issue it addresses. Indeed, the attorney may organize her notes as she goes by initially recording the fruits of her research in separate computer files identified by corresponding issues, or by recording her notes in separate places within a file. Similarly, an attorney who dictates her notes into a recording device in the library can then ask her assistant to type the dictation into a computer file, after which the attorney can make notes on the hard copy to direct the assistant to reorganize the notes on the computer file.

A law student preparing for final examinations has a special need to summarize, reorganize, and analyze his notes in outline form. In the course of a semester, a typical law student will amass several notebooks full of case briefs and notes of class discussion. Although these notes represent summaries of the thousands of pages of reading and hundreds of hours of class discussion and lecture for several courses, they are still too massive and disorganized to permit effective review and analysis for exam preparation. A well-organized summary of these notes in outline form can enable the student to stand back from the trees formed by cases and to see the broad outline of the legal forest.

The real value of a course outline, however, is not in the final product as a study aid, but in the student's activities of reviewing and synthesizing material and of drafting the outline. These tasks develop important skills of organization, analysis, and expression. A method of reasoning essential to the entire process of outlining is inductive reasoning.

II. INDUCTIVE REASONING

Through two variations of inductive reasoning, you can use information from a series of specific cases to reach a conclusion about either

1. the outcome of another specific case, or
2. the likelihood of the truth of a general proposition.[1]

A. Analogy

The process of using inductive reasoning to predict the outcome of a specific case by comparing it to other cases is one of analogy. For example, a series of cases has permitted warrantless searches of automobiles and similar vehicles, if the searches were supported by probable cause, because (1) the mobility of the vehicles created exigent circumstances that made it impracticable to obtain a warrant before searching, and (2) the owner of each vehicle had only limited expectations of privacy in its contents because the vehicle was subject to extensive administrative regulation. From those cases, you could use inductive reasoning to conclude that police may search a motor home without a warrant because (1) the motor home is similar in mobility to the vehicles that were the subjects of the prior cases, and (2) government regulation of all licensed motor vehicles gives the owner of the motor home

---

1. *See, e.g.*, Irving M. Copi, INTRODUCTION TO LOGIC 24-28, 469-73 (10th ed. 1998).

reduced expectations of privacy similar to those of the owners of the vehicles in the prior cases:

**Four cases permitted warrantless searches of the
following kinds of vehicles, because each vehicle
was mobile and subject to administrative regulation:**

Case #1: car on highway
Case #2: delivery truck in a private driveway
Case #3: family van in a shopping center parking lot
Case #4: four-wheel drive truck on unpaved desert

One reasonable conclusion from the prior cases:

In Case #5, a warrant should not be required to search a motor
home parked on the street in a residential neighborhood,
because it is mobile and subject to administrative regulation,
as were the vehicles in Cases 1-4.

As with all inductive reasoning, this conclusion about the motor home does not necessarily follow from the outcomes of the previous cases. Rather, the strength of the supporting cases simply makes the truth of the conclusion more or less likely. Indeed, you might argue that government regulation of licensed vehicles is less significant to the scope of privacy expectations than is the range and nature of activities for which a vehicle is designed. If that argument were accepted, you might use inductive reasoning to generalize from a different series of cases, each of which held that police could not search a house, apartment, or other dwelling without a warrant even if they had probable cause to search. From those cases, you could conclude that the occupant of a motor home would enjoy protection from warrantless searches similar to that enjoyed by the occupant of a house, because each structure is designed for residential uses such as sleeping, eating, and storing personal effects:

**Four cases required a warrant to search the following
kinds of dwellings, partly because the expectation of
privacy in the contents of dwellings is so high:**

Case #1: unattached house on its own lot
Case #2: rented unit of apartment complex
Case #3: weekend cabin in the mountains
Case #4: natural cave on private land used as a dwelling

One reasonable conclusion from the prior cases:

In Case #5, a warrant should be required to search a motor home
parked on the street in a residential neighborhood, because it is used
as a dwelling during vacation travel and contains the kinds of personal
items normally stored in a fixed dwelling.

Thus, depending on the relative weight that you assigned to competing factors and values, you would find one of the two competing lines of authority more nearly analogous to your case. This flexibility in inductive reasoning explains why judges can reasonably differ on the proper application and extension of precedent.[2]

B. Generalizing from Particulars

The second variation of inductive reasoning allows you to construct a general proposition from specific cases. By using this process to prepare a course outline, you can begin making the transition from daily briefing of cases to solving problems on a final examination. With this type of reasoning, you attempt to construct a general rule that is consistent with the facts and outcomes of past cases. You can then apply the general rule to other cases with similar facts.

For example, you may have briefed four cases in which courts denied punitive damages on claims for various breaches of contract: innocent breach of a construction contract, intentional breach of a contract for the sale of real estate, malicious breach of a contract to supply water, and intentional breach of a lease. Although a universal rule would not necessarily follow from the cases, you could reasonably induce from the cases a general rule that punitive damages are not available for breach of contract. You could then apply that rule to a new case, such as the intentional breach of an employment contract. The new case is not identical to any of the prior cases but is nonetheless encompassed by the general rule derived from the prior cases through inductive reasoning:

Four cases denied punitive damages for the following kinds of breach of contract:

Case #1:   innocent breach of a construction contract
Case #2:   intentional breach of a realty contract
Case #3:   malicious breach of a water-supply contract
Case #4:   intentional breach of a lease

General rule derived from the prior cases:

Punitive damages are not available for breach of contract, regardless of the breaching party's state of mind.

Application of general rule to new case:

In Case #5, punitive damages will not be available for intentional breach of an employment contract.

---

2. *See, e.g.*, California v. Carney, 471 U.S. 386 (1985) (disagreeing with the California Supreme Court's conclusion that a warrant was required to search a motor home).

The degree of confidence that you have in the general rule will depend on the strength of the supporting cases. If one of the previous decisions had awarded punitive damages for breach of a marriage contract, the general rule stated above would be a less reliable guide to the outcome of other kinds of disputes within its terms, and you would apply the rule with caution. You could improve the reliability of the rule by modifying it to achieve consistency with all the previous cases: Punitive damages are not available for breach of contract, except for breach of marriage contracts.

Exercise **8-1**

Imagine that a parent, Carmen, is developing family rules for the social activities of her teenage daughter, Monica, during the school year. Carmen states that she wants Monica to set aside adequate time for sleep and home-work, but Carmen has not clearly articulated specific rules. Instead, she provides guidance to Monica by reacting to specific events, or "cases," with expression of approval or disapproval. In each of the following four cases, identify one or more reasonable interpretations of the "holding" of each case. By comparing each new holding to previous ones, and by generalizing from the particles of the cases, can Monica include in a specific rule or rules?

1. CASE #1: THE PIZZA HANGOUT

On Friday, October 1, Monica attended a high school football game, which ended at 9:45 P.M. She then joined some friends for pizza and arrived home at 11:15 P.M. Carmen scolded her for being late, saying, "It's after 11 o'clock. Where have you been?" When Monica responded that she had "hung out" with a friend at the pizza parlor after eating pizza, Carmen stated: "Well, next time, after the game, don't *hang out* at the pizza parlor. You need your sleep, and you've got plenty of homework to do."

2. CASE #2: PIZZA REPRISE

On Friday, October 8, Monica attended a high school football game, which ended at 9:45 P.M. She then joined some friends for pizza and arrived home at 10:55 P.M. Carmen greeted her at the door cheerfully and stated, "Hi. How was your evening? It's just about 11. If you hurry, you can get to bed by 11:30."

3. CASE #3: SATURDAY NIGHT AT THE MOVIES

During the week of October 11-17, Monica attended a school volleyball game on Tuesday night and a high school musical production on Friday night, returning home by 11:00 P.M. on each night. Carmen expressed no disapproval. On Saturday afternoon, Monica asked Carmen whether she could go out with a friend to an early evening showing of a movie. Carmen responded, "No. You've been out twice already this week, and that's enough for one week. You need to catch up on your sleep and your homework."

4. CASE #4: THE OBLIGATORY BIRTHDAY PARTY

During the week of October 18-25, Monica went to a movie with friends on Thursday evening and to the school dance on Friday night, returning home by 11:00 P.M. on each night. When Monica returned on Friday night, Carmen announced that Monica would be joining Carmen and other family members to attend the fiftieth birthday party of Monica's uncle. Monica expressed surprise, expecting her mother to insist that Monica stay focused on homework all weekend. Carmen responded, "Well you probably should, but the whole family is going. We can't miss an event like this."

C. Relationship to Deductive Reasoning

Both forms of inductive reasoning described in Sections A and B above can be applied to the broad framework of deductive reasoning described in Chapter 6. In that framework, after identifying an issue, you state the applicable rule and apply it to the relevant facts to reach a conclusion:

> Issue
> Rule   {Major Premise}
> Application to Facts   {Minor Premise}
> Conclusion

1. FORMULATING THE RULE

The process of synthesizing cases was introduced in Chapter 7, Section II.B.7. The immediately preceding discussion of inductive reasoning provides a fuller explanation and extension of one form of synthesis. You can use inductive reasoning to construct a general rule from a series of cases; in turn, you can use that rule to form the major premise of your deductive analysis, as discussed in Chapter 6. In an office memorandum or a brief, you could represent this process comprehensively in several paragraphs or pages of in-depth analysis of case law that shows how you arrived at your understanding of the current form of a developing legal principle. The discussion of law in the first sample memorandum toward the end of Chapter 11 illustrates moderately in-depth analysis.

Alternatively, you could state the rule as a simple proposition in a single sentence, followed by citation to the authority or authorities from which you derived the rule:

A promise does not satisfy the consideration requirement if it allows the promisor to refrain from performing at his unfettered whim or discretion. *See Strong v. Sheffield,* **144 N.Y. 392, 39 N.E. 330 (1895).**

Because of time limitations and other constraints, when you state a rule in an examination answer, you will tend toward this simpler example, almost always without any citation to authority.

2. APPLYING THE RULE TO THE FACTS

To help you apply the legal rule to the facts of your dispute, you can invoke the inductive process of analogizing between the facts of previous cases and the facts of your own case. In an office memorandum or brief, you may represent this process comprehensively in several paragraphs or pages in which you compare the facts and reasoning of previous cases to the facts of your own case. Again, the fact analysis in the first sample memorandum toward the end of Chapter 11 illustrates such explicit analogy and distinction.

Alternatively, you could analyze the facts more simply by directly explaining why the facts of your case do not satisfy the legal rule:

In this case, the lender's promise to forbear until he "needs" the money appears to condition the length of his forbearance on financial events that are at least partly outside his control. As long as his income and expenses create no need for the money, the lender has committed himself to forbear from demanding payment. Therefore, the lender's promise satisfies the consideration requirement, and the guarantor's promise is enforceable.

As with the statement of the legal rule, your fact analysis in an exam answer will often tend toward this simpler example. In developing even a simple fact analysis, however, you may implicitly compare the facts of your case with the facts and reasoning of the cases that you have earlier analyzed. Thus, although you may not always have time during an examination to express the details of your comparison, the inductive process of analogizing and distinguishing cases nonetheless informs your fact analysis.

3. ROLE OF THE COURSE OUTLINE

By preparing a course outline, you can use inductive reasoning to help bridge the gap between your case briefs and the deductive analysis called for in a law school examination. As discussed more fully below, your outline should be organized around general legal rules, some of which you have constructed through inductive reasoning from groups of cases. These are rules that you can later recall and restate in an examination answer.

Moreover, your outline should illustrate these rules with brief summaries of the cases from which you derived the rules. Your familiarity with the facts and reasoning of these cases will help you apply the general rules to the facts of your examination questions, even if you do not always have time during the examination to fully express your process of analogizing and distinguishing cases.

III. TECHNIQUES OF OUTLINING COURSE MATERIALS

To transform your case briefs and class notes to a useful outline, you must reorganize, analyze, and summarize. The finished product will be an infinitely more useful study guide than your original notes, but the real value of a course outline is in the process of constructing it rather than in the finished product. Expressing your understanding of the law in outline form forces you to identify and resolve lingering areas of confusion that a less rigorous form of review might conceal. Moreover, outlining develops skills of organization and expression that you must summon and apply in the examination room and the law office. A commercial outline might contain information that you can understand and even remember, but it does not provide an effective means of developing important skills.

A. Fundamental Principles of Outlining

The format for a course outline is largely a matter of personal style for each student. The techniques of outlining described in this chapter are not the only ones that you might find helpful. The techniques described here, however, have the benefit of developing skills that can be readily employed in drafting office memoranda and briefs, as well as exam answers. These outlining techniques require you to

1. classify cases to facilitate a reorganization that focuses on general principles rather than on individual cases, and
2. display the proper relationships among points in the outline.

1. CLASSIFICATION

Your course outline should not simply present a series of case briefs or even of case brief summaries. Instead, it should emphasize general rules of law and should subordinate the case briefs to the role of illustrating the rules.

a. Topics and Subtopics

The first step in organizing such a course outline is to classify the kinds of problems or rules addressed in the case briefs and class notes and to recognize which kinds of problems are subsets of more general topics. Depending on the volume and complexity of the material to be outlined, you may identify several levels of classifications of problem areas or principles. If so, the most logical way to proceed is first to identify the classifications that have the broadest scope, and then to identify the subsidiary classifications that form subsets of the major classifications.

For example, an outline of legal remedies might encompass two broad categories of relief: (1) specific relief, in the form of an injunction to perform as promised, and (2) substitutional relief, or money damages. Within each of those two major topics, the course material would undoubtedly present subsidiary problem areas, each of which encompasses another set of subsidiary problem areas, and so on. The following sequence of headings traces a single, descending line of such classifications leading to the topic of the availability of punitive damages in tort and contract actions.

I. Specific Relief
   • • • •
II. Substitutional Relief—Money Damages
   A. Nominal Damages
   • • • •
   B. Compensatory Damages
   • • • •
   C. Punitive Damages
     1. Purpose and Measure
   • • • •
     2. Availability
       a. Torts
   • • • •
       b. Contracts
   • • • •

Each of the classifications in this outline identifies a subset of the area of law encompassed by the subject of remedies and identifies the subject matter of disputes that have required the application of legal rules to facts. Moreover, each major classification in the outline first addresses a topic at the most general level and then separately examines more specific problems within the topic.

b. Transitions and Overviews

To clearly signal the organizational procession from the general to the specific, you may wish to begin each significant section and subsection with a brief paragraph or a separate introductory section that presents an overview of the subsections that follow:

I. Overview
     A successful claimant may be entitled to either or both of two basic kinds of relief: (1) specific relief, in the form of an injunction that orders the defendant to take, or refrain from taking, some action; (2) substitutional relief, in the form of an award of money damages.
II. Specific/Injunctive Relief
   • • • •
III. Substitutional Relief
     Depending on the circumstances, courts may award any of three kinds of money damages: nominal, compensatory, or punitive.
   A. Nominal Damages
   • • • •
   B. Compensatory Damages
   • • • •
   C. Punitive Damages
   • • • •

c. Revealing Comprehension or Confusion About Relationships Between Points

By displaying the proper relationships among points in your outline, you demonstrate a full understanding of its analytic content. For example, the excerpts presented above accurately identify some topics as subsets of more general topics.

Conversely, the topic and subtopic headings of an outline may reveal confusion that the author may recognize at a glance and seek to clear up. For example, the following outline erroneously classifies compensatory damages as an element of specific relief. It also misleadingly suggests that the topics of the availability and measure of punitive damages are no more closely related to one another than either is to questions about nominal damages:

   I. Specific Relief
     A. Compensatory Damages
     • • • •

  II. Substitutional Relief—Money Damages
     A. Nominal Damages
     • • • •

     B. Availability of Punitive Damages
     • • • •

     C. Measure of Punitive Damages
     • • • •

If you are not sure whether your outline headings reflect a solid grasp of the course material, you might ask a classmate or classroom instructor to glance at them and provide you with a quick evaluation.

2. GETTING STARTED

a. Working from a Disorganized "Laundry List"

If you have trouble starting your outline, you might set organizational considerations aside until you clearly identify the points that you later will display in logical structure. For example, you might start by glancing through your notes and the table of contents of your coursebook and by making a "laundry list" of rules or problem areas that the cases have presented:

injunctions
expectation interest
nominal damages
adequacy of remedy at law
compensatory damages
mitigation of damages
punitive damages
unique goods
specific performance of personal services

Once you have identified the topics that you want to address in the outline, you can classify the problems presented in the list and can determine their proper relationships to one another.

b. Illustration: Everything in Its Place

When they were younger, my two sons used a remarkably similar process when they cleaned their playroom. Scattered throughout the room were such things as stuffed animals and dolls, fiction and nonfiction books, and toy dinosaurs and cars. They knew that the stuffed animals and dolls belonged on the window box, the dinosaurs belonged in the red toy bin, the cars belonged in a special box, and the books belonged on one of two shelves. Their nonfiction reference books, such as those on science and nature, belonged on a shelf in their bedroom closet. All other books were stored between bookends on top of a bedroom dresser. When putting away these belongings, they typically waded through the scattered objects, picking out all the objects within a single category or subcategory, such as all cars, and putting them in their proper place before gathering objects from another category or subcategory. The organizational structure of their activity could be represented in the following way:

I. Proper Places for Dolls, Toys, and Books
   A. Dolls and Stuffed Animals
      {together as single category on window box}
   B. Toys
      1. Dinosaurs
         {red toy bin}
      2. Cars
         {special box}
   C. Books
      1. Nonfiction Reference Books
         {bedroom closet shelf}
      2. All Other Children's Books
         {between bookends on dresser}

---

c. Special Challenges of Organizing Course Materials

Of course, my children's chore was relatively simple. Their playthings were concrete, simple, and readily distinguished from one another. Moreover, my wife and I devised the categories and the corresponding storage areas.

As a law student, however, you must work with more abstract principles and must devise your own categories and subcategories. Your casebook's table of contents may provide some hints on categories and organization, but you should not hesitate to depart from it. A casebook occasionally adopts an unusual organizational structure for pedagogic purposes, and you may prefer a more straightforward structure that translates more readily to a guide for problem-solving.

Organizing an outline of legal points is not an exact science. The flexibility and uncertainty inherent in the analysis of much of the material that you encounter in the first year of law school make it impossible to identify a single "correct" method of organizing an outline of that material. Nonetheless, your diligent efforts leading to a reasonable outline will develop skills of organization that you can transfer directly to more formal legal documents such as briefs, memoranda, and contracts.

B. Content of the Outline

1. IDENTIFYING, CONSTRUCTING, AND STATING RULES

As a means of preparing to apply general legal rules to the facts of an exam problem, you should identify or even construct legal rules from the statutes and cases that you have studied. This process does not compel an unduly simplistic and mechanical approach to the law. The legal rules are simply shorthand representations of more complex sets of information that you can explore in greater detail when you refer to the case law from which the rules are drawn.

On some topics, a legislature supplies a statutory rule or a court states a general rule derived from earlier case law. Even dictum from a judicial opinion may provide a reliable guide to a tentative statement of a general rule. Although you must identify the narrow holding of a decision to evaluate the effect of the case as precedent, you may safely look to dictum for aid in constructing general rules that you can profitably apply in an examination.

In many instances, however, you will not find concise statements of general rules on a particular legal topic in statutes or in the holdings or dicta of judicial decisions. Instead, you must identify the cases that address issues related to the topic, and you must use techniques of synthesis, such as inductive reasoning, to construct a general rule from the individual cases. To use the example presented in Section II.B. above, you might study the holdings in a series of decisions denying punitive damages in different kinds of contracts cases and construct a general rule that punitive damages are not available for breach of contract, even if none of the decisions stated such a rule of general application. Indeed, your synthesis at the outline stage may lead you to revise your earlier, more tentative generalizations about a series of cases.

2. ILLUSTRATING RULES WITH EXAMPLES

a. Case Summaries as Examples or Exceptions to a Rule

Regardless of the method that you use to identify a general legal rule, your statement of the rule should not stand alone. You should illustrate and give more definite shape to the rule by

1. summarizing the case law from which the rule was derived and
2. identifying competing rules or exceptions to the rule:

V. Punitive Damages
  A. Purpose and Measure
  • • • •
  B. Availability
    1. Torts— . . . .
  • • • •
    2. Contracts—Courts generally do not award punitive damages for breach of contract.

    a. Example: In *White v. Benkowski*, CB at 12, the court affirmed a trial court's denial of punitive damages for even a malicious breach of an agreement to supply water.

    b. Exception to Rule: In dictum, the *White* court suggested that it might retain a traditional exception allowing punitive damages for breach of a marriage agreement.

    c. Minority Approach for Malicious Breaches: A few jurisdictions have followed the lead of *Jordan v. Ash*, CB at 16, which granted punitive damages for an employer's "malicious and oppressive" breach of an employment agreement, even though the employee had not proved all the elements of an independent tort.

The concise statement of the general rule in Subsection B.2 of the outline above represents the kind of information that you must recall and express on a law school examination. To apply that rule to the facts of an exam question, however, you must have a more concrete understanding of the law than is reflected in the abstract statement of the general rule. For this, you must analyze individual cases, as illustrated in Subsections a, b, and c in the above example.

Subsections a and b illustrate a student's understanding of the parameters of the rule in most jurisdictions: Pursuant to a traditional exception, some courts might still award punitive damages in the case of breach of a marriage agreement; otherwise, even a finding of malice on the part of the breaching party will not cause the court to depart from the general rule against punitive damages. Subsection c reflects the student's judgment that *Jordan* represents a minority approach: In a few jurisdictions, courts might be disposed to grant punitive damages for breach of any kind of contract, if the breach is accompanied by the kind of malicious intent sometimes associated with the most egregious of intentional torts. By identifying the factual context of *Jordan*, the student can remain sensitive to the possibility that this minority approach is limited to employment contracts or other contracts in which the parties have disparate bargaining power.

In adding case summaries to the outline, you should retain a basic structure that organizes the subject matter around legal rules and that subordinates the cases to illustrations of those rules. For example, a case that addresses distinct issues relating to the proper measure of compensatory damages and to the availability of punitive damages might appear in summarized form in two places in the outline: (1) a summary of the court's first holding would illustrate a rule about compensatory damages, and (2) a summary of the second holding would illustrate a rule about punitive damages stated in a different section of the outline.

b. Adding Policy Analysis

A more sophisticated outline of the same material might incorporate a policy analysis of the rule and the cases that illustrate it, perhaps reflecting the student's evaluation, as well as her synthesis, of the cases:

2. Contracts—Courts generally do not award punitive damages for breach of contract.
   a. Possible Policy Justifications—A breach of a private contract may not injure community interests as much as would a tort or a crime. Indeed, in some instances a breach may benefit the community by permitting reallocation of the freed resources to more productive uses. Compensatory damages would permit this reallocation while making the victim of the breach whole, but punitive damages would discourage the reallocation.
   b. Example: In *White v. Benkowski*, CB at 12, the court affirmed denial of punitive damages for even a malicious breach of a contract to supply water. This decision doesn't seem to further any important policy, however, because the supplier did not reallocate the water to a more urgent use.
   c. Exception: In dictum, the *White* Court suggested that it might retain a traditional exception allowing punitive damages for breach of a marriage agreement, presumably because "community resentment" may once have been greater in such cases.
   d. Minority Approach: In *Jordan v. Ash*, CB at 16, the court approved punitive damages for an employer's "malicious and oppressive" breach of an employment agreement, even though the employee had not proved all the elements of an independent tort. Deterrence through punitive damages is appropriate in such cases, because the injurious conduct is designed to harm others rather than to reallocate resources or serve any other business needs.

The policy analysis may be suggested in the opinions themselves, may be the topic of class discussion, or may be the product of your original analysis. In this example, Illustration c does more than simply identify possible limitations to the rule. It also implicitly raises questions about the continued viability of an exception that arguably is rooted in outdated values. Similarly, Illustration d does more than identify a minority approach as a different kind of qualification to the general rule. In conjunction with Illustration b, it implicitly compares the merits of maintaining certainty in a broad rule of general application (Illustration b) with the case-specific fairness achieved by narrowly shaping rules so that they apply no further than the reasons that support them (Illustration d).

If time permits, you may wish to consult a treatise for clarification or for ideas that enrich your outline. However, you will develop skills best by preparing outlines from course materials and class notes with minimum reference to study aids and with only occasional reference to respected treatises to help clear up areas of confusion.

c. Examples on Either Side of the Line Defined by the Rule

Often, you can best illustrate the parameters of a rule by comparing two factually distinguishable, legally consistent cases that reach different results. By identifying a set of facts that satisfies the legal rule and by contrasting them with a set of facts that does not, the outline helps to bring concrete meaning to an otherwise abstract rule.

For example, an outline of statutory liability for civil rights violations might address the subtopic of a judge's defense of absolute immunity from money damages. More particularly, an outline prepared in 1987 might compare the following opinions in which the same court had twice in 1986 addressed the rule that a judge enjoys immunity for acts performed in a "judicial function":

VI. Immunity Defenses
   [overview]
   A. Absolute Immunities—Legislators, judges, and prosecutors must make sensitive policy decisions on controversial matters and are conspicuous targets for retaliatory suits. Absolute immunity allows them to exercise discretion without fear of reprisal.
      1. Legislators— . . . .
      • • • •
      2. Judges—A state judge is absolutely immune from liability for money damages, even for allegedly malicious unconstitutional acts, if the judge (a) had subject-matter jurisdiction, and (b) was acting in a judicial function.
         a. Subject-Matter Jurisdiction— . . . .
         b. Judicial Function—A judge enjoys immunity only for actions taken within a judicial function, as contrasted with the judge's administrative function. | **Rule**
            (1) Example: In *Forrester v. White,* CB 423 (7th Cir. 1986),[3] a judge enjoyed absolute immunity from liability for alleged discrimination in firing a probation officer. Because the probation officer's duties included advising the judge on substantive matters, hiring or firing the officer was a judicial function that "directly implicated the exercise of the judge's discretionary judgment." | **Facts that satisfy the rule**
            (2) Example: In *McMillan v. Svetanoff,* CB 425 (7th Cir. 1986), a judge was not absolutely immune from liability for alleged race discrimination in firing a court reporter, who recorded proceedings but did not perform legal analysis. Hiring and firing such employees was an administrative task because it did not require exercise of the judge's legal knowledge or experience. | **Facts that do not satisfy the rule**

---

3. *Rev'd,* 484 U.S. 219 (1988). Although the circuit decision was reversed in 1988, the state of the law in the Seventh Circuit in 1986 provides a good vehicle for illustrating factually contrasting decisions in the same jurisdiction.

In this outline, Subsections b(1) and b(2) give concrete meaning to the abstract rule stated in subsection b by providing examples of facts that satisfy the rule stated in Subsection b and facts that fail to satisfy the rule.

Exercise 8-2

---

1. OUTLINING EXERCISE—RULES OF THE HOUSE

Imagine that parents, Gerald and Janice, are teaching their toddler, Debbie, good habits and behavior. Debbie can't fully understand abstract rules, so Gerald and Janice teach her through positive or negative feedback in specific situations. In the last few weeks, Debbie remembers the following experiences for which she received praise or admonishment:

The Case of the Hand in the Cookie Jar: Debbie reached into a cookie jar and helped herself to a cookie shortly before dinner. Janice and Gerald admonished Debbie that the cookie would spoil her appetite for dinner.

The Case of the Broken Vase: Debbie climbed onto a chair, reached a vase on a table top, and threw the vase to the floor, breaking it. Janice and Gerald sent Debbie to her room, admonishing her that she should not play with her parents' possessions.

The Case of the Chocolate Ice Cream: After dinner one night, Debbie asked for some chocolate ice cream. To her surprise, her parents served her a dish of ice cream, praising her for having finished her vegetables.

The Case of the Mistreated Teddy Bear: Anxious to test her parents' limits one evening, Debbie climbed onto a chair with her favorite teddy bear and threw the teddy bear onto the living room carpet. Debbie's parents saw this event but had no reaction; they continued reading the newspaper and watching TV.

The Case of the Bouncing Ball: Emboldened by the teddy bear incident, Debbie brought out her favorite rubber ball and began kicking it around the living room, causing it to bounce off the TV set and to narrowly miss Janice's glass of wine sitting on the coffee table. Janice flashed Debbie an angry glance, and Gerald sternly said, "Outside with that ball!"

Assignment: From these cases, derive at least two general rules governing Debbie's behavior in her home. Illustrate each of your rules with brief summaries that show what kinds of behavior either satisfy or violate the rules. If appropriate, draft an overview statement that captures the essence of all the rules and examples. When you have completed your outline, compare it with the sample outline toward the end of Chapter 9.

2. OUTLINING EXERCISE—ADVERTISEMENTS AS OFFERS

Review the case briefs that you prepared for Exercise 7-1(3) near the end of Chapter 7. Prepare an excerpt of a contracts outline that addresses the question of whether a store's newspaper advertisement amounts to an offer.

Derive a general legal rule from the two cases and use summaries of the cases as illustrations of the rule.

3. OUTLINING EXERCISE—RULES FOR MONICA

Review Exercise 8-1 near the beginning of this chapter. From the four cases, derive rules, or several elements of a single rule, that describe limitations that Carmen imposes on Monica's social activities. Prepare an outline of this topic, organizing the outline around the rules or elements of a rule. Illustrate each statement of a rule or element of a rule with a one-sentence summary of one of the cases or with an observation of your own.

C. The Outline as a Study Tool

Although the process of preparing an outline is more valuable than the finished product, a thoughtful outline makes an excellent study tool. When reviewing for exams, you can put your voluminous notes aside and use the brief references to cases in the outline to trigger your memory about the fuller case analysis that you performed earlier in the semester.

In the few hours before an exam, you may want to take a broader view of the course by skimming the legal rules stated in the major sections and subsections of your outline. The factual context provided by case summaries will easily come to mind if you have earlier analyzed those cases, expressed the analysis in the outline, and read the entire outline once or twice after preparing it. Indeed, you may find it helpful to prepare a brief outline of the outline by writing down the major headings of the outline on a separate sheet of paper. From this list of headings, you might develop a checklist of the issues most likely to be addressed in a final examination.

IV. SUMMARY

To outline course material, follow these steps:

1. Analyze and synthesize by briefing the cases and reflecting on class discussion.
2. Identify topics that you intend to address in the outline. You should identify significant general rules that are stated in the course materials or that you can construct from the course materials through a process of inductive reasoning.
3. State those rules in an organized fashion that shows the proper relationships among the rules.
4. Finally, illustrate the general rules with brief summaries of the cases from which the rules are derived.

Exercise 8-3

This and previous chapters of this book have introduced you to an integrated process of case analysis and synthesis and summary and reorganization of information in an outline. The next chapter addresses flexible application of deductive reasoning in applying principles to new sets of facts, such as those in examination questions.

The following exercises introduce you to these processes on a level that should require no formal training or knowledge of special legal rules. Follow the directions of the exercises, use your common sense, and express your answers in simple, concise language. For practice in outlining traditional course material, perform Assignment 2 in Appendix III, near the end of this book.

1. CASE ANALYSIS

In each of the three cases below, try to derive a lesson or a rule from the case that would help guide the central character, Han Li, in his future actions regarding speed limits on streets and highways. State this point in a simple sentence or two, including a brief statement of the probable policy justifications for the rule. If you wish, you may also briefly describe special facts that help illustrate the rule. In the second and third cases, you may also consider commenting briefly on ways in which the case compares or contrasts with the preceding case or cases.

In this exercise, do not concern yourself with the question of whether Mr. Li obeyed or violated the speed limit. Instead, focus on the facts and policies that justify the establishment of different speed limits in different settings.

In the first case analysis below, the exercise is completed as an example.

a. The Case of the School Zone

Han Li recently immigrated to the United States, enrolled in a community college in Phoenix, Arizona, and obtained a driver's permit. While driving throughout the state, he carefully surveyed his surroundings so that he could quickly learn the customs and rules of driving in the United States.

When approaching an elementary school on a two-lane residential street at 8:15 on Monday morning, Li noticed dozens of children laughing and running in the schoolyard, as well as a few children walking on the sidewalk toward the school. He also noticed a sign stating "15 mph when school is in session." Before Li could slow down, however, a police officer pulled him over and cited him for driving 25 miles per hour.

Sample Statement of Lesson: The speed limit in an elementary school zone in a residential neighborhood is 15 mph when school is in session, probably because the risk of children running into the road is particularly great at that time and place. In this case, that risk was underscored by presence of numerous children in the playground and on the sidewalk.

b. The Case of the Urban Freeway

Later that morning, Li entered the interstate freeway from the center of Phoenix. Within the city limits, the divided freeway meandered through the city in gentle curves, varying in width from three to four lanes in each direction. It was heavily traveled, with cars and trucks frequently changing lanes and merging near the numerous freeway entrances and exits, some of which were only one mile apart from the next set of entrances and exits.

Li was traveling 60 miles per hour but slowed down when he noticed a sign stating "55 mph." He was not anxious to repeat his experience in the school zone.

Lesson?

c. The Case of the Rural Freeway

As Li proceeded south on the freeway toward Tucson, he left the Phoenix city limits and passed through nearly 100 miles of rural, nonresidential desert. The freeway was mostly straight and level, varying in width from two to three lanes in each direction. Traffic was light, and several consecutive sets of freeway entrances and exits were separated by 10 to 15 miles. Li noticed a sign posting a speed limit of 65 miles per hour, and he increased his speed accordingly.

Lesson?

2. SYNTHESIS AND OUTLINING

Use the three cases in Problem 1 above to generalize about legislative policy in setting speed limits on different roads. As an example of one approach, try the following:

First, think about the factors that seem to influence the setting of speed limits. Your stated policy justifications in each of the cases should help you here. Then, try to make a single statement that helps to explain all of the speed limits described in the cases. As an example, you might complete the following sentences:

Speed limits on streets and freeways range from 15 mph to 65 mph, depending on such factors as . . . . These factors reflect general policy concerns for . . . .

For this exercise, you should not concern yourself with the question whether Li obeyed or violated the speed limits in each of the cases. To keep this exercise simple, focus your attention only on the speed limits and the justifications for them. Of course, quite apart from Li's obeying or violating the speed limits, the particular circumstances of each case will help you identify the justifications for the speed limits.

Once you have constructed your statement, illustrate it with a series of three examples. Each example should be a brief summary of the critical information in each of the three cases. The information is critical if it helps to illuminate the point that you make in your general statement.

For example, your series of illustrations could take the following form:

Speed limits on streets and freeways range from 15 mph to 65 mph, depending upon such factors as . . . . These factors reflect an overarching policy concern for . . . .

1. *Example*—In The Case of the School Zone, the speed limit in a residential elementary school zone is set at 15 mph while school is in session, because . . . .
2. *Example*—In contrast, in The Case of the Rural Freeway . . . .
3. *Example*—In The Case of the Urban Freeway . . . .

---

3. PREDICTING THE OUTCOME OF A NEW CASE

Just before reaching Tucson, Li exits the freeway and drives on a straight, level two-lane undivided highway through desert. Side roads intersect the highway every few miles. The traffic is light, and the area is sparsely populated, but several homes border the highway over a 10-mile stretch.

One hundred yards ahead, a police officer sits in his car at a stop sign where a side road intersects the highway. Li is traveling 50 mph. He is eager to obey the speed limit but has forgotten to note the posted speed limit a few miles back.

In the face of uncertainty about the speed limit, Li prudently slows down as he approaches the officer. However, the incident stimulates his curiosity about the speed limit.

Place yourself in Li's position. Use your general statement in Problem 2 above as a guide for guessing the speed limit for the highway. Apply the factors that you derived from each of the previous cases to the facts of this new case. Then, reach some reasonable conclusion about the probable speed limit. Do not look for some magic number as the single correct answer. Simply make a reasonable estimate based on the other cases and support your estimate with good analysis of the policies and the facts.

Chapter 9

Essay Examinations

I. OVERVIEW—PERSPECTIVE AND GENERAL FORMAT

The answer to a law school essay examination is generally similar to the discussion section of an office memorandum, which is discussed in detail in Chapters 11 and 12. When you reach those chapters, you should reflect on the parallels between an office memorandum and an essay examination answer. To better prepare you for the comparison, this chapter occasionally pauses to note which facets of examination answers have counterparts in office memoranda and to point out the differences in styles appropriate to each document.

A. Perspective

Most essay examinations ask for a balanced analysis of a problem with a direction such as the following: "Discuss the claims and defenses that the parties may reasonably assert. Be sure to discuss arguments on both sides of each issue." Like an actual office memorandum assignment, the exam

149

problem may identify one of the parties as your client. Nonetheless, the exam presumably requests that you adopt an objective perspective rather than advocate only your client's claims and defenses. In addition to developing arguments for your own client, you must anticipate and demonstrate an understanding of the counterarguments that the opposing party likely will raise.

Indeed, many exam problems do not even identify one of the parties as your client. Your perspective then will be even more strictly neutral than it would be for an office memorandum, which at least anticipates advocacy on behalf of an identified client.

Finally, a few exam problems may ask you to advocate only the claims and defenses of an identified client. If so, your answer will take the partisan approach of a brief to a court. Such exams, however, are rare.

B. General Format

As introduced in Chapter 6, an answer to an essay examination and the discussion section of an office memorandum typically share a general structure: After (1) identifying the *issue,* you should (2) summarize the applicable *legal rule* or rules, (3) *apply* the rule to the relevant *facts* to determine whether the facts satisfy the legal rule, and (4) state a reasonable *conclusion.*

Some of the more formal components of other legal documents are notably missing from a good exam answer. For example, professors normally do not require you to formally state all the issues at or near the beginning of your answer, as you would in an office memorandum or in some briefs. Even more important, you should never waste time drafting an introduction that separately restates all the facts of the problem. In all but the most unusual examinations, the problem will state the facts for you. Accordingly, your professor will test your ability to analyze groups of those facts in the context of specific issues, but not your ability to restate all the facts at the outset.

II. ELEMENTS OF THE ANSWER

A. Issues

1. IDENTIFYING ISSUES

Occasionally, a professor will identify examination issues by asking you to respond to specific questions, such as, "Did Seller make an offer to Buyer?" More commonly, the exam problem will end with a very general question about the rights and obligations of the party, and it will require you to identify the relevant issues.

To identify the issues, you must apply the skills and knowledge that you have acquired from briefing cases and outlining course material throughout the semester. By briefing countless cases, you have learned to sift through complicated fact patterns and to recognize the kinds of facts that have potential legal significance. Moreover, by briefing and synthesizing cases and by outlining the course material, you have armed yourself with a general knowledge of relevant legal rules and policies. With this preparation, by carefully studying the facts of the exam problem, you can determine what claims and defenses the parties can reasonably assert and which elements of those claims and defenses are placed in doubt.

For example, suppose that an exam problem asks you to assume that the relevant jurisdiction has retained the common law definition of burglary. Part of the problem describes Robert Glass just before dawn opening the door of the cab of a VW bus and reaching inside to steal stereo equipment lying on the driver's seat. It also states that the owner of the bus, Leova Rosales, is sleeping in the back of the vehicle while on a road trip, with curtains drawn between her and the cab of the bus. The problem also asks you to assume that theft of the stereo equipment would constitute felony larceny in the jurisdiction.

You know from your studies that the common law crime of burglary requires proof of the breaking and entering of a dwelling of another at night with the intent to commit a felony. Armed with this knowledge, you can see that the facts provide a nonfrivolous basis for prosecuting Robert Glass for common law burglary. For example, Robert's opening the closed cab door and reaching into the VW bus to steal the stereo equipment are almost certainly a "breaking and entering" with an "intent to commit a felony." These elements of the crime probably do not raise issues warranting substantial discussion. At most, you might briefly argue that Leova's leaving the window wide open invited entry to an extent that negated a "breaking."

Other elements of the crime, however, are in greater doubt. Even though Leova had drawn her curtains to permit her to sleep late, the moments "just before dawn" are only arguably "during the night." Moreover, the cab of Leova's bus is not clearly part of "a dwelling." Thus, whether Robert committed a burglary is subject to some debate and is a general issue in the problem.

Moreover, each element of the crime that is in doubt forms the basis of a subissue. For example, the VW bus may be unlike the more conventional houses that satisfied the "dwelling" requirement in the common law cases that you have studied. Although Leova is temporarily using the bus as sleeping quarters, the vehicle is arguably primarily a means of transportation, and the cab is physically separated from the sleeping quarters. Because you can reasonably argue either side of this topic, whether Leova's bus is a "dwelling" for purposes of common law burglary is a subissue warranting discussion. Other elements of the crime and possible defenses may be placed in issue by the facts summarized above or by other facts in the problem.

2. SCOPE OF ANALYSIS

Because the process of identifying issues requires you to exercise judgment, you can never determine with complete certainty which questions your professor thinks are sufficiently clearly raised by the facts to warrant discussion. Moreover, some professors directly examine your ability to identify as many issues as possible, including those related to novel or particularly creative legal theories. When in doubt, therefore, you should identify and at least briefly discuss even marginal issues. If the professor expects some discussion of a marginal issue, you will earn valuable points for even a conclusory discussion. On the other hand, if the professor disagrees that a particular matter warrants analysis, you will have minimized the lost time by keeping the discussion brief.

3. EXPRESSING YOUR IDENTIFICATION OF ISSUES

You need not state each of the issues and subissues of an examination problem in polished detail. However, your answer should leave no doubt about which issue you are analyzing in any passage in the answer. To guide your reader through your analysis, you can use the same techniques that help convey organization to the reader in the discussion section of an office memorandum. You should discuss major issues in separate sections and should precede each discussion with a section heading that generally identifies the issue analyzed in that section.

A section heading introducing an issue or subissue can simply be a word or phrase that refers to a claim, a defense, or one element of a claim or defense. Unless the question raises the possibility of claims of only one party against one other, section headings also should identify which party is bringing a claim against which other in each section.

For example, an examination problem might raise issues about various tort claims among three parties: Smith, Jones, and King. A student might display the general organization of his answer with section headings such as the following:

    I. *Smith v. Jones*
      A. Battery
      • • • •
      B. Infliction of Emotional Distress
      • • • •
   II. *Smith v. King*
      A. Negligence
      • • • •
      B. Strict Products Liability
      • • • •
 III. *Jones v. Smith—Defamation*
      • • • •

In some cases, you may wish to illuminate the issue that is denoted by a section heading by using an introductory sentence or two to refer briefly to a potential argument of one of the parties, to facts that raise the issue, or to a preliminary legal conclusion that sets up the issue. For example, immediately under Section II.A in the example above, you might provide this orientation: "Smith may claim that King negligently hired Jones, proximately causing Smith's injuries at Jones's hands."

Alternatively, you can replace the word or phrase in the section heading with a question stated in a full sentence: "Is King liable to Smith for negligently hiring Jones, proximately causing Smith to suffer injury at Jones's hands?" If you adopt this approach, however, remember that the professor reading the examination answer typically will not expect the precision and specificity appropriate for the formal statement of issues in a case brief, office memorandum, or brief to a court. Therefore, you should not waste valuable time trying to meet those standards in framing your issue in an exam answer.

If your analysis of an issue is lengthy or complex, you may want to use subsection headings to identify your discussions of subissues, with or without section numbers and letters:

I. *Smith v. Jones*
  A. Battery
  • • • •
  B. Intentional Infliction of Emotional Distress
    [overview of elements of claim]
    1. Extreme and Outrageous Conduct
  • • • •
    2. Intent or Recklessness
  • • • •
    3. Severe Emotional Distress
  • • • •
    4. Causation
  • • • •

In simpler cases, however, subtler guides to the reader often will be sufficient to identify subissues. You can separate your discussions of distinct subissues into separate paragraphs, and you can use a topic sentence to identify the subissue addressed in each paragraph:

Intentional Infliction of Emotional Distress:
  [overview of elements of claim]
  "Extreme and outrageous" conduct is limited to . . . . Viewed in isolation, Principal Jones's method of questioning Schoolboy Smith about illegal drugs. . . .
  Reckless disregard for the risk of causing severe distress can be established through. . . . In this case, Principal Jones was aware . . . .
  Severe emotional distress means more than . . . .
  Principal Jones's conduct will be viewed as the legal cause of Schoolboy Smith's injuries if . . . .

In response to a complex essay question that raises multiple issues, you may help orient the reader by beginning your response with an introductory sentence or two that briefly identifies all the major issues that you plan to discuss. However, you should not compose a lengthy introduction that makes the subsequent discussion redundant.

B. Legal Rule

1. PRESENTATION OF LEGAL RULES

At the broadest level, the statement of a legal rule may consist of a summary of the elements of a claim that a party in the examination problem may reasonably pursue:

Intentional Infliction of Emotional Distress:
 Principal Jones may be liable to Schoolboy Smith for intentional infliction of emotional distress if he engaged in extreme and outrageous conduct that caused Smith severe emotional distress, and if Jones either intended to cause such distress or recklessly disregarded the near certainty of causing such distress.

If you divide the discussion of this claim into subsections or paragraphs to address separate subissues, you might state a subrule in the form of a definition or other illumination of one of the elements of the claim:

"Extreme and outrageous" conduct is limited to shocking conduct that is beyond all possible bounds of decency. The defendant's conduct is more likely to satisfy this standard if he occupies a position of power or authority over the plaintiff.

Some examination problems may raise questions about choice of law or the precise formulation of the applicable rule. For example, a problem in a contracts examination may raise the question of whether the Uniform Commercial Code or the common law applies to a transaction.[1] Other examination problems may raise questions about the choice between traditional rules and progressive trends, or between majority rules and minority approaches. If you have time to discuss such problems, consider briefly discussing each of the competing rules. Then, in the fact analysis that follows, you can discuss the likelihood of success of a claim or defense under each legal rule.

2. DEPTH AND FORMALITY OF ANALYSIS

When writing an office memorandum, you normally must discuss specific statutes and case law from a particular jurisdiction that apply to the dispute, and you must carefully cite to the authority on which you rely. Moreover, you often will present the in-depth case analysis and synthesis from which you derive a legal rule.

In contrast, most law school examinations will require you to discuss

---

1. "Unless the context otherwise requires," article 2 of the Uniform Commercial Code applies "to transactions in goods." U.C.C. § 2-102 (2000).

general legal principles that you must memorize for a closed-book examination. Additionally, you ordinarily will not have time to describe the process of synthesizing cases from which you have derived legal rules for your outlines. Instead, you may simply present the kind of concise statements of law that you have previously constructed for your outlines.

In an examination answer, moreover, unless your professor instructs otherwise, you ordinarily need not cite to authority in your discussion of legal rules. You may earn an extra point or two by identifying the names of particular cases that illustrate issues or rules, but that practice is productive only if you remember the case name quickly and accurately. The extra point or two is not worth a significant investment of time, and the possibility of losing points or precious time by naming an irrelevant case reduces the appeal of guessing.

Your professor's expectations may be greater if she gives an open-book examination or provides statutory materials for the examination. If you have legal authority at your disposal during the examination, you can more easily cite to statutes and cases, quote relevant portions of statutes, and explain how two or more cases combine to contribute to the development of a legal principle.

C. Fact Analysis—Application of Law to Facts

1. PRESENTATION OF FACT ANALYSIS

In each section or subsection devoted to an issue or subissue, you should identify facts relevant to the issue and should briefly explain whether the facts satisfy the legal rule that you have summarized. In most cases, you have identified a matter as an issue because the facts of the problem suggest uncertainty about whether a legal rule is satisfied. Therefore, you usually can find some facts that support each side of the dispute, and you should take care to argue both sides:

Intentional Infliction of Emotional Distress:
    Principal Jones may be liable . . . .
    Viewed in isolation, Principal Jones's method of questioning Schoolboy Smith about illegal drugs probably was not "extreme and outrageous" in itself, because Jones "addressed Smith politely" and "never raised his voice." On the other hand, Jones was inherently intimidating to Smith, a ten-year-old child, because of Jones's status as an adult and as the highest authority at the elementary school. Moreover, it was common knowledge in the school that Jones had suspended two other students that semester for forging false notes excusing absences. By asking Smith to empty his pockets and to reveal the contents of his desk and locker, Jones implicitly accused Smith of lying when Smith denied any involvement with illegal drugs. In light of Jones's position of authority, his request to search Smith may have been unusually shocking and intimidating, particularly because the request immediately followed Smith's sincere denials.

---

2. DEPTH AND FORMALITY OF ANALYSIS

In an office memorandum, you will explore in depth the application of legal rules to facts by carefully comparing the facts and reasoning of previous cases to the facts of your own case. Through this process of analogizing and distinguishing precedent, you can thoroughly analyze the facts of your case to determine whether they satisfy the applicable legal rules.

In contrast, few professors will expect you to describe particular cases studied in class and to expressly analogize them to, or distinguish them from, the dispute presented in an exam problem. If you have conscientiously briefed your cases throughout the semester, you will recall cases that help you to spot issues and to analyze the problem, and you may mentally draw direct distinctions and analogies. However, you will seldom have sufficient time to express those distinctions and analogies in thorough case analysis in your examination answer. Instead, you should directly explain how relevant facts support or undermine the application of a legal rule.

As with statements of legal rules, professors who give open-book examinations may have higher expectations. If class materials are readily available to you during the exam, you may be expected to compare cases in your fact analysis. This may be true also for a closed-book exam in an exceptional area of law dominated by a manageable number of conspicuous cases, such as the Supreme Court case law governing personal jurisdiction. If you have mastered a relatively small number of important cases that define an area of law, you can feasibly refer to them by name and develop factual analogies and distinctions, even if you do not have access to your course materials during the examination.

D. The Conclusion

1. TAKING A POSITION

Some professors will examine you on your ability to apply settled law to familiar facts to reach a certain "correct" conclusion on several issues. In such cases, you should use the IRAC method of organization to explain how the law and facts lead you to a single, correct answer.

More typically, however, professors will examine you on the kinds of issues that actually would be litigated, ones that do not have a certain answer because of uncertainty in the law or in the application of the law to novel facts. In such a case, the professor expects you to argue both sides of the dispute and will not require you to identify a single "correct" answer. Nonetheless, just as your supervising attorney will expect you to reach conclusions, in the form of predictions, on even close questions in an office memorandum, most law professors will expect you to state a conclusion for each issue that you discuss in an examination answer. On close questions, you can hedge the conclusion with qualifying terms, such as "probably." Furthermore, the professor may accept any of several reasonable positions as an acceptable conclusion. Still, she will expect some resolution of each issue and subissue:

Intentional Infliction of Emotional Distress:

Principal Jones may be liable to Schoolboy Smith . . .

Extreme Conduct—
[rule and fact analysis on this subissue]
Principal Jones's questioning and request to search constituted extreme and outrageous conduct.

Subsidiary conclusion

Intent or Recklessness—
[rule and fact analysis on this subissue]
Although Principal Jones may not have intended to inflict severe emotional distress, he probably acted recklessly.

Subsidiary conclusion

Severe Emotional Distress—
[rule and fact analysis on this subissue]
Schoolboy Smith's transitory fear probably did not amount to severe emotional distress.

Subsidiary conclusion

Causation—
[rule and fact analysis on this subissue]
Any fear that Schoolboy Smith suffered over the incident was directly caused by Principal Jones's reckless actions.

Subsidiary conclusion

Conclusion—
Because Schoolboy Smith probably did not suffer extreme emotional distress, I conclude that Principal Jones is not liable for intentional infliction of emotional distress.

General conclusion

2. COMPREHENSIVE CONCLUSIONS

In an office memorandum, you should not only state conclusions at the end of your discussion of each issue and subissue, you should also summarize all your major conclusions and express your recommendations in a separate conclusion section.

In contrast, few law professors will expect you to summarize all previous major conclusions in a general summary of claims and defenses at the end of your answer to an exam problem. For example, in the illustration in the immediately preceding subsection, if the examination also raised issues of battery and false imprisonment, you would state a general conclusion for each of the three tort claims (battery, false imprisonment, and intentional infliction of emotional distress), but you ordinarily would not be expected to end your discussion of the problem with a comprehensive restatement of your conclusions on all three claims. Such a consolidated restatement of conclusions will score few points in an examination unless it adds new information or enhances the clarity of the discussion that precedes it. In most cases, accordingly, you will benefit by using the last few minutes allocated to a problem to look for additional issues that you might have missed rather than to summarize conclusions that you have already clearly communicated in your discussions of individual issues.

III. TECHNIQUES FOR WRITING EXAM RESPONSES

A. Effective Use of Time

At the beginning of the examination, you should determine how much time you will allocate to each problem, and you should adhere to that schedule. Adequate discussions of all the problems in an examination will score more points than unusually thorough discussions of some of the problems at the cost of inadequate treatment of others. The same holds true for treatment of issues within a problem: Adequate discussions of all the major issues will score more points than an unusually thorough discussion of only half the issues. Thus, if an exam problem raises an unusual number of issues, the professor may expect only superficial discussion of each.

Although law school examinations require quick thinking, uninterrupted concentration, and rapid writing, you should not begin writing prematurely. You are more likely to write sensible responses and to avoid wasted effort if you spend up to a quarter of the time allotted for each problem in mastering the assignment and in "prewriting."

B. Mastering the Assignment

You should read an exam problem once at a moderately quick pace to get a general picture of the events described, to classify the general nature of the probable claims and defenses, and to discover the particular question or questions posed by the professor, usually at the end of the problem. You should then read the problem at least once again, this time at a much more deliberate pace, to spot specific issues and to make marks or margin notes that highlight important facts.

C. Prewriting

A few students have such well-developed skills of organization, such good memories, and such powers of concentration that they can write their examination answers without first outlining their analyses. The rest of us, however, will benefit greatly if we devote a few minutes to analysis and outlining before beginning to write.

The outline on scratch paper should be nothing more than a skeletal construction of the issues that you intend to address and the significant facts relating to each of those issues. The outline becomes your primary vehicle for analysis and organization. Before you begin writing, you can use it to decide which issues you will address, what order of presentation is most logical or efficient, and what facts support each side of the dispute in each section:

Q1—

    I. *Smith v. Jones*
        A. Battery—injurious contact, and no consent, but requisite intent? Jones stumbled but was already reaching for the purpose of . . . .
        B. Intent. Inflic. of Emot. Distress
            1. Extreme Conduct—Jones—polite, but great authority. Request to search suggests disbelief and possibility of discipline.
            2. Intent or Reckless—
        • • • •
        C. Defamation
        • • • •

If the legal rules associated with an issue are unusually complex, or if you desire to discuss alternative legal theories, you may wish to include some reference to the law in the outline as well.

By scribbling a quick outline, you can examine your complete analysis at a glance and can determine whether it makes sense. If the analysis appears to be faulty, incomplete, or illogically organized, you can easily change your plans at the outlining stage. You would find it much more difficult to change your approach after you have written half of your response.

Finally, after completing your outline, you should quickly read the problem once again before beginning to write. Because you have fully analyzed the problem in the outline, you can then more effectively recognize the legal significance of facts in the problem. Indeed, facts that appeared to be insignificant in earlier readings may now reveal themselves as material.

D. Writing the Answer

If you have prepared an outline of your answer, writing the answer in the answer booklet should be a fairly mechanical process. Your task is simply to express in full sentences the ideas that are represented in your examination outline, taking care to cover all the elements of a complete answer: issue, rule of law, application of law to facts, and conclusion. Your outline provides a guide that will keep you on track even when you momentarily lose sight of the main issues because of nervousness or temporary devotion to the details of a subissue.

Because of the intense time pressures of most essay examinations, law professors do not expect polished writing or perfect organization, and you should not waste precious time thinking about the best possible way to express your ideas. Nonetheless, you will have an advantage if you have worked conscientiously in your legal writing class to develop the skills of organization and clear, concise writing for office memoranda that are addressed in Chapters 12 and 13 of this text. You will score more points by clearly expressing many relevant ideas than will students whose verbose and repetitious prose expresses fewer ideas in the same space or whose writing is so unclear that the professor simply cannot understand it.

If you discover near the end of an exam that you have insufficient time to complete your analysis in full prose, you should simply outline the remainder of your response in your examination answer booklet. Most professors will give more points for a clear overview of all the remaining issues than for a fuller development of only one of several remaining issues.

IV. SUMMARY AND REVIEW

To prepare for law school essay examinations,

1. brief and synthesize cases; and
2. prepare a course outline by further synthesizing cases, reorganizing materials to highlight legal principles, and illustrating the principles with summaries of the case briefs.

To write a good essay examination answer,

1. read and analyze each examination problem, taking care to allocate your time wisely;
2. quickly and briefly outline your response to a problem; and
3. express your response in a clear, well-organized fashion, taking care to discuss both sides of each issue within the framework of IRAC: Issue, Rule, Application to facts, and Conclusion.

Below are study and exam materials that illustrate the process of studying law, from briefing cases to taking an exam. Because this example is taken from a family setting, the summary of cases is much less formal than a series of briefs of judicial opinions. With a bit of imagination, however, you can draw an analogy between these sample materials and those that you will prepare in law school.

Notice that the legal rules stated in the exam answer are taken directly from the student's outline, which the student has committed to memory. Moreover, the student's knowledge of the case illustrations in the outline helps the student engage in the fact analysis in the examination answer. Finally, one issue in the exam requires the student to develop new rules by extrapolating from the familiar rules and the policies that support them.

CASE SUMMARIES WITH SYNTHESIS

The Case of the Hand in the Cookie Jar: Debbie reached into a cookie jar and helped herself to a cookie shortly before dinner. Janice and Gerald admonished Debbie that the cookie would spoil her appetite for dinner.

The Case of the Broken Vase: Debbie climbed onto a chair, reached a vase on a table top, and threw the vase to the floor, breaking it. Janice and Gerald sent Debbie to her room, admonishing her that she should not play with her parents' possessions.

The Case of the Chocolate Ice Cream: After dinner one night, Debbie asked for some chocolate ice cream. To her surprise, her parents served her a dish of ice cream, praising her for having finished her vegetables. Unlike in the cookie jar case, Debbie did not spoil her appetite by eating the ice cream.

The Case of the Mistreated Teddy Bear: Anxious to test her parents' limits one evening, Debbie climbed onto a chair with her favorite teddy bear and threw the teddy bear onto the living room carpet. Debbie's parents saw this event but had no reaction; they continued reading the newspaper and watching TV. Unlike in the broken vase case, Debbie's actions here did not jeopardize her parents' possessions.

The Case of the Bouncing Ball: Emboldened by the teddy bear incident, Debbie brought out her favorite rubber ball and began kicking it around the living room, causing it to bounce off the TV set and to narrowly miss Janice's glass of wine sitting on the coffee table. Janice flashed Debbie an angry glance, and Gerald sternly said, "Outside with that ball!" This is more similar to the broken vase case than to the teddy bear case, because Debbie's bouncing ball threatened to cause harm to her parents' television set and wine glass.

OUTLINE

Rules for Debbie

I. Overview—Debbie's parents try to restrict Debbie's activities to those that are beneficial to her health and that protect her parents' possessions from harm.

II. Dietary Rules—Debbie is permitted to eat sweets, but only at times that won't spoil her appetite for more healthful foods.

A. Example: In *The Case of the Chocolate Ice Cream,* Debbie's parents gladly served her ice cream after dinner, because she had eaten all her vegetables.

B. Example: In *The Case of the Hand in the Cookie Jar,* Debbie was not permitted to eat a cookie shortly before dinner, because it would ruin her appetite for dinner.

III. Rules about Toys—Debbie is permitted to play only with her own toys and not in a way that will endanger her parents' possessions.

A. Example: In *The Case of the Broken Vase,* Debbie was disciplined for breaking her parents' vase.

B. Example: In *The Case of the Bouncing Ball,* Debbie was admonished for playing with her own rubber ball in a way that endangered her parents' possessions, such as the TV set and wine glass.

C. Example: In *The Case of the Mistreated Teddy Bear,* Debbie was permitted to play with her own teddy bear, even by throwing it onto the floor, apparently because such conduct did not harm any of her parents' possessions.

EXAMINATION PROBLEM

On Saturday morning, Debbie began coloring in her coloring book with a box of crayons. She soon expanded her artistic activity to drawing a multicolored mural on one of the walls of her room. Displeased with the quality of her drawing, Debbie broke each of her 24 crayons in half and threw them into her wastebasket. Indeed, she was so displeased with her artistry that she decided to wash her drawing off the wall. To that end, Debbie opened the cupboard under the kitchen sink and took a bottle of liquid drain cleaner, which she thought was a form of soap but was in fact a toxic chemical capable of burning her eyes and skin. At that moment, Debbie's parents intercepted her and discovered each of her activities during the day. Fully discuss whether Debbie has violated any rules of her house.

EXAMINATION ANSWER

Issue[2]	*I. Harm to Parents' Possessions*
Rule	Debbie's parents permit her to use and even abuse her own toys, but they do not allow Debbie to harm their possessions.
Application	Debbie did not harm her parents' property by drawing in her coloring book. And she probably did not harm their property by breaking her crayons, because those presumably were her own toys. However, Debbie almost certainly violated her parents' rules by drawing on her bedroom wall. Although the wall was in her room, her parents probably view it as part of their possessions, because they undoubtedly are responsible for maintaining it. Debbie did not physically break the surface of the wall as she might break a vase. However, a crayon drawing on the wall might require vigorous scrubbing or even repainting. Therefore, it probably represents actual harm to the wall.
Conclusion	Debbie has violated her parents' rule against harming their possessions.
Issue	*II. Promotion of Debbie's Health and Protection of Parents' Possessions*
Rule	In addition to prohibiting Debbie from harming their possessions, Debbie's parents forbid her to eat sweets if they will spoil her appetite for more healthful foods.
Application	Debbie has not tried to eat sweets at an inappropriate time. However, she has endangered her health by carrying a dangerous chemical, the drain cleaner,

2. The margin labels are included in this sample to remind you that a complete legal analysis should include four basic elements. Those labels should not appear in the margins of an actual examination answer; some professors may be offended by such a mechanical approach.

with the intention of opening the bottle and using the chemical to clean her wall. The policy behind the dietary rule is apparently to help maintain Debbie's health. Therefore, Debbie's parents likely would disapprove of other activities that endanger her health, particularly activities that would cause more serious harm than simply eating unhealthful foods.

Similarly, Debbie's parents may admonish her under an extension of their rule prohibiting harm to their possessions. Debbie is unlikely to do any harm to the drain cleaner. On the other hand, the drain cleaner is one of her parents' possessions rather than one of Debbie's toys. Moreover, if Debbie spilled the drain cleaner, she would waste it, and she might harm other possessions of her parents that came in contact with the chemical. Therefore, Debbie's parents are likely to disapprove of Debbie's taking the drain cleaner out of concern for their possessions as well as concern for Debbie's safety.

Because the chemical could cause serious harm to Debbie and to her parents' possessions, I conclude that her parents will admonish her and will adopt a general rule prohibiting her from taking such bottles from cupboards.

Conclusion

SAMPLES

1. SAMPLE EXAMINATION ANSWER

Read Sample Memorandum 1 toward the end of Chapter 11. Imagine that an examination problem raises several issues, one of which is similar to the consideration issue discussed in that sample memorandum. The general structure of the discussion of that issue in the examination answer would be similar to that of the Discussion section of the sample memorandum. Nonetheless, even a thorough examination answer would be less formal than the memorandum. For example, the examination answer would omit citations and in-depth case analysis:

Q1   Issue
    Lender v. Borrower
    • • • •
    Lender v. Guarantor
    • • • •
    Consideration—Illusory Promise:

    This lender's promise to refrain from asserting   **Rule**
his claim and demanding payment until he "needs

the money" arguably is illusory, thus creating doubt whether the guarantor's promise is enforceable.

An enforceable contract requires a bargained-for exchange in which a promisor exchanges his own promise for a return promise or performance. The requirement of an exchange is not satisfied if one party gives only an illusory promise, which does not commit the promisor to any future performance. Even if a promise leaves open the possibility that the promisor will escape obligation, however, the promise is valid if the promisor does not have complete control over the events on which the promisor's obligation is conditioned.

Application

The lender's promise to forbear until he "needs" the money appears to condition the length of his forbearance on financial events that are at least partly outside his control: As long as his income and expenses created no need for the money, the lender had a commitment to forbear from demanding payment. In an effort to escape obligations, the guarantor could argue that the word "need" refers to a subjective perception of deprivation that is inseparable from one's desires, which are subject to the promisor's unfettered discretion. However, "need" is distinguishable from "want."

Conclusion

Because the formality of the written agreement suggests that the parties must have intended to create binding obligations, a court probably would interpret the word "need" to impose objective restrictions on the lender's rights and conduct, thereby satisfying the consideration requirement and making the guarantor's promise enforceable.

2. SAMPLE EXAMINATION PROBLEM AND RESPONSE

Examine the following contracts problem and response. Although the fact analysis is fairly simple, the internal organization is more complex than that in the sample answer in Problem 1 above, because the issue of recovery under quasi-contract invites discussion of two subissues in separate paragraphs, each with its own subrule, fact analysis, and preliminary conclusion.

Problem

While jogging one morning, realtor Maria Reyes came upon the victim of an auto accident that had occurred a few minutes earlier. The victim was unconscious and was bleeding profusely from a severed artery. Reyes saved the victim's life by flagging down a motorist and by applying direct pressure to the severed artery during the ten-minute ride to the hospital. A paramedic would have charged $300 for providing a similar lifesaving technique. Reyes's clothes were covered with blood, but they washed clean. Reyes herself was shaken and exhausted for a few hours after the incident. Reyes later demanded compensation from the victim. Discuss the potential liability and remedies.

Sample Answer

Liability for Unjust Enrichment:[3]

The unconscious victim could not expressly or through conduct communicate a promise to pay Reyes. Therefore, Reyes cannot recover on the basis of contract or promissory estoppel.[4]

Reyes likely will bring an action in quasi-contract for restitution of the reasonable value of the benefit that she conferred on the victim. To recover on this theory, she must prove that she unjustly enriched the victim.[5]

Enrichment is a measurable benefit. Reyes enriched the victim by rendering tangible first aid services and summoning help, thus saving the victim's life.[6]

Reyes must prove that it would be unjust for the victim to retain the benefits of the first-aid services without compensating Reyes for them. Reyes could prove this by showing that she had some relationship with the victim that led Reyes reasonably to expect compensation. However, the courts ordinarily presume that emergency services at the scene of an accident are provided gratuitously. Reyes could overcome that presumption if she could show that she acted in a professional capacity when rendering the services or that the services she rendered were unusually burdensome or hazardous.

Reyes cannot establish any expectation of compensation based on her profession: She is a realtor and is not in the business of charging for medical services. She might have a better chance of rebutting the presumption of gratuitous emergency services by showing that her services were so burdensome that she expected compensation. After all, she engaged in the physically demanding task of cradling an accident victim in a moving car for ten minutes while applying direct pressure to a bleeding artery. The physical and emotional distress of this event caused her to suffer exhaustion and distress for several hours. On the other hand, Reyes's actions posed little risk to her own safety, took relatively little time, and did not require special knowledge, skill, or training. Moreover, she likely would have felt distressed by the accident even if she had only witnessed the injury and had not acted to treat the victim.[7]

---

3. This heading reflects the exam writer's decision to discuss issues of liability separately from those of remedies. Within the section addressing liability, the writer introduces and separately analyzes the elements of quasi-contract: (1) enrichment that is (2) unjust. She could have begun each of those analyses with a subsection heading, but good paragraphing appears to be a sufficient guide to organization within the two major sections, particularly because the facts raise no significant issue about enrichment.

4. This paragraph makes an introductory point about claims not in issue by stating the facts and conclusion and leaving the rules implicit. This paragraph could be omitted, but it might be good for an extra point or two because it explains how the student selected some issues for discussion and excluded others.

5. This paragraph identifies the main issue and states the applicable rule on the broadest, most general level.

6. This paragraph introduces a minor subissue, "enrichment," states the applicable rule, and reaches a conclusion on that subissue by applying the rule to the facts. Because this element of the claim is not seriously in doubt, it does not warrant fuller discussion. The brief discussion of this subissue serves primarily to introduce a more substantial issue in the next paragraph.

7. The preceding paragraph identifies a subissue and states the law applicable to that subissue. This paragraph reaches a conclusion on that subissue by applying the law to the facts. Notice how this paragraph argues both sides of the facts on this close question.

Although this is a close question, the facts suggest that Reyes could not reasonably have expected compensation for her emergency services. Therefore, I conclude that Reyes cannot recover.[8]

Remedies

Assuming that Reyes could prove a claim for quasi-contract, she would be entitled to restitution measured by the reasonable value of the benefit that she bestowed on the victim. The purpose of such relief would be to deny the unjust enrichment to the recipient of the benefit; therefore, whenever feasible, damages ought to be measured by the value that the recipient places on the benefit. If that is not feasible, a court may award damages based on the general market value of the benefit or, as a last resort, on the out-of-pocket costs incurred by the provider of the benefit.[9]

In this case, from the perspective of the victim, the value of the benefit bestowed by Reyes arguably is the value of the victim's life. A court would not use this value as the measure of the restitutionary relief, because it is relatively difficult to fix and because it is disproportionately greater than the effort expended by Reyes. Instead, the court probably would award the damages based on the general market value of Reyes's services. That measure is more nearly proportionate to Reyes's efforts, and it can easily be established by reference to the $300 fee that would have been charged by a paramedic. Alternatively, a court might award damages based on the actual costs incurred by Reyes, as measured by such things as inconvenience to Reyes and the cost of cleaning her jogging clothes. However, because the market-value remedy is more consistent with restitution, I conclude that a court would award $300 in damages if Reyes could establish a claim based on quasi-contract.[10]

Exercise 9-1

1. THE SURFING BURGLAR

Review Exercise 6-1 at the end of Section III.A of Chapter 6. Treat it as a closed-book examination question and write a response in essay form that identifies the issues, summarizes the law, applies the law to the facts relevant to each issue, and arrives at a conclusion on each issue. You may supplement the statements of law in Exercise 6-1 with any common law of burglary that you have studied in your criminal law course. Otherwise, base your analysis on the general legal rules provided in Exercise 6-1.

---

8. This paragraph states a conclusion on the entire issue of liability. A student undoubtedly could have received equal credit for reaching the opposite conclusion, so long as the student discussed all the facts and arguments.

9. This paragraph discusses the legal rules for computing damages.

10. This paragraph reaches a conclusion on the question of damages by applying the legal standards to the facts.

2. RULES FOR MONICA

Review Chapter 8 at Exercises 8-1 and 8-2(3). Using your own outline or one supplied by your professor as a study aid prior to a closed-book test, or as an in-exam guide in an open-book test, draft an answer to the following essay question:

Question

On Wednesday night, Monica, who is a junior in high school, attended an evening volleyball competition at her school. She returned home by 10:30 P.M. On Friday night, Monica went to the school dance with a date, Pat. When Monica and Pat returned from the dance at 10:55 P.M., they parked in the driveway at Monica's house within view of Monica's mother, Carmen, who was sitting in the living room. While parked in the driveway, they talked, laughed, and held hands for 20 minutes. After Pat kissed Monica goodbye and drove away, Monica entered her house and greeted Carmen at 11:15 P.M. On Saturday afternoon, Monica asked Carmen whether Monica could go with friends to the high school basketball game, to watch Monica's brother, Mike, play in the first of more than a dozen home games in the basketball season. Carmen plans to attend some home games during the season, although not this first one.

Fully discuss whether Monica's action on Friday and request on Saturday are consistent with Carmen's rules regarding her daughter's social activities. For every issue that you identify, summarize the rule or subrule that helps to resolve that issue, apply the rule to the relevant facts, and reach a conclusion. Whenever possible, discuss both sides of the question.

Part V

Neutral Analysis—The Office

Memorandum of Law

Chapters 10-14 discuss various stages of preparing an office memorandum of law, including researching the problem, organizing and drafting the memorandum, and citing to authority. In many first-semester legal writing programs, the office memorandum will be your primary vehicle for studying legal method and writing. Nonetheless, remember that the previous nine chapters lay the foundation for Part V; you should not hesitate to review them when that would be helpful.

In an actual assignment in a law office, your first task in preparing an office memorandum will be to spend substantial time in a law library researching the law that applies to the issues raised in your assignment. Accordingly, the first chapter in Part V introduces basic research techniques and strategies.

On the other hand, many first-semester writing programs introduce students to the challenges of preparing law office memoranda gradually, initially assigning first a "closed-universe" problem in which the instructor supplies the necessary legal materials for the students. In such a closed-universe assignment, students will not need to research the law, and they may even be prohibited by the assignment from supplementing the research supplied by the instructor.

If you begin with a closed-universe assignment, you can safely skip Chapter 10 until you are faced with a research assignment. Even so, you may want to begin thinking about the research process by glancing through Chapter 10 and contemplating how you might have used research tools to find the legal materials that your instructor supplied to you.

Once you have completed your study of Part V, you will be ready to perform one or more of the office memorandum assignments in Appendix IV, near the end of this book.

Chapter 10

Introduction to the Law Library

I. MASTERING THE ASSIGNMENT

The surest way to disappoint a supervising attorney is to misunderstand the assignment. Even a thoroughly researched and beautifully written memorandum will fall flat if it fails to address the matters that the supervisor wanted the associate to analyze.

Unfortunately, many supervising attorneys are too busy to communicate their assignments clearly and thoroughly. Even worse, most will not accept blame for confusion about the assignment. Instead, they expect you to assume responsibility for clarifying vague or confusing points. Consequently, you should not be shy about demanding additional information from the supervising attorney. Indeed, even at the risk of momentarily causing inconvenience to your supervising attorney, you should aggressively dig out the information that you need to master your assignment so that you can draft a memorandum that precisely meets the attorney's needs. On reading such a memorandum, the delighted supervising attorney will remember little about the minor inconvenience.

Confusion about the topics that your supervising attorney expects you to address may take various forms. In some cases, you may be unable to

171

identify narrow, precise issues because the assignment is unavoidably general or abstract. Supervising attorneys occasionally request office memoranda on general, abstract questions of law, such as the likely scope and effect of a new statute. Although they are not yet working on any disputes relating to the assigned issues, they expect that the general legal analyses developed in such memoranda will help them counsel clients who are concerned about their rights or obligations under the new law. You can tailor such a memorandum to your supervisor's needs by requesting clarification on (1) the kinds of topics that your supervisor deems to be essential and (2) the kinds of disputes in which the firm's clients likely would become embroiled.

In many cases, abstraction in the assignment is unnecessary because the supervising attorney intends to use the legal analysis in the memorandum to help represent a client in a currently active, concrete dispute. In such a case, if your supervising attorney does not provide you with sufficient information to enable you to thoroughly understand the factual context, you should ask her for further factual details or for a convenient source of such information. By anticipating the application of legal standards to facts, you can frame the issues precisely and narrowly, and you can tailor the research and analysis to your supervisor's real needs.

Vagueness in an assignment often is attributable to precisely the analytic uncertainty on which the memorandum is intended to shed light. Therefore, you may benefit from secondary meetings with the supervising attorney after receiving the initial assignment but before writing the memorandum. In some cases, your supervising attorney will not even attempt to identify issues but will instead supply the factual context and ask you to define and analyze the issues. In other cases, the supervisor may state the issues in general and preliminary form, expecting you to refine and supplement them. Even if the supervisor has no such expectation, you may be able to acquire information that allows you to focus the assigned issues more sharply. With a thorough knowledge of the factual context, you can clarify the essential issues as your research deepens your understanding of the legal standards.

As you do so, questions may arise about appropriate limits on the range of topics that you should address or about the depth to which the supervisor would like you to analyze a tangential issue. If so, you should determine whether the supervisor can conveniently give brief guidance on these questions before you begin writing. Although you should not become dependent on such guidance, neither should you give credence to a popular assumption on the part of clerks and associates that supervisors are universally hostile to such contacts. Most supervisors will recognize the benefit of a brief follow-up meeting and will welcome the opportunity to help you sharpen the focus of your analysis.

II. RESEARCH TOOLS

Effective research skills are the product of long hours in the library, for which no primer on research techniques can substitute. Nonetheless, a few tips on research strategy may help you avoid inefficient or unproductive activity. The following discussion provides a preliminary guide to selected research tools available in virtually any law library.[1]

A. Traditional Research Tools

As suggested in Chapters 3 and 4, most research assignments require research of primary law in state or federal constitutions, statutes, or judicial decisions. The judicial decisions establish case law, some of which develops common law principles and some of which interprets and applies constitutional or statutory provisions.

1. STATUTES—CODE SERVICES

Most state and federal statutes are published in codes, in which statutory enactments are organized by subject matter. For example, the multivolume official United States Code reproduces the text of the United States Constitution, federal statutes enacted by Congress, and rules governing federal judicial proceedings, such as the Federal Rules of Civil Procedure and the Federal Rules of Evidence.

To illustrate, the following excerpt from Title 18 of the United States Code sets forth the one-sentence text of section 3290, which you might have found by using the subject-matter index of the Code. That statute states an exception to the general rule that the government must prosecute a federal crime, if at all, within a certain period of time after the commission of the crime. The statutory text is followed by notes on historical background and by statutory cross-references:

§ 3290. Fugitives from justice

No statute of limitations shall extend to any person fleeing from justice.

(June 25, 1948, ch. 645, 62 Stat. 829.)

HISTORICAL AND REVISION NOTES

Based on Title 18, U.S.C., 1940 ed., § 583 (R.S. § 1045).

Said section 583 was rephrased and made applicable to all statutes of limitation and is merely declaratory of the generally accepted rule of law.

CROSS REFERENCES

Absence from district as tolling limitation for prosecution for internal revenue violations, see section 6531 of Title 26, Internal Revenue Code.

SECTION REFERRED TO IN OTHER SECTIONS

This section is referred to in title 26 section 6531.

---

1. This discussion does not address techniques for researching agency rules and regulations or local ordinances, nor does it examine special research services for certain subject areas, such as tax, labor law, and American Indian tribal codes and case law. For more comprehensive guides to research tools and techniques, you can consult textbooks such as Christina L. Kunz, Deborah A. Schmedemann, Matthew P. Downs & Ann L. Bateson, THE PROCESS OF LEGAL RESEARCH (5th ed. 2000); Amy E. Sloan, BASIC LEGAL RESEARCH: TOOLS AND STRATEGIES (2000).

Particularly useful as a research tool is an annotated code service, such as United States Code Annotated, United States Code Service, or any of the various annotated state code services. The annotated codebooks are updated fairly frequently, with new developments published in paperback supplements or pocket parts that insert into the main volume. Moreover, the annotated codebooks cite to related agency regulations and to law review articles about the statute, and they briefly summarize judicial decisions that interpret the statute.

Examine, for example, the excerpts from West Group's United States Code Annotated reproduced on page 175 of this textbook. Those excerpted annotations supplement the text of section 3290 with an indexed summary of cases in which the statute has been interpreted and applied. Under category 9, entitled "Constructive Flight," an annotation cites to and describes a holding of *United States v. Catino*[2] regarding the theory of "constructive flight."

2. WEST'S CASE REPORTERS WITH HEADNOTES AND KEY NUMBERS

Using the citation in the annotated codebook as a guide, you can find the full text of the judicial decision that interprets the constitution, statute, or rule. Normally, you will find the decision in a multivolume service known as a "reporter" system, such as Federal Reports 2d. In a reporter published by West Group, the text of the judicial decision is preceded by consecutively numbered "headnotes," which summarize critical points of law or application of fact in the opinion. To help you find the portion of the text of the opinion that corresponds to a particular headnote, the West reporter inserts within the text a bracketed number that matches the corresponding headnote number. More important for further research purposes, each headnote refers to one or more topics with "key numbers" that refer to a section of a West case digest that collects other cases addressing the same issue.

An example is on page 176 of this textbook, reproducing excerpts of the court's opinion in *United States v. Catino* from pages 718, 719, and 722 of volume 735 of West's Federal Reporter 2d. The text of the opinion begins immediately after the designation of the authoring judge: "LUMBARD, Circuit Judge:". After reviewing the facts and discussing preliminary points of law, the opinion states a rule about intent to flee, immediately after the numbers "4, 5" within brackets. The number "4" within the brackets corresponds to the fourth headnote preceding the opinion itself. That headnote not only summarizes the point about intent to flee stated in the opinion, it assigns that point to a category that is designated as "Criminal Law 153."

---

2. The annotation cites to the case in an unconventional manner. A more widely accepted citation form would read "United States v. Catino, 735 F.2d 718 (2d Cir. 1984)," with the case name italicized or underscored if cited in a memorandum or brief.

§ 3290. Fugitives from justice

No statute of limitations shall extend to any person fleeing from justice.

(June 25, 1948, c. 645, 62 Stat. 829.)

Historical and Revision Notes

Reviser's Note. Based on Title 18, U.S.C., 1940 ed., § 583 (R.S. § 1045).

Said section 583 was rephrased and made applicable to all statutes of limitation and is merely declaratory of the generally accepted rule of law.

Cross References

Internal revenue criminal prosecutions, presence outside United States or status of fugitive from justice as affecting periods of limitations, see section 6531 of Title 26, Internal Revenue Code.

Library References

Criminal Law ⬯153.
C.J.S. Criminal Law § 230.

Notes of Decisions

Absence from jurisdiction 8
Authorities, flight from 10
Burden of proof 16
Construction 1
Constructive flight 9
Escapees, persons within section 4
Extradition 2
Flight from
    Authorities 10
    Unrelated charges 11
Good faith effort to surrender 13
Motive and intent 14
Persons entitled to plead limitations 15
Persons within section
    Gene~ 3

Ship's personnel, persons within section 6
Sufficiency of evidence 17
Termination of fugitive status 12
Unrelated charges, flight from 11
Visitors, persons within section 7
Waiver 19
Weight and sufficiency of evidence 17

---

1. Construction

Congressional policies underlying thi~ chapter and the "fleeing from justi~ ~ion to it are harmonized by i~

~583~ [now this ~ ~ is not ne~~ry that the party charged should have left jurisdiction in which crime was allegedly committed, after an indictment found, or for purpose of avoiding a prosecution anticipated or begun, but simply that, having within the jurisdiction committed that which by its laws constituted a crime, he had left its jurisdiction. McGowen v. U.S., 1939, 105 F.2d 791, 70 App.D.C. 268, 124 A.L.R. 1047, certiorari denied 60 S.Ct. 98, 308 U.S. 552, 84 L.Ed. 464. See, also, King v. U.S., C.C.A.Ark.1944, 144 F.2d 729, certiorari denied 65 S.Ct. 711, 324 U.S. 854, 89 L.Ed. 1413.

"Fugitive from justice" is person who, having committed a crime in violation of laws of United States, flees from jurisdiction of court

reside~ ~ce ~ th~ trict, or a ~oncealing ~ therein, avoid detection or puni~ ~t for some of fense against the United States, to constitute a "fleeing from justice." U.S. v. O'Brian, C.C. Kan.1873, Fed.Cas.No.15,908.

9. Constructive flight

Fact that defendant, who was in French prison awaiting trial on french charges, actively resisted extradition request throughout proceedings instead of consenting to return to United States, coupled with his letter expressing a desire to resist all further extradition requests, constituted a constructive flight from justice, thereby tolling limitations period under section 3282 of this title. U.S. v. Catino, C.A.N.Y.1984, 735 F.2d 718, certiorari denied, 105 S.Ct. 180, 83 L.Ed.2d 114.

677

⌐ɪn jurɪsu..   where an offense ιι⌐ɔ ɒeen committed with intent of avoiding arrest or prosecution. 18 U.S. C.A. §§ 3282, 3290.

3. Criminal Law ⬥⟞153

A person can be "fleeing from justice" in one jurisdiction for purposes of tolling provision for five-year limitations period, even though in prison in another. 18 U.S. C.A. §§ 3282, 3290.

4. Criminal Law ⬥⟞153

Intent to flee from prosecution or arrest may be inferred from a person's failure to surrender to authorities once he learns that charges against him are pending, whether defendant leaves jurisdiction intending to avoid prosecution or, having learned of charges while legally outside jurisdiction, constructively flees by deciding not to return.

5. Criminal Law ⬥⟞153

⟋⟍⟍ that author⟋⟍ knew of⟋⟍ ᴅᴅ-

UNITED STATES of America, Appellee,

v.

Alfred CATINO, Defendant-Appellant.

No. 956, Docket 83–1419.

United States Court of Appeals,
Second Circuit.

Argued March 22, 1984.

Decided May 24, 1984.

Certiorari Denied Oct. 1, 1984.
See 105 S.Ct. 180.

Defendant was convicted in the United States District Court for the Southern District of New York, Lee P. Gagliardi, J., for ᶠailinɡ ⟋⟍⟍⟍ to beɡⱱⱱⱱ ᶢ a sen- ⟋⟍port

e⟋⟍ɪply proⱱ⟍⟍esst⟍ C.A. §§ 3282, 3290.

9. Criminal Law ⬥⟞113

The term "first brought" within meaning of statute providing that for offense alleged to have been committed outside jurisdiction of any district, venue lies only in the district where offender is arrested or first brought applies only in situations where offender is returned to United States already in cust⟋⟍ 18 U.S.C.A ⟋⟍§ 322⟍

⟋⟍⟍ (stat-
⟋⟍ith effort to
· Catino had

⟋guendo that
extradition in
ιake a factual
ts view, the
ⁿced by his
ιno obviously
ιt returning to
· as new charges
December 14,
ιdition request
· and contin-
, was denied
court reasoned
ιtus from March
his resistance to
District made
ɴ justice" with
ᶠeast until the
Since tolⁱ⟍

Be⟍ARD; ⟍ɴAN an⟍
PRATT, ⟍ⁱt Judges.

LUMBARD, Circuit Judge:

Alfred Catino appeals from his conviction entered June 4, 1983, in the Southern District of New York, Gagliardi, J., following his conditional guilty plea. Catino pleaded guilty to two counts: failing to a⟍⟍ⁱon ⟍rch 17, 1975⟍ ᵉegin serⱱ⟍ ⟍e imp⟍ ⁱor ⟍

⟍ana⟍ ⁱⁱⱱ
la⟍⟍ⁱted States⟍ als he los⟍ protection of Speedy Trial Act). However, he argues that a non-fugitive cannot *become* a fugitive by virtue of his resistance to extradition. We disagree.

[4, 5] The intent to flee from prosecution or arrest may be inferred from a person's failure to surrender to authorities once he learns that charges against him are pending. *Matter of Assarsson*, 687 F.2d 1157, 1161–62 (8th Cir.1982); *United States v. Ballesteros-Cordova*, 586 F.2d 1321, 1324 (9th Cir.1978). This is true whether the defendant leaves the jurisdiction intending to avoid prosecution, or, having learned of charges while legally outside the jurisdiction, "constructively flees" by deciding not to return. *Jhirad v. Ferrandina*, 536 F.2d 478, 483–84 (2d Cir.), *cert. denied*, 429 U.S. 833, 97 S.Ct. 97, 50 L.Ed.2d 98 (1976) (*Jhirad II*). The fact that the authorities know of the defendant's whereabouts outside of the jurisdiction does⟍ not of itself start the st⟍te runniⁿ⟍ ⟍ *II*
⟍ra⟍

U.S. ....nt, 774 F.2d 8.... ....ari
den.... ..6 S.Ct. 1190, 475 U.S. 1012, 89
L.Ed.2d 305.

...itation period for
...ersonal income
...ning false cor-
...uring 60–day
...mmons en-
...een taken,
... 26 U.S.C.A.
...).
...304.

...ing to enforce
...l full compli-
...until 60–day
...f judicial en-
...so that six-year
...ied and IRS could
...ully making and
...eturns. 26 U.S.
...7609(a)(1), (b),
...R.A.P. Rule

...1283, certiorari
...482 U.S. 927, 96

...ugh nuclear
...employees
...iod for
...tat...

...culative.... ....that
...it to avoid be...g contin-
agent was insufficient to
...stimony lacked circumstan-
...ustworthiness. Fed.Rules
U.S.C.A.
...6 F.2d 896.

...ception stating that
...eriod in criminal cases
...or of any person fleeing
...rehensive, in that a person
...in one jurisdiction loses
...of limitations for all
...dictions. 18 U.S.C.A.

...d 718, certiorari
...469 U.S. 855, 83

five-year limitations
...a person absents him-
...ere an offense has
...f avoiding ar....
...§ 3282

☞153. —— Fugitives from Justice.

C.A.D.C. 1983. U.S. v. Singleton, 702 F.2d
1159, 226 U.S.App.D.C. 422, appeal after remand 759 F.2d 176, 245 U.S.App.D.C. 156, re-
hearing denied 763 F.2d 1432, 246 U.S.App.D.C.
171.

C.A.Cal. 1982. U. S. v. Gonsalves, 675
F.2d 1050, certiorari denied 103 S.Ct. 83, 459
U.S. 837, 74 L.Ed.2d 78, appeal after remand
731 F.2d 1409.

C.A.7 (Ill.) 1988. Defendant's intent to
avoid arrest or prosecution must be proven to
trigger tolling of applicable statute of limitations because defendant was a fugitive from
justice. 18 U.S.C.A. § 3290.
U.S. v. Marshall, 856 F.2d 896.

To invoke fugitive from justice tolling statute, Government must demonstrate that defendant fled jurisdiction with intent to avoid arrest or prosecution by a preponderance of the
evidence. 18 U.S.C.A. § 3290.
U.S. v. Marshall, 856 F.2d 896.

District cour...'s determination that defen-
...t fled jur.... ...to avoid pr.... ....tion was
...learl.... .....d a.... .....of

...ane.... .....from
...ed State.... ....ial on crim.... ....he
was not re....u.d of a duty to do a.... ....could to
return.
> U.S. v. Catino, 735 F.2d 718, certiorari
> denied 105 S.Ct. 180, 469 U.S. 855, 83
> L.Ed.2d 114.

Fact that defendant, who was in French
prison awaiting trial on French charges, actively resisted extradition request throughout proceedings instead of consenting to return to
United States, coupled with his letter expressing a desire to resist all further extradition
requests, constituted a constructive flight from
justice, thereby tolling statute of limitations
period. 18 U.S.C.A. §§ 3282, 3290.
> U.S. v. Catino, 735 F.2d 718, certiorari
> denied 105 S.Ct. 180, 469 U.S. 855, 83
> L.Ed.2d 114.

Tolling statute of limitations period on
ground that defendant's resistance to extradition request constituted a constructive flight
from justice did not impermissibly penalize
defendant for asserting his right to oppose
extradition, On theory that to claim benefit of
statute of limitations, he would.... ....had to
give up his right to resist unl.... ....n.
....that the.... ....thing

3. WEST'S CASE DIGESTS

The designation "Criminal Law 153" includes a picture of a key. "Criminal Law" is the "Digest Topic," and "153" is the "Key Number" corresponding to a subtopic within the Criminal Law topic. Together, they correspond to a subsection of the multivolume West's Federal Practice Digest 4th, which is essentially an enormous outline of federal case law, similar in form and design to the kind of course outline described in Chapter 8. Your library will have similar digests for state law, collecting decisions by state or region.

By pulling the appropriate volume on "Criminal Law" in West's Federal Practice Digest 4th and turning to section 153, you will find summaries of judicial decisions, as shown in the excerpts on page 177 of this text. There, you will see citations not only to *United States v. Catino*, but also to other cases addressing the same or similar issues. In addition to the citations, the digest often summarizes the point in each opinion that relates to the Key Number topic.

Even without the annotated codebook that cited to *United States v. Catino*, you could find that case and others on point by searching through the index of the West Federal Practice Digest 4th. As shown in the excerpt reproduced below, under the heading "FUGITIVES FROM JUSTICE" and the subheading "LIMITATION of prosecution, suspension," the index refers you to Digest Topic and Key Number "Crim Law 153," which will lead you directly to the relevant cases.

FRIENDLY   98 F P D 4th—76

References are to Digest Topics and Key Numbers

FRIENDLY SUIT SUBMISSION of controversy, see this index Submission of Controversies	**FUGITIVES** DETAINERS. Extrad 54 SLAVES. Slaves 9
FRIENDSHIP CONSIDERATION for contract. Contracts 60	**FUGITIVES FROM JUSTICE** EXTRADITION in general. Extrad 30, 37 HARBORING or concealing. Comp Off 3.5
FRIGHT DAMAGES, fright as element. Damag 51, 52	LIMITATION of prosecution, suspension. Crim Law 153 **FULL FAITH AND CREDIT**
FRINGE BENEFITS WORKERS' compensation, computation of wages, see this index Workers' Compensation	APPELLATE jurisdiction of cases involving Federal Constitution. Courts 219.8(4) JUDGMENT, foreign judgments, see this index Foreign Judgments
FRISK ..OP and frisk......ally, see this index Stop and Frisk	STATE court judgment, affect in Federal court— Chil....... Judgm 828(3.2) S.....ts, records, et...f every other st..

Reprinted with permission from Federal Practice Digest 4th. Copyright © by West Publishing Company.

Alternatively, if you had sufficient experience to identify "Criminal Law" as the digest topic, you might find Key Number 153 by glancing through the table of contents at the beginning of the Criminal Law section in the digest, as shown in the excerpt on page 179 of this textbook.

If you proceeded in this manner, you would find *United States v. Catino* through the digest and only then discover the statute by reading the case. In those circumstances, you should also find the statutory text in the annotated codebook. Although the codebook annotations and the West digest entries will inevitably refer to many of the same cases, the overlap may not be perfect,

CRIMINAL LAW   27 F P D 4th—350

Reprinted with permission from Federal Practice Digest 4th. Copyright © by West Publishing Company.

and the two services often organize and categorize their case summaries differently. You will not unreasonably duplicate your efforts by looking for helpful cases in both services.

Of course, if you are researching a question governed exclusively by common law, you can bypass the legislative materials and focus your attention on case law. You might initially find a case in the West digest, perhaps after consulting its index or the table of contents preceding a major topic in the digest. Alternatively, you might find a citation to a helpful case while studying a secondary authority, such as an article or treatise. Although such secondary authorities are not sources of primary law that directly bind any government official, they may help you understand the contours of a legal topic and find citations to cases that can act as a springboard for further research.

4. USING A CITATION SERVICE TO CHECK SUBSEQUENT HISTORY AND FIND MORE CASES

You must check the "subsequent history" of any judicial decision on which you rely in your analysis. Using an online computer citation service, or using

Shepard's multivolume citation service, you should determine whether the decision has been affirmed, overruled, followed, distinguished, or questioned, or simply whether it has been accepted or rejected for future appellate review. Secondarily, you can use such a citation service as you would a case digest to find other cases on point. The service will identify subsequent decisions that have cited to the decision you are checking, and some of those subsequent decisions will offer useful holdings or discussions.

Unless an issue is tightly controlled by a significant decision and its progeny, however, a citation checking service is a relatively clumsy means of finding helpful case law and should not be your tool of first resort. Aside from revealing the subsequent history of a judicial decision, the service may be useful primarily as a method of cross-checking your previous research in annotated codebooks and case digests; on rare occasions it will turn up a useful subsequent decision that you missed with your primary case-finding tools.

The kind of information that has made Shepard's bound volumes a standard tool for lawyers is now available through computer research tools. The passages below, however, describe the bound volumes.

To use Shepard's most efficiently for such cross-checking, pay attention to a superscript number set within the citation to a subsequent decision. It refers to a West headnote number in the decision whose citation you are checking. The superscript in a Shepard's subsequent citation means that the subsequent decision cites the earlier decision on a particular issue. The superscript is the same as the headnote number corresponding to that issue in the earlier decision. If you intend to use the earlier decision in your analysis only with respect to the issue corresponding to a particular headnote number, you can limit your search in Shepard's to subsequent decisions whose citations contain the same superscript in their Shepard's citation.

For example, in this excerpt from Shepard's Federal Cases citation service, the entries below the designation "Vol. 735" identify decisions that have cited to cases published in volume 735 of the Federal Reports 2d. More specifically, the entries below the number 718 identify subsequent decisions that cite to *United States v. Catino*, which appears in volume 735 of Federal Reports 2d, starting on page 718. Many of those subsequent decisions cite to *United States v. Catino* for different points. However, the ones with the superscript "4" after the "F2d" designation might be of particular interest to you. According to Shepard's, those subsequent decisions cite to *United States v. Catino* on the topic corresponding to headnote 4 in *Catino*, the general definition of intent to flee from prosecution. If

Vol. 735

827F2d²1570
827F2d⁴1573
j827F2d1577
836F2d¹⁹539
848F2d1574
23ARF691s

—488—
US cert den
in469US1018
105S

66
63BRW¹540
64BRW²835

—718—
US cert den
in469US855
in105SC180
Cir. 2
739F2d⁴796
635FS¹²766
638FS⁴620
686FS²85
686FS⁴85
Cir. 4
787F2d949
Cir. 5
f809F2d¹²248
628FS⁴1476

Cir. 11
765F2d⁴1050
765F2d⁷1050
24ARF365s
33ARF716s

—725—
US cert den
in469US1110
105

you were interested in researching that proposition only, you could examine only those cases cited in Shepard's with the superscript "4."

Of course, you should not forget to note the subsequent history of *United States v. Catino*. The Shepard's notation "U.S. cert den" shows that the United States Supreme Court rejected an invitation to review the federal appellate court's decision in *Catino*.

5. LEGISLATIVE HISTORY

As discussed in Section II.B of Chapter 4, scholars and judges disagree on the manner and extent to which courts should consult legislative history as an aid in interpreting ambiguous statutory language. Controversial or not, however, legislative history finds its way into many briefs and judicial decisions.

Techniques for finding legislative history will vary, depending on the resources available in your library and the jurisdiction that produced the legislation. Historically, for example, many state legislatures have not published as much information about the legislative history of a bill as has been typical with federal legislation. In some states, for example, you may need to consult with the clerk of the state Senate or House of Representatives to obtain a legislative committee report or an audio tape or written transcript of committee proceedings or floor debates. A few states, on the other hand, have long published legislative reports and proceedings in library resources similar to those available for federal legislative history. Increasingly, moreover, such information is becoming available on state legislative Internet sites. If you have any question about the status of state legislative history in your jurisdiction, ask your law librarian for guidance.

A number of research tools in bound volumes can help you find *federal* legislative history, especially for legislation enacted in recent decades. Moreover, a few states have analogous resources for state legislation. A brief overview of some of these resources will suffice to get you started.

a. Codebooks

In Subsection 1 above, this chapter introduced you to one simple research tool for finding legislative history: codebooks. If you have already located a statute in a codebook, the codebook will provide the public law numbers of the legislation, the dates of legislative amendments, and citations to Statutes at Large, which will set forth the text of the legislation as it appeared at its original enactment or at a later stage of amendment.

If the codebook is annotated, it also will refer you to sources of pre-enactment legislative history, such as congressional committee reports. For example, following the text of a section of Title VII of the Civil Rights Act of 1964, 42 U.S.C.A. § 2000e-2 (1994), United States Code Annotated refers to Senate Report No. 872 and House Report No. 914, representing the findings, explanations, and recommendations of congressional committees prior to consideration of the Civil Rights Act of 1964. The annotated codebook states that these reports are published beginning on page 2355 of 1964 United States Code Congressional and Administrative News (USC-CAN), a set of bound volumes that you should have in your library. The annotated codebook contains similar citations to a House Report and a Conference Report on the 1972 amendments to the Civil Rights Act, and to a House Report, an Interpretive Memorandum, and a Statement by the President on the 1991 amendments to the Civil Rights Act. Once again, these citations in the annotated codebook are to USCCAN, which selectively compiles useful documents and other proceedings regarding significant federal legislation enacted since 1945.

b. Congressional Information Service

For federal legislation enacted since 1970, a more complete legislative research tool is provided by the Congressional Information Service (CIS). Once you get the public law number of the statute in question from the CIS Index, a bound volume of CIS will set forth annotations briefly identifying the legislative history of the statute, such as congressional committee reports, legislative hearings, and floor debates. The annotation may also refer to an "Abstract" in yet another CIS volume, which will describe the legislative history in slightly greater detail, such as by listing the witnesses who testified at legislative hearings, or by providing a synopsis of committee reports. Finally, CIS provides the full text of the reports and hearings in microfiche form, separately stored in your library. CIS's new electronic index, "Congressional Universe," makes it an even more useful tool for researching legislative history.

c. Individual Compiled Legislative Histories

Of course, if a scholar has compiled and analyzed the legislative history of a particular statute, you may find the legislative history to be most accessible in that specific compilation. You can find such individual compilations through Nancy P. Johnson's SOURCES OF COMPILED LEGISLATIVE HISTORIES: A BIBLIOGRAPHY OF GOVERNMENT DOCUMENTS, PERIODICAL ARTICLES, AND BOOKS, 1ST CONGRESS—102ND CONGRESS (1996). For example, page B195 of this bibliography cites to resources relating to the Omnibus Trade and Competitiveness Act of 1988. One of the cited resources is a ten-volume legislative history of the Act, prepared by Bernard D. Reams, Jr., and Mary A. Nelson, and published in 1991. Johnson's bibliography notes that the ten-volume compilation includes congressional reports, hearings, and debates.

You should feel particularly lucky if you find such a compilation for legislation predating 1945, for which neither CIS nor USCCAN will provide legislative history. Researching the history of such early legislation is much more difficult, and you will benefit greatly from the work of any scholars who have already undertaken the task and published the fruits of their labors.

B. Computer-Assisted Research

In a world increasingly geared to electronic information, computer terminals may eventually render obsolete most of the stacks of bound volumes that now take up great space in law libraries. A law office with limited library space can use computers to find the text of judicial decisions and statutes that are stored on commercially available CD-ROMs or in electronic databases such as the popular online computer research services, LEXIS-NEXIS and WESTLAW, now available also on the Internet through their Web sites.

The vast databases of LEXIS-NEXIS and WESTLAW include the text not only of legislation and case law but also of such things as agency rules and regulations, Restatements of the Law, law review articles, news and business periodicals, and public notices. Some users may prefer WESTLAW for its integration of the West topic and key number system into its computer search software. Others may prefer LEXIS-NEXIS for the manner in which its word-search software operates or for some element of its database, such as its extensive international law resources. You can best learn LEXIS-NEXIS or WESTLAW computer search techniques through hands-on training from your law school librarian or a LEXIS-NEXIS or WESTLAW representative, or by consulting a book that is devoted to computer research techniques.[3]

Other sources of legal information are accessible by computer on the Internet. Still relatively unrefined as a research tool, the Internet often contains transient sources or unreliable information, and it can be a clumsy, unfocused research tool. However, universities, government agencies, and established providers of online research services, including LEXIS-NEXIS and WESTLAW, are increasingly making their databases available on Internet sites,[4] steadily improving the utility of the Internet as a research tool. Moreover, many of these sites provide reliable information without charging any user fees.[5]

To the extent that you use a computer research tool that charges a fee, you should develop a sense of the relative efficiency of different kinds of research tools in different kinds of searches. For example, even though the trustworthy and efficient LEXIS-NEXIS and WESTLAW computer research services have revolutionized legal research, they are not the exclusive answer to your research problems in this era of transition from bound volumes to electronic information. You can still accomplish some research tasks with great efficiency in the stacks of bound volumes. Moreover, LEXIS-NEXIS and WESTLAW charge their subscribers by the minute, search, or transaction. As a student, you may be entitled to free access to these computer research tools for law school assignments; outside that academic context, however, your clients ultimately will pay for your access to LEXIS-NEXIS and WESTLAW. You may inflate your bills to your clients if you spend precious time online searching for or reading text that you could readily locate in a bound volume a few feet from your office.

To ensure cost-effective use of expensive computer research tools, you should also master the traditional library resources in bound volumes. As you supplement this knowledge with computer research skills, you will probably determine that some kinds of computer searches will be cost-effective, because they will significantly reduce your research time, freeing you for work

---

3. *See, e.g.*, Adam J. Piacente, Computer-Assisted Legal Research Unplugged: The User-Friendly Guide to LEXIS-NEXIS and WESTLAW (2000); Christopher G. Wren & Jill Robinson Wren, Using Computers in Legal Research: A Guide to LEXIS and WESTLAW (1994).

4. For a comprehensive guide to Internet research, see Herbert N. Ramy & Samantha A. Moppett, Navigating the Internet: Legal Research on the World Wide Web (2000).

5. For just two examples of such sites, see Cornell Law School's site at *http://www.law.cornell.edu* and the United States Supreme Court's site at *http://www.supremecourtus.gov.* For more, see Antje Mays, Legal Research on the Internet: A Compendium of Websites to Access United States Federal, State, Local and International Laws (1999).

on other cases and offsetting the computer research expense with fewer hours billed for the client. Conversely, you may find that you can accomplish other research tasks more effectively and inexpensively with bound volumes in your office or at a local library, because traditional research tools are quick and comprehensive. With some care and experience, you can acquire a sense of balance between traditional and computer-assisted research tools.

III. RESEARCH STRATEGY

Before setting your sights on specific primary authority in the library, you should acquire a general grasp of the fundamental legal principles in the relevant subject areas so that you can more effectively identify issues and exclude unproductive lines of inquiry. A general survey course on the subject in law school should be sufficient to enable you to define issues and to delve immediately into specific, primary authority such as statutes or case law. If you have not taken a course on the subject matter of the assignment, you should consider beginning your research with a secondary source that provides general background information. As their labels suggest, primary authority within the relevant jurisdiction takes analytic precedence over secondary authority. Nonetheless, you will often find and use the primary authority more effectively if you first consult a secondary source, such as a reputable treatise, to enhance your understanding of the broad outlines of the subject.

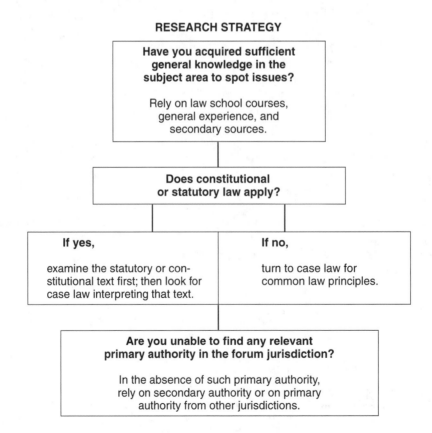

RESEARCH STRATEGY

Have you acquired sufficient general knowledge in the subject area to spot issues?

Rely on law school courses, general experience, and secondary sources.

Does constitutional or statutory law apply?

If yes,

examine the statutory or constitutional text first; then look for case law interpreting that text.

If no,

turn to case law for common law principles.

Are you unable to find any relevant primary authority in the forum jurisdiction?

In the absence of such primary authority, rely on secondary authority or on primary authority from other jurisdictions.

Once you have begun to explore primary authority, you should look for relevant legislation before digging too deeply into case law. A single statute can diminish or even destroy the authoritative value of a whole line of case law that developed common law doctrines or that interpreted previously effective legislation. Thus, you can avoid hours of marginally productive reading by immediately finding the latest applicable legislation.

Even when you know that a body of case law interprets currently effective legislation, you should turn first to the statute itself. At least a glance at the statutory language will provide valuable context for the case law that interprets the statute. Moreover, an annotated codebook may help you dig up interpretive case law that you missed with other case-finding tools. If you can find no judicial decisions that interpret the statutory language in question, you should look for helpful legislative history, if any.

Of course, if you find no statute or constitutional provision on point, you may safely turn to case law as primary authority for applicable common law. In the absence of any relevant primary authority in the jurisdiction, you can rely on the persuasive authority provided by secondary sources or by primary authority from other jurisdictions.

IV. USING THE LIBRARY

A. Taking Notes

You should take thorough notes on any authority that may be helpful. Even marginally applicable cases may warrant note; their relevance may become clear only after further research and analysis. To avoid the need for frequent returns to the library, your notes should include any information that you may later need in drafting the office memorandum, including

1. the full citation,
2. the specific page on which relevant material appears,
3. a sufficient summary of the facts to provide necessary context and to define the holding,
4. a careful summary of the holding and reasoning, including helpful dictum, on any issues relevant to your research assignment, and
5. the verbatim language of any passage that you think might be worth quoting; you may want to photocopy any part of an opinion that warrants special or extended study.

Moreover, to facilitate further research, you should record data provided by the publisher designed to be used with formal research tools. For example, an opinion that is reproduced in a reporter published by West Publishing Company will begin with West "headnotes," each of which includes at least one key number. As discussed in Section B above, these headnotes and key numbers are worth recording in your notes, because they will help you find other cases on point. For example, the following library notes incorporate these West features:

Osterholt v. St. Charles Drilling Co., 500 F. Supp. 529 (E.D. Mo. 1980).

pp. 530-32. Landowner sued drilling company for damages stemming from installation of defective well and water system. pp. 534-35—Judgment for P on K.

p. 536 [9] (Fraud 61)—punitive damages denied for alleged misrepresentation, because of absence of "aggravating circumstances" such as willful, wanton, reckless, or malicious conduct.

Court refers to other case at 582 F.2d at 1087—should look this up.

In this example, the researcher is particularly interested in the passage on page 536 discussing punitive damages. The shorthand citation at the end of the notes refers to an opinion cited in *Osterholt* that the researcher will examine. The phrase "(Fraud 61)" refers to a West key number that will help the researcher use the West digest system to find other cases discussing the same issue. Indeed, that key number may lead to other cases reported in the West system that will supply the researcher with other West key numbers that are productive on the topic of punitive damages. The number "9" in brackets refers to the headnote number associated with the relevant passage. As illustrated in Section B above, that headnote number will help the researcher use Shepard's citation service as a tool for finding subsequent cases that cite *Osterholt* on the issue of punitive damages for tort.

B. Library Courtesy

In light of the scarcity of resources in any law library, discourtesy in the library can lead to frustration and wasted time for all. Rather than pile three dozen books on a table for an afternoon's reading, you should take only one or two books off the shelves at a time, take notes, and immediately reshelve the books. If you follow a methodical approach, you can efficiently exhaust the research possibilities with minimum duplication of effort.

For example, after finding an applicable statute in an annotated codebook, you may use the annotations to find interpretive case law. Because the descriptive paragraphs in the annotations provide only general guidance, you may not be able to determine whether a reported opinion contains noteworthy information until you have glanced at the opinion itself. You can do that while standing at the stacks. If the opinion warrants close reading, you can take the reporter to a library carrel for note taking. If the opinion appears to be unhelpful, you can return the reporter to the shelves without having taken it from the vicinity.

V. REORGANIZATION AND OUTLINING

As summarized at the beginning of Chapter 8, the process of transforming library notes into a well-organized office memorandum is similar to that of summarizing and reorganizing case briefs in a student course outline. Both processes require you (1) to synthesize cases to arrive at general principles and (2) to classify cases to show which of them illustrates each principle. With this synthesis and reorganization, you can highlight ideas and illuminate them with illustrative cases, rather than simply present a laundry list of individual cases whose relationships to one another are unclear.

If you produce voluminous library notes for a complex assignment, you may wish to begin the process of reorganization by indexing your notes in the manner described at the beginning of Chapter 7. For example, a researcher has assigned a number to each authority summarized in the following library notes:

---

1. Statute of frauds—Ariz. Rev. Stat. Ann. § 44-101 (West 1967).

"No action shall be brought in any court in the following cases unless the promise or agreement upon which the action is brought . . . is in writing and signed by the party to be charged . . . 5. Upon an agreement which is not to be performed within one year from the making thereof."

2. *Tiffany Inc. v. W.M.K. Transit Mix, Inc.*, 16 Ariz. App. 415, 493 P.2d 1220 (1972).

P.2d at 1221-22—Tiffany prepared a bid to state agency to complete work on highway project; before bidding, it received oral price quote from Transit Mix for the supply of sealcoat chips for the project. Tiffany used that quote in its bid, the state awarded the bid to Tiffany, Transit refused to perform, Tiffany sues, and Transit raises statute of frauds as defense.

1222-23—UCC statute of frauds applies

a. 1224-25 [5-7] (Estoppel 52, 85, 99)—distinction between equitable and promissory estoppel: equitable—reliance on misrepresentation of fact; used as a "shield" or defense against a claim. Promissory—reliance on a promise; used as a defense or as basis for cause of action for damages.

b. 1225 [8, 9] (Estoppel 85)—If proved at trial, following facts would support application of promissory estoppel: Transit promised to supply sealcoat chips at certain price in event that Tiffany got the main bid; Tiffany relied by using quote in its own bid; Transit should have foreseen that Tiffany would use its quote if it were the lowest. (dictum?)

1225-26 [10] (Frauds, stat. of 144)—nonetheless, statute of frauds bars enforcement of promise. Court recognizes estoppel to avoid statute if promisee relies on misrepresentation about requirements of statute (equitable estoppel?) or on promise to satisfy or not to rely on statute—but can't avoid statute by relying on other party's underlying oral promise to perform.

3. *Mac Enters. v. Del E. Webb Dev. Co.*, 132 Ariz. 331, 645 P.2d 1245 (Ct. App. 1982).

P.2d at 1250 [6] (Frauds, stat. of 144)—no estoppel to avoid statute of frauds, because Webb made no promise upon which Mac could reasonably rely.

4. *Kiely v. St. Germain*, 670 P.2d 764 (Colo. 1983) (en banc).
768-69—[7] (Frauds, stat. of 119(1))—good discussion of liberal
Rest. 2d use of promissory estoppel to avoid statute of frauds and case
law that prompted it—*Tiffany* cited as example of narrower approach.

. . . .

After analyzing the problem, the researcher then developed a rough
outline to express a proposed organization for each office memorandum.
As illustrated at the beginning of Chapter 8, the outline of the discussion
section is organized around legal principles and identifies which authority
supports and illustrates each principle:

III. DISCUSSION

A. Applicability and Satisfaction of Statute of Frauds

Rules: requires writing signed by party to be charged if cannot be performed
in 1 year [ARS § 44-101(5), #1]

Facts: K is for 2 years, and no writing at all

Conclusion: statute applies & is not satisfied

B. Estoppel to Avoid Statute

　　1. Misrep. or Promise about Statute's Requirements

Rules: equitable estoppel and promissory estoppel relating to requirements
of statute [*Cress*, #6; and *Johnson*, #10, or *Tiffany*, #2a]

Facts: no representation or promise about statute's requirements

Conclusion: trad. forms of avoidance through estoppel not available

　　2. Reliance on Underlying Promise to Perform

Rules: Introduce liberal doctrine [Rest. 2d, #5, *Kiely*, #4]. Discuss whether
AZ likely to adopt liberal rule [*Cf. Fremming*, #9, with *Tiffany*, #2b]—Some
cases have assumed theory, but found elements not satisfied [*Trollope*, #8, and
Mac, #3]—Distinguish *Tiffany?* [Wallach, #13 and U.C.C. sections it cites;
Trollope, #8, *Dean*, #7, and *Johnson*, #10]

Facts: Williams' actions probably constitute detrimental, foreseeable
reliance

Conclusion: If AZ court adopts liberal view of avoidance of statute through
promissory estoppel, facts probably support claim for damages.

Some authorities appear more than once and in different parts of the
outline because those authorities contain information relevant to more than
one topic or subtopic in the discussion. Each shorthand reference to an
authority is followed by the index number to the place in the author's library

notes where that authority is summarized. As illustrated at the beginning of Chapter 8, the index number helped the author quickly locate the authority in his notes when he drafted the memoranda. Also, as discussed at the beginning of Chapter 8, you can facilitate this process of reorganizing library notes by taking your notes on a portable computer or by summarizing the discussions of different issues from a single source on separate note cards.

When researching a problem, you should avoid the temptation to include every idea and authority that you have encountered in the library. The outlining stage provides a good opportunity to exclude marginally relevant material as well as to reorganize and analyze.

VI. WRITING THE MEMORANDUM

Once you are satisfied with the organization and analysis reflected in your outline, you can use the outline as a general guide when writing the memorandum. Some law firms encourage their attorneys to dictate their first drafts into hand-held tape recorders, but many new associates find it difficult to display good style in dictation. Consequently, if you dictate the first draft, you may want to work from a particularly detailed written outline so that you can focus your attention on sentence structure rather than on organizational matters.

The remaining chapters in Part V thoroughly explore the process of writing and organizing an office memorandum, as well as citing to legal authority. The next chapter describes the general content of an office memorandum so that you can get a clearer idea of your goal. Once you have that goal in mind, you can better absorb the detailed information in the remaining three chapters regarding writing style, organization, and citation form.

VII. SUMMARY

Before drafting an office memorandum, you should

1. master the assignment,
2. research and analyze the problem, and
3. reorganize your research notes into a rough outline of the discussion section of your memorandum.

In researching the problem, use secondary authority to help you identify issues and important lines of primary authority, but rely on applicable primary authority for your final analysis whenever it is available. In researching primary authority, look first for statutes or constitutional provisions that may apply, and then look for judicial decisions that interpret and apply the statute or constitution. Whether a judicial decision interprets statutory law or develops common law, check its subsequent history before relying on it.

If you need help identifying or locating the best research tool for your assignment, do not hesitate to ask your librarians for assistance. They have great expertise, and they usually will gladly take the time to share it with you.

Chapter 11

Content of the Office Memorandum of Law

I. AUDIENCE, PURPOSE, AND PERSPECTIVE

An office memorandum of law is one of the most effective means with which a new associate or a summer law clerk can directly help a supervising attorney represent a client. The supervising attorney may be preparing a more formal document, such as a pleading or brief to a court, an opinion letter to a client, or a demand letter to an opposing party. To help her prepare any of these documents, the supervising attorney may use the office memorandum as a source of information, or even as a partial rough draft. In other cases, the supervising attorney may use the information in an office memorandum to develop a tax strategy for a business client or a settlement strategy for negotiations on behalf of a litigation client.

An office memorandum informs rather than advocates. To effectively represent the client, the supervising attorney must know both the weaknesses and the strengths of the client's claims and defenses. If you present a balanced analysis of the dispute in your office memorandum, you will enable your supervising attorney to focus her attention on her strongest arguments, to anticipate the counterarguments of the opposing party, and to develop an effective strategy. On the other hand, if you selectively bear only good news

191

to your supervising attorney, you will mislead her. Indeed, your unbalanced analysis may cause her embarrassment when further proceedings expose problems in her client's case, problems that she might have avoided or at least anticipated had the law firm confronted them at an earlier stage.

On the other hand, an office memorandum is not entirely neutral; in most cases, it anticipates advocacy on behalf of a client. Therefore, even though you explore arguments on both sides of a dispute in your memorandum, you should not convey a detached indifference to the outcome. Many supervising attorneys complain that student law clerks and recent graduates of law school tend to treat office memoranda as purely academic exercises and to abandon a client's cause too readily after identifying obstacles to the client's claims or defenses. To avoid such criticism, you should do more than identify weaknesses in a client's case; you should also recommend the best means of overcoming them. You must neither conceal such weaknesses nor surrender to despair over them. Instead, you should identify the best means to exploit the strengths of the client's case and suggest creative solutions to the problems raised by the weaknesses.

II. GENERAL FORMAT FOR AN OFFICE MEMORANDUM

Like alternative formats for student case briefs, a number of formats for office memoranda have earned popularity. If your law firm or individual supervising attorney expresses a preference for a particular format, you should respect the wishes of your intended audience. Otherwise, you can choose any reasonable format, such as either of the following:

Format A	Format B
I. Issue(s)	I. Overview
II. Brief Answer(s)	II. Facts
III. Facts	III. Issue(s) & Brief Answer(s)
IV. Discussion	IV. Discussion
V. Conclusion	V. Conclusion

Format A presents the issues first so that the reader can appreciate the legal significance of the facts when she reads them. Following the statement of issues are brief answers that tersely preview the final conclusion. As discussed below, the brief answers and the conclusion serve different purposes.

In some cases, complex multiple transactions and confusing relationships between multiple parties may make a single-sentence statement of the issues incomprehensible to one who has not first read the facts. As discussed in Section III.A below, you can address such confusion by stating your issue, along with its premises, in more than one sentence. Alternatively, format B provides a special format for such cases: In a paragraph or two, a brief overview identifies the general nature of the dispute and the issues, and it summarizes the writer's conclusions. Such an introduction enables the reader to appreciate the legal significance of the facts, and it allows the writer to simplify the issues and brief answers. In turn, the statement of facts gives the reader sufficient information to comprehend a detailed statement of the issues, permitting the author of the memorandum to follow the facts with a more formal, specific statement of the issues than was feasible in the overview.

III. ELEMENTS OF AN OFFICE MEMORANDUM

The heading of a memorandum is simple and requires only brief discussion. The heading should identify the author of the memorandum; the recipient of the memorandum; the subject matter, stated in a manner that facilitates filing and later retrieval; and the date:

To: Susan Elias
From: James Nelson
Re: Enforceability of Julie Week's Promise to Act as Guarantor for Loan
        Obligation; File 02-127
Date: September 16, 2002

The following subsections examine the more substantive elements of Format A for an office memorandum: Issues, Brief Answer(s), Facts, Discussion, and Conclusion.

A. Issues—Identification and Expression

1. REVIEW

Section III of Chapter 6 discusses the general process of identifying issues for analysis. Section II.B.2.a of Chapter 7 discusses the process of framing issues for statement in a case brief. Section II.A of Chapter 9 discusses the process of identifying issues for discussion in an essay examination. These sections lay the foundation for identifying and framing issues in an office memorandum, and you should review them now.

Your task of identifying issues for analysis in an office memorandum is similar to that of identifying issues on a law school examination: You must have at least a general knowledge of the law governing the dispute so that you can recognize the legal problems raised by the facts. In many cases, courses that you have taken in law school will enable you to identify the general nature of the issues and to direct your research efforts; if not, a secondary source such as a good treatise may provide the necessary background information.

You should not finally identify and express the issues until the final stages of drafting. When you prepare a case brief for class discussion, you ordinarily cannot state with particularity the issues discussed in the judicial decision until you have completed your analysis of the entire opinion. Similarly, when preparing an office memorandum, you ordinarily cannot state with particularity the issues raised by the facts of the dispute until you have finished your research and have fully analyzed the problem. At that time, you must decide which elements of a claim or defense are sufficiently in doubt that they warrant identification and discussion as issues.

2. EXAMPLE: IDENTIFYING ISSUES IN A TITLE VII SUIT

For example, Title VII of the Civil Rights Act of 1964 imposes liability on employers for engaging in "unlawful employment practices," and it defines "employer" in part as "a person engaged in an industry affecting commerce."[1] Although engagement "in an industry affecting commerce" is always an element of employer liability, in many cases the facts known to all parties leave no doubt that the employer's activities satisfy the statutory rule under any reasonable interpretation. In such a case, the party charged with discrimination could not credibly dispute its status as an "employer" on grounds relating to commerce, and you should not identify that matter as an issue in your memorandum. At most, you might briefly state this conclusion in an introduction to the discussion of a substantial issue.

In the same case, however, unusual facts and uncertainty in the applicable legal standards might raise doubts about whether the employer has committed an "unlawful employment practice." Because the employee plausibly claims that the employer committed an unlawful employment practice, and because the employer plausibly denies it, the parties reasonably dispute that matter, and you should identify it as an issue for discussion.

3. EXPRESSING ISSUES WITH PARTICULARITY

Once you have identified and analyzed issues for discussion in your memorandum, you should state them with the same specificity and attention to facts that would be appropriate in the statement of issues in a case brief prepared for class discussion. To review these techniques, you may want to return briefly to Section II.B.2 of Chapter 7.

For example, you should not state the issue in such general terms as "whether the employer committed an unlawful employment practice under Title VII of the Civil Rights Act of 1964." The author of the memorandum might be tempted to state such a general issue if he anticipates that other attorneys will consult the memorandum for general guidance when analyzing Title VII claims brought by other clients in different factual contexts. The author may fear that the other attorneys will fail to recognize the value of the memorandum as a general resource if the issue in the memorandum is so specific that it reveals the narrow factual context of the dispute, a context

---

1. 42 U.S.C. §§ 2000e(b) (definition of "employer"), 2000e-2(a) (unlawful employer practices) (1994); *see also id*. at §§ 2000e(g) and (h) (definitions of "commerce" and "industry affecting commerce").

that differs from the ones confronted by the other attorneys. But this fear is misplaced. The other attorneys will recognize instantly that the memorandum in the file will likely set forth general standards about Title VII that will be useful in most Title VII claims, and they will be grateful for an issue statement that tips them off quickly about the precise ways in which their cases differ from the one analyzed in the memorandum.

Accordingly, after researching the law and analyzing the facts, you should more precisely identify the contours of the dispute likely to be raised by the parties:

Did Salerno create a hostile working environment for his female employees by repeatedly asking them for dates, thus making Salerno liable for sex discrimination under Title VII by altering the employees' terms or conditions of employment?

If your question becomes tangled with excessively complex factual or legal details, you can make it simpler by leaving some of those details for the brief answer:

I. ISSUE

Did Salerno create a hostile working environment for his female employees by repeatedly making unwelcome sexual advances, in violation of Title VII of the Civil Rights Act of 1964?

II. BRIEF ANSWER

Probably yes. Salerno allowed his male employees to work unmolested, but he repeatedly and aggressively asked three female employees for dates, long after the employees expressed their discomfort with the advances. In light of the intrusive and sexually charged manner in which Salerno made his requests, he probably created a hostile working environment for the employees. If so, he is liable under Title VII for engaging in sex discrimination that altered the employees' working conditions.

Section II.B.2.b of Chapter 7 discusses a similar technique, that of drafting a case brief so that the statements of issue and holding share the burden of expressing important details. Alternatively, one author recommends that students and attorneys state the premises of an issue in separate sentences within the issue statement.[2] For example, you could state the Title VII issue in the following way:

---

2. *See* Bryan A. Garner, THE WINNING BRIEF: 100 TIPS FOR PERSUASIVE BRIEFING IN TRIAL AND APPELLATE COURTS 77-79 (1999) ("Rule 12: Weave facts into your issues to make them concrete."); Bryan A. Garner, *The Deep Issue: A New Approach to Framing Legal Questions*, 5 Scribes J. Legal Writing 1 (1994-95).

I. ISSUE

Title VII imposes liability on an employer that discriminates on the basis of sex in a way that alters conditions of employment. One way to alter employment conditions is by creating a hostile working environment for employees. In our case, the employer repeatedly directed sexually charged requests for dates to three female employees, even though the employees complained that the advances were unwelcome. The employer discriminated on the basis of sex because he allowed his male employees to work unmolested. Did the employer's discriminatory conduct also amount to a hostile working environment for the female employees sufficient to alter their conditions of employment?

This format for a multisentence issue statement may not meet with the approval of every supervising attorney, and it may not be perfectly consistent with some court rules governing the statement of issues in a brief. Still, when supervisors and court rules permit, you may want to experiment with this approach for particularly complex issues.

B. Brief Answer

Each brief answer should be a succinct response to the question presented in each issue. The precise form of the answer may depend on the degree of specificity that you have achieved in the statement of the issue, just as the appropriate form for the statement of the holding in a case brief may depend on the degree of specificity of the issue statement.

In some cases, the issue may be sufficiently simple and the statement of the issue sufficiently specific to justify limiting the brief answer to a word or two, such as "yes," "no," "probably yes," or "probably no." If so, each brief answer can appear immediately after the statement of the corresponding issue without any separate section heading.

In most cases, however, you may find it difficult to state all the elements of a complex issue in a single, graceful sentence. In those cases, you can supply additional information in a brief answer of one or more sentences under a separate section heading. Even so, you should not use the brief answer to explore analytic justifications in great depth; the reader can more easily absorb a complex summary of the analysis after she has read the discussion section of the memorandum. For example, the medical malpractice dispute discussed on pages 91-92 might raise the following issues and brief answers:

I. ISSUES

A. Does the phrase "any toxic material" in New Maine's strict liability statute encompass a generally safe anesthetic that produced a fatal reaction in a patient with a rare nerve disorder?

B. Is Humane Hospital liable to Souza's estate for negligent administration of the anesthetic?

1. Did Humane's anesthesiologist breach a duty of care by administering the anesthetic without assistance and by failing to monitor Souza's reactions to anesthesia?

2. Did Souza's nerve disorder constitute a supervening cause that broke the chain of causation between the anesthesiologist's conduct and Souza's death?

II. BRIEF ANSWERS

A. Probably not. A restrictive interpretation is supported by the legislative history and by a general public policy in New Maine encouraging the provision of affordable medical services. The legislature probably did not intend the statutory phrase "toxic material" to include medically prescribed substances that ordinarily produce a beneficial result or otherwise facilitate medical treatment.

B. Probably yes.

1. Probably yes. Under generally accepted hospital procedures, at least two trained medical personnel must monitor the administration of anesthesia, with at least one person monitoring the patient's reactions. A jury likely will find that the anesthesiologist breached a duty of care to the patient by administering the anesthesia alone.

2. No. The jury likely will also find that the patient's nerve disorder was not a supervening cause and that the anesthesiologist's negligence proximately caused the patient's death.

C. Facts

Some new associates in a law firm regularly omit statements of facts in their legal memoranda. The associates often explain that a supervising attorney obviously knows the facts of an assigned case because she gave the facts to the associate in some oral or written form when she assigned the memorandum.

For several reasons, however, you should include at least a brief statement of facts in a legal memorandum unless your supervising attorney specifically authorizes you to omit it. The supervising attorney may have been familiar with the facts when she assigned the memorandum, but she may need a brief review to refresh her memory when she later reads your memorandum. Alternatively, she may simply want reassurance that you share her understanding of the facts. Furthermore, the memorandum should be a self-contained document that is helpful to any member of the firm who may be called on to take over the file, including an attorney who knows nothing about the case and does not have time to glean the facts from the file. Finally, a statement of the factual premises on which you based your legal analysis helps you focus your research and analysis, and it protects you from criticism if that analysis later becomes obsolete or misleading in light of newly discovered facts.

In selecting facts for statement, you should focus on material facts and background facts with attention to the considerations that you would apply in preparing a case brief for class. However, you should hesitate less in an office memorandum than in a case brief to mention a marginally significant fact. When briefing a case, you must rely on the court's summary of the facts as a complete record on which the court based its decision; moreover, you can test your analytic abilities by attempting to isolate the material facts and helpful background facts and by omitting the others. In contrast, when preparing an office memorandum at an early stage of a dispute, you know that the facts on which you rely for your analysis are incomplete. Subsequent proceedings may reveal other facts that support new claims, defenses, or arguments. Moreover, previously known facts that appeared to be unimportant when you drafted the memorandum may take on new legal significance as a consequence. In your statement of facts, therefore, you should recite all material facts in detail, and you should summarize any other information that either provides helpful background material or appears to have the potential to take on new significance as the litigation proceeds.

D. Discussion

1. INTRODUCING YOUR ANALYSIS

In the discussion section of your legal memorandum, you will express your complete legal analysis of each issue stated at the beginning of the memorandum. If your memorandum addresses a single issue that you have formally stated at or near the beginning of the memorandum, your discussion of the issue need not begin with any descriptive heading beyond the major section heading "Discussion."

However, if you address multiple issues, you should separately analyze each issue under a descriptive section heading. Although the heading need not restate the issue in full detail, it should link your analysis to an issue that is more formally and narrowly stated earlier in the memorandum:

IV. DISCUSSION
    A. Strict Liability for Use of Toxic Materials
    • • • •
    B. Negligence
    • • • •
        1. Negligent Act
    • • • •
        2. Proximate Cause
    • • • •

Immediately after you identify an issue with a section heading, you may want to illuminate the issue in an introductory sentence or two that refers briefly to facts, arguments, or theories that help to explain the significance of the issue. For example, the following opening sentence expands on the section heading by explaining the significance of the theory of strict liability:

A. Strict Liability for Use of Toxic Material

If a statute or the common law imposes strict liability for Souza's death, then Souza's estate can establish liability without proving negligence.

In some cases, the opening paragraph of a section may even draw subsidiary legal conclusions as a means of pinpointing the narrow question in dispute. For example, the following paragraph concludes that a proposed transaction would include a sale of goods. Coupled with other observations, that subsidiary conclusion leads to the primary issue of the section:

A. Choice of Law—UCC or Common Law

Whether Maldonado accepted Weinstein's offer depends in part on whether the common law of contracts or the Uniform Commercial Code (UCC) applies to the transaction. The UCC applies only to "transactions in goods." U.C.C. § 2-102 (2000). Weinstein's offer to supply specifically identified, separately priced, movable plumbing parts clearly contemplates a sale of goods as part of the transaction. See U.C.C. § 2-105(1) (2000). His proposed transaction, however, also involves the service of installing the fixtures, raising a question about the applicability of the UCC to mixed transactions for both services and the sale of goods.

The UCC applies to such a mixed transaction only if. . . .

Of course, if an issue is adequately represented in a section heading and needs no further elaboration, the discussion can proceed immediately to an analysis of the legal standards:

A. Applicability and Satisfaction of the Statute of Frauds

The Arizona statute of frauds bars enforcement of "an agreement which is not to be performed within one year from the making thereof," unless it, "or some memorandum thereof, is in writing and signed by the party to be charged." Ariz. Rev. Stat. Ann. § 44-101(5) (West 1994) (copy of full text attached). . . .

2. ANALYZING THE LAW AND THE FACTS

After you have drafted the section heading and the optional elaboration of the issue, you ordinarily should follow the "IRAC" pattern of deductive reasoning developed in Chapter 6: For each issue or subissue, analyze the law and apply the law to the facts to reach a conclusion. The nature of the analysis in a discussion section obviously will vary with each issue. If the clearly applicable abstract legal rule is simple, you can present the rule and supporting authority directly and concisely, permitting you to direct most of your attention to fact analysis. Other issues may require a choice among competing rules or a clarification of the content of the applicable legal rule. If so, you may need to discuss the abstract legal rule in depth before applying it to the facts. Of course, determining the content of the rule and applying it to the facts are often related tasks: Your discussion of the question of whether particular facts satisfy the legal standard may help to clarify the content of a vague or uncertain rule.

a. Example: Statutory Analysis

Reproduced below is a portion of the discussion section of a sample office memorandum set in the fictitious state of New Maine, whose case law we will assume is published solely in the New Maine Reporter, abbreviated "N. Me." It analyzes the issue of statutory liability for administering anesthesia. The statutory analysis in the passage focuses on defining the legal rule in a simple factual context, thus requiring relatively little independent fact analysis. In contrast, the memorandum must engage in original statutory analysis because no judicial decision has yet interpreted the statutory language in question. Accordingly, after refining the issue in an introduction, the author of the discussion presents the statutory analysis on three levels in descending order of priority: the language of the statute, its legislative history (often difficult to find for state legislation, but easily accessible in published materials in this fictitious jurisdiction), and general policy considerations. In this example, the author has applied the law to the relevant facts at each level of the statutory analysis rather than in a single consolidated fact analysis at the end of the discussion; other means of organizing the discussion, however, are presented in the next chapter.

IV. DISCUSSION

A. Strict Liability for Use of Toxic Materials

Introduction

 If a statute or the common law imposes strict liability for Souza's death, then Souza's estate can establish liability without proving negligence. New Maine's common law doctrine of strict liability for injuries caused by ultrahazardous activities does not apply to noncriminal medical practices engaged in by licensed physicians. *Stanislaus v. Good Samaritan Hosp.*, 212 N. Me. 113, 115 (1989). New Maine has recently enacted a statute, however, that imposes strict liability for injuries stemming from the use of "any toxic material": "A commercial enterprise is liable for injuries proximately caused by its use of any toxic material, without regard to the degree of care exercised by the enterprise." 12 N. Me. Rev. Stat. Ann. § 242 (Supp. 2001) (effective Jan. 1, 2002). As a profit-making hospital, Humane presumably is a "commercial enterprise" within the meaning of the statute. It is less certain, however, that the anesthetic administered to Souza would qualify as a "toxic" material.

Narrow issue

The common meaning of the word "toxic" is "poisonous." *E.g., The Random House Dictionary of the English Language* 1500 (unabridged) (1970). Souza's estate might plausibly argue that the anesthetic was a toxic material because it was poisonous to Souza, even though it would not have been poisonous to most others. The word "toxic," however, applies more naturally to substances that are universally harmful to humans, such as cyanide, DDT, or sulfuric acid. It strains the common meaning of "toxic" to apply it to an anesthetic that might occasionally be harmful to persons with unusual allergies or other extraordinary conditions.

Analysis of statutory language

Preliminary fact

Legislative history also supports a restrictive interpretation of the statutory term "any toxic material." The report of the New Maine Senate Committee on Health and Welfare suggests that the legislature was concerned only with the most deadly of substances:

Legislative history

> The purpose of this bill is to reallocate the cost of unavoidable accidents from victims to industry and its consumers, to discourage unnecessary use of deadly chemicals and other hazardous materials, and to encourage the development and use of substitute materials that are generally safe for human contact.

N. Me. Sen. Rep. No. 112, 1996-1997 Sess. 2 (2001). The anesthetic in this case probably is closer to the materials "generally safe for human contact" condoned by the legislature than it is to the "deadly chemicals and other hazardous materials" condemned by it.

Fact analysis

Finally, general state policy appears to support an interpretation that excludes medically prescribed substances from the reach of the statute. The legislature and judiciary of New Maine have recognized a policy of restricting the liability of physicians to encourage the ready availability of affordable medical services. For example, under the New Maine "Good Samaritan" statute, physicians who provide certain emergency medical services are not liable for adverse consequences unless they engage in culpable conduct amounting to at least gross negligence. 12 N. Me. Rev. Stat. Ann. § 229 (1992). This protective policy is also reflected in the courts' refusal to

Policy analysis

extend common law strict liability for ultrahazardous activities to even experimental medical practices.
See Stanislaus, 212 N. Me. at 115. The legislature
presumably was aware of these laws when it enacted
the toxic materials statute in 2001.

Souza's estate may argue that the legislature
intended to retreat from the protective policies of
these laws by imposing strict liability on a limited
segment of the activities of commercial medical
practices. Absent more specific evidence of legislative intent to depart from existing legal policies,
however, it is probably more likely that the legislature retained its protective attitude and assumed
that the term "toxic material" would not include
routinely prescribed medicines or anesthetics.

Fact analysis

In this case, the prescribed anesthetic, ethane,
was not the safest available at the time of Souza's
operation. Nonetheless, it is a frequently prescribed
substance that produces beneficial results with only
minor side effects in all but the most unusual cases.

Conclusion

The strict liability statute almost certainly does not
apply to Souza's death.

b. Example: Established Common Law

In contrast to the previous example, the sample discussion below briefly
summarizes noncontroversial legal standards and places greater emphasis on
fact analysis. After illuminating the issue of negligence and summarizing
general principles, the discussion separately addresses distinct subissues in
different subsections. Within the first of those subsections, devoted to "negligent act," the author has consolidated the relatively simple legal standards
in a single paragraph, leading to a single, uninterrupted line of fact analysis.
She has divided the fact analysis itself into two paragraphs, presenting opposing factual arguments.

IV. DISCUSSION

A. Strict Liability for Use of Toxic Materials

• • • •

B. Negligence

Introduction

Assuming that Humane Hospital is not strictly
liable for Souza's death, it may nonetheless be liable
to Souza's estate if its agent caused the death
through negligence. *See Kityama v. Mercy Hosp.,*
183 N. Me. 752, 759-60 (1974) (hospital liable for
negligence of its nurse). An action for negligence
requires proof of a negligent act or omission that

proximately causes injury. *Baker v. Bruce*, 153 N. Me. 817, 820 (1967).

In our case, the injury to Souza is obvious. In greater doubt are the elements of negligent act and proximate cause.

1. Negligent Act

A negligent act or omission consists of the breach of a duty of care owed to another. *Id.* at 821. A medical specialist owes a duty to patients to exercise at least the ordinary skill and care that is reasonable and customary nationwide in that medical specialty. *Kityama*, 183 N. Me. at 760. Furthermore, under the "thin-skulled plaintiff" rule, that duty of care encompasses the special care necessary to address increased risks created by a patient's unusual susceptibility to injury. *Id.* In this case, Humane's anesthesiologist, Unger, may have breached duties of care in her unassisted administration of general anesthesia in the face of Souza's known nerve condition.

Unger exercised care in determining Souza's disorder of the nervous system and in informing her of the risks presented by each of the most suitable anesthetics. Moreover, when administering the anesthetic selected by Souza, Unger took care to provide the prescribed dosage by monitoring the anesthetic intake gauge.

However, Unger's intense concentration on the anesthetic intake gauge may have been an act of carelessness, rather than enhanced care, because it diverted Unger's attention from Souza and from equipment monitoring Souza's vital signs. Faced with Souza's known nerve disorder, Unger probably had a duty to follow the standard medical practice of summoning a nurse to assist her in administering the anesthesia. Had she done so, the team could have monitored both Souza's vital signs and the intake gauge, and a team member undoubtedly would have detected signs of distress at least 10 seconds before death, arguably enough time to cease anesthesia and take corrective measures.

On these facts, a jury could find that Unger was negligent in her administration of the anesthetic.

2. Proximate Cause

. . . .

Narrow issues

Legal rules

Fact analysis favoring Humane

Fact analysis favoring Souza's estate

Conclusion

E. The Conclusion

Even though the questions addressed in an office memorandum may be close, and even though your supervising attorney will not feel bound by your advice, she will expect you to take a position by stating your conclusions. A thorough memorandum will include both (1) a brief resolution of each issue within the part of the discussion section devoted to that issue, and (2) a more general summary of conclusions in a separate section at the end of the memorandum.

In the conclusion section, you can summarize the individual conclusions that you have reached in the discussion section of the memorandum. In addition, you may wish to summarize the analytic support for the conclusions in a depth that would have been inappropriate in the brief answers stated earlier.

Finally, you should use the conclusion section to express any strategic recommendations that your analysis inspires. For example, you may recommend that the law firm file a complaint, settle a weak case, investigate certain facts, or concentrate its efforts on a particular legal theory.

Although you may express more information in the conclusion section than in the brief answers, your conclusion should nonetheless represent a selective summary of your analyses and recommendations. In a simple case, a few sentences may suffice; even moderately complex cases require no more than a few paragraphs.

For example, the following passage concisely synthesizes the conclusions previewed above in Section B as brief answers, and it adds strategic recommendations:

V. CONCLUSION

Summary of analyses

In light of legislative and judicial policies favoring limits on physicians' liability, the strict liability statute regulating toxic materials probably will not apply to the administration of anesthetic in this case. The courts will be even less likely to retreat from precedent by applying the common law doctrine of strict liability for ultrahazardous activities. A jury may find, however, that Humane's anesthesiologist was negligent in failing to summon assistance to administer the anesthesia or to monitor the patient closely. We can try to characterize Souza's nerve condition as a supervening cause, but *Rainbow Landscaping* will not be easy to distinguish.

Strategic recommendation

Because the risk of substantial liability is great, I recommend that we advise Humane to settle. Souza's estate may be willing to compromise; its negligence claim is not appropriate for summary disposition and thus is subject to the unpredictability of a jury.

IV. SUMMARY

Choose a suitable format for your office memorandum, such as the following:

    I. Issues
   II. Brief Answers
  III. Facts
  IV. Discussion
   V. Conclusion

As you draft your office memoranda, remember your audience and purpose. Your goal is to inform a supervising attorney who typically is preparing to represent a client. The supervisor usually needs an analysis that is balanced but that creatively explores means of overcoming obstacles to the client's claims or defenses. Be certain to cover the elements of IRAC in the discussion section on your memorandum: For each issue, or subissue, analyze the legal rule and apply the rule to the facts to reach a conclusion.

SAMPLES

1. SAMPLE MEMORANDUM 1

Imagine that an attorney from the fictitious state of Calzona drafted the following office memorandum using only authority from the Calzona Supreme Court. Study the memorandum and consider the questions that follow it.

MEMORANDUM

TO: Susan Elias
FROM: James Nelson
RE: Enforceability of Julie Week's Promise to Act as Guarantor for Her Cousin's Loan Obligation; File 02-127
DATE: September 16, 2002

I. ISSUE

By stating that he would refrain from demanding payment from Borrower on a loan obligation until he "needs the money," did Lender state a promise that provided consideration for Guarantor's promise to pay the obligation in the event that Borrower failed to pay on demand?

II. BRIEF ANSWER

Probably yes. Although the Lender's promise arguably is illusory, it probably satisfies the consideration requirement by committing the Lender to a performance, subject only to economic events not entirely within the Lender's control.

III. FACTS

One of our regular business clients, Julie Week (Guarantor), asserted the following facts in an interview.

On December 15, 2001, Guarantor's cousin, Don Caslin (Borrower), purchased a used Mercedes Benz sports coupe from a private owner, Thomas Beatty (Lender), for $20,000. In a self-financing arrangement, Borrower paid $8,000 on delivery and agreed in writing to pay the remainder of the purchase price in 12 monthly installments of $1,000 each, beginning January 1, 2002.

From January to June 2002, Borrower timely paid Lender a total of $6,000 in monthly installments. In late June, however, Borrower suffered unusual losses in his private business, and he failed to pay the installments due on July 1 and August 1. After Lender threatened to sue for the return of the automobile, Guarantor and Lender entered into a written agreement (the Guarantee Agreement) designed to give Borrower time to recover from his temporary financial difficulties. Dated August 5, 2002, the Guarantee Agreement refers to the agreement between Lender and Borrower as the "CREDIT/SALE AGREEMENT," and it contains the following statement of mutual obligations:

> 1. LENDER will refrain from asserting his claim against BORROWER and from demanding payment on the CREDIT/SALE AGREEMENT until LENDER needs the money.
> 2. In the event that BORROWER fails to pay all amounts due under the CREDIT/SALE AGREEMENT upon demand by LENDER, GUAR-ANTOR will pay those amounts immediately and will pay further install-ments as they become due under the CREDIT/SALE AGREEMENT.

On August 25, 2002, Lender demanded payment from Borrower, and Borrower explained that he could not yet pay. On September 2, 2002, Lender demanded immediate payment of $3,000 from Guarantor; he also stated that he expects either Borrower or Guarantor to pay the remaining three installments as they become due on the first of each month.

We do not yet have any evidence that Lender engaged in fraud during formation of the Guarantee Agreement or that he did not in fact have a "need" for the money on August 25. You have asked me to analyze the question whether the Guarantee Contract is unenforceable on its face for lack of consideration.

IV. DISCUSSION

Lender's promise to refrain from asserting his claim and demanding payment until he "needs the money" arguably is illusory. If so, Guarantor's promise is not supported by consideration and is unenforceable.

An enforceable contract requires a bargained-for exchange in which a promisor exchanges his own promise for a return promise or performance. *Smith v. Newman*, 161 Calz. 443, 447, 667 P.2d 81, 84 (1984). The requirement of an exchange is not satisfied if one party gives only an illusory promise, which does not commit the promisor to any future performance. *Atco Corp. v Johnson*, 155 Calz. 1211, 627 P.2d 781 (1980).

In *Atco Corp.*, the manager of an automobile repair shop purportedly promised to delay asserting a claim against the owner of an automobile for $900 in repairs. Specifically, he promised to forbear from asserting the claim "until I want the money." In exchange, a friend of the owner promised to act as guarantor of the owner's obligation. *See id.* at 1212, 627 P.2d at 782. The word "want" stated no legal commitment because it permitted the manager at his own discretion to refuse to perform any forbearance at all. Because the manager incurred no obligation, the guarantor's promise was gratuitous and unenforceable. *See id.* at 1213-14, 627 P.2d at 782-84.

On the other hand, even if a promise leaves open the possibility that the promisor will escape obligation, the promise is valid if the promisor does not have complete control over the events on which the promisor's obligation is conditioned. *Bonnie v. DeLaney*, 158 Calz. 212, 645 P.2d 887 (1982). In *Bonnie*, an agreement for the sale of a house provided that the buyer could cancel the agreement if the buyer "cannot qualify for a 30-year mortgage loan for 90% of the sales price" with any of several banks listed in the agreement. *Id.* at 213, 645 P.2d at 888. In enforcing the agreement against the seller, the court distinguished *Atco Corp.* on the ground that the word "cannot" referred to the buyer's ability to obtain a loan rather than to his desire. Because his ability to obtain a loan was partly controlled by events and decisions outside his control, the promises in the sale agreement were nonillusory and binding. *See id.* at 214-15, 645 P.2d at 889-91.

Our client's case probably is more nearly analogous to *Bonnie* than it is to *Atco Corp.* Lender's promise to forbear until he "needs" the money appears to condition the length of his forbearance on financial events that are at least partly outside his control: As long as his income and expenses create no need for the money, Lender has a commitment to forbear from demanding payment.

To convince a court to draw an analogy to *Atco Corp.* rather than to *Bonnie*, we should argue that the word "need" refers to a subjective perception of deprivation that is inseparable from one's desires. Lender arguably can control his financial needs through his personal spending decisions, subject only to his own discretion.

Unfortunately, the analogy to *Bonnie* is stronger because financial needs are almost certainly controlled partly by external factors. Lender's promise probably is not illusory.

V. CONCLUSION

The promises stated in the Guarantee Agreement appear to satisfy the consideration requirement because Lender assumed a legal obligation by promising to refrain from asserting his claim and demanding payment until he "needs" the money. Unless we discover other serious defects in the Guarantee Agreement, Guarantor appears to be obligated to pay, and her defenses will not be worth litigating. We should urge Guarantor to settle Lender's claim, and we should try to persuade Borrower to indemnify Guarantor and to assume responsibility for further payments.

Questions on Sample Memorandum 1

a. Did the substantive labels assigned to the parties serve as helpful reminders of the respective roles of the parties, or would you have retained the parties' last names as less distracting references?

b. Does the statement of facts include any facts that you would omit or summarize further? Does it omit any important facts to which the author likely had access?

c. Identify the parts of the "Discussion" section that illuminate the issue, discuss the legal standards, analyze the facts, and state a conclusion.

d. Do you agree with the author's analysis? Does it adequately explore both sides of the dispute? Is it too pessimistic?

2. SAMPLE MEMORANDUM 2

The following memorandum, which is set in a fictitious jurisdiction, borrows from examples set forth in previous sections of this chapter addressing individual elements of office memoranda.

MEMORANDUM

TO: James Clapton
FROM: Ginger Jackson
RE: Souza v. Humane; strict liability and negligence—File No. 02-123
DATE: September 9, 2002

I. ISSUES

A. Does the phrase "any toxic material" in New Maine's strict liability statute encompass a generally safe anesthetic that produced a fatal reaction in a patient with a rare nerve disorder?

B. Is Humane Hospital liable to Souza's estate for negligent administration of the anesthetic?

1. Did Humane's anesthesiologist breach a duty of care by administering the anesthetic without assistance and by failing to monitor Souza's reactions to anesthesia?

2. Did Souza's nerve disorder constitute a supervening cause that broke the chain of causation between the anesthesiologist's conduct and Souza's death?

II. BRIEF ANSWERS

A. Probably not. A restrictive interpretation is supported by the legislative history and by a general public policy in New Maine encouraging the provision of affordable medical services. The legislature probably did not intend the statutory term "toxic material" to include medically prescribed substances that ordinarily produce a beneficial result or otherwise facilitate medical treatment.

B. Probably yes.

1. Probably yes. Under generally accepted hospital procedures, at least two trained medical personnel must monitor the administration of anesthesia, with at least one person monitoring the patient's reactions. A jury likely will find that the anesthesiologist breached a duty of care to the patient by administering the anesthesia alone.

2. No. The jury likely will also find that the patient's nerve disorder was not a supervening cause and that the anesthesiologist's negligence proximately caused the patient's death.

III. FACTS

On February 17, 2002, our client, Humane Hospital, Inc. (Humane), admitted 22-year-old Teresa Souza to its facility in Greenville, New Maine, for surgery to correct a bone deformity in her foot. Souza's bone deformity was not life-threatening, but it severely hampered her mobility. The planned surgery required general anesthesia.

Dr. Roberta Unger, an anesthesiologist for Humane, studied Souza's medical history and discovered that she suffered from a rare nerve disorder that slightly increased the risk that she would suffer an adverse reaction from anesthesia. Unger carefully informed Souza of the advantages and risks associated with each of the three safest and most effective general anesthetics. Souza decided to proceed with the operation and with the administration of general anesthesia. Unger and Souza ultimately agreed that Unger would administer ethane, a widely used and generally safe form of ether. Unger had initially recommended Forane, a potent muscle relaxant that maintains a stable heart rate. Souza, however, rejected Forane because of its greater cost.

At 10:00 A.M. on February 18, Souza was prepared for surgery. While the circulating nurse was occupied with another patient, and before the surgical team arrived, Unger began administering the prescribed anesthetic to Souza. Unger and Souza were alone in the room. Apparently because she was concerned that an overdose might trigger an adverse reaction, Unger concentrated intensely on the anesthetic intake gauge, which monitored the flow of anesthetic. As a consequence, she failed to watch either Souza or the equipment monitoring Souza's reactions. Approximately one minute after Unger began administering the anesthetic, the monitoring equipment sounded an alarm, and Souza died. Efforts to revive her failed. According to computer records, the monitoring equipment reflected growing signs of distress in Souza beginning approximately 10 seconds before her death and before the alarm sounded.

An autopsy showed that the anesthetic combined with Souza's nerve disorder to trigger a reaction that caused cardiac arrest. Mary L. Richards, Ph.D., a professor at the University of New Maine School of Nursing, has told us that hospitals throughout the nation ordinarily require the anesthesiologist to be accompanied by a nurse during the administration of anesthesia.

Both the nurse and the anesthesiologist are expected to continuously assess the patient's reaction to anesthesia by reading monitoring equipment and by observing the patient directly. Although she cannot be certain, Richards guesses that the fatal reaction was triggered largely by the final 10 seconds of Unger's administration of anesthesia.

Souza's estate has sued Humane in tort for wrongful death. It advances two theories of tort liability: (1) statutory strict liability for use of toxic materials and (2) negligence in the administration of the anesthetic.

IV. DISCUSSION

A. Strict Liability for Use of Toxic Materials

If a statute or the common law imposes strict liability for Souza's death, then Souza's estate can establish liability without proving negligence. New Maine's common law doctrine of strict liability for injuries caused by ultrahazardous activities does not apply to noncriminal medical practices engaged in by licensed physicians. *Stanislaus v. Good Samaritan Hosp.*, 212 N. Me. 113, 115 (1989). New Maine has enacted a statute, however, that imposes strict liability for injuries stemming from the use of "any toxic material": "A commercial enterprise is liable for injuries proximately caused by its use of any toxic material, without regard to the degree of care exercised by the enterprise." 12 N. Me. Rev. Stat. Ann. § 242 (Supp. 2001) (effective Jan. 1, 2002).

The New Maine courts have not yet had an opportunity to interpret the strict liability statute in a published opinion. As a profit-making hospital, Humane presumably is a "commercial enterprise" within the meaning of the statute. It is less certain, however, that the anesthetic administered to Souza would qualify as a "toxic" material.

The common meaning of the word "toxic" is "poisonous." *E.g., The Random House Dictionary of the English Language* 1500 (unabridged) (1970). Souza's estate might plausibly argue that the anesthetic was a toxic material because it was poisonous to Souza, even though it would not have been poisonous to most others. The word "toxic," however, applies more naturally to substances that are universally harmful to humans, such as cyanide, DDT, or sulfuric acid. It strains the common meaning of "toxic" to apply it to an anesthetic that might occasionally be harmful to persons with unusual allergies or other extraordinary conditions.

Legislative history also supports a restrictive interpretation of the statutory term "any toxic material." The report of the New Maine Senate Committee on Health and Welfare suggests that the legislature was concerned only with the most deadly of substances:

> The purpose of this bill is to reallocate the cost of unavoidable accidents from victims to industry and its consumers, to discourage unnecessary use of deadly chemicals and other hazardous materials, and to encourage the development and use of substitute materials that are generally safe for human contact.

N. Me. Sen. Rep. No. 112, 1996-1997 Sess. 2 (2001). The anesthetic in this case probably is closer to the materials "generally safe for human contact" condoned by the legislature than it is to the "deadly chemicals and other hazardous materials" condemned by it.

Finally, general state policy appears to support an interpretation that excludes medically prescribed substances from the reach of the statute. The legislature and judiciary of New Maine have recognized a policy of restricting the liability of physicians to encourage the ready availability of affordable medical services. For example, under the New Maine "Good Samaritan" statute, physicians who provide certain emergency medical services are not liable for adverse consequences unless they engage in culpable conduct amounting to at least gross negligence. 12 N. Me. Rev. Stat. § 229 (1992). This protective policy is also reflected in the courts' refusal to extend common law strict liability for ultrahazardous activities to even experimental medical practices. *See Stanislaus*, 212 N. Me. at 115. The legislature presumably was aware of these laws when it enacted the toxic materials statute in 2001.

Souza's estate may argue that the legislature intended to retreat from the protective policies of these laws by imposing strict liability on a limited segment of the activities of commercial medical practices. Absent more specific evidence of legislative intent to depart from existing legal policies, however, it is probably more likely that the legislature retained its protective attitude and assumed that the term "any toxic material" would not include routinely prescribed medicines or anesthetics.

In this case, the prescribed anesthetic, ethane, was not the safest available at the time of Souza's operation. Nonetheless, it is a frequently prescribed substance that produces beneficial results with only minor side effects in all but the most unusual cases. The strict liability statute probably does not apply to Souza's death.

B. Negligence

Assuming that Humane is not strictly liable for Souza's death, it may nonetheless be liable to Souza's estate if its agent caused the death through negligence. *See Kityama v. Mercy Hosp.*, 183 N. Me. 752, 759-60 (1974) (hospital liable for negligence of its nurse). An action for negligence requires proof of a negligent act or omission that proximately causes injury. *Baker v. Bruce*, 153 N. Me. 817, 820 (1967).

In our case, the injury to Souza is obvious. In greater doubt are the elements of negligent act and proximate cause.

1. Negligent Act

A negligent act or omission consists of the breach of a duty of care owed to another. *Id*. at 821. A medical specialist owes a duty to patients to exercise at least the ordinary skill and care that is reasonable and customary nationwide in that medical specialty. *Kityama*, 183 N. Me. at 760. Furthermore, under the "thin-skulled plaintiff" rule, that duty of care encompasses the special care necessary to address increased risks created by a patient's unusual susceptibility to injury. *Id*. In this case, Humane's anesthesiologist, Unger, may have breached duties of care in her unassisted administration of general anesthesia in the face of Souza's known nerve condition.

Unger exercised care in determining Souza's disorder of the nervous system and in informing her of the risks presented by each of the most suitable anesthetics. Moreover, when administering the anesthetic selected by Souza, Unger took care to provide the prescribed dosage by monitoring the anesthetic intake gauge.

On the other hand, Unger's intense concentration on the anesthetic intake gauge may have been an act of carelessness, rather than enhanced care, because it diverted Unger's attention from Souza and from the equipment monitoring Souza's vital signs. Faced with Souza's known nervous disorder, Unger probably had a duty to follow the standard medical practice of summoning a nurse to assist her in administering the anesthesia. Had she done so, the team could have monitored both Souza's vital signs and the intake gauge, and a team member undoubtedly would have detected signs of distress at least 10 seconds before death, arguably enough time to cease anesthesia and take corrective measures.

On these facts, a jury could find that Unger was negligent in her administration of the anesthetic.

2. Proximate Cause

Even if its agent was negligent, Humane will not be liable to Souza's estate unless the negligence proximately caused Souza's death. *See, e.g., Baker v. Bruce*, 153 N. Me. 817, 821 (1967). Proximate cause is a flexible doctrine that precludes liability if the relationship between negligence and an injury is so attenuated that it would be unfair to hold the negligent party responsible for the injury. *Id.* at 821-22.

In this case, Humane can argue that the 10-second warning appearing on the monitoring equipment would not have given even two observant medical workers sufficient time to reverse Souza's fatal reaction. If so, even careful administration of anesthesia would have resulted in death, suggesting that Souza's reaction was truly an unforeseeable accident rather than the proximate result of any negligent act. Unfortunately, the factual premise of this argument may be unsound: According to our own expert, the marginal effects of the final 10 seconds of anesthesia probably were critical. We may want to investigate this further with other experts.

As a fall-back position on proximate cause, Humane could try to characterize Souza's rare nerve condition as a supervening cause. Such an intervening cause may break the chain of causation between the negligence and the injury, particularly if the intervening event was unexpected. *See Safehouse Ins. Co. v. Rainbow Landscaping Co.*, 223 N. Me. 29, 31, 35 (1987) (dictum). Unfortunately, a court may be reluctant to analyze this issue within the framework of supervening cause. Under the more conventional approach, a court would simply apply the "thin-skulled plaintiff" rule to expand Unger's duty of care to encompass responsibility for increased risks of injury created by Souza's known nerve condition. However, if we can persuade the court to depart from the conventional approach and to analyze the increased risk within the less clearly applicable framework of supervening cause, we will gain the opportunity to develop an additional argument to avoid liability.

To develop a supervening-cause argument, we must distinguish *Rainbow*

Landscaping, which liberally allocates the risks of some intervening causes to the tortfeasor. In *Rainbow Landscaping*, a landscaping company agreed in writing with a general contractor to install a sprinkler system in the yards surrounding a new house in its final stages of construction. The written contract specifically obligated the landscaper to perform its work "in a manner that does not interfere with the ongoing work of other subcontractors or deface their finished product." *Id.* at 32. On the day that the landscaper began its work, its employees knew that another subcontractor was painting the interior of the house. While welding a sprinkler pipe to a house water line, an employee of the landscaper ignited paint fumes that had accumulated in a room recently painted by the painting subcontractor. The resulting fire entirely destroyed the nearly completed house.

In a suit brought against the landscaper by the owner's insurer, the landscaper argued on its motion for a directed verdict that, even if the landscaper had acted negligently, the paint fumes constituted an intervening cause that precluded a finding of proximate cause. The trial court denied the motion, and the jury returned a verdict for the insurer. The New Maine Supreme Court affirmed. It held that the landscaper was responsible for the consequences of the combustion of paint fumes that it had triggered because its employee should have been aware of the paint fumes and the danger they posed. *Id.* at 35. In dictum, the court stated that it might have reached a different result had the landscaper reasonably failed to foresee that the welding could trigger such a blaze. *See id.*

We can try to distinguish our case from *Rainbow Landscaping* by arguing that the landscaper's agreement to accommodate the work of other subcontractors justified the finding that the landscaper should have known of the hazard. Under this reasoning, the agreement was critical to the allocation of responsibility to the landscaper for the consequences of igniting the paint. That contract has no direct counterpart in our case. Moreover, in light of New Maine's policy of limiting the liability of medical care providers, a court might be willing to apply the doctrine of proximate cause more stringently in a hospital setting than in a construction setting.

On the other hand, although Souza's adverse reaction to the anesthetic was not highly probable, it was certainly foreseeable as a possible consequence; Unger's intense concentration on the intake gauge shows that she indeed specifically anticipated such a reaction. The absence of a contract such as the one in *Rainbow Landscaping* might be viewed as a technical and immaterial distinction.

Therefore, even if we can persuade a court to analyze Souza's nerve condition within the framework of supervening cause, the court probably will not find the doctrine satisfied on the facts of this case. If Souza's estate can prove that Unger was negligent, it almost certainly can show proximate cause as well.

V. CONCLUSION

In light of legislative and judicial policies favoring limits on physicians' liability, the strict liability statute regulating toxic materials probably will not apply to the administration of the anesthetic in this case. The courts will be even less likely to retreat from precedent by applying the common law doctrine imposing strict liability for ultrahazardous activities. A jury may find, however, that Humane's anesthesiologist was negligent in failing to summon assistance for the administration of the anesthesia and to monitor Souza more closely. We can try to characterize Souza's nerve condition as a supervening cause, but *Rainbow Landscaping* will not be easy to distinguish.

Because the risk of substantial liability is great, I recommend that we advise Humane to settle. Souza's estate may be willing to compromise; its negligence claim is not appropriate for summary disposition and thus is subject to the unpredictability of a jury.

Questions on Sample Memorandum 2

a. Distinguish between the statutory and common law claims discussed in Sample Memorandum 2. How does the legal method of analyzing one claim differ from that of the other?

b. Review the statutory analysis in Section IV.A of Sample Memorandum 2. Its original analysis of language, legislative history, and policy is indispensable precisely because no court had yet interpreted the statute. Imagine instead that the author of the memorandum had found a New Maine case that discusses the applicability of the strict liability statute to a restaurant that sold raw oysters infected with the Vibrio vulnificus bacteria. Most oysters naturally absorb this bacteria, and almost all persons who ingest the bacteria after eating raw oysters suffer no ill effects. However, in a tiny percentage of persons, particularly those with liver or kidney problems, the bacteria can lead to septicemia, which often results in death. In the New Maine case, *Spratt v. Shuck*, a man developed a bacterial infection and died after eating raw oysters served in a restaurant.[3]

Imagine that the New Maine Supreme Court examined the language, legislative history, and policy of the New Maine statute governing strict liability for toxic materials. Imagine further that it found that a raw oyster infected with the Vibrio vulnificus bacteria is not a "toxic material" within the meaning of the statute. Would the author of the memorandum discuss the issue of statutory liability in the same manner if a case like *Spratt v. Shuck* were available? Would he rely as heavily on his own analysis of language, legislative history, and policy? How would the analysis differ if it focused on case law such as *Spratt v. Shuck*?

c. Review the subsection discussing the element of proximate cause in a negligence action. Note how the author of the memorandum seeks to manipulate the analytic framework within which to address the legal consequences of Souza's unusual nerve condition. Is this a fair method of argument? Can it be used in other contexts? Most professors of tort law readily conclude that a court would analyze Souza's nerve condition within the "thin-skulled plaintiff" rule regarding the scope of duties and not within the framework of proximate cause. In that light, is the argument in the

---

3. The facts for this fictitious case are inspired by those of Simeon v. Doe, 618 So. 2d 848 (La. 1993).

memorandum a welcome exercise in creative argument, or is it a misleading waste of time for the reader?

d. Notice the frequent use of the word "we" in the section on proximate cause. Should the author of a memorandum avoid using such first-person pronouns in a legal analysis? Are first-person pronouns appropriate when referring to the law firm's development of facts or legal theories? Are they better than passive voice or other abstractions?

Chapter 12

Organization of Office Memoranda and Briefs

One of the most important features of effective legal analysis and writing is good organization. Techniques of organization are also among the most difficult to develop and to teach. With a few months of practice, however, you can steadily improve your skills. Regular outlining of course material in law school is an excellent way to build basic skills.

Although the focus of Part V is objective analysis in office memoranda, the techniques of organization described in this chapter apply directly to both office memoranda and legal briefs. Accordingly, this chapter uses examples from both memoranda and briefs. The following sections explore problems of organization on four different levels, progressing from broader problems of (1) format and (2) relationships among multiple issues, to narrower problems of (3) progression within sections and (4) effective paragraphing.

I. FORMAT

Before drafting any legal document, you must select an appropriate format for the document. The format will determine the essential content of the document and the order in which you present the different parts of that content.

Rules of procedure and local court rules prescribe formats for appellate briefs. With somewhat less detail, they also prescribe or suggest formats for trial pleadings, motions, and briefs. You should take care to follow these rules, because they presumably reflect the court's views about effective content and administrative efficiency. If you depart from the prescribed format, you may irritate the judge or judges who must read the document. Indeed, you may even lead the judge or the clerk's office to reject the document for filing or to impose other sanctions.[1]

The most appropriate format for other documents, such as a contract or office memorandum, is partly a matter of judgment or style for you or your law firm. For example, Section II of Chapter 11 outlines two different formats for an office memorandum; whether one is more appropriate to an assignment than another will depend on the complexity of the memorandum, the preferences of your supervising attorney, and your own personal style. Before beginning to write such a document, you should take a few moments to determine which format will best suit your audience, your personal style, and the purposes of the document.

II. RELATIONSHIPS AMONG MULTIPLE ISSUES AND SUBISSUES

Your statement of the issues and your discussion or argument section of an office memorandum or legal brief should reflect the proper relationships among multiple issues and subissues. Good organization at this broad level requires a thorough understanding of the substantive analysis as well as attention to techniques of effective writing. Therefore, if you experience unusual difficulty with this level of organization, you may wish to supplement your research before proceeding further. By reviewing basic principles in a secondary source, you can gain a broad perspective that will help you organize your material.

A. Proper Relationships Among Topics

Stated most simply, the section headings of the discussion or argument section of a document should show which topics are distinct and indepen-

---

1. *See, e.g.*, N/S Corp. v. Liberty Mutual Ins. Co., 127 F.3d 1145 (9th Cir. 1997) (striking appellant's briefs and dismissing appeal, and citing to similar actions in other cases); Westinghouse Elec. Corp. v. NLRB, 809 F.2d 419, 424-25 (7th Cir. 1987) (imposing $1,000 penalty on counsel for evading federal rule limiting the number of pages of its opening brief).

dent, and which are subsets of a more general topic. The statement of the issues should show the same relationships. These relationships are a function of the elements of the legal claims or defenses in question.

For example, suppose that you are preparing an office memorandum to discuss the following theories of employer liability for the discharge of an employee: (1) violation of a promise expressed in the company policy manual to invoke specified hearing procedures before terminating any employee, (2) wrongful discharge for a reason that violates public policy, and (3) intentional infliction of emotional distress.

The following information about the legal content of these claims in one state will help you devise an appropriate organizational structure. The elements of a contract action for breach of promise in a policy manual are (1) a promise in the manual by the employer to restrict the circumstances justifying discharge of the employee; (2) a basis for enforcing the promise, such as incorporation of the manual into the employment contract; and (3) breach of the promise.[2] The elements of the tort of wrongful discharge of an at-will employee in violation of public policy are (1) discharge of the employee (2) for a reason that contravenes a legislative public policy.[3] Finally, the elements of the tort of intentional infliction of emotional distress are (1) extreme and outrageous conduct (2) that is taken with the intent to cause emotional distress or with reckless disregard for the possibility of those consequences and (3) that causes (4) severe emotional distress.[4]

Although organization of these topics is a matter of judgment rather than an exact science, most legal writers will agree that the following section headings of the discussion section of the memorandum leave room for improvement:

IV. DISCUSSION
    A. Wrongful Discharge—Violation of Public Policy or Breach of Promise in Employee Manual
    B. Intentional Infliction of Emotional Distress
        1. Remedies

First, section A inappropriately encompasses two distinct kinds of claims. True, both claims represent theories of liability in an emerging field known generically as wrongful discharge. Under this state's law, however, wrongful discharge in violation of public policy is a tort whose elements have little in common with those of a claim for breach of a contractual promise to restrict the circumstances of terminating the employment contract.

Second, section B inappropriately includes a single subsection on remedies. If remedies were the only topic in section B, a subsection designation would be unnecessary. On the other hand, if section B discusses a theory

---

2. *See* Ariz. Rev. Stat. Ann. § 23-1501(2) (West Supp. 2000); Leikvold v. Valley View Community Hosp., 688 P.2d 170 (Ariz. 1984) (common law predecessor to § 23-1501(2)).
3. *See* Ariz. Rev. Stat. Ann. § 23-1501(3)(b) (West Supp. 2000); Wagenseller v. Scottsdale Mem'l Hosp., 710 P.2d 1025, 1031-36 (Ariz. 1985) (common law predecessor to § 23-1501(3)(b)).
4. *See, e.g.*, Watts v. Golden Age Nursing Home, 619 P.2d 1032 (Ariz. 1980).

of liability as well as remedies, both subtopics should be represented in subsection headings if either is. Finally, if the topic of remedies encompasses all of the theories of liability, it should not be buried within a section that addresses only the theory of intentional infliction of emotional distress.

By applying principles discussed in Section III.A of Chapter 8, you could address these defects and adopt an improved organizational structure such as the following:

IV. DISCUSSION
    A. Breach of Contract
    B. Wrongful Discharge in Violation of Public Policy
    C. Intentional Infliction of Emotional Distress
    D. Remedies

Of course, this sample outline represents only one of many reasonable organizational structures for the memorandum in question. Other organizational structures may reflect different ways of presenting the analyses of remedies. For example, you might recognize that sections A through C present various theories of liability and could be consolidated in a section that is on the same level as the separate topic of remedies. Because the remedies for breach of contract are significantly different from those available for either of the tort claims, the section on remedies could discuss them separately:

IV. DISCUSSION
    A. Theories of Liability
        1. Breach of Contract
        2. Wrongful Discharge in Violation of Public Policy
        3. Intentional Infliction of Emotional Distress
    B. Remedies
        1. Contract
        2. Tort

Alternatively, you might decide to discuss remedies within each of the sections that introduces a theory of liability, rather than in a separate comprehensive section devoted to remedies. Under this organizational scheme, you might consolidate the two tort theories into a single section if you concluded that the remedies for each would be governed by the same tort principles. Depending on the depth of discussion in the memorandum, you could discuss remedies either in a paragraph at the end of each major section or, as shown below, in separate subsections.

IV. DISCUSSION
    A. Breach of Contract
        1. Breach of Promise in an Employee Manual
        2. Remedies

    B. Tort
       1. Wrongful Discharge in Violation of Public Policy
       2. Intentional Infliction of Emotional Distress
       3. Remedies

B. Order of Topics

1. LOGICAL ORGANIZATION IN AN OFFICE MEMORANDUM

In an office memorandum, you should organize your topics in a logical order that permits early topics to build a foundation for subsequent topics. The clearest example of this is a multiple-issue discussion in which some issues are "threshold issues" in the sense that the resolution of those issues affects the analysis of other issues. Logically, you should discuss the threshold issues before you discuss the issues that are dependent on the outcome of the threshold issues.

For example, suppose that Maya Tortilla Co. alleges that Bakeway Supermarkets (1) formed a contract with Maya; (2) breached its contractual obligations, at least under Maya's interpretation of the contract; (3) and is liable to Maya for $20,000 in damages. If Bakeway disputes each of these allegations, the parties have raised three entirely separate issues.

Logically, you should discuss issue #1 first because contract formation is a threshold issue: Bakeway did not assume any contractual obligations and consequent potential liability if it did not form a contract with Maya. Similarly, you should discuss issue #2 before issue #3 for two reasons. First, Bakeway is not liable in damages unless it breached. Second, to determine whether Bakeway breached, you must interpret the contract and define Bakeway's obligation; in turn, the scope of Bakeway's obligation will determine Maya's expectation interest, on which damages will be based.

2. STRATEGIC ORGANIZATION IN A BRIEF

If you are drafting a brief rather than an office memorandum, you might organize your arguments differently, because strategic considerations may lead you to depart from a purely logical ordering of arguments. Like other people, judges are strongly influenced by first impressions. In many cases, the first argument in a brief influences the judge more strongly than later ones. Also, if pressed for time, a busy trial judge may not reach the last few pages of a pretrial motions brief before oral argument. Accordingly, if one of your arguments is much stronger than the others, you can exercise discretion to present it first in your brief, even though another issue is logically prior.

3. DISCUSSING OR ARGUING THE FULL RANGE OF ISSUES

Finally, you should apply all these considerations only to order your topics effectively, not to cut off discussion of any of the issues. In a close case, you cannot predict with certainty how a court will resolve a threshold issue. Accordingly, if a threshold issue raises a question sufficiently doubtful to warrant full discussion in an office memorandum or a brief, you should address all of the other substantial issues, even if you tentatively resolve the threshold issue in a way that logically would cut off discussion. In an office memorandum, for example, if you conclude that Bakeway did not breach the contract, you should nonetheless discuss the question of the amount of damages for which Bakeway would be liable if it had breached.

C. Technique

As illustrated in Section V of Chapter 10, the most efficient way to organize the topics of a memorandum or brief is to outline them after you have researched and analyzed the problem but before you begin to write. Even when you are working under severe time pressure, you should take a few minutes to organize your notes, think deeply and creatively about the analysis, and explore the relationships among topics by comparing different outlines of the discussion or argument. You can much more easily modify your analytic approach and writing strategy at the outline stage than you can midway through the first draft.

If you do not prepare an outline before writing the first draft, and if the first draft appears hopelessly disorganized, you can still derive benefits from outlining techniques, albeit with less efficiency than at the prewriting stage. By writing out the section and subsection headings of your first draft in outline form, you can expose and evaluate the organization of your draft and can improve the organization by modifying the outline.

Finally, once you have chosen an organizational structure, you should clearly communicate that structure to the reader with descriptive section and subsection headings that are at least roughly parallel to the structure of the statement of issues. In an answer to a law school examination, such headings may even take the place of more formal statements of the issues.

III. PROGRESSION WITHIN SECTION OR SUBSECTION

Once you have divided your topics into separate sections, you are ready to organize the discussion or argument within each section. At the most general level, your analysis should follow the familiar "IRAC" pattern of deductive reasoning: After introducing the issue or argument with a heading and perhaps with a brief introduction in the text, you should discuss or argue the law, apply that law to the facts, and reach a conclusion.

Effective progression within a section also requires attention to one or more of five considerations:

1. hierarchy of authority,
2. progression from general to specific,

3. progression from fundamental to uncertain, and
4. separation or consolidation of logical discussions or arguments.

The first three of these considerations deal mainly with the development of legal standards. The fourth deals with methods of combining legal and factual analysis.

A. Hierarchy of Authority

In statutory analysis, the hierarchy of authority leads to a convention of organization. You should analyze, or at least present, the statutory language in question before analyzing cases that either interpret the statute or that discuss supplemental common law:

C. Commercial Impracticability

The Uniform Commercial Code (UCC) provides that, in limited circumstances, a seller's failure to deliver goods is not a breach of contract "if performance as agreed has been made impracticable by the occurrence of a contingency the non-occurrence of which was a basic assumption on which the contract was made." U.C.C. § 2-615(a) (2000). The UCC's use of the term "impracticable" suggests a more liberal standard for discharging obligations than the traditional common law standard of "impossibility of performance." *See Bjorn v. Borg* . . .

The normal convention of starting with the statutory language will occasionally apply with less force in the analysis of some of the more commonly litigated provisions of a constitution. Because constitutional provisions are typically even more general than statutory provisions, the enormous body of case law interpreting a provision may take on a life of its own, overshadowing the actual words of the provision. Thus, you need not quote the language of the Fourth Amendment before asserting a well-established proposition about the need to obtain a warrant before searching a dwelling; reference to case law interpreting the Fourth Amendment in most cases will be sufficient. Nonetheless, you should begin the analysis by at least identifying the Fourth Amendment as the source of the restriction on searches. Moreover, some constitutional issues, like most issues of statutory interpretation, will be sufficiently novel to require original analysis, in which case you should begin the analysis with the language of the constitutional provision.

B. Progression from General to Specific

Reading a legal analysis or argument should be like viewing a large painting that covers a third of the wall of a museum exhibit room. As the viewer enters, he sees the general outlines of the whole painting, and he becomes curious about a few provocative parts of the whole. He then moves closer to the painting to separately examine each of these parts. Finally, when he steps back to view the painting again as a whole, he may appreciate it more fully than he did when he had not yet explored some of the details.

Similarly, a legal document should

1. provide an overview to the document,
2. separately explore important matters in some detail, and
3. conclude with a summary or with general insights that are easier to appreciate after the discussion of details.

On a broad level, a memorandum or brief performs these functions with (1) the statement of issues or other introduction, (2) the discussion or argument, and (3) the conclusion. On a narrower level, this kind of progression is often appropriate within a section of the discussion or argument.

For an example of progression within a section, suppose that the plaintiff in a tort action alleges that the defendant intentionally inflicted emotional distress. If the defendant, your client, contends that the facts in the record fail to satisfy two of the elements of that tort, your brief for the defendant might address each of those two elements separately, either in separate paragraphs or in separate subsections of the argument. If so, you can orient the reader by beginning with a paragraph that introduces each of the elements:

II. ARGUMENT

A. Lew's Allegations in Count II Fail to State a Claim for Intentional Infliction of Emotional Distress.

General overview

To establish a right to relief for intentional infliction of emotional distress, Lew must plead and prove that (1) Smith engaged in extreme and outrageous conduct (2) with the intent to cause severe emotional distress or with reckless disregard for the possibility of those consequences, and that (3) his actions caused Lew to suffer (4) severe emotional distress. *See Watts v. Golden Age Nursing Home,* 127 Ariz. 255, 619 P.2d 1032 (1980). Even assuming the truth of Lew's allegations about the manner in which Smith terminated Lew's employment contract, the complaint does not properly allege either the extreme conduct or the severe distress required for liability. Therefore, Lew has failed to state a claim for relief in Count II.

1. Smith's Alleged Conduct Was Not "Extreme and Outrageous."

Specific argument

Only the most deplorable and shocking conduct satisfies the narrow definition of "extreme and outrageous conduct." *Beers v. Bolton* . . . In *Beers,* . . .

In this case, the complaint alleges only that Smith was a blunt manager who exercised his contractual privilege to fire Lew without advance notice and who stated his reasons for firing him with utmost candor. . . .

2. Lew's Alleged "Depression" Does Not Amount to Severe Emotional Distress.

Proof of severe emotional distress . . .

The introduction in the first paragraph above not only provides an overview of the legal standards, it summarizes the overall argument of the section. That argument appears elsewhere as well: The brief (1) states it concisely in the heading for section A; (2) develops it in greater detail in each of the subsections; and (3) should repeat it in general terms at the end of section A, in a separate conclusion section at the end of the document, or both.

At a different level within a section, you might introduce a general principle in a topic sentence before exploring it in greater detail within the same paragraph:

Even if a promise leaves open the possibility that the promisor will escape obligation, however, the promise is valid if the promisor does not have complete control over the events on which the promisor's obligation is conditioned. *Bonnie v. DeLaney*, 158 Calz. 212, 645 P.2d 887 (1982). In *Bonnie*, an agreement for the sale of a house provided that the buyer could cancel the agreement if the buyer "cannot qualify for a 30-year mortgage loan for 90% of the sales price" with any of several banks listed in the agreement. *Id.* at 213, 645 P.2d at 888. In enforcing the agreement against the seller, the court distinguished *Atco Corp.* on the ground that the word "cannot" referred to the buyer's ability to obtain a loan rather than to his desire. Because his ability to obtain a loan was partly controlled by events and decisions outside his control, the promises in the sale agreement were nonillusory and binding. *See id.* at 214-15, 645 P.2d 889-91.	**Topic sentence** **Specific case analysis**

In the preceding example, the opening sentence of the paragraph summarizes the general point that the *Bonnie* decision illustrates. That introduction prepares the reader for the detailed analysis of *Bonnie* that follows.

C. PROGRESSION FROM FUNDAMENTAL TO COMPLEX POINTS

Some legal discussions or arguments may lend themselves to a related method of organization within a section or subsection: progression from fundamental or undisputed points to complex or disputed points. In some cases, the preliminary points may address matters that are not even ultimately in issue; they may simply provide helpful background information or establish legal premises to the main topic of discussion.

For example, the following passage from a brief provides background information about statutory policies. That information helps support the ultimate argument that a contractual provision attempting to fix damages for breach is not enforceable:

C. The Liquidated Damages Clause Is Void as a Penalty

Fundamental premises

The contract for the sale of the engine parts is a "transaction in goods" and thus is covered by the Uniform Commercial Code (UCC). U.C.C. §§ 2-102, 2-105 (2000). UCC remedies for breach of contract are designed to compensate the victim of the breach for the loss of the value of the expected performance. *See* U.C.C. § 1-106(1) (2000). They do not permit imposition of a penalty that is designed to discourage breach or to punish the breaching party. *See id.;* U.C.C. § 2-718(1) (2000).

Transition to disputed point

Within limited parameters, the UCC permits parties to agree to fix damages for breach in advance by including a provision for "liquidated damages" in their sales contract. However, such damages must be limited to

> an amount which is reasonable in the light of the anticipated or actual harm caused by the breach, the difficulties of proof of loss, and the inconvenience or nonfeasibility of otherwise obtaining an adequate remedy. A term fixing unreasonably large liquidated damages is void as a penalty.

U.C.C. § 2-718(1) (2000). In this case, section 5.4 of the contract attempts to fix damages at an amount that is disproportionate to any anticipated or actual harm. Thus, it is an unenforceable penalty clause. . . .

The first paragraph of the preceding passage addresses fundamental matters of statutory policy that are technically not in issue because the opposing party will not dispute them. It provides a general orientation, however, that will help to place in perspective the argument relating to the hotly disputed question: Does the liquidated damages clause constitute an impermissible penalty under the UCC?

D. Separation or Consolidation of Analyses

1. OVERVIEW

In analyzing an issue in a memorandum or a brief, you ordinarily should follow the general structure of the syllogism of deductive reasoning:

1. major premise—rule of law,
2. minor premise—application of law to facts,
3. conclusion.

At the simplest level, you can present all the elements of a single syllogism in a single, undivided section of your discussion or argument:

A. Topic or Argument
Introduction
Legal Rule
Application to Facts
Conclusion

Many topics of discussion or argument, however, are not so simple. If a topic is unusually complex, you might separately present the elements of a single syllogism in several subsections:

A. Topic or Argument
Introduction
1. Legal Rule
   a. Analysis of Persuasive Authority
   b. Policy Analysis
2. Application to Facts
   a. Analysis of Facts Relating to One Transaction
   b. Analysis of Facts Relating to a Second Transaction
3. Conclusion

Conversely, if your main topic of discussion or argument encompasses closely related subtopics that do not warrant separation into formal subsections, you might exercise discretion to discuss more than one topic within an undivided section or subsection. If so, you can present your analysis in either of two ways. First, you can separate the topics into several smaller syllogisms within the section, each syllogism with its own legal and factual analyses set forth in separate paragraphs:

A. Topic or Argument
Introduction
Legal Rule 1
Facts 1
Conclusion 1
Legal Rule 2
Facts 2
Conclusion 2

Alternatively, you can consolidate the related topics into a single syllogism:

A. Topic
Introduction
Legal Rules 1 & 2
Application to Facts 1 & 2
Conclusions

Most writers tend to react to these problems of organization on a subconscious, intuitive level. However, the decision to separate or consolidate is sufficiently important to warrant conscious analysis.

2. SINGLE SYLLOGISM IN UNDIVIDED SECTION

At the broadest level, if a topic or argument is sufficiently important and discrete to warrant a separate section or subsection heading, you ordinarily should develop it completely and resolve it within that section or subsection. In the following excerpts from a brief, an advocate divides the arguments about two elements of a tort into subsections. In each of these subsections, the advocate analyzes an element in a single, complete syllogism. For example, in subsection A.1 below, she presents her view of the law for that element, applies the law to the facts relating to that element, and states a conclusion about the sufficiency of the allegations relating to that element:

II. ARGUMENT

Major argument

A. Lew's Allegations in Count II Fail to State a Claim for Intentional Infliction of Emotional Distress.

To establish a right to relief . . .

First subargument

1. Smith's Alleged Conduct Was Not "Extreme and Outrageous."

General rules of law

Only the most deplorable and shocking conduct satisfies the narrow definition of "extreme and outrageous conduct." *See* . . . Conduct that simply reflects normal social and economic adversities is not extreme or outrageous. *See, e.g., Frank v. Boswell,* . . .

In-depth analysis of case law

In *Frank,* a landlord's eviction notice did not reflect extreme and outrageous conduct, even though it was "rude, threatening, and intimidating." *Id.* at 289. The court reasoned that . . .

Facts of current dispute

In this case, Lew's complaint alleges conduct that is even less extreme than the conduct in *Frank.* It alleges that Smith "fired Lew without severance pay and with full knowledge that Lew's family was facing a desperate financial crisis." Plaintiff's Second Amended Complaint ¶ 7. It further alleges that Smith communicated his decision in a "terse, unfriendly, and unsympathetic conversation, without advance notice." *Id.* at ¶ 8.

Analysis of facts

These allegations state only that Lew was the victim of his own economic distress and that Smith acted to protect the interests of his business. Although some business owners might take it upon themselves to offer personal counseling and financial aid to their employees or ex-employees, Smith has no legal duty to do so.

Thus, the complaint does not allege circumstances that could establish the requisite "extreme and outrageous conduct."

| | Conclusion |

2. Lew's Alleged "Depression" Does Not Amount to Severe Emotional Distress.

| | Second subargument |

Proof of severe emotional distress . . .

3. SEPARATION OF ELEMENTS OF SINGLE SYLLOGISM INTO MULTIPLE SUBSECTIONS

In a particularly complex analysis, you might depart from the most basic organizational structure by developing only one element of a complete analysis within a section or subsection. For example, you could develop the legal rules in one section and analyze the facts in a separate section, perhaps dividing the fact analysis into subsections:

A. Officer Bates Could Not Lawfully Arrest Jones Without Probable Cause to Believe That Jones Had Committed a Felony.

| | Legal rules |

Although a police officer may arrest a suspect without a warrant in some circumstances, he may not place a suspect under full arrest without probable cause to believe that the suspect has committed a crime. *See* . . . A police officer does not have probable cause unless . . .

B. Officer Bates Did Not Have Probable Cause.

| | Application to facts |

At the suppression hearing, Officer Bates asserted that Jones matched the description of the burglar and that Jones volunteered incriminating statements. Whether taken separately or together, however, these factors did not create probable cause.

1. Jones Did Not Match the Description of the Burglar.

| | First subset of facts |

A written transcript of the radio report shows that Officer Bates received the following description of the burglary suspect: white male, six feet tall, 180 lbs., short brown hair, wearing a navy blue windbreaker. . . .

2. Jones's Statements Did Not Create Probable Cause.

Second subset of facts

The combined testimony of Jones and Officer Bates creates a clear and consistent picture of their conversation on Washington Street. . . .

Under this approach, the discussion of the law appears primarily in section A of the brief, and section B addresses the fact analysis. It would not be uncommon, however, for the author of such a passage to refer briefly to legal authority within section B when helpful to support the fact analysis.

4. MULTIPLE SYLLOGISMS WITHIN SINGLE, UNDIVIDED SECTION

Conversely, you may have occasion to present more than one complete analysis in a discrete section or subsection. If so, you can either (1) fully develop and resolve one syllogism before analyzing the next, or (2) combine the related legal rules of arguably distinct syllogisms and apply them to all the relevant facts.

a. Separation of Multiple Syllogisms

Within an undivided section, you may occasionally address several closely related topics, none of which is sufficiently important and discrete to warrant further subdivision into subsections. In many such cases, you can develop these related topics separately within the section or subsection.

For example, you can completely develop and resolve an introductory analysis before moving on to the main topic, as in the following excerpt from a legal memorandum:

A. Option Contract Under UCC

General statutory rules

In some circumstances, a merchant's promise not to revoke an offer to buy or sell goods is enforceable even if gratuitous:

> An offer by a merchant to buy or sell goods in a signed writing which by its terms gives assurance that it will be held open is not revocable, for lack of consideration . . . ; but any such term of assurance on a form supplied by the offeree must be separately signed by the offeror.

U.C.C. § 2-205 (2000).

Complete syllogism on preliminary matter

"Merchant" includes "a person who deals in goods of the kind." U.C.C. § 2-104 (2000). Stillwell regularly sells computers as part of her wholesale office supply business. Therefore, she is a merchant of the goods that she offered to supply to Azoulay, and section 2-205 thus governs the revocability of her offer.

A more difficult question is whether Stillwell "separately signed" the promise not to revoke contained in the form supplied by Azoulay, the offeree. The purpose of the statutory requirement for a separate signing is . . .

> Transition to
> main topic of
> discussion

The second paragraph of this example quickly resolves the question of merchant status in a complete syllogism, with a statement of the law, an analysis of the facts, and a conclusion. Because that issue is simple and noncontroversial, it does not warrant presentation in a separate subsection with its own heading. On the other hand, it is sufficiently independent from the analysis of the requirement for a separate signing that you should develop and resolve it in a separate paragraph before analyzing other topics raised by the general standards in the first paragraph.

Some legal writers strain this form of separation when using it within a section that features in-depth case analyses of a series of cases. Rather than synthesize these cases and apply the synthesized law in consolidated form to the facts, the writer pauses briefly after each case analysis and applies the holding of that case to the relevant facts. Although this is a popular form of argument, it sometimes results in repetition and a rambling, piecemeal effect. You should not use it as a substitute for effective expression of synthesis of authority, as explored in Chapter 14, Section II.B.

b. Consolidation of Multiple Syllogisms

In other cases, you may prefer to combine closely related legal standards and apply them as a group to all the relevant facts. This approach is illustrated by the second and third paragraphs of the following excerpt of a brief:

II. ARGUMENT

A. Bennett Will Prove That Tippett Is Liable Under 42 U.S.C. § 1983 for Violating Bennett's Civil Rights.

Federal law imposes civil liability on a person who acts under the color of state law to deprive another of a federal right:

> General
> statutory rules

> Every person who, under the color of any [state law or custom], subjects, or causes to be subjected, any citizen of the United States or other person within the jurisdiction thereof to the deprivation of any rights, privileges or immunities secured by the Constitution and laws, shall be liable to the party injured. . . .

42 U.S.C. § 1983 (1994).

Consolidated discussion of rules for three subarguments

A private party acts "under the color of state law" if he acts in concert with a state official acting in his official capacity. *See Dennis v. Sparks,* 449 U.S. 24, 27-29 (1980). State action denying a litigant a fair and impartial hearing in civil litigation constitutes a deprivation of due process under the Fourteenth Amendment. *See Catchpole v. Brannon,* 42 Cal. Rptr. 2d 440, 443 (Ct. App. 1995). Although section 1983 implicitly incorporates the common law doctrine of absolute immunity for judges, that immunity does not protect private parties who conspire with the judge. *See Dennis,* 449 U.S. at 29-32.

Consolidated application of three rules to facts

In this case, Bennett will prove all the elements of his claim under section 1983. First, the evidence will show that Tippett conspired with Judge Bell by bribing Judge Bell to rule against Bennett on his motion for a preliminary injunction; Tippett therefore acted under the color of state law. Second, Tippett's bribe denied Bennett an impartial hearing and therefore deprived Bennett of his federal right to due process. Finally, even though Tippett acted under the color of state law, he has no official state function and therefore does not enjoy the protection of any official immunity.

Conclusion

Thus, the evidence will show that Tippett is liable to Bennett for violating Bennett's due process rights.

c. Discretion to Separate or Consolidate

The decision to separate or consolidate legal analyses often is a matter of judgment on which reasonable writers can disagree. As a general rule, a more superficial treatment of the topics lends itself to consolidation, as in the example above. On the other hand, if you analyze closely related topics in greater depth, you could divide the same discussion of a brief into separate syllogisms that are fully developed and resolved in separate paragraphs within the section:

II. ARGUMENT

A. Bennett Will Prove That Tippett Is Liable Under 42 U.S.C. § 1983 for Violating Bennett's Civil Rights.

General statutory rules

Federal law imposes civil liability on a person who acts under the color of state law to deprive another of a federal right:

Every person who, under the color of any . . .

42 U.S.C. § 1983 (1994). In this case, Bennett will prove all the elements of his claim under section 1983.

A private party acts "under the color of state law" if he acts in concert with a state official acting in his official capacity. *See Dennis v. Sparks,* 449 U.S. 24, 27-29 (1980). In *Dennis,* a state judge . . . Similarly, the evidence in this case will show that Tippett conspired with Judge Bell by bribing Judge Bell to rule against Bennett on his motion for a preliminary injunction. Therefore, Tippett acted under the color of state law.

Full syllogism on first subargument

The Fourteenth Amendment's guarantee of due process in state proceedings is a federal substantive right, the deprivation of which is remediable under section 1983. *See generally Carey v. Piphus,* 435 U.S. 247 (1978). State conduct denying a litigant a fair and impartial hearing in civil litigation constitutes a deprivation of due process under the Fourteenth Amendment. *See Catchpole v. Brannon,* 42 Cal. Rptr. 2d 440, 443 (Ct. App. 1995). In this case, Tippett's bribing the judge directly affected the outcome of the hearing on Bennett's request for a preliminary injunction; therefore, Tippett caused a deprivation of Bennett's right to due process.

Full syllogism on second subargument

Finally, Tippett is not immune from liability for money damages. Bennett agrees that state judges are absolutely immune from liability for damages for their judicial acts taken within their jurisdiction. *See Stump v. Sparkman,* 435 U.S. 349 (1978). However, such immunity does not extend to a private party who conspires with a state judge, even though by so conspiring the private party acts under the color of state law. *See Dennis,* 449 U.S. at 29-32 (1980). In this case, Tippett has no official status as an officer of the court; instead, he is a private party who therefore enjoys no official immunity.

Full syllogism on third subargument

Thus, the evidence will show that Tippett is liable to Bennett for violating Bennett's due process rights.

General conclusion

Of course, if the topics are truly independent and warrant extended discussion, you may wish to adopt the conventional approach of presenting each analysis in a separate subsection and under a separate heading:

II. ARGUMENT

A. Bennett Will Prove That Tippett Is Liable Under 42 U.S.C. § 1983 for Violating Bennett's Civil Rights.

General statutory rules

    Federal law imposes civil liability. . . . 42 U.S.C. § 1983 (1994). In this case, Bennett will prove all the elements of his claim under section 1983.

1. Tippett Acted Under the Color of State Law.

Full syllogism in several paragraphs within first subsection

    A private party acts "under the color of state law" if he acts in concert . . .
    In *Dennis,* . . .
    In this case, the evidence will show that Tippett conspired with Judge Bell . . .
    Therefore, Tippett acted under the color of state law.

2. Tippett Denied Bennett Due Process.

Full syllogism in several paragraphs within second subsection

    The Fourteenth Amendment's guarantee of due process in state proceedings is a federal substantive right, . . .
    In *Catchpole,* . . .
    In this case, Bennett will prove that Tippett bribed Judge Bell to rule against Bennett on his motion for a preliminary injunction. . . .
    Therefore, Tippett violated Bennett's rights to due process.

3. Tippett Is Not Immune from Suit.

Third subsection

    Bennett agrees that . . .

d. Separate Analysis of Adverse Authority in Responsive Brief

A special organizational structure is sometimes appropriate for responsive briefs. In the ordinary three-stage briefing procedure, the answering brief will respond directly to the opening brief, and the reply brief will respond to the answering brief. In responding to an argument in a preceding brief, you can affirmatively develop a legal theory and apply it to the facts, and you can then separately address authority on which the preceding brief relies. You should analyze each adverse authority and discredit or distinguish it. You can use the same technique in an opening brief that anticipates a counterargument.

For example, in the following sample passage, the brief writer has affirm-atively and confidently argued that Tippett denied Bennett due process under a mainstream legal theory. Only after completing that argument does he seek to persuade the judge to reject an approach based on *Parratt v. Taylor*, on which the opposing party relied in a previous motion:

II. ARGUMENT

A. Bennett Will Prove That Tippett Is Liable Under 42 U.S.C. § 1983 for Violating Bennett's Civil Rights.

1. Tippett Acted Under the Color of State Law.

• • • •

2. Tippett Denied Bennett Due Process.

The Fourteenth Amendment's guarantee of due process in state proceedings is a federal . . .

In *Catchpole*, . . .

In this case, Bennett will prove that Tippett bribed Judge Bell to rule against Bennett on his motion for a preliminary injunction. . . . There-fore, Tippett violated Bennett's rights to due process.

Tippett argued in the reply brief to his motion to dismiss that Bennett has an adequate remedy under state tort law and that section 1983 therefore affords him no relief, citing *Parratt v. Taylor*, 451 U.S. 527 (1981). *Parratt* is distinguishable . . .

Full syllogism in several paragraphs within second subargument

Separate paragraphs distinguishing adverse authority

In this example, *Parratt v. Taylor* does not clearly address a distinct topic; instead, it helps define the limits of due process in certain contexts. Thus, in a neutral analysis, you might consolidate your discussion of *Parratt* with your discussion of other authorities that establish the legal rule, even though you ultimately distinguish *Parratt* from your case.

In a responsive brief, however, you can invite the judge to analyze your case initially without the distraction of distinguishable adverse authority. By delaying your analysis of the adverse case law in this manner, you are free to develop the initial argument strongly and positively, without the qualifica-tions inherent in the subsequent discussion of adverse authority.

5. SUMMARY

These examples have primarily illustrated two issues of organization: (1) whether to present topics in separate sections or within a single, undivided section and (2) whether to separate or consolidate analyses within a section. These issues illustrate the role of judgment in legal writing and particularly in developing organizational structures. Many problems of this nature have no single, clearly correct solution; your resolution will depend on the nature and the depth of the analyses or arguments and on your personal style preferences.

IV. PARAGRAPHS

A. The Role of Paragraphs Within a Section

Just as descriptive headings and subheadings communicate the division of a discussion or argument into sections or subsections, good paragraphing helps to communicate the organizational structure within a section or subsection. For instance, the paragraphing in the following passage signals the transition from (1) an analysis of the statutory requirements of conduct "under the color of state law" to (2) an analysis of Fourteenth Amendment guarantees:

Statute	A private party acts "under the color of state law" if he acts in concert with a state official acting in his official capacity. *See Dennis v. Sparks,* 449 U.S. 24, 27-29 (1980). In *Dennis,* a state judge . . . Similarly, the evidence in this case will show that Tippett conspired with Judge Bell . . .
Constitution	The Fourteenth Amendment's guarantee of due process in state proceedings is a federal substantive right . . .

A second presentation of the same arguments assumes a greater depth of analysis. Imagine that each of five topic sentences begins a new paragraph. The five topic sentences represented by the phrases and clauses in the following example signal the transitions between (1) general legal rules, (2) in-depth case analysis, (3) fact analysis, (4) conclusion, and (5) analysis of potentially adverse authority.

Law	The Fourteenth Amendment's guarantee of due process in state proceedings is a federal substantive right . . . *See Catchpole v. Brannon,* . . .
	In *Catchpole,* . . .
Facts	In this case, Bennett will prove . . .
Conclusion	Thus, Tippett is liable to Bennett . . .
Adverse authority	Tippett has argued . . . , citing *Parratt v. Taylor,* 451 U.S. 527 (1981). *Parratt* is distinguishable . . .

B. Paragraph Content and Development

To say that each paragraph should present a single topic or idea oversimplifies the matter, for the appropriate scope of the subject matter of each paragraph may depend on the relationship between the paragraph and the remainder of the discussion. For example, the following analysis of merchant status is superficial, conclusory, and preliminary to the main topic for discussion. Accordingly, you could combine the legal standard, fact analysis, and conclusion in a single paragraph:

"Merchant" includes "a person who deals in goods of the kind." U.C.C. § 2-104(1) (2000). Jones regularly sells computers as part of her wholesale office supply business. Therefore, she is a merchant of the goods that she offered to supply to Azoulay, and section 2-205 thus governs the revocability of her offer.

In contrast, the reader can most easily absorb the typically more thorough analysis of the main topic if you divide the statement of legal rules and the fact analysis into at least two separate paragraphs. At the simplest level, each paragraph could correspond to one of the three elements of deductive reasoning. For example, after it explains the issue, a sample exam answer analyzes a problem in three paragraphs that (1) summarize the applicable legal rules, (2) apply the rules to the facts, and (3) state a conclusion:

An enforceable contract requires a bargained-for exchange in which a promisor exchanges his own promise for a return promise or performance. The requirement of an exchange is not satisfied if one party gives only an illusory promise, which does not commit the promisor to any future performance. A promise is illusory if it leaves the promisor free to perform or not according to his unfettered whim or discretion, such as . . .	**Legal rules**
Guarantor should argue that Lender's promise to forbear until he "needs" the money permits Lender to decide at his own whim and unfettered discretion when to demand payment, because he has some control of his own needs. However, that argument would prevail only if the word "need" refers to a subjective perception of deprivation that is inseparable from Lender's purely personal wants or desires. Lender can argue . . .	**Application to facts**
Unfortunately for our client, Lender's promise in the guarantee agreement probably is not illusory, because the word "need" provides some substance to Lender's commitment to forbear. Therefore, Guarantor's promise probably is supported by consideration and is enforceable.	**Conclusion**

In more complex analyses, the development of legal standards alone may progress through several paragraphs, perhaps beginning with an overview of general standards in one paragraph, followed by two or more additional paragraphs, each of which explores a significant case or a policy argument.

Similarly, the fact analysis may progress through several paragraphs, perhaps displaying different levels of fact analysis or different categories of facts. For example, the five paragraphs represented by the following phrases and clauses help to signal the transitions between (1) general legal standards, (2) in-depth case analysis, (3) identification of relevant facts, (4) analysis of those facts, and (5) conclusion:

	A. Smith's Alleged Conduct Was Not "Extreme and Outrageous."
Law	. . . Conduct that simply reflects normal social and economic adversities is not extreme or outrageous. *See, e.g., Frank v. Boswell,* . . .
	In *Frank,* . . .
Facts	In this case, Lew's complaint alleges conduct that is even less extreme than the conduct in *Frank.* . . .
	These allegations state only that . . .
Conclusion	Thus, the complaint does not allege circumstances that could establish the requisite "extreme and outrageous conduct."

C. The Role of Sentences Within a Paragraph

A paragraph does not contain some magic number of sentences. The appropriate number of sentences depends in part on the relationship between the paragraph and the topics addressed in surrounding paragraphs.

Of course, if you find that you have set off a single sentence as a separate paragraph, you should always question whether the isolated sentence would better serve as the concluding sentence of the previous paragraph or the topic sentence of the next one. As illustrated by the concluding paragraph of the illustration above, just before Section C, however, a single sentence may stand by itself as a separate paragraph if it completely addresses a discrete topic or if presentation in a separate paragraph achieves important goals of clarity or emphasis. If you blindly adhere to a "rule" against single-sentence paragraphs, you may find yourself composing an unnecessary, empty sentence to accompany an informative sentence that could have stood alone.

Whenever possible, your first sentence in a multiple-sentence paragraph should communicate your strategy by introducing the topic of the paragraph, expressing a transition, or both. For example, the first sentence in the following example signals the transition from the analysis of precedent to the identification of the relevant facts of the current dispute, and it provides an overview of the case comparison:

In this case, Lew's complaint alleges conduct that is even less extreme than the conduct in *Frank.* It alleges that Smith "fired Lew without severance pay and with full knowledge that Lew's family was facing a desperate financial crisis." Plaintiff's Second Amended Complaint ¶ 7. It further alleges . . .

In this sample paragraph, the topic sentence introduces fact analysis. Topic sentences or thesis statements are at least as important in introducing discussions of legal authority. To present legal authority effectively, you must use such topic or transition sentences or paragraphs to introduce statutes and case law and to express your syntheses of authority. Section II of Chapter 14 thoroughly discusses and illustrates this critical element of legal writing.

After you have composed an effective topic sentence, you should organize other sentences within a paragraph to develop information in a logical, organized fashion. For example, the paragraph below is designed to define the limits of the scope of the Uniform Commercial Code and to raise a question about the applicability of the Code to a particular transaction. The awkward placement of the second and third sentences of the paragraph disrupts continuity by stating an intermediate conclusion before establishing its premise:

Whether Maldonado accepted Weinstein's offer depends in part on whether the common law of contracts or the Uniform Commercial Code (UCC) applies to the transaction. Weinstein's offer to supply specifically identified, separately priced, movable plumbing parts clearly contemplates a sale of goods as part of the transaction. *See* U.C.C. § 2-105(1) (2000). The UCC applies only to "transactions in goods." U.C.C. § 2-102 (2000). His proposed transaction, however, also involves the service of installing the fixtures, raising a question about the applicability of the UCC to mixed transactions for both services and the sale of goods.	**General issue** **Application to facts** **Legal premise** **Specific issue**

Reversing the order of the second and third sentences develops points in a more logical order and retains the coherence of transitions:

Whether Maldonado accepted Weinstein's offer depends in part on whether the common law of contracts or the Uniform Commercial Code (UCC) applies to the transaction. The UCC applies only to "transactions in goods." U.C.C. § 2-102 (2000). Weinstein's offer to supply specifically identified, separately priced, movable plumbing parts clearly contemplates a sale of goods as part of the transaction. *See* U.C.C. § 2-105(1) (2000). His proposed transaction, however, also involves the service of installing the fixtures, raising a question about . . .	**General issue** **Legal premise** **Application to facts** **Specific issue**

Many organizational approaches may result in a logical and coherent presentation of information in a paragraph. Nonetheless, one simple technique is worth highlighting: You can lead a reader from familiar to new information in a paragraph by beginning each sentence with a previously established idea and linking it to a new idea. For example, the phrases in capital letters in the following passage represent new information, and the italicized phrases represent previously introduced information. In each sentence after the first one, previously introduced information is linked to a new idea.

An enforceable contract requires a bargained-for EXCHANGE in which a promisor exchanges his own promise for a return promise or performance. The requirement of an *exchange* is not satisfied if one party gives only an ILLUSORY PROMISE, which does not commit the promisor to any future performance. A *promise is illusory* if it leaves the promisor free to perform or not according to his unfettered whim or discretion, such as. . . .

This technique of consistently linking a familiar idea with a new one is only one of many approaches that you may use in developing a paragraph. You should always retain maximum flexibility to adapt your organizational approach to the particular characteristics of a passage. The final two chapters of Part V provide further guidance. They (1) continue to explore paragraphing and paragraph content in the context of presentation of authority and (2) address good organization of words and clauses within a sentence to enhance the clarity or persuasive force of the sentence.

V. SUMMARY

When organizing the topics or arguments in an office memorandum or brief, you should

1. with few exceptions, discuss separate issues in separate sections or subsections,
2. arrange your sections and subsections so that they reflect the proper relationships among topics and subtopics, and
3. present your topics or arguments in a logical order, subject to considerations of strategy.

Within a section or subsection, you should

1. explain the legal rule,
2. apply the rule to the facts, and
3. reach a conclusion.

If the topic or argument within a section or subsection is governed by several closely related rules, you should exercise judgment to either

1. consolidate your statement of all the rules before applying them to all the relevant facts or

2. separately apply some preliminary legal rules to facts before progressing to other rules within the section or subsection.

When organizing material within a section or subsection, you should consider

1. the hierarchy of authority and
2. progression from general to specific and from fundamental to uncertain.

Chapter 13

Legal Writing Style in the Office
Memorandum

Chapter 1's introduction to writing style identified clarity and conciseness as the principal characteristics of effective legal writing. This chapter more comprehensively examines those topics, and Chapter 14 addresses special problems of citing to legal authority.

This chapter uses selected writing problems as vehicles for developing a method for legal writing. The method it promotes is a flexible approach that provides general guidance in any legal writing assignment. It seeks to show you that effective legal writing style to a great extent is analogous to the sound practices of legal method and analysis discussed in the preceding chapters. Accordingly, it invites you to treat rules and conventions of writing very much like legal rules: To use them well, you must understand their purposes and policies. For further practice in recognizing the policies underlying conventions of writing, perform the problems in Appendix V, near the end of this book.

Although this chapter primarily addresses writing style for office memoranda, most of the principles discussed apply equally to briefs, and some of the examples are taken from briefs. Special techniques of persuasive writing are explored in Chapter 16.

I. CLARITY

You cannot write clearly unless you first develop clear ideas. In many cases, muddled legal writing reflects an incomplete understanding of the substantive legal analysis and suggests the need for further research and reflection. Only when you have fully mastered your analysis can you clearly communicate the analysis to a comprehending reader.

Beyond sound analysis, an important element of clarity in any legal document is effective organization on all the levels discussed in Chapter 12. Other elements of clarity, discussed below, are simplicity, effective sentence structure, and precision in word selection.

A. Simplicity and Plain English

For centuries, the public has complained about lawyers' fondness for legal jargon: stuffy, peculiar, archaic legal terminology. People have good reason to complain. For example, some lawyers still refuse to end a witness's sworn and notarized written statement with the perfectly descriptive word "signed." Instead, they insist on inserting the archaic phrase "Further affiant sayeth not."

Although the extent to which you stray from plain and simple terms is partly a matter of personal style, you should tend toward simplicity. If a simple, familiar word will clearly express your idea, your reader may find that a peculiar, complex, or unfamiliar word or phrase in its place is distracting or even unintelligible.

Moreover, simplicity in writing does not condemn you to expressing only simple ideas. Rather, it helps you to express even complex and abstract ideas in such clear, concrete, and simple terms that your reader easily grasps your ideas on first reading.

You can best appreciate the virtues of simplicity by recognizing the ultimate purpose of your document. A legal memorandum should efficiently communicate ideas, and a brief should persuade. A document cannot perform either of these functions if the reader must pause at every sentence to ponder its meaning.

Unfortunately, unnecessary abstraction, complexity, and peculiarity found in some legal writing suggests that the writer's objective is to "sound like a lawyer" or to impress his supervising attorney or a judge with the breadth of his vocabulary. One judge describes the effect of such writing:

> [T]he use of legalese or "six-bit" college words may help convince your client that you are worth the hourly fee being charged, but it does not help win his case. Indeed, it actually interferes in your communication with the court when the judge is constantly shifting attention from the brief to either a Webster's, Black's Law, or a Latin-to-English dictionary. I know you received a high dollar education. Instead of trying to impress me with some high-brow vocabulary, use your education to figure out how to simplify what you are saying with plain language. After all, the simpler you make it, the easier it is for me to understand.[1]

1. Brian Quinn, *Dispelling Misconception*, 62 Tex. B.J. 890, 891 (1999).

Occasionally, a peculiar word or phrase earns its place in legal writing as a shorthand term for an unavoidably complex or unfamiliar concept. For example, Chapter 5 uses the term "stare decisis" to refer to a complex set of principles that help to define legal method in the United States. Although this Latin term is unfamiliar to most students entering law school, it qualifies as a useful "term of art" because it is widely accepted among trained lawyers as convenient shorthand for a set of ideas that the more familiar term "precedent" does not fully convey. Surprisingly few forms of peculiar legal language, however, are justified as necessary terms of art. Therefore, you should critically evaluate any unusual language in your writing to ensure that it informs more than distracts.[2]

Legal jargon is particularly inappropriate in a document that is addressed to a layperson, perhaps a client, who may be unfamiliar with even rudimentary legal terminology. When addressing such an audience, not only should you exercise special care to avoid unnecessary jargon, you should explain in plain English the meanings of legal terms of art that other attorneys would easily recognize.

E x e r c i s e **13-1**

A simple contract should (1) introduce the parties to the contract, (2) recite any background facts that explain the motivations of the parties and thus help to explain their bargain, (3) define the parties' rights and obligations by setting forth their mutual promises, and (4) signify each party's agreement to the terms of the contract.

The following contract is written in antiquated jargon. Parts of the contract are taken from the contract interpreted in *McMichael v. Price*, 58 P.2d 549 (Okla. 1936). Contract language from formbooks provided further inspiration.

Simplify all or part of the structure and language of the contract so that it expresses the terms of the parties' agreement in plain English. Feel free to use subject headings, section numbers, and paragraphing. Compare your revision with the sample contracts at the end of Chapter 23.

REQUIREMENTS CONTRACT

This contract for the purchase and sale of sand entered into on this, the _____ day of _____, by and between Sooner Sand Co., a general partnership of which Harley T. Price and W. M. McMichael are partners, hereinafter known as the party of the first part, and Bassi Distributing Co., a joint venture of Bassi Trucking Co. and Hardcore Rock & Gravel, Inc., hereinafter known as the party of the second part, Witnesseth:

---

2. *See* Richard C. Wydick, Plain English for Lawyers 61-63 (4th ed. 1998).

Whereas, the party of the first part is engaged in the business of selling and shipping sand from Phoenix to various customers in the State of Arizona but has not developed markets outside of Arizona and desires to supply sand wholesale to a distributor with customers outside the state; and

Whereas, the party of the second part has an established business in Phoenix selling and shipping sand to various customers in several states outside Arizona, including California, Nevada, Utah, and Colorado, and desires a stable source of supply of sand for that business;

Now, therefore, in consideration of the mutual covenants herein contained, and other good and valuable consideration the receipt of which is hereby acknowledged, the parties hereby represent, warrant, affirm, promise, covenant, and agree that the said party of the first part will, upon receipt of periodic written orders submitted by the said party of the second part, furnish all of the sand which the said party of the second part requires for shipment to various and sundry points outside of the State of Arizona, for a period of five (5) years from the date hereinabove, said sand to be of a grade and quality at least equal in quality and comparable with the sand of various grades sold by other sand companies in the City of Phoenix, Arizona; furthermore, the said party of the second part agrees to pay as payment and compensation for said sand so furnished a sum per ton which represents sixty percent (60%) of the current market price per ton of concrete at the place of destination of said shipment.

In witness whereof, the said parties have hereunto set their hands and seals the day and year first above written.

Sooner Sand Co.—Authorized Agent

Bassi Distributing Co.—Authorized Agent

B. Sentence Structure

1. STRUCTURING AND PUNCTUATING LONG OR COMPLEX SENTENCES

Short, crisp sentences can be powerful:

Jenkins lived to tell his side of the story. Roberts did not.

On the other hand, a succession of very short sentences may sound stilted or may require empty or repetitive transitional phrases to link the sentences together:

It was 1:00 A.M. John left the party. He went home. He drove his BMW.

Moreover, long sentences that convey numerous thoughts in multiple clauses are not necessarily problematic; if punctuated and constructed sensibly, they may be clear and readable.

Unfortunately, however, legal writing often suffers from unnecessarily long and complex sentences that are poorly constructed. The reader of such a sentence must assimilate too much information at once and guess at the proper relationships of the ideas.

Two characteristics of the process of legal writing may account for many excessively long and complex sentences. First, the writer has researched and pondered his analysis before verbalizing it, and he may have forgotten the difficulty that another lawyer encounters when exposed to the concepts for the first time. If so, he may attempt to convey a greater number of difficult concepts in a single sentence than the reader is prepared to digest. Second, some lawyers dictate their first drafts on a tape recorder and neglect to revise the transcribed draft adequately. Dictation may encourage long and complex sentences, because the speaker is deceived into believing that his inflection, dynamics in volume, and pauses provide adequate guides to sentence structure. In fact, transcripts of trials and presidential press conferences reveal that such oral guides to structure often do not transcribe adequately to the written page.

a. Closure Through Punctuation

You can use two devices to avoid or revise unmanageable sentences: closure and visual guides to structure.

Closure usually refers to punctuation that allows a reader to pause to assimilate one or more ideas before moving to the next. For example, the following passages illustrate three levels of closure. The first presents at least three distinct ideas in a single sentence punctuated only by commas:

Although punitive damages are designed to punish the wrongdoer rather than compensate the victim for actual injury, many courts will award punitive damages only if the plaintiff proves actual injury, and some courts will limit punitive damages to an amount that bears a reasonable relationship to the award of compensatory damages.

The sentence above is constructed reasonably well. However, the commas in the sentence invite only brief pauses between ideas, leaving the reader breathless if she is unfamiliar with the subject matter. Periods dividing the passage into three sentences encourage the reader to pause more substantially and to digest each idea before facing the next:

Punitive damages are designed to punish the wrongdoer rather than compensate the victim for actual injury. Nonetheless, many courts will award punitive damages only if the plaintiff proves actual injury. Moreover, some courts will limit punitive damages to an amount that bears a reasonable relationship to the award of compensatory damages.

If you desire to link the second and third ideas to one another more closely than to the first idea in the paragraph, you can replace the second period with a semicolon. The semicolon provides such a conceptual link with nearly the same level of closure as provided by a period:

Punitive damages are designed to punish the wrongdoer rather than compensate the victim for actual losses. Nonetheless, many courts will award punitive damages only if the plaintiff proves actual injury; moreover, some courts will limit punitive damages to an amount that bears a reasonable relationship to the award of compensatory damages.

In some passages, visual guides to the structure of a long sentence may effectively substitute for the closure provided by multiple short sentences. The following passages illustrate both techniques. The first sample passage takes advantage of closure by limiting each sentence to a single idea:

The evidence supports three critical factual conclusions. First, the marijuana, cocaine, and heroin all belonged to Carson and Klein. Second, Rivers was unaware of the presence of those drugs in the house when he entered the living room. Third, when Klein offered to sell the marijuana to Rivers, Rivers declined and attempted to leave the house.

The closure is welcome in this example, because two of the factual conclusions set forth in separate sentences are sufficiently complex to require punctuation within those conclusions.

In the next sample passage, the series of conclusions in the first passage progresses through a single sentence without the disruption of substantial closure. It retains some of the qualities of closure by using numbers as the equivalent of road signs[3] to identify the end of one element of the series and the beginning of the next:

The evidence supports three critical factual conclusions: (1) the marijuana, cocaine, and heroin all belonged to Carson and Klein; (2) Rivers was unaware of the presence of those drugs in the house when he entered the living room; and (3) when Klein offered to sell the marijuana to Rivers, Rivers declined and attempted to leave the house.

---

b. Repetition of Prepositions or Other Linking Words or Phrases

If the elements of the series are less complex, you can provide a subtler guide to sentence structure by repeating an introductory word or phrase, such as "that" in the following example:

---

3. One author calls this technique "tabulation." Wydick, *supra* note 2, at 46-47.

Top Notch Co. is not liable on this contract theory unless Jackson can prove that the personnel manual was part of Jackson's employment contract, that the manual contained a promise of job security, and that Top Notch breached such a promise when it discharged Jackson for refusing to shave his beard.

Some writers balk at repeating "that" in this manner, or even at using it in the first instance. In some sentence structures, their point is well taken. For example, the word "that" is unnecessary in the following sentence:

I knew that he would come back.

Although the sentence above does not display any errors of grammar or syntax, a writer could exercise discretion to omit the word "that," thus adopting a more concise style with no appreciable loss of clarity:

I knew he would come back.

In other cases, however, the word "that," although unnecessary, may help the reader to distinguish quickly between two possible sentence structures. Consider, for example, the following sentences:

The court held two principles above all others.

The court held the defendant in custody without bail.[4]

The court held the defendant had not consented to the search.

In the first two sentences, the word "held" is used, at least figuratively, in the sense of possessing or retaining some thing, tangible or intangible. In those two sentences, the word "that" has no place; the writer could not insert it without adding other words. In the third sentence, however, the word "held" is used in a different sense and syntax. Like the word "said" or "concluded" in similar contexts, it introduces a holding or ruling of the court. In this context, a writer could exercise discretion to insert "that" after "held":

The court held that the defendant had not consented to the search.

Indeed, although not necessary, adding the word "that" in the final sample sentence helps the reader to instantly change gears from the structure of the first two sample sentences to the different structure of the third. Without the "that" as a guide to the structure of the third sentence, the reader might

---

4. This sentence would be more precise if it stated that the court ordered the sheriff to hold the defendant without bail, but it suffices to illustrate the point under consideration.

momentarily assign the same meaning to "held" that it had in the first two sentences, relying later on context to dispel the confusion.

Thus, one should not too quickly adopt an inflexible rule against inserting "that" in such contexts. The decision whether to employ such a guide to structure is a matter of judgment, style, and context in these examples.

c. Complex Series

Chapter 1 examined the serial comma rule and its relationship to the goal of clarity in writing. To ensure clarity in complex as well as simple contexts, adherents to the traditional approach consistently insert the final comma in any series of two or more things:

We encountered high winds, driving rain, and dense fog.

The elements of a series, however, need not be limited to simple nouns, such as "wind, rain, and fog." They may be verb phrases, such as "washed the car, mowed the lawn, and repaired the roof." They may even be independent clauses, each of which could stand alone as a complete sentence with a subject and verb.

Particularly troublesome is a series in which at least one element contains a subsidiary series presenting subelements. The first challenge in such a sentence is to clearly distinguish among the elements and subelements at various levels in the series and subsidiary series. Unfortunately, legal writers frequently confuse these relationships:

The defendant had left his car at a garage for repairs, repainting, other maintenance, and lacked money for public transportation to another city.

The writer has punctuated this sentence as a single series with four elements: "repairs," "repainting," "other maintenance," and "lacked money." The series is not parallel in structure because the first three elements are objects and the fourth is a verb with an object. Along with the content of the sentence, that lack of parallelism helps to reveal the intended sentence structure. If retained as a single sentence, the passage is best structured as a compound sentence with two independent clauses as the major elements and with a series of three subelements within the first major element:

1. The defendant had left his car at a garage for
   a. repairs,
   b. repainting, **and**
   c. other maintenance, and
2. **he** lacked money for public transportation to another city.

The seemingly minor revisions in the corrected sentence are significant. The addition of the conjunction "and" between the second and third element of the subsidiary series signals the end of that series. Moreover, the addition of the subject "he" in the second major element of the compound sentence transforms that element into an independent clause, parallel with the first major element.

d. Toward a Flexible, Policy-Oriented Approach to Punctuation

Many routine conventions of punctuation provide guides to sentence structure and should be applied flexibly to achieve that goal. For example, the insertion of a comma to separate independent clauses joined by a conjunction[5] is not arbitrary; it often avoids temporary confusion in sentence structure, as illustrated by the following unpunctuated sentence:

Coastal Bank breached its loan commitment to the owner and the contractor threatened to terminate its performance.

Halfway through the sentence, many readers assume that the conjunction "and" joins "owner" to "the contractor." Thus, on encountering "the contractor," those readers conclude for a fraction of a second that the bank owed its loan commitment to the contractor as well as to the owner. By the time they reach the verb "threatened," they realize from context that "the contractor" is the subject of a new independent clause rather than the second in a series of two objects of the prepositional phrase "to the." By that time, however, the ambiguity in sentence structure has caused readers to hesitate for a moment and perhaps even to regress by rereading part of the sentence. This momentary confusion may be even more pronounced in a more complicated compound sentence.

A comma inserted before the conjunction more instantly identifies "the contractor" as the beginning of a new independent clause:

Coastal Bank breached its loan commitment to the owner, and the contractor threatened to terminate its performance.

This example illustrates two general principles of style. First, the reader of a brief or memorandum may be able to glean the meaning of the first sample sentence from context; however, if multiplied in the course of a document, the additional labor and frequent instances of momentary confusion can leave the reader weary. Some conventions of punctuation or other matters of style may not be critical to the reader's ultimate comprehension, but they enhance the efficiency and ease with which the reader comprehends.

Second, you should apply rules or conventions of writing style the way that you apply rules of law: Apply and extend them as far as necessary to vindicate their underlying purposes or policies, but no further. For example, the following compound sentence is perfectly readable without a comma separating the independent clauses:

---

5. *See* William Strunk, Jr. & E. B. White, THE ELEMENTS OF STYLE 5 (4th ed. 2000).

The robber ran and the police gave chase.

Because this sentence is short and simple, the reader can recognize its structure at a glance, arguably making the comma unnecessary as a guide to structure.

You can avoid the comma question and raise others by placing a period after the first independent clause:

The robber ran. And the police gave chase.

This punctuation gives special emphasis to the action in each clause, but many writers recoil at the idea of beginning a sentence with the simple conjunction "and" or "but." Such usage is not grammatically incorrect; it is simply stylistically questionable in many cases. If the clauses are simple and short, they will normally flow more smoothly if combined in a single sentence with a conjunction in the middle of the sentence. On the other hand, if you want to divide the clauses into two sentences to emphasize each clause or to provide your reader with closure after a long clause, you probably will prefer a stronger transition word than "and" or "but." When writers decide to begin a sentence with a conjunction, most prefer to use a more substantial conjunctive adverb, such as "Moreover," "Furthermore," "In contrast," "However," or "Nonetheless":

Mr. Blumquist survived the initial explosion. Nonetheless, he died a short time later of smoke inhalation.

Section III of Chapter 1 explains why you should reject an inflexible rule against starting sentences with a conjunctive adverb, such as "however," helping you to minimize the need to begin a sentence with "and" or "but" to achieve important objectives in legal writing. But you should not conclude that this construction is universally incorrect. It will simply be a rare passage in legal writing that benefits from such construction. In this entire book, only a handful of sentences begin with "and" or "but." And the two in this paragraph are included primarily to underscore the theme of this subsection: Many rules of composition should be viewed as general guides to style rather than absolute prohibitions on unconventional usage.

A few more examples will further underscore this point. Consider, for example, the question whether to insert a comma after a subordinate phrase or clause to separate it from the main clause that follows it:

After reviving the victim at poolside{,} the paramedic transported her to the hospital emergency room.

Some writers, including this author, normally insert such a comma, even after a relatively short and simple introductory phrase or clause. By analogy to the justification for the traditional serial comma rule, we reason that the comma almost never hurts and that it may be a helpful guide to sentence structure if the introductory phrase or clause is long or complex.

Other writers, however, prefer to avoid unnecessary punctuation. They may prefer to insert a comma after an introductory phrase or clause only when necessary for clarity. Such an exercise of discretion is perfectly legitimate, although it requires the writer to determine the degree of complexity or length that would cause a reader to stumble in the absence of a comma.

For example, each of the following five sentences or excerpts begins with a subordinate word, phrase, or clause. The word or phrase beginning the main clause is printed in bold. In which of the examples would you insert a comma before the main clause?

(i) Later **he** mowed the lawn.
(ii) On January 1, 1997 **he** resolved to quit smoking.
(iii) After she examined the patient **Dr. Ong** requested a conference with the chief surgeon.
(iv) In light of Hart's conduct and his oral representations regarding the policy manual **the judge** ruled that . . .
(v) Although few courts have addressed the question whether a member of a city council enjoys the absolute immunity conferred on state legislators **the policy** of protecting the legislative process from . . .

As stated above, a writer could reasonably choose to insert a comma in each of the five examples. Others might exercise discretion to withhold further punctuation from example (i) and perhaps example (ii) because readers can recognize the relatively simple structures of those examples at a glance. Even those inclined to preserve ink, however, should begin adding a comma at the level of complexity of example (iii) or (iv). The dependent clause at the beginning of example (iii) includes a subject, verb, and object. Moreover, the object, "the patient," might be confused with the subject of the main clause, "Dr. Ong," unless separated by a comma:

After she examined the patient, Dr. Ong requested a conference . . .

In examples (iv) and (v), the introductory phrases or clauses are sufficiently long and complex that readers will appreciate a comma, because it invites them to pause to assimilate the information in the introduction before proceeding to the main clause.

A final example will serve to emphasize the role of style and judgment in punctuation and to illustrate the limits of inflexible rules. In the following sentence, a common convention of punctuation justifies each of the commas, viewed in isolation:

The contract is written, signed, and dated, and, therefore, the statute of frauds does not apply.

The first two commas appropriately separate three elements of a series. The third comma appropriately separates the two independent clauses joined by the conjunction "and." The last two commas at least represent a defensible judgment that "therefore" is parenthetic and should be set apart from the rest of the clause with commas.

Nonetheless, most writers would be dissatisfied with the sentence, because the concentration of five commas within six words of text is distracting. In response, many writers simply omit one or more commas without changing the structure of the sentence:

The contract is written, signed, and dated and, therefore the statute of frauds does not apply.

Although this revision is less cluttered, it omits commas that served important functions.

An honest appraisal of the original sentence should reveal structural flaws. None of the five commas are incorrect; however, the sentence structure concentrates the commas in a manner that is stylistically displeasing. You can directly respond to this problem by changing the location of "therefore," thus decreasing the need for commas around it by lessening its parenthetic qualities:

The contract is written, signed, and dated, and the statute of frauds therefore does not apply.

Alternatively, you can replace one of the commas with a semicolon by omitting the conjunction "and" between the two independent clauses:

The contract is written, signed, and dated; therefore, the statute of frauds does not apply.

In sum, if you understand the policy justifications for conventions of punctuation, you can more confidently recall them, apply them, and even depart from them when the context justifies an unconventional approach. Conversely, even technically correct writing may display problems of style that invite you to exercise judgment and to consciously choose among alternative sentence structures.

Appendix V describes other common conventions of punctuation and asks you to analyze them.

Exercise 13-2

1. CARE WITH COMMAS

Which of the following sentences requires further punctuation? Should you address these sentences with an inflexible rule of punctuation or with attention to principles of good writing underlying conventions of punctuation?

    a. Two pieces of evidence link Jones to the crime: A witness observed Jones strike the victim with his fist and a glove recovered from the crime scene matches the one found in Jones's car.

    b. The court dismissed the action and Romero appealed.

    c. The judge dismissed the action because the limitations period had expired.

    d. Because the limitations period had run the court dismissed the action.

    e. In some cases even perfectly relevant evidence should be excluded if it would seriously confuse the jury because the prejudicial effect of such evidence outweighs its probative value.

    f. The court rejected the defendant's argument that the action should be dismissed because the limitations period had run reasoning that the plaintiff had established grounds for tolling the limitations period.

2. CLOSURE AND ROAD SIGNS

Redraft the following sentence to make it easier to read. Break it into multiple sentences or clauses, or use any other device to lead the reader gracefully through the ideas it expresses.

> Plaintiff American Continental Can Co. brought this action against Defendants Conco Sheet Metal Co., Bassi Distributing Co., and Miller Trucking Co., alleging that Conco Sheet Metal Co. had sold it defective sheet metal, that Bassi Distributing Co. had fraudulently misrepresented the description and quality of Conco Sheet Metal Co.'s products, and that Miller Trucking Co. had negligently damaged sheet metal that it agreed to transport from the warehouse of Conco Sheet Metal Co. to the factory of American Continental Can Co., and requesting compensatory and punitive damages.

3. THE AMBIGUOUS SERIES

Identify the major elements of the series in the sentence set forth below. Where does the last element of the series begin? What different interpretations does the sentence permit? How would you use a comma to advance either interpretation over the other?

> In the event of default, the Lessee must vacate the premises, forfeit the security deposit and pay Lessor's actual damages or pay liquidated damages under section 12 of this Lease.

2. CONCRETE VERBS AND ACTIVE CONSTRUCTION

a. Concrete Verbs

Lawyers often sacrifice vigor and clarity in their legal writing by employing vague and abstract verbs such as "involve," "exist," or "occur":

A modification to the contract occurred on July 1.

Even more frequently, lawyers drain the strength from verbs by building sentences around a form of the phrase "there is":

There was a modification to the contract on July 1.

The author of the preceding sentence has converted the active verb "modify" into the noun "modification," creating a need for the verb "was," a form of the relatively abstract and passive infinitive "to be." Unless you really intend to focus attention on the mere existence or absence of modification, you could improve this sentence by identifying the actors, abandoning the "be" verb, and focusing on the real action word in the sentence, "modify":

Nelson and Kubichek modified their contract on July 1.

In some cases, replacing abstract wording such as "there is" with a more concrete, active verb will enable you to add new meaning as well as vigor. For example, the following sentence abstractly comments on the absence of critical evidence:

There is no evidence in the record that Robert Emery intended to kill the bank teller.

A more concrete verb can emphasize the absence not only of direct evidence of intent but also of circumstantial evidence from which a factfinder might infer intent:

No evidence in the record even suggests that Robert Emery intended to kill the bank teiler.

b. Active and Passive Construction

Avoidance of forms of "there is" in legal writing is simply a special branch of a more general preference for active voice in sentence structure. A clause in active voice presents its principal parts in the normal order of actor, verb, and object of the action, such as "curiosity killed the cat."

In contrast, the following sentence features three clauses in passive voice, each of which places the object before the verb and dispenses with the actor altogether:

The *Allen* doctrine has been criticized, but it continues to be applied because it has been approved in dictum.

The following revision identifies the actors associated with each verb, but it still uses passive voice throughout, as revealed by the inverted order of object, verb, and actor:

The *Allen* doctrine has been criticized by a few appellate judges, but it continues to be applied by trial judges because it has been approved in dictum by the Supreme Court.

Active voice is more informative than the first example above, and it more directly and concisely conveys all the information presented in the second example:

A few appellate judges have criticized the *Allen* doctrine, but trial judges continue to apply it because the Supreme Court has approved it in dictum.

The vigor of active construction can be especially useful in composing strong statements in persuasive writing. For example, the following sentence in passive voice fails to assign responsibility for the repair of the air conditioning:

The air conditioning was not repaired until 60 days after the tenant gave written notice of the defect.

In contrast, the next sentence uses active voice to identify the landlord as the responsible party and to characterize the landlord's inaction as a culpable omission:

The landlord neglected to repair the air conditioning until 60 days after the tenant gave written notice of the defect.

Although active voice generally is more direct, concise, or informative than passive voice, you may occasionally have reason to prefer passive voice. For example, you may use passive voice to deliberately omit reference to an actor or actors whose identities are unknown or unimportant:

The bridge was erected in 1923.

Even in this case, some writers so strongly prefer active voice that they refer to the actor or actors generically:

Workers built the bridge in 1923.

However, most writers would reasonably adopt the passive construction to avoid diverting the reader's attention to unimportant information.

In some cases, you may be aware of the identity of the actor but use passive construction to avoid drawing attention to that identity. For example, a defense attorney might desire to emphasize mitigating factors in a crime while avoiding any reminder to the jury that her client stands accused of the wrongdoing:

The hostage was not harmed in any way.

Conversely, you may deliberately use passive voice to place unusual emphasis on the actor by placing the actor at the end of the sentence, as in the second of the following sentences:

The defense wants you to believe that Mr. Cass committed suicide by injecting himself with a lethal dose of heroin. To the contrary, the evidence shows that the heroin was injected by the defendant, Ms. Borden.

In some sentences, if you place the actor or actors at the beginning of the sentence, you will unduly delay introducing the verb:

Ms. Williams, the firm's top expert in tax law, and Mr. Scales, an eloquent oral advocate with 20 years of experience before the state appellate courts, argued the case.

With passive voice, you can introduce the simple verb and its object early in the sentence:

The case was argued by Ms. Williams, the firm's top expert in tax law, and by Mr. Scales, an eloquent oral advocate with 20 years of experience before the state appellate courts.

In summary, you should prefer vigorous, concrete verbs in active construction unless you have a specific purpose for a vague, abstract, or passive verb.

Exercise 13-3

1. BENEFITS OF ACTIVE, CONCRETE VERBS

Replace the passive, abstract verbs in the following sentences with more active, concrete verbs.

    a. There are only two Supreme Court decisions that address this issue.
    b. It was argued by government counsel that the tax regulation was applicable to the land exchange.
    c. The landlord was ordered by the court to achieve completion of the repairs within 30 days.
    d. There was a conspiracy among four distributors to effect an immediate price increase.

2. BENEFITS OF PASSIVE CONSTRUCTION

By replacing the active verb with a passive verb, restructure the following sentence to minimize the number of words separating the subject, verb, and object and to emphasize the "clearly erroneous" standard.

> Federal Rule of Civil Procedure 52(a), which provides that a federal trial court's findings of fact in a nonjury trial "shall not be set aside unless clearly erroneous," limits our review.

3. EFFECTIVE PLACEMENT OF MODIFIERS

For clarity, you should place a modifying word, phrase, or clause close to the part of the sentence that it modifies. On the other hand, to ensure a smooth flow in your writing, you should avoid interrupting important parts of a sentence with a lengthy modifier. The following sample sentences illustrate how these principles relate to one another.

The first sample sentence below attempts to describe the effects of cross-examination on a witness. Unfortunately, it subjects the reader to a classic dangling modifier:

Withering under relentless cross-examination, the prosecutor forced the witness to recant his earlier testimony.

The first five words of this sample sentence form a subordinate phrase. It is subordinate because, unlike the clause that follows it, it cannot stand alone as a full sentence; rather, it provides further information about an element of the clause. The subject of the independent clause, "the prosecutor," is positioned next to the modifying phrase and thus receives the impact of that phrase. But it is the witness, not the prosecutor, who withered under

the cross-examination. You can remedy this defect in the sentence by changing the modifying phrase so that it addresses the action of the prosecutor:

With relentless cross-examination, the prosecutor forced the witness to recant his earlier testimony.

But this alters the focus of the sentence. If you want to retain the focus on
the witness, you can restructure the sentence so that the original modifying
phrase is adjacent to the object that it modifies, "the witness":

The witness, withering under the prosecutor's relentless cross-examination, recanted his earlier testimony.

That sentence structure leaves no doubt that the witness is the one who
has withered. Unfortunately, it places the modifying phrase between the
subject and the verb, separating important parts of the sentence. This separation will not be objectionable if the modifier is very short and simple. Indeed,
it creates only a minor inconvenience in the sample sentence above. However,
a longer, more complex modifier in that position can be distracting:

The witness, who had testified on direct examination that he was walking toward the intersection and therefore was in a position to see the signal, admitted on cross-examination that he had his back to the intersection at the time of the accident.

To eliminate the separation of subject and verb in the shorter sample
sentence, you might consider gathering all the parts of the main clause and
moving them to the beginning of the sentence:

The witness recanted his earlier testimony, withering under the prosecutor's relentless cross-examination.

In other sentences, this structure is often quite successful. Unfortunately,
in this sample sentence, it introduces the recantation before the withering,
producing a sense of anticlimax. The structure also creates ambiguity about
whether the witness or his earlier testimony was withering.

Perhaps the best revision of the sample sentence places the modifying
phrase or clause at the beginning of the sentence, paving the way for an
uninterrupted main clause:

Withering under the prosecutor's relentless cross-examination, the witness recanted his earlier testimony.

Some might object to this structure on the ground that a long subordinate phrase or clause at the beginning of a sentence unduly delays introduction of the main clause. That objection may be valid in some contexts with the following qualification: A moderately long or complex subordinate phrase or clause ordinarily will be less distracting if it is placed at the beginning of the sentence than if it appears in the middle of the sentence and separates important parts of the main clause.

The following passages are sample revisions of a sentence with long and multiple subordinate clauses. When read with the previous examples, these alternative revisions suggest that the best solutions to the problems discussed above sometimes differ with the circumstances of each sentence.

Unlike the more moderate introduction in the last sample revision above, the subordinate clauses in the following sentence inconveniently delay introduction of the main clause:

Because the consumer fraud statute applies to misrepresentations in either the "advertisement or sale" of merchandise, and because the "sale" of merchandise normally is associated with the passing of title from the seller to the buyer, *see* U.C.C. § 2-106(1) (2000), the statute appears to apply to a seller's misrepresentations made during the delivery of merchandise under a preexisting contract.

You would only increase the reader's frustration by moving the subordinate clauses to the middle of the sentence, between the subject and the verb:

The consumer fraud statute, because it applies to . . . , and because the "sale" of merchandise normally is . . . , appears to apply to a seller's misrepresentations. . . .

You could reveal the information in the sentence more gracefully by starting with the main clause:

The consumer fraud statute appears to apply to a seller's misrepresentations made during the delivery of merchandise under a preexisting contract, because the statute applies to misrepresentations in either the "advertisement or sale" of merchandise, and because the "sale" of merchandise normally is associated with the passing of title from the seller to the buyer, *see* U.C.C. § 2-106(1) (2000).

In the context of this sample sentence, this structure does not produce the ambiguity or inappropriate sense of anticlimax that it produced in one of the revisions of the first sample sentence above.

Of course, this revised sentence is nonetheless too long and complex. You can solve all the problems in this passage simply by breaking it into shorter sentences, as recommended in the discussion of closure in Section B.1.a above:

The consumer fraud statute applies to misrepresentations in either the "advertisement or sale" of merchandise. The "sale" of merchandise normally is associated with the passing of title from the seller to the buyer. *See* U.C.C. § 2-106(1) (2000). Therefore, the statute appears to apply to . . . .

Exercise 13-4

1. PRECISE PLACEMENT OF MODIFIERS

Consider the different positions into which you could insert the word "only" in the following sentence: Officer Jones fired his gun three times at the suspect.

Which of the positions is most consistent with the information in each of the following?

    a. Officer Jones fired his gun three times, not five times as reported by a witness.

    b. Officer Jones fired his gun three times, but no other officer fired his gun more than once.

2. MODIFYING CLAUSES AND SENTENCE STRUCTURE

Revise the following sentences. Which of several possible revisions do you prefer, and why?

    a. The trial judge, after reviewing the evidence and considering the arguments of the parties, ruled that the contraband was the product of an illegal search.

    b. Protesting that he had not finished his testimony, the bailiff escorted the witness from the courtroom.

4. RESTRICTIVE AND NONRESTRICTIVE CLAUSES

Most writers confess to difficulty in identifying restrictive and nonrestrictive clauses and in choosing between the relative pronouns "that" and "which" once they have identified the clause. Most critical for clarity is your remembering to insert a comma before a nonrestrictive clause (and after the clause if it does not end the sentence) and to omit such a comma before a nonrestrictive clause. If you wish to go beyond popular usage and satisfy purists in your circle, you will also remember to introduce a restrictive clause with the relative pronoun "that," saving "which" for nonrestrictive clauses.

a. The Role of the Comma

To illustrate the distinction between restrictive and nonrestrictive clauses, imagine that you and a supervising attorney are standing next to a large conference table in a meeting room of your law firm. The conference table is the only table in the room, and eight chairs are placed around it. Your supervisor makes a statement that is reproduced below without internal punctuation:

This table *which we just purchased a year ago* is already showing signs of wear.

Now, imagine the inflection and timing of your supervisor's oral statement. She probably stressed the main clause: "This table is already showing signs of wear." On the other hand, you can imagine that her voice lowered in pitch and volume when she interjected the italicized clause: "which we just purchased a year ago." You can imagine her pausing after "table" and "ago," lending a parenthetic quality to the information between the pauses.

The italicized clause is parenthetic because it is not needed to identify the subject, "this table." Your supervisor was clearly referring to objects in the room, and those objects include only one table. She has directed your attention to that unique object simply by referring to "this table." Her statement about the firm's recently purchasing the table helps to reinforce her point about the table's rapid deterioration, but that statement is not needed to identify the table and distinguish it from all others within the range of your perception. Thus, you could naturally treat the italicized clause as an "aside," an interruption of the main clause. The clause provides interesting additional information, but the rest of the sentence would coherently stand alone without it. The italicized clause is "nondefining" because it is not necessary to define the subject. Stated otherwise, it is "nonrestrictive" because it is not necessary to restrict the universe of tables to the conference table in this meeting room; the phrase "this table" had already accomplished that task.

In an oral statement, you would normally pause before and after such a nonrestrictive clause. In a written statement, you achieve the same effect by setting the clause apart with commas:

This table, which we just purchased a year ago, is already showing signs of wear.

Imagine now that your conversation turns to the eight chairs surrounding the conference table. You would undoubtedly experience confusion if your supervisor made the following statement without pointing to a particular chair:

The chair has several small holes in its upholstery.

The subject "the chair" is not sufficiently precise to identify the one chair among eight to which your supervisor is referring. She could avoid the confusion by adding a clause that directs your attention to a single chair. Each of the following revisions contains such a clause:

The chair next to the potted cactus has several small holes in its upholstery.
The chair which sits next to the potted cactus has several small holes in its upholstery.
The chair that sits next to the potted cactus has several small holes in its upholstery.

Regardless of which version your supervisor spoke, she did not pause before the italicized passage; instead, she plowed straight through the sentence at least until she had singled out one of the chairs. The italicized information is not parenthetic; rather than interrupting the main clause, it is a direct continuation of the subject, necessary to identify or to define the chair to which she is referring. In that sense, it is a "defining" or "restrictive" clause because it restricts the universe of eight chairs in the room to the single chair to which your supervisor intends to refer. Just as such a clause would not inspire a pause in an oral statement, it would not require commas in a written statement.

So far, your reaction to these examples is probably a resounding "Who cares?" The following sample sentences, however, illustrate that the distinction between a restrictive and a nonrestrictive clause occasionally materially affects the content of a sentence in legal writing. The construction of the first sample sentence suggests that all reckless driving constitutes a felony and that a new statute therefore applies to all reckless driving:

The new statute mandates a jail term only for reckless driving, which constitutes a felony violation of the vehicle code.

The meaning of this sentence is conveyed partly by the comma, which suggests to the reader that the sentence would be perfectly sensible if it ended at "reckless driving" and that the clause following the comma simply adds additional, parenthetic information. The clause following the comma is nonrestrictive, or nondefining, because it does not purport to identify a subset of the general category of things within the term "reckless driving."

Even without any changes in wording, the second sample sentence suggests by the absence of a comma that only some forms of reckless driving rise to the level of a felony and that the statute applies only to those forms of reckless driving:

The new statute mandates a jail term only for reckless driving which constitutes a felony violation of the vehicle code.

The absence of a comma invites the reader to rush to the end of the sentence to discover what kind of reckless driving is covered, suggesting that the sentence could not sensibly stop at the term "reckless driving." In this sentence, the clause following "reckless driving" is restrictive, or defining, because it identifies a subset of the things in the general category of reckless driving.

b. The Choice between "That" and "Which"

Both sentences, however, use the relative pronoun "which" to introduce the restrictive or nonrestrictive clauses, leaving the burden of conveying the restrictive or nonrestrictive nature of the clause to the presence or absence of a comma. To partially relieve the comma of that burden, careful writers—or at least the purists among them—use the relative pronoun "that" in a restrictive clause to emphasize the restrictive nature of the clause and to more clearly distinguish it from a nonrestrictive clause:

The new statute mandates a jail term only for reckless driving that constitutes a felony violation of the vehicle code.

Similarly, in the earlier example of the chair with the holes in its upholstery, a sentence that uses a relative pronoun should use "that" rather than "which":

The chair that sits next to the potted cactus has several small holes in its upholstery.

Because many writers do not have a natural ear for the purist's use of "that," they tend to use "which" in both restrictive and nonrestrictive clauses. In fact, this practice is so widespread that some might characterize it as the popular approach. Nonetheless, many supervising attorneys will go "which hunting" when reviewing the work of associates.

In most cases, any ambiguity or uncertainty resulting from using "which" in a restrictive clause will be insignificant. For example, the difference in meaning between the following two sentences is insignificant to the analysis that the writer intends to convey:

The court applied a fairness test, which inquires whether a transaction was consummated through fair dealing and at a fair price.

The court applied a fairness test that inquires whether a transaction was consummated through fair dealing and at a fair price.

Because the sentence refers to only one of many possible formulations of a test that incorporates considerations of fairness, the final clause probably should be restrictive, as in the second example. However, because emphasis of the restrictive nature of the clause is not necessary for analytic clarity, the following popular choice of words would be inoffensive:

The court applied a fairness test which inquires whether a transaction was consummated through fair dealing and at a fair price.

Nonetheless, at least when the choice of relative pronouns will affect clarity, you should follow the example of the Supreme Court, which clearly distinguished between restrictive and nonrestrictive clauses in the following excerpt from an opinion:

Although the Court of Appeals' construction of the Act and of Regulation Z is shared by three of the four other Courts of Appeals *that* have ruled on the question, this view, *which* is essentially a claim that the plain language of the statute and the regulation requires the result reached by the court below, has recently been challenged on several fronts.[6]

c. Procedural Labels

You may also raise questions about restrictive and nonrestrictive clauses when you join procedural labels, such as "plaintiff," to the names of parties to litigation. In that context, you need not worry about a choice between "that" and "which," but you may pause before choosing between the insertion or omission of a comma.

For example, if Robert Jones is one of three plaintiffs in an action, then a phrase that uses his name to define "plaintiff" is restrictive and should omit any comma:

Plaintiff Robert Jones moves for summary judgment . . .

6. Anderson Bros. Ford v. Valencia, 452 U.S. 205, 211-12 (1981) (emphasis added).

In this example, "Robert Jones" restricts the universe of "plaintiffs" to one of the three plaintiffs in the litigation.

In contrast, if Jones is the only plaintiff, you could treat a similar reference as nonrestrictive and include commas:

Plaintiff, Robert Jones, moves for summary judgment . . .

In this example, "Robert Jones" arguably supplies parenthetic information about a party who is already identified by the label "Plaintiff."

Alternatively, even if Jones is the only plaintiff, you could reasonably eliminate the commas by characterizing "Plaintiff" as a title that is joined with a name, as in "Dr. Long" or "Secretary-Treasurer Richard King":

Plaintiff Robert Jones . . .

This is probably the least distracting stylistic option. However, you cannot adopt this usage of "plaintiff" as a title if you treat "plaintiff" as a common noun by preceding it with an article, such as "the." In that case, you must treat the party's name as a nonrestrictive modifier if he is the only plaintiff:

The plaintiff, Robert Jones, moves for summary judgment against the defendant, Cecelia Ynez . . .

Exercise 13-5

Relative Pronouns and Wealthy Relatives

Compare the following alternative provisions of a will:

I leave to my daughter my bank account that is in Western Savings.
I leave to my daughter my bank account, which is in Western Savings.

After drafting the will, but before death, the testator closed the bank account at Western Savings and used the funds from that account to open a new one at First Interstate Bank.[7] Which provision would most likely bequeath the First Interstate Bank account to the daughter?

---

7. The source of this problem is Rebecca W. Berch, *Words That/Which Cause Problems in Legal Writing*, 25 Ariz. Bar Briefs No. 9 (1987).

C. Precision

1. CAREFUL EXPRESSION OF ANALYSIS

Once you clearly understand the idea that you want to communicate, you must select the words and phrases that precisely convey your intended meaning. As suggested in Chapter 1, achieving precision in writing may require you to subordinate other potential goals, such as entertaining your reader. For example, many writers believe that they will bore their readers if they repeatedly use a single word or phrase to refer to the same idea throughout a passage. They often address this concern by engaging in "elegant variation": varying the word or phrase used to refer to the same idea. However, any entertainment value of the variation will fail to justify the confusion that typically results.

For example, perhaps to elegantly vary their phrasing, many legal writers intermittently use "while" as a synonym for "although," and they use "when" or "where" as a synonym for "if." The following construction is common:

While the court declined to decide the issue of retroactivity in *Fleming*, its dictum in subsequent cases suggests that it has always assumed that the *Fleming* principle applies retroactively.

The primary meaning of "while" in this syntax is duration or simultaneity. But, of course, the writer does not mean that the court offered dictum in subsequent cases *at the same time* that it declined to decide the issue in a previous case. "Although" would more precisely convey the contrast or tension between the court's actions. In the context of the entire sentence, the less precise version does not cause serious confusion or inconvenience. By displaying care with details, however, the more precise wording strengthens the credibility of the writer on more substantive matters.

More substantial risks of confusion arise in the use of synonyms for "because." "Since" is particularly popular:

Since the employer invited the applicant to read the policy manual at the initial interview, the manual became part of their bargain.

Let's assume that the writer meant to say that the manual became part of the bargain *because* the employer introduced the manual into the negotiations, not simply that the manual became part of the bargain sometime after the initial interview. Although the multiple dictionary definitions of "since" typically include "because," the primary dictionary definition relates to time frame or sequence of events:

> From then till now; in the interval; before this; before now; ago; after that time.—*prep.* Continuously from the time of; as, *since* yesterday; subsequent to; after.—*conj.* In the interval after the time when, as: I have been ill twice

since I saw you last. Without interruption, from the time when; as, *since* we saw you last; because; seeing that; inasmuch as.[8]

Therefore, most readers fail to recognize "since" as a signal for a causal relationship when they first encounter it in a sentence such as the example above. Although the reader may later discover the intended meaning of "since" from context, that process may produce momentary hesitation or even regression in reading. The ambiguity is most serious when the sentence otherwise refers to a time frame:

Since Rabin breached the contract on January 1, 1985, the three-year limitations period expired before Smith filed suit on January 10, 1988.

This sentence will appear to some readers to make the marginally useful point that the limitations period expired after the breach of contract as well as before the filing of suit. The word "because" in place of "since" would more clearly convey the intended causal relationship: The breach of contract triggered the commencement of the running of the limitations period; therefore, the period expired before suit was filed.

You create an even greater risk of confusion if you replace "because" with "as," because causation is not a readily recognized connotation of "as":

Plaintiff is entitled to the equitable remedy of injunctive relief as his legal remedy is inadequate.

One popular dictionary does not even clearly list "because" as a definition for "as"; the closest it comes is listing "since" as a definition of "as" in its conjunctive form.[9] As explained above, even this reference to "since" is ambiguous.

In each of these three examples, "because" would more precisely and unambiguously convey the writer's intended meaning of causal relationship, because it has no other meaning.[10] Moreover, "because" is self-descriptive: The root word "cause" within it suggests its meaning.

2. BEYOND DOGMA

Popular use of synonyms for "because" illustrates the range of considerations that often influence nuances in writing style. Despite the precision that "because" permits, many writers depart from it in the interests of elegant variation, or they reject it altogether because they think that it has an unsophisticated ring to it. However, few readers demand variation or stimulation from every word in a sentence. As with many other words—such as "the,"

8. NEW WEBSTER'S DICTIONARY 902 (encyclopedic ed. 1981).
9. *Id.* at 58.
10. *See id.* at 86.

"with," and "a"—"because" precisely and unobtrusively performs its function without diverting the reader's attention from more substantively important parts of the sentence. Indeed, the text of this section has used each of those words repeatedly, presumably without offending the average reader.

The most interesting reason that writers give for substituting "since" or "as" for "because" is their recollection of an admonition in grade school never to begin a sentence with "because." Of course, if beginning a sentence with "because" offended some principle of syntax or other consideration of composition, replacing it at the beginning of the sentence with a synonym, and a poor one at that, would not cure the defect. In fact, however, some grade school teachers may have invented or repeated such a rule in reaction to students' early tendencies to write incomplete sentences, such as: "Because I missed the bus." Those teachers probably should have explained the requisite components of a complete sentence rather than place undeserved blame on the word "because."

One defense of "as" and "since" as expressions of causal relationship has greater merit. Some writers believe that "as" and "since" are not synonymous with "because" in that context but express slightly different shades of causation. Those writers reasonably use "because" to refer to a direct causal relationship and "since" or "as" to refer to a more attenuated relationship.[11] A style that carefully recognizes such a distinction arguably enhances precision. Unfortunately, few writers use "since" or "as" to connote a causal relationship in such a principled manner. Moreover, to a greater extent than in literary writing, legal writing tends to describe causal relationships that are sufficiently direct to justify use of "because" in place of the softer "since" or "as."

As with Chapter 1's discussion of the proper placement of "however" in a sentence, this discussion illustrates once again the importance of avoiding unthinking adherence to inflexible and arbitrary rules of composition, such as a "rule" against starting a sentence with "because." If you understand the reasoning supporting a convention of writing style, you will be better equipped to evaluate that convention. You may then opt to apply the convention universally, reject it completely, or apply it selectively to those situations in which application furthers the reasoning.

II. CONCISE WRITING

When you concisely express clear and persuasive ideas in vivid, active, and precise prose, you can strive to convey the ideas with maximum efficiency and effect, as described by a character in Tom Stoppard's play, *The Real Thing*:

---

11. *See generally* Strunk & White, supra note 5, at 23-24 ("because" presented as concise replacement for the verbose phrase "the reason why is that," and "since" presented as primary replacement for "owing to the fact that"); E. B. White, THE SECOND TREE FROM THE CORNER 17 (1984) ("Parnell was not a playmate of mine, as he was a few years older. . . .").

> *Henry:*   . . . This thing here, which looks like a wooden club, is actually
> several pieces of particular wood cunningly put together in a
> certain way so that the whole thing is sprung, like a dance floor.
> It's for hitting cricket balls with. If you get it right, the cricket
> ball will travel two hundred yards in four seconds, and all you've
> done is give it a knock like knocking the top off a bottle of stout,
> and it makes a noise like a trout taking a fly . . . (*He clucks his
> tongue to make the noise.*) What we're trying to do is to write
> cricket bats, so that when we throw up an idea and give it a little
> knock, it might . . . *travel.* . . .[12]

A legal document that effectively conveys its message in 10 pages is more
like Henry's cricket bat than one that rambles on for 20 pages to convey
the same message.

Still, you must not achieve brevity in your writing by omitting important
ideas or sacrificing clarity of expression. You should strive first to express all
important ideas in sufficient detail to successfully communicate or persuade.
With that accomplished, you can streamline your writing by omitting extra-
neous ideas and expressing the important ones efficiently. Overworked supervisors and judges will thank you for it, as reflected in one state appellate
judge's advice:

> First and foremost, more is not always better. . . .
> • • • •
> Conversely, avoid being overly "brief and concise." . . .
> In effect, you are being asked to strike a balance between too much
> and too little. Including needless matter poses the risk of distracting the
> court while being conclusory may result in the court holding the argument
> waived. Exercise your judgment with appropriate regard for the possible
> consequences when striking the balance.[13]

When you are satisfied that you have expressed all critical points and
you have turned to the task of omitting needless matter, you should control
the length of your document through content, form, and style. You can
control content primarily through the scope and depth of analysis. You
can achieve concise form and style through efficient organization, sentence
structure, and phrasing.

A. Content: Scope and Depth of Analysis

"Scope of analysis" refers to the range of issues or topics that you address
in your legal document. "Depth of analysis" refers to the level of detail with
which you address a topic.

1. SCOPE OF ANALYSIS

The range of ideas that you address in your document can dramatically affect
the document's length. In analyzing a problem, you need not develop

---

12. Tom Stoppard, THE REAL THING 51 (1984).
13. Brian Quinn, *Dispelling Misconception*, 62 Tex. B.J. 890, 891 (1999).

every theory that you have encountered in the library. Instead, you can (1) thoroughly discuss the most important and clearly relevant topics, (2) exclude distracting tangents that are unlikely to affect the outcome of the dispute, and (3) determine whether to discuss topics between the two extremes, perhaps in less detail than would be appropriate for a mainstream theory.

As discussed more fully in Section III.B of Chapter 6, you may find that you tend to apply different scopes of analysis to different kinds of documents. The scope of analysis ordinarily can be quite broad in your examination answers, because most of your professors will specifically test your ability to identify a wide range of issues. The scope of analysis should be much narrower in a brief, because briefs generally are most persuasive if they focus only on the strongest available arguments. The scope of analysis in a typical office memorandum is somewhere between the scope of analysis of an examination and that of a brief. An office memorandum should not fail to at least briefly discuss a theory or approach that may ultimately be helpful. On the other hand, to a greater extent than an examination answer, an office memorandum should focus on thorough development of the most helpful theories rather than on identification of every conceivable approach.

2. DEPTH OF ANALYSIS

By properly balancing varying depths of analysis in the discussion or argument section of your memorandum or brief, you can make the document more concise and readable. For convenience, this book will use the terms "light analysis" and "in-depth analysis" to refer to the opposite extremes on the spectrum. You engage in light analysis when you simply state a proposition of law and cite to supporting authority. You engage in in-depth analysis when you analyze legal authority more thoroughly, such as by discussing the facts, holding, and reasoning of case law. You may also control the depth of analysis by choosing between (1) expressing a full deductive argument and (2) expressing an incomplete syllogism, leaving a premise of your deductive argument implicit.

a. Depth of Analysis of Legal Authority

Sample Memorandum 1 near the end of Chapter 11 provides an example of balance between light analysis and in-depth analysis of authority from the fictitious state of Calzona. The second paragraph of the discussion section briefly outlines fundamental principles, which provide helpful background information and which almost certainly will not be disputed by the parties. For this purpose, the author of the memorandum has used light analysis by simply stating propositions of law and citing to supporting authority:

An enforceable contract requires a bargained-for exchange in which a promisor exchanges his own promise for a return promise or performance. *Smith v. Newman*, 161 Calz. 443, 447, 667 P.2d 81, 84 (1984). The requirement of an exchange is not satisfied if one party gives only an illusory promise, which does not commit the promisor to any future performance. *Atco Corp. v. Johnson*, 155 Calz. 1211, 627 P.2d 781 (1980).

However, the memorandum also raises the more difficult issue of whether a particular promise made by a lender was illusory, an issue the parties obviously dispute. An adequate discussion of that issue requires more thorough analysis of case law to determine which precedent is more nearly analogous to the facts of the current dispute. Such in-depth analysis explores the facts, holding, and reasoning of each significant case:

In *Atco Corp.*, the manager of an automobile repair shop promised to forbear "until I want the money" from asserting a claim against the owner of an automobile for $900 in repairs; in exchange, a friend of the owner promised to act as guarantor of the owner's obligation. *Id.* at 1212, 627 P.2d at 782. The word "want" stated no legal commitment, because it permitted the manager at his own discretion to refuse to perform any forbearance at all. Because the manager incurred no obligation, the guarantor's promise was gratuitous and unenforceable. *See id.* at 1213-14, 627 P.2d at 782-84.	**In-depth analysis of *Atco***
On the other hand, even if a promise leaves open the possibility that the promisor will escape obligation, the promise is valid if the promisor does not have complete control over the events on which the promisor's obligation is conditioned. *See Bonnie v. DeLaney*, 158 Calz. 212, 645 P.2d 887 (1982). In *Bonnie*, an agreement for the sale of a house provided that the buyer could cancel the agreement if the buyer "cannot qualify for a 30-year mortgage loan for 90% of the sales price" with any of several banks listed in the agreement. *Id.* at 213, 645 P.2d at 888. In enforcing the agreement against the seller, the court distinguished *Atco Corp.* on the ground that the word "cannot" referred to the buyer's *ability* to obtain a loan rather than to his *desire*. Because his ability to obtain a loan was partly controlled by events and decisions outside his control, the promises in the sale agreement were nonillusory and binding. *See id.* at 214-15, 645 P.2d at 889-91.	**In-depth analysis of *Bonnie***

The light analysis in the first sample paragraph in this subsection quickly establishes noncontroversial points without weighing the reader down with unnecessary detail. The more detailed analysis in the second and third sample paragraphs provides the reader with a fuller understanding of a specific legal doctrine, the illusory promise, thus creating a solid legal foundation for the fact analysis that will follow.

Sample Memorandum 2 near the end of Chapter 11 also displays a combination of light and in-depth analyses. Section IV.A of that sample memo presents an in-depth analysis of a new statute, including discussion of the statutory language, the legislative history, and the general policies reflected in other legislation and common law. In contrast, many of the settled principles of tort law explored in section IV.B of that sample memo were appropriately established with light analysis.

You must strike an effective balance between light and in-depth analyses to achieve the dual goals of clarity and conciseness. Unless the issue is extremely simple, if you use only light analysis to discuss a point in an office memorandum, you may not define the applicable legal principles with sufficient clarity to permit thoughtful fact analysis. Moreover, if you use only light analysis to argue a disputed point of law in a brief, you probably will fail to persuade. On the other hand, if you use in-depth analysis excessively, you may cause the reader to grow weary and to lose sight of the general legal theory while wandering endlessly among individual cases.

To help strike this balance, you can use citations with parenthetic explanations as a middle ground between light and in-depth analyses. For example, the following passage uses parenthetic explanations to explain how the cited authorities support the proposition for which they are cited:

In other decisions, Arizona courts have assumed that the statute of frauds may be mitigated to protect a party's reliance on the promise to perform, but they have refused to apply the doctrine because the normal requirements of estoppel were not satisfied. *See, e.g., Trollope v. Koerner,* 106 Ariz. 10, 17, 18, 470 P.2d 91, 98-99 (1970) (insufficient reliance); *Mac Enters. v. Del E. Webb Dev. Co.,* 132 Ariz. 331, 336, 645 P.2d 1245, 1250 (Ct. App. 1982) (no promise).

The brief reference to facts or holdings in the parentheses following the citations provides helpful information for the reader. A full paragraph of in-depth analysis of each case, on the other hand, would simply distract from the fuller discussion of the cases that are more nearly on point.

Another example uses a parenthetic explanation to state the holding of nonbinding case law from another jurisdiction:

The Arizona Statute of Frauds applies to "an agreement which is not to be performed within one year from the making thereof." Ariz. Rev. Stat. Ann. § 44-101(5) (West 1994) (copy of full text attached). The statute probably applies to any employment contract with a fixed term that exceeds one year without qualification. *See, e.g., Waddell v. White,* 51 Ariz. 526, 539-40, 78 P.2d 490, 495-96 (1938). *But cf. Doyle v. Dixon,* 97 Mass. 208 (1867) (holding that death of promisor could result in early full performance of promise not to compete for five years). Williams and Kramer agreed that their employment contract would remain in effect unconditionally for two years; therefore, it falls within the statute.

In this example, the author of an office memorandum cited *Doyle* to help define the limits of the proposition for which *Waddell* is cited as affirmative support. *Doyle* does not warrant a full paragraph of in-depth analysis because it is a century-old case that interprets a different state's statute of frauds in a different factual context. The parenthetic explanation, however, takes up little space and helpfully warns of a possible limitation or counterargument to the main proposition.

b. Incomplete Syllogisms

So far, this section has discussed depth of analysis of legal principles. You may apply the same considerations to the complete deductive syllogism of major premise, minor premise, and conclusion. Normally, a memorandum or brief presents even a simple legal argument in a full syllogism with a discussion of the applicable legal rule, an application of the rule to the facts, and a conclusion:

Under the Uniform Commercial Code (UCC), the term "merchant" includes any person who "deals in goods of the kind." U.C.C. § 2-104(1) (2000). Wilson deals in used cars because he regularly buys and sells used cars as an adjunct to his car rental business. Therefore, he is a merchant of used cars under the UCC.

Alternatively, particularly if the argument is minor or tangential, you can present it in an incomplete syllogism, leaving the legal rule implicit:

Wilson is a "merchant" of used cars under the UCC because he regularly buys and sells used cars as an adjunct to his car rental business. *See* U.C.C. § 2-104(1) (2000).

A more detailed statement could mention the statutory definition, still without tying it directly to the statutory term "merchant":

Wilson is a "merchant" of used cars under the UCC because he regularly buys and sells used cars as an adjunct to his car rental business and thus "deals in goods of the kind." *See* U.C.C. § 2-104(1) (2000).

In each of these examples of incomplete syllogisms, the single textual sentence states a conclusion and the facts supporting it. The legal rule that forms the major premise is implicit or incomplete; the reader assumes that the cited authority supplies an abstract rule that permits the conclusion to follow from the facts. In some cases, a brief parenthetic explanation after the citation helps to define the abstract legal rule and to show how the citation supports the fact analysis. With or without such an explanation, you can use this technique to make a minor point without disrupting the flow of the main analysis or distracting the reader's attention from more important discussions of authority.

B. Form: Efficient Organization, Sentence Structure, and Phrasing

1. ORGANIZATION AND REPETITION

By applying the principles of organization discussed in Chapter 12, you can write more concisely as well as more clearly. With good organization, you can eliminate unnecessary repetition and present ideas efficiently by building each subsection on the foundations laid in the previous ones.

You need not adopt an organizational framework that eliminates all repetition. Indeed, typical formats for office memoranda and briefs contemplate a form of repetition. Using an office memorandum format recommended in Chapter 11, for example, you can

1. introduce your analysis in a statement of the issues and in brief answers at the beginning of the memorandum,
2. explore your analysis fully in the discussion, and
3. summarize your analysis and recommendations in a final conclusion.

In the same memorandum, you would

1. state all the relevant facts near the beginning of the memorandum and
2. analyze the facts relating to each issue in each corresponding section of the discussion.

This overlap in the elements of a legal document is not wasteful, particularly if you recognize the distinct purposes of the elements.

Nonetheless, needless repetition within such a framework may add pages without adding clarity. Good organization on all levels should minimize this problem.

2. SENTENCE STRUCTURE AND PHRASING

You can often trace verbosity within a sentence to unnecessary repetition, loose verb structure, and expression of implicit information. In such sentences, the words expressing useful ideas are lost among words that convey marginally useful ideas or that simply connect substantive ideas to one another.[14] In editing surplus words from your writing, however, you must not shave your writing so close that you sacrifice clarity.

a. Repetition

As discussed in the previous section, some repetition is built into the general format of a legal document. Moreover, even at the level of words and phrases, carefully planned repetition may be justified on rare occasions as a guide to complex sentence structure or as a means of gaining unusual emphasis:

Jack Bailey has declared his guilt with his own actions. He declared his guilt when he fled the murder scene on the arrival of neighbors; he declared his guilt when he later tried to conceal the murder weapon; and he declared his guilt at trial by offering incredible and inconsistent testimony.

---

14. One author recommends that writers maximize the ratio of "working words" to "glue words" in a sentence. *See* Wydick, *supra* note 2, at 9-24.

However, needless repetition of words or phrases serves only to add words that contribute nothing to the substance of a sentence. Even worse, it may cause the reader to pause and wonder whether the repetitive words are intended to convey slightly different ideas:

Section 24 of the lease is null, void, invalid, completely unenforceable, and of no legal force or effect whatsoever.

With a much shorter, cleaner sentence employing only one of the adjectives, you can precisely convey the intended meaning:

Section 24 of the lease is void.

On the other hand, even closely related terms are not repetitive if they convey meanings that are different in a way that is significant to the analysis. For example, state and federal statutes prohibit various kinds of discrimination based on "race, color, or national origin." Although the classes encompassed by these terms may overlap, they are not identical. Thus, an employer who discriminates against a dark-skinned African American in favor of a light-skinned African American arguably discriminates on the basis of color, even though not necessarily on the basis of race or national origin.[15]

b. Verb Structure

You will often add extra words to your sentences when you transform verbs into nouns or use verbs in the passive voice. For example, the author of the following clause added unnecessary bulk to his writing by transforming the verb "objected" into the noun "objection," and substituting "presented" as the verb:

Defense counsel presented an objection to the testimony.

You add further unnecessary bulk by using the passive voice, adding the words "was" and "by":

An objection to the testimony was presented by defense counsel.

If you employ the verb "objected" to express the action in active voice, you eliminate surplus words and lead the reader more directly to the main point:

Defense counsel objected to the testimony.

15. *See generally* Walker v. Secretary of Treasury, I.R.S., 713 F. supp. 403 (N.D. Ga. 1989).

c. Implicit Information

Legal writers frequently express implicit information by referring to procedure when defining a substantive legal principle:

If a party proves that a contract requires a performance that would violate a criminal statute, the court will strike down the contract as illegal and unenforceable.

Unless you really intend to emphasize burdens of proof and court procedures, you can convey all the necessary information in fewer words by focusing exclusively on substance:

A contract is illegal and unenforceable if performance of its obligations would violate a criminal statute.

---

d. Tension between Clarity and Conciseness

In your quest to eliminate surplus words, you should remain sensitive to the tension between clarity and conciseness, taking care to retain words and phrases that communicate important information. For example, the following sentences reflect each kind of verbosity cited at the beginning of this section:

Robert Jones, who is the plaintiff, brought this action against Mary Smith, the defendant. In this action, Jones filed a complaint that alleges that Smith committed a breach of the contract of employment between Smith and Jones.

You can combine these sentences into a single, much more concise sentence. At the margin, however, further revisions for conciseness may sacrifice important information, depending on your intended connotation and emphasis.

An initial revision reduces the number of words from 37 to 17, arguably without sacrificing clarity on any level:

Plaintiff Robert Jones brought this action against Defendant Mary Smith, alleging that Smith breached their employment contract.

Among other things, this revision eliminates the repetition of "this action," recognizes that the filing of a complaint is implicit in other phrases, uses "breached" as a direct verb, and replaces wordy clauses and phrases such as "who is the plaintiff" and "between Smith and Jones" with single but equally precise words.

By treating "Plaintiff" and "Defendant" as implicit, and by replacing "brought this action" with "sued," you can trim another five words from the sentence:

Robert Jones sued Mary Smith, alleging that Smith breached their employment contract.

This revision, however, may achieve conciseness at the expense of other considerations of style. To many readers, "sued" carries the negative connotation of harassing litigation; therefore, counsel for Jones might prefer the softer, though less concise, phrase "brought this action." Also, if you wish to refer to the parties subsequently only as "Plaintiff" and "Defendant" or only as "Jones" and "Smith," you may prefer to emphasize the relationship of each party's name with his or her procedural title by initially using the full phrases "Plaintiff Robert Jones," and "Defendant Mary Smith."

If you do not object to the last revision above, you could trim two more words from the sentence and achieve a more direct flow by eliminating the reference to "alleging":

Robert Jones sued Mary Smith for breaching their employment contract.

Sticklers for precision, however, might argue that you should use the preposition "for" to introduce a description of the requested relief rather than the ground for liability.

To summarize, revisions for conciseness are matters of judgment that require sensitivity to considerations of emphasis, precision, connotation, and other elements of clarity.

Exercise 13-6

Rewrite the following sentence to make it more direct and concise.

> The Federal Rules of Civil Procedure, Rule 26(c), provides that the issuance of protective orders to the effect that certain matters ought not to be inquired into in the course of discovery is within the authorization of the court.

III. REVIEW AND REVISION

To polish your writing, you must critically review and revise early drafts. The need for revision is particularly evident in first drafts dictated into a tape recorder. Moreover, you may need to revise successive drafts several times to produce the best possible final document.

To critically review and revise your own writing, you must approach writing analytically rather than purely intuitively: You must become suffi-ciently familiar with style problems that you can spot them in your own writing, even when the familiarity of your own prose tends to make you comfortable. You can best develop these editing skills by studying writing style in books or workshops, by reviewing and critiquing your own work and that of others, and by asking others to review and critique your writing.

Unfortunately, time pressures and limits on the client's resources will sometimes compel you to produce a final draft after only one or two opportu-nities for revision. The minimally acceptable level of review and revision is easily stated: At the very least, you must proofread your first draft and make necessary changes, particularly if you have dictated the draft. Every judge has a horror story about an atrociously written brief, one that obviously was dictated and never proofread. No limitation on time or resources justifies such shoddy work.

The appropriate level of review and revision beyond the minimum is a matter of priorities and economics. A client with ample resources and with a great deal at stake in an important pretrial motion or appeal might expect its legal counsel to spare no expense in writing the best possible brief. You and your colleagues undoubtedly would begin work on the brief as early as possible, subject it to particularly critical review, and polish it through many drafts.

In all but unusual cases, however, you would waste your client's money by spending as much time polishing a preliminary office memorandum or a letter to the client. Such a document should be clear, complete, and concise, but limits on resources may preclude more than one or two rewrites. Moreover, even if you ordinarily avoid procrastination, you will occasionally be stuck with an emergency "rush job" that leaves you little time for revision.

Consequently, you should strive to produce the best possible written product on the first draft. You can do this by learning to avoid style problems common to your writing and by devoting appropriate attention to the prewriting stage.

Ironically, to develop the ability to avoid common style problems on the first draft, you must identify and analyze your writing habits by initially devoting extra time and attention to multiple drafts. Perhaps with the aid of a colleague or a writing manual, you will gradually become sufficiently conscious of your writing problems and their solutions that you can begin to avoid those problems on first or second drafts, reducing the need for substantial editing.

For example, one summer associate in a major law firm learned from a writing consultant that he tended to overuse the passive, abstract verb form "there is." He resolved to use his word processing program to highlight this and related phrases in his first drafts, to revise the highlighted passages on second drafts, and eventually to become sufficiently sensitive to the problem to avoid it on first drafts.

You can further minimize the need for redrafting, and thus save time in the long run, by carefully formulating and organizing your analysis before beginning to write. You should prepare an outline of your document and consider discussing the outline with your supervising attorney or a peer. Because most people are less articulate when speaking than when writing, a careful outline is particularly important if you intend to dictate your first draft. Once satisfied with the broad outlines of your analysis, you can devote greater attention to the details when you begin writing or dictating.

One final note of caution: Word processing provides attorneys with the luxury of blocking and moving passages of text from one computer file to another, such as from a contract for one client to a similar contract for another client. Although this process can reduce the time needed to prepare the initial draft of the second document, it also underscores the need for careful proofreading and revision. The passage in the first document may be helpful as a starting point, but it may not be perfectly tailored to the transaction in the second document. Moreover, the imperfection may be sufficiently subtle to require special diligence in evaluating and revising initial drafts of the second document.

IV. SUMMARY

Your two most important goals in legal writing style are clarity and conciseness. These two goals ordinarily are consistent and complementary. When they conflict, give priority to clarity. More specifically:

To write clearly,

1. use simple, plain English unless a legal term of art will inform more than distract;
2. flexibly use effective sentence structure and punctuation, with adequate closure and guides to structure;
3. use concrete verbs in the active voice, unless passive construction serves a specific purpose;
4. distinguish between restrictive and nonrestrictive clauses when necessary for clarity; and
5. select the word or phrase that precisely conveys your meaning.

To write concisely,

1. maintain reasonable limitations on scope and depth of analysis; and
2. avoid verbosity by adopting efficient organization, sentence structure, and phrasing.

To polish your writing,

1. revise early drafts; and
2. create the best possible product on first draft.

Finally, avoid applying conventions of composition mechanically. Instead, adopt an approach to writing that is analogous to legal method: Strive to understand the purposes and policies of conventions of composition, and apply those conventions flexibly to satisfy the purposes and policies.

Chapter 14

Presenting, Quoting, and Citing to Authority

When you assert your analysis or interpretation of the law in a memorandum or a brief, you must support your assertions with legal authority, as illustrated in various examples in previous chapters. One author refers to the process as one of providing "proof and explanation that the rule exists and that you have stated it accurately."[1] As explored in Section II.A.2 of Chapter 13, the manner in which you support your assertions of a legal rule will depend on the depth of analysis that is appropriate to the issue. For example, you might safely support a simple, noncontroversial assertion of law with a single citation to authority, while a less settled assertion might warrant several pages of analysis and synthesis of multiple authorities.

This chapter examines three elements of effective legal writing that you should keep in mind when you support your assertions of law with legal authority: (1) citing to authority in proper form, (2) presenting the law and citations effectively, and (3) quoting from legal authority effectively and sparingly. As with Chapter 13's discussion of legal writing style, this chapter occasionally refers to special techniques of advocacy, but it primarily addresses

---

1. Richard K. Neumann, Jr., LEGAL REASONING AND LEGAL WRITING 95 (4th ed. 2001).

the balanced, nearly neutral analysis that is appropriate for an office memorandum. Techniques of advocacy are explored in greater detail in Parts VI-VIII.

I. CITATION FORM

You should cite to authority in a manner that clearly and concisely identifies the source of the authority and that helps the reader find the authority in a library. These goals are met, sometimes in different ways, by two popular guides to citation form: THE BLUEBOOK: A UNIFORM SYSTEM OF CITATION,[2] a citation manual published and distributed by the Harvard Law Review Association, and the ALWD CITATION MANUAL,[3] authored by the Association of Legal Writing Directors and Darby Dickerson. The BLUEBOOK has long been the "bible" of citation style and probably will remain the standard mandated by some local court rules and journals for several years to come. The ALWD CITATION MANUAL, however, may be destined to overtake the BLUEBOOK as the next citation manual of choice for the simple reason that legal writing faculty drafted it with the specific goal of responding to perceived deficiencies or unnecessary complexities of the BLUEBOOK.

Because this textbook was written and first published before the ALWD CITATION MANUAL was conceived, its citations in text and footnotes are set forth in BLUEBOOK form, except when it reproduces without substantial editing a brief or judicial opinion that uses a different citation form, or when the author consciously departs from BLUEBOOK format for reasons of personal taste, or when this section provides contrasting examples from the ALWD CITATION MANUAL.

The following subsections summarize a few of the more important citation rules of both the ALWD CITATION MANUAL and the seventeenth edition of the BLUEBOOK. You should view the summaries below as only

---

2. THE BLUEBOOK: A UNIFORM SYSTEM OF CITATION (Columbia Law Review Ass'n et al. eds., 17th ed. 2000) [hereinafter, "BLUEBOOK"].

3. Association of Legal Writing Directors & Darby Dickerson, ALWD CITATION MANUAL (Aspen L. & Bus. 2000). The preceding citation is in the form required by the cited work. *Id.* at 8. The BLUEBOOK, on the other hand, requires typeface of large and small capitals for the book's author and title when cited in a footnote of a treatise such as this one, and it omits reference to the publisher as in the following: ASS'N OF LEGAL WRITING DIRECTORS & DARBY DICKERSON, ALWD CITATION MANUAL (2000) [hereinafter, "ALWD CITATION MANUAL"]. Although this author applauds the ALWD's format for citing to books, further references to the BLUEBOOK and the ALWD CITATION MANUAL generally will be in BLUEBOOK form to maintain consistency with the citations in the remainder of this textbook, which were composed before introduction of the ALWD CITATION MANUAL. Even when generally using BLUEBOOK form, however, this author refrains—other than in the example above—from setting the author of a book in large and small capitals. Even before the ALWD adopted a style that helped to set the author and book title apart, this author did so as a matter of personal preference by slightly altering BLUEBOOK format. The extent to which you may similarly substitute your carefully considered personal preferences for the form prescribed by a citation manual may depend on the requirements of your intended audience, whether it be a court, supervisor, or law school instructor.

an overview and not as a substitute for careful study of your assigned citation manual.

The sample citations in this section are for a legal memorandum or brief rather than a printed book or article. Accordingly, this section does not discuss or provide examples of special typefaces or citation forms that the BLUEBOOK reserves for more formal publications.

A. Constitutions, Codes, and Federal Regulations

Under either of the leading citation manuals, when citing to a specific constitutional provision that is currently in force, refer to the article or amendment number and, if appropriate, to a section number:[4]

U.S. CONST. art. III, § 1.
U.S. CONST. amend. XIV.
ARIZ. CONST. art. VI, § 1.

The first citation above refers to section 1 of article III of the United States Constitution. The second citation refers to the Fourteenth Amendment to that constitution. The third citation refers to section 1 of article VI of the Arizona Constitution.

A simple citation to a codified statute includes the volume or title number, code abbreviation, section number, and date of the code edition cited:[5]

---

42 U.S.C. § 1983 (1994).

The citation above refers to section 1983 in title 42 of the official United States Code, published in 1994. In some code systems, the title or volume immediately precedes the section number, as in the next example.

If the code cited is not published under the supervision of governmental officials, both citation manuals require identification of the publisher in the parenthetic phrase that contains the year of publication:[6]

ARIZ. REV. STAT. ANN. § 47-2207 (West 1997).

The citation above refers to section 2207 of title 47 of the Arizona Revised Statutes Annotated, the title that encompasses Arizona's commercial code. It was published by West Group in 1997. Interestingly, many practicing

---

4. ALWD CITATION MANUAL, *supra* note 3, R. 13.2, at 98; BLUEBOOK, *supra* note 2, R. 13.2, at 98. If the constitutional provision is no longer in force, you should add a parenthetic explanation stating the fact and date of repeal or suspension. ALWD CITATION MANUAL, *supra* note 3, R. 13.3, at 99 (referring to repeal or suspension); BLUEBOOK, *supra* note 2, R. 11, at 75 (referring to repeal).
5. ALWD CITATION MANUAL, *supra* note 3, R. 14.2, at 102; BLUEBOOK, *supra* note 2, R. 12, at 76.
6. ALWD CITATION MANUAL, *supra* note 3, R. 14.2(e), at 104; BLUEBOOK, *supra* note 2, R. 12.3.1(d), at 80.

attorneys in Arizona depart from the citation manuals by using the shortened abbreviation "A.R.S." when citing to the Arizona Revised Statutes Annotated.

Both the BLUEBOOK and the ALWD CITATION MANUAL mandate the year of publication as part of every full citation to a statute.[7] In practice, however, attorneys and courts frequently omit the year of publication unless it is significant or necessary to avoid confusion. When citing to the *Code of Federal Regulations* (C.F.R.), however, attorneys should more conscientiously follow the manuals' mandate to specify the date of the most recent edition because the Code is frequently revised. For example, the ALWD CITATION MANUAL cites to a federal regulation by its title number, abbreviation for the code, section number, and date of edition cited:

---

42 C.F.R. § 422.206(a) (1999).[8]

BLUEBOOK format is consistent with the citation above.[9]

B. Case Law

1. BASIC CITATION FORM

When citing to case law, specify the case name, the volume and page of the reporter, the court, and the year of decision:[10]

Bell v. United States, 349 U.S. 81 (1955).
Bundy v. Jackson, 641 F.2d 934 (D.C. Cir. 1981).
Wagenseller v. Scottsdale Mem'l Hosp., 147 Ariz. 370, 710 P.2d 1025 (1985).
Tucson Med. Ctr. v. Zoslow, 147 Ariz. 612, 712 P.2d 459 (Ct. App. Div. 2 1985).

The first case cited above is a decision of the United States Supreme Court, found at page 81 of volume 349 of the official United States Reporter.

The second is a decision of the District of Columbia Circuit of the United States Court of Appeals, found at page 934 of volume 641 of the Federal Reporter, second series.

The third is a decision of the Arizona Supreme Court, found at page 370 of volume 147 of the official Arizona Reports, and also found at page

---

7. ALWD CITATION MANUAL, *supra* note 3, R. 14.2(f), at 104; BLUEBOOK, *supra* note 2, R. 12.3.2, at 80.

8. ALWD CITATION MANUAL, *supra* note 3, R. 19.1, at 160.

9. BLUEBOOK, *supra* note 2, R. 14.2, at 97.

10. ALWD CITATION MANUAL, *supra* note 3, R. 12, at 58; BLUEBOOK, *supra* note 2, R. 10, at 55.

1025 of volume 710 of West Publishing Company's[11] unofficial regional Pacific Reporter, second series. Because a decision in the official Arizona Reports is assumed to be that of the Arizona Supreme Court unless otherwise designated, no further identification of the court is needed next to the date within the parentheses.[12]

In contrast, the fourth citation includes the notation "Ct. App." within the parentheses to identify the source of the authority as the Arizona Court of Appeals in BLUEBOOK form;[13] however, the full BLUEBOOK designation for that court, Ariz. Ct. App., is unnecessary next to the date in this example, because the reference to the official Arizona Reports in the parallel citation identifies the forum as an Arizona court. The ALWD CITATION MANUAL would further omit "Ct." on the apparent ground that "App." is a fully descriptive court designation for the Arizona Court of Appeals when the state of Arizona is identified in the abbreviation of the reporter.[14]

Reference to the department, district, or division of the authoring court, such as "Div. 2" in the fourth citation above, is required by the BLUEBOOK only if it "is of particular relevance."[15] In contrast, that information is mandated by the ALWD CITATION MANUAL for all citations to state cases "to inform readers whether the case is binding within a certain jurisdiction or to reflect the weight of the case."[16]

2. ABBREVIATIONS OF CASE NAMES

The BLUEBOOK calls for abbreviation of many words in case names in citations. For example, in the sample Arizona citations in subsection 1 above, the BLUEBOOK requires "*Memorial Hospital*" to be abbreviated to "*Mem'l Hosp.*" and "*Medical Center*" to be abbreviated to "*Med. Ctr.*"[17] The BLUE-BOOK, however, does not permit abbreviation of "United States" when used as the name of a party.[18] The ALWD CITATION MANUAL, on the other hand, calls for abbreviation of many common terms in the case name of a citation,[19] including abbreviation of "United States":[20]

Bell v. U.S., 349 U.S. 81 (1955).

11. West Publishing is related to the West Group identified in Section A above as the publisher of the 1997 edition of the ARIZONA REVISED STATUTES ANNOTATED. According to West Group's Web site, West Publishing merged with Thomson Legal Publishing in June 1996, producing West Group, which is a division of The Thomson Corporation. *About West Group*, at http://www.westgroup.com/aboutus/history.asp (last visited Nov. 10, 2001); http://www.westgroup.com/aboutus/overview.asp (last visited Nov. 10, 2001).
12. *See* ALWD CITATION MANUAL, *supra* note 3, R. 12.4(c)(3)(f), at 72; BLUEBOOK, *supra* note 2, R. 10.4(b), at 66.
13. BLUEBOOK, *supra* note 2, T.1., at 190.
14. ALWD CITATION MANUAL, *supra* note 3, app. 1, at 337.
15. BLUEBOOK, *supra* note 2, R. 10.4(b), at 66.
16. ALWD CITATION MANUAL, *supra* note 3, R. 12.6(b)(2), at 74.
17. BLUEBOOK, *supra* note 2, R. 10.2.2, at 62, T6, at 302-03.
18. *Id.* R. 10.2.2, at 62. The BLUEBOOK, however, requires abbreviation of "United States" to "U.S." when it is part of the name of the institutional author of a book. *Id.* at R. 15.1.3(c), 109.
19. ALWD CITATION MANUAL, *supra* note 3, R. 2.1(a), at 17.
20. *Id.* R. 12.2(g), at 62.

3. PARALLEL CITATIONS

Most case law appears in more than one published form. For example, the Arizona decisions cited above appear in both the official Arizona Reports and in the unofficial Pacific Reports, second series, published by West Publishing Company. The BLUEBOOK and ALWD CITATION MANUAL instruct you to use parallel citations in briefs if preferred or required by local court rules.[21] In the illustrations in section B.1. above, the Arizona decisions are set forth in parallel citations, because Arizona rules for appellate briefs provide that "[c]itations of authorities shall be to the volume and page number of the official reports and also when possible to the unofficial reporters and selected cases."[22]

In office legal memoranda, or in briefs if parallel citation is not required by local rules, however, the ALWD CITATION MANUAL calls for citation to only one source, with a West reporter normally preferred over other print reporters,[23] except in the case of decisions of the United States Supreme Court, for which citations to the official United States Reports are preferred.[24] Similarly, for office memoranda, the BLUEBOOK advises you to cite "to the relevant regional reporter" and to the official public domain citation, if one is available.[25] As a practical matter, however, if your legal memorandum may serve as the partial blueprint for a brief or other court filing that you or your supervisor will later draft, and if the local court rules will require parallel citations in the future brief, parallel citations in your office memorandum—though not required by citation manuals—may be helpful to the author of the brief.

4. SUBSEQUENT HISTORY

Your case citation should include any significant subsequent history:[26]

Scott v. Sears, Roebuck & Co., 605 F. Supp. 1047 (N.D. Ill. 1985), *aff'd*, 798 F.2d 210 (7th Cir. 1986).

In the example above, the author of a memorandum has cited to a decision of the United States District Court for the Northern District of Illinois to support a proposition. She has noted in her citation that the United States Court of Appeals for the Seventh Circuit affirmed the district court's decision. We may assume that she cited primarily to the district court's opinion because it included some language or reasoning not expressed in the appellate court's

---

21. *Id.* R. 12.4(c)(2), at 60 (only if "required by local rule"); BLUEBOOK, *supra* note 2, P.3, at 14 (cite to reporters, including parallel citations, "preferred by local rules").
22. ALWD CITATION MANUAL, *supra* note 3, app. 2, at 379 (quoting Ariz. R. Civ. App. P. 13(a)(6)).
23. *Id.* R. 12.4(a)(2), at 67, 12.4(c)(2), at 70.
24. *Id.* R. 12.4(b), at 69.
25. BLUEBOOK, *supra* note 2, R.10.3.1(b), at 62.
26. *See* ALWD CITATION MANUAL, *supra* note 3, R. 12.8, at 77; BLUEBOOK, *supra* note 2, R. 10.7, at 68.

opinion; otherwise, she could have cited directly to the appellate court's opinion to support her proposition.

According to both the BLUEBOOK and the ALWD CITATION MANUAL, a case citation need not include the denial of certiorari or other discretionary appeal from a decision that is at least two years old, unless the denial is "particularly relevant"[27] or "particularly important."[28] In practice, however, many attorneys routinely note all denials of certiorari in their citations.

5. ORDER OF AUTHORITIES WITHIN A STRING

You can string multiple citations in succession, separating them with semicolons:

Bundy v. Jackson, 641 F.2d 934 (D.C. Cir. 1981); *Barnes v. Costle*, 561 F.2d 983 (D.C. Cir. 1970); *Scott v. Sears, Roebuck & Co.*, 605 F. Supp. 1047 (N.D. Ill. 1985), *aff'd*, 798 F.2d 210 (7th Cir. 1986).

The BLUEBOOK and ALWD CITATION MANUAL list various kinds of authorities in hierarchical order, specifying the order of citation to different kinds of authority or to case law from different courts.[29] You should cite to cases decided by the same court in reverse chronological order.[30] In an often overlooked statement, however, the BLUEBOOK sensibly instructs authors to override the other rules for ordering citations if more substantive criteria support giving priority to one or more authorities.[31] An author, for example, might cite to cases in descending order of strength of authority based on the breadth of their statements of helpful rules or based on the strength of factual analogy.

6. SPECIFIC PAGE CITES

When citing to a passage within a decision, cite to the specific page or pages on which the passage appears:[32]

---

27. BLUEBOOK, *supra* note 2, R. 10.7, at 68.
28. ALWD CITATION MANUAL, *supra* note 3, R. 12.8(a)(7), at 78, & Sidebar 12.6, at 79.
29. *Id.* R. 46, at 305; BLUEBOOK, *supra* note 2, R. 1.4, at 25.
30. ALWD CITATION MANUAL, *supra* note 3, R. 46.3(h), at 307; BLUEBOOK, *supra* note 2, R. 1.4(d), at 26.
31. In the second and third sentences of R. 1.4, the BLUEBOOK states:

> If one authority is considerably more helpful or authoritative than the other authorities cited within a signal, it should precede the others.

> Absent this or some other substance-related rationale for placing one authority before another, cite authorities in the order in which they are listed below.

BLUEBOOK, *supra* note 2, R. 1.4, at 25. This textbook follows this recommendation in more than once instance.
32. ALWD CITATION MANUAL, *supra* note 3, R. 5, at 25, & 12.5, at 72; BLUEBOOK, *supra* note 2, R. 3.3(a), at 34, & 3.3(d), at 36.

Bundy v. Jackson, 641 F.2d 934, 936-37 (D.C. Cir. 1981).
Wagenseller v. Scottsdale Mem'l Hosp., 147 Ariz. 370, 380 n.5, 710 P.2d 1025, 1035 n.5 (1985).

In the first citation above, the cited passage appears on pages 936 to 937. In the second citation, the cited passage appears in footnote 5, which is found on page 380 of the Arizona Reports and on page 1035 of the Pacific Reporter. Alternatively, as discussed in subsection 8.a below, you may cite to a specific paragraph in a public domain citation.

7. SHORT-FORM CITATION

If you have fully cited to a case in a brief or legal memorandum, you may refer to it within the same general discussion by a shortened case name, volume, reporter, and specific page cite:[33]

Bundy, 641 F.2d at 938.
Wagenseller, 147 Ariz. at 381, 710 P.2d at 1036.

You may use "*Id.*" in subsequent citations to a case first cited in a single source, if no other citations intervene:

Bundy, 641 F.2d at 938. The court also held . . . . *Id.*

When using "*Id.*," add new specific page cites if appropriate:

Bundy, 641 F.2d at 938. The court also held . . . . *Id.* at 939.

The Bluebook also permits the use of "*Id.*" to refer to the first source in a parallel citation:[34]

Wagenseller v. Scottsdale Mem'l Hosp., 147 Ariz. 370, 710 P.2d 1025 (1985). The court held that . . . . *Id.* at 381, 710 P.2d at 1036.

---

33. ALWD Citation Manual, *supra* note 3, R. 12.21(b), at 92; Bluebook, *supra* note 2, R. 10.9(a)(i), at 72.
34. Bluebook, *supra* note 2, P.4(a), at 16.

The ALWD CITATION MANUAL, however, reasons that each reporter in the parallel citation is a separate source, requiring a short-form citation to each of those sources, rather than *"id."*:[35]

Wagenseller v. Scottsdale Mem'l Hosp., 147 Ariz. 370, 710 P.2d 1025 (1985). The court held that . . . . *Wagenseller*, 147 Ariz. at 381, 710 P.2d at 1036. It reasoned that . . . . *Wagenseller*, 147 Ariz. at 380-82, 710 P.2d at 1035-37.

---

8. CITATIONS TO ALTERNATIVE SOURCES OF CASE LAW

a. Public Domain Citations

The citations for case law in subsections 1-4 above are based on the publication of judicial opinions in bound reporter systems. The citations accordingly refer to specific volume and page numbers in those systems. The same case law, however, is increasingly available from electronic sources, such as CD-ROMs, online computer research services, or Internet sites. Partly to facilitate citation to decisions that may appear in a number of formats, some jurisdictions have adopted or proposed "public domain citation forms," also known as "universal," "vendor-neutral," or simply as "neutral" citation forms. Neutral citations allow the reader to locate a judicial opinion, as well as a paragraph within the opinion, in any case law reporter system, without reference to pagination in a bound volume.

Courts that adopt a public domain citation system typically will sequentially number their opinions issued in a given year, and will sequentially number the paragraphs in each opinion. A neutral citation should include the following information at a minimum: case name, year of decision, abbreviation of authoring court, number assigned to the opinion, and parallel citation to a reporter or online source, if available, as in this example from the ALWD CITATION MANUAL:

Johnson v. Traynor, 1998 N.D. 115, 579 N.W.2d 184.[36]

If you wish to cite to a specific paragraph in the opinion, you should add the paragraph number, as in this example from the BLUEBOOK:

---

35. ALWD CITATION MANUAL, *supra* note 3, R. 12.21(f), at 95. If the textual sentences after the initial citation refer to the case name, the short-form citation could omit the case name: "The *Wagenseller* court held that . . . 147 Ariz. at 381, 710 P.2d at 1036." *Id.* R. 12.21(c)(1). One might stretch that rule to omit the case name as well in the short-form citations in the text associated with this footnote, which refer to "the court," in a context that clearly equates "the court" with the *Wagenseller* court and its decision in that case.

36. ALWD CITATION MANUAL, *supra* note 3, R. 12.16(c), at 88 (presenting alternative format adopted by the North Dakota Supreme Court, which omits the familiar periods in "N.D." and "N.W.2d").

Beck v. Beck, 1999 ME 110, ¶ 6, 733 A.2d 981, 983.[37]

Although jurisdictions proposing or adopting neutral citation forms are currently in the minority, the movement is likely to gain momentum in light of endorsements by the American Bar Association (ABA) and the American Association of Law Libraries (AALL). Proponents of this movement have recommended a variety of forms for neutral citations, so general consensus on a uniform citation form has not yet taken hold.[38] Of course, if the courts in your jurisdiction have adopted a particular format for neutral citations, you can safely adopt that format, and indeed must do so for court filings if mandated by local rules.

b. LEXIS, Westlaw, Slip Opinions, and Internet Sites

Even if the relevant jurisdiction has not yet adopted a public domain citation system, you may occasionally need to cite to an electronic source or to a court's official slip opinion for case law, simply because the decision is so recent that it has not yet been published in a traditional reporter system. For example, even before a decision appears in print in the paperback supplement to a West's regional reporter system, it may be available on the LEXIS-NEXIS or Westlaw electronic databases, or in the court's own "slip opinions" published either in a printed hard copy or in electronic form at an Internet site. If so, you may wish to cite solely to one of these sources. Alternatively, if the jurisdiction has adopted a public domain citation system, you may wish to include an electronic source or slip opinion as a parallel citation after a neutral citation:

State v. Robinson, 1999 Me. 86, 1999 WL 353072 (June 3, 1999).[39]

The BLUEBOOK presents the following example of a citation to a court's official slip opinion, this one from a jurisdiction that does not separately paginate each slip opinion, so that the slip opinion begins on page 3458 and contains a relevant passage on page 3465:

Charlesworth v. Mack, No. 90-567, slip op. 3458, 3465 (1st Cir. Jan. 19, 1991).[40]

---

37. BLUEBOOK, *supra* note 2, R. 10.3.3, at 64 (adopting state's postal code to identify state's highest court).

38. Compare, for example, different ways of identifying the authoring court in the citations discussed *supra* note 35 and in the examples in the text accompanying notes 36 and 37. The AALL publishes its own citation manual for vendor-neutral citations to cases, statutes, regulations, and other sources: Comm. on Citation Formats, Am. Ass'n of Law Libraries, Universal Citation Guide (1999).

39. ALWD CITATION MANUAL, *supra* note 3, R. 12.16(c), at 88.

40. BLUEBOOK, *supra* note 2, R. 10.8.1 (b), at 70.

The following would be an acceptable short-form citation:

Charlesworth, slip op. at 3466.[41]

If you are citing to the case generally, and not to a particular page number, you could omit the reference to the slip opinion page number:

Charlesworth v. Mack, No. 90-567 (1st Cir. Jan. 19, 1991).[42]

Alternatively, if you wish to cite to a particular page within the slip opinion, and the court's slip opinions are separately paginated so that each begins with page 1, you should refer only to the specific page within:

Charlesworth v. Mack, No. 90-567, slip op. at 6 (1st Cir. Jan. 19, 1991).[43]

The ALWD citation rules for slip opinions are consistent with the BLUEBOOK examples above.[44]

The ALWD CITATION MANUAL recommends the following format for citations to LEXIS-NEXIS and Westlaw: case name, computer identifier (typically, the year, database, and document number), court abbreviation, and precise date:

Young v. Apfel, 1999 WL 325026 (N.D. Ind. May 19, 1999).[45]

To the extent that the reference to the database clearly identifies the court, all or part of the court abbreviation may be omitted within the parentheses:

White v. C.J. Coakley Co., 1999 Va. App. LEXIS 261 (May 4, 1999).[46]

To cite to a particular screen or page number within the case, insert an asterisk and the screen or page number after the database identifier:

White v. C.J. Coakley Co., 1999 Va. App. LEXIS 261 at *3 (May 4, 1999).[47]

---

41. *See generally id.* at R. 10.9(a), at 72-73 (presenting short-form citations for cases reported in reporters and electronic databases).
42. *See id.* R. 10.8.1, at 70 (presenting example that is similar but that is set in a different jurisdiction and that refers to a date of "filing" rather than a "date of decision").
43. *Id.*
44. ALWD CITATION MANUAL, *supra* note 3, R. 12.18, at 89, 12.21(e), at 95.
45. *Id.* R. 12.12(a), at 86.
46. *Id.*
47. *See id.*

Subsquent citations in short form may the omit the date and part of the case name:

White, 1999 Va. App. LEXIS 261 at *3.[48]

The BLUEBOOK is generally consistent with the preceding examples, but it instructs you to include the docket number after the case name, and it inserts a comma before the reference to a particular screen or page number:

Albrecht v. Stanczek, No. 87-C9535, 1991 U.S. Dist. LEXIS 5088, at *1 n.1 (N.D. Ill. Apr. 18, 1991).[49]

The docket number, as well as the date and part of the case name, would be omitted from the short-form citation in BLUEBOOK format:

Albrecht, 1991 U.S. Dist. LEXIS 5088, at *2.[50]

If no other source is available, cite to a case published on the Internet by substituting the Uniform Resource Locator (URL) for the computer database, as in this example from the ALWD CITATION MANUAL:

West v. Buchanan, <http://www.alaska.net/~akctlib/sp5134.txt> (Alaska June 11, 1999).[51]

Once again, BLUEBOOK format is similar, but it includes the docket number of the case and leaves the URL for the end of the citation:

Minnesota v. McArthur, No. C4-99-502 (Minn. Ct. App. Sept. 28, 1999), http://www.courts.state.mn.us/library/archive/ctapun/9909/502.htm.[52]

C. Basic Citation Form for Books and Articles

The BLUEBOOK advises you to cite to books or treatises by the full name of the author, followed by the title, the edition number if beyond the first edition, and the year of publication:[53]

---

48. *Id.* R. 12.21(d), at 94.
49. BLUEBOOK, *supra* note 2, R. 18.1.1, at 130.
50. *Id.* R. 18.7(a), at 143.
51. ALWD CITATION MANUAL, *supra* note 3, R. 12.15, at 87.
52. BLUEBOOK, *supra* note 2, R. 18.2.1(b), at 134 (italics added for case name, as it would be if cited in a brief or legal memorandum, rather than in BLUEBOOK format for footnotes).
53. *Id.* R. 15, at 107.

Richard C. Wydick, *Plain English for Lawyers* (4th ed. 1998).[54]

The ALWD CITATION MANUAL additionally calls for identification of the publisher:[55]

Richard C. Wydick, *Plain English for Lawyers* (4th ed. N.C. Acad. Press 1998).

Under the rules of either citation manual, you should cite to articles in law journals by the full name of the author, title, volume of the journal, page number on which the article begins, and year of publication:[56]

Roscoe Pound, *Common Law and Legislation*, 21 Harv. L. Rev. 383 (1908).

For either kind of authority, if you refer to a specific passage within the authority, cite to the specific page or pages on which the passage appears:[57]

Richard C. Wydick, *Plain English for Lawyers* 53-55 (4th ed. 1998).
Roscoe Pound, *Common Law and Legislation*, 21 Harv. L. Rev. 383, 387 (1908).

D. Citation Within a Citation

If you support your proposition with authority that itself relies on other authority, you may express such reliance with a parenthetic explanation:[58]

Meritor Sav. Bank v. Vinson, 477 U.S. 57, 65 (1986) (quoting 29 C.F.R. § 1604.11(a)(3) (1985)). Moreover, the Court referred approvingly to . . . *Id.* at 65-66 (describing holding of *Rogers v. EEOC*, 454 F.2d 234, 238 (5th Cir. 1971)).

To reverse the emphasis, you can cite first to the authority that above was viewed as parenthetic:[59]

54. The typeface above is consistent with BLUEBOOK format for citation to a book in court documents or legal memoranda. BLUEBOOK, *supra* note 2, P.1, at 11. The BLUEBOOK calls for a typeface of small capitals for the author and title of a book when cited in an article or book, such as this textbook. *Id.* R. 15.1.1, at 107, 15.2, at 109. The ALWD CITATION MANUAL sensibly avoids this distinction and calls for the typeface shown in the text above for citations in all documents. ALWD CITATION MANUAL, *supra* note 3, R. 22, at 186.
55. ALWD CITATION MANUAL, *supra* note 3, R. 22.1(i), at 193.
56. *Id.* R. 23, at 200; BLUEBOOK, *supra* note 2, R. 16, at 117.
57. ALWD CITATION MANUAL, *supra* note 3, R. 22.1(c)(1), at 189, R. 23.1(e)(2), at 203; BLUEBOOK, *supra* note 2, R. 15, at 107, R. 16, at 117.
58. ALWD CITATION MANUAL, *supra* note 3, R. 47, at 311; BLUEBOOK, *supra* note 2, R. 1.6(d), at 29.
59. *See* BLUEBOOK, *supra* note 2, R. 1.6(d), at 30.

29 C.F.R. § 1604.11(a)(3) (1985), *quoted in Meritor Sav. Bank v. Vinson*, 477 U.S. 57, 65 (1986).

E. Citation Signals

The following citation signals describe the relationship between the cited authority and either (1) the proposition for which it is cited or (2) other authority. In each of many of the sample citations below, a parenthetic explanation at the end of the citation supplements the signal by more specifically describing the relationship between the cited authority and the stated proposition or other authority. You may prefer to use parenthetic explanations even more liberally than suggested in the examples below. According to the BLUEBOOK, "[p]arenthetical information is generally recommended when the relevance of a cited authority might not otherwise be clear to the reader."[60] The ALWD CITATION MANUAL goes further by "strongly encourag[ing]" you "to include an explanatory parenthetical after the cited source to describe the force or meaning of the authority" in any citation introduced with a signal.[61]

1. NO SIGNAL

Use no signal to introduce a citation if the proposition for which authority is cited (1) quotes from the cited authority, (2) names the authority or otherwise refers to it, or (3) is directly supported by the authority, often because the proposition is a paraphrase or summary of a passage in the authority.[62] Each of these types of propositions is illustrated, in the order set forth above, in the following passage. The second and third citations use "*id.*" to refer to the previously cited authority, *Oncale*, but none of the citations begins with a citation signal:

> Sexual harassment constitutes sex discrimination if "members of one sex are exposed to disadvantageous terms or conditions of employment to which members of the other sex are not exposed." *Oncale v. Sundowner Offshore Servs., Inc.*, 523 U.S. 75, 80 (1998) (quoting *Harris v. Forklift Sys., Inc.*, 510 U.S. 17, 25 (Ginsburg, J., concurring)). The *Oncale* court held that same-sex harassment could meet this standard and thus constitute sex discrimination under Title VII. *Id.* at 80, 82. Such discrimination, however, does not trigger liability under the statute unless it so degrades the working environment that it alters terms or conditions of employment. *Id.* at 78, 81.

---

60. *Id.* R. 1.5, at 28.
61. ALWD CITATION MANUAL, *supra* note 3, R. 45.4, at 303.
62. *Id.* R. 45.2(a), at 301; BLUEBOOK, *supra* note 2, R. 1.2(a), at 22.

2. "See"

Introduce a citation with "*see*" if the cited authority supports your proposition, but only indirectly, thus requiring the reader to infer an unstated logical link between the proposition and the authority.[63] For example, your proposition may not appear in the cited authority, but it may follow directly from it if you tailor the holding of the cited authority to the facts of your own case. In the following example, Gracy's, Inc., Bailey, and Johnson are nowhere mentioned in the cited authority, *Oncale*. Therefore, even though the *Oncale* decision clearly supports the proposition about Johnson's claim, it does so only indirectly, requiring the reader to infer that the proposition regarding Johnson's claim follows from the application of general principles in *Oncale* or from an analogy to *Oncale*'s application of general principles to the facts of Oncale's claim:

Gracy's, Inc., will be liable for sex discrimination under Title VII if its general manager, Bailey, selectively harassed Johnson because of his sex and if the harassment was so severe or frequent that it altered Johnson's conditions of employment. *See Oncale v. Sundowner Offshore Servs., Inc.,* **523 U.S. 75, 78-82 (1998).**

---

3. "Accord"

According to the BLUEBOOK, if a proposition quotes or names an authority, you should cite to the quoted or named authority without any signal, and you may then use "*accord*" to introduce citations to additional cases that directly support the proposition but are not named or quoted in the proposition as is the first authority.[64] You can also use "*accord*" to introduce authority from other jurisdictions that adopt the same rule as is stated by the authority to which you cite without any introductory signal.[65] The ALWD CITATION MANUAL does not include "accord" among its approved signals.[66]

4. "See generally"

Use "*see generally*" to signify that the cited authority provides general background information related to the proposition for which the authority is cited:[67]

63. BLUEBOOK, *supra* note 2, R. 1.2(a), at 22; *see* ALWD CITATION MANUAL, *supra* note 3, R. 45.3, at 302 (use when authority "supports the stated proposition implicitly"). The ALWD CITATION MANUAL also recommends using "*see*" when the cited authority "contains dicta that support the proposition." ALWD CITATION MANUAL, *supra* note 3, R. 45.3, at 302. Another way to handle dicta, however, is to use whatever signal would be appropriate with a holding and simply identify the cited passage of the authority as dictum in a parenthetic explanation. For example, if a statement in dictum directly supports a proposition for which the dictum is cited, a writer might appropriately use no signal but signify with the term "(dictum)" at the end of the cite that the support, though direct, is less persuasive or binding than would be a holding of the same content.

64. BLUEBOOK, *supra* note 2, R. 1.2(a), at 22.

65. *Id.*

66. ALWD CITATION MANUAL, *supra* note 3, R. 45.3, at 302.

67. ALWD CITATION MANUAL, *supra* note 3, R. 45.3, at 302; BLUEBOOK, *supra* note 2, R. 1.2(d), at 24.

In Arizona, an employer may be liable in some circumstances for breach of a promise in a company policy manual. *See Leikvold v. Valley View Cmity. Hosp.*, 141 Ariz. 544, 546, 688 P.2d 170, 172 (1984); *see generally* Michael A. Di Sabatino, Annotation, *Modern Status of Rule that Employer May Discharge At-will Employee for Any Reason*, 12 A.L.R. 4th 544 (1982) (examining erosion of doctrine that employer may terminate without liability an employee hired for an indefinite period of time).

The annotation cited above does not provide direct support for the proposition about Arizona law, because the annotation predated the *Leikvold* case, which firmly established the Arizona law on point. Instead, the annotation provides general background information about a national trend of expanding employee rights under tort and contract law, background information that can give the reader a fuller understanding of the general topic raised in the proposition.

5. *"Cf."* and *"COMPARE . . . with"*

Use "*cf.*" to introduce an authority that supports the stated proposition by analogy or distinction, followed by parenthetic explanation:[68]

The "Proposal to Purchase Real Estate" probably is not an offer to buy a lot within the subdivision, because it does not clearly identify which lot would be purchased. *Cf. Craft v. Elder & Johnston Co.*, 38 N.E.2d 416 (Ohio Ct. App. 1941) (holding that a newspaper ad for indefinite quantity of sewing machines was only an invitation to negotiate); *Lefkowitz v. Great Minneapolis Surplus Store*, 86 N.W.2d 689 (Minn. 1957) (holding that a newspaper ad was an offer, but only because it was unusually specific and definite).

Neither of the authorities cited above directly supports your proposition about the real estate proposal, because the authorities address the specialized factual context of newspaper advertisements. Nonetheless, the first citation above supports the stated proposition by showing how analogous facts in the context of a newspaper advertisement supported the same result as the one proposed for a personalized real estate transaction. The second citation indirectly supports the stated proposition by explaining that a different result from the one proposed depended on materially different facts, also in the specialized context of a newspaper advertisement. To directly compare these two different kinds of support, or to contrast different legal approaches, you can use "*Compare . . . with*," along with parenthetic explanations.[69] The following example compares two different kinds of support for a proposition:

---

68. ALWD CITATION MANUAL, *supra* note 3, R. 45.3, at 302; BLUEBOOK, *supra* note 2, R. 1.2(a), at 23.
    69. ALWD CITATION MANUAL, *supra* note 3, R. 45.3, at 302, 45.4, at 303; BLUEBOOK, *supra* note 2, R. 1.2(b), at 23.

A newspaper ad is an offer only if it is sufficiently complete and definite that it leaves no important terms open for further negotiation. *Compare Craft v. Elder & Johnston Co.*, 38 N.E.2d 416 (Ohio Ct. App. 1941) (newspaper ad for indefinite quantity of sewing machines was only an invitation to negotiate), *with Lefkowitz v. Great Minneapolis Surplus Store*, 86 N.W.2d 689 (Minn. 1957) (newspaper ad was an offer because it was unusually specific and definite).

6. "See also"

As an alternative to the signals discussed in subsections 3-5 above, the BLUEBOOK invites you to introduce additional supporting authority with "*see also.*" The BLUEBOOK defines "*see also*" so that it arguably lies roughly between no signal, "*accord,*" and "*see,*" on the one hand, and "*cf.*" or "*see generally*" on the other:

> Cited authority constitutes additional source material that supports the proposition. "*See also*" is commonly used to cite an authority supporting a proposition when authorities that state or directly support the proposition already have been cited or discussed. The use of a parenthetical explanation of the source material's relevance . . . following a citation introduced by "*see also*" is encouraged.[70]

If you follow this advice, you likely will use the "*see also*" signal to introduce additional supporting authority that follows authority introduced with a "*see*" signal, or perhaps with no signal. You typically will use "*see also*" to introduce authority that supports your proposition less directly than does the authority preceding it, thus justifying a parenthetic explanation.

For example, suppose the first authority in a citation sentence is introduced with "*see*" because it clearly supports your proposition, but only indirectly, requiring some inference on the reader's part.[71] You might introduce the second authority with "*see also,*" rather than with no further signal if the second authority states or supports your proposition, but not so clearly or obviously that you can dispense with a parenthetic explanation. Of course, in some contexts "*see generally*" or "*cf.*" would be appropriate to signify such an attenuated relationship between the authority and the proposition. Consequently, "*see also*" should be reserved for supporting authority that is not so far removed from the specific topic of your proposition that it provides only general background information, a level of support that is better signified by "*see generally.*" Nor should you use "*see also*" to introduce authority that is so contextually different from your proposition that it supports the proposition only by analogy, a relationship better signified by "*cf.*"

For example, the first authority in the following passage, *Rite Realty, Inc. v. Simmons*, is introduced with "*see*" presumably because the court in

---

70. BLUEBOOK, *supra* note 2, R. 1.2(a), at 23.
71. *See supra* subsection 2.

Rite Realty found no offer on facts very similar to those of the "Proposal to Purchase Real Estate," which is the subject of the office memorandum or brief. In contrast, the second authority is introduced with "*see also*" because it provides slightly less certain support:

The "Proposal to Purchase Real Estate" probably is not an offer to buy a lot within the subdivision, because it does not clearly identify which lot would be purchased. *See Rite Realty, Inc. v. Simmons*, . . . (1968); *see also Frost v. Baker* . . . (finding no offer because document proposed to sell a working farm without identifying the farm, its location, or the price).

In this example, *Frost v. Baker* requires parenthetic explanation, because its facts raised more obvious problems in finding an offer than does the "Proposal to Purchase Real Estate" in the case at hand.[72] Nonetheless, *Frost* provides more than general background information. Moreover, neither its reference to a proposal to sell rather than buy nor the more obvious indefiniteness in the terms of its proposal suggest that its support requires the reader to draw an analogy to find support. Accordingly, "*see also*" is a more appropriate introductory signal than "*see generally*" or "*cf.*"

Many writers more naturally and intuitively use "*see also*" in a slightly different context, suggested by the BLUEBOOK's statement that "*see also*" might follow the citation to an authority that has already been *discussed*. For example, if you have engaged in an in-depth discussion of a case and applied it to the facts to reach a conclusion, you might end your discussion with a "*see also*" citation to provide additional, albeit less telling, support:

Officer Caruso's warrantless search of Kelly's motor home is squarely supported by the Supreme Court's decision in *California v. Carney*, 471 U.S. 386 (1985). In *Carney* . . . . Similarly, in this case, Kelly had parked his motor home at a parking strip along a state beach. . . . Thus, Officer Caruso needed only probable cause to search Kelly's motor home. *See id.*; *see also Wisconsin v. Snide* . . . (upholding warrantless search of fishing boat with sleeping berths while it was docked at lakeside and subject to administrative regulation of government authorities).

The ALWD CITATION MANUAL dispenses with "*see also*," leaving its function to be performed by other signals, such as "*see*," "*cf.*," and "*see generally*." In light of the subtlety and complexity of the discussion above regarding the proper use of "*see also*," the approach of the ALWD CITATION MANUAL is appealing.

---

72. Of course, a parenthetic explanation following the citation to *Rite Realty* might be helpful as well. Indeed, the ALWD CITATION MANUAL "strongly encourage[s]" a parenthetic explanation for any citation preceded by a signal of any sort. ALWD CITATION MANUAL, *supra* note 3, R. 45.4, at 303. Still, in the example above, the need for a parenthetic explanation is much stronger in the second citation, suggesting its more attenuated relationship to the stated proposition.

7. *"But"* and *"contra"*

Introduce an authority that opposes your proposition with a new citation sentence beginning with *"but,"* combined with another signal, such as *"see"* or *"cf.,"* as in *"But see"* or *"But cf.":*[73]

The "Proposal to Purchase Real Estate" probably is not an offer to buy a lot within the subdivision, because it does not clearly identify which lot would be purchased. *Cf. Craft v. Elder & Johnston Co.,* 38 N.E.2d 416 (Ohio Ct. App. 1941) (newspaper ad for indefinite quantity of sewing machines was only an invitation to negotiate). *But cf. Buntz v. Great Calzona Surplus Store,* 251 Calz. 188 (1957) (newspaper ad may be an offer even though it leaves quantity and description of goods uncertain).

In this example, the fictitious opinion in *Buntz* plays a different role than did the *Lefkowitz* case in subsection 5 above. Although *Lefkowitz* reached a different result than stated in your proposition, its reasoning and materially different facts nonetheless supported your proposition by analogy. In contrast, *Buntz* reaches a different result than the one you propose because it adopts contrary reasoning on similar facts. Because the author viewed the context in Buntz as only analogous to that of her factual context, she appropriately introduced it with the signal *"But cf."* If an authority contradicted your proposition indirectly, requiring some inference but not analogy to a different context, you would introduce it with *"But see."* If an authority directly contradicted your proposition, you would introduce it with *"Contra."*[74]

8. *"E.g."*

Use *"e.g.,"* combined with another signal if necessary, to show that the cited authority is simply an example of numerous cases that might be cited to support the proposition:[75]

See, e.g., Dothard v. Rawlinson, 433 U.S. 321, 323-32 (1977) (height and weight requirement for prison guards).

Alternatively, you may cite to multiple authorities without the *"e.g."* signal:

See Dothard v. Rawlinson, 433 U.S. 321, 323-32 (1977) (height and weight requirement for prison guards); *Griggs v. Duke Power Co.,* 401 U.S. 424 (1971)

---

73. ALWD CITATION MANUAL, *supra* note 3, R. 45.3, at 302; BLUEBOOK, *supra* note 2, R. 1.2(c), at 23.
74. *See* ALWD CITATION MANUAL, *supra* note 3, R. 45.3, at 302; BLUEBOOK, *supra* note 2, R. 1.2(c), at 23.
75. BLUEBOOK, *supra* note 2, R. 1.2(a), at 22; ALWD CITATION MANUAL, *supra* note 3, R. 45.3, at 302. Contrary to the BLUEBOOK and the example given in the text above, the ALWD CITATION MANUAL does not set off *"e.g."* with commas. *Id.*

(high school diploma or intelligence test); *Blake v. City of L.A. Police Dep't*, 595 F.2d 1367 (9th Cir. 1979) (height and physical abilities test for police officers).

As a matter of style, however, you should avoid long string citations of multiple authorities unless you have good reason to cite to more than two or three strong, illustrative authorities. For example, to establish that six circuits of the United States Court of Appeals have agreed that the same ambiguous statute should be interpreted in a certain manner, you might reasonably cite to a decision in each of six circuits in a long string citation. In most other contexts, however, you can save your reader time and effort by citing to your best one, two, or three authorities and using the *"e.g."* signal to signify that numerous other authorities hold similarly.

E x e r c i s e 14-1

1. EDITING CITATIONS

Using the citation manual designated by your professor, correct the errors in the following citations.

   a. Article III, Federal Constitution, sec. 1.
   b. U.S. Code, section 1983, title 42 (1994).
   c. *Crane Co. v. American Standard, Inc.*, C.A.2d, 1973, 490 F.2d 332 at 335 through 336.
   d. *Michigan Sugar Co. v. Jebavy Sorenson Orchard Co.*, Mich. Ct. App., 1976, 239 N.W.2d 693, 66 Mich. App. 642. {cited in a brief to a Michigan court}.

2. CONSTRUCTING CITATIONS

Express the correct citation for the following authorities in a brief to a Connecticut court:

   a. In 1980, the Connecticut Supreme Court issued a decision in *Cherwell-Ralli, Inc. v. Rytman Grain Co.* It appeared in volume 180 of the Connecticut Reporter, the official reporter for the Connecticut Supreme Court, beginning at page 714. It also appeared in volume 433 of the unofficial, regional Atlantic Reporter, second series, beginning at page 984.
   b. You wish to cite in full to the decision described in *a* above at page 716 of the official reporter and page 986 of the unofficial reporter. After an additional sentence of text, you wish to cite to the same authority at page 715 of the official reporter and page 985 of the unofficial reporter. No other citations have intervened.

c. You wish to cite to the decision described in *a* above at page 717 of the official reporter and page 987 of the unofficial reporter. You last cited to this authority in the previous page of your document, as described in *b* above; since then, several citations to other authorities have intervened.

3. SELECTING CITATION SIGNALS

In each excerpt below, select the appropriate citation signal, or mark an "x" to designate that no signal is appropriate.

a. At a minimum, due process requires a hearing before a disinterested, unbiased judge. _____ *Bracy v. Gramley*. . . . {*Bracy* directly states this proposition, although in slightly different words.}

b. At a minimum, due process requires a hearing "before a judge with no actual bias against the defendant or interest in the outcome of his particular case." _____ *Bracy v. Gramley*. . . {*Bracy* is the source of the quote.}

c. Except in special circumstances, police officers cannot search a residence without a warrant. _____ *Agnello v. United States*. . . ; _____ *California v. Carney*. . . (permitting warrantless search of a motor home because of its mobility and because of reduced expectation of privacy stemming from administrative regulation of all motor vehicles). Because no special circumstances justified a warrantless search in this case, the discovery of the marijuana was the product of an illegal search. _____ *Agnello v. United States*. . . {*Agnello* directly states the opening proposition, though in other words, and it is only the first of many Supreme Court decisions to directly affirm this proposition. *Carney* supports a different result in a context that shares sufficient factual elements to be arguably analogous, though the Supreme Court ultimately found it to be distinguishable. *Agnello* indirectly supports the second proposition, because—in the context of a different case, not involving the discovery of the marijuana in the present case—it stated that failure to obtain a warrant in similar circumstances could make a search illegal}.

II. PRESENTING YOUR AUTHORITY EFFECTIVELY

A. Subordinating Your Citations

1. CITATION CLAUSES AND SENTENCES

Authors of law journal articles or treatises can gracefully insert case names at the beginning or in the middle of textual sentences, because they customarily drop the remainder of the citations to footnotes. Some attorneys and judges are beginning to advocate a similar style for office memoranda and briefs to courts.[76] According to current convention, however, most citations in briefs and in office memoranda remain in the text, raising issues about the best way to combine the citations with the propositions for which they are cited.

Occasionally, a citation to authority is so short that you can unobtrusively insert it into the middle of a sentence as a citation clause:

Because the employer is potentially liable for punitive damages, 42 U.S.C. § 1981a(a)(1) (1994), we should seriously consider the plaintiff's offer to settle for reasonable compensatory damages.

Longer citations at the beginning or middle of a sentence in an office memorandum or brief, however, can divert attention from substantive ideas in the text of the sentence:

In *Tucson Med. Ctr. v. Zoslow,* 147 Ariz. 612, 614, 712 P.2d 459, 461 (Ct. App. 1985), the court held that, in the absence of an express restriction by contract or statute, a tenant generally has the unrestricted right to assign or sublet.

The passage above draws the reader's attention first to the authority, and only then to the proposition for which the authority is cited. Because the case citation has little independent significance in the example, you could improve this passage by moving the citation to a separate citation sentence, permitting you to reserve the main text for the ideas for which the authority is cited. If you do not wish to emphasize the identity of the authoring court, you can make the strongest substantive statement by presenting the legal proposition as an unqualified statement of truth that at least one court has incidentally discovered:

In the absence of an express restriction by contract or statute, a tenant generally has the unrestricted right to assign or sublet. *Tucson Med. Ctr. v. Zoslow,* 147 Ariz. 612, 614, 712 P.2d 459, 461 (Ct. App. 1985).

On the other hand, if the decisions of the authoring court are controlling on the court adjudicating the current dispute, you may want to identify the authoring court in the textual sentence, while continuing to subordinate the case name and the rest of the citation:

The Arizona Court of Appeals has held that, in the absence of an express restriction by contract or statute, a tenant generally has the unrestricted right

---

76. *See, e.g.,* William Glaberson, *Legal Citations on Trial in Innovation v. Tradition,* N.Y. Times, July 8, 2001, at A1 (footnote notation in title of article omitted).

to assign or sublet. *Tucson Med. Ctr. v. Zoslow,* 147 Ariz. 612, 614, 712 P.2d 459, 461 (Ct. App. 1985).

On rare occasions, you might appropriately retain a full citation to authority in a textual sentence if the citation itself has such great independent significance that it warrants such emphasis:

> In *Brown v. Board of Education,* 347 U.S. 483 (1954), the Supreme Court unanimously held that state-sponsored racial segregation in public schools violates the equal protection guarantee of the Fourteenth Amendment.

In this example, the case name, the identity of the authoring court, and even the date of the decision all trigger recognition in most readers. Alternatively, you could refer to the instantly recognizable case name in the textual sentence, saving the remainder of the citation for a separate citation sentence:

> In *Brown v. Board of Education,* the Supreme Court unanimously held that state-sponsored segregation in public schools violates the Equal Protection guarantee of the Fourteenth Amendment. 347 U.S. 483 (1954).

This form, however, is unconventional if it represents the initial citation to this authority in the memorandum or the brief.

2. IN-DEPTH CASE ANALYSIS

You will have even greater reason to subordinate your citations when you present an in-depth case analysis. The following introduction to the analysis of a fictitious case not only inappropriately begins a textual sentence with a full citation, it also begins exploring the details of the case without first explaining generally why the case warrants in-depth analysis:

> In *Bonnie v. DeLaney,* 158 Calz. 212, 645 P.2d 887 (1982), an agreement for the sale of a house provided that the buyer could cancel the agreement if the buyer "cannot qualify for a 30-year mortgage loan for 90% of the sales price" with any of several banks listed in the agreement. *Id.* at 213, 645 P.2d at 888. In enforcing the agreement against the seller, the court distinguished
> . . .

The reader trudges through such a passage with little interest and at least moderate irritation, because he doesn't discover the point of the case until the end of the passage. A series of such paragraphs presenting a laundry list of cases can produce a rambling effect that causes the reader to lose track of the principles that the cases are meant to illustrate.

You can greatly improve the passage quoted above by introducing it with an overview of the point that the in-depth case analysis will illustrate:

On the other hand, even if a promise leaves open the possibility that the promisor will escape obligation, the promise is valid if the promisor does not have complete control over the events upon which the promisor's obligation is conditioned. *Bonnie v. DeLaney,* 158 Calz. 212, 645 P.2d 887 (1982). In *Bonnie,* an agreement for the sale of a house provided that the buyer could cancel the agreement if the buyer "cannot qualify for a 30-year mortgage loan for 90% of the sales price" with any of several banks listed in the agreement. *Id.* at 213, 645 P.2d at 888. In enforcing the agreement against the seller, the court distinguished . . . .

The preceding passage uses a topic sentence to present an overview of the case analysis. In more complex analyses, you might precede the case analysis with a paragraph that provides the appropriate overview in two or more sentences.

This method of presenting authority enables you to introduce the case citation in a separate citation sentence and to begin the in-depth case analysis with an unobtrusive, short-form reference to the case name:

. . . is conditioned. *Bonnie v. DeLaney,* 158 Calz. 212, 645 P.2d 887 (1982). In *Bonnie,* . . . .

Moreover, if you intend to analyze several cases on the same issue, you can use the topic sentence or overview paragraph to help you to express your synthesis of the case law. As first discussed in Section II.B.7 of Chapter 7, which you may wish to review now, synthesis of authority is a critical component of legal method, warranting further exploration of writing techniques that effectively display synthesis.

B. Synthesis of Case Law

Many legal rules are the products of synthesis of two or more legal authorities. In an office memorandum or a brief, you should present such legal rules with clear guides to your synthesis rather than with isolated and unconnected analyses of the authorities.

1. LACK OF SYNTHESIS BURDENS THE READER

For example, suppose that a section of an office memorandum analyzes the issue whether a federal civil rights act addresses employment discrimination against a person because he is French Canadian. The following sample passage presents a "laundry list" of case briefs. It is ineffective because it provides insufficient guidance to the author's synthesis, or perhaps because it betrays the author's failure to synthesize:

I. RACIAL CLASSIFICATIONS
UNDER SECTION 1981

Section 1981 of title 42 of the United States Code provides in part as follows:

> All persons within the jurisdiction of the United States shall have the same right in every State and Territory to make and enforce contracts . . . as is enjoyed by white citizens. . . .

General statutory rules

In *Runyon v. McCrary*, 427 U.S. 160 (1976), African-American applicants to private, commercially operated, nonsectarian schools sued the schools through their parents. They alleged that the schools refused to admit them because of their race in violation of section 1981. A divided Supreme Court ruled that the school's discriminatory admissions policy violated the statute. It held that the statute applied to private contracts and that application of the statute to the school's admissions policy did not infringe upon the constitutional interests of the students or their parents in association, privacy, and parental control.

In-depth analysis without topic sentence to express an overview

In *McDonald v. Santa Fe Trail Transp. Co.*, 427 U.S. 273 (1976), white employees sued their employer and their union under section 1981 and Title VII of the Civil Rights Act of 1964. They alleged that their discharge for misappropriation of property was racially motivated because an African-American employee similarly charged was not dismissed. The Supreme Court acknowledged that the "immediate impetus" for the 1866 predecessor to section 1981 was "the necessity for further relief of the constitutionally emancipated former Negro slaves." *Id.* at 289. Nonetheless, on the strength of legislative history indicating that the bill would protect all races, the Supreme Court held that section 1981 imposes liability for discrimination aimed at any race, including whites. *Id.* at 289-96.

In-depth analysis without topic sentence to express overview or synthesis

In *St. Francis College v. Al-Khazraji*, 481 U.S. 604 (1987), a college professor of Arab ancestry sued his employer under section 1981 and other civil rights statutes. He alleged that the denial of his application for tenure was racially motivated because similarly situated Caucasians fared better in the tenure process. The trial court dismissed the section 1981 claim on the ground that it failed to state a

In-depth analysis without topic sentence to express overview or synthesis claim of race discrimination because Arabs were not a race distinct from Caucasians. *See id.* at 606. The court of appeals reversed and remanded for further proceedings, and the Supreme Court affirmed the decision of the court of appeals.

The Supreme Court held that scientific knowledge and cultural attitudes at the time of enactment of the 1866 and 1870 predecessors to section 1981 shaped the racial classifications addressed by the statute. Legislative history and popular dictionary and encyclopedic sources of the era reflect the view that groups with relatively narrowly defined ancestral roots and ethnic characteristics, such as "Germans," "Greeks," "Jews," and "Gypsies," represent distinct races. The Supreme Court concluded that Arabs would be viewed as a separate race under those standards and that section 1981 therefore addresses discrimination based on Arab ancestry. *See id.* at 610-13.

In our case . . . .

2. THE BENEFITS OF EXPRESSING YOUR SYNTHESIS

The preceding passage does not give adequate notice of the points or issues that each case brief is intended to illustrate, nor does it explain how the authorities relate to one another. The following passage provides a better guide to the author's synthesis. It uses a transition sentence or paragraph to provide a preview of the point illustrated by each case brief and to explain how each authority relates to previously analyzed authorities. The passage below also flows more coherently because it limits its in-depth analysis to the announced topic of the section and refers only tersely to other potential problems in the scope of the statute.

I. RACIAL CLASSIFICATIONS UNDER SECTION 1981

Federal civil rights legislation prohibits certain kinds of racial discrimination in contractual relations:

Statutory language

All persons within the jurisdiction of the United States shall have the same right in every State and Territory to make and enforce contracts . . . as is enjoyed by white citizens. . . .

42 U.S.C. § 1981 (1994).

General guides from case law interpreting the statute

As suggested by the statutory reference to rights "enjoyed by white citizens," the "immediate impetus" for the 1866 predecessor to section 1981 was

"the necessity for further relief of the constitutionally emancipated former Negro slaves." *McDonald
v. Santa Fe Trail Transp. Co.*, 427 U.S. 273, 289
(1976). Consequently, section 1981 applies most
clearly to race discrimination against African Americans. *See, e.g., Runyon v. McCrary*, 427 U.S. 160
(1976).

    Section 1981's prohibition of discrimination,
however, extends beyond discrimination against African Americans and applies more generally to discrimination based on any racial classification. *See
McDonald*, 427 U.S. 273. In *McDonald*, white employees sued their employer and their union under
section 1981 and Title VII of the Civil Rights Act
of 1964. They alleged that their discharge for misappropriation of property was racially motivated because an African-American employee similarly
charged was not dismissed. On the strength of legislative history indicating that the bill would protect
all races, the Supreme Court held that section 1981
imposes liability for discrimination against members
of any race, including whites. *See id.* at 289-96.

    McDonald did not attempt to identify all the
racial classifications protected under section 1981.
More recently, the Supreme Court held that the
applicable classifications are not those recognized
by many contemporary scientific theories, but are
the narrower and more numerous classifications
generally recognized when Congress enacted the
predecessors to section 1981. *See St. Francis College
v. Al-Khazraji*, 481 U.S. 604 (1987).

    In *St. Francis*, the Supreme Court reinstated
the civil rights claims of a college professor of Arab
ancestry who alleged that he was discriminatorily
denied tenure because similarly situated Caucasians
fared better in the tenure process. The Supreme
Court held that scientific knowledge and cultural
attitudes at the time of enactment of the 1866 and
1870 predecessors to section 1981 shaped the racial
classifications addressed by the statute. Legislative
history and popular dictionary and encyclopedic
sources of the era reflect the view that groups with
relatively narrowly defined ancestral roots and ethnic
characteristics, such as "Germans," "Greeks,"
"Jews," and "Gypsies," represent distinct races.
The Supreme Court concluded that Arabs would
be viewed as a separate race under those standards
and that section 1981 therefore addresses discrimination based on Arab ancestry. *See id.* at 610-13.

    In our case . . . .

**Topic sentence
introducing in-
depth analysis of
*McDonald***

**Transition
paragraph
expressing (1)
relationship of
McDonald to *St.
Francis* and (2)
overview of *St.
Francis***

**In-depth
analysis of *St.
Francis***

3. PARALLELS TO EFFECTIVE STUDY TECHNIQUES

The two passages quoted above illustrate the parallels between effective law school study techniques and techniques for preparing documents in a law office. The first passage resembles one of a series of only loosely connected case briefs, such as those you might prepare for class discussion. The case briefs contain useful information, but you can more effectively apply that information to an examination problem if you synthesize the cases and then reorganize them in a course outline. Moreover, as explained in Section III of Chapter 8, the outline will help you most if it emphasizes controlling principles and relegates the discussion of cases to the role of illustrating those principles.

In a law office, you will use a similar analytic process in presenting case law in a memorandum or brief. As illustrated in the second passage above, topic sentences or paragraphs introducing each case discussion emphasize principles and often act as transitions that convey case syntheses. The detailed discussion of each case simply illustrates a principle or qualification to a principle that you have already identified in a topic sentence. You should construct such a topic sentence or paragraph to introduce each in-depth case analysis. Your reader can then make her way through the series of individual case briefs without losing sight of the broader outlines of the analysis.

4. CONSOLIDATED STATEMENT OF SYNTHESIS

In some analyses, you can state an overview of the complete synthesis in a single introductory sentence or paragraph rather than set it forth incrementally in the topic sentences of several paragraphs. For example, the third paragraph in the following passage from an office memorandum prepared in 1986 provides a synthesized overview of two cases that are subsequently discussed in detail:

> Federal civil rights legislation imposes liability for deprivation of constitutional rights by agents of the state:

General statutory rules

> Every person who, under color of [state law], subjects . . . any citizen of the United States . . . to the deprivation of any rights . . . secured by the Constitution and laws, shall be liable to the party injured.

> 42 U.S.C. § 1983 (1994).

General immunity rules from interpretive case law

> Although section 1983 does not expressly limit its remedies, it implicitly incorporates a variety of common law immunity defenses. *See City of Newport v. Fact Concerts, Inc.,* 453 U.S. 247, 258 (1981). A state judge, for example, is absolutely immune from liability for money damages even for allegedly unconstitutional judicial acts taken within the

judge's subject matter jurisdiction. *See Stump v. Sparkman*, 435 U.S. 349 (1978). This immunity defense protects the independence of the judiciary by encouraging judges to make controversial decisions to the best of their abilities, uninhibited by the fear of suit. *See id.* at 355-56, 363.

Not all work-related tasks performed by a judge are judicial functions covered by absolute immunity. For example, a judge's hiring or firing a judicial employee may be a purely administrative act to which absolute immunity does not apply. *See, e.g., McMillan v. Svetanoff*, 793 F.2d 149 (7th Cir. 1986). In the Seventh Circuit, a judge's action relating to personnel is "judicial" rather than purely "administrative" only if the action implicates the judicial decision making process that the immunity defense is designed to protect. *Compare id.* (holding that firing court reporter was an administrative act unprotected by absolute immunity) *with Forrester v. White*, 792 F.2d 647 (7th Cir. 1986) (holding that firing probation officer was judicial function protected by absolute immunity).[77]

In *McMillan*, a newly elected trial judge discharged his entire courtroom staff upon taking office and rehired only one of the dismissed employees. A discharged court reporter alleged that the judge had fired her because of her race and her political affiliation, in violation of her constitutional rights under the First and Fourteenth Amendments. The Seventh Circuit characterized the function of hiring and firing employees as "typically an administrative task." 793 F.2d at 155. It concluded that the act of firing a court reporter did not implicate the judicial decision making process, because it did not involve judicial discretion requiring the exercise of the judge's "education, training, and experience in the law." *Id.* at 154-55. The act was therefore unprotected by the defense of absolute immunity in a section 1983 suit.

In contrast, in *Forrester*, the same court approved the defense of absolute immunity for a state appellate judge's allegedly discriminatory demotion and discharge of a juvenile and adult probation officer. 792 F.2d at 648. The probation officer's duties included preparing pre-sentencing reports, recom-

Specific immunity rules from case law

Synthesis of *McMillan* with *Forrester*

In-depth analysis of *McMillan*

In-depth analysis of *Forrester*

---

77. Two years after the Seventh Circuit issued its decision in *Forrester*, the United States Supreme Court overruled it. Forrester v. White, 484 U.S. 219 (1988). However, if you can imagine the passage in the main text as part of a memorandum written in 1986, it serves well to illustrate the process of synthesis.

> mendations for disposition of juvenile cases, and recommendations for revocation of juvenile and adult probation and parole. *See id.* at 648-49. The information that the probation officer provided "directly implicated the exercise of the judge's discretionary judgment." *Id.* at 657. Thus, maintenance of judicial independence required absolute immunity to protect the judge's ability to demote and discharge the probation officer without fear of suit. *See id.* at 657-58.
>
> In our case . . . .

III. QUOTATIONS

A. Using Quotations Selectively

If the interpretation or application of a statute or contract is disputed by the parties, the starting point of your analysis is the actual language of the statute or contract. Accordingly, when presenting such an analysis in a memorandum or brief, you should quote the relevant statutory or contractual provisions.

You should generally quote more sparingly from case law. Supervising attorneys and judges are primarily interested in your original synthesis of case law and your analysis of the facts within the legal framework. They are not impressed by your demonstrated ability to cut and paste page-long passages written by others.

Occasionally, a passage from case law is so clear, concise, powerful, and narrowly tailored to your dispute that paraphrasing cannot improve it. By quoting such a passage, you obviously will enhance the memorandum or brief. Often, however, a passage from case law will seem out of context if quoted, perhaps because it clashes with your writing style or because its relevant portions are unavoidably intermingled with distracting references to points not relevant to your dispute. In such a case, you can help focus the attention of your reader on important ideas, rather than on sudden shifts in style or context, by stating the rule or analysis of a case in your own words.

This general admonition against excessive quotation probably applies most strongly to appellate briefs. Although their workload is heavy, most appellate judges or their law clerks have sufficient time to study the important cases cited in appellate briefs. Moreover, appellate courts have the power to overrule at least some of the precedent likely to be cited in the briefs. Consequently, appellate judges in particular tend to look for original analysis, including policy analysis, rather than extensive quotation from authorities that a judge or a law clerk can easily secure from the library.

In contrast, busy trial judges preparing for hearings on motions may not have time to study carefully all the important cases cited in the briefs.[78] Additionally, they must follow, and cannot overrule, applicable appellate decisions within their jurisdiction. For both these reasons, some trial judges may appreciate passages in briefs that quote arguably controlling holdings from appellate case law. Similarly, some supervising attorneys ask their law clerks or associates to quote extensively from important case law in office memoranda, presumably because they want to second-guess the writer's analysis of the case law or because they want to determine whether portions of the quoted materials are suitable for quotation in their own briefs.

> Still, when you do decide to quote authority in a brief or an office memorandum, you need not quote at epic length. Indeed, a sure way to induce skimming is the back-to-back employment of two quotes of more than ten lines each. . . . Select a short helpful quote, and show its application to your case. Give enough to make your point but not so much as to sink your brief from excess weight.[79]

If you believe that a trial judge or supervising attorney might want to read the full text of some statute or case law that is not readily available in her office or chambers, you need not clutter up the body of your document with lengthy quotation. You can simply attach photocopies of the authority as an appendix to your document.[80]

B. Presenting Block Quotations

1. BASIC TECHNIQUES

If you quote a substantial portion of any authority, you should set the quoted passage apart in a single-spaced, indented block, without quotation marks other than those that appear within the original quoted text. This blocking technique helps the reader to distinguish the lengthy quotation from the original text. The BLUEBOOK citation manual calls for block quotation only if the quoted passage exceeds 49 words.[81] The ALWD CITATION MANUAL instructs you to block any quotation that exceeds either 49 words or four lines of text in your document.[82] In the opinion of this author, however, the visual benefits of blocking are evident in shorter passages, and you should exercise discretion about whether to block any quotation that takes up all or part of at least three lines of text.

The principles stated in Section II above about subordinating citations and introducing case analyses with topic sentences apply equally to block quotations. Unless the citation to a block quotation has independent significance, you should relegate it to the end of the quote by placing it at the left-hand margin on a new line below the block. You should also introduce

---

78. *See generally* Noel Fidel, *Some Do's and Don'ts of Motion Writing*, Ariz. B.J., Aug. 1983, at 9.
79. *Id.* at 10-11.
80. *Id.*
81. BLUEBOOK, *supra* note 2, R. 5.1(a); at 43.
82. ALWD CITATION MANUAL, *supra* note 3, R. 48.5(a), at 320.

the quoted passage with a thesis statement, a substantive overview that summarizes the point that you intend the passage to convey to the reader.

The following passage inappropriately introduces a block quotation of a statutory provision with a citation that has little independent significance. Moreover, the absence of a substantive introduction induced the writer to convey the point of the quote with distracting underlining:

Title 42 U.S.C. § 2000e-2(a)(1) provides:

> It shall be an <u>unlawful</u> employment practice for an employer—
> (1) to fail or refuse to hire or to discharge any individual, or otherwise <u>to discriminate against any individual</u> with respect to his compensation, terms, conditions, or privileges of employment, <u>because of such individual's</u> race, color, religion, <u>sex</u> or national origin.

Using a substantive introduction, you could revise this passage to subordinate the citation, provide the reader with helpful orientation, and minimize the need for underlining as a means of emphasis:

Federal law prohibits sex discrimination in employment:

> It shall be an unlawful employment practice for an employer—
> (1) to fail or refuse to hire or to discharge any individual, or otherwise to discriminate against any individual with respect to his compensation, terms, conditions, or privileges of employment, because of such individual's race, color, religion, sex or national origin.

42 U.S.C. § 2000e-2(a)(1) (1994) [Title VII § 703(a)(1)].

Alternatively, you may want to acknowledge that the title and name of the original legislative act in this example is familiar to most lawyers and therefore has independent significance. You can refer to the act in the introduction, while continuing to subordinate the code citation:

Title VII of the Civil Rights Act of 1964 makes it unlawful for an employer to engage in sex discrimination:

> It shall be an unlawful employment practice for an employer—
> (1) to fail or refuse . . . .

42 U.S.C. § 2000e-2(a)(1) (1994) [Title VII § 703(a)(1)].

Finally, if you want to refer repeatedly to this section of the statute throughout your brief or memorandum, you can emphasize the section number within Title VII, which is more familiar to most lawyers than the code number, by referring to it in the introduction:

Section 703(a) of Title VII of the Civil Rights Act of 1964 makes it unlawful for an employer to engage in sex discrimination:

> It shall be an unlawful employment practice for an employer—
> (1) to fail or refuse . . .

42 U.S.C. § 2000e-2(a)(1) (1994). Section 703(a) identifies two principal elements of unlawful discrimination . . . .

Even after judicious editing, you may find that a quoted passage is exceptionally long or complex. Particularly if the quotation addresses multiple themes, you can lead the reader through such material by breaking the quotation into parts and preceding each part with a substantive introduction:

Under the Uniform Commercial Code, a response to an offer may be an acceptance even though it varies the terms of the offer:	Introduction to U.C.C. § 2-207(1)
A definite and seasonable expression of acceptance or a written confirmation which is sent within a reasonable time operates as an acceptance even though it states terms additional to or different from those offered or agreed upon	Text of U.C.C. § 2-207(1)
U.C.C. § 2-207(1) (2000). However, a proviso to the same statute provides that the offeree may avoid acceptance and state a counteroffer if "acceptance is expressly made conditional on assent to the additional or different terms." *Id.*	Proviso to U.C.C. § 2-207(1)
If the original offeree's response is an acceptance, the statute provides that some of the new terms in the acceptance may be added to the contract without the express assent of the original offeror:	Introduction to U.C.C. § 2-207(2)
The additional terms are to be construed as proposals for addition to the contract. Between merchants such terms become part of the contract unless: (a) The offer expressly limits acceptance to the terms of the offer; (b) they materially alter it; or (c) notification of objection to them has already been given or is given within a reasonable time after notice of them is received.	Text of U.C.C. § 2-207(2)

U.C.C. § 2-207(2) (2000).

2. SPECIAL TECHNIQUES FOR ADVOCACY

You can use a substantive introduction to a block quotation as effective preliminary advocacy in a brief. Your introduction will emphasize the point of the quote by presenting it in summary form. Indeed, because some judges tend to skim over block quotations, your substantive introduction may be the only statement of the point that the judge reads carefully.

Moreover, quotations from contracts, statutes, or case law often are reasonably subject to varying interpretations, and a substantive introduction can encourage the reader to interpret the quoted passage in a favorable manner. For example, the following passage from an employment contract lists several grounds for discharging an employee, but it doesn't expressly state whether the list is exclusive:

> XI. Ajax Co. reserves the right to discharge any employee who
>
> 1. fails to perform satisfactorily,
> 2. commits gross insubordination, or
> 3. commits a criminal act on the work site.

Assuming that an employee hired under this contract is employed for an indefinite term, the traditional common law at-will rule would permit the employer to discharge the employee for any reason if the contractual list of grounds for discharge is not intended to be exclusive. On the other hand, if the contract provision quoted above is interpreted to include an implicit promise by the employer to refrain from discharging an employee except for the listed reasons, then the contract would override the otherwise applicable common law rule.

When quoting this passage in the argument section of the brief for either the employer or a discharged employee, you will achieve the least impact with a stock introduction such as:

Section XI of the Employment Contract provides, in relevant part, as follows:

Instead, as counsel for the discharged employee, you should use an argumentative introductory sentence to characterize the provision as a restriction on the employer's freedom to terminate the employment contract:

The Employment Contract expressly identifies only three grounds for discharge, all relating to poor performance or serious misconduct:

> XI. Ajax Co. reserves the right to discharge any employee who
>
> 1. fails to perform satisfactorily,
> 2. commits gross insubordination, or
> 3. commits a criminal act on the work site.

Employment Contract § XI. The parties obviously intended this list to be the exclusive . . . .

Conversely, as counsel for the employer, you can use an argumentative introduction to characterize the provision as an affirmation of the employer's common law freedom to terminate:

No provision of the contract expressly limits Ajax Co.'s common law right to discharge any employee at Ajax's will. Indeed, the only provision addressing termination selects three particularly strong grounds for illustration and emphasis:

XI. Ajax Co. reserves the right to discharge any employee who

    1. fails to perform satisfactorily,

    2. commits gross insubordination, or

    3. commits a criminal act on the work site.

Employment Contract § XI.

Vargas argues that the parties intended this list to be exclusive. On the contrary . . . .

You can always begin arguing for a favorable interpretation after neutrally presenting the quoted passage. However, the reader is more likely to adopt your proposed interpretation if a substantive introduction prepares him for the interpretation before he reads the quoted passage.

Exercise 14-2

Rewrite the following passage to subordinate citations and to introduce the block quotation with a brief substantive overview. You may assume that the case names are not sufficiently independently significant to warrant emphasis in textual sentences.

DISCUSSION

A. Liability for Discrimination under Section 1981

1. First Amendment Defense

Lilly Prep School has asserted in a letter to our client that it has a First Amendment right to teach and practice racial segregation in its classrooms. We expect it to raise this as a defense in any lawsuit that we file.

In *NAACP v. Alabama*, 357 U.S. 449 (1958), the Supreme Court recognized a First Amendment right "to engage in association for the advancement of beliefs and ideas." *Id.* at 460. In *Runyon v. McCrary*, 427 U.S. 160 (1976), however, the Court stated:

From this principle it may be assumed that parents have a First Amendment right to send their children to educational institutions that promote the belief that racial segregation is desirable, and that the children have an equal right to attend such institutions. But it does not follow that the *practice* of excluding racial minorities from such institutions is also protected by the same principle.

Id. at 176.

IV. SUMMARY

To present authority effectively,

1. subordinate citations, emphasize ideas, and express your syntheses in topic sentences or paragraphs;
2. use quotations selectively, subordinate the citations to the quotations, and introduce quotations with substantive overviews; and
3. use effective citation form and citation signals.

Part VI

Introduction to

Advocacy

Written advocacy is a special branch of legal method and writing that combines creative analysis, persuasive writing, and attention to local rules, special formats, and ethical considerations. Part VI provides an overview of advocacy at all stages of litigation, ending with an exercise that explores a motion to dismiss a complaint.

Parts VII and VIII examine written advocacy in the context of four other kinds of pleadings or briefs: (1) complaints and an answer, (2) briefs on a motion for summary judgment, (3) briefs on a motion to exclude evidence, and (4) appellate briefs. Each of those chapters includes at least one full sample pleading or brief. By studying this chapter and some or all of the documents in the following chapters, you will develop a general grasp of the methods and purposes of brief writing, enabling you to prepare a brief for any stage of litigation.

Chapter 15

Advocacy: Overview and Ethics

I. OVERVIEW—GENERAL FORMAT AND PROCEDURE

A. Procedure

In a typical dispute, you will advocate your client's case in various written documents through several stages of litigation. If correspondence between the parties fails to resolve the dispute in its early stages, the parties may commence formal litigation by filing pleadings, typically a complaint and an answer. Before trial, you might file or respond to "motions" that request the judge to take certain actions, such as to make advance rulings on the admissibility of evidence or to rule on the merits of some or all of the claims and defenses without a trial. During a trial with a jury, you may submit or respond to briefs that request the judge to instruct the jury on the law in a certain way or even to decide the case "as a matter of law" without the jury. At the outset of a trial without a jury, you may submit a trial brief that invites the judge to find certain facts and to apply your interpretation of the law to the facts to reach certain conclusions. Finally, if either party appeals the judgment of the trial court, you will draft one or more briefs to one or more appellate courts, inviting the appellate court to either affirm or reverse the judgment of the court immediately below it.

Throughout these proceedings, the pleadings, motions, and appeals will follow similar briefing schedules:

1. The party seeking relief or seeking reversal of the judgment of a lower court files a complaint, petition, or opening brief.
2. The opposing party responds with an answer, response, or answering brief.
3. Finally, the party who filed the petition or opening brief generally has the opportunity to file a reply brief that addresses points raised in the opposing party's answering brief or response. Under federal pleading rules, the drafter of a complaint may file a reply to the answer only if the court orders a reply or if the defendant has asserted a counterclaim in the answer, in which cases the reply is mandatory.[1]

B. Basic Formats

The format of a pleading differs significantly from that of a brief. Various pretrial, trial, and appellate briefs, however, have much in common. Each will include some statement of the background of the case, followed by an argument and a conclusion.

In some ways, an appellate brief may be more detailed and formal than a pretrial brief. By the time a case reaches an appellate court, the litigants have developed some record of the facts or factual allegations, and they have advanced the dispute through significant procedural steps. Accordingly, an appellate brief's description of the background of a case typically includes a formal statement of facts and a summary of the procedural history. On the other hand, when the parties litigate a pretrial motion, the facts may be sketchy and the procedural history brief. Consequently, many pretrial briefs combine the procedural history and statement of relevant facts in an "Introduction," "Background," or "Statement of Facts." As explored later in Chapter 19, briefs on a motion for summary judgment are exceptional in their unusually formal pretrial presentation of facts.

An appellate brief may be more formal than a pretrial brief in other ways as well. For example, rules of procedure and local court rules typically require an appellate brief to include a table of contents, table of authorities, and formal statement of issues. These are customarily omitted from all but the most complex pretrial briefs.[2]

These differences, however, are relatively superficial in light of the universality of the heart of any brief: the argument. Unlike an office memorandum, your brief will not explore the strengths and weaknesses of both sides of

---

1. *See* Fed. R. Civ. P. 7(a).
2. *Cf.* Cal. R. Super. Ct. 313(d) (motions brief exceeding ten pages must include a table of contents and table of authorities).

the dispute. Instead, you will use the brief to advocate the legal and factual analysis that best supports the claims or defenses of your client.

This perspective of a brief is reflected not only in the subtler facets of writing style but also in fundamental elements of format such as section headings. In the discussion section of an office memorandum, a section heading may be a neutral phrase that generally describes a topic of discussion and helps your reader recall an issue stated more formally at the beginning of the memorandum. In contrast, you will use a "point heading" in the argument section of a brief to state the conclusion that you want the judge to adopt on each issue. In each point heading, you will assert a point in a complete sentence as a prelude to your full deductive argument on that issue.

Chapters 16 and 17 address these and other techniques of written and oral advocacy in greater depth. First, however, Section II introduces you to a few of the many ethical obligations that you assume as an advocate.

II. GOOD FAITH, REASONABLENESS, AND FULL DISCLOSURE

A. Assertion of Claims and Defenses

As an attorney, you owe a duty to your client to advocate her case vigorously.[3] In carrying out this duty, you will often argue for creative extension of existing law or for replacement of existing law with new rules.[4] Fundamental principles of professional responsibility, however, impose limits on your advocacy.[5] For example, Federal Rule of Civil Procedure 11 requires attorneys to certify that their written advocacy is supported by a reasonable investigation of the law and facts and is not advanced for an improper purpose:

> (b) Representations to Court. By presenting to the court (whether by signing, filing, submitting, or later advocating) a pleading, written motion, or other paper, an attorney or unrepresented party is certifying that to the best of the person's knowledge, information, and belief, formed after an inquiry reasonable under the circumstances,—
> (1) it is not being presented for any improper purpose, such as to harass or to cause unnecessary delay or needless increase in the cost of litigation;
> (2) the claims, defenses, and other legal contentions therein are warranted by existing law or by a nonfrivolous argument for the extension, modification, or reversal of existing law or the establishment of new law;

---

3. *See, e.g.,* MODEL CODE OF PROF'L RESPONSIBILITY EC 7-4 (1980); *id.* at Canon 7.
4. *See generally infra* subsection C.
5. *See, e.g.,* MODEL RULES OF PROF'L CONDUCT R. (hereafter "MODEL RULE") 3.3(a)(1) (2000) (proscribing knowingly false statements of material fact or law).

(3) the allegations and other factual contentions have evidentiary support or, if specifically so identified, are likely to have evidentiary support after a reasonable opportunity for further investigation or discovery; and

(4) the denials of factual contentions are warranted on the evidence or, if specifically so identified, are reasonably based on a lack of information or belief.[6]

Rule 11 authorizes a judge to impose "an appropriate sanction upon the attorneys, law firms, or parties that have violated [Rule 11] or are responsible for the violation."[7] The sanction may include "directives of a nonmonetary nature, an order to pay a penalty into court, or . . . an order directing payment to the movant of some or all of the reasonable attorneys' fees and other expenses incurred as a direct result of the violation."[8]

Rule 11 also contains a controversial "safe harbor" provision that permits a person responsible for a Rule 11 violation to escape sanctions by withdrawing the offending claim or defense after receiving notice of a motion for sanctions:

> A motion for sanctions under this rule . . . shall not be filed with or presented to the court unless, within 21 days after service of the motion . . . the challenged paper, claim, defense, contention, allegation, or denial is not withdrawn or appropriately corrected.[9]

Critics have complained that this "safe harbor" provision and the discretionary nature of sanctions threaten to "render the Rule toothless."[10] As explored more fully in the following sections, however, perhaps the best guide to responsible advocacy is the desire shared by most advocates to maintain their reputations for candor and quality work.

B. Disclosure of Adverse Authority

As an advocate, you have no duty to argue your opponent's case or even to present a balanced analysis such as would be appropriate in an office memorandum. Nonetheless, every advocate is also an officer of the court[11] and owes a general duty of candor and fairness to the court and to other lawyers.[12] Within this framework, the American Bar Association (ABA) Model Rules of Professional Conduct specifically require every advocate to disclose significant authority adverse to the advocate's arguments:

> A lawyer shall not knowingly: . . .
> (3) fail to disclose to the tribunal legal authority in the controlling

---

6. FED. R. CIV. P. 11(b).
7. *Id.*
8. *Id.*
9. *Id.*
10. Amendments to the Federal Rules of Civil Procedure and Forms, 113 S. Ct. 89, 194 (orders preface) (1993) (Scalia, J., dissenting).
11. *See, e.g.*, Ex parte Garland, 71 U.S. (4 Wall.) 333, 378 (1867), *cited in* ABA Formal Opinion 146 (1935).
12. *See* MODEL RULE 3.3 (2000) (candor to court); ABA Formal Opinion 146 (1935).

jurisdiction known to the lawyer to be directly adverse to the position of the client and not disclosed by opposing counsel.[13]

The scope of this duty depends in large part on the interpretation of the phrase "directly adverse." However, the most sensible approach to disclosure is one that maintains your credibility as an advocate. If adverse authority within the forum jurisdiction is sufficiently analogous that the court would consider it in deciding a case, the judge or the judge's law clerk likely will discover the authority sometime before the end of the proceedings, even if it has escaped the notice of the opposing counsel. You can minimize the impact of such adverse authority by acknowledging it early in the proceedings and distinguishing or discrediting it.[14]

The reference to "controlling jurisdiction" in the disclosure rule appears to flatly exclude authority from other than the forum jurisdiction, even if it is squarely on point. In some circumstances, however, your desire to maintain credibility may be a better guide than a specific ethical rule. For example, if the question before the court is so novel that no authority within the forum jurisdiction addresses it, and if adverse authority from another jurisdiction would be particularly persuasive, then the court might expect you to disclose the nonbinding adverse authority and to squarely address it.

If an adverse authority does not meet these standards, you need not address it unless the other party relies on it or the court raises a question that encompasses it. In an opening brief, for example, you should not waste time by distinguishing marginally analogous adverse case law or by criticizing poorly reasoned persuasive authority on which the opposing counsel is unlikely to rely. Instead, you should concentrate on affirmatively presenting your own arguments and supporting authority, and you should attack only the most obvious adverse authority. Then, you can wait to see which authority the opposing counsel advances in the answering brief, and you can attack that adverse authority in your reply brief. Of course, if the court asks you broadly about adverse precedent, you "should make such frank disclosure as the question seems to warrant,"[15] regardless of the scope of ethical duties or strategic considerations that might otherwise apply.

C. Misleading Legal Argument

The ABA Model Rules of Professional Conduct prohibit a lawyer from knowingly making "a false statement of . . . law to a tribunal."[16] However, a legal analysis will not amount to a false statement about the law unless it clearly falls outside the range of plausible interpretations of the legal authorities.

For example, defining the holding of a judicial opinion and determining its effect as precedent is an exercise in legal realism that produces disagreement among able jurists. Thus, as an advocate, you often have room to take

---

13. MODEL RULE, 3.3(a)(3) (2000) (taken from MODEL CODE OF PROF'L RESPONSIBILITY DR 7-106(B)(1) (1969)).
14. *See* Charles W. Wolfram, MODERN LEGAL ETHICS § 12.8, at 682 (1986).
15. ABA Formal Opinion 280 (1949).
16. MODEL RULE, 3.3(a)(1) (2000).

an aggressive stance in identifying facts that appear to have been material to a decision and in characterizing the holding and reasoning of the decision.

As with other ethical questions, practical considerations of effective advocacy may provide the best guide to responsible conduct. Published precedent on which you rely is readily accessible to the opposing counsel and to the court. Careless or fraudulent analyses that cross the line separating creative advocacy from misrepresentation almost certainly will be brought to the court's attention. Few things can damage your credibility and effectiveness more than a reputation for stretching legal authority beyond the limits of plausible interpretation.

III. SUMMARY

In shifting from neutral analysis to advocacy, you must adopt a suitable format for your document and make the transition from an objective writing style to a persuasive one, as explored in the following chapters. Take care to satisfy ethical duties in asserting claims and defenses, in disclosing adverse authority, and in representing the content of legal authority.

Chapter 16

Developing Your Legal Arguments

By performing some or all of the exercises throughout Parts I-IV of this book, you have steadily developed your skills in spotting and analyzing legal issues and developing legal arguments. You now should be ready to select, organize, and express your legal arguments in a brief.

Your statements of issues, facts, and procedural history will vary greatly in style and content depending on the stage of the litigation at which you draft a legal document. Consequently, this book separately examines those elements of a pleading or a brief in Parts VII and VIII. Many techniques of advocacy, however, apply broadly to all kinds of briefs and are appropriately introduced in Part VI, Chapters 16 and 17. Specifically, this chapter examines methods of (1) organizing arguments, (2) introducing arguments, and (3) developing the elements of a deductive argument. Chapter 17 examines techniques of persuasive writing and oral argument.

I. ORGANIZING LEGAL ARGUMENTS

As discussed in Section II of Chapter 12, you ordinarily should discuss or argue discrete issues in separate sections of your office memorandum or brief. Moreover, your section and subsection headings should show the proper relationships among your topics and subtopics. Beyond these considerations, you also must decide (1) which arguments to advance, (2) the order in which to present your arguments, and (3) the internal organization of each argument.

As you examine these matters in the following sections, reflect on the value of preparing an outline of the argument section of your brief before you begin writing it. The same techniques discussed in Chapter 8 for outlining course materials, and in Section V of Chapter 10 for outlining the discussion section of an office memorandum, will help you outline the argument section of your brief.

A. Choosing a Theme and Supporting Arguments

1. SELECTING ARGUMENTS

As explained in Section III.B of Chapter 6, you should be more selective in choosing arguments to advance in a brief than in choosing issues to discuss in an essay examination or an office memorandum. For example, a federal appellate judge advises you to "[f]orce yourself to omit fringe issues and far-out theories; they will only dull the thrust of your appeal and obscure the potentially winning point."[1] A professor of trial practice and advocacy emphasizes that this

> means making choices. You throw out arguments that aren't plausible. You pick between the inconsistent legal theories. You cull out the weak points. You toss out whatever gets in the way. You discard what doesn't need to be said, even if it doesn't hurt.
>
> What's left is tight. Lean. Spare. It crackles with power because it's undiluted with stuff that doesn't matter.[2]

2. DEVELOPING A THEME

When making these choices at the outlining stage, try to develop a theme for your brief, a thread that runs through the brief from the Statement of Facts to the Argument. If possible, your theme should reflect some facet of the dispute that shows "that your client's position is not only legally correct but also equitably, ethically, and morally 'right.'"[3] Your best arguments are likely to be ones that not only are analytically sound but also that help you advance your underlying theme throughout your brief.

For example, in litigation of a products liability suit, the injured plaintiff's brief might consistently advance a theme that highlights a dangerous defect in the product used by the plaintiff. In contrast, the defendant manufacturer's brief might consistently advance a theme that emphasizes the weakness of

---

1. Hon. Jacques L. Wiener, Jr., *Ruminations from the Bench: Brief Writing and Oral Argument in the Fifth Circuit*, 70 Tul. L. Rev. 187, 194 (1995).

2. James W. McElhaney, *The Art of Persuasive Legal Writing: Briefs Come Alive When Every Word Sings to the Reader*, ABA J., Jan. 1996, at 76.

3. Wiener, *supra* note 1, at 190.

the causal link between the product's defect and the plaintiff's injuries. Although each brief may necessarily address matters that do not directly advance the theme, each authoring attorney should endeavor to bring the brief's theme to the fore in various parts of the brief, from the issue and fact statements to the argument.

3. MOOD AND METAPHOR

A theme might also consist of a mood or perspective that forms a backdrop to the arguments. For example, one attorney used the metaphor of a lawless frontier to convey a theme in a motion for summary judgment.[4] Although you must avoid careless or distracting metaphors when a straightforward explanation would be clearer, sometimes a telling metaphor repeated occasionally as a thread that runs through a brief can effectively convey a persuasive theme.

The motion for summary judgment challenged an arbitration decision interpreting a collective bargaining agreement, a decision to which a reviewing court would grant substantial deference.[5] Accordingly, the author of the brief bore the burden of showing that even that deferential standard of review imposed meaningful limits on the arbitrator's interpretation and that the arbitrator had exceeded those limits as a matter of law. Throughout the brief, the author argued those points with sound analysis of the law and facts and with traditional policy arguments. But the author of the brief wanted to create a mood as well, and the case itself invited the author to draw allusions to unrestrained frontier justice in the lawless Wild West: The workplace was a coal mine, and the arbitrator's last name was West. To introduce this theme, the first sentence of the argument suggested that failure to curb the arbitrator's discretion would render labor relations as chaotic and lawless as in some frontier outpost in the Wild West:

Despite the deference arbitrators are granted in reaching their decisions, one principle stands clear: the federal labor policy of promoting arbitration of industrial disputes does not create a lawless frontier where arbitrators are free to impose their own brand of "industrial justice."

The phrase "industrial justice" by itself is not pejorative, but the author linked it to an image of arbitrariness and lawlessness associated with untamed frontiers. The brief did not belabor this metaphor; however, it reminded readers of this image every time it named the arbitrator, West, and every time that it referred to West's "own brand of industrial justice." Finally, both these reminders combined with a new play on words at the beginning of the third subsection of the argument:

---

4. The examples in this subsection were supplied in 2000 by Christopher Mason, an attorney with the Phoenix office of the law firm of Bryan Cave LLP.
5. *See* United Paperworkers Int'l Union v. Misco, Inc., 484 U.S. 29, 36-38 (1987).

. . . Arbitrator West also shot holes through another provision of the [agreement], enforcing his own brand of "industrial justice."

In his response to the opposing party's cross-motion for summary judgment in the same case, this author argued that the arbitrator had refused to choose between two different plausible interpretations of the collective bargaining agreement and instead had compromised inappropriately by choosing an interpretation somewhere between the plausible meanings, arguably an interpretation that no language in the agreement supported. For this argument, the author developed a different theme, one that compared and then contrasted the arbitrator's interpretation with King Solomon's fabled solution:

Just as King Solomon threatened to do, the arbitrator in this dispute split the baby and imposed an irrational solution to achieve his desired result. . . . Of course, King Solomon ultimately revealed his wisdom by vacating his irrational decision. Here, the Court should likewise vacate Arbitrator West's irrational decision.

Such colorful metaphors or similes to create a theme are a matter of personal style and can never substitute for sound analysis of the law, facts, and social policies. They may, however, create an effective backdrop for the analysis, encouraging your reader to develop a gut reaction in favor of your client.

B. Determining the Order of Your Arguments

Consider beginning your argument with a paragraph that states the theme of your brief or that provides an overview or roadmap to multiple arguments that follow. Such an overview paragraph would appear at the beginning of the Argument section of your brief, even before the subsection heading for the first of several arguments.

Of course, you cannot set forth an effective roadmap without first deciding on an effective ordering of your arguments. If your brief includes a formal statement of the issues, the organization of that statement should mirror the organization of your arguments. To determine the most appropriate order of arguments, you may need to balance neutral analytic considerations against strategic considerations. Moreover, in a responsive brief, you must decide whether to adopt or depart from the organizational structure of the opposing counsel's preceding brief.

1. LEADING WITH YOUR STRONGEST ARGUMENT

As discussed in Section II.B of Chapter 12, neutral analytic considerations will lead you to argue threshold issues first and then to argue the issues that are dependent on the outcome of the threshold issues. Strategic considerations, however, may lead you to place your strongest argument first, even if that organization requires you to depart from a purely logical ordering of arguments.

The strategic considerations are based on the varying levels of emphasis associated with different parts of the argument section of the brief. In a sentence, an idea generally will receive greater emphasis if placed at the beginning than if placed in the middle, but the place of greatest emphasis ordinarily is the end of the sentence. The same might be true of a short brief submitted to a judge who has plenty of time to study it. The first argument in such a brief would receive the emphasis associated with any initial encounter that makes a first impression. Ideas in the middle of the brief might capture slightly less attention, but they could help lay the foundation for a forceful climax. Presumably, the climactic argument would leave a lasting impression on the judge because it is the last argument that the judge would read.

Unfortunately, briefs are seldom brief, and judges often lack time to read them carefully. Indeed, a trial judge with a full pretrial motions calendar may have time only to skim through your motions brief before oral argument. Far from occupying the place of greatest emphasis, the end of your brief may not be read at all, or at least it may not be read with the same care that the judge devoted to the beginning of the brief.

Consequently, advocates usually begin their briefs with their strongest arguments. In fact, aware of this practice, judges have come to expect that the first argument in a brief is the strongest argument, and they accordingly may be tempted to prejudge an entire brief on the basis of the merits of the first argument. This phenomenon, of course, simply reinforces the belief among advocates that they should lead with their strongest arguments. Consequently, if one of your arguments is much stronger than the others, you can exercise discretion to present it before the others even though another issue is logically prior.

2. SPECIAL CONSIDERATIONS FOR RESPONSIVE BRIEFS

When you write a responsive brief, the organization selected by the opposing counsel for the preceding brief is yet another factor in your own deliberations about organization. In a complex case, you can conveniently respond to each point in a preceding brief by simply adopting the preceding brief's organizational structure and methodically knocking down each of your opponent's arguments. On the other hand, if you can more persuasively argue your case with a different organizational structure, you should not hesitate to depart from the structure adopted by your opponent.

For example, suppose that Maya Tortilla Co. has sued Bakeway Supermarkets, alleging that Bakeway (1) formed a contract with Maya; (2) breached its obligations, at least under Maya's interpretation of the contract; (3) and is liable to Maya for $40,000 in damages. Maya has filed a pretrial motion requesting the trial court to grant it summary judgment, which is judgment as a matter of law without a full trial on the facts. Maya has supported its motion with a preliminary showing of facts and with a brief that argues each of the issues in the order presented above. Bakeway can escape summary judgment on any issue by creating a genuine dispute of material fact on that issue, a dispute that must be resolved in a full trial.

As counsel for Bakeway, you could logically begin the argument of your answering brief with Maya's issue #1 because contract formation is a threshold issue: Bakeway did not assume any contractual obligations and consequent potential liability if it did not form a contract with Maya. Moreover, the opening brief begins with issue #1, and you could simplify your task by simply adopting the organizational structure of the opening brief.

However, suppose that you can most easily avoid summary judgment against Bakeway on issue #2. Although you cannot easily refute formation of a contract, you can point to admissible evidence of contract negotiations that supports Bakeway's interpretation of the contract. Moreover, under Bakeway's interpretation of the contract, Bakeway performed rather than breached the contract. Thus, you are confident that you can create a triable issue of fact about the meaning of the contract provision that states Bakeway's obligations. In those circumstances, you could reasonably begin your argument with issue #2, even though that organization departs from a purely logical ordering and from the structure of the opening brief. If you persuade the judge in your first argument that she should deny summary judgment on issue #2, she may then be more strongly disposed to order a trial on other issues as well.

Of course, a responsive brief should not fail to meet the arguments of the preceding brief "head-on, issue for issue, as they are posited."[6] Nonetheless, the responsive brief can do so on its own terms, within an organizational and analytic framework that places its arguments in the best light.

C. Internal Organization: Deductive Arguments

Once you decide the order of your arguments, you must adopt an effective scheme of internal organization for each argument. You should exercise the flexibility and creativity to adopt any method of internal organization and advocacy that will present your client's argument most effectively. Unless you have good reason to adopt some other approach, however, you should start with the elements and organization of a deductive argument.

"IRAC," which represents the form of deductive reasoning appropriate to an objective analysis in an office memorandum, is thoroughly discussed in Chapter 6. Moreover, Sections III and IV of Chapter 12 examine various techniques for organizing points within a deductive argument of a memorandum or a brief. Before writing your brief, you should review those passages.

The following section in this chapter emphasizes one difference between the deductive reasoning appropriate to an objective office memorandum and the deductive argument appropriate to a brief: An argument in a brief leads with the advocate's desired conclusion rather than with a neutral identification of an issue. Thus, each argument in a brief should include four major elements: Conclusion, Rule, Application of the legal rule to facts, and Conclusion. The acronym "CRAC" may help you remember these elements.

6. Wiener, *supra* note 1, at 197.

II. INTRODUCING LEGAL ARGUMENTS

A. Point Headings

For each issue in the argument section of your brief, you will discuss the law and apply the law to the facts to reach a conclusion. Before you begin your full argument, however, you will introduce it in an argumentative section heading, or "point heading." In each section or subsection that addresses a discrete issue, your point heading previews the conclusion.

Thus, while a section heading in an office memorandum can neutrally identify the issue addressed in that section, the section heading of an argument in a brief advocates a position by asserting a point and inviting the judge to reach a particular conclusion. It thus sets the tone for the full argument.

If a section or subsection of your argument develops a full deductive argument, its point heading should be tailored to the facts of your case, much like the statement of an issue and holding in a student case brief. Indeed, you may view your point headings as statements of the holdings in your case that you want the court to adopt:

II. ARGUMENT

    A. O'Gorman is not liable for medical costs associated with Wallace's heart failure, because O'Gorman's conduct did not proximately cause that injury.

    B. O'Gorman is not liable for punitive damages because he did not act with the requisite "evil mind."

Because these point headings refer to the parties and incorporate important facts, they convey a clear, concrete point, even when read in isolation. The bold letters and the indentation help the point headings stand out on the page, providing conspicuous road signs for the reader. You may flexibly adopt any technique or combination of techniques that helps your point headings stand out on the page, although this author believes that the older style of underlining and using all capital letters provides more distraction than emphasis in any heading that runs for more than a few words.

In some cases, as discussed in Section III.D.3 of Chapter 12, you may develop only one element of a deductive argument, such as an abstract legal principle, within a section or subsection. In such cases, of course, each point heading should be limited to stating a conclusion on the point developed in the section or subsection:

II. ARGUMENT

    A. O'Gorman is not liable for punitive damages because he lacked the requesite scienter.

        1. O'Gorman is not liable for punitive damages unless he acted with an "evil mind."

2. The evidence at trial will show that O'Gorman did not act
   with an "evil mind."

The advantages of point headings are obvious in multiple-issue briefs, in which you must divide the argument into sections and subsections. Within the argument section of the brief, the point headings pop up periodically as road signs that signal an entrance to a new street or highway of your argument. Additionally, at least in an appellate brief, you will set forth your point headings together in the table of contents near the beginning of the brief, providing a quick summary of all your points, a concise road map of the judge's journey through your brief.

Even in a single-issue brief, however, you should begin your argument with a point heading. It will simply stand alone in the argument section without any number or letter denoting division of the argument into sections:

II. ARGUMENT
The alleged agreement is unenforceable because it was not signed by the party against whom enforcement is sought.

B. Introductory Paragraphs

Immediately after the point heading but before discussing the legal authority, you may want to use an introductory sentence or paragraph to illuminate the issue and to expand on the point heading:

A. The UCC requires the alleged agreement to be in writing, because the alleged subject matter was priced at more than $500.

Scott Paper Supply alleges that Sun Printing Co. breached a contract to purchase a shipment of bond paper priced at $11,200. Sun Printing Co. denies that it ever agreed to such a purchase. This is precisely the kind of groundless contract claim that statutes of frauds are designed to bar.

The Uniform Commercial Code statute of frauds generally bars . . .

Such an introductory paragraph can be particularly helpful in a responsive brief. Rather than abstractly addressing the issues, an answering or reply brief should respond directly to each of the preceding brief's arguments. In a responsive brief, the introductory paragraph following a point heading can set up your full response by (1) summarizing the opposing party's argument and (2) explaining generally why the opposing argument lacks merit, usually saving citation to authority for the more detailed discussion of law that follows:

A. Scott Paper Supply's timely confirmation of the agreement satisfied the UCC statute of frauds, because Sun Printing Co. failed to object to it.

Scott Paper Supply argues that the Uniform Commercial Code statute of frauds bars enforcement of the purchase agreement because the agreement is not memorialized in a written document signed or expressly adopted by Scott. Scott's argument is meritless because the confirmation signed by Sun Printing Co. satisfied the requirements of the statute and because the UCC deems Scott to have implicitly adopted that confirmation by failing to object to it.

The UCC provides that . . . .

Such an opening paragraph will accomplish its purpose only if it, as a whole, affirmatively advances your own argument. You will surely defeat its purpose if you simply lead with your opponent's argument and give it special emphasis. Accordingly, you should begin with a summary of your opponent's argument only as a means of putting your own argument in its best light. Specifically, after you summarize your opponent's argument, you must immediately and convincingly refute it with a summary of your response. In one brief, an advocate identified opposing counsel's argument and dismissed it in a single sentence, leaving the reader no opportunity to dwell on the opposing argument:

Plaintiffs' claim that the Subpoena seeks "wholly irrelevant" information is simply not supported by the facts and governing law in this case. The Ninth Circuit has held . . . .

Such an opening sentence or paragraph presents a condensed pattern of point and winning counterpoint that you hope the judge will see in the broader outlines of the competing briefs.

In some cases, you can use an opening paragraph to particularly strong advantage by "setting up" your opponent's argument for an easy response. Specifically, you should try to restate your opponent's argument fairly and accurately but in a way that fully reveals its weaknesses. For example, suppose that your opponent's opening brief on appeal argues that the trial judge erred in denying injunctive relief, but it acknowledges the trial judge's broad discretion in such matters only in a vague passage buried in the middle of a lengthy section. In your answering brief, you will take greater pains to emphasize the discretionary nature of such relief. You might begin that emphasis not only in your point heading but also in an opening paragraph that summarizes your opponent's argument in a way that immediately reveals its weakness:

A. The trial court properly exercised its discretion to deny the extraordinary remedy of injunctive relief.

Redrock Co. bears the heavy burden of showing that Judge Norris abused her discretion by denying Redrock's demand for an injunction against further construction on the Big River Project. In fact, the record establishes a balance of equities that tip sharply against injunctive relief. Judge Norris's careful decision was a routine and proper exercise of discretion.

Injunctive relief is . . . .

III. DEVELOPING THE DEDUCTIVE ARGUMENT

A. Arguing the Law

Chapters 6 and 12-15 have provided you with the legal method and the techniques of organization and writing with which you can construct an argument about the content of applicable law on a particular issue or subissue. An outline of these principles will illustrate the range of considerations that may enter into your strategic decisions when arguing the law within the argument portion of your brief.

1. HIERARCHY OF AUTHORITY

First, you must be sensitive to the hierarchy of authority. For example, suppose that (1) your client is not liable under common law standards for actions that he took as an employer, but (2) a federal statute will impose liability if it applies to your client's business. If applicable, the statutory law will supersede the common law. Therefore, you must analyze the statute and determine whether you can argue either that it is unconstitutional or that it does not apply to your case. This statutory analysis might include arguments concerning the statutory language, the legislative history, the policy underlying the statute, or the limitations imposed by constitutional provisions.

2. STRENGTH OF CASE LAW AS PRECEDENT

Second, in analyzing case law, regardless of whether it interprets a statute or applies common law, you must appreciate the relative strength of different kinds of authorities. Case law from a higher court within the forum jurisdiction is mandatory law and potentially controlling on the facts of your case, and you must argue for a broader or narrower interpretation of its holding, depending on whether it supports or undermines your position. Case law from other jurisdictions may have persuasive value, but only in the absence of controlling law within the jurisdiction.

For example, in the following passage of an argument, the counsel for Beatty, a lender, encourages the court to synthesize mandatory precedent in a favorable manner and to brush aside adverse persuasive authority from another jurisdiction:

Weeks cites to authorities from other jurisdictions to argue that Beatty's promise is illusory and therefore does not satisfy the consideration requirement. However, her position is inconsistent with Calzona Supreme Court cases. As discussed below, the principles derived from a synthesis of the Calzona cases establish that Beatty's promise is not illusory and that Weeks's promise is enforceable.

Introduction to argument

Even if a promise leaves open the possibility that the promisor will escape obligation, the promise is not illusory if the promisor does not have complete control over the events on which the promisor's obligation is conditioned. *Bonnie v. DeLaney,* 158 Calz. 212, 645 P.2d 887 (1982). In *Bonnie,* an agreement for the sale of a house provided that the buyer could cancel the agreement if the buyer "cannot qualify for a 30-year mortgage loan for 90% of the sales price" with any of several banks listed in the agreement. *Id.* at 213, 645 P.2d at 888. In enforcing the agreement against the seller, the court emphasized that the word "cannot" referred to the buyer's ability to obtain a loan rather than to his desire. Because his ability to obtain a loan was partly controlled by events and decisions outside his control, the promises in the sale agreement were nonillusory and binding. *See id.* at 214-15, 645 P.2d at 889-91.

In-depth analysis of favorable case law

The *Bonnie* court distinguished its earlier decision, *Atco Corp. v. Johnson,* 155 Calz. 1211, 627 P.2d 781 (1980). In *Atco Corp.,* the manager of an automobile repair shop promised to forbear "until I want the money" from asserting a claim against the owner of an automobile for $900 in repairs. In exchange, a friend of the owner promised to act as guarantor of the owner's obligation. *Id.* at 1212, 627 P.2d at 782. The word "want" stated no legal commitment because it permitted the manager at his own discretion to refuse to perform any forbearance at all. Because the manager did not incur even a conditional obligation, the guarantor's promise was gratuitous and unenforceable. *Id.* at 1213-14, 627 P.2d at 782-84.

In-depth analysis of adverse case law

Together, these cases show that any limitation on the promisor's freedom will validate his promise. A promise is illusory only if it leaves the promisor complete control over his actions.

Synthesis that emphasizes favorable case law

Under these controlling principles, the parties in this case each assumed valid obligations. . . .

Application to facts

Argument against application of nonbinding authority

> Thus, *Atco* is distinguishable from our case, and *Bonnie* is controlling.
>
> Weeks attempts to salvage his flawed analogy to *Atco* by interpreting it in light of authority from New Maine. The New Maine cases, however, are not binding on this court and are inconsistent with the reasoning of the controlling authority in *Bonnie.* . . .

In this example, counsel for Beatty summarized her argument in the first paragraph. In the second and third paragraphs, she synthesized local case law by reconciling two decisions with apparently contrasting holdings. In the fourth paragraph, she concluded her synthesis with a form of inductive reasoning in which she derived a legal rule by generalizing from the two cases. In the fifth paragraph, as illustrated more fully in Section B below, counsel for Beatty applied this rule to the facts of her case, taking care to analogize the favorable precedent and to distinguish the adverse precedent. In the final paragraph, she protected this analysis by explaining why case law from another jurisdiction should not be used to interpret the local case law in a different manner.

The persuasive influence of authority from a lower court or from a court in another jurisdiction may be stronger in the absence of any applicable mandatory authority from the forum state. If persuasive authority undermines your client's position, you can try to distinguish it from the facts of your case or to discredit its reasoning as unworthy of adoption as the rule of law in the forum jurisdiction. Conversely, if persuasive authority supports your position, you should argue that its reasoning is sound and is consistent with the policy of the forum jurisdiction.

For example, in the following passage, an advocate attempts to persuade a court in the imaginary state of New Maine to adopt the reasoning of fictitious California case law and to reject fictitious precedent from Washington and Florida:[7]

Complementary in-depth analysis of favorable case law

> The Federal Gun Control Act (FGCA) preempts more stringent state gun control legislation. *California v. Biggs,* 567 P.2d 765 (Cal. 1987). In *Biggs,* state officials sought to confiscate a private collection of automatic pistols under the authority of a California statute that bans private ownership of all automatic guns. The California Supreme Court found that the FGCA's registration requirements for most varieties of automatic guns implicitly authorize private, registered ownership of such guns. It therefore held that the FGCA barred the state from prohibiting such ownership.
>
> In reaching its decision, the California Supreme

---

7. All the arguments, authorities, and citations in this example are fictitious.

Court exhaustively analyzed the legislative history of the FGCA. It noted that . . . .

Two courts had previously rejected the preemption argument adopted in *Biggs,* but each of them overlooked the critical legislative history so carefully analyzed in *Biggs. Arzani v. Matlock,* 332 So. 2d 234 (Fla. 1986); *Washington v. Smedley,* 558 P.2d 777 (Wash. 1986). For example, in *Arzani,* the Court summarily held that . . . .

Critical analysis of adverse case law

The advocate obviously hopes that the preceding passage will persuade the court to adopt the reasoning of *Biggs.* In the fact analysis, the advocate can argue further that *Biggs* is analogous to the facts of her case and that the rule of law it represents thus applies to those facts.

3. DEPTH OF ANALYSIS

In presenting your legal arguments and authority, you must exercise firm control over depth of analysis, as introduced in Section IV.B.1 of Chapter 6 and discussed more thoroughly in Section II.A.2 of Chapter 13. You should review those sections, which examine three different levels or depths of analysis:

1. "light analysis" to present fundamental and undisputed propositions with direct statements of law and citation to authority,
2. in-depth analysis of statutes or case law to explore policy and reasoning, and
3. direct statements of law and citation to authority with parenthetic explanations for an intermediate level of analysis.

A good brief typically will employ the full range of depths of analysis. If a dispute reaches a court without a negotiated settlement, the issues are presumably substantial and reasonably contested by both parties. Consequently, neither party will be able to prevail on crucial issues with conclusory statements of the law and application to the facts. Instead, the brief likely will advance "in-depth" arguments of the law, the facts, or both for all but general background points.

Nonetheless, general legal background may be necessary to set the context for your more specific legal analyses. Rather than jump too quickly to the details of a complex argument, first provide your reader with necessary foundational points.

4. PRESENTING YOUR AUTHORITY

Finally, you must lead your reader through each of your arguments and support your assertions of law with supporting authority. Three techniques explored in Sections II and III of Chapter 14 are particularly important: You should

1. express your syntheses of authorities or other thesis statements in topic sentences or paragraphs;
2. unless the citations are independently significant, focus attention on your ideas and relegate citations to subordinate citation sentences; and
3. introduce quotations with substantive overviews that invite the judge to adopt your interpretation of the quoted material.

B. Analyzing the Facts

As discussed in greater detail in Chapter 22 in the context of appellate briefs, the opening statement of facts in a brief is most effective if it does not prematurely argue the law or the application of the law to the facts. In contrast, when you analyze the relevant facts in the argument section of a brief, you should explicitly reach a conclusion by relating the facts to the previously discussed legal standards. You may accomplish this by (1) directly applying the law to the facts or (2) using a form of inductive reasoning to analogize or distinguish precedent by comparing the facts and reasoning of the precedent to your own case.

To illustrate the first technique, suppose that you have established in your discussion of the law that a state police officer can be liable for punitive damages for recklessly depriving a citizen of her right to be free from arrest without probable cause. In the fact analysis of your argument, you could directly apply that rule of law to the facts by showing how the defendant police officer acted recklessly. In the following sample passage, the notations within brackets refer to pages of the trial court reporter's transcript on which critical testimony of witnesses is found.

Substantial evidence in the record supports the jury's finding that Officer Mullins acted with at least reckless disregard for Wong's clearly established Fourth Amendment rights. Mullins's actions show that even he did not believe that Wong fit the dispatcher's description of the robbery suspect. According to his own testimony, when he initially spotted Wong moments after receiving the robbery report, he passed by her and continued looking for the suspect. [RT at 324.] Only after failing to find a suspect who fit the dispatcher's description did he relocate Wong and summarily arrest her. [RT at 326.] An experienced officer such as Mullins obviously knew that he did not have probable cause to arrest Wong.

The jury could infer from these facts that Officer Mullins felt compelled to arrest somebody for the robbery and that he recklessly gambled that Wong might have been involved simply because of her proximity to the robbery. This is precisely the kind of reckless disregard for constitutional rights that an award of punitive damages is designed to deter. . . .

Alternatively, your discussion of the law may include in-depth case analysis and synthesis of arguably controlling, analogous, or distinguishable authority. If so, you may want to use the second technique of inductive reasoning to compare those cases directly to your dispute in your fact analysis:

Bonnie is closely analogous to our case and thus supports the conclusion that Beatty's promise was not illusory. In both *Bonnie* and our case, the promised performance was conditioned on events not entirely within the control of the promisor. In *Bonnie*, the buyer could escape his obligations only if market conditions rendered him *unable* to obtain a satisfactory mortgage loan. Similarly, in our case, Beatty could terminate his obligation to refrain from collecting on the debt only if economic conditions affected his income and expenses so as to create a *need* for the money.

Analogizing favorable case law on the facts

Conversely, *Atco Corp.* is distinguishable from our case. The promisor in that case retained the freedom to escape all contractual obligations if, at his own discretion, he *wanted* to. In contrast, the Guarantee Agreement in this case did not permit Beatty to demand his money whenever he *wanted* it. Instead, ...

Distinguishing adverse case law on the facts

C. Conclusions

Immediately after your fact analysis in each argument of your brief, you should briefly repeat the conclusion that you previewed in the point heading for that section or subsection:

Scott Paper Supply timely objected to Sun Printing Co.'s written confirmation of the alleged agreement. Therefore, the confirmation does not satisfy the requirements of the statute of frauds.

Additionally, every brief should end with a formal conclusion section. Many attorneys squander this opportunity to summarize their analyses. The following boilerplate is typical:

III. CONCLUSION

For the foregoing reasons, Appellant respectfully requests this Court to reverse the judgment of the superior court.

Although this style is conventional, a more substantive conclusion ordinarily is more satisfying, particularly if the brief presents more than one argument.

A substantive conclusion need not take up much space. If your arguments are simple, your conclusion need only briefly and generally repeat the request for relief and the supporting grounds, as in this closing to a brief in support of a motion to exclude evidence before trial:

III. CONCLUSION

Under Rule 403, Powell is entitled to pretrial exclusion of all evidence of his membership in the Black Panthers organization. The prejudicial effect of the evidence substantially outweighs its probative value, and the prejudice can be avoided only through exclusion of the evidence before trial.

In a more complex case, the conclusion might briefly summarize multiple arguments:

III. CONCLUSION

Yazzi's statement to the police officer is inadmissible on three grounds. First, it is not relevant to any issue in this suit. Second, even if it were relevant, it would be excludable because its prejudicial value substantially outweighs its probative value. Finally, it is inadmissible hearsay not falling within the exception for statements for purposes of medical treatment. This evidence should be excluded before trial to avoid exposing it to the jury and causing irremediable prejudice.

IV. SUMMARY

To effectively advocate your client's case in a written document,

1. organize your legal arguments in logical order, subject to overriding considerations of strategy;
2. introduce each of your arguments with an effective point heading and, if helpful, an introductory paragraph; and
3. present your analysis of the law, apply the law to the facts, and state the conclusion that you want the court to reach.

The next chapter examines persuasive writing style, as well as oral argument.

Chapter 17

Expressing Your Advocacy: Persuasive Writing Style and Oral Argument

I. PERSUASIVE WRITING STYLE

Supervising attorneys often complain that law students or recent graduates from law school do not use sufficiently strong language to write persuasively. Admittedly, advocacy calls for a writing style different from the more nearly neutral style appropriate for an office memorandum. Unfortunately, however, many supervising attorneys equate persuasive writing style with hyperbole, and they advise writers to pepper every sentence of a brief with exaggerated modifiers. Such a style may grab a judge's attention, but it does not often persuade. Judges recognize overstatement and tend to take everything in such a brief with an extra pinch of salt. Even worse, a writing style that is too obvious in its advocacy tends to divert the judge's attention from the substance of the argument and to focus it on the style itself.

The most persuasive writing style may be one that the judge never notices, one that keeps her attention riveted on the substance of the arguments and that presents those arguments so reasonably and clearly as to give

343

her the impression that the brief merely confirms her own independent conclusions. The most important element of such writing is good substantive analysis; a few extra hours of research and reflection may lead to an argument that is easily written in a persuasive manner. Beyond that, persuasive legal writing is distinguished by (1) strong, but not exaggerated, language and (2) effective emphasis through sentence structure, specificity, and concreteness.

A. Persuasive Language

1. THE ADVERSARIAL APPROACH

To clearly communicate your legal analysis to a supervising attorney in an office memorandum, you must candidly reveal uncertainties in the law and weaknesses in your client's case. In contrast, a brief in the same litigation generally should not explore the weaknesses of a client's case except as necessary to satisfy ethical duties or maintain credibility. The adversary system ensures that opposing counsel will test your arguments.

Thus, in an office memorandum, you might candidly admit the weakness of the support for a client's argument, as with the following fictitious analysis of a client's preemption argument:

Only one state court has held that the Federal Gun Control Act preempts more stringent state gun control legislation. *See California v. Biggs*, 567 P.2d 765 (Cal. 1987). Two other courts have interpreted the act to permit, or even encourage, more stringent state controls that are consistent with its policy. *See Arzani v. Matlock*, 332 So. 2d 234 (Fla. 1986); *Washington v. Smedley*, 558 P.2d 777 (Wash. 1986). To support our argument that the federal act preempts the New Maine gun registration legislation, we should emphasize the thorough reasoning of *Biggs* and try to discredit or distinguish *Arzani* and *Smedley*.

In *Biggs*, . . .

In contrast, in a brief to the court in the same case, you must state your client's argument more positively, while acknowledging and attempting to distinguish or discredit the contrary authority:

The Federal Gun Control Act preempts more stringent state gun control legislation. *See California v. Biggs*, 567 P.2d 765 (Cal. 1987). In *Biggs*, state officials sought to confiscate . . . .

Two courts had previously rejected the preemption argument adopted in *Biggs*, but each of them overlooked the critical legislative history so carefully analyzed in *Biggs*. *See Arzani v. Matlock*, . . . ; *Washington v. Smedley* . . . . For example, in *Arzani*, ...

The proposition for which *Biggs* is cited in the second example illustrates the power of the simple, unqualified statement:

The Federal Gun Control Act preempts more stringent state gun control legislation.

You should avoid unnecessary qualifiers that weaken arguments, such as the following introduction to the argument of your client, Mason:

Mason contends that the Federal Gun Control Act preempts more stringent state gun control legislation.

Because the argument section of your brief obviously comprises a series of legal contentions, specific introductions to that effect are superfluous. You may set up a response to your opponent's propositions by referring to them as "arguments" or "contentions," but such a characterization of your own conclusions or statements of law tends to weaken them.

2. CLICHÉS THAT WEAKEN OR OFFEND

Ironically, modifiers that are designed to reinforce a proposition sometimes sap the strength from an otherwise powerful statement. For example, comments such as "it is abundantly clear that" have little effect on the judge except to make him wonder whether the words were added to shore up a shaky proposition that in fact is subject to great debate. Along with other forms of exaggeration, clichés such as these tend to make the advocacy in the writing too obvious and distracting. Most judges will accept your conclusions more readily if you offer persuasive arguments than if you invoke stock phrases that describe your arguments as persuasive.

The line between strong advocacy and overstatement is most delicate when referring directly to a matter within the court's discretionary power. For example, the word "should" in the following argument reflects lack of confidence in the argument:

This court should exclude evidence of Jenkins' subjective intentions regarding the lease.

On the other hand, a stronger verb suggests a presumptuous challenge to the power of the court:

This court must exclude evidence of Jenkins' subjective intentions regarding the lease.

On reading such an argument, the judge might be subconsciously inclined to demonstrate that she does indeed have the discretionary power to admit the evidence, the exercise of which would not likely be overturned on appeal.

Restating the proposition in passive voice tends to soften and depersonalize the challenge:

Evidence of Jenkins' subjective intentions regarding the lease must be excluded.

Nonetheless, the challenge to the judge's power remains implicit in this construction. Perhaps the best statement is one that focuses directly on the character of the evidence rather than on the power of the judge:

Evidence of Jenkins' subjective intentions regarding the lease is inadmissible.

This proposition is strong and unqualified, yet it avoids expressing or directly implying a personal challenge to the judge.

3. PERSONAL ATTACKS

Equally important to avoid are personal attacks on opposing counsel. Although you may become exasperated with apparently unreasonable or offensive conduct by your opponent, judges do not appreciate being caught in a crossfire of personal insults. Unless misconduct by a party or his attorney is properly the subject of a motion, judges are far more interested in your response to the opposing counsel's arguments than in your personal opinion of your opponent's intelligence, research skills, or personality. Thus, you may safely characterize the opposing counsel's argument as internally inconsistent, but you should not comment that he is unable to write a coherent brief. Similarly, if your statement of the procedural history unemotionally records events that reflect the opposing counsel's intransigence or bad faith, the judge will undoubtedly draw negative conclusions about his advocacy without any further comment from you.

B. Sentence Structure

To preserve your credibility and ethical standards, you often must candidly acknowledge law that is adverse to your client's case and that you can neither discredit nor distinguish. You can minimize the resulting damage by using techniques of persuasive writing style to de-emphasize the adverse law and to focus attention on more helpful points.

One such technique consists of placing helpful information in the main clause and relegating adverse information to a dependent subordinate clause, a clause that cannot stand by itself as a complete sentence. For example, as counsel for the plaintiff in a contract action, you can de-emphasize the general rule against damages for emotional distress by disposing of it in an opening subordinate clause:

Although damages for emotional distress are not often awarded for breach of contract, Jones is entitled to such an award because of the exceptional nature

of his case: The central purpose of his contract with Runyon Pet Cemetery was to alleviate his grief over the loss of his dog. *See generally* . . .

You maintain credibility with this passage by facing, rather than evading, the general rule. Moreover, by placing the general rule in a subordinate clause, you invite the reader to give it only brief pause, as you might invite a guest at a restaurant to dine lightly on appetizers in anticipation of the main course.

Location of information within a sentence also affects emphasis. Generally, the end of a sentence conveys the greatest emphasis, the beginning of a sentence conveys secondary emphasis, and a parenthetic phrase or clause at a natural breaking point in the middle of the sentence conveys the least emphasis. For example, if you represent the defendant in the example above, you can emphasize the general rule by placing it at the end of the sentence:

In demanding an award of damages for emotional distress, Jones runs afoul of the general rule that such damages are not awarded for breach of contract.

In this example, as in the first, the general rule is stated in a subordinate clause. Nonetheless, the order of clauses within the sentence emphasizes the general rule.

Generally, you will emphasize the general rule least by placing it in a parenthetic clause at a natural breaking point in the middle of the sentence:

Jones is entitled to an award of damages for emotional distress in this exceptional case, even though such awards are rare in contract actions, because the central purpose of his contract with Runyon Pet Cemetery was to alleviate his grief over the loss of his dog.

This passage may be the best of the three for the plaintiff because it places favorable information in the positions of greatest emphasis.

Of course, if you are willing to sacrifice other style objectives, you can create unusual emphasis in the middle of the sentence with an abrupt, dramatic, or unnatural interruption of the sentence:

Jones unreasonably demands—and he admits that such damages generally are not awarded in contract actions—an award of damages for emotional distress.

II. ORAL ARGUMENT TO THE COURT

In many appeals and pretrial or trial motions, you will argue your client's case orally to the court after submitting your written brief. In most cases, your written brief will influence a judge more strongly than will your oral argument. Indeed, before oral argument, most judges read both parties' briefs and come to a tentative decision on the merits.

Nonetheless, oral argument is not yet a meaningless formality in our courts. It provides you with a final opportunity to emphasize critical points, respond to judges' questions, change the mind of a judge who had tentatively decided to rule in favor of the opposing party, or strongly influence a judge who has not formed a tentative opinion.

A. General Format

The typical oral argument follows a pattern similar to that of a briefing schedule: The advocate seeking relief or reversal of a judgment in a lower court argues first, the opposing advocate responds, and the first advocate has an opportunity for rebuttal. In some courts, the advocate arguing first must tell the court before she begins her argument whether she wishes to divide her time between opening argument and rebuttal.

Rebuttal is a powerful weapon. It provides the advocate who opens the oral argument with an opportunity to respond directly to the oral argument of the opponent. It also permits the advocate with the opening argument to have both the first and last word on the issues. Therefore, if you give the opening oral argument, you should always preserve the opportunity for rebuttal.

B. Formality and Demeanor

Appropriate courtroom attire is mandatory for any oral argument. Beyond that, the level of formality of the proceedings will vary among courts.

For pretrial and trial motions, some state trial court judges hold oral arguments in their chambers rather than in the courtroom. After friendly, informal introductions, all are seated. As the judge listens from behind his desk, you and the opposing counsel will deliver your arguments while seated in office chairs.

Other trial judges and virtually all appellate panels of judges, however, conduct oral arguments with greater formality. In those courts, you deliver your oral argument from a lectern in the courtroom.

If you are uncertain about the customs in a court or the expectations of a particular judge, you should not hesitate to seek advice from the staff of the clerk's office or from the judge's personal law clerk. To consult with them, you can use the telephone or simply arrive early on the day of the argument.

Your demeanor in oral argument should be as formal as your attire. You should be confident and relaxed but respectful of the judge. If you disagree with a judge during the argument, you need not make him defensive by being disagreeable. For example, if he asks you whether your formulation of a legal rule will have certain adverse policy ramifications, you should answer the question confidently but without arrogantly suggesting that the question is silly.

Thus, you should not respond to a judge's question or assertion with a challenge to his analytic skills, such as the following:

No, your Honor, that is incorrect.

Instead, you should answer the question without casting doubt on the questioner:

Your Honor, the court should be able to avoid those potential problems of line-drawing by stating its holding in this appeal narrowly. I suggest the following formulation: . . . .

In some cases, you may even want to validate the question before answering it:

That question has occupied the attention of a number of courts and scholars, your Honor. To answer it, I must review the rationale for the exclusionary rule.

C. Content of the Argument

1. INTRODUCTION OF THE ARGUMENT

In a formal courtroom argument, you should begin your presentation by introducing yourself and your representative capacity:

Good morning, your Honors. I am Terry Malloy. I represent Bakeway Stores, the appellant on this appeal and the defendant in the trial court.

Many advocates still begin their arguments with the traditional phrase,

---

May it please the court, I am Terry Malloy. . . .

This phrase sounds a little silly, because it suggests that you hope that your name "pleases the court." However, it also signals respect to the court and a willingness to allow the judges to set the agenda for the dialogue through their questions and comments. When in doubt, you probably should introduce yourself in this or some equally deferential manner.

After the personal introduction, you can capture the judges' attention with a brief characterization of the motion or appeal. If the facts are compelling, you can describe the general nature of the case in a sentence or two that conveys the theme of your argument. For example, suppose that a state is prosecuting prison inmates for possessing weapons materials in prison in violation of prison regulations and the state criminal code. The attorney for the defendant inmates has filed a motion to exclude evidence obtained in an allegedly illegal search. He might introduce his oral argument at the suppression hearing with the following characterization of the case:

Your Honor, the evidence in question is the product of a series of intrusive, physically brutal, and medically unsound body cavity searches of nearly a dozen unconsenting inmates, some of whom sustained permanent injuries as a result.

Alternatively, you can introduce your advocacy strongly by stating the issue in a way that invites a favorable response. In the criminal prosecution of the prison inmates, the prosecutor might begin her oral argument with the following:

Your Honor, this motion presents the question of whether prison officials may constitutionally conduct emergency searches to maintain prison security against the threat of a planned, armed insurrection by inmates.

2. BODY OF THE ARGUMENT

a. General Strategy

Many courts impose a time limit on each oral argument. Although the limits in some courts of last resort may be as long as 60 minutes for each side in a complex case, 15 to 30 minutes is more typical, and arguments on simple pretrial motions may be limited to 5 minutes. In most motions or appeals, you will not have time to address all the issues in the depth in which you explored them in your brief. Consequently, you should carefully study the arguments presented in both parties' briefs to determine the most effective strategy for oral argument.

Your strategy will differ depending on the circumstances of each case. In one appeal, for example, you may rely on multiple arguments that are both complex and interdependent. You may fear that, even with a well-organized brief to guide them, the judges may not fully appreciate how the arguments fit together to form the larger picture. You may thus decide to present an oral outline of all the arguments and their relationships, leaving the detail of each to your brief. More commonly, you can identify an argument in your brief that you wish to emphasize, perhaps because it addresses a critically important threshold issue, because it is your strongest theory, or even because it is the weakest link in your argumentative chain and needs extra support.

Whatever strategy you choose, you should communicate your intentions immediately after the introduction to your argument. For example, at a hearing to suppress evidence obtained in an allegedly illegal search, the prosecutor may try to justify the search on several grounds. Although she will introduce evidence at the hearing supporting each of the grounds and will advocate each ground in her brief, she might use her oral argument to focus on the determinative issue of consent to search. If so, she should reveal her plans to the court:

This hearing presents three major issues, all of which the briefs examine in detail. I will be happy to answer questions on any of the issues. However, I would like to focus my presentation on the issue of consent to search. If the facts show that the inmates consented to the searches, this court need not address the more difficult questions related to expectations of privacy in prison and to reasonableness of the search methods.

---

b. Using the Facts

Many judges will advise oral advocates before argument that the judges are familiar with the facts of the case and that the advocates should proceed with their legal analyses. Even absent such an instruction, you ordinarily should not begin your argument with a lengthy recitation of the facts beyond a general characterization of the nature of the case. You might depart from this advice if the facts are particularly compelling and your legal arguments are not. In most cases, however, you will make better use of your limited time by arguing the law and applying the law to the facts without a separate introductory recitation of facts.

Whenever you rely on facts in an oral argument, be certain of the source of the facts. Be prepared to cite to the portion of the record that establishes the facts.

c. Responding to Questions

Questions from the bench constitute the most uncertain variable in oral argument. They ensure that oral advocacy in most cases is not a series of speeches but a dialogue, primarily between each advocate and the judges, and secondarily between the advocates as they respond to one another. Ironically, oral argument also permits judges on a panel to establish a coy dialogue among themselves, as they attempt to persuade each other with comments and questions ostensibly directed to the advocates.

You should genuinely welcome the opportunity to respond to questions. A judge's questions may reveal areas in which she has doubts, permitting you to directly influence her thinking on those points.

Occasionally, a judge will press you for a concession on your weakest among several alternative arguments. Your waiving the argument might be the most effective way to turn the judge's attention to your stronger arguments. However, you should not too quickly waive a major argument that you had earlier determined was sufficiently meritorious to warrant discussion in your brief. If you are arguing before a panel of judges, the other panel members may not share the doubts of the questioning judge; yet, if you waive the controversial point during oral argument, none of the judges will take up your cause on that theory. Thus, even though it appears that you must waive the argument to preserve your credibility, you should first try to shift to a more productive topic of discussion without making the concession:

> Your Honor, I prefer not to waive our argument that the prison officials lacked probable cause to search, but I admit that our other arguments are stronger. Both in the trial court and on appeal, the defendant inmates have most strongly complained of the unreasonable method of the searches. On this issue, the law is clear: . . . .

Except when trying to avoid a waiver of an argument, you should not give the appearance of evading questions from the bench. You should confront and answer the questions directly. To answer judges' questions effectively, you must come to the argument thoroughly prepared. In particular, you should be ready to

- discuss the facts, holding, and reasoning of any case that you seek to rely on or to distinguish;
- cite to the record to identify the source of facts on which you rely; and
- discuss the policy implications of alternative holdings among which the court must choose.

An excellent method of preparing for the oral argument is to hold practice sessions with colleagues acting as judges. Your colleagues can give you constructive criticism on your performance. Moreover, the questions they ask during the practice rounds will help you anticipate the questions likely to be asked by the judges in the actual oral argument.

Even with excellent preparation, you may not always anticipate every question that a judge may ask you. If you cannot formulate a satisfactory answer to a truly unexpected and excessively challenging question, you probably will do better to acknowledge the difficulty of the question and to offer to address it in your rebuttal or in a supplementary brief than to simply bluff or brush the question aside.

Because you cannot always predict the number of questions from the bench, you must build maximum flexibility into your argument. You should be prepared to do either of the following or anything in between:

- present your arguments without interruption until your time elapses or you otherwise finish your argument; or
- present a brief introduction, respond without break to a series of questions that takes up all your allotted time, and request that the court permit you to end with a prepared conclusion no longer than a few sentences.

3. THE CONCLUSION

You should end your argument on a strong note, perhaps with a summary of your strongest points. A carefully planned conclusion will be particularly helpful if persistent questioning from the bench prevents you from covering all the points that you had planned to address in your oral argument. Faced with the impending expiration of your allotted time, you can fall back on the conclusion as a quick means of stating your points, if only in summary fashion.

D. Nervousness and Verbal Stumbling

All but the most experienced oral advocates feel some anxiety at the prospect of facing an inquisitive panel of judges in a public setting. If you feel such anxiety, you may be concerned that your nervousness will interfere with your speech patterns, causing your voice to shake or causing you to stumble over your words or to pause to collect your thoughts. You need not worry excessively about such problems for two reasons.

First, as long as the judge can understand you, the substance of your arguments and of your responses to questions will be more important than your charisma and stage presence. Some law school moot court programs may exalt form over substance: You may earn points if you can glibly respond to a judge's questions without pause, or lose points if you occasionally stumble over a difficult word. In actual oral arguments, however, judges will be more concerned with establishing a genuine dialogue with you. They will not be uncomfortable with a few moments of silence from you; indeed, most will expect you to pause to think deeply before answering a particularly difficult question. Moreover, if you speak sufficiently slowly and clearly to make yourself understood, most judges will forgive you for the occasional verbal stumbling that nervousness may produce.

Second, you can minimize distracting imperfections in your delivery caused by nervousness. Perhaps the best way to bring such nervousness under control is to approach your oral argument with the confidence that comes from thorough preparation. If you have carefully prepared your analysis, mastered the facts and the record, anticipated questions, and rehearsed your argument before colleagues playing the role of inquisitive judges, you can confidently assume that you will bring an expertise to the courtroom that the judge will appreciate.

To deal with nervousness at the beginning of your argument, you can prepare a carefully worded introduction that you can commit to memory, so that you will not find yourself groping for words at the outset. Then, after you have warmed up your speaking voice, you can speak more flexibly from a rough outline of your main argument before closing with a carefully planned conclusion.

III. SUMMARY

Effective advocacy requires sound analysis, sensible organization, and effective writing style. In addition to the matters examined in Chapter 16, you should adopt a persuasive writing style and carefully prepare an oral argument that strategically supplements your brief.

The following chapters examine further techniques of persuasive writing in the context of particular legal documents.

Exercise 17-1

MOTION TO DISMISS

Under Federal Rule of Civil Procedure 12(b)(6) a defendant may move to dismiss a complaint "for failure to state a claim upon which relief can be granted." Many states have adopted identical provisions in their state rules of civil procedure.

The imaginary state of Calzona has adopted the language of Rule 12(b)(6) in a state rule of civil procedure, Calz. R. Civ. P. 12(b)(6). You may also assume that the Calzona courts agree with the standards for evaluating Rule 12(b)(6) motions that are set forth in *Greenwood v. Taft, Stettinius & Hollister*, 663 N.E.2d 1030, 1031 (Ohio Ct. App. 1995). Finally, imagine that the following Arizona decision is in fact a decision of the Supreme Court of Calzona: *Wagenseller v. Scottsdale Mem'l Hosp.*, 710 P.2d 1025 (Ariz. 1985). You may assume that pages 1031-36 of *Wagenseller* state the current law in Calzona regarding the tort of wrongful discharge for violation of public policy, that no statute or more recent case law applies, and that you may cite to *Wagenseller* as though it were a Calzona decision by replacing "Ariz." with "Calz." in the parenthetic identification of state and year.

Find these authorities in your law library and study them. Then read Assignment 4 in Appendix IV, near the end of this book. Assume that George Bryant has filed a complaint against Marie Jardon, doing business as Chez Marie, alleging only that Jardon's agent fired Bryant from his employment at Chez Marie for a reason that violated Calzona public policy. Using the authorities described above and the information from Assignment 4 about the public policies in Calzona, draft a short brief supporting or opposing a motion to dismiss Bryant's complaint in the Calzona Superior Court. You may rely on any authority cited in Chapter 4, Section III.A, of this book to support your interpretation of the employment discrimination statutes cited in Assignment 4 of Appendix IV.

Your brief will support or oppose the following motion:

[Your Name]
[Your Address]

CALZONA SUPERIOR COURT
WARMS SPRINGS COUNTY

George BRYANT, Plaintiff,	
v.	No. CIV-9X-79
	MOTION TO DISMISS
Marie JARDON, d.b.a. Chez Marie, Defendant.	(Oral argument requested)

Defendant, Marie Jardon, moves this Court to dismiss Plaintiff's Complaint for failure to state a claim for which relief can be granted. *See* Calz. R. Civ. P. 12(b)(6) (1995). Plaintiff has failed to allege a violation of public policy, a required element of his claim for relief. This motion is supported by the attached Memorandum of Law.

[Your Name]

Attorney for Defendant, Marie Jardon

[Date]

If you draft a supporting brief, you should staple the above motion on top of your supporting brief. A brief in support of a motion was traditionally titled "Memorandum of Points and Authorities" and is now more commonly titled "Memorandum of Law." You may begin your brief with the following heading:

MEMORANDUM OF LAW IN SUPPORT OF MOTION TO DISMISS

The body of your brief should include three parts:

  I. Facts [or "Introduction," or "Background," or "Statement of the Case"]
 II. Argument
III. Conclusion

If you draft a brief opposing the motion, begin with a cover page that includes the same identification of the author of the brief, the court, and the parties, but replace "Motion to Dismiss" with "Opposition to Defendant Jardon's Motion to Dismiss." Below that, without stating a motion of your own, you can simply state the plaintiff's intent to oppose the motion, perhaps with a very brief reference to the nature of your argument. You can then begin your brief with the same heading as above, except with the phrase "IN OPPOSITION TO" in place of "IN SUPPORT OF."

Use the above format and the skills that you have acquired from Part VI to draft a short, simple brief supporting your motion, or one opposing the motion submitted by a classmate. In addition, be prepared to orally argue your position before an instructor or classmate posing as the trial judge.

For a similar exercise, perform Assignment 1 in Appendix VI, near the end of this book.

Part VII

Pretrial Advocacy—Pleadings and Motions

You may file different kinds of pleadings and briefs to a court from the inception of a lawsuit to its final disposition in a court of last resort. Part VI of this book ended with an exercise that introduced you to a motion to dismiss a complaint. This part of the book explores other kinds of pretrial pleadings and briefs with the aim of preparing you to initiate or respond to any form of written advocacy. Part VIII will examine appellate briefwriting.

The following three chapters introduce you to three kinds of pretrial written advocacy: pleadings, motions for summary judgment, and pretrial motions to exclude evidence. When combined with the Motion to Dismiss exercise at the end of Part VI, and with the discussion of appellate briefs in Part VIII, Part VII should provide you with the skills and confidence you need to perform any task of written advocacy.

Chapter **18**

Pleadings

I. THE COMPLAINT

"A civil action is commenced by filing a complaint with the court."[1] One might suppose that any lawyer would graduate from law school with a solid grasp of the mechanics of such a fundamental and significant document. However, few law students draft a complaint before leaving law school, and many graduate without having seen one. Not surprisingly, when faced with the task of preparing a complaint, you may be tempted to turn for guidance to the forms in formbooks or in your office files.

Forms may provide general guidance in some cases. In fact, many jurisdictions have officially authorized pleading forms for certain kinds of suits. The California Judicial Council has even approved pleading forms that invite the user to choose among standard allegations by checking boxes.[2]

Nonetheless, you will more quickly and thoroughly master the skills of artful pleading if you understand the components of a complaint well enough

---

1. FED. R. CIV. P. 3.
2. *See* Barbara Child, DRAFTING LEGAL DOCUMENTS: PRINCIPLES AND PRACTICES 10-14 (2d ed. 1992).

to draft one "from scratch." Your primary tools in such a task are the results of your investigation of facts and your knowledge of the applicable law. Beyond that, rules of procedure and local court rules provide the necessary guidance.

A. Format

Local court rules on pleading often specify a form for a caption that identifies the case and the nature of the document. For example, the Rules of Practice for the United States District Court for the District of Arizona specify the precise location in the caption on the cover sheet for, among other things, the following information: (1) the name, address, state bar attorney number, and telephone number of the representing attorney; (2) the title of the court; (3) the names of the parties; and (4) a designation of the nature of the document.[3]

More substantively, the Federal Rules of Civil Procedure require a complaint, or any other pleading setting forth a claim for relief, to contain three elements:

1. A short and plain statement of the grounds upon which the court's jurisdiction depends . . . .
2. A short and plain statement of the claim showing that the pleader is entitled to relief.
3. A demand for judgment for the relief the pleader seeks . . . .[4]

Each of these elements warrants further examination.

1. JURISDICTIONAL STATEMENT

The jurisdictional statement is particularly important in a complaint filed in federal court, because the subject matter jurisdiction of federal courts is limited to that authorized by Article III of the United States Constitution and by federal statutes.[5] Therefore, in the initial paragraphs of a complaint in federal court, you should allege facts establishing subject matter jurisdiction based on a federal question,[6] diversity of citizenship,[7] or a special statutory grant of jurisdiction.[8] Although the jurisdictional statement is sufficient if it alleges facts that support the court's exercise of jurisdiction,[9] federal pleaders customarily cite to the specific statutes that grant jurisdiction:

3. D. ARIZ. R. 1.9(a).
4. FED. R. CIV. P. 8(a).
5. *See, e.g.,* Mayor v. Cooper, 73 U.S. (6 Wall.) 247, 252 (1868).
6. *See* 28 U.S.C. § 1331 (1994).
7. *Id.* § 1332.
8. *See, e.g.,* 42 U.S.C. § 2000e-5(f)(3) (1994) (granting jurisdiction of actions brought under Title VII of the Civil Rights Act of 1964).
9. Aguirre v. Automotive Teamsters, 633 F.2d 168, 174 (9th Cir. 1980).

3. This claim arises under Title VII of the Civil Rights Act of 1964; therefore, this court has subject matter jurisdiction under 42 U.S.C. § 2000e-5(f)(3) and 28 U.S.C. § 1331.[10]

Some jurisdictional statements in federal complaints also include allegations that establish that the court has personal jurisdiction over the defendant, if that is not apparent from the body of the complaint. Assuming that lack of personal jurisdiction is treated as an affirmative defense for pleading purposes, however, a complaint will not be insufficient for failure to affirmatively plead personal jurisdiction over the defendant.

Pleading subject matter jurisdiction is less important in state court than in federal court, because most state trial courts are courts of general jurisdiction. When state pleaders address subject matter jurisdiction at all, it is often with simple introductory allegations that the amount in controversy exceeds that reserved for state courts of limited jurisdiction, perhaps coupled with a citation to the state constitutional or statutory provision that authorizes the court's exercise of general trial jurisdiction.

Nonetheless, some state legislatures have adopted all the elements of the governing federal rule of civil procedure, thus requiring a jurisdictional statement in state court complaints.[11] Because a special allegation of subject matter jurisdiction is less clearly necessary in a state court complaint, state pleaders often begin their complaints with allegations of *personal* jurisdiction over the defendants. Such statements typically introduce the parties and allege in fairly conclusory fashion that the defendant has engaged in conduct in the state out of which the claim arises or has otherwise established the requisite contacts with the state.

2. CLAIM FOR RELIEF

Early state pleading codes that required allegations of "material facts" or "ultimate facts" supporting a cause of action generated considerable controversy over the intended meaning of the word "facts."[12] Perhaps to avoid that controversy, Federal Rule of Civil Procedure 8(a)(2) omits any reference to "facts" in its requirement of a statement of the claim for relief. Nonetheless, "Rule 8(a)(2) envisages the statement of circumstances, occurrences, and events in support of the claim presented."[13] Most people would use the word "fact" to describe allegations of that nature. Similarly, this book will use "fact" in this context while attempting to avoid the historical confusion surrounding the term.

10. *See also* FED. R. CIV. P., app. Form 2(b), (c) (providing form allegations for federal question jurisdiction).
11. *See, e.g.,* ARIZ. R. CIV. P. 8(a).
12. *See, e.g.,* Walter W. Cook, *"Facts" and "Statements of Fact,"* 4 U. Chi. L. Rev. 233, 233-34, 235-39, 241-42, 246 (1937), *reprinted in* William R. Bishin & Christopher D. Stone, LAW, LANGUAGE, AND ETHICS 277-81 (1972).
13. Advisory Committee on Rules for Civil Procedure, *Report of Proposed Amendments to the Rules of Civil Procedure for the United States District Courts* 18-19 (1955), *reprinted in* Richard H. Field, Benjamin Kaplan & Kevin M. Clermont, MATERIALS FOR A BASIC COURSE IN CIVIL PROCEDURE 524 (7th ed. 1997).

Thus, in the main body of the complaint, you will allege facts and conclusions of liability that establish entitlement to relief. This may require preliminary legal research as well as fact investigation. Your knowledge of the law will enable you to identify legally significant facts, and your knowledge of the case will help you to determine what facts you can allege in good faith.

To draft your claim for relief artfully, you must determine

1. the extent, if any, to which you should supplement fact allegations with references to the law;
2. the specific content of the fact allegations; and
3. the appropriate level of specificity of the allegations.

a. Allegations of Fact and Citations to Law

Your complaint should allege facts and ultimate conclusions establishing a claim for relief; you need not cite to supporting legal authority.[14] Thus, you need allege only two of the three elements of the syllogism of deductive reasoning:

Major premise	Rule of Law
Minor premise	Allegations of Fact
Conclusion	Allegation of Liability or Other Ultimate Conclusion

A complaint with the minimum necessary elements will explicitly set forth the minor premise and the conclusion, and it will leave the major premise implicit.

For a simple example, a form complaint appended to the Federal Rules of Civil Procedure states a claim for debt that alleges subsidiary facts and the ultimate conclusion that the defendant "owes" money to the plaintiff:

> 2. Defendant on or about June 1, 1935, executed and delivered to plaintiff a promissory note . . . whereby defendant promised to pay to plaintiff or order on June 1, 1936 the sum of _____ dollars with interest thereon at the rate of six percent per annum.
> 3. Defendant owes to plaintiff the amount of said note and interest.[15]

These sample allegations do not explicitly state the major premise that a promise to pay money expressed in a written promissory note is enforceable under the common law of contracts or under some other legal authority. Whether the alleged facts state a claim for relief under applicable legal authority can be addressed in subsequent proceedings, such as on a motion to dismiss.[16]

Thus, in practice, citation to specific legal authority is much less common in the claim for relief than in the jurisdictional statement. The only references to legal authority commonly found in claims for relief are descriptive headings that introduce counts with general legal theories of relief, such as "Negli-

---

14. *E.g.*, Doss v. South Cent. Bell Tel. Co., 834 F.2d 421 (5th Cir. 1987).
15. FED. R. CIV. P., app. Form 3 (brackets and footnote deleted).
16. *See* FED. R. CIV. P. 12(b)(6).

gence," "Wrongful Discharge," "Employment Discrimination," or "Breach of Contract."

Nonetheless, a pleader will sometimes cite to authority in the claim for relief for a strategic purpose. For example, in cases in which the plaintiff wants a settlement at the outset of litigation, his attorney may briefly cite to authority in the complaint to demonstrate to the defendant that the claim is substantial and that further litigation is unlikely to reduce the risk of liability. In most cases, however, the attorney could achieve the same result less subtly, and perhaps more effectively, with a demand letter that explains the merits of the claim. Such a letter could either precede or accompany the complaint.

When the allegations or implicit legal theories are unusually complex, some attorneys recommend a middle ground: You can limit your allegations to factual matters but can explain the nature of the claims and allegations in a short "Introduction" or "Overview" that precedes the specific factual allegations. In one or two paragraphs, you can help the reader see the whole forest before entering the confusing stands of trees by (1) briefly identifying any novel legal theories on which your claims depend, or (2) summarizing how numerous complicated transactions or other facts relate to one another, or both.[17]

b. Substance of Allegations

One writer has recommended that pleaders pay heed to the journalist's five Ws when stating a claim for relief: who, what, where, when, and why.[18]

Who—In some complaints, you will introduce the parties in the jurisdictional allegations. Otherwise, your statement of the claim for relief should identify them and their relationship to one another. It should also identify any other significant actors.

What, Where, When—The statement of the claim should describe the events that give rise to the claim. You should take care to allege all facts or conclusions needed to support the request for relief. For example, you should support a request for specific performance with an allegation that the legal remedy is inadequate.

Why—You should allege any state of mind that is material to the claim or to the availability of special relief. For example, a request for punitive damages in a common law tort claim must be supported by an allegation of malice, willful misconduct, or at least recklessness, depending on the jurisdiction.

You need not allege all matters that may ultimately be in dispute; you need allege only the elements of your client's prima facie case. Affirmative defenses must be pleaded in the answer,[19] and the complaint need not anticipate them. The federal rules list 19 affirmative defenses;[20] statutes and case law may help you define the burdens of pleading on other matters. In case of doubt, you should plead a matter as part of the claim for relief.

17. *See generally* e-mail from Peter Friedman, Director of Research, Analysis, and Writing Courses and Legal Skills Courses, Case Western Reserve Univ. School of Law (Sept. 10, 2000) (discussing practice of inserting "introductory, non-numbered text into the beginnings of complaints in complex cases").
18. Delmar Karlen, PROCEDURE BEFORE TRIAL IN A NUTSHELL 41-42 (1972).
19. *See* FED. R. CIV. P. 8(c).
20. *Id.*

For example, suppose that the jurisdiction in which the complaint is filed recognizes a cause of action for intentional infliction of emotional distress on proof of four elements: (1) The defendant engaged in extreme and outrageous conduct (2) with the intent to cause severe emotional distress or with reckless disregard for the possibility of those consequences, and (3) the conduct caused the plaintiff to suffer (4) severe emotional distress.[21] After introductory allegations establishing personal jurisdiction and identifying Jansen as the plaintiff and Bostich as one of the defendants, the count for this claim should allege facts supporting each of the four elements of the prima facie case:

COUNT I
Infliction of Emotional Distress

Relationship of parties

3. Jansen worked on an assembly line at the Zydeco Radio factory under the direct supervision of Bostich. As Jansen's supervisor, Bostich had the authority to impose production quotas on Jansen and to impose discipline, including termination, for failure to meet quotas.

Conduct

4. From April 1 to June 10, 2001, Bostich engaged in the extreme and outrageous conduct of imposing impossible production quotas on Jansen and causing Jansen to believe that his job security depended on his meeting the quotas.[22]

State of mind

5. Bostich maliciously engaged in this conduct for the purpose of causing Jansen to suffer severe emotional distress. Alternatively, Bostich recklessly disregarded the likelihood that Jansen would suffer such distress.[23]

Causation and distress

6. On June 10, 2001, as a direct result of Bostich's conduct, Jansen suffered a complete nervous breakdown requiring bed rest for three weeks and extensive medical care.

Injuries

7. Jansen continues to suffer insomnia, headaches, inability to concentrate at work, general nervousness, and other emotional distress as a result of Bostich's conduct. In an effort to address these symptoms, Jansen has frequently consulted a general physician and a psychological counselor, incurring substantial medical expenses.

Jansen therefore requests the following relief:
. . .

---

21. *See, e.g.*, Watts v. Golden Age Nursing Home, 619 P.2d 1032, 1035 (Ariz. 1980) (citing Restatement (Second) of Torts § 46).

22. Whether the allegations of paragraphs 3 and 4 establish "extreme and outrageous conduct" will depend on the law of that jurisdiction and could be litigated on a motion to dismiss for failure to state a claim. *See, e.g.*, Fed. R. Civ. P. 12(b)(6).

23. This allegation of scienter should suffice not only to satisfy the second element of the tort but to support a request for punitive damages as well.

In contrast, even if the allegations raise some question of whether the statute of limitations has expired, the complaint need not affirmatively allege that the statute of limitations has not expired or has been tolled. Instead, expiration of the statute of limitations is an affirmative defense that the defendant has the burden of pleading.[24]

c. Specificity of Fact Allegations

The early, rigid common law forms of action gave way in this country in the nineteenth century with widespread enactment of versions of the Field Code, which required complaints to set forth a "statement of the facts constituting the cause of action, in ordinary and concise language."[25] In the twentieth century, the federal system and most states replaced their versions of the Field Code with rules permitting pleadings that give the court and the opposing party more general, less fact-specific notice of most claims and defenses.[26] Federal Rule of Civil Procedure 8(a)(2) requires the main portion of a complaint to include only a "short and plain statement of the claim showing that the pleader is entitled to relief." Revelation of specific evidentiary details is left to the discovery and disclosure process, motions for summary judgment, and the pretrial conference.[27]

Of course, a bare allegation of liability without any supporting facts would be insufficient even under the federal rules: "[Rule 8(a)(2)] requires the pleader to disclose adequate information as the basis of his claim for relief as distinguished from a bare averment that he wants relief and is entitled to it."[28] Nonetheless, the rules permit fact allegations that are fairly general and conclusory.

The appropriate level of generality can be illustrated by a continuum that represents varying degrees of specificity in fact allegations. The continuum begins with allegations of conclusions based on the analysis of implicit subsidiary facts. It gains steadily in specificity until it presents specific evidence that establishes subsidiary facts:

CONCLUSION	SPECIFIC EVIDENCE
negligence	eyewitness estimate of speed; analysis of skid marks

As an example of extreme specificity, a complaint could state a claim for negligent operation of an automobile by alleging each bit of evidence with which the plaintiff hopes to prove negligence at trial:

---

24. *See* FED. R. CIV. P. 8(c).

25. *See* Richard L. Marcus, *The Puzzling Persistence of Pleading Practice*, 76 Tex. L. Rev. 1749, 1753 & n.28 (1998) (discussing and quoting the Field Code).

26. *See id.* at 753-54.

27. *See* FED. R. CIV. P. 12, 16, 26-37, 56.

28. Advisory Committee on Rules for Civil Procedure, Report of Proposed Amendments to the Rules of Civil Procedure for the United States District Courts 18-19 (1955), *reprinted in* Field, Kaplan & Clermont, *supra* note 13, at 524, 525.

3. . . . Jill Graham and Ben Cooper were standing at the corner of 7th Avenue and Washington Street at noon and observed the defendant driving his automobile at high speed west on Washington Street toward 9th Avenue. Each of them estimated that the defendant was traveling at approximately twice the posted speed limit of 35 miles per hour. An expert who examined skid marks at the accident scene estimated that the defendant's automobile was traveling at more than 60 miles per hour when it entered the intersection of Washington Street and 9th Avenue. . . .

Nearer to the other extreme, the complaint could allege the ultimate conclusion of negligence with only general supporting factual information:

2. On January 1, 1998, defendant negligently drove a motor vehicle in the intersection of Washington Street and 9th Avenue, striking plaintiff in the crosswalk.
3. As a result, ...

This second example is adapted from a sample form in the Federal Rules of Civil Procedure,[29] illustrating the acceptability of general, conclusory allegations on most matters.

In states that retain the more fact-oriented pleading requirements of the Field Code, the appropriate level of specificity probably would lie somewhere in the middle of the continuum. The complaint in such a state would allege the "ultimate facts" supporting the conclusions of liability, but it would not give a detailed account of all the evidence from which the facts and conclusions are derived. For example, the complaint might allege that the defendant operated the car negligently by exceeding the speed limit and by weaving between lanes, but it would not require allegations of the subsidiary evidence of speeding, such as the analysis of skid marks.[30]

Whether your complaint is governed by the federal standard of notice pleading or by more traditional rules, you may reap strategic advantages from alleging your claim for relief with the maximum generality allowed. Unnecessarily specific allegations, for example, might prematurely commit the plaintiff to a particular factual theory of the case. In one suit to recover a commission, an attorney specifically alleged that her client, the plaintiff, acted as agent for the defendant in a real estate transaction. That allegation was unnecessary to the client's claim for relief, which would have been supported by a more general allegation of contractual liability. Subsequent discovery revealed that the plaintiff probably did not act as the defendant's agent. The plaintiff's earlier allegations of agency, however, supported a defense and counterclaim for the defendant based on breaches of an agent's fiduciary duties. The plaintiff was forced to move to amend the complaint to delete the allegation of agency, an amendment necessary to avoid summary judgment for the defendant.

29. FED. R. CIV. P., app. Form 9 ¶¶ 2, 3.
30. *See generally* Field, Kaplan & Clermont, *supra* note 13, at 525-26.

Despite the potential pitfalls of detailed allegations, few complaints are as conclusory as the passage above quoted from the sample federal negligence pleading. In some cases, greater specificity is required by applicable rules or statutes. For example, the Federal Rules of Civil Procedure provide that allegations of certain "special matters," such as "fraud or mistake," must state the circumstances with particularity.[31] Moreover, even the general notice pleading standards of the federal rules are subject to interpretation, and courts in some jurisdictions have developed a reputation for demanding greater specificity than might seem to be required by the plain language of the rules.[32]

Even when particularity is not required, some attorneys allege events with greater specificity than is required by notice pleading rules because they wish to present a more vivid and sympathetic story to help the reader understand the relationships between complex transactions.

In summary, the specificity of your allegations is partly a matter of style and strategy. As long as you take care to allege facts supporting every element of your prima facie case, you can tailor the specificity of your allegations to your strategic needs. Even so, you should start with general allegations and add specificity only if you have good reason to do so. If excessively detailed allegations unnecessarily transform your pleading into a cumbersome tool for its intended audiences, you may face a court that is receptive to a motion to strike your pleading.[33]

3. REQUEST FOR RELIEF

Your complaint should end with a simple statement of the relief sought by your client. The main request for relief typically is for an injunction, an award of money damages, or both. Consult local rules to determine whether you must request a specific dollar amount of some kinds of damages and an unspecified amount of other kinds. Although a request for a specific amount of damages will seldom be mandatory under local rules, you more likely will exercise discretion to allege a specific amount of damages in a suit for a certain sum of money, such as money due on a loan: "$10,000 plus interest."

Additionally, you should request an award of reasonable costs and attorneys' fees if your client has a legal basis for such an award. Finally, you can

31. FED. R. CIV. P. 9(b); *see also* 15 U.S.C. § 78u-4(b) (1994 ed., Supp. V) (requiring complaints in securities fraud actions to allege certain facts with particularity); Ziemba v. Cascade Int'l, Inc., 256 F.3d 1194, 1202 (11th Cir. 2001) (explaining purposes of Rule 9(b) but noting that it is not intended to abrogate the concept of notice pleading).

32. *See, e.g.*, Marcus, *supra* note 25, at 1774 ("courts sometimes construct dubious new pleading barriers," such as when they "apparently still strain to justify the application of [Rule 9(b)'s particularity requirements] outside their natural sphere"); Patricia M. Wald, *Summary Judgment at Sixty*, 76 Tex. L. Rev. 1897, 1941-42 (1998) (partly "fueled by the overloaded dockets of the last two decades," courts are increasingly using summary judgment to weed out marginal cases, and "appear to be requiring plaintiffs to plead facts with ever greater detail in order to survive motions to dismiss").

33. *See* Anserve Ins. Serv., Inc. v. Albrecht, 960 P.2d 1159, 1161 (Ariz. 1998) (en banc) ("Early on, the trial judge should have granted the motion to strike" a 269-page complaint.); McHenry v. Renne, 84 F.3d 1172, 1180 (9th Cir. 1996) (a complaint that was "written more as a press release, prolix in evidentiary detail, yet without simplicity, conciseness and clarity . . . fails to perform the essential functions of a complaint").

retain flexibility by closing the request for relief with a catch-all request for "other appropriate relief":

Jansen therefore requests judgment granting the following relief:

1. an award of compensatory damages in an amount to be set at trial;
2. an award of punitive damages in an amount to be set at trial;
3. an award of reasonable costs and attorney's fees; and
4. such other relief as the court deems appropriate.

B. Style and Organization

1. WRITING STYLE

Some of lawyers' stuffiest jargon can be found in antiquated pleadings:

Comes now the plaintiff before this honorable court and, through his attorneys, Jenkins, Brown, and Little, alleges, pleads, and avers as follows:

3. That the defendant did employ said plaintiff as a designer of clothes . . . ;

4. That on July 6, 1927, said defendant did . . . ;

Wherefore, the plaintiff prays that this honorable court grant judgment for the plaintiff and award . . .

The federal rules reject jargon in favor of plain English: "Each averment of a pleading shall be simple, concise, and direct."[34] Stated in plain English, the allegations in the preceding example are unquestionably simpler and more concise:

Plaintiff alleges:

3. The defendant employed the plaintiff as a designer of clothes . . . .

4. On July 6, 1927, the defendant . . . .

Plaintiff requests the following relief: . . . .

---

2. ORGANIZATION

To facilitate analysis of the claims by the court and the parties, set forth the allegations of your complaint in consecutively numbered paragraphs. Separation of the statements of different claims for relief into separate counts may be permissible or required, depending on the circumstances.

If you have joined separate claims for relief based on different transactions, federal rules require a statement of the claims in separate counts

---

34. FED. R. CIV. P. 8(e)(1). Ironically, the sample forms in the appendix to the federal rules contain their share of jargon.

"whenever a separation facilitates the clear presentation of the matters set forth."[35] Otherwise, presentation of allegations in separate counts appears to be discretionary.

Even if your client's claims arise out of a single transaction, separate counts may be helpful if you rely on distinct legal theories that are based on different fact allegations. For example, a consumer injured by a faulty electrical appliance may have a cause of action against the retailer on two legal theories: products liability in tort and breach of a contractual warranty. If you divide the allegations into separate counts, you can identify which fact allegations are material to each theory of relief. If some facts are common to both theories, one count can incorporate some of the allegations of the other:

COUNT I

Products Liability

4. On January 1, 2002, Green purchased a microwave oven from Retailer.
5. The microwave oven had an unreasonably dangerous defect . . .
• • • •

COUNT II

Breach of Warranty

8. Green realleges the allegations in paragraphs 4-7.
9. Babcock Appliance Center warranted the microwave oven to be free of defects. . . .

You must also exercise discretion to determine whether to follow each count with a separate request for relief or to consolidate them in a single request after presenting all counts. As with separation of theories into counts, separation of requests for relief to accompany different counts may be helpful if the available remedies vary with each count. For example, if punitive damages are available only on the products liability count and if attorney's fees are available only on the count for breach of warranty, separate requests for relief after each count may facilitate subsequent analysis of the claims. On the other hand, if the requests for relief on different counts are identical, consolidation in a single request obviously avoids pointless repetition.

II. THE ANSWER

To avoid judgment against him by default, the defendant must respond to a complaint by filing an answer or other appropriate response.[36] The answer

35. FED. R. CIV. P. 10(b).
36. See FED. R. CIV. P. 12(a). The defendant may move to dismiss the complaint on its face before filing an answer. See FED. R. CIV. P. 12(b).

must admit or deny each allegation of the complaint.[37] In addition, the answer may set forth affirmative defenses,[38] assert counterclaims against the plaintiff,[39] or both.[40] If the answer asserts a counterclaim, the original plaintiff must file a reply that admits or denies each allegation of the counterclaim and that may set forth affirmative defenses to the counterclaim.

A. Admissions and Denials

If a defendant contests liability, he obviously is prepared to deny in good faith some of the material allegations of the complaint. On the other hand, nearly every complaint will contain some allegations that the defendant admits. Therefore, when drafting an answer, you should not generally deny all allegations of the complaint; instead, you should address each paragraph of the complaint and identify areas of dispute.[41] For example, an answer to the complaint partially set forth earlier in this chapter might admit and deny allegations in the following manner:

ADMISSIONS AND DENIALS

1. Defendant Bostich admits the allegations in paragraphs 1-3 of Plaintiff Jansen's complaint.

2. Bostich denies the allegations in paragraph 4 of the complaint that he set impossible goals for Jansen and that he intimidated Jansen in his work. Bostich admits that he warned Jansen of the possibility of termination for failing to meet goals.

3. Bostich denies the allegations in paragraph 5 of the complaint.

4. Bostich has no information on which to form a belief in the truth of the allegations in paragraph 6 of the complaint, and he therefore denies them.

If the complaint is more than a few paragraphs long, it may help to match up the paragraphs of the complaint and answer, rather than admitting several paragraphs of allegations in the first paragraph of the answer:

---

1. Defendant Bostich admits the allegations in paragraph 1 of Plaintiff Jansen's complaint.

2. Defendant Bostich admits the allegations in paragraph 2 of the complaint.

3. Defendant Bostich admits the allegations in paragraph 3 of the complaint.

---

37. *See* FED. R. CIV. P. 8(b).
38. *See* FED. R. CIV. P. 8(b), 8(c).
39. *See* FED. R. CIV. P. 7(a), 8(a).
40. An answer may also assert a cross-claim against an originally named codefendant or a third-party claim against a new "third-party defendant" that the defendant impleads. *See id.*
41. *See generally* FED. R. CIV. P. 8(b) (form of denials).

4. Bostich denies the allegations in paragraph 4 of the complaint that . . . .

One attorney even recommends that each paragraph of the answer restate or summarize the corresponding allegation of the complaint before admitting or denying it. The judge might be disposed to refer repeatedly to such a self-contained answer, rather than to refer to the complaint, which would not include the defendant's denials.[42]

B. Affirmative Defenses

In a separate section of your answer, you should allege facts and conclusions supporting any affirmative defenses that your client, the defendant, may reasonably assert.[43] Even if the allegations of the complaint are true and are legally sufficient to state a claim for relief, a meritorious affirmative defense to the prima facie case will justify judgment for the defendant.

For example, in the litigation between Jansen and Bostich, suppose that the statute of limitations for tort actions in the jurisdiction is one year, that Jansen filed his complaint on June 9, 2002, and that Bostich last communicated a supervisory ultimatum to Jansen on June 6, 2001. Bostich may be prepared to argue that the statute of limitations has expired on the ground that Jansen's cause of action accrued at the latest on June 6, 2001, the date of Bostich's last act, rather than on June 10, 2001, the date of Jansen's nervous breakdown. If so, Bostich could assert this in fairly conclusory fashion as an affirmative defense:

AFFIRMATIVE DEFENSE

5. Bostich last exercised any supervisory control over Jansen on June 6, 2001. Therefore, Jansen's cause of action accrued more than one year before the filing of his complaint, and the statute of limitations bars his action.

C. Counterclaims

The defendant named in a complaint may himself wish to assert an independent claim for relief against the plaintiff. If so, the roles of the parties are reversed for purposes of the counterclaim, and the principles of pleading discussed in Section I above apply to the counterclaim.[44]

For example, in the litigation between Jansen and Bostich, additional facts might support a claim against Jansen for battery:

---

42. Benjamin R. Norris, *Writing Pleadings*, Ariz. Att'y, Dec. 2000, at 37.
43. *See* FED. R. CIV. P. 8(b), 8(c).
44. *See* FED. R. CIV. P. 8(a).

COUNTERCLAIM

Battery

6. On the evening of July 16, 2001, Jansen struck Bostich over the head with a baseball bat as Bostich left the Zydeco Radio factory.

7. Jansen acted maliciously and for the specific purpose of causing serious injury to Bostich.

8. As a result of Jansen's malicious attack, Bostich lost consciousness, required treatment in a hospital emergency room, and suffered debilitating pain for 24 hours.

Therefore, Bostich requests the following relief: . . . .

III. SUMMARY

When drafting pleadings, follow the format prescribed by applicable rules. For example, federal rules require the drafter of a complaint to allege

1. jurisdiction,
2. a claim for relief, and
3. a demand for judgment.

In an answer, you

1. must admit or deny the allegations of the complaint, and
2. may also assert affirmative defenses or a counterclaim.

Generally, pleadings should allege ultimate conclusions and supporting facts but not legal standards. Although the claim for relief must allege all elements of the prima facie case, most allegations may be general and need not develop specific, evidentiary facts.

Exercise 18-1

Compare and critically evaluate the following three versions of a complaint in the same wrongful discharge action. Which level of specificity of allegations do you prefer? What other differences in style do the complaints reflect? Which styles do you prefer?

For further practice with pleadings, perform Assignments 2-4 in Appendix VI, near the end of this book.

Thomas Sanchez
Simpson, Sanchez & Summers
303 North Central Avenue
Phoenix, Arizona 85002
(602) 229-1111
Bar No. 28371
Attorney for the plaintiff

IN THE SUPERIOR COURT
MARICOPA COUNTY, ARIZONA

GEORGE BRYANT, Plaintiff, v. MARIE JARDON, d.b.a. Chez Marie, Defendant.	No. _____ COMPLAINT

Plaintiff alleges:

COUNT 1

I

Plaintiff George Bryant is a resident of Phoenix, Arizona. Defendant Marie Jardon owns and operates Chez Marie, a restaurant located in Phoenix, Arizona.

II

Bryant worked for Jardon as a waiter at Chez Marie from August 16, 1992 to September 28, 1993.

III

At the time of his discharge on September 28, 1993, Bryant had an employment contract with Chez Marie that imposed substantive and procedural restrictions upon Jardon's right to terminate Bryant's employment.

IV

Acting through her agent, Mario Prieto, Jardon discharged Bryant on September 28, 1993, in breach of her employment contract with Bryant.

V

As a result of Jardon's breach of contract, Bryant has suffered lost wages and other incidental and consequential losses.

COUNT 2

VI

Bryant realleges and incorporates paragraphs I-V above.

VII

Acting through her agent, Jardon maliciously and unlawfully discharged Bryant for reasons that violate public policy, causing Bryant lost wages and other injuries.

Bryant therefore requests judgment granting the following relief:

1. an order reinstating Bryant to his position as waiter at Chez Marie;

2. an award of compensatory and punitive damages;

3. an award of costs and attorney's fees; and

4. other appropriate relief.

Dated _____

by _____,
    Thomas Sanchez
    Simpson, Sanchez & Summers
    303 North Central Avenue
    Phoenix, AZ 85002
    Attorneys for Plaintiff

Thomas Sanchez
Simpson, Sanchez & Summers
303 North Central Avenue
Phoenix, Arizona 85002
(602) 229-1111
Bar No. 28371
Attorney for the plaintiff

ARIZONA SUPERIOR COURT
MARICOPA COUNTY

GEORGE BRYANT, Plaintiff, v. MARIE JARDON, d.b.a. Chez Marie, Defendant.	No. _____ COMPLAINT

Plaintiff alleges:

I
BREACH OF PROMISE

1. Plaintiff George Bryant is a resident of Phoenix, Arizona. Defendant Marie Jardon owns and operates Chez Marie, a restaurant located in Phoenix, Arizona.

2. Bryant worked for Jardon as a waiter at Chez Marie from August 16, 1992 to September 28, 1993. Mario Prieto acted as the maître d' and supervisor of waiters at Chez Marie during Bryant's employment at Chez Marie. In all the events alleged below, Prieto acted on behalf of Jardon.

3. At the time of his discharge on September 28, 1993, Bryant had an employment contract with Chez Marie that included the terms of an "Employee Handbook." Bryant foreseeably relied to his detriment on promises contained in the Handbook.

4. The Employee Handbook contains promises of job security, including promises that (i) Jardon will not discharge any waiter except for inadequate performance and (ii) any waiter recommended for discharge has the right

to meet with Jardon and Prieto to persuade them that the waiter should not be discharged. The Handbook also provides that Jardon will make the final determination in the event of disagreement between Prieto and Jardon on a discharge matter.

5. At all times during his employment at Chez Marie, Bryant performed his job in a manner that met the highest standards at Chez Marie. Despite the adequacy of Bryant's performance, Prieto discharged Bryant on September 28, 1993. Although Bryant immediately requested a meeting with Prieto and Jardon to discuss the discharge, both Prieto and Jardon refused to convene such a meeting.

6. As a result of Jardon's breach of promises in the Handbook, Bryant has suffered lost wages and other incidental and consequential losses.

7. Jardon's breach of promises in the Handbook constitutes a breach of her employment contract with Bryant and has created an injustice that can be avoided only by enforcing the promises.

II
WRONGFUL DISCHARGE

8. Bryant realleges and incorporates paragraphs 1-7 above.

9. In discharging Bryant, Prieto was motivated by malice, by an invidiously discriminatory animus, and by concerns unrelated to the successful operation of Chez Marie. Jardon's termination of Bryant's employment therefore violated public policy.

III
REQUEST FOR RELIEF

10. Bryant requests:
   i. an order reinstating Bryant to his position as waiter at Chez Marie;
   ii. an award of compensatory damages in an amount to be set at trial;

    iii. an award of punitive damages in an amount to be set at trial;

    iv. an award of costs and attorney's fees; and

    v. such other relief as the court deems appropriate.

Dated _____

                by _____,
                     Thomas Sanchez
                     Simpson, Sanchez & Summers
                     303 North Central Avenue
                     Phoenix, AZ 85002
                     Attorneys for Plaintiff

Thomas Sanchez
Simpson, Sanchez & Summers
303 North Central Avenue
Phoenix, Arizona 85002
(602) 229-1111
Bar No. 28371
Attorney for the plaintiff

IN THE SUPERIOR COURT OF THE STATE OF ARIZONA
IN AND FOR THE COUNTY OF MARICOPA

GEORGE BRYANT, Plaintiff, v. MARIE JARDON, d.b.a. Chez Marie, and MARIO PRIETO, Defendants.	No. _____ COMPLAINT (JURY TRIAL REQUESTED)

Plaintiff George Bryant, by and through his attorneys, Simpson, Sanchez and Summers, alleges the following:

1. This is an action for injunctive relief and for compensatory damages exceeding $50,000. This court has original jurisdiction pursuant to the Arizona Constitution, Article 6, § 14(3).

2. Plaintiff is a resident of Phoenix, Arizona. Defendant Marie Jardon owns and operates Chez Marie, a restaurant located in Phoenix, Arizona. Defendant Mario Prieto acted as the maître d' and supervisor of waiters at Chez Marie during Bryant's employment at Chez Marie. All material events alleged below took place in Maricopa County.

I
FIRST CLAIM FOR RELIEF
(Breach of Contract)

3. Plaintiff worked for Defendants as a waiter at Chez Marie from August 16, 1992 to September 28, 1993. In all the events alleged below, Defendant Prieto acted on his own behalf as well as on behalf of Defendant Jardon.

4. On January 1, 1993, Defendants modified Plaintiff's employment contract to include promises of job security contained in the terms of an "Employee Handbook" and in oral assurances.

5. Among other things, the Employee Handbook contains the following

promises of job security: (i) Defendants will not discharge any waiter except for inadequate performance and (ii) any waiter recommended for discharge has the right to meet with Defendants to persuade them that the waiter should not be discharged. The Handbook also provides that Defendant Jardon will make the final determination in the event of disagreement between Defendants on a discharge matter. (Copy of text of excerpts of Handbook is attached and incorporated by this reference.)

6. At all times during his employment at Chez Marie, Plaintiff performed his job in a manner that met the highest standards at Chez Marie. Despite the adequacy of Plaintiff's performance, Defendants discharged Plaintiff on September 28, 1993. Although Plaintiff immediately requested a meeting with Defendants to discuss the discharge, Defendants refused to convene such a meeting.

7. As a result of Defendant's breach of contract, Plaintiff has suffered lost wages and other incidental and consequential losses.

THEREFORE, Plaintiff demands judgment granting the following relief:

i.   an order reinstating Plaintiff to his former position at Chez Marie;
ii. an award of compensatory damages for all consequential and incidental losses;
iii. an award of costs and attorney's fees; and
iv. such other relief as the court deems appropriate.

II
SECOND CLAIM FOR RELIEF
(Promissory Estoppel)

8. Plaintiff realleges paragraphs 1-7 above and incorporates them by this reference.

9. On January 1, 1993, Defendants gave Plaintiff promises of job security by making oral assurances and by distributing the Employee Handbook. Plaintiff relied to his detriment on those promises by performing extraordinary services and by forbearing from taking other job opportunities. That reliance was reasonably foreseeable by Defendants.

10. Defendants' termination of Bryant's employment on September 28,

1993 constituted a breach of their promises of job security and has created an injustice that can be avoided only by enforcing the promises.

THEREFORE, Plaintiff demands judgment granting the following relief:

    i. an order reinstating Plaintiff to his former position at Chez Marie;

    ii. an award of compensatory damages for all consequential and incidental losses;

    iii. an award of costs and attorney's fees; and

    iv. such other relief as the court deems appropriate.

III
THIRD CLAIM FOR RELIEF
(Wrongful Discharge)

11. Plaintiff realleges paragraphs 1-10 above and incorporates them by this reference.

12. Defendants maliciously discharged Plaintiff because of his sexual orientation and because Plaintiff's exemplary performance made Defendant Prieto jealous. Those reasons for discharge reflect bad faith and violate the public policy of state laws.

THEREFORE, Plaintiff demands judgment granting the following relief:

    i. an order reinstating Plaintiff to his position as waiter at Chez Marie;

    ii. an award of compensatory damages in an amount to be set at trial;

    iii. an award of punitive damages in an amount to be set at trial;

    iv. an award of costs and attorney's fees; and

    v. such other relief as the court deems appropriate.

Dated _____

                by _____,
                    Thomas Sanchez
                    Simpson, Sanchez and Summers
                    1303 North Central Avenue
                    Phoenix, AZ 85002
                    Attorneys for Plaintiff

Chapter **19**

Motion for Summary Judgment

Motion for Summary Judgment

I. PROCEDURAL CONTEXT

A pretrial motion for summary judgment is a popular means of determining whether the court should dispose of all or part of a dispute before the parties try the case to a jury. In most cases, you will have no difficulty alleging facts that state a claim for relief; therefore, your complaints will seldom be susceptible to attack for failure to state a claim. On the other hand, even if you allege a claim or defense in good faith, you may fail to gather substantial admissible evidence supporting the claim or defense. In such cases, the opposing party's motion for summary judgment exposes the absence of a triable issue of fact. It compels you to choose between making at least a preliminary showing of the evidence supporting your allegations or suffering adverse judgment before trial. In other cases, both parties concede the absence of any dispute of fact, stipulate to the facts, and use the motion for summary judgment to argue unsettled questions about the law and its application to the stipulated facts.

Summary judgment litigation often takes place only after each party has thoroughly investigated the case through the discovery and disclosure process.[1] Indeed, the trial judge may delay resolution of a motion for summary judgment if further discovery is needed to permit the nonmoving party to support its opposition. Nonetheless, if you successfully move for summary judgment, you will avoid the greater burdens of a full trial.

On the other hand, if the trial court denies your motion for summary judgment, your unsuccessful motion may hamper your ability to settle the case before trial. If the opposing counsel initially expected to settle the case, he may have only minimally prepared the case prior to summary judgment litigation. Your motion for summary judgment, however, will have forced your opponent to organize his facts and legal arguments. If the motion fails, he likely will be much more demanding in settlement negotiations for three reasons. First, the denial of the motion will strengthen his belief in the potential merits of his client's claims or defenses. Second, he will be more nearly prepared for trial after researching the law and gathering the facts to oppose your motion for summary judgment. Finally, his client will have invested significant resources in opposing the motion, expenditures that his client will likely incorporate into the client's new settlement position.[2] Consequently, you should not move for summary judgment unless you have a reasonable chance of success.

Summary judgment litigation provides you with a stimulating vehicle for developing briefwriting skills. You must remain constantly sensitive not only to the merits of the underlying claims or defenses but also to the standards for summary judgment. Moreover, the local rules of many courts prescribe a special format for summary judgment briefs, providing you a valuable opportunity to examine the role of procedural rules in written advocacy.

II. STANDARDS FOR SUMMARY JUDGMENT

The federal rules authorize a court to grant summary judgment if the parties do not genuinely dispute any material facts and if the moving party is entitled to judgment as a matter of law.[3] In some cases, the court may use summary judgment proceedings to grant final judgment "as to one or more but fewer

1. The federal procedures for discovery and disclosure are set forth in Federal Rules of Civil Procedure 26-37. *See also* Roger W. Kaufman, *Amending the Disclosure Amendments*, Ariz. Att'y, Mar. 1997, at 16 (summarizing history of Arizona's precocious disclosure rules and subsequent changes in the sanctions for violations of those rules).

2. *See, e.g.*, Raymond L. Ocampo, Jr., *Moving Violations*, Cal. Law., Aug. 1984, at 47, 48.

3. *See* FED. R. CIV. P. 56(c), 56(e). Beyond the scope of this discussion are state standards for summary disposition that deviate from the federal rules. Many states follow the federal standards closely. *See, e.g.*, Orme Sch. v. Reeves, 802 P.2d 1000 (Ariz. 1990) (en banc) (interpreting ARIZ. R. CIV. P. 56); Aguilar v. Atlantic Richfield Co., 24 P.3d 493, 512-14 (Cal. 2001) (amending California summary judgement rules are similar, though not identical to, federal standards).

than all of the claims or parties,"[4] or to identify some uncontested material facts without granting any final judgment.[5]

When moving for summary judgment, you have the initial burden of showing that the pretrial record supports judgment in your favor. If you move for summary judgment on the strength of a claim or defense on which you would have the burden of proof at trial, you must support your motion for summary judgment with credible evidence tending to prove all the elements of the claim or defense.[6] You could make such a showing with deposition testimony, answers to interrogatories, admissions, or other information and documents obtained during discovery or disclosure, or with affidavits prepared specifically for the motion.[7]

As an alternative basis for summary judgment, you may demonstrate that the opposing party lacks factual support for an element of her claim or defense. If so, you need not affirmatively produce evidence tending to negate that element. Instead, you may satisfy your initial burden simply by reviewing the existing record and demonstrating that it contains no evidence supporting the critical element.[8]

Once you have satisfactorily supported your motion, the opposing party can avoid summary judgment by setting forth "specific facts" that establish a genuine issue of material fact for trial.[9] She may not rely on the allegations or denials in her own pleading but must point to the moving party's admissions or to facts in affidavits, deposition testimony, or other documentary evidence or fruits of discovery.[10]

Moreover, to warrant a trial, the factual issue must be both genuine and material.[11] For an illustration of the materiality requirement, suppose the record on summary judgment establishes without dispute that the defendant intentionally struck the plaintiff with a baseball bat. The defendant could not successfully respond to the plaintiff's motion for summary judgment by establishing even a genuine dispute of fact about the color of the shoes worn by the defendant on the day of the attack. Once the identity of the attacker and the nature of the attack have been established, a factual dispute about the attacker's footwear would not be material to the plaintiff's tort claim, because it would have no bearing on liability.

The court must not resolve genuine issues of material fact on summary judgment. To determine the genuineness of a factual issue, however, the court may undertake a limited evaluation of the strength of the facts pre-

4. FED. R. CIV. P. 54(b).
5. *See* FED. R. CIV. P. 56(d).
6. *See* Celotex Corp. v. Catrett, 477 U.S. 317, 331 (1986) (Brennan, J., dissenting).
7. *See* FED. R. CIV. P. 56(c).
8. *See* Celotex Corp. v. Catrett, 477 U.S. 317, 322-24 (1986) (majority opinion); *id.* at 329-31 (Brennan, J., dissenting). *But see* Aguilar v. Atlantic Richfield Co., 24 P.3d 493, 513-14 (Cal. 2001) (California summary judgment rules depart from federal standards on this point).
9. FED. R. CIV. P. 56(e). Alternatively, the nonmoving party may concede the absence of any issue of material fact and simply argue that it, rather than the moving party, is entitled to judgment. In such a case, the parties typically file cross-motions for summary judgment, and each party asserts entitlement to judgment as a matter of law.
10. *See* FED. R. CIV. P. 56(e); *see also* Southern Rambler Sales, Inc. v. American Motors Corp., 375 F.2d 932, 937 (5th Cir. 1967) ("Rule 56 [is] saying in effect, 'Meet these affidavit facts or judicially die.' ").
11. *See* FED. R. CIV. P. 56(c).

sented by the nonmoving party. A factual issue is not genuine if the nonmoving party's factual support is so trivial that "the record taken as a whole could not lead a rational trier of fact to find for the non-moving party."[12] In short, the nonmoving party "must do more than simply show . . . some metaphysical doubt as to the material facts."[13]

If the materials establish grounds for summary judgment, the court ordinarily will grant judgment to the moving party, but the rules arguably do not require it to do so.[14] For example, if a case presents a difficult and novel issue of law, the appellate courts may be better equipped to review the case and develop the new legal standard in the context of a full record after trial. In such a case, the trial court might exercise discretion to deny summary judgment even though the moving party has established grounds for judgment as a matter of law.[15]

III. FORMAT FOR SUMMARY JUDGMENT BRIEFS—OVERVIEW

Rules of procedure, local court rules, and custom suggest that materials supporting a motion for summary judgment should include the following:

1. a motion requesting action by the court;
2. a statement of material facts;
3. affidavits, or other materials not already in the record, that support the fact statement and the motion; and
4. a supporting brief, sometimes referred to in court rules as a "memorandum of law" or "memorandum of points and authorities."

The requirements for the response are similar except that the nonmoving party need not file a formal motion opposing the motion for summary judgment. At most, the nonmoving party may wish to file a cover page that announces the response and briefly introduces the supporting brief and other materials. The moving party's reply, if any, consists solely of a brief that replies to the arguments raised in the nonmoving party's response.

Some local rules describe parts of the required format in surprising detail. For example, local rules for some United States District Courts specify the information required on designated lines of the caption of the title page of each document filed in support of the motion.[16] The most interesting of the local rules addressing summary judgment, however, are those specifying formats for the statements of facts.

12. Matsushita Elec. Indus. Co. v. Zenith Radio Corp., 475 U.S. 574, 587 (1986).
13. *Id.* at 586.
14. *See* Orme Sch. v. Reeves, 802 P.2d 1000, 1008 n.11 (Ariz. 1990) (en banc).
15. *See generally* Haydon v. Rand Corp., 605 F.2d 453, 455 (9th Cir. 1979).
16. *See, e.g.,* D. ARIZ. R. 1.9(a).

IV. STATEMENTS OF FACTS

Before the advent of local rules governing motions for summary judgment, briefs and supporting materials often failed to pinpoint areas of factual dispute. Often, counsel for the moving party summarized the materials supporting the motion in a general narrative fact statement, and counsel for the nonmoving party summarized supporting materials in a general counterstatement of the facts. Worse yet, in some cases, one or both advocates omitted any consolidated statement of the facts and simply referred to the record in fact analyses dispersed throughout the argument section of the brief.

To help trial judges identify the potential areas of factual dispute, many courts have enacted local rules specifying special formats for briefs on motions for summary judgment. For example, the Arizona Rules of Civil Procedure require the moving party to state the facts in numbered paragraphs, similar to allegations in a complaint:

> Any party filing a motion for summary judgment shall set forth, separately from the memorandum of law, the specific facts relied upon in support of the motion. The facts shall be stated in concise numbered paragraphs.[17]

Unlike allegations in a complaint, this fact statement must include citations to supporting materials: "As to each fact, the statement shall refer to the specific portion of the record where the fact may be found."[18] If you represent the moving party, you could reasonably entitle this section "[Moving Party's] Statement of Material Facts."

Interpreting another court's local rules, one judge has stated that a statement of material facts supporting a motion for summary judgment should "contain only factual allegations . . . limited to material facts," and should "be short," containing "only one or two individual allegations, thereby allowing easy response."[19]

The Arizona rules instruct the nonmoving party to respond to the moving party's statement of material facts by identifying areas of factual dispute in much the same way that an answer sets forth denials of allegations in a complaint:

> Any party opposing a motion for summary judgment shall file a statement in the form prescribed by this Rule, specifying those paragraphs in the moving party's statement of facts which are disputed, and also setting forth

---

17. ARIZ. R. CIV. P. 56(c)(2). *See also* Malec v. Sanford, 191 F.R.D. 581, 583 (N.D. Ill. 2000) (quoting and interpreting Local Rule 56.1(a) for the United States District Court for the Northern District of Illinois, setting forth a similar format for the moving party's statement of material facts).

18. ARIZ. R. CIV. P. 56(c)(2).

19. *Malec*, 191 F.R.D. at 583.

those facts which establish a genuine issue of material fact or otherwise preclude summary judgment in favor of the moving party.[20]

If you represent the nonmoving party, you might reasonably entitle this section "Response to {Moving Party's} Statement of Material Facts," or "[Nonmoving Party's] Statement of Undisputed and Disputed Material Facts" because you obviously hope that the court will rule that your documents establish a dispute with respect to at least some of the material facts.

Fact statements following this format provide the court with a clear guide to the opposing parties' positions on summary judgment. For example, the following represents excerpts from the plaintiff's statement of facts on his motion for summary judgment in a suit alleging race discrimination in violation of federal law:

---

1. Defendant, Irma Barnes, owns and operates "Irma's Diner," a restaurant and bar located in Mesa, Arizona. Barnes employs more than 15 employees in this business. (Exh. D, Barnes Dep. at 3-4.)

2. Plaintiff, Michael Powell, is African American. He worked as the night manager of the bar at Irma's Diner from January 1, 1993 to June 17, 1994. (Exh. B, Personnel Record for Michael Powell.) . . .

3. . . .

4. On June 17, 1994, Barnes confronted Powell about Powell's selection of a rhythm and blues band as musical entertainment for the bar. After using several racial slurs in the ensuing discussion, she fired Powell solely because of his race. (Exh. A, Powell Aff. ¶ 8.) . . .

Barnes's response to the motion for summary judgment should specifically identify which portions of Powell's statement of facts she disputes. To highlight areas of dispute with maximum clarity, you probably should respond to each of the moving party's paragraphs with a corresponding, identically numbered paragraph:

---

1. Barnes does not dispute paragraph 1 of Powell's Statement of Facts.

2. Barnes does not dispute paragraph 2 of Powell's Statement of Facts.

3. Barnes does not dispute paragraph 3 of Powell's Statement of Facts.

4. Barnes does not dispute the assertions in paragraph 4 that Barnes fired Powell on June 17, 1994, after confronting Powell about his selection of musical entertainment. Barnes disputes that she used racial slurs or that race played any factor in her termination of Powell's employment. . . .

In addition, Barnes should identify the specific facts that reflect a genuine factual dispute on the material issue of Barnes's racial animus. Unless these

20. ARIZ. R. CIV. P. 56(c)(2). *See also Malec,* 191 F.R.D. at 583-84 (quoting and interpreting N.D. Ill. R. 56.1(b), setting forth a similar format for the opposing party's statement of undisputed and disputed facts). The Arizona rules also permit the nonmoving party to join with the moving party in stipulating to facts not in dispute. ARIZ. R. CIV. P. 56(c)(2).

facts appear in Powell's fact statement, Barnes normally would state them as "Additional Facts" in a separate section that follows her identification of areas of dispute:

STATEMENT OF UNDISPUTED AND DISPUTED FACTS

1. Barnes does not dispute . . . .

• • • •

4. Barnes does not dispute the assertions . . . musical entertainment. Barnes disputes . . . Powell's employment.

• • • •

ADDITIONAL FACTS

1. Barnes never used racial slurs in Powell's presence, and she fired Powell solely because he displayed insubordination in the face of direct instructions by Powell to replace the band Barnes had hired. (Plaintiff's Exh. D, Barnes Dep. at 24-25.)

Some court rules permit the moving party to respond to the nonmoving party's statement of additional facts.[21]

Most court rules governing fact statements for summary judgment can be interpreted to permit you to attach the statement of facts under the same title sheet that states the motion and covers the supporting brief, or that presents the opposition and supporting brief, as long as you set forth the statement of facts separately from the brief itself. Nonetheless, most attorneys prefer to file the formal statement of facts under a caption as a separate document.

V. SUPPORTING EVIDENTIARY MATERIALS

You must support each assertion in your statement of facts with admitted alleged facts from the opposing party's pleading or with facts reflected in affidavits, materials generated through discovery and disclosure, or other evidence. Federal Rule of Civil Procedure 56 specifically provides that the affidavits must "be made on personal knowledge"[22] and must "set forth

---

21. *See Malec*, 191 F.R.D. at 584 (citing to N.D. Ill. R. 56.1(a)(3) (final unnumbered paragraph)).

22. FED. R. CIV. P. 56(e); *see also* Vandventer v. Wabash Nat'l Corp., 867 F. Supp. 790, 798 (N.D. Ind. 1994) (rejecting and expressing displeasure at affidavit that was prepared by attorney and that did not reflect personal knowledge of party who signed affidavit); Sherman v. Community Consol. Sch. Dist. 21, 758 F. Supp. 1244, 1250 (N.D. Ill. 1991) (rejecting father's affidavit because it did not assert father had personal knowledge of retaliation against his son because of his son's refusal to pledge allegiance to the flag).

such facts as would be admissible in evidence."[23] More broadly, you should assume that the court will consider only evidence that would be admissible at trial when it determines whether all the materials supporting and opposing summary judgment create a genuine issue of fact for trial.[24] Therefore, even though your opponent may overlook this matter,[25] your summary judgment materials should preliminarily establish the admissibility of (1) documents included in the summary judgment materials or (2) the expected trial testimony represented in the materials, such as in affidavits or deposition testimony.[26]

For example, the following excerpt from an affidavit asserts the admissibility of other documents under the "business records" exception to the "hearsay rule" of evidence:[27]

---

5. The Payroll Action forms in Exhibits B and C are true copies of records that I prepared and kept in the course of my regularly conducted business activity, which includes maintaining such employment records as a uniform practice. Those forms include information within my own knowledge and information that my supervisor transmitted to me on matters within his knowledge.

Some attorneys separately file supporting affidavits and other evidence. If those materials are not voluminous, however, you can more conveniently and appropriately attach them to the formal statement of facts.

VI. THE MOTION

As with every document that you separately file with the trial court, you should begin your motion with a caption identifying the case and the nature of the document. In the motion itself, you should simply and clearly state your request for action and should briefly introduce the grounds supporting the request.

Unfortunately, many lawyers have developed a tradition of loading motions with abstract boilerplate that says almost nothing about the motion or the dispute:

23. FED. R. CIV. P. 56(e). The Federal Rules of Evidence and their state counterparts govern the admissibility of evidence at trial.
24. *See* Malec v. Sanford, 191 F.R.D. 581, 585 (N.D. Ill. 2000) ("[A]lthough the evidence supporting a factual contention need not be admissible itself, it must represent admissible evidence. For example, a deposition transcript is not usually admissible at trial but (obviously) may be used in support of summary judgment . . .").
25. *See, e.g.,* Catrett v. Johns-Manville Sales Corp., 826 F.2d 33, 37 (D.C. Cir. 1987) (regardless of whether letter qualified as a business records exception to the hearsay rule, trial court properly considered it on summary judgment because other party failed to object to its use).
26. *See* Andrews v. R.W. Hays Co., 998 P.2d 774 (2000) (court disregarded hearsay statements in affidavit because neither the affidavit nor other materials established exception to hearsay rule); *cf.* Olympic Ins. Co. v. H.D. Harrison, Inc., 418 F.2d 669, 670 (5th Cir. 1969) (document produced in ordinary course of business was sufficiently reliable to form basis for summary judgment).
27. *See* FED. R. EVID. 803(6).

> Defendant, Sun Printing Co., by and through its undersigned attorneys, Jenkins, Powell, and Smith, P.C., hereby moves, pursuant to the Arizona Rules of Civil Procedure, Rule 56, for an order granting summary judgment against Plaintiff, Scott Paper Supply, on the grounds that there exists no genuine issue of material fact and that Defendant is entitled to summary judgment as a matter of law. This motion is supported by the attached memorandum of law, the Statement of Material Facts separately filed with this Court, and the documents and exhibits filed with this court.

A judge skims such boilerplate with glassy eyes. She does not need a superfluous reference to the legal representation; your identity as legal counsel is revealed at the top of the cover page and in your signature at the end of the motion. In addition, the judge is well aware of the basic abstract standards for summary judgment;[28] repeating those standards in the motion adds nothing to her knowledge about your case.

The judge will read your motion with greater interest if you clearly and concisely state what relief your client wants and why he is entitled to it. In particular, you should convey new information to the court by tailoring the abstract standards to the facts:

> Pursuant to Arizona Rule of Civil Procedure 56, the defendant, Sun Printing Co. ("Sun"), moves for summary judgment against the plaintiff, Scott Paper Supply ("Scott"). Sun is entitled to judgment under the UCC Statute of Frauds because Scott cannot genuinely dispute that the agreement alleged by Scott was for paper priced at more than $500 and was never reduced to writing.
>
> This motion is supported by the attached memorandum of law, by the separately filed Statement of Undisputed Facts and accompanying exhibits, and by the record in this case.

By conveying the theme of the full argument, such a motion whets the judge's appetite for the supporting memorandum of law. An even crisper motion could state the first paragraph more concisely:

> Defendant, Sun Printing Co., moves for summary judgment against Plaintiff, Scott Paper Supply. *See* Ariz. R. Civ. P. 56. Sun Printing Co. is entitled to judgment because the oral agreement alleged by Scott Paper Supply is unenforceable under the UCC Statute of Frauds as a matter of law. This motion is supported by . . . .

As terse as this passage may sound, it contains more useful information than the longer string of boilerplate in the first example.

When opposing a motion, you need not state a formal countermotion in the title page of your opposition materials. You may follow the caption

---

28. *See* Noel Fidel, *Some Do's and Don'ts of Motion Writing*, Ariz. B.J., Aug. 1983, at 8, 9 (advising legal writers to omit "canned" recitations of basic summary judgment standards).

immediately with your responsive brief. At the most, you might include a cover page with a brief statement of opposition parallel to the motion:

> Plaintiff, Scott Paper Supply ("Scott"), opposes Defendant's motion for summary judgment. Defendant, Sun Printing Co. ("Sun"), is not entitled to judgment as a matter of law, because Scott's supporting materials show that Sun adopted Scott's written and signed confirmation of the agreement, satisfying the UCC Statute of Frauds under Ariz. Rev. Stat. Ann. § 47-2201(B) (West 1997). This opposition is supported by the attached memorandum of law, by the . . . .

VII. THE BRIEF

Your brief, or legal memorandum, is your tool of persuasion. With it, you argue for a favorable interpretation of the law and analysis of the facts. A motions brief typically includes three sections:

1. an introduction,
2. an argument, and
3. a conclusion.

In a complex case, you should consider adding a formal statement of the issues at the beginning of your brief. Such a statement of issues would not be typical in a motions brief but could be helpful in unusual circumstances.

A. The Introduction

The first section of your supporting brief should summarize the facts, with the brief opposing summary judgment sometimes emphasizing material disputes of facts. In either party's brief, you might reasonably title this section "Introduction" or "Summary of Facts." In this introductory section, you can summarize the facts in a more concise and less formal manner than is possible in the separate, formal statement.

For each statement of a fact in this introduction, you should cite to a source—either to (1) the underlying evidentiary sources already in the record or added to the record in your summary judgment materials, or (2) paragraphs in your separately filed statement of facts, which in turn will cite to underlying evidentiary sources. Some courts prefer, or even require, the brief to cite only to paragraphs in the separately filed statement of facts.[29] When court rules or other judicial pronouncements do not specify a preference or requirement, you can exercise discretion to cite either to the original source or to your separately filed fact statement. If, for example, each of the fact statements in the Introduction is supported by a single underlying evidentiary source, such as an affidavit or deposition testimony, citation to

---

29. *See, e.g.,* Malec v. Sanford, 191 F.R.D. 581, 586 (N.D. Ill. 2000).

that original source could be concise, informative, and helpful to the reader. On the other hand, if each of many fact statements is supported by several underlying sources, or if the citation to some underlying sources is quite lengthy, citation to those sources could impede the flow of the Introduction, and your reader will probably prefer more concise citations to your separately filed statement of facts.

In addition, you may use an introductory section to present a summary of your argument or a combination of facts, procedural history, and summary of your argument. For example, you might begin your Introduction with a paragraph-long overview of your arguments or the issues in the case, to provide a context for a subsequent summary of the facts in chronological order. Section IV.C.2 of Chapter 22 advises against premature legal argument in a statement of facts in an appellate brief. However, this admonition applies with less force in the introduction to your summary judgment brief, because you will separately file a formal statement of facts for summary judgment.

Accordingly, the Introduction may be a suitable place to advance any theme that you have developed for your brief. Alternatively, you can express your theme or brief overview of your arguments in the first paragraph of your Argument section.

B. The Argument

Chapters 6 and 16 discuss techniques of legal argument. Indeed, some of the examples in Chapter 16 are taken from sample summary judgment briefs. This section addresses techniques of persuasion peculiar to summary judgment briefs.

Argument of purely legal questions can be crucial in some summary judgment litigation: If the court determines that material facts are not in dispute, or if the parties have stipulated to the absence of factual dispute, the court will decide whether a moving party is entitled to judgment as a matter of law.

Typically, however, the parties will also argue about the presence or absence of a genuine dispute of fact. In such a case, once you have established the law on an issue or subissue, you should thoroughly analyze the facts. As discussed in greater detail in the immediately preceding section, when you argue the facts, remember to cite to your formal, separately filed statement of facts or to the original evidentiary sources that are already in the record or are included in your supporting materials. The samples in this chapter suggest several ways to cite to either kind of source; any reasonable citation form is acceptable.

Also, remember to incorporate the standards for summary judgment into your argument. For example, if you are moving for summary judgment, you should not argue that "the preponderance of the evidence shows that Sun Printing Co. objected to the contents of the confirmation within ten days after receipt." Such an argument gives the impression that you are inappropriately asking the judge to resolve a factual issue without a trial. Instead, your brief should refer to the "undisputed evidence" and the inferences that can be drawn from it, thus properly asserting the absence of a factual dispute.

Conversely, if you are opposing summary judgment, your brief should remind the judge periodically that nothing more than a genuine and material question of fact is needed to defeat summary judgment. In making this point, you should not simply reiterate the abstract standard; rather, you should identify issues of fact that make summary judgment inappropriate:

Opposition facts	Scott Paper Supply's letter confirming the purchase agreement is dated September 1 [Exh. 2], and Scott's Distribution Manager personally mailed it that day [Exh. 3, Connor Aff. ¶ 3]. Scott Paper Supply never received any objection to the terms of the confirmation. [*Id.* ¶ 4.] Moreover, Sun Printing Co. concedes that it has no record of making any such objection. [Exh. 4, Sun's Ans. to Scott's First Set of Inter., No. 23.]
Dispute of fact	In direct opposition to Sun Printing Co.'s assertions, this evidence shows that Sun Printing Co. received the confirmation and failed to object to it. At the very least, this evidence raises a genuine dispute of fact that must be resolved at trial.

C. The Conclusion

You should end each section of the argument of your brief with a conclusion about the topic of that section, similar to the conclusion stated in the point heading that introduces the argument. Together, the point heading and the conclusion provide maximum emphasis in their positions as the first and last things the judge reads within a section. Finally, as illustrated in Chapter 16, the entire brief should end with a section entitled "Conclusion" that encompasses all the arguments of the brief.

VIII. SUMMARY

To prepare a motion for summary judgment,

1. draft a motion that requests summary judgment and briefly introduces the judge to the grounds for your motion;
2. prepare evidentiary materials that will support your statement of facts, if they are not already in the record;
3. draft a separate statement of facts that cites to the supporting materials; and
4. draft a supporting brief that
   a. summarizes the facts and procedural history,
   b. argues the law and facts relating to the issues, with attention to the standards for summary judgment, and
   c. states your conclusions.

When opposing a motion for summary judgment, you should prepare a brief and a separate statement of facts with supporting materials. To oppose a motion or to reply to an opposition brief, you need not file a separate motion. Instead, you should submit a brief that responds to the arguments presented in the preceding brief.

For further practice with summary judgment, perform Assignment 5 in Appendix VI, near the end of this book. Study the following sample and think about the law and facts that you would need to respond successfully to it.

SAMPLE

Lisa Hall
Kendricks, Hall, & Oats, P.C.
3310 Alma School Rd., Suite 200
Mesa, Arizona 85283
(602) 839-0365
Bar No. 0076089

ARIZONA SUPERIOR COURT
MARICOPA COUNTY

CHARLOTTE REMBAR, Plaintiff, v. ALEXANDER HART d.b.a. COMCON, Defendant.	No. C732431 Defendant Hart's Motion for Summary Judgment (Judge Wisdom)

Defendant Alexander Hart d.b.a. Comcon moves for summary judgment on all claims in this action. Under Arizona Rule of Civil Procedure 56, Hart is entitled to judgment as a matter of law because the undisputed facts show that Hart did not promise Rembar job security and did not discharge Rembar for an unlawful reason or in a wrongful manner.

This motion is supported by the attached Memorandum of Law, the separately filed Statement of Material Facts, and the entire record before the Court.

March 3, 2002

Lisa Hall for
Kendricks, Hall, & Oats, P.C.
3310 Alma School Rd., Suite 200
Mesa, Arizona 85283

MEMORANDUM OF LAW IN SUPPORT OF MOTION FOR SUMMARY JUDGMENT

I. INTRODUCTION

As documented and set forth more fully in Defendant Hart's Statement of Material Facts ("Hart SofF"), Alexander Hart employed Charlotte Rembar as a computer systems consultant for Hart's sole proprietorship, Comcon. [Hart SofF ¶ 2.] Although Hart distributed an employment manual to Rembar, their employment contract permitted either party to terminate the contract at will. [Hart SofF ¶¶ 2-5.]

On November 1, 2001, Hart discharged Rembar because of her "negative attitude." [Hart SofF ¶¶ 7-8.] During her employment, Rembar often flirted with Hart, and Hart sometimes returned the flirtations; however, Hart and Rembar did not have a romantic relationship, and Hart never made any unwelcome advances toward Rembar. [Hart SofF ¶ 6.]

Rembar has asserted four claims for relief in her complaint: (1) breach of an alleged promise of job security, (2) sex discrimination in violation of the Arizona Civil Rights Act ("the ACRA"), (3) wrongful discharge in violation of public policy, and (4) intentional infliction of emotional distress. Because the record shows that Hart employed Rembar at will and that Hart discharged Rembar for a legitimate business reason in an a proper manner, Hart is entitled to judgment as a matter of law on all these claims.

II. ARGUMENT

A. Hart did not breach his employment contract with Rembar by discharging Rembar for her negative attitude.

"The employment relationship is severable at the pleasure of either the employee or the employer unless both the employee and the employer have signed a written contract to the contrary. . . ." Ariz. Rev. Stat. Ann. § 23-1501(2) (West Supp. 1996). In some circumstances, an employee manual can become part of the employment contract, and promises of job security in the manual can restrict the employer's freedom to terminate the contract. *See id.* Nonetheless, even assuming for purposes of summary judgment that Hart and Rembar's employment contract included the terms of the Comcon Policy Manual, Hart did not breach those terms for two reasons. First, neither the Policy Manual nor any other term of the contract imposed any restriction on Hart's freedom to terminate Rembar's employment. Second, even if the contract permitted Hart to fire Rembar only for unsatisfactory performance, her negative attitude created such grounds for discharge.

1. *The Employment Contract Remained Terminable at Will.*

Even assuming the Comcon Policy Manual was incorporated into the employment contract, the manual did not change the at-will nature of the contract because it did not contain requisite "provisions of job security."

Leikvold v. Valley View Comty. Hosp., 141 Ariz. 544, 547, 688 P.2d 170, 173 (1984) (quoting *Pine River State Bank v. Mettille*, 333 N.W.2d 622, 628 (Minn. 1983)). Because the terms of the contract "are clear and unambiguous, the construction of the contract is a question of law for the court" and thus is appropriate for summary judgment. *Id.* at 548, 688 P.2d at 174.

Comcon hired Rembar for an indefinite term of employment, rather than for a fixed term. [Hart SofF ¶ 2.] The terms of Comcon's Policy Manual unambiguously left Hart free to terminate his contract with Rembar at his will. No provision of the Policy Manual purports to restrict the grounds for discharge of an employee. [Hart SofF ¶ 3.] Instead, the only provisions relating to termination affirmatively reserve Hart's right to discharge employees. [Hart SofF ¶¶ 4-5.] Because Rembar had worked at Comcon for more than 60 days, she was classified as a nonprobationary employee at the time of her discharge. [Hart SofF ¶¶ 2, 4-5.] Under the heading "Nonprobationary Employment," the Policy Manual especially emphasizes a particular ground for discharge: "Comcon reserves the right to terminate the employment of any employee who is not performing satisfactorily." [Hart SofF ¶ 5.] However, it does not state or even suggest that unsatisfactory performance is the exclusive ground for discharge. Absent such a stated restriction, Hart remains free under the general rule to terminate the contract for any reason or for no reason at all.

Hart's employment contract with Rembar was terminable at will.

2. Hart Validly Fired Rembar for Unsatisfactory Performance.

Even if the Policy Manual had identified unsatisfactory performance as the sole ground for discharging nonprobationary employees, Hart would not have breached such a provision.

Hart discharged Rembar because of her "negative attitude." [Hart SofF ¶¶ 7-8.] Because Rembar's position required her to work closely with clients, a pleasant personality and a positive attitude were indispensable qualities for satisfactory job performance. [Hart SofF ¶ 7.] Therefore, even assuming that the employment contract provided for limited job security, Hart did not breach the contract because the undisputed facts show that he discharged Rembar for unsatisfactory performance.

B. Hart did not engage in sex discrimination in violation of the ACRA.

Because Comcon has always employed fewer than fifteen employees [Hart SofF ¶ 1], Rembar has no claim against Hart under federal employment discrimination law. *See* 42 U.S.C. § 2000e(b) (1994) (defining employers covered by Title VII of the Civil Rights Act of 1964). Although Comcon is a covered employer under the ACRA, Ariz. Rev. Stat. Ann. § 41-1461(2) (West 1999), he did not violate its provisions.

The ACRA makes it an "unlawful employment practice for an employer: 1. To . . . discharge any individual or otherwise to discriminate against any individual with respect to his compensation, terms, conditions or privileges of employment because of such individual's . . . sex. . . ." Ariz. Rev. Stat.

Ann. § 41-1463.B (West 1999). Rembar alleges that Hart discriminated against her by subjecting her to unwelcome sexual advances and discharging her in retaliation for her refusal to submit to the alleged advances. The record, however, contradicts these allegations.

Rembar's own frequent flirtations with Hart showed that she welcomed Hart's harmless flirtations and attentions. Hart never made advances that were not welcomed by Rembar, and he never conditioned benefits of employment on Rembar's acquiescing to his flirtations. [Hart SofF ¶ 6.] Most important, Rembar's discharge had nothing to do with any flirtations between Hart and Rembar; Hart discharged Rembar solely because of her unsatisfactory job performance. [Hart SofF ¶¶ 7-8.]

As a matter of law, Hart did not engage in sexually discriminatory conduct in violation of the ACRA.

C. Hart is not liable in tort for wrongfully discharging Rembar, because the Arizona Civil Rights Act provides the exclusive remedy for such alleged misconduct.

Before its statutory modification, the common law tort of wrongful discharge imposed liability for a violation of an important public policy reflected in the state's constitution, its statutes, or, in limited circumstances, its judicial decisions. *See Wagenseller v. Scottsdale Mem'l Hosp.*, 147 Ariz. 370, 378-89, 710 P.2d 1025, 1033-34 (1985). Rembar's complaint demands tort damages for common law wrongful discharge in violation of the public policies reflected in the ACRA, a tort claim recognized in this state until recently. *See Broomfield v. Lundell*, 159 Ariz. 349, 767 P.2d 697 (Ct. App. 1988). Her claim fails as a matter of law, however, both on the facts in this record and through statutory preemption.

First, as stated in arguments A and B above, Hart did not engage in sexual harassment or any other sexually discriminatory employment practice that would violate the policies of the ACRA. Second, even if Rembar can genuinely dispute those facts, her wrongful discharge claim is preempted by the Employment Protection Act ("the EPA"), Ariz. Rev. Stat. Ann. § 23-1501 (West Supp. 2000).

The EPA provides that an employer may be liable for discharging an employee "in violation of a statute of this state." Ariz. Rev. Stat. Ann. § 23-1501(3)(b) (West Supp 2000). If the violated statute provides its own civil remedies, however, those remedies are exclusive; indeed, the EPA lists the ACRA as its first example of a source of such exclusive remedies:

> [T]he remedies provided to an employee for a violation of the statute are the exclusive remedies for the violation of the statute or the public policy set forth in or arising out of the statute, including the following:
>   (i) The civil rights act prescribed in title 41, chapter 9.

Id.; *see also* Ariz. Rev. Stat. Ann. § 41-1481 (West 1999) (setting forth enforcement procedures and remedies for violations of the ACRA). Because Rembar bases her wrongful discharge claim on alleged violations of the ACRA, her remedy is limited to the relief available in the ACRA. *See Cronin v. Sheldon*, 195 Ariz. 531, 991 P.2d 231 (1999) (finding that the EPA constitutionally preempted the tort remedy recognized in *Broomfield*).

Accordingly, regardless of whether Rembar can establish a factual dispute about the reasons for her discharge, Hart is entitled to summary judgment on Rembar's tort claim of wrongful discharge.

D. Hart did not engage in extreme and outrageous conduct and therefore is not liable for infliction of emotional distress.

The EPA would not preempt a claim of intentional infliction of emotional distress for an unlawfully discriminatory discharge. *Cronin*, 195 Ariz. at 541, 991 P.2d at 241 (dictum). However, Hart is not liable for intentional infliction of emotional distress unless his conduct was so "extreme and outrageous" that it fell "within that quite narrow range" of conduct "at the very extreme edge of the spectrum." *Watts v. Golden Age Nursing Home,* 127 Ariz. 255, 258, 619 P.2d 1032, 1035 (1980). As discussed above, Hart discharged Rembar for legitimate business reasons. [Hart SofF ¶¶ 7-8.] Moreover, Hart communicated his decision in a normal professional matter. [Hart SofF ¶ 8.] Because of its economic consequences, termination of employment is often an extremely distressing event for the discharged employee. However, discharge for business reasons is an economic fact of life and hardly amounts to a basis for tort liability.

Moreover, even if Rembar could establish a dispute of fact regarding the reason for her discharge, the dispute would not be material. "[I]t is extremely rare to find conduct in the employment context that will rise to the level of outrageousness necessary to provide a basis for recovery for the tort of intentional infliction of emotional distress." *Mintz v. Bell Atl. Sys. Leasing Int'l, Inc.*, 183 Ariz. 550, 554, 905 P.2d 559, 563 (Ct. App. 1995) (quoting *Cox v. Keystone Carbon Co.*, 861 F.2d 390, 395 (3d Cir. 1988)).

In *Mintz*, an employee was hospitalized after a suffering a nervous breakdown as the alleged result of gender discrimination in the workplace. The employer terminated her disability benefits, ordered her to return to work, and then—while the employee was again hospitalized after returning to work for one day—notified her of a reassignment of her duties by a letter delivered to the hospital. *Id.* at 552, 905 P.2d at 561. The Arizona Court of Appeals affirmed a finding that, as a matter of law, this alleged conduct was not extreme and outrageous, even assuming that the employer had failed to promote the employee because of gender discrimination and that it knew that the employee was unusually susceptible to emotional distress. *Id.* at 553-54, 905 P.2d at 564-65.

In light of cases such as *Mintz*, a federal district court has characterized Arizona's standard for extreme and outrageous conduct as one requiring "extraordinary" conduct. *Tempesta v. Motorola, Inc.*, 92 F. Supp. 2d 973, 987 (D. Ariz. 1999). Applying *Mintz*, the *Tempesta* court granted summary judgment for the defendant employer on the employee's claim of intentional infliction of emotional distress, even after assuming the truth of the employee's allegations that he had suffered harassment and wrongful termination because of his sex. *Id.* at 986-87.

It is even clearer in this case that Hart did not engage in extreme and outrageous conduct. Even if Rembar's allegations of mild sexual advances and retaliatory discharge were supported by the record, that conduct would not satisfy the demanding test of egregiousness applied in Arizona courts. As a matter of law, Hart is not liable for intentional infliction of emotional distress.

III. CONCLUSION

Rembar cannot genuinely dispute Hart's showing on the facts that Hart promised Rembar no job security, that Hart discharged Rembar for performance, and that Hart did not engage in sexual harassment. Therefore, Hart is entitled to summary judgment on all claims.

March 3, 2002

Lisa Hall for
Kendricks, Hall, & Oats, P.C.
3310 Alma School Rd., Suite 200
Mesa, Arizona 85283

COPY OF THE FOREGOING MAILED
March 3, 2002 to:

Roberts and Cray
101 E. Washington St., Suite 600
Phoenix, Arizona 85001

Lisa Hall
Kendricks, Hall, & Oats, P.C.
3310 Alma School Rd., Suite 200
Mesa, Arizona 85283
(602) 839-0365
Bar No. 0076089

ARIZONA SUPERIOR COURT
MARICOPA COUNTY

CHARLOTTE REMBAR, Plaintiff, v. ALEXANDER HART d.b.a. COMCON, Defendant.	No. C732431 Defendant Hart's Statement of Material Facts and Exhibits Supporting Motion for Summary Judgment (Judge Wisdom)

For purposes of summary judgment only, Defendant Alexander Hart d.b.a. Comcon presents the following material facts:

1. Alexander Hart is the sole owner and manager of Comcon, a firm that provides expert consulting on computer systems to businesses in the Phoenix metropolitan area. From January to November 2001, Comcon employed eight employees other than Hart himself; Comcon has never employed a greater number of employees before or since. [Hart Aff. ¶ 1 (Exh. D).]

2. On January 1, 2001, Hart hired Charlotte Rembar for the position of Comcon consultant at a salary of $5,000/month. [Jan. 1, 2001 Payroll Action (Exh. B).] The only written record of Rembar's contract with Comcon is a Payroll Action form that states her date of hire and her salary. *Id.;* [Hart Aff. ¶ 2 (Exh. D)]. The term of Rembar's employment was left indefinite. *Id.*

3. At or before the time of Rembar's hiring, Alexander Hart gave Rembar a Policy Manual that summarizes many of the personnel procedures at Comcon. [Policy Manual (Exh. A).] The Policy Manual includes one example of a ground for discharging a nonprobationary employee, but it does not explicitly limit Comcon's right to discharge an employee for any other reason. *Id.* at § IV.

4. Under the heading *"Probationary Employment,"* section IV.A of the policy manual provides that "Each employee will work on probationary status during his or her first 60 days of employment. During this probationary

period, Comcon reserves the right to terminate the employee for any reason or for no reason at all." *Id.* at § IV.A.

5. Under the heading *Nonprobationary Employment*, section IV.B of the policy manual provides that "Comcon reserves the right to terminate the employment of any employee who is not performing satisfactorily." *Id.* at § IV.B.

6. From the beginning of her employment at Comcon, Rembar sought to attract Hart's attentions with casual flirtations, such as references to his appearance and suggestive smiles. Hart returned the flirtations in a similar manner, but no sexual relationship developed between them. Any flirtations directed by Hart toward Rembar were welcomed, and even invited, by her. Hart never demanded sexual favors from Rembar, and he never conditioned any benefits of employment on Rembar's submitting to a sexual demand or otherwise reacting to a flirtation. [Hart Aff. ¶ 3 (Exh. D).]

7. In the fall of 2001, Hart became dissatisfied with Rembar's performance. Specifically, she displayed a negative attitude in her work. Because Comcon consultants must work closely with their clients, a consultant with a negative attitude severely hampers Comcon's business relationships. [Hart Aff. ¶ 4 (Exh. D).]

8. Effective November 2, 2001, Hart terminated Rembar's employment because of her negative attitude. [Nov. 1, 2001 Payroll Action (Exh. C).] Hart communicated the discharge to Rembar in a normal, professional manner. [Hart Aff. ¶ 4 (Exh. D).]

March 3, 2002

Lisa Hall for
Kendricks, Hall, & Oats, P.C.
3310 Alma School Rd., Suite 200
Mesa, Arizona 85283

E X H I B I T   A

POLICY MANUAL
for Employees of Comcon

I. INTRODUCTION

The success of Comcon lies in its ability to recruit and retain the best employees available nationally. To promote a stable and productive work-force, Comcon endeavors to provide attractive terms and conditions of employment, as reflected in the following policies.

II. SALARY

A. Initial Salary . . .

B. Change in Salary . . .

III. HOLIDAYS, VACATIONS, SICK LEAVE

A. Holidays . . .

B. Personal Leave . . .

IV. TERMINATION

A. Probationary Employment

Each employee will work on probationary status during his or her first 60 days of employment. During this probationary period, Comcon reserves the right to terminate the employee for any reason or for no reason at all.

B. Nonprobationary Employment

Comcon reserves the right to terminate the employment of any employee who is not performing satisfactorily.

E X H I B I T   B

PAYROLL ACTION

NATURE OF ACTION

___X___ New Hire   _____ Change in Pay   _____ Termination

PREVIOUS PAY ___N.A.___

NEW PAY ___$5,000/mo___

EFFECTIVE DATE ___Jan. 1, 2001___

REASON FOR CHANGE OR TERMINATION

COMMENTS

Consultant

DATE ___Jan. 1, 2001___

PROCESSED BY ___Leslie West___

E X H I B I T   C

PAYROLL ACTION

NATURE OF ACTION

_____ New Hire   _____ Change in Pay   _X_ Termination

PREVIOUS PAY _$5,000/mo_

NEW PAY _N.A._

EFFECTIVE DATE _Nov. 2, 2001_

REASON FOR CHANGE OR TERMINATION
      Negative Attitude

COMMENTS

DATE _Nov. 1, 2001_

PROCESSED BY _Leslie West_

E X H I B I T   D

AFFIDAVIT OF ALEXANDER HART
IN SUPPORT OF MOTION FOR SUMMARY JUDGMENT

Maricopa County,
Arizona

Alexander Hart, under oath, swears to the following information from personal knowledge:

1. I am the sole owner and manager of Comcon, a firm that provides consulting services to businesses on the development and use of computer systems. From January to November 2001, I employed eight employees, the largest workforce that I have employed since I formed Comcon in 1999. Specifically, during that period I employed a secretary, an accountant, and six consultants.

2. On January 1, 2001, I hired Charlotte Rembar for the position of consultant. The Payroll Action form identified in this motion as Exhibit B is the only written record of Rembar's hiring and her terms of employment. Rembar and I understood at the time of hiring that her term of employment was indefinite. On or before the time of her hiring, I gave her a Comcon Policy Manual, which reaffirms that Rembar had no definite term of employment or guarantee of continued employment.

3. From the beginning of her employment at Comcon, Rembar sought to attract my attentions with casual flirtations such as suggestive smiles and compliments on my grooming and appearance. She made it clear that she welcomed reciprocation, and I often returned her flirtations with similar smiles and comments. Our personal relationship never advanced beyond these casual flirtations. Specifically, we never had a sexual relationship, and I never made any unwelcome sexual advances toward Rembar, nor did I ever condition any benefits of employment on Rembar's submitting to any sexual demands or otherwise reacting in any way to my flirtations.

4. Sometime in the fall of 2001, I began to notice that Rembar displayed a negative attitude about me, about herself, and about her work. I find it extremely important to maintain a workforce with positive attitudes and pleasant personalities, because the consultants work closely with clients, and our business thus depends on maintaining good personal relationships with clients. To ensure that we maintained those relationships, I discharged Rembar effective November 2, 2001, to rid our workforce of her negativism. I communicated the discharge to Rembar in a normal, professional manner in an office meeting on November 1, 2001.

5. The Payroll Action forms in Exhibits B and C are true copies of records that were prepared and kept under my direction by my personal secretary, Leslie West, in the course of her regularly conducted business activity, which includes maintaining such employment records as a uniform practice. Those forms include information within Ms. West's own knowledge and information that I transmitted to her on matters within my knowledge. The Policy Manual in Exhibit A is a true copy of a manual that I drafted and printed in June 2000 and have since distributed to all employees.

I swear under oath that the foregoing is true:

_____

Alexander Hart

_____

Date

Chapter 20

Motion to Exclude Evidence Before Trial

BLACK'S LAW DICTIONARY defines "in limine" as: "On or at the threshold; at the very beginning; preliminarily."[1] Simply put, the typical motion in limine is a motion to exclude evidence before trial, or at least to require opposing counsel to raise the question of admissibility outside the presence of the jury during trial. Conversely, but much more rarely, an advocate may use it to move for admission of evidence before trial if she anticipates an objection to the evidence.[2]

Thus, in contrast to the typical motion for summary judgment, a motion to exclude evidence seeks to define the scope of the trial litigation rather than finally dispose of the case before trial. It generally is simpler than a motion for summary judgment. If you can strip the mystery away from the popular Latin phrase, you should have little trouble supporting or opposing the motion.

---

1. BLACK'S LAW DICTIONARY 791 (7th ed. 1999).
2. *See* Hon. Robert E. Bacharach, *Motions in Limine in Oklahoma State and Federal Courts*, 24 Okla. City U. L. Rev. 112, 114 (1999).

I. PRETRIAL EXCLUSION OF EVIDENCE

The Federal Rules of Civil Procedure expressly authorize "advance rulings from the court on the admissibility of evidence" in pretrial conferences.[3] Additionally, those rules and the Federal Rules of Evidence implicitly authorize a trial court to rule on pretrial motions to exclude evidence other than in pretrial conference, or they at least leave undisturbed the court's inherent power to do so.[4]

During trial, attorneys can and do object to evidence offered for admission.[5] However, pretrial rulings on complex, potentially prejudicial, or particularly significant evidentiary matters tend to improve the efficiency and quality of the trial proceedings.[6]

For example, suppose a visitor to your client's factory sues your client for injuries sustained at the factory. At trial, the plaintiff's counsel asks a defense witness in front of the jury to confirm that your client offered to pay the plaintiff's medical expenses. You can immediately object that the question seeks a response that may lead the jury to find liability on an improper ground.[7] In most jurisdictions, the judge will sustain your objection and will order the witness not to provide the solicited testimony.[8] However, the damage to your client's case may be irreparable if the question alone improperly influences the jury's deliberations, despite the court's admonishments to the jury to ignore it. You could have protected your client more effectively had you earlier persuaded the judge to exclude the evidence before trial and to order the parties to refrain from referring to the evidence in any way at trial.

Additionally, pretrial litigation of complex evidentiary matters permits more thorough written and oral argument by the parties and more considered deliberation by the court, all without disrupting an ongoing trial. Moreover, pretrial disposition of objections to particularly significant evidence gives the parties an opportunity to modify their trial strategies or to reassess their settlement positions.[9]

---

3. FED. R. CIV. P. 16(c)(3).

4. *See generally* FED. R. EVID. 103(c) ("In jury cases, proceedings shall be conducted, to the extent practicable, so as to prevent inadmissible evidence from being suggested to the jury by any means, such as making statements or offers of proof or asking questions in the hearing of the jury."); Charles W. Gamble, *The Motion* In Limine: *A Pretrial Procedure That Has Come of Age*, 33 Ala. L. Rev. 1, 2 & n.6 (1981).

5. *See* FED. R. EVID. 103(a) (unnumbered paragraph following subsections (1) & (2)) (referring to rulings "admitting or excluding evidence, either at or before trial").

6. *See* FED. R. CIV. P. 16(a) (stating objectives of pretrial conference).

7. *See* FED. R. EVID. 409, Advisory Committee's Note. Exclusion of such evidence also promotes a generally humanitarian policy of encouraging such assistance, regardless of liability. *Id.*

8. See FED. R. EVID. 409.

9. *See* Gamble, *supra* note 4, at 8-10.

II. FORMAT—OVERVIEW

Local rules addressing motions typically provide for a motion and supporting brief, an opposing brief, and an optional reply brief.[10] However, unlike local rules that require a special format for some parts of a motion for summary judgment,[11] rules of procedure and local court rules of most jurisdictions specify no detailed format for a motion to exclude evidence beyond the general requirements for all motions.[12] Instead, the common format is a product of custom and common sense. As with any legal document, you can best support or oppose a motion to exclude evidence if you understand the purposes of your document and draft it accordingly.

III. THE MOTION

In a motion to exclude evidence, you should simply and clearly state the action requested and briefly summarize the grounds for the motion. In describing the relief requested, you probably should go beyond generally asking for exclusion of certain evidence. To ensure effective protection, you should describe the objectionable evidence as inclusively as possible and should request an order specifically prohibiting the opposing party from referring to the evidence:

> The defendant, Axxon Corp., moves for a pretrial order excluding all evidence that Axxon Corp. offered to provide medical care and pay the medical expenses of the plaintiff, Herb Taylor. The evidence is inadmissible under Federal Rule of Evidence 409.
> Specifically, Axxon Corp. requests an order directing Taylor and his counsel (1) to refrain from referring to such an offer in any way in the presence of the jury during voir dire and all subsequent proceedings, and (2) to take all necessary steps to ensure that their witnesses avoid such references.

To oppose a motion to exclude evidence, you need not file a separate motion; you can simply file a brief that opposes the original motion. At the most, you might want to draft a cover page for your brief that parallels the motion in summarizing the ruling you seek and the supporting grounds:

> Plaintiff Herb Taylor opposes Defendant Axxon Corp.'s motion to exclude evidence of Axxon Corp.'s offer to provide and pay for medical care. The

---

10. *See, e.g.*, D. ARIZ. R. 1.10.
11. *See* Chapter 19.
12. *See, e.g.*, ARIZ. R. CIV. P. 7.1 (setting forth general requirements for motions, including a written statement of grounds and the relief or order sought, supplemented by a legal memorandum).

evidence is admissible to show the extent of Taylor's injuries. The court should not exclude the evidence for this purpose.

IV. THE BRIEF

A brief supporting or opposing a motion to exclude evidence, or any other motion, is often referred to as a "Memorandum of Law." When preparing a brief supporting a motion to exclude evidence, you ordinarily should follow the familiar pattern of Introduction, Argument, and Conclusion. The party opposing your motion should file a responsive brief that directly answers the arguments of your supporting brief. Similarly, in your reply brief, if any, you should respond to the points made in the opposing brief.

On a motion for summary judgment, you will address at least some of the claims or defenses of the litigation on their merits. In contrast, on a motion to exclude evidence, you will typically focus more narrowly on the admissibility of certain evidence. Consequently, in your supporting or opposing briefs, you should address the merits of claims or defenses only to the extent necessary to address some element of admissibility, such as relevance. This narrow focus affects the scope of the introduction and argument sections of the briefs.

A. The Introduction

In the introductory section of a brief supporting a motion to exclude evidence, you need not include a full statement of facts and procedural history. In light of the motion's focus on an evidentiary issue, your introduction need summarize only those portions of the facts and procedural history necessary to an understanding of that issue. You should accompany your motion with any necessary factual support for your assertions, such as affidavits or documents. Additionally, you should cite to such attachments or to other parts of the record. Any reasonable citation form is acceptable; two examples are presented below. Finally, your introduction should explain why you expect the nonmoving party to attempt to introduce the evidence at trial and why the court should resolve the matter before trial, unless you choose to address those matters in the Argument section.

For example, the brief supporting the motion might begin with the following introductory points:

MEMORANDUM IN SUPPORT OF
MOTION TO EXCLUDE EVIDENCE

I. INTRODUCTION

Nature of the case　　　Herb Taylor, a sales representative for Corbin Heavy Equipment Co., brought this tort action against Axxon Corp. He alleges negligence in the maintenance of the Axxon manufacturing plant in Albuquerque, New Mexico.

Specifically, Taylor alleges that, while touring the Axxon plant in January 2000 with Axxon General Manager Jerry Olshon, Taylor lost his footing, fell backwards, and struck his head against a forklift. [Compl. ¶¶ 3, 4.] According to Olshon's deposition testimony, as a humanitarian gesture, Olshon immediately offered on behalf of Axxon to provide transportation to the nearest hospital and to pay for Taylor's medical expenses. [Olshon Dep. 18.] Taylor later developed difficulties with his eyesight, which he alleges are the result of his accident at the Axxon plant. [Compl. at ¶ 6.]

Facts

The critical issue in this case is whether Axxon negligently maintained its plant, causing Taylor to fall. Taylor's counsel has examined Olshon extensively during deposition about Olshon's offer to pay medical expenses, leading Axxon to believe that Taylor's counsel will attempt to introduce that evidence at trial.

Belief that evidence will be introduced

Evidence of Olshon's offer to pay medical expenses is inadmissible to establish Axxon's liability, and Axxon will not introduce it for other purposes. The evidence must be excluded before trial, because reference to it even in a question to a witness would indelibly and improperly influence the jury.

Need for pretrial exclusion

When opposing a motion, you should state any facts and procedural history that are material to your argument and that are not fairly stated in the opening brief:

I. INTRODUCTION

Plaintiff Taylor is prepared to prove that Defendant Axxon Corp.'s negligence proximately caused Taylor to lose nearly all sight in his right eye. Axxon apparently seeks to show that Taylor's injuries at the Axxon factory were slight and that Taylor's partial blindness must be unrelated. *See* Answer ¶ 6. Thus, the extent of Taylor's injuries at the factory is in issue.

Issues for trial

Taylor plans to introduce Axxon Corp.'s offer to provide and pay for medical care as evidence that Axxon's agent at the scene of the accident determined Taylor's injuries to be serious. The evidence is admissible for this purpose and should not be excluded.

Relevance of evidence on particular issue

B. The Argument

1. LEGAL RULES

The argument section of a motion to exclude evidence follows the same general pattern discussed in Chapters 6 and 16. Each section or subsection within the argument should state a contention in a point heading, analyze the law and the facts, and restate or summarize the contention in a conclusion.

In the statement of legal standards in the opening brief supporting a motion to exclude evidence, you typically will focus on rules of evidence that restrict admissibility. If you prefer a thorough analysis, you may choose to develop the legal standards carefully:

Even relevant evidence is inadmissible "if its probative value is substantially outweighed by the danger" that it will cause "unfair prejudice." Fed. R. Evid. 403. Evidence presents such a danger if it has "an undue tendency to suggest a decision on an improper basis, commonly, though not necessarily, an emotional one." *Id.*, Advisory Committee Note.

In this case, evidence of Powell's membership in the Black Panthers organization more than 20 years ago has little, if any, probative value. . . .

On the other hand, the general standards for some of the more commonly invoked evidentiary rules are familiar to judges and attorneys. Therefore, you could exercise stylistic discretion to present those standards summarily, or even implicitly, and to move more quickly to the fact analysis:

Evidence of Powell's former membership in the Black Panthers organization should be excluded because it presents a danger of unfair prejudice that greatly outweighs its probative value. *See* Fed. R. Evid. 403. The F.B.I. file report shows that Powell was a member of the Black Panthers more than 30 years ago for the brief period of eight months. During that time, Powell participated in peaceful demonstrations and political rallies, and he met with other members in "strategy meetings." . . .

---

2. APPLICATION OF RULES TO FACTS

As in any legal argument, the fact analysis should lead to a conclusion by relating the facts to the legal standard:

Little relevance	Purely political and social activities such as these have little or no probative value on the question of the likelihood that Powell provoked Beatty's assault. As a member of the Black Panthers organization, Powell did not espouse violence or engage in any violent activities.
Unfair prejudice	The primary effect of the evidence would be to inflame the passions of the jury. Despite the nonvio-

lent role that Powell played as a member of the organization, many view the Black Panthers as a radical organization that actively sought violent confrontation with established institutions such as police agencies. Some jurors undoubtedly would react emotionally to the controversial image of the Black Panthers.

The evidence of Powell's membership in the Black Panthers organization therefore should be excluded on the ground that it presents a danger of unfair prejudice that substantially outweighs its probative value.

The argument section of an opposing brief or a reply brief will contain similar elements, except that each will be narrowly tailored to respond directly to contentions advanced in the brief that preceded it.

C. The Conclusion

Chapter 16's discussion of conclusions includes examples from sample motions in limine. In summary, you should

1. end each argument in a brief with a conclusion on that argument, and
2. end the entire brief with a general summary of all the arguments and of your request for relief.

V. SUMMARY

To prepare a motion to exclude evidence before trial,

1. draft a motion that simply and clearly requests the court to exclude specified evidence and to prohibit the parties from referring to the evidence at trial;
2. draft a supporting brief that
   a. introduces the facts and procedural history relevant to the motion,
   b. argues the law and facts relating to the evidentiary issues, and
   c. states your conclusions; and
3. attach any documentary evidence or affidavits necessary to support your motion or refer to evidence already in the record.

To oppose a motion to exclude evidence, or to reply to an opposition brief, you need not file a separate motion. Instead, you should submit a brief that responds to the arguments presented in the preceding brief.

For further practice with motions to exclude evidence, perform Assignment 6 in Appendix VI, near the end of this book.

SAMPLE

Deborah E. Driggs
State Bar No. 6081
David L. Keily
State Bar No. 12345
SACKS, TIERNEY, KASEN & KERRICK, P.A.
3300 North Central Avenue, Suite 2000
Phoenix, Arizona 85012-1576
Telephone: (602) 279-4900
Attorneys for Defendants Rayner

SUPERIOR COURT OF ARIZONA
MARICOPA COUNTY

AGUA FRIA SAND & ROCK, INC., an Arizona corporation, Plaintiff, v. Estate of DALE FAY RAYNER, Deceased; JACK RAYNER, JR., Personal Representative of the Estate of DALE FAY RAYNER, Deceased; Estate of JACK RAYNER, JR., Personal Representative of the Estate of JACK RAYNER, SR., Deceased; JACK RAYNER, JR., Defendants.	No. C-531100 MOTION IN LIMINE TO EXCLUDE TESTIMONY AS TO TRANSACTIONS WITH OR STATEMENTS BY JACK M. RAYNER, SR. AND DALE FAY RAYNER (Oral Argument Requested) (Hon. Gloria G. Ybarra)

Defendants Rayner move for an order excluding testimony by the plaintiff or its agents, or questions or statements by its counsel, about transactions with or statements by Jack M. Rayner, Sr., and Dale Fay Rayner. This motion is made pursuant to Arizona's Deadman's statute, Ariz. Rev. Stat. Ann. 12-2251 (Supp. 1985), and is supported by the attached Memorandum of Points and Authorities.

DATED December 29, 1986.

By _____
Deborah E. Driggs
David L. Keily, for
SACKS, TIERNEY, KASEN & KERRICK, P.A.
Attorneys for Defendants

MEMORANDUM OF POINTS AND AUTHORITIES

I. FACTUAL BACKGROUND

Plaintiff Agua Fria Sand & Rock, Inc. (Agua Fria) brought this suit against defendants for fraud, breach of a duty of due care, and breach of a lease. Agua Fria was the assignee of a leasehold interest in certain real property owned by defendants. On this property, Agua Fria operated a sand and gravel mine. In February 1980, Agua Fria's plant and equipment were destroyed by a flood. After the flood, Agua Fria moved its operations to a new site on the property.

Agua Fria alleges that the defendants wrongfully evicted them from the new site. Although Agua Fria occupied the land as a tenant at will, it alleges that the defendants promised to execute and deliver a written lease for a term of 20 years.

The defendants deny that they had promised to execute and deliver a written lease for a term of 20 years to Agua Fria. They allege that Agua Fria was evicted because it had failed to make rental payments and to satisfy other lease obligations.

Jack M. Rayner, Sr., died on October 14, 1982. Dale Fay Rayner died on April 17, 1984. Jack M. Rayner, Jr., is the Personal Representative of the Estates of Jack M. Rayner, Sr., and Dale Fay Rayner. Agua Fria has sued Jack M. Rayner, Jr., in his capacity as Personal Representative of the estates of Jack M. Rayner, Sr., and Dale Fay Rayner.

Questions, argument, or testimony before the jury regarding alleged oral promises made by either testator will improperly influence the jury, even if objection at trial or related proceedings is sustained. Therefore, this Court should exclude all such references before trial.

II. ARGUMENT

The Arizona Deadman's Statute bars admission of testimony of transactions with, or statements by, Jack M. Rayner, Sr., and Dale Fay Rayner.

To reduce the danger of fraudulent testimony, the Arizona Deadman's statute restricts the admission of testimony about transactions with, or about statements made by, the testator in certain suits:

> In an action by or against personal representatives, administrators, guardians or conservators in which judgment may be given for or against them as such, neither party shall be allowed to testify against the other as to any transaction with or statement by the testator, intestate or ward unless called to testify thereto by the opposite party, or required to testify thereto by the court. The provisions of this section shall extend to and include all actions by or against the heirs, devisees, legatees or legal representatives of a decedent arising out of any transaction with the decedent.

Ariz. Rev. Stat. Ann. § 12-2251 (Supp. 1985).

The statute clearly applies to this case. First, Agua Fria has filed suit against Jack M. Rayner, Jr., in his capacity as personal representative of the estates of Jack M. Rayner, Sr., and Dale Fay Rayner. Judgment may be granted for or against Jack M. Rayner, Jr., in his capacity as personal representative. Finally, Agua Fria plans to introduce evidence of an alleged oral agreement by the deceased, Jack M. Rayner, Sr., and Dale Fay Rayner, to execute a written lease with a term of 20 years.

The statute authorizes admission of testimony of transactions with or statements by the deceased if "required . . . by the court." Therefore, such admission ultimately lies within the discretion of the trial court. *Mahan v. First Nat'l Bank,* 139 Ariz. 138, 140, 677 P.2d 301, 303 (Ct. App. 1984). The trial court's determination to admit testimony of transactions with or statements by the decedent will be upheld only if (1) independent evidence corroborates the transaction with the decedent, and (2) an injustice will result if the testimony is rejected. *Id.*

Agua Fria has no independent evidence to support its claims that the deceased promised to execute and deliver a written lease of the premises for a term of 20 years. Instead, Agua Fria rests on the bald assertion that the deceased made such promises. This type of uncorroborated testimony is exactly what the statute was intended to proscribe.

Second, no injustice will result from exclusion of testimony of transactions with or statements by Jack M. Rayner, Sr., and Dale Fay Rayner. The exclusion will apply equally to both parties. Moreover, exclusion of the testimony comports strongly with public policy to render incompetent as witnesses persons who will gain from distortion of transactions with the decedent when death has rendered the decedent incapable of refuting these inaccuracies. *See Carrillo v. Taylor,* 81 Ariz. 14, 299 P.2d 188 (1956). The exclusion will simply preclude Plaintiff Agua Fria from making use of self-serving, uncorroborated declarations about what the deceased supposedly said. Agua Fria should not be able to manufacture lease obligations out of the alleged representations of those who are no longer able to refute them.

III. CONCLUSION

The objectionable testimony in this case is uncorroborated, and its exclusion will not result in an injustice. Therefore, this testimony should be excluded under the applicable Deadman's statute. To prevent evasion of the statute, this Court's order should apply broadly to comments or questions of counsel in front of the jury, as well as to testimony.

December 29, 1986.

SACKS, TIERNEY & KASEN, P.A.

Deborah E. Driggs
David L. Keily
3300 North Central Avenue
Phoenix, Arizona 85012-1576
Attorneys for Defendants

Part VIII

Appellate

Briefs

Writing appellate briefs differs from most pretrial briefwriting in three respects. First, if you have fully tried your case before appeal, you will analyze the issues on appeal on a more complete factual record than was available during the litigation of pretrial motions. Second, in developing your arguments on appeal, you must consider standards of appellate review, which require varying levels of deference to trial court rulings and findings. Third, rules of procedure and local rules typically prescribe a more formal and detailed format for appellate briefs than for most pretrial or trial briefs.

Chapter 21

Standards of
Appellate Review

I. THE RECORD ON APPEAL

Aside from physical exhibits and some kinds of documentary evidence admitted into court, the proceedings in the trial court are recorded in two records: the trial court clerk's record and the reporter's transcript.[1] The trial history of a case can usually be most easily traced in the trial court clerk's record, which contains litigation documents filed with the trial court, from the initial pleadings to the notice of appeal. It also includes the written judgment of the court, along with orders reflecting the court's rulings on procedural and other preliminary matters. A docket sheet attached to the clerk's record contains a brief entry for each document in the record. This provides a convenient index to the record and a summary of the history of the litigation.

The reporter's transcript is a record of all the statements made "on the record" in court during the litigation process. It includes oral arguments

---

1. *See, e.g.,* FED. R. APP. P. 10(a).

of the parties on motions, testimony of witnesses, rulings from the bench, and instructions to the jury.

Shortly after a disappointed litigant has filed notice of appeal from the judgment of the trial court, the parties on appeal designate the portions of the clerk's record and reporter's transcript that are necessary for the appeal.[2] In some circumstances, other original documents and physical exhibits admitted into evidence may also be forwarded to the appellate court.[3]

Before writing an appellate brief, you must master the record on appeal because the evidence and arguments presented to the trial court help to define the scope of the appellate court's inquiry. Indeed, when referring in your brief to testimony, arguments, rulings, or other portions of the trial history, you should carefully cite to the pages of the clerk's record or reporter's transcript that reflect that information. Although rules of procedure or local rules may specify a different citation form, common abbreviations for citation to page 134 of the clerk's record are "CR at 134," for "clerk's record" or "CT at 134," for "clerk's transcript." The reporter's transcript is commonly cited as "RT at 383," or simply "R at 383." If either record is bound in multiple volumes, you must also cite to the volume number in some reasonable fashion. For example, you might cite to page 115 of the third volume of the reporter's transcript as "III RT at 115" or "3 RT at 115." In any of these citations, one could omit the "at," or replace it with an abbreviation for "page," depending on your style or applicable rules; for example, CR 134; 3 RT p. 115; III RT pg. 115. Finally, if the opening brief is accompanied by an appendix containing relevant parts of the record, appellate rules of procedure or local court rules may require citation to the appendix rather than to the underlying record.[4] One might cite to such an appendix in any of several reasonable ways, such as Appendix p. 42; Appendix at 42; or App. 42.

II. STANDARDS OF REVIEW IN THE FEDERAL COURTS

A. Overview

An appellate court will apply different standards of review to different kinds of trial court findings or rulings. For example, on a motion for summary judgment or a motion to dismiss an action for failure to state a claim, a trial court does not resolve any factual disputes; instead, it decides as a matter of law whether alleged or undisputed facts satisfy the applicable legal standards. When reviewing a trial court's granting of such a motion, the appellate court will place itself in the position of the trial court and decide, without deference

---

2. *See, e.g.,* FED. R. APP. P. 10(b), 11(a).
3. *See, e.g.,* FED. R. APP. P. 11(b)(2).
4. *See, e.g.,* FED. R. APP. P. 28(e).

to the trial court's analysis, whether the moving party satisfied its burden on the motion.[5]

In contrast, a jury's verdict or a trial judge's findings of fact rendered after trial represent the factfinder's resolution of factual disputes. When reviewing such findings, an appellate court will restrict its review, deferring to some extent to the factfinder's resolution of conflicting evidence.

Thus, to effectively argue your case on appeal, you must consider the standard of review, or the degree to which the appellate court will defer to a finding or ruling made in the trial court. Indeed, the outcome of some appeals will depend directly on the standard of review that the appellate court chooses to apply.[6]

Appellate standards of review in the federal court system will serve as a starting point for your understanding standards that apply in a state court. Under the two most important standards—and subject to a "constitutional facts" exception discussed at the end of this chapter—an appellate court restricts its review of questions of fact but not of questions of law.

B. Restricted Appellate Review of Findings of Fact

1. REVIEW OF JURY FINDINGS

The Seventh Amendment to the United States Constitution guarantees the right to a jury trial "in suits at common law," and it provides that "no fact tried by a jury shall be otherwise re-examined in any court of the United States, than according to the rules of the common law." Accordingly, a federal appellate court generally will uphold the factual findings of a jury in a civil case unless those findings are not supported by "any substantial evidence."[7] Federal statutes prescribe the same standard of review for the findings of some administrative agencies.[8]

Even though a different set of constitutional considerations applies, an appellate court will also restrict its review of a jury's findings of fact resulting in conviction in a criminal case. Specifically, rather than reweigh all the evidence, an appellate court may constitutionally uphold a criminal convic-

---

5. *See* Experimental Eng'g, Inc. v. United Technologies Corp., 614 F.2d 1244, 1246 (9th Cir. 1980) (reviewing dismissal of action for failure to state a claim); Heiniger v. City of Phoenix, 625 F.2d 842, 843-44 (9th Cir. 1980) (discussing standards of review for summary judgment).

6. *See, e.g.*, Chaline v. KCOH, Inc., 693 F.2d 477, 480 n.3 (5th Cir. 1982); Walsh v. Centeio, 692 F.2d 1239, 1241 (9th Cir. 1982).

7. *See, e.g.*, Aetna Life Ins. Co. v. Kepler, 116 F.2d 1, 4 & n.1 (8th Cir. 1941). Interestingly, a finding of negligence is not a pure finding of fact, because it requires the jury to define and apply a standard of care, resulting in a mixed conclusion of law and fact. For purposes of appellate review, however, such jury verdicts are treated as findings of fact. Appellate courts distinguish more finely between a trial judge's findings of fact and conclusions of law.

8. *See, e.g.*, 29 U.S.C. § 160(f) (1994) (appellate review of findings of the National Labor Relations Board); 5 U.S.C. § 706(2)(E) (standards for reviewing administrative agency findings, as set forth in the Administrative Procedure Act); In re Gartside, 203 F.3d 1305 (Fed. Cir. 2000) (under the Administrative Procedure Act, "substantial evidence" standard of review applies to review of findings of fact of Patent and Trademark Office Board of Appeals).

tion if "the record evidence could reasonably support a finding of guilt beyond a reasonable doubt."[9]

The Seventh Amendment does not apply to state courts. Therefore, some states may permit broader appellate review of jury findings, particularly review of a jury's calculation of damages in a civil suit. New York, for example, has legislatively authorized its state appellate courts to overturn a jury's calculation of damages as excessive or inadequate if the jury award materially deviates from reasonable compensation. More typically, however, a state or federal trial court will set aside a jury's calculation of compensatory damages only if the damages are so excessive as to shock the conscience of the court, and an appellate court typically will overturn the trial court's determinations whether to set aside jury awards only if the trial court abused its discretion.[10]

2. REVIEW OF A JUDGE'S FINDINGS OF FACT

In civil suits in which the parties have no constitutional or statutory right to a jury, or in suits in which the parties have waived their right to a jury, the trial judge will both find the facts and rule on the law. Under Federal Rule of Civil Procedure 52(a), a federal court of appeals will not overturn the factual findings of a federal trial judge unless the findings are "clearly erroneous." Although Rule 52(a) applies only to civil proceedings and does not directly apply to a trial judge's factual findings on preliminary rulings in a criminal trial, some courts have adopted Rule 52(a)'s "clearly erroneous" standard by analogy for the criminal context.[11]

Under Rule 52(a), a trial judge trying a case without a jury will divide his findings into findings of fact and conclusions of law. For example, he may state as a conclusion of law that a federal antidiscrimination statute requires proof of intent to discriminate, and he may state as a finding of fact that the evidence shows no discriminatory intent. On appeal, the appellate court could review without restriction the trial judge's interpretation of the statute to require proof of intent to discriminate; accordingly, it would reverse the trial court's conclusion on that question if it interpreted the statute differently. In contrast, the appellate court would not overturn the trial judge's factual finding of absence of discriminatory intent unless the record showed that finding to be clearly erroneous,[12] even if the appellate judges might have found discriminatory intent had they been the initial factfinders.

9. Jackson v. Virginia, 443 U.S. 307, 318 (1979).
10. *See* Gasperini v. Center for Humanities, Inc., 518 U.S. 415, 422 (1996) (comparing earlier judicial standards in New York courts to N.Y. Civ. Prac. L. & R. § 5501(c) (McKinney 1995)). In *Gasperini*, the Court held that the Seventh Amendment is satisfied in a federal diversity action applying New York substantive law if the federal district court reviews the jury's award under the New York statutory standard and if the federal appellate court reviews the district court's determination only for abuse of discretion. *Id.* at 419, 432-39.
11. *See, e.g.*, Ornelas v. United States, 517 U.S. 690, 699 (1996) (in reviewing determinations of reasonable suspicion and probable cause in suppression hearing, appellate court reviews district court's findings of historical fact for clear error). Of course, the defendant has a right to a jury determination of the ultimate facts regarding criminal liability. *See* U.S. CONST. amend. VI.
12. *See* Pullman-Standard v. Swint, 456 U.S. 273, 287-88 (1982).

One court has defined the clearly-erroneous standard of appellate review in a colorful manner that seems to require great deference to the trial court's findings of fact: "To be clearly erroneous, a decision must . . . strike us as wrong with the force of a five-week-old, unrefrigerated dead fish."[13] Under a more conventional measure of clear error, however, the reviewing court simply asks "whether 'on the entire evidence,' it is 'left with the definite and firm conviction that a mistake has been committed.'"[14] At least in theory, the clearly erroneous standard permits broader appellate review than does the substantial-evidence standard typically applied to findings of juries and some administrative agencies:[15]

> Under the substantial-evidence standard, a reviewing court must uphold the findings of a jury or administrative agency if the record contains sufficient evidence to permit a reasonable person to make those findings. In contrast, the clearly-erroneous standard permits the reviewing court to review the entire record, and to overturn a finding of fact if it is convinced that the finding is clearly wrong, even though a reasonable person could have made the finding.[16]

An appellate court's deference to factual findings made in the trial court is supported by practical and policy considerations that recognize distinctions in the roles of trial and appellate courts. The factfinder in the trial court, either the judge or the jury, is generally in a better position than the appellate court to evaluate the evidence. This advantage is strongest when factual findings are based partly on the factfinder's evaluation of the credibility of witnesses: The mannerisms of the witness on the stand may be much more revealing than the cold print of the reporter's transcript. Accordingly, Rule 52(a) specifically directs appellate courts to give "due regard" to "the opportunity of the trial court to judge of the credibility of the witnesses."

Conversely, the trial court's advantage is weakest when factual findings are based largely on documentary evidence that is available in identical form to both the trial and appellate courts. Nonetheless, Rule 52(a) applies to "[f]indings of fact, whether based on oral or documentary evidence," suggesting that restrictions on appellate review must be at least partly based on policies other than a practical advantage enjoyed by the trial court.

In fact, restricted appellate review of findings of fact is independently justified by the importance of an appellate court's role in developing general principles of law relative to its role of correcting error in the judgment in a particular case. Admittedly, appellate courts should perform a limited

---

13. Parts & Elec. Motors, Inc. v. Sterling Elec. Inc., 866 F.2d 228, 233 (7th Cir. 1988).

14. Hunt v. Cromartie, 121 S. Ct. 1452, 1458 (2001) (quoting United States v. United States Gypsum Co., 333 U.S. 364, 395 (1948)).

15. See, e.g., Dickinson v. Zurko, 527 U.S. 150, 162-64 (1999) (recognizing that the "clearly erroneous" standard allows for more searching review, but characterizing the difference as subtle, and observing that the choice between the two standards will not often determine the outcome); Loehr v. Offshore Logistics, Inc., 691 F.2d 758, 760-61 (5th Cir. 1982).

16. Charles Richard Calleros, *Title VII and Rule 52(a): Standards of Appellate Review in Disparate Treatment Cases—Limiting the Reach of* Pullman-Standard v. Swint, 58 Tul. L. Rev. 411 n.40 (1983) (citations omitted); *see also Zurko*, 527 U.S. at 162 (distinguishing between the "definite and firm conviction" required for clear error and the "reasonable mind" standard for the substantial evidence test).

"corrective" function by subjecting each trial judgment to some review for error and thus reducing the risk of injustice.[17] At least as important, however, is the appellate court's "institutional" function of "developing and declaring legal principles that will have application beyond the case that serves as the vehicle for expression of the principles."[18] This institutional function is strongest in the highest appellate court in a jurisdiction.[19] It emphasizes the development of a cohesive body of legal standards rather than the review of evidence supporting findings of fact.

C. Conclusions of Law: Mixed Conclusions of Fact and Law in a Nonjury Trial

In contrast to restricted appellate review of findings of fact, appellate review of a trial judge's conclusions of law is unrestricted. The appellate court may freely correct the trial court's formulation of legal standards.[20]

Often, however, classifying a finding as more nearly one of law than of fact in a nonjury trial is a difficult task.[21] Without doubt, Rule 52(a)'s clearly erroneous standard applies to appellate review of a trial judge's findings of historical fact, such as findings about events and actions.[22] It also applies to review of "factual inferences" drawn by a trial court from "undisputed basic facts."[23] However, some trial court determinations fall between the two extremes of formulation of abstract legal standards and findings of historical fact or factual inference. For example, a trial judge's determination of whether the historical facts satisfy an abstract legal standard is a mixed finding of fact and law, which may contain elements of both factual inference and refinement of the legal standard.

Appellate review of a narrow class of such mixed findings is restricted under a special standard of review. Specifically, an appellate court will severely restrict its review of certain "discretionary" rulings of a trial judge, such as discovery and evidentiary rulings, the granting or denial of injunctive or declaratory relief, or the determination whether to grant a new trial. Assuming that the trial judge formulated the correct legal rule before applying it to the facts, the appellate court generally will not overturn such a mixed finding of the trial judge unless she abused her discretion.[24]

17. Calleros, *supra* note 16, at 421-22.
18. *Id*. at 420-21.
19. Indeed, under its "two-court rule," the United States Supreme Court will give particular deference to a finding of fact made by a trial judge and upheld on appeal in the intermediate court of appeals. *See, e.g.*, Rogers v. Lodge, 458 U.S. 613, 622-27 (1982).
20. *See* Pullman-Standard v. Swint, 456 U.S. 273, 287 (1982).
21. *See id*. at 288.
22. *See, e.g.*, Washington v. Watkins, 655 F.2d 1346, 1352 (5th Cir. 1981).
23. Commissioner v. Duberstein, 363 U.S. 278, 291 (1960) (citing United States v. United States Gypsum Co., 333 U.S. 364, 394 (1948)).
24. *See, e.g.*, General Elec. Co. v. Joiner, 522 U.S. 126 (1997) (district court's evidentiary rulings—including those on admission or exclusion of scientific evidence—are reviewed only for abuse of discretion); Browning-Ferris Indus. of Vt. v. Kelco Disposal, Inc., 492 U.S. 257, 279 (1989) (district court's decision whether to grant new trial or remittitur after jury award is reviewed for abuse of discretion), *cited with approval in* Gasperini v. Center for Humanities, Inc., 518 U.S. 415, 435 (1996) (review of district court's decision whether to set aside jury award of damages in a diversity suit); Wilton v. Seven Falls Co., 515 U.S. 277, 289-90 (1995) (abuse of discretion standard for reviewing district court's decision whether to entertain a declaratory judgment action); Los Angeles Mem'l Coliseum Comm'n v. National Football

Most mixed findings, however, do not fall within this narrow class of discretionary rulings. Instead, for purposes of appellate standards of review, appellate courts must classify the findings under Rule 52(a) as findings of fact or conclusions of law. The proper means of accomplishing this classification is a matter of continuing debate.[25] However, the practical and policy considerations underlying restrictions on appellate review provide some guidance in the debate.

If a mixed question of fact and law requires the application of a simple, noncontroversial legal rule to complex historical facts, its resolution may primarily require the trial judge to refine her understanding of the facts rather than to engage in substantial legal reasoning. The trial judge is in the best position to make such a determination, and review of the resulting mixed finding requires exercise primarily of the appellate court's corrective function. Therefore, an appellate court should view the finding as more nearly a finding of factual inference than a conclusion of law, and it should restrict its review accordingly.

Consider, for example, a dispute about whether numerous statements and actions by an employer reflected an intent to discriminatorily deny promotions to female employees, in violation of Title VII. Although resolution of that question inevitably requires some refinement of the statutory term "discriminate,"[26] it primarily requires an analysis of the facts. Thus, an appellate court undoubtedly would treat it as a question of fact for purposes of restricted appellate review.

Conversely, if a mixed question of fact and law requires the application of complex, uncertain, or highly controversial legal standards to simple historical facts, the trial judge's resolution of the question may primarily reflect refinement of her understanding of the content of the legal rules. The appellate court is at least equally capable of making such a determination, and it will primarily exercise its institutional function on review. Therefore, an appellate court should view the finding as more nearly a conclusion of law than one of factual inference.[27]

Consider, for example, the question in one United States Supreme Court case of whether the government presented "clear, unequivocal and convincing" proof that a naturalized citizen had fraudulently procured his certificate of naturalization during World War II by falsely renouncing his allegiance to Nazi Germany and falsely swearing allegiance to the United States. The technical nature of the special standard of proof and the uncertainty and political sensitivity of the legal concept of "allegiance" made this mixed question primarily one of law. Therefore, the appellate courts could review the trial court's determination without restriction.[28]

Similarly, courts will freely review the mixed question of whether a jury

League, 634 F.2d 1197, 1200 (9th Cir. 1980) (abuse of discretion standard for reviewing district court's decision whether to grant injunctive relief).

25. *See* Pullman-Standard v. Swint, 456 U.S. 273, 287 (1982).

26. 42 U.S.C. § 2000e-2(a)(1) (1994).

27. *See generally* United States v. McConney, 728 F.2d 1195, 1204 (9th Cir. 1984) (in a criminal case, adopting a "functional analysis that focuses on the nature of the inquiry required when we apply the relevant rule of law to the facts as established"); Calleros, *supra* note 16, at 425-32 (using different definitional framework to develop similar analysis).

28. Baumgartner v. United States, 322 U.S. 665 (1944).

award of punitive damages violates constitutional guarantees of due process[29] or whether particular speech falls within a category protected by the First Amendment.[30] Indeed, to safeguard constitutional guarantees of freedom of speech, courts have adopted a limited "constitutional facts" exception to the normally restricted review of findings of historical fact discussed above in Section II.B. In such cases, courts may examine the underlying record and freely review even some purely factual findings of a jury or trial court judge, if the facts are critical to the First Amendment analysis.[31] Even when freely reviewing findings of constitutional fact, however, the appellate court will defer to the factfinder's determinations of witness credibility.[32]

TRIAL COURT DETERMINATION	APPELLATE STANDARD OF REVIEW
Finding of fact by jury and some administrative agencies	Affirmed if supported by substantial evidence
Findings of jury in criminal conviction	Affirmed if rational basis or reasonable support in the evidence for a finding that prosecution met its burden of proof
Trial judge's exercise of discretion	Affirmed unless judge abused discretion
Trial judge's finding of fact	Affirmed unless clearly erroneous
Trial judge's ruling on the law	Reviewed without restriction and rejected if appellate court disagrees on the merits
Trial judge's mixed finding of law and fact	Treated as finding of fact or finding of law by trial judge, depending on whether legal or factual questions predominate

29. Cooper Indus. v. Leatherman Tool Group, Inc., 121 S. Ct. 1678 (2001).
30. See, e.g., Bose Corp. v. Consumers Union, 466 U.S. 485, 504-06 (1984).
31. Id. at 499-514 (freely reviewing district court's finding of actual malice in defamation case and referring to other cases and contexts, including independent review of the record in jury cases); see also id. at 515 (White, J., dissenting) (interpreting majority's analysis as applying to a pure question of fact); id. at 515 (Rehnquist, J., dissenting) (same); id. at 518 n.2 (Rehnquist, J., dissenting) (arguing that full independent review of constitutional facts found by state jury is less controversial than freely reviewing the careful written findings of a district court judge), Adam Hoffman, Corralling Constitution Fact: De Novo Fact Review in the Federal Appellate Courts, 50 Duke L.J. 1427 (2001).
32. Id. at 499-500; Harte-Hanks Communications, Inc. v. Connaughton, 491 U.S. 657, 688 (1989).

Chapter 22

The Brief—Effective
Appellate Advocacy

I. OVERVIEW OF APPELLATE BRIEFS: FORMAT

Rules of procedure and local court rules typically prescribe formats for appellate briefs that are more formal and detailed than those for motions memoranda and other briefs. When you represent the "appellant," the party bringing the appeal, you will file the opening brief. At a minimum, typical rules will require this brief to include the following substantive components:

1. a statement of the issues raised on appeal;
2. a statement of the procedural history of the case, usually entitled "Statement of the Case";
3. a statement of the facts relevant to issues raised on appeal;
4. an argument (sometimes preceded by a summary of the argument); and
5. a conclusion.

In addition, rules often require other substantive and formal components such as a table of contents, an alphabetically arranged table of authorities, and statements of jurisdiction and of standards of review. For example, Federal Rule of Appellate Procedure 28 specifies the following components for the appellant's opening brief:

Rule 28. Briefs

(a) *Appellant's Brief.* The appellant's brief must contain, under appropriate headings and in the order indicated:

(1) a corporate disclosure statement if required by Rule 26.1;

(2) a table of contents, with page references;

(3) a table of authorities—cases (alphabetically arranged), statutes, and other authorities—with references to the pages of the brief where they are cited;

(4) a jurisdictional statement, including: [the basis of the trial court's subject-matter jurisdiction and the appellate court's jurisdiction, complete with references to relevant statutes and facts; filing dates showing timely filing of appeal; and a statement that appeal is taken from a final order or otherwise from a ruling that the appellate court may review];

(5) a statement of the issues presented for review;

(6) a statement of the case briefly indicating the nature of the case, the course of proceedings, and the disposition below;

(7) a statement of facts relevant to the issues submitted for review with appropriate references to the record (see Rule 28(e));

(8) a summary of the argument, . . . ;

(9) the argument, which must contain:

(A) appellant's contentions and the reasons for them, with citations to the authorities and parts of the record on which the appellant relies; and

(B) for each issue, a concise statement of the applicable standard of review (which may appear in the discussion of the issue or under a separate heading placed before the discussion of the issues);

(10) a short conclusion stating the precise relief sought; and

(11) the certificate of compliance, if [the brief satisfies length requirements through word or line count under Rule 32(a)(7), rather than through page limitations].

If you represent the "appellee," the party seeking a ruling affirming the judgment of the trial court, you must file an answering brief. Subsection (b) of Rule 28 provides that the appellee's answering brief should include all the components listed for the appellant's opening brief, except for subsection (a)(10). The appellee may adopt the statements of jurisdiction, issues, case, facts, and standard of review presented in the appellant's brief if the appellee is satisfied with them.

According to subsection (c) of Rule 28, the appellant may respond to appellee's answering brief with a reply brief, but the reply brief can dispense with most of the statements set forth in the appellant's opening brief. In addition to an argument responding to the answering brief, it need contain only a table of contents and a table of authorities.

Rules of procedure or local court rules typically specify additional formal requirements regarding such things as typeface, line spacing, margins, overall length, and the color of the cover sheets for the opening, answering, and reply briefs.[1] The specified form for the information on the cover of an appellate brief varies in different jurisdictions. In some jurisdictions, the cover sheet includes the caption of the case in the same basic format as it appeared in trial pleadings and briefs, as illustrated by the sample briefs at the end of this chapter and Chapters 18-20. In other jurisdictions, including the United States Courts of Appeals, rules of procedure simply require the cover to include certain identifying information, which attorneys usually present on several widely spaced lines that are centered on the cover page.[2]

Court rules have traditionally contemplated that appellate advocates will provide multiple copies of briefs in "hard copy," printed or typewritten on paper. The rules of procedure and local court rules of some jurisdictions, however, also permit parties to file briefs by electronic means, which might include electronic files on a computer disk, on a CD-ROM, or transferred over the Internet. If authorized by rule, an electronic brief on CD-ROM may include "hyperlinks," which can connect citations in the brief to "hypertext" setting forth the text of the cited authorities or passages in the record.[3]

II. STATEMENT OF ISSUES

The art of stating issues in a student case brief or an office memorandum is discussed in detail in Section II.B.2 of Chapter 7 and Section III.A of Chapter 11. You should review those principles now as a starting point for drafting the statement of issues in your appellate brief. When drafting an issue statement in a brief, however, you should additionally strive to phrase the issue in a way that suggests a favorable response or otherwise serves to advocate your client's case.

A. Issue Statements as Preliminary Advocacy

Your statement of the issue can invite the court to apply an analytic framework or standard of review that best suits your client's arguments. Of course, you should develop that strategy primarily in the argument section of the brief. In addition, however, you can make the judge more receptive to your approach by initially exposing her to the theme of your brief in your statement of the issues.

For example, suppose that you represent an appellant who appeals from

1. *See, e.g.*, FED. R. APP. P. 32(a).
2. *See* FED. R. APP. P. 32(a)(2).
3. *See, e.g.*, FED. R. APP. P. 25(d) (authorizing federal courts of appeals to adopt local rules permitting electronic filing); 8th CIR. R. 25(A) (authorizing electronic filing in the Eighth Circuit); *compare* 11th CIR. R. 31-5 (permitting electronic briefs on floppy disk, CD-ROM, or Internet upload, with the possibility of hyperlinks to other materials on the latter two) *with* 5th CIR. R. 31.1 (authorizing an attorney to file an electronic brief on a "computer readable disk copy" that includes only the brief and not other materials).

a trial judge's decision to deny a preliminary injunction. You know that the appellate court will overturn that decision only if the trial judge abused her discretion, provided that the trial judge applied the proper legal standards to the facts.[4] However, you believe that her ruling leaves some room for question about the content of the legal rules governing injunctions that she applied to the facts. Accordingly, you might use the statement of the issue to invite the appellate court to find error in the trial judge's formulation of the legal rules, which formulation would be subject to unrestricted review, as discussed in Chapter 21:

In denying Surge Corp.'s request for a preliminary injunction, did the trial judge apply an incorrect legal rule by requiring a showing of likelihood of success on the merits, rather than using a "sliding-scale" test that would justify a preliminary injunction upon a showing of especially great irreparable harm and at least substantial questions on the merits?

The opposing counsel may argue that the trial judge in fact applied a sliding-scale test and that the judge's balancing of the facts does not reflect an abuse of discretion under the most flexible of legal rules. Nonetheless, he might frame the issue so that it emphasizes the restricted standard of review of the ultimate ruling and refers only abstractly to potential questions about choices among legal rules:

Did the trial judge properly exercise her discretion to deny preliminary injunctive relief on the ground that Surge Corp. failed to make the requisite showing on the merits under applicable legal rules?

Of course, the nature of the opportunity to promote a favorable approach in the statement of the issue will vary with the circumstances of each appeal. For example, an appeal in a contracts dispute might raise a purely legal question about whether the peculiar facts of an exceptional case justify a special exception to the general common law requirement of consideration for contracts formation. If so, the parties might use their statements of the issue, as well as their arguments, to appeal either to the appellate judges' senses of fairness and justice or to their appreciation of the benefits of certainty in the law.

In those circumstances, if you represent the party who would benefit from an exception to the general rule, you might use the statement of the issue to promote the value of fairness by vividly and concretely emphasizing the peculiar facts of the case:

Does McGowin's moral obligation to perform his promise to pay Webb for past services give rise to a legal obligation in light of the serious physical

4. *See, e.g.*, Los Angeles Mem'l Coliseum Comm'n v. National Football League, 634 F.2d 1197, 1200 (9th Cir. 1980).

injuries suffered by Webb and the immeasurable benefit he gave to McGowin in heroically saving McGowin's life?

This statement of the issue appeals to the appellate court's corrective function: reaching a just result on the unique facts of the particular case before it, even if that requires a departure from general principles.[5]

In contrast, if you represent the party who would benefit from application of the general rule, you would advance a different theme. Specifically, you might use the statement of the issue to promote the consideration rule in its abstract form or to emphasize the general policies supporting the rule:

Did the trial court correctly reject a vague and uncertain "moral obligation" exception to the fundamental principle that a promise made in recognition of past services lacks consideration and therefore is unenforceable?

This issue appeals to the appellate court's institutional function: the wisdom of applying the rule in nearly every context, the importance of maintaining the vitality of a long-standing rule, and the need for certainty and predictability in the law.[6]

B. Credibility of the Advocate

In phrasing the statement of the issue to advocate an approach or a conclusion, you should not be so anxious to invite a favorable response that you state a false issue. For example, assume that you represent a criminal defendant who appeals from a state conviction for illegal possession of cocaine. The applicable criminal statute defines "possession" as contemporaneous intent and ability to exercise physical control over the substance. If the trial judge correctly instructed the jury on the applicable legal rules and definitions, you might still argue that substantial evidence did not support the jury finding of ability to exercise control over the cocaine. If so, the following statement of the issue would not effectively advance your client's cause:

Is proof of ability to control an illegal substance a requisite element of a conviction for illegal possession of that substance?

Under currently accepted legal definitions in the state, an appellate judge would readily agree that the question presented by this statement of the issue must be answered affirmatively. However, she would object that the question does not fairly characterize any nonfrivolous issue on appeal. Because the trial judge correctly instructed the jury on the applicable legal standards, your implicit attack on the completeness of the instructions would

5. *See generally* Webb v. McGowin, 168 So. 196, 199 (Ala. Ct. App. 1936) (Samford, J., concurring) (departing from "strict letter of the rule" in the interests of justice).
6. *See generally* Mills v. Wyman, 3 Pick. 207 (Mass. 1825) (rejecting "moral obligation" exception in the interests of maintaining universal application of the consideration doctrine).

be futile. Instead, your issue statement must fairly address your client's true contention on appeal:

> **Is the jury's finding of Wade's ability to control the cocaine unsupported by substantial evidence in light of undisputed testimony that the officers found Wade standing outside the locked automobile containing the cocaine, without a key to the automobile?**

Thus, you must recognize limits to your efforts to invite a favorable response to a statement of the issue. Specifically, you must maintain credibility and must fairly link the statement of the issue to your genuine argument on appeal.

III. STATEMENT OF PROCEDURAL HISTORY

Rules of procedure or local court rules will specify whether you must state the procedural history in a separate section or combine it with the historical facts. If the rules require you to state the procedural history in a separate section, they typically designate the section as the "Statement of the Case." If the rules instead require you to combine the facts and procedural history, they typically designate the combined section as either the "Statement of the Case" or the "Statement of Facts." With either format, the essential elements of a statement of procedural history are brief descriptions of "the nature of the case, the course of the proceedings, and its disposition in the court below,"[7] with citations to the record.

In the opening paragraph of the statement of procedural history, you should introduce the parties and generally describe the claims and defenses that they presented in the trial court. Next, you should chronologically recite the portions of the trial history and the rulings of the court that are relevant to the issues on appeal, including the trial court's final judgment and the appellant's filing notice of appeal. In a brief to a second-level court of appeal, you should also summarize the ruling of the intermediate appellate court. As described in Section I above, court rules in some jurisdictions may require you to discuss additional matters.

Once you have identified parties as the appellant and the appellee in your brief, you would do well in any jurisdiction to follow federal appellate rules for referring to parties:

> *References to Parties.* In briefs and at oral argument, counsel should minimize use of the terms "appellant" and "appellee." To make briefs clear, counsel should use the parties' actual names or the designations used in the lower court or agency proceeding, or such descriptive terms as "the employee," "the injured person," "the taxpayer," "the ship," "the stevedore."[8]

7. FED. R. APP. P. 28(a)(6).
8. FED. R. APP. P. 28(d).

IV. STATEMENT OF FACTS

A. Format

Your statement of facts on appeal is subject to two limitations. First, except for matters within common knowledge or otherwise subject to judicial notice,[9] the appellate court and the litigants are constrained by the trial court record as the exclusive source of the facts of the dispute. In a fully tried case, those facts are reflected in testimony recorded in the reporter's transcript, in documentary evidence admitted at trial, and in any physical evidence admitted at trial and retained by the trial court clerk. If the trial court disposed of the case on the pleadings or on summary judgment, the facts are reflected in the allegations of the pleadings or in the preliminary presentation of evidence on the motion for summary judgment. Rules of procedure and local court rules will set forth the responsibilities of the parties, primarily the appellant, in forwarding all or part of the trial court record to the appellate court and in filing relevant portions in an appendix to the appellate briefs.[10]

Second, if findings of fact are made by a jury or by the trial court, those findings take on greater significance than the underlying record of testimony and other evidence because of the restricted appellate review of such findings, as discussed in Chapter 21. If the appellant wishes to challenge the findings of fact, the appellant should refer to the underlying record of evidence to support the challenge; however, the findings normally will stand unless clearly erroneous or unsupported by substantial evidence. If the appellant instead chooses to limit the attack to a challenge of the trial judge's formulation of legal standards or the judge's application of those standards to facts, the appellant must rely on the findings of fact, perhaps with supplementary references to illuminating evidence that is consistent with the findings. The appellee, of course, should focus on either the findings or the underlying evidence supporting the findings, depending on which response most appropriately meets the appellant's challenge. These strategic considerations are illustrated in Section V.C.1. below.

As discussed in Chapter 21, Section I, when you refer to facts or procedural history in any section of your appellate brief, you must cite to the source. Applicable rules may require you to cite directly to the underlying record on appeal or to an appendix that contains excerpts of the record.[11]

---

9. *See, e.g.*, FED. R. EVID. 201 and advisory committee note on subdivision (f) (judicial notice of adjudicative facts in trial and on appeal); United States v. Pink, 315 U.S. 203, 216 (1942) (appellate judicial notice of record in other case); Ellie Margolis, *Beyond Brandeis: Exploring the Uses of Non-Legal Materials in Appellate Briefs*, 34 U.S.F.L. Rev. 197 (2000) (arguing for effective use of nonlegal materials to establish "legislative facts" on appeal, as well as at trial).

10. *E.g.*, FED. R. APP. P. 10 (the record on appeal), 11 (forwarding the record), 30 (appendix to the briefs), 32(b) (form of appendix).

11. *E.g.*, FED. R. APP. P. 28(e), 30(c)(2); *see also* Han v. Stanford Univ., 210 F.3d 1038 (9th Cir. 2000) (appeal dismissed for failure to correct opening and reply briefs' omission of citations to the record). For a guide to preparing an appellate appendix containing excerpts of the record on appeal, see Roger J. Miner, *Essay: Common Disorders of the Appendix and Their Treatment.* 3 J. App. Prac. & Process 39-54 (2001).

B. The Power of Facts

The opening statement of facts in a brief can play a surprisingly important role in your advocacy. In many cases, applicable legal standards are sufficiently general, flexible, or unclear to support any of several conclusions on the application of the law to facts. Indeed, a judge's determination of whether the facts satisfy the applicable legal standard helps to further refine the legal standard.

A persuasive statement of facts near the beginning of your brief may incline a judge to rule in favor of your client even before the judge has considered the legal analysis. If so, the judge may take advantage of the flexibility or uncertainty in the legal principles to reach the result that the facts have persuaded her to define as just, provided that she can do so without departing from clearly controlling precedent or otherwise upsetting the orderly development of a coherent body of law. A persuasive opening statement of facts will help make the judge receptive to the legal and factual analyses in the argument section of your brief.

C. Persuasive Presentation of Facts

To present the facts persuasively, you may be tempted to slant the record misleadingly in favor of your client's case or to introduce legal arguments and conclusions in the statement of facts. Neither technique will succeed.

1. ADVOCACY WITH CREDIBILITY

If you riddle your statement of facts with exaggerations or misleading omissions, you will simply diminish your credibility. Instead, your statement of facts should display your client in a favorable light while reflecting a concern for completeness and accuracy. If the judge is convinced that your statement is accurate and complete, she may repeatedly consult it as a fair summary of the record, resulting in maximum exposure of the subtle advocacy of your statement.

Rather than omit unfavorable facts, you should place them in a context that minimizes their impact and that helps you emphasize favorable facts. In addition to the techniques of persuasive writing discussed in Chapter 17, you can use the organization of the entire fact statement to emphasize the favorable facts. Chronological order of facts may be the clearest and most logical; it is certainly the order most often recommended by judges. However, you can increase the impact of favorable events by describing them in the places of greatest emphasis: the beginning and end of the fact statement. If you can do so without unduly sacrificing clarity and continuity, you can justify departing from chronological order or at least supplementing a chronological statement with a second reference to a critical and favorable fact at the beginning or end.

You can also emphasize favorable facts by using specific, concrete descriptions and strong verbs in active voice. Conversely, you can lessen the impact of unfavorable facts by describing them in general, abstract terms. For example, suppose that Samuel Hughes, the defendant in a prosecution for first-degree murder, seeks to mitigate the offense by showing that he was intoxicated at the time of the crime and therefore could not have premeditated the killing. As the prosecutor, you can de-emphasize his intoxication by referring to it generally, and you can emphasize his aggressive conduct by describing it in gruesome detail:

While under the influence of self-induced intoxication, the defendant murdered Grace Smith by bludgeoning her from behind with a baseball bat.

This statement relegates the defendant to anonymity by referring to him with a procedural label. In contrast, it names the victim, thus inviting the reader to recognize her as a person, rather than a statistic. Moreover, the description of the attack as one from behind tends to portray the victim as particularly sympathetic and defenseless. The statement not only refers to the defendant's impaired state of mind abstractly and in a subordinate phrase, it invites the reader to reject the intoxication as a mitigating factor by characterizing it as self-induced. Finally, strong, vivid words such as "murdered" and "bludgeoning" convey the horror of the assault.

As counsel for the defendant, you might refer to the same incident with opposite emphasis, even though you must concede that Hughes struck the fatal blow:

When he fatally injured the decedent, Samuel Hughes was staggering from the effects of a full pint of whiskey.

In contrast to the prosecutor's statement, this one refers to the killing and the victim in abstract terms and in a subordinate clause. Moreover, it humanizes the defendant in the main clause by referring to him by name and describing his intoxication vividly.

2. PREMATURE LEGAL ARGUMENT

If you prematurely introduce legal or factual argument into your statement of facts, you may undermine the effectiveness of your fact statement as a vehicle for making the judge receptive to your main argument. A judge knows that the legal argument of a brief will be one-sided, and he generally reserves judgment on legal conclusions until he has read both briefs. But he may be more willing to draw his own conclusions from an apparently complete and accurate statement of facts.

For example, if your statement of facts specifically characterizes a driver's operation of an automobile as negligent, it may produce a defensive reaction in the judge; he may warn himself that he should resist such a mixed conclusion of law and fact until he has thoroughly studied the arguments in both briefs. On the other hand, if your statement of facts vividly describes the automobile veering from lane to lane at an excessive speed, it will implicitly invite the judge to draw his own conclusion that the driver acted negligently. Even if tentative or subconscious, that conclusion will predispose the judge toward accepting your explicit legal arguments and conclusions in the argument section of your brief.

Thus, when the judge reaches the argument section of the brief, he may resist arguments supporting conclusions that you had bluntly attempted to force on him in the statement of facts. He will be more comfortable with arguments that seem to confirm conclusions he had reached on his own after reading apparently nonargumentative facts.

D. Summary and Perspective

To ensure that your opening statement of facts makes the judge more receptive to your main argument, you should

1. state the facts completely and accurately;
2. emphasize favorable facts and de-emphasize unfavorable ones through sentence structure, varying levels of specificity and concreteness, and general organization; and
3. avoid premature argument.

V. THE ARGUMENT

Earlier chapters and exercises have provided you with the basic information and skills you need to formulate, organize, and express your arguments in any brief. In summary, for each issue you should

1. state the conclusion you want the court to adopt in an argumentative point heading,
2. argue for a favorable interpretation of legal authority,
3. apply the legal rules to the facts, and
4. state the conclusion that you want the appellate court to reach.

This section will supplement the earlier chapters by examining some characteristics that are peculiar to appellate arguments.

A. Summary of Argument

Some rules of procedure and local court rules will require, or at least permit, appellate advocates to include a summary of the argument immediately before the main argument.[12] If applicable rules do not require a summary, you should include one in a separate section only if your brief is sufficiently complex that a summary will substantially enhance your reader's comprehension. If a summary in a separate section is neither required nor appropriate, you still should consider beginning your argument with an overview paragraph that outlines your arguments and conveys the theme of your brief.

---

12. *E.g.*, FED. R. APP. P. 28(a)(8).

If you do include a summary of argument in a separate section of your brief, you should place it under a section heading entitled "SUMMARY OF ARGUMENT," but you must keep it short. A summary of argument should do no more than briefly explain your major points in a few paragraphs, citing only to the most significant authorities. Along with the collection of point headings in your Table of Contents, the summary of argument can help you provide your reader with a general road map of her journey through your brief. If the summary delves into your argument in even moderate detail, however, it will make the main argument seem repetitive, to the irritation of your reader.

The discussion below addresses fully developed arguments in the main argument section.

B. Arguing the Law—The Role of Policy Analysis

Appellate briefs differ in style from pretrial and trial briefs in the greater extent to which they examine the underlying policies of legal standards. Depending on the procedural posture and other circumstances of a particular appeal, this difference in approach may reflect such factors as the restrictions on appellate review of factual findings, the appellate court's institutional function of developing a cohesive body of law, and the varying degrees to which stare decisis controls decisions at various levels of the court system.

Unless the appellant assumes the difficult burden of challenging factual findings made in the trial court, the appellate briefs likely will explore questions about the content of legal rules, either in the abstract or in the process of determining whether the accepted facts satisfy the rules. Because the appellate court can overrule its own precedents, it will consider policy arguments that favor or oppose extending, modifying, or overruling those precedents.

The institutional function of the appellate courts further encourages policy analysis in appellate briefwriting. For two reasons, this effect is greatest in the highest court of a jurisdiction. First, unlike an intermediate court of appeals, the highest court is not bound by the precedent of any court within that jurisdiction.[13] Second, the highest courts in many jurisdictions will accept review of some kinds of lower court decisions only after a discretionary determination that appellate resolution would help develop a cohesive body of law or otherwise would significantly affect the outcome of many cases other than the one that serves as the vehicle for addressing the questions.

Thus, more often than in trial briefs, appellate advocates will allocate substantial portions of their arguments to the policies underlying legal rules and to the social and jurisprudential consequences of retaining or abandoning those rules. Moreover, these characteristics typically will be even more pronounced in a court of last resort than in an intermediate court of appeals.

For example, the following two passages are excerpts of arguments about the proper application of precedent of the state supreme court, the highest

---

13. Of course, decisions of a state court of last resort on a question of federal law could be reviewed by the United States Supreme Court, and the state court would be bound by United States Supreme Court precedent on such questions.

court in the state. The first argument could be addressed to the trial court or even to the intermediate court of appeals. Because neither court can overrule the state supreme court precedent, the argument focuses on the applicability of the law of the precedent to the facts of the dispute:

B. The trial judge erred in instructing the jury that Bramwell could be liable for the tort of wrongful discharge if he discharged Kirkeide in "bad faith" rather than in violation of public policy.

Introduction to argument

The trial court's instruction on the tort of wrongful discharge fails to distinguish between conduct that violates a public policy and conduct that is simply unfair or retaliatory in the context of a particular employment relationship. This instruction permitted the jury to award damages against Bramwell for conduct that is not a tort in this state.

General legal rule

The New Maine Supreme Court has recently recognized a cause of action in tort for wrongful discharge. However, it carefully limited its holding to discharges that violate public policy:

> Thus, an employer is liable in tort for wrongful discharge if it discharges an employee for a reason that violates an important public policy of the state. Pronouncements of public policy will most often be found in our state's constitution and its legislation.

In-depth case analysis

Blass v. Arcon Co., 337 N. Me. 771, 776 (1996).

In *Blass,* the employer discharged a truck driver in retaliation for the driver's refusal to transport toxic wastes in unsafe containers. The employer was liable in tort for wrongful discharge because its conduct violated the policies of state environmental and occupational safety statutes. *See id.* at 777.

Application to facts

In contrast to *Blass,* Bramwell's discharge of Kirkeide in this case did not violate any public policy. At most, Bramwell acted hastily and exercised poor business judgment, but not in a way that implicates public policy. Yet, the trial court's instruction permitted the jury to impose liability . . . .

In the preceding illustration, the *Blass* decision did not need to address whether a discharge can be tortious for reasons other than a violation of public policy; therefore, it does not preclude future extensions of the new tort of wrongful discharge. Nonetheless, the briefwriter has reasonably assumed that a trial court or intermediate court of appeals would not readily extend a newly recognized tort beyond the terms of the Supreme Court's holding. Thus, the briefwriter concentrates on explaining the holding of the *Blass* decision and distinguishing it.

In contrast, the following passage is addressed to the New Maine Supreme Court, the mythical author of the *Blass* decision. Because that court can overrule, limit, or extend its own precedent, the argument spends more time on policy analysis. Specifically, it argues that, as a matter of policy, the court should not broaden the tort of wrongful discharge beyond the holding of the *Blass* decision.

B. The trial judge erred in instructing the jury that Bramwell could be liable . . . .

The trial court's instruction on the tort of wrongful discharge fails to distinguish between conduct that violates a public policy and conduct that . . . .

Introduction to argument

Although this Court has recently recognized a cause of action in tort for wrongful discharge, it carefully limited its holding to discharges that violate public policy:

General legal rule

Thus, an employer is liable . . . .

Blass v. Arcon Co., 337 N. Me. 771, 776 (1996).

In *Blass,* the employer discharged a truck driver in retaliation for the driver's refusal to transport toxic wastes in unsafe containers. . . .

In-depth case analysis

This court should reject Kirkeide's invitation to extend the tort of wrongful discharge beyond the holding of *Blass.* This state has long promoted the policy of freedom of contract, permitting contracting parties to shape their own rights and obligations. *See, e.g., Snell v. Abundes,* 128 N. Me. 217, 221 (1970). Even if limited to violations of public policy, the tort of wrongful discharge effectively limits the parties' freedom to create a contract that is terminable at the will of either party. Any further restriction on the freedom to contract would require courts to review nearly every contested business decision that affects the tenure of an employee. To preserve freedom of contract and to conserve judicial resources, this Court should narrowly tailor the tort of wrongful discharge to impose liability only for discharges that offend the values of society as a whole, and not for discharges that merely reflect ill will between two private parties.

Policy analysis

In our case, the trial court's instruction, approved by the court of appeals, extended the tort of wrongful discharge beyond the holding of *Blass.* By permitting an award of damages for a bad-faith discharge, ...

Application to facts

C. Arguing the Law and the Facts

1. STRATEGIC CHOICES

The appellant will seek to overturn unfavorable findings or conclusions of the trial court. Thus, as explained in Section II above, the appellant will benefit from unrestricted appellate review of such findings or conclusions. Accordingly, if you represent the appellant, you should try to characterize unfavorable mixed findings of fact and law in a nonjury trial as conclusions of law, which are reviewable on appeal without restriction. On this matter, neither party is bound by the trial court's characterization of a finding as one of fact or law. In a jury trial, on the other hand, a jury's mixed finding of fact and law normally will be treated as a finding of fact for purposes of restricted appellate review.

If an unfavorable finding is undeniably one of fact, you must make some strategic choices among alternative approaches on appeal. As counsel for the appellant, you must decide whether to challenge the unfavorable finding of fact under a restricted standard of review or to argue that the trial court applied the wrong legal rule to the facts, or both.

For example, suppose the plaintiff in a federal civil rights suit successfully sought compensatory and punitive damages against your client, a police officer, for false arrest in violation of the Fourth Amendment. At trial, the trial judge gave the following instructions to the jury over your objection:

If you find that Officer Mullins arrested Ms. Wong without probable cause, you must find that Officer Mullins violated Ms. Wong's clearly established constitutional rights, and you must award Ms. Wong compensatory damages in the amount of her actual injuries. Furthermore, if you find that Officer Mullins was grossly and inexcusably careless with regard to Ms. Wong's constitutional rights, you may exercise discretion to award Ms. Wong punitive damages in an amount that will punish Officer Mullins and discourage him and others from similar violations.

Applying these instructions to the facts, the jury found Officer Mullins liable and awarded Ms. Wong $5,000 in compensatory damages and $25,000 in punitive damages. The trial court also awarded Ms. Wong her reasonable attorney's fees.

Your client, Officer Mullins, has appealed. As one of your arguments on appeal, you wish to challenge the award of punitive damages, which is necessarily premised on a jury finding that Officer Mullins was "grossly and inexcusably careless." You can attack the award in either or both of two ways.

First, to take advantage of unrestricted appellate review of matters of law, you can try to persuade the appellate court that the trial judge incorrectly instructed the jury on the law:

A. Officer Mullins is entitled to a new trial because the trial judge erroneously instructed the jury that it could award punitive damages for conduct less culpable than reckless disregard for constitutional rights.

The United States Supreme Court has established a recklessness standard for punitive damages in federal civil rights actions:

> We hold that a jury may be permitted to assess punitive damages in an action under § 1983 when the defendant's conduct is shown to be motivated by evil motive or intent, or when it involves reckless or callous indifference to the federally protected rights of others.

Smith v. Wade, 461 U.S. 30, 56 (1983).

A standard based on reckless misconduct requires a greater showing of culpability than simple negligence. *See Johnson v. Lundell* . . . . In *Johnson,* . . . .

The extraordinary nature of punitive damages justifies close scrutiny of the trial judge's instructions to ensure that they recognize even fine distinctions in culpability. Otherwise, ...

In this case, the trial court instructed the jury that it could award punitive damages if it found that Officer Mullins was "grossly and inexcusably careless." III R.T. 52. This instruction did not adequately convey the requisite standard: reckless or callous disregard of constitutional rights.

Even when coupled with the adjective "grossly," the word "careless" connotes only a breach of duty rising to the level of negligence. . . .

The trial court improperly instructed the jury on the standard for punitive damages. Officer Mullins is entitled to a new trial so that the jury may apply the proper legal standard to the facts.

Marginal annotations:
- General legal rule
- Related legal rules
- Policy analysis
- Application to facts: The instruction
- Further analysis of instruction
- Conclusion

Alternatively, if you are prepared to labor against a restricted standard of review, you can try to persuade the appellate court to overturn the jury's implicit finding that Officer Mullins was "grossly and inexcusably careless." Under this approach, you must review the underlying evidence, such as the testimony at trial, and explain why the jury's finding is not supported by substantial evidence:

B. Alternatively, this court should vacate the award of punitive damages because substantial evidence does not support the jury's finding

that Officer Mullins acted with the requisite culpability to justify punitive damages.

Introduction to argument

Even if the trial court's instructions adequately conveyed the culpability required for an award of punitive damages, the jury did not properly find such culpability on the part of Officer Mullins. At most, the evidence supports the conclusion that Officer Mullins made a reasonable mistake in judgment in chaotic circumstances. Therefore, the trial judge erred in denying Mullins's Motion for Judgment Notwithstanding the Verdict on the issue of punitive damages, and this court should overturn the jury's award of punitive damages.

Rules governing review of jury's findings

This court may overturn a finding of the jury if the finding is unsupported by substantial evidence in the record so that no reasonable juror could have made the finding on the evidence. *See* . . . . This substantial-evidence standard permits appellate courts to review jury findings to guard against verdicts based on bias, passion, or incompetence. *See* . . . . To satisfy the purposes of such review, this court should scrutinize the record for . . . .

Examination of facts: The testimony

Officer Mullins's uncontradicted testimony establishes the reasonableness of his actions. He testified that the report over his squad car radio identified the robbery suspect only as a young man of slight build with dark, shoulder-length hair. II RT at 335-36. One block from the robbery site, Officer Mullins spotted Ms. Wong walking at a very brisk pace away from the robbery site. *Id.* at 336. He initially passed her by because he was looking for a male suspect. *Id.* at 337. However, when he found no other suspects in the vicinity, he realized that Ms. Wong fit the description of the robbery suspect except for her gender. *Id.* at 339. He remembered that Ms. Wong was wearing jeans and a sweatshirt, and he realized that an agitated witness might have been mistaken about her gender. *Id.* at 339-40. Consequently, he turned his squad car around, found Ms. Wong again, and stopped her for questioning. *Id.* at 340.

Other testimony supports Officer Mullins's version of the events. Ms. Wong herself testified that she had been walking at an unusually brisk pace. I RT at 327. She also admitted that she had trouble answering Officer Mullins's questions. *Id.* at 331. Although in her testimony Ms. Wong offered innocent explanations for her hurried pace and her inability to communicate effectively with Officer Mullins,

Analysis of testimony: Permissible inferences

nothing in the record shows that these explanations were apparent to Officer Mullins at the time of the arrest. . . .

In sum, the evidence leads inescapably to one conclusion: In his eagerness to fulfill his duties as a police officer, Officer Mullins mistakenly arrested the wrong person, but he did not recklessly disregard anyone's constitutional rights in doing so. Quite the contrary, he took steps at several stages to safeguard Ms. Wong's rights.

The record simply does not contain substantial evidence supporting the jury's finding of sufficient culpability to justify an award of punitive damages. Apparently, the jurors misunderstood or ignored the trial court's instructions and based their verdict on irrelevant factors.

Conclusion

For these reasons, even if this Court affirms the jury's finding of lack of probable cause, it must overturn the jury's award of punitive damages. The evidence does not support this extraordinary award.

Counsel for the appellee can respond to either of these arguments directly. In response to the first sample argument, she can argue either that (1) the law permits an award of punitive damages for culpability less than recklessness, or (2) the trial judge's instructions adequately conveyed the requisite standard of recklessness. In response to the second sample argument, she can (1) emphasize the restricted standard of appellate review, (2) describe evidence in the record that supports a jury finding of recklessness, and (3) explain why that evidence should be viewed as "substantial."

2. VARIETIES OF FACT ANALYSIS

As illustrated in the preceding subsection, the appropriate nature and depth of fact analysis on appeal will depend in part on two factors: (a) the nature of the appellant's challenge to the trial court's judgment, and (b) the procedural posture of the case when the trial court disposed of it.

a. Nature of Appellant's Challenge

For an example of the first factor, suppose that you represent the appellant and that you choose to challenge not the jury's findings of fact but only the trial judge's instructions on the law, as in the first sample passage in Subsection 1. above. Your arguments on such a challenge will often focus on the law and include only modest fact analysis. Specifically, even if "fact" is expansively defined to include the trial judge's actual instructions, your application of the law to the facts could include no more than a comparison of the correct legal rule to the actual instruction and a statement about the need for a new trial with proper instructions to the jury:

In this case, the trial court instructed the jury that it could . . . . This instruction did not adequately convey . . . .

. . . Officer Mullins is entitled to a new trial so that the jury may apply the proper legal standard to the facts.

In contrast, detailed fact analysis will be mandatory if the appellant challenges the findings of fact of the trial judge or jury, as did the appellant in the sample briefs at the end of this chapter. As illustrated in the second sample passage in Subsection 1. above, the parties then must review the record and argue whether the evidence supports the finding of fact under the applicable standard of review:

Officer Mullins's uncontradicted testimony establishes the reasonableness of his actions. He testified that . . . .

Other testimony supports Officer Mullins's version of the events. Ms. Wong herself testified that . . . .

In sum, the evidence leads inescapably to one conclusion: . . . .

The record simply does not contain substantial evidence supporting the jury's finding . . . .

---

b. Procedural Posture

Your fact analysis may also vary with the second factor: the procedural posture of the case at the time of trial disposition. Specifically, dispositions at different pretrial and trial stages will lead to appellate analyses of different kinds of facts.

For example, suppose that the trial court dismissed the action for failure of the complaint to state a claim for relief. On appeal, you can argue the law, but you will have no findings of fact or even underlying evidence in the record to which to apply the law. Instead, you must argue whether the factual allegations of the complaint state a claim for relief under the correct interpretation of the law.

In summary judgment litigation, on the other hand, you ordinarily will develop a record of preliminary showings of fact with documents, affidavits, and other discovery materials. Therefore, on appeal, you can argue whether the evidentiary materials submitted by both parties create a genuine issue of fact for trial under the applicable law.

Finally, the record will include formally introduced evidence if either party has appealed from the trial judge's denial of a motion for a directed verdict or for a judgment notwithstanding the verdict after presentation of the evidence in a jury trial. Moreover, on appeal from judgment after a full trial, the record will include both the evidence and the findings of the judge or jury. As explored above, the record in either case may provide a fertile source for fact analysis, depending on the appellant's strategic choices and the nature of her challenge to the ruling or judgment in the trial court.

VI. THE CONCLUSION

The discussion in Section III.C. of Chapter 16 about the conclusion section of a brief applies with full force to appellate briefs. At the least, your conclusion must briefly restate the action that your client requests the appellate court to take. In a complex case, your conclusion may also include a brief summary and synthesis of the arguments presented in your brief.

Exercise 22-1

In addition to responding to the appellant's arguments on appeal, an appellee may file its own "cross-appeal" to affirmatively challenge aspects of a lower court's decision. The following appellate briefs are the Opening Brief, Answering Brief, and Reply Brief on a cross-appeal filed by the appellee of the main appeal. The briefs reproduced below appear in their original form, with the exception of corrections of minor typographical errors, the deletion of some references to the main appeal, and the omission of a procedural issue and a portion of the arguments on punitive damages.

The briefs depart in many ways from the citation form and writing style recommended in this book, perhaps illustrating that a variety of styles can effectively communicate or persuade. As you read these briefs, consider what changes you would make to conform the writing to your own style, and consider the following questions.

1. STATEMENTS OF THE CASE

Study the procedural history traced in the statements of the case in the opening brief and the answering brief. Identify the trial court rulings challenged by each party. Is it clear why both Koepnick and Sears were dissatisfied, resulting in cross-appeals? What standard did the trial court apply in reaching its decision on the point appealed from on the cross-appeal? What standard of review should the appellate court apply?

2. STATEMENTS OF FACT

Study the statements of fact in the opening and answering briefs. Could you identify the author of each statement if you read no other parts of the briefs? Does each fact statement successfully present an apparently complete and neutral summary of the facts while placing the advocate's client in the best possible light?

Consider the points of conflict between the two fact statements. In what instances is the apparent conflict simply a reflection of each advocate using techniques of writing style to emphasize some facts and de-emphasize others? In what instances is the conflict rooted in genuine disagreement about the factual conclusions that find support in the record? What is the legal significance on appeal of conflicting evidence in the record on a material point, given the procedural posture of this case?

3. STATEMENTS OF ISSUES

Study the statements of the issues in the opening and answering briefs. Does each advocate successfully phrase each issue in a way that invites a favorable response for his client? Does either state a false issue that easily invites a favorable response but that does not fairly identify the real issue on appeal?

4. ARGUMENTS

Study the arguments in all three briefs. How important is fact analysis to the arguments in each brief? Would the allocation of resources between fact analysis and discussion of legal rules be different if the appellant were appealing from the trial court's rejection of a novel legal theory of recovery?

5. RESPONSIVE ARGUMENTS

Does the answering brief effectively respond to the opening brief? Does the reply brief effectively respond to the answering brief?

6. WRITING STYLE

How would you change the writing style or presentation of authority in any of the briefs? Explain the reasons for your editing.

7. FORMAT

How well do the briefs conform to the following formats for appellate briefs that were prescribed by the version of the Arizona Rules of Civil Appellate Procedure in effect when the briefs were filed?

> **Rule 13. Briefs**
> *13(a) Brief of the Appellant.* The brief of the appellant shall concisely and clearly set forth under appropriate headings and in the order here indicated:
>
> 1. A table of contents with page references.
> 2. A table of citations, which shall alphabetically arrange and index the cases, statutes and other authorities cited, with references to the pages of the brief on which they are cited.
> 3. A statement of the case, indicating briefly the basis of the appellate court's jurisdiction, the nature of the case, the course of the proceedings and the disposition in the court below.
> 4. A statement of facts relevant to the issues presented for review, with appropriate references to the record. . . .
> 5. A statement of the issues presented for review. . . .
> 6. An argument, which shall contain the contentions of the appellant with respect to the issues presented, and the reasons therefor, with

citations to the authorities, statutes and parts of the record relied on. The argument may include a summary. . . .

7. A short conclusion stating the precise relief sought.
8. An appendix if desired.

13(b) Brief of the Appellee. The brief of the appellee shall conform to the requirements of the preceding subdivision, except that a statement of the case, a statement of the facts or a statement of the issues need not be included unless the appellee finds the statements of the appellant to be insufficient or incorrect.

13(c) Reply Brief. The appellant may file a reply brief, but it shall be confined strictly to rebuttal of points urged in the appellee's brief. No further briefs may be filed except as provided in Rule 13(e) or by leave of court. . . .

13(e) Briefs in Cases Involving Cross-Appeals. A party who files a cross-appeal may combine in one brief his brief as appellee and his brief as cross-appellant. If the appellant wishes to file a further brief, he may combine in one brief his reply brief as appellant and his brief as cross-appellee. The cross-appellant may file a reply brief on the issues of the cross-appeal.

Fred Cole
Roger W. Perry
Gust, Rosenfeld, Divelbess & Henderson
3300 Valley Bank Center
Phoenix, Arizona 85073
Attorneys for Defendant-Appellee/Cross-Appellant

**IN THE
COURT OF APPEALS
STATE OF ARIZONA**
Division One

MAX KOEPNICK,
        Plaintiff-Appellant
        Cross-Appellee,
 	
    v.
 	
SEARS, ROEBUCK & COMPANY,
        Defendant-Appellee
        Cross-Appellant.
	1 CA-CIV 9147
	
	MARICOPA County
	Superior Court
	No. C-502081

OPENING BRIEF ON CROSS-APPEAL

TABLE OF CONTENTS

TABLE OF AUTHORITIES

APPELLEE'S OPENING BRIEF ON CROSS-APPEAL

STATEMENT OF THE CASE

Plaintiff-appellant Max Koepnick ("Koepnick") commenced this action by filing a complaint on December 5, 1983 (C.T. at 1). The defendants named in the complaint were defendant-appellee Sears, Roebuck & Company ("Sears") and the City of Mesa ("Mesa"). The complaint set forth claims in six counts, which were all alleged to have arisen out of an incident that occurred at the Sears store at Fiesta Mall in Mesa, Arizona on December 6, 1982. Sears was named as defendant in only four of the counts. These were Count One for false arrest, Count Four for trespass to chattel, Count Five for invasion of privacy and Count Six for malicious prosecution. Mesa was named as defendant in Count Two for false arrest and Count Three for assault and battery. Mesa was also named as a co-defendant with Sears in Counts Five and Six.

Prior to trial, Mesa moved for summary judgment on Count Two for false arrest (C.T. at 55). The court granted Mesa's motion on that count based on the court's determination that probable cause existed for Mesa to detain Koepnick (Minute entry dated January 9, 1986).

Trial to a jury on the other counts of Koepnick's complaint commenced on January 10, 1986. At the close of Koepnick's case-in-brief, Sears moved for a directed verdict on all counts asserted against it (7R.T. at 13). Plaintiff stipulated to the dismissal of Count Six for malicious prosecution against Sears, and the court granted Sears a directed verdict on Count Four for invasion of privacy (Minute entry dated January 21, 1986). Mesa made a similar motion and was granted directed verdicts on Count Two for false arrest, Count Five for invasion of privacy, Count Six for malicious prosecution and all plaintiff's claims for punitive damages (Minute entry dated January 21, 1986).

At the close of evidence, Sears and Mesa again moved for directed verdicts on all the remaining claims against them. These motions were denied (8R.T. at 84-92). The remaining claims were submitted to the jury. The jury returned verdicts against Sears for $25,000.00 in compensatory damages and $500,000.00 in punitive damages on Count One for false arrest and $100.00 in compensatory damages and $25,000.00 punitive damages on Count Four for trespass to chattel (9R.T. at 101-03). The jury also returned verdicts against Mesa for $50,000.00 on Count Three for assault and battery and $100.00 on Count Four for trespass to chattel (9R.T. at 101-03). Judgment was entered on the verdicts on February 25, 1986 (C.T. at 97; Appendix A).

Sears filed motions for judgment notwithstanding the verdicts and for a new trial on Counts One and Four on March 11, 1986 (C.T. at 100). Mesa filed a motion for a new trial on March 11, 1986 (C.T. at 101) and a motion for judgment notwithstanding the verdict or, in the alternative, for a new trial and for remittitur on March 12, 1986 (C.T. at 104). An amended motion for judgment notwithstanding the verdicts and for new trial was filed by Sears on April 16, 1986 (C.T. at 113).

A hearing on the post-trial motions was held on April 17, 1986. Upon consideration of the motions, the court granted Sears' and Mesa's motions for judgment N.O.V. on Count Four for trespass to chattel and granted Sears' motion for new trial on Count One for false arrest. The court granted judgment N.O.V. for defendants on the trespass to chattel claim as Koepnick failed to present evidence that the alleged trespass caused any damage or injury, which is an essential element of an actionable claim. The court granted a new trial on the false arrest claim as the court determined that reasonable cause to detain Koepnick existed as a matter of law and that, therefore, it had erred in instructing the jury on the issue of reasonable cause (Minute entry dated May 14, 1986; Appendix B).

A second hearing occurred on June 24, 1986 pertaining to further post-trial motions, and the court clarified its minute entry of May 14, 1986 (Minute entry dated June 27, 1986; Appendix C). (The trial court's attempt at clarification did not completely succeed in that the minute entry repeatedly refers to the "assault" claim when the court actually means to refer to the false arrest claim.) The final order setting forth the court's disposition of the post-trial motions, including the granting of judgment on Count Four for trespass to chattel and the granting of Sears' motion for new trial on Count One for false arrest, was entered July 23, 1986 (C.T. at 125; Appendix D).

Koepnick filed a notice of appeal on July 24, 1986, with respect to the trial court's order granting Sears' motion for judgment notwithstanding the verdict on Count Four for trespass to chattel and for a new trial on Count One for false arrest (C.T. at 124). Sears filed a notice of cross-appeal with respect to the portions of the judgment dated February 24, 1986, granting judgment in favor of Koepnick and the portions of the order dated July 18, 1986, denying Sears' motion for judgment notwithstanding the verdict on Count One for false arrest and conditionally denying defendant Sears' motion for new trial on the Count Four for trespass to chattel (C.T. at 128). No appeal was taken by either Koepnick or Mesa with respect to the adjudications of the claims asserted by Koepnick against Mesa. Accordingly, Mesa is not a party to this appeal.

The parties stipulated to waiving the posting of cost bonds on the appeals. This court has jurisdiction of the appeal and cross-appeal pursuant to A.R.S. § 12-1201 B and F.

STATEMENT OF FACTS

On December 6, 1982, Koepnick drove to the Sears store located at Fiesta Mall to get some screwdrivers (4R.T. at 145-47). He arrived at approximately 5 P.M. (4R.T. at 145). Once in the store, he was assisted by Mara Thomas, a sales clerk in the hardware department (4R.T. at 147; 8R.T. at 36). After Koepnick selected the tools he wanted, Thomas carried them to the cash register (4R.T. at 148). Koepnick was waited on at the cash register by Bruce Rosenhan, another sales clerk, who rang up the tools for Koepnick (4R.T. at 150-51; 7R.T. at 88). These tools consisted of a set of screwdrivers, a wrench set, a nut-driver set, an open-end wrench set and a set of pliers (7R.T. at 88-89; Ex. 11). Koepnick asked Rosenhan for an itemized receipt

(4R.T. at 151; 7R.T. at 88). Rosenhan bagged Koepnick's purchases, stapling the bag closed with the receipts on the outside (4R.T. at 151; 7R.T. at 89). Koepnick left the cash register area (4R.T. at 171; 7R.T. at 89).

After waiting on Koepnick, Rosenhan went out to work on the sales floor (7R.T. at 90). Rosenhan saw Koepnick again in the hardware department approximately 15 minutes after he had waited on him (7R.T. at 90-91). Koepnick came over to where he and Thomas were in the back of the department (7R.T. at 90). Rosenhan saw Koepnick speak to Thomas and pull a large wrench out of the shopping bag Rosenhan had earlier stapled closed (7R.T. at 91). At that time, Koepnick's bag was open and there were no receipts in view on it (7R.T. at 91). Rosenhan realized that the wrench Koepnick pulled out of the bag was not one of the wrenches from the sets that he sold to Koepnick (7R.T. at 91). When Rosenhan finished with the customer he was helping, he asked Thomas if Koepnick put the wrench back in his bag and whether she had sold it to him (7R.T. at 92). Thomas told him that Koepnick put it back in his bag and that she had not sold that wrench to him or had anything to do with it (7R.T. at 92). Rosenhan asked all the other employees present in the department whether they had sold that particular wrench to Koepnick and learned that none of them had either (7R.T. at 92).

Rosenhan went to the front register and used the phone to call security (7R.T. at 92). He spoke with Steve Lessard, one of the security agents on duty at that time in the store (4R.T. at 77). It was approximately 5:35 to 5:40 when Lessard received the call from Rosenhan (4R.T. at 83). He informed Lessard that he believed that there was a customer in the store who was a shoplifter (4R.T. at 77). Lessard told him to meet in the sewing machine department, which is located next to hardware (4R.T. at 77-78). When Rosenhan and Lessard met, Rosenhan explained what had occurred with the purchase of the tools and the subsequent incident of the large wrench being observed in the bag (7R.T. at 93; 4R.T. at 78-79). Lessard radioed to Dave Pollock, another security agent on duty at Sears, and requested that he come and assist him (4R.T. at 79).

When Pollock arrived, Lessard explained what he had learned from Rosenhan and asked him to watch Koepnick while he spoke with the other employees (4R.T. at 79-80). Lessard went around the hardware department and spoke with each of the employees present there (4R.T. at 80). Among the employees he spoke with was Mara Thomas, who informed Lessard of her contacts with Koepnick and confirmed the fact that she did not sell or help Koepnick with the large wrench he had in his bag (4R.T. at 80-81; 8R.T. at 41).

After Lessard had spoken with all of the employees in the hardware department and confirmed that none of them sold the wrench in question, he observed Koepnick in the socket aisle (4R.T. at 82). Koepnick picked out some sockets and then put the bag he was carrying down at the cash register (4R.T. at 82). Koepnick went back to the socket aisle and picked up another socket (4R.T. at 82). While Koepnick was away from the cash register area, Lessard instructed Pollock to go by the shopping bag and confirm that the large wrench in question was still in it (4R.T. at 82). When Pollock went over to the bag, he observed that the bag was pulled open and the wrench was inside (7R.T. at 41). No receipts were seen in or on the bag by Pollock (7R.T. at 41, 84). Pollock reported back to Lessard and told him what he saw (7R.T. at 41).

Lessard and Pollock observed as Koepnick returned to the cash register and purchased some sockets (7R.T. at 42; 4R.T. at 82-83). As Koepnick began to leave the store, Lessard went to the clerk at the cash register and asked what items had been purchased, verifying that Koepnick had not paid for the crescent wrench in question at that time (7R.T. at 83-84). Lessard and Pollock followed Koepnick out of the store (4R.T. at 84). At no time did either observe Koepnick take any receipts off the shopping bag he was carrying (4R.T. at 84). As they followed Koepnick out of the store, they discussed the information they had and decided to stop Koepnick with respect to the large wrench in question (4R.T. at 84).

Koepnick estimated that it was approximately 6:15 P.M. when he exited the east door of the store (5R.T. at 72). Lessard approached Koepnick as he walked into the parking lot area approximately 20 to 25 feet from the door of the store (4R.T. at 87). Koepnick refused to stop when Lessard first spoke to him (5R.T. at 178; 4R.T. at 87-88). Koepnick testified that Lessard then came around in front of him, pulled the wrench in question out of the bag and told him that he did not have a receipt for it (4R.T. at 178). Koepnick was also told he was under arrest for shoplifting (4R.T. at 178). Both Koepnick and Lessard testified that Koepnick was shown identification by Lessard, although Koepnick testified that he did not see it clearly (4R.T. at 179-80; 4R.T. at 87-88). Koepnick did not show a receipt for the wrench when Lessard stopped him (4R.T. at 91; 5R.T. at 63).

Koepnick initially refused to return to the store with Lessard and Pollock (4R.T. at 179). Koepnick was informed that he had to return to the store with them (4R.T. at 180). After some further discussion, Koepnick was escorted up to the security office in the Sears store (4R.T. at 179-81; 5R.T. at 70-72). He was not handcuffed or physically injured in any way by the Sears employees (5R.T. at 70, 72). Once in the security office, Koepnick was instructed to sit down to wait for the police to arrive (4R.T. at 183).

In the security office, Lessard examined the shopping bag Koepnick had been carrying and found receipts for the purchase of the sockets (4R.T. at 94; 5R.T. at 72-73). No other receipts were found in or on the bag (4R.T. at 95). Although Koepnick had the receipts for his other purchases in his front shirt pocket, he never attempted to show them to the Sears employees (5R.T. at 63, 66). While waiting for the police to arrive, Koepnick asked if he could get a drink of water or go down to his truck, but those requests were refused (4R.T. at 183).

While Pollock watched Koepnick, Lessard continued his investigation and began to prepare his report of the incident (4R.T. at 97-98). Lessard telephoned the hardware department and spoke to Kim Miller, the hardware department manager. Lessard called the hardware department as he needed the stock number for the wrench in question (8R.T. at 72). He also wanted to have the audit tape on the cash register checked as there were no receipts in the shopping bag for the tool sets that Rosenhan had told him he had rung up for Koepnick (8R.T. at 72).

Officer Michael Campbell of the Mesa Police Department arrived at 6:30 P.M., approximately 15 minutes after Koepnick had been brought to the security office (6R.T. at 67; 4R.T. at 186). Campbell and Lessard stepped across the hall to permit Lessard to inform the officer as to what he had observed (4R.T. at 186; 4R.T. at 101-02). As Lessard was talking with Officer Campbell, Koepnick attempted to walk out of the security office (4R.T. at 187; 4R.T. at 58). Officer Campbell came out into the hallway and met Koepnick at the door to the security office (4R.T. at 187; 4R.T. at 59). Koepnick and Officer Campbell became involved in an altercation, resulting in Koepnick striking his head against the back wall of the security office (4R.T. at 187-88; 4R.T. at 60-64). After that occurred, Officer Campbell was able to handcuff Koepnick (6R.T. at 96-98).

Officer Campbell had made the decision to arrest Koepnick when the altercation started (6R.T. at 93). While he was being handcuffed by Officer Campbell, Koepnick took the receipts that had been in his shirt pocket and stuffed them inside his shirt (4R.T. at 189; 6R.T. at 96-97). Once Koepnick was handcuffed, Officer Campbell removed the receipts he had observed Koepnick stuffing inside his shirt (4R.T. at 66; 6R.T. at 100). The receipts that were found on Koepnick were examined and matched to the various tools Koepnick had in his shopping bag (4R.T. at 191; 4R.T. at 68).

During the altercation, Officer Campbell had instructed Pollock to use his radio to call for assistance (6T. 981). Sergeant Reynolds and Officer Gates came to the Sears security office in response to the request (6R.T. at 108).

Lessard learned after the altercation that another sales clerk, Jeff Ward, had also been working in the hardware department that day (4R.T. at 103-04). Ward, however, had left the sales floor before Rosenhan observed Koepnick with the wrench in the shopping bag and called Lessard down to investigate the situation (8R.T. at 9-10). When Ward later returned to the hardware department, Miller informed him of the call from Lessard and that security had some questions about whether a customer paid for a certain wrench (8R.T. at 110). Ward told Miller that he had rung up such a wrench for a customer (8R.T. at 11). Miller took Ward up to the security office (8R.T. at 11). They arrived about the time the altercation occurred between Koepnick and Officer Campbell (4R.T. at 103; 8R.T. at 12).

Once Lessard became aware of Ward's contact with Koepnick, he interviewed Ward (4R.T. at 104). Ward stated that he had first observed Koepnick as Koepnick walked up to the cash register and pulled the receipt off a shopping bag that was lying on the counter (4R.T. at 104; 8R.T. at 6). Ward asked him if that was his package and Koepnick said it was (4R.T. at 104; 8R.T. at 6). Koepnick had a large combination wrench and a smaller set of wrenches with him to purchase (4T. 104; 8T. 6). Ward rang these items up, and Koepnick paid for them (4R.T. at 104). Ward then bagged these wrenches in a smaller brown bag, which Koepnick placed inside the larger shopping bag he already had (4R.T. at 104; 8R.T. at 104; 8R.T. at 8). Koepnick then placed the receipts Ward had prepared for the wrenches in his shirt pocket and left (8R.T. at 8). Ward did not see Koepnick again on the sales floor that night (8R.T. at 9). After Ward finished ringing up the other customers at the cash register, he left the sales floor (8R.T. at 9, 24). Ward told Lessard he had been on a break (4R.T. at 72). Ward could not recall at trial exactly where he went when he left the sales floor (8R.T. at 9).

After questioning Ward, Lessard discussed with the police officers the possibility that Koepnick had taken the wrench he purchased from Ward out to his truck and brought the shopping bag back in and put another wrench in it (4R.T. at 69-70). Lessard was familiar with this method of shoplifting through his work as a security agent (4R.T. at 105). The information Lessard had that caused him to believe that this was a possibility was (1) Ward's statement that he had bagged the large wrench in a separate brown bag that was not present in the large shopping bag Koepnick had when he was stopped, (2) Rosenhan's statement that there was a period of 15 minutes from the time he last saw Koepnick after his first purchase until he saw him again in the hardware department with the wrench, and (3) Koepnick's actions in not exhibiting the receipts for his purchases when he was detained (4R.T. at 105-06, 111).

The police officers made the decision to search Koepnick's truck (6R.T. at 101-02; 6R.T. at 128). Officer Campbell testified that he asked Koepnick for permission to search the truck and Koepnick consented (6R.T. at 130). Koepnick testified that he consented to the search only on the condition that he be allowed to go with them (4R.T. at 194). Lessard accompanied Officer Gates down to Koepnick's truck (4R.T. at 107). Officer Gates opened the vehicle and Lessard assisted him in looking in the truck (4R.T. at 107). No Sears merchandise was found (4R.T. at 107). The search of the truck lasted about two minutes (4R.T. at 72-73). Nothing was taken or damaged in the search (4R.T. at 110-11, 197).

Once Officer Gates and Lessard returned to the security office, the police officers discussed what action they would take (4R.T. at 197-98). Sergeant Reynolds made the decision to cite Koepnick for disorderly conduct for his actions in striking Officer Campbell (6R.T. at 130). After Koepnick received the citation, he was released by the Mesa Police Department (4R.T. at 198).

ISSUES PRESENTED

1. Did the trial court err in denying Sears' motion for judgment notwithstanding the verdict on the claim for false arrest when the evidence is insufficient to support a finding by the jury that plaintiff was detained by Sears in an unreasonable manner or for an unreasonable length of time?

2. Did the trial court err in denying Sears' motion for judgment notwithstanding the verdict on the punitive damage claims where the evidence fails to establish a *prima facie* case for such damages?

ARGUMENT

I. SEARS' MOTION FOR JUDGMENT NOTWITHSTANDING THE VERDICT ON THE CLAIM FOR FALSE ARREST SHOULD HAVE BEEN GRANTED BY THE TRIAL COURT.

A. Applicable Standard of Review.

The standard of review for determining the appropriateness of the granting of a judgment N.O.V. is whether the evidence is sufficient that reasonable men could discern facts to support the verdict. *Rancho Pescado, Inc. v. Northwestern Mutual Life Insurance Co.,* 140 Ariz. 174, 680 P.2d 1235 (App. 1984). In reviewing a judgment N.O.V., the appellate court views the evidence most favorably to sustaining the verdict. *Lerner v. Brettschneider,* 123 Ariz. 152, 598 P.2d 515 (App. 1979). When the evidence is insufficient to meet the burden of proof to establish the claim, entry of judgment N.O.V. is proper. *Rancho Pescado, Inc. v. Northwestern Mutual Life Insurance Co.,* 140 Ariz. at 186, 680 P.2d at 1247; *Lerner v. Brettschneider,* 123 Ariz. at 155, 598 P.2d at 518.

B. There Was Insufficient Evidence to Justify Any Finding of Liability on the Claim of False Arrest.

A.R.S. § 13-1805C sets forth the statutory shopkeeper's privilege for detaining a suspected shoplifter. A detention is deemed privileged under this statute if it is made with reasonable cause for a proper purpose and done in a reasonable manner and for reasonable time. *Gortarez v. Smitty's Super Valu, Inc.,* 140 Ariz. 97, 680 P.2d 807 (1984). The undisputed evidence established the existence of all the elements necessary for this privilege. Therefore, Sears' motion for judgment notwithstanding the verdict on plaintiff's claim of false arrest should have been granted by the trial court.

1. Reasonable Cause.

The existence of reasonable cause and the reasonableness of the detention, both as to time and manner, are for the court to decide as a matter of law where there is no conflict in the evidence. *Id.* at 104. The trial court determined as a matter of law that reasonable cause did exist for plaintiff's detention in granting of the motion for new trial. The propriety of that decision is discussed in Section I.E of Sears' response brief, which is incorporated herein by reference to avoid duplication.

The remaining elements of A.R.S. § 13-1805C that must be established for the privilege to exist are (1) a proper purpose for the detention, (2) the reasonableness of the time of the detention, and (3) the reasonableness of the manner of the detention. *Id. Gortarez,* 140 Ariz. at 104.

2. Proper Purpose.

A.R.S. § 13-1805C sets forth two purposes for which a privileged detention may be made under the statute. They are (1) questioning the subject, or (2) summoning a law enforcement officer. Given Koepnick's testimony at trial, which must be accepted for the purposes of deciding a motion for judgment N.O.V., there is plainly a dispute in the evidence as to what questioning, if any, occurred during Sears' detention of him. Koepnick's testimony was that he was not questioned at all (4R.T. at 184-85). There is, however, no question about the existence of the alternative purpose authorized by the statute for Koepnick's detention—summoning a law enforcement officer. It is undisputed that the Mesa Police Department was contacted by Sears and requested to respond to where plaintiff was being detained (Opening brief, p. 8). Thus, this element of the privilege is unquestionably present in this case.

3. The Length of Detention.

The reasonableness of the length of Koepnick's detention is also undis-putedly established by the evidence. There is no evidence in the record that creates any issue of fact as to the reasonableness of the length of Sears' detention of Koepnick. The undisputed evidence is that plaintiff was taken to the Sears security office and the police called without any undue delay on the part of Sears. No evidence of anything to the contrary is present in the record. Upon Officer Campbell's arrival, Lessard immediately began to explain the situation to him. Even before he could even finish, the altercation between Koepnick and Officer Campbell occurred. At that time, Koepnick was placed under arrest by Officer Campbell independently of any shoplifting and taken into the custody of the Mesa Police. From that point on plaintiff was no longer in Sears' custody.

These facts are undisputed. There is nothing in the evidence which would permit the jury to conclude that the length of Koepnick's detention by Sears for the express statutory purpose of summoning a law enforcement officer was unreasonable. Indeed, there was no way Sears could make Koep-nick's detention for that purpose any shorter. The length of that detention was determined by the amount of time it took the Mesa Police to respond to the Sears store. This is something that Sears had no control over; in any event, there is no evidence to permit a jury to find that the actual amount of time it took the officer to respond was in any way unreasonable. Accord-ingly, the trial court should have determined that the length of Koepnick's detention by Sears was reasonable as a matter of law.

4. The Manner of Detention.

Neither is there any evidence in the record that creates any issue of fact as to the reasonableness of the manner of Koepnick's detention by Sears. The evidence is again undisputed that Koepnick was stopped by Lessard, escorted up to the Sears security office and detained there until the police arrived. The Arizona Supreme Court in *Gortarez* stated that reasonable force may be used to detain a suspected shoplifter. 140 Ariz. at 104, 680 P.2d at 814. There is no evidence that any unreasonable force was ever used on plaintiff by Sears employees. Sears employees never struck or fought with Koepnick (5R.T. at 70-72). They did not even handcuff or search him (4R.T. at 96; 5R.T. at 70). Koepnick confirmed in his testimony that he was not physically injured in any manner by Sears employees (5R.T. at 72). In short, there is absolutely no evidence to indicate that the manner of plaintiff's detention by Sears was unreasonable.

As indicated above, the reasonableness of the detention, both as to time and manner, is one for the court to decide as a matter of law where there is no conflict of the evidence. *Id.* As there was no conflicting evidence presented at trial as to these elements that would support a finding that the manner and length of Sears' detention of Koepnick was unreasonable, the trial court should have determined that the detention was reasonable as a matter of law and not submitted any issue of this claim to the jury. Accord-ingly, Sears' motion for judgment notwithstanding the verdict on the claim of false arrest should have been granted by the trial court.

II. SEARS' MOTION FOR JUDGMENT NOTWITHSTANDING THE VERDICT ON THE CLAIMS OF PUNITIVE DAMAGES SHOULD HAVE BEEN GRANTED BY THE TRIAL COURT

A. The Applicable Standard.

The Arizona Supreme Court has recently modified the standard for determining whether there has been a *prima facie* showing permitting the assessment of punitive damages. The decisions discussing and applying this new standard include *Filasky v. Preferred Risk Mutual Insurance Co.*, No. CV-86-0237-T (filed March 2, 1987); *Gurule v. Illinois Mutual Life and Casualty Co.*, No. CV-86-0488-PR (filed March 2, 1987); *Rawlings v. Apodaca*, 151 Ariz. 149, 726 P.2d 565 (1986); and *Linthicum v. National Life Insurance Co.*, 150 Ariz. 326, 723 P.2d 675 (1986). The portion of the *Linthicum* decision setting forth the new standard is quoted at length in Section IV.B of Appellee's response brief, which is incorporated herein by reference to avoid duplication.

Although the trial court denied Sears' motion for judgment N.O.V. with respect to punitive damages before the Supreme Court announced the more stringent standard in *Linthicum v. National Life Insurance Co.*, that standard applies to cases upon appellate review. *See, e.g., Hawkins v. Allstate Insurance Co.*, No. CV-86-0010-PR (filed February 26, 1987) (applying standard announced in *Linthicum* to trial court's pre-*Linthicum* ruling on motion for judgment notwithstanding the verdict).

Under the new standard, plaintiffs are not automatically entitled to an instruction on punitive damages upon the showing of a *prima facie* intentional tort. To recover punitive damages, something more is required over and above the "mere commission of a tort." *Rawlings v. Apodaca*, 151 Ariz. at 162, 726 P.2d at 587. There must be a showing of either an intent to injure the plaintiff or a conscious pursuit of a course of conduct knowing that it creates a substantial risk of significant harm to others. *Linthicum v. Nationwide Life Insurance Co.*, 150 Ariz. at 330, 723 P.2d at 679. The requirement of this "something more" or "evil mind" is to assure that punitive damages are awarded only where the purposes of deterrence are furthered. *Gurule v. Illinois Mutual Life and Casualty Co.*, slip op. at 3. The punishment resulting from punitive damage is appropriate only where there is "some element of outrage similar to that usually found in crime." *Rawlings v. Apodaca*, 151 Ariz. at 161, 726 P.2d at 578, *quoting* Restatement (Second) of Torts, § 908, comment b (1979).

B. The Evidence Fails to Show a *Prima Facie* Case for Punitive Damages with Respect to the Claim of False Arrest

As discussed in Section I.B of this cross-appeal brief, the evidence in the record is insufficient to make out a prima facie case of false arrest, let alone rise to the level necessary to permit the assessment of punitive damages. There is absolutely no evidence that suggests that Sears intended to injure Koepnick or that it consciously pursued a course of conduct knowing that it created a substantial risk of tremendous harm to him. As the trial court

determined, the facts are uncontradicted that Lessard actually and reasonably believed that when Koepnick left the store he had merchandise for which he had not paid. Acting on that reasonable belief, Lessard stopped Koepnick
.   .   .   .

C. The Evidence Fails to Establish a *Prima Facie* Case for Punitive Damages with Respect to the Claim of Trespass to Chattel

.   .   .   .

CONCLUSION

The trial court was correct in finding that reasonable cause existed as matter of law for Sears' detention of Koepnick. The court erred, however, in ruling that there was sufficient evidence to submit to the jury the issues of the reasonableness of the time and manner of the detention. Accordingly, the trial court's order of July 23, 1986 should be reversed to the extent that it provides for a new trial on these issues. The trial court should be instructed to enter judgment notwithstanding the verdict in favor of Sears on the false arrest claim.

The evidence was also insufficient to submit the issue of punitive damages to the jury on either of the claims of false arrest or trespass to chattel. Accordingly, Sears is entitled to judgment notwithstanding the verdict on the issue of punitive damages as well.

Respectfully submitted this 13th day of April, 1987.

GUST, ROSENFELD, DIVELBESS & HENDERSON

By _____
    Fred Cole
    Roger W. Perry
    Attorneys for Defendant-Appellee/Cross-Appellant

Thomas J. Quarelli, Esq.
1832 E. Thomas
Phoenix, Arizona 85016

William J. Monahan, P.C.
340 E. Palm Lane, Suite 130
Phoenix, Arizona 85004

Paul G. Ulrich, P.C.
3030 N. Central, Suite 310
Phoenix, Arizona 85012

Attorneys for Plaintiff-Appellant/Cross-Appellee

IN THE COURT OF APPEALS
STATE OF ARIZONA
DIVISION ONE

MAX KOEPNICK,
    Plaintiff-Appellant,
    Cross-Appellee,
 	
    v.
 	
SEARS ROEBUCK & COMPANY,
    Defendant-Appellee,
    Cross-Appellant.
	No. CA-CIV 9147
	
	MARICOPA County
	Superior Court
	No. C-502081

APPELLANT'S CROSS-APPEAL ANSWERING BRIEF

TABLE OF CONTENTS

TABLE OF AUTHORITIES

APPELLANT'S CROSS-APPEAL ANSWERING BRIEF

STATEMENT OF THE CASE

On December 5, 1983, Plaintiff/cross-appellee Max Koepnick sued Defendant/cross-appellant Sears, Roebuck & Co. ("Sears") and the City of Mesa ("Mesa") for false arrest, assault, trespass to chattel (by further detaining him while searching his truck), invasion of his right of privacy and malicious prosecution. These claims all arose out of Koepnick's arrest for alleged shoplifting on December 6, 1982 (Appendix A, C.T. at 1). The counts in Koepnick's complaint alleging invasion of privacy against both defendants and malicious prosecution, false arrest and punitive damages against Mesa were all disposed of by directed verdicts (Appendix B, C.T. at 97). Those issues are not involved in this appeal.

The remaining portions of Koepnick's complaint were tried to a jury on January 13-22, 1986. The jury awarded Koepnick $25,000 in compensatory damages and $500,000 in punitive damages against Sears for false arrest. It awarded him $100 in compensatory damages against both Sears and Mesa and $25,000 in punitive damages against Sears for trespass to Koepnick's personal property. The jury also awarded Koepnick $50,000 in compensatory damages against Mesa for assault (9R.T. at 101-03). Judgment was entered against both defendants pursuant to those jury verdicts on February 25, 1986 (Appendix B, C.T. at 97).

On March 11, 1986, Sears filed motions for judgment notwithstanding the verdicts and for new trial (C.T. at 100). Mesa also filed a motion for a new trial on March 11, 1986 (C.T. at 101). Mesa then also moved for judgment notwithstanding the verdict and, in the alternative, for new trial and for remittitur on March 12, 1986 (C.T. at 104). Sears thereafter filed an amended motion for judgment notwithstanding the verdicts and for new trial on April 16, 1986 (C.T. at 113). Koepnick filed responses to Mesa's and Sears' motions on March 20 and 25, 1986, respectively (C.T. at 107, 108, 109). Both Sears and Mesa filed reply memoranda in support of their respective motions on April 16, 1986 (C.T. at 114, 115).

On May 14, 1986, the trial court entered the following minute orders: (1) granting Sears' motion for new trial on Koepnick's false arrest claim; (2) granting Sears' and Mesa's motions for judgment N.O.V. with respect to Koepnick's claim of trespass to personal property; and (3) denying Mesa's motion for new trial or for judgment N.O.V. with respect to Koepnick's assault claim. On June 27, 1986, the trial court clarified its May 14, 1986 minute order by denying Sears' motion for judgment N.O.V. on Koepnick's false arrest claim to the extent it granted Sears' motion for a new trial concerning that issue. Having granted a new trial on Koepnick's false arrest claim, the trial court also vacated his judgment against Sears for punitive damages. A formal written order incorporating all those rulings and directing that it be entered as a final judgment was filed on July 23, 1986 (C.T. at 124).

On July 24, 1986, Koepnick filed a notice of appeal only from the portions of the trial court's order granting Sears' motion for new trial on his false arrest claim and for judgment N.O.V. on his claim of trespass to chattel (C.T. at 124). The portion of the litigation involving Mesa has been settled. Mesa is therefore not a party to this appeal and has not filed a cross-appeal. Sears filed a notice of cross-appeal with respect to other portions of the judgment on August 5, 1986 (C.T. at 128). The parties have stipulated that the cost bonds for their respective appeals are waived. This Court has jurisdiction concerning this appeal pursuant to A.R.S. § 12-2101(F)(1).

STATEMENT OF FACTS

I. KOEPNICK AND HIS PURCHASES.

A. Max Koepnick was a manager, foreman, and mechanic for a large Queen Creek farming operation whose assets exceed $2,500,000 (4R.T. at 145, 6R.T. at 21). His lawsuit resulted from his detention and arrest for shoplifting while he was purchasing tools for the farm at the Sears store in Fiesta Mall, Mesa, Arizona, on December 6, 1982 (4R.T. at 145-47). Koepnick paid cash for those tools and had the receipts for all of them in his possession when he was arrested, including the receipt for a 1 5/16" open-end crescent wrench. That wrench was the precipitating cause of his arrest.

Koepnick drove to Sears in the farm pickup truck he used for business purposes (4R.T. at 145-46). He entered the store at approximately 5:00 P.M. (4R.T. at 145, 5T 68). Business in the Sears store happened to be slow at that particular time (3R.T. at 13). Koepnick proceeded to the hardware department. He first purchased a five-wrench set, a nut-driver, an open-end wrench set, a plier set, and a set of screwdrivers (Ex. 11). Bruce Rosenhan, Sears hardware department manager, rang up those purchases on a cash register and stapled portions of the Sears seven-part handwritten receipt used at customers' requests for cash purchases to the outside of the bag (4R.T. at 149, 173). Sears' policy was to staple the register receipt and the original of the seven-part receipt to the outside of the bag (3R.T. at 22, 4R.T. at 45). The customer's purchases were also recorded automatically on the cash register tape (3R.T. at 18-19). The other six copies of the handwritten receipt may have been placed in a trash can on one of the shelves below the cash register (3R.T. at 21).

Koepnick then left his purchases at the cash register counter to look for a wrench (4R.T. at 151). During this time he flirted with a sales person, Mara Thomas, who showed him various tools. Ms. Thomas then escorted him to the register where he purchased a 1 5/16" open-end crescent wrench. Sales clerk Jeff Ward made this sale. At that time, Ward prepared another handwritten seven-part form, since this sale was also for cash (8R.T. at 8-9, Ex. 12). As had occurred with Koepnick's first purchases, the crescent wrench was bagged and stapled together with the receipt. This bag was placed inside the first, with the wrench handle sticking out (4R.T. at 173). At trial, Koepnick denied the wrench was ever put into a separate brown bag (4R.T. at 173, 174). He also testified all the receipts were stapled onto the original bag (4R.T. at 17). Jeff Ward then left the hardware department to take a break (3R.T. at 12, 8R.T. at 9).

Koepnick picked up the bag from the register counter and started to leave. However, he then remembered he needed some spark plug sockets (4R.T. at 174). He therefore went back to the register, set the bag down and proceeded to look for the sockets (4R.T. at 175).

During this time, manager Rosenhan contacted Sears security guards Steve Lessard and Dave Pollock, who began observing Koepnick. Lessard spoke with all four hardware department employees then on the floor about whether there was a receipt for the open-end crescent wrench (3R.T. at 9). None could remember ringing it up. However, Lessard failed to ask those employees if anyone else was then on a break (*id.*). He simply assumed those four employees were the only ones on duty (3R.T. at 10-11). Moreover, no one checked either the register tape or the receipts tray behind the counter (3R.T. at 34). Doing so would have confirmed that Koepnick had in fact paid for the crescent wrench, since the cash register tape could have been checked against the wrench's stock number (3R.T. at 19-20). Lessard also admitted at trial that he also could have searched for the six discarded copies of Koepnick's three sets of receipts that were probably in the trash container below the cash register (3R.T. at 21-22).

Meanwhile, Lessard had Pollack walk past the bag on the counter to confirm visually that the wrench in the bag was a Sears product (3R.T. at 28). Pollack could see a price tag sticker on the end of the wrench. However, although the stapled receipts on the bag were also in plain view, they were not checked against the merchandise (4R.T. at 175). Lessard himself admitted that Pollack had an "easy view" of the receipts (3R.T. at 29-30).

Lessard himself also saw the bag on the counter. However, he did not notice the handwritten receipts and cash register tape stapled to the top of the bag (3R.T. at 27). He also testified at trial he could not dispute testimony that the register receipts and handwritten receipts were stapled to the top of the bag (*id.*). He "didn't recall" whether anyone bothered to look for those receipts on the bag before Koepnick was stopped, although he conceded that it would have been a "fairly reasonable thing to do" (3R.T. at 30).

While this "investigation" was occurring, Koepnick located and purchased the sockets, returned to the register counter, picked up his bag from the counter, tore off all the receipts, placed them in his shirt pocket and left the store. Lessard and Pollack followed him (4R.T. at 177). Lessard estimated that he had between 20 and 25 minutes to make his investigation before he stopped Koepnick outside the store (3R.T. at 14). He even had time to discuss with Pollack that they had "done a thorough investigation" (3R.T. at 34).

II. KOEPNICK'S DETENTION, ARREST, ASSAULT, AND EVENTUAL RELEASE.

Koepnick placed the time and location of his stop and arrest by Lessard and Pollack at 6:15 P.M., in a dark, dimly lighted area of the Sears parking lot (5R.T. at 72). Koepnick's version of the facts was that in that dimly lighted area two punks accosted him, yelled "Hey," and positioned themselves on each side of him (4R.T. at 178). They then jerked the wrench out of the bag stating, "You don't have a receipt, do you?" (4R.T. at 180-81).

Koepnick thought he was being hustled. He asked who his captors were. Their response was, "We're security guards." (4R.T. at 179). Koepnick asked them to "prove it." In response, one of the guards flashed his badge (*id.*). However, Koepnick could not see it clearly (4R.T. at 179-80). Koepnick was then told that he was going with the guards and that he was under arrest for shoplifting (4R.T. at 180).

Koepnick was escorted to an upstairs security room, denied a drink of water, and seated, with no inquiry as to whether he had a receipt for the wrench (4R.T. at 180). The Mesa police were called. When Koepnick attempted to enter the hallway to obtain a drink of water, he and Officer Campbell (who was wearing a bulletproof vest) got into a pushing match. As a result, Koepnick fell or was thrown head first through the wall of the security room, causing him to incur neck and other injuries (4R.T. at 60-64).

Koepnick was then handcuffed. While he was recovering from the blow to his head, the Mesa police and the Sears security staff verified every item he had purchased against every receipt on the table of the security room (4R.T. at 68). Lessard had also verified with Jeff Ward that Koepnick had in fact purchased the crescent wrench. The bag which supposedly contained the wrench had already been accounted for in the security office. However, despite all of Koepnick's purchases being fully accounted for, the Mesa police continued to detain him at Sears' insistence while Lessard conducted a non-consensual, unescorted search of his truck, looking for an alleged "brown bag" (4R.T. at 71). Koepnick had approximately $1,200-1,400 in cash and all of his business records in the truck (4R.T. at 197). The search, which required approximately 15 to 20 minutes, proved fruitless (4R.T. at 197-98). During this time, Koepnick remained under detention. Had Lessard not decided to search Koepnick's truck, Koepnick would simply have been cited immediately for disorderly conduct and then released (6R.T. at 115). Instead, after the search, Koepnick was then freed of his handcuffs and cited for disorderly conduct (4R.T. at 198). He was finally permitted to leave the Sears security room at about 7:00 P.M. (4R.T. at 199).

ISSUES PRESENTED

1. Did the trial court properly deny Sears' motion for judgment notwithstanding the verdict on Koepnick's false arrest claim where the evidence, viewed most favorably to him, was disputed as to each element of the statutory shopkeeper's privilege, A.R.S. § 13-1805(C)?

2. Did the trial court properly deny Sears' motion for judgment notwithstanding the verdict on Koepnick's false arrest punitive damage claim where the evidence presented reasonably established a *prima facie* case for such damages?

3. Was the evidence supporting punitive damages as to Koepnick's trespass to chattel claim sufficient to submit that issue to the jury as well?

ARGUMENT

I. THE TRIAL COURT PROPERLY DENIED SEARS' MOTION FOR JUDGMENT NOTWITHSTANDING THE VERDICT WITH RESPECT TO KOEPNICK'S FALSE ARREST CLAIM.

A. The Applicable Standards of Review.

In reviewing the trial court's denial of a motion for judgment notwithstanding the verdict, the appellate court will review the evidence to determine whether it was of sufficient character that reasonable minds could differ as to inferences to be drawn from the facts. *Adroit Supply Co. v. Electric Mutual Liability Insurance Co.,* 112 Ariz. 385, 542 P.2d 810 (1975); *Marcal Limited Partnership v. Title Insurance Co. of Minnesota,* 150 Ariz. 191, 722 P.2d 359 (App. 1986). In doing so, this Court will view the evidence in the light most favorable to sustaining the verdict. It then must review the evidence to determine whether the evidence would permit a reasonable person to reach the challenged verdict. *Maxwell v. Aetna Life Insurance Co.,* 143 Ariz. 205, 693 P.2d 348 (App. 1984).

When the sufficiency of evidence to sustain the jury's verdicts is questioned on appeal, every conflict in the evidence and every reasonable inference therefrom will be resolved in favor of sustaining the verdict and judgment. *See McNelis v. Bruce,* 90 Ariz. 261, 367 P.2d 615 (1962). On appeal, a reviewing court must take the evidence in the light most favorable to upholding the jury's verdict. *Miller v. Schaffer,* 102 Ariz. 457, 432 P.2d 585 (1967). Applying these standards to the evidence in this record, Koepnick submits the trial court properly denied Sears' motion for directed verdict with respect to his false arrest claim.

B. Requirements to Sustain the Statutory Shopkeeper's Privilege.

A.R.S. § 13-1805(C) provides that a merchant "with reasonable cause may detain on the premises in a reasonable manner and for a reasonable time any person suspected of shoplifting . . . for questioning or summoning a law enforcement officer." The statute thus states four elements, all of which must be established to sustain the shopkeeper's privilege: (1) reasonable cause for detention; (2) reasonable manner for detention; (3) reasonable time; and (4) proper purpose (for questioning or summoning a law enforcement officer). Koepnick submits that a directed verdict in Sears' favor with respect to his false arrest claim would not be justified unless the evidence satisfied the applicable standard of review previously stated with respect to all four elements required to establish the statutory privilege. Viewing the evidence most favorably to Koepnick, this record simply does not permit that conclusion.

Each of the elements of Sears' defense also required Sears to prove the affirmative of the issue. *E.g., Black, Robertshaw, Frederick, Copple & Wright, P.C. v. United States,* 130 Ariz. 110, 634 P.2d 298 (App. 1981); *Yeazell v. Copins,* 98 Ariz. 109, 402 P.2d 541 (App. 1965). Unless Sears could persuade a jury by a preponderance of the evidence and reasonable inferences therefrom that each statutory element had been satisfied, Sears thus could not prevail.

1. Reasonable Cause.

Given the facts and reasonable inferences therefrom most favorable to Koepnick, he was clearly entitled to have the reasonable cause issue submitted to the jury. In the first place, Lessard testified he had 20 to 25 minutes to make an investigation before Koepnick left the Sears store and stated that he had made a thorough investigation. He therefore did not have to make a "snap" decision based on incomplete evidence to detain someone who might be hurriedly leaving. Koepnick testified that all of the handwritten receipts for the tools he bought were stapled to the outside of his shopping bag in plain view. However, neither Lessard nor Pollack ever attempted to read them to determine whether the open-end crescent wrench was listed. Lessard was also unable to dispute Koepnick's testimony in this regard, and admitted that looking at the receipts would have been a reasonable thing to do.

Lessard also failed to make the basic inquiry whether there were other hardware department employees then on duty other than the four he interviewed. The possibility that another employee might have been on a break was certainly a reasonable one to be explored. The security guards also never looked for the extra copies of the seven-part receipt, although they might well have been found either in the receipts tray behind the counter or in a trash container on one of the shelves below the cash register. No one ever checked the register tape which would have shown the stock number for the open-end wrench Koepnick had paid for. Given all these deficiencies in the security guards' investigation, there was certainly a reasonable basis for disputing Sears' position that it had reasonable cause to detain Koepnick. Moreover, pursuant to A.R.S. § 13-1805(d), "reasonable cause" is a defense to a false arrest claim. Sears therefore had the burden of proving the affirmative of this issue. *E.g., Black, Robertshaw, Frederick, Copple & Wright, P.C. v. United States,* 130 Ariz. 110, 634 P.2d 298 (App. 1981); *Yeazell v. Copins,* 98 Ariz. 109, 402 P.2d 541 (1965). Unless it could persuade a jury by a preponderance of the evidence and reasonable inferences therefrom that the nature and extent of its investigation was appropriate under the circumstances, Sears could not prevail. Given all the deficiencies in the security guards' investigation and in view of the relatively lengthy time available for them to pursue the simple additional inquiries that could have been made, the trial court could not properly remove the "reasonable cause" issue from the jury in Sears' favor.

2. Proper Purpose.

Sears' Cross-Appeal Opening Brief at p. 3 concedes there was a factual dispute concerning what questioning, if any, occurred during Sears' detention of Koepnick. The statutory purpose of "questioning the subject" was thus admittedly not satisfied for purposes of obtaining a directed verdict. The other possible proper purpose permitted by A.R.S. § 13-1805(C) for privileged detention is "summoning a law enforcement officer." Koepnick acknowledges that Sears did contact the Mesa Police Department, but only after he was detained by Sears employees. He was not necessarily detained for that purpose. Moreover, after Officer Campbell's investigation, the officer testified he would simply have cited Koepnick immediately for disorderly conduct and then let him go (6R.T. at 115). Instead, Lessard, Sears employee, insisted that Sears search Koepnick's truck even after all the receipts for his purchases had been accounted for (6R.T. at 101, 102). Koepnick remained in detention for at least 15 to 20 minutes more while Lessard and Officer Gates searched his truck (4R.T. at 197). His handcuffs were not removed until this search had been completed (4R.T. at 197). Koepnick submits that this continuation of his detention was improper because it was motivated by Lessard's desire to search his truck, not for any legitimate reasons connected with the police officers' investigation. There was therefore an issue presented as to whether a proper purpose existed throughout the entire period of time in which Koepnick was detained.

3. Length of Detention.

Koepnick contends that the length of his detention was reasonable only until the Sears employees and Mesa police officers had completed their investigation. Once that occurred, Koepnick should have been released immediately. Instead, he was then detained for an additional 15 to 20 minutes at Lessard's request so Lessard could search his truck. Although Koepnick technically may have been in the police officers' custody during that additional period of time, the evidence clearly established that this additional period of detention would not have occurred but for Lessard's request. Under these circumstances, there is also a factual issue as to the propriety of the length of time Koepnick was detained so far as Sears is concerned.

4. Manner of Detention.

Factual disputes were also presented as to the manner in which Koepnick was detained by Sears. To begin with, he was accosted by Lessard and Pollack in an accusatory manner. Koepnick testified they stated, "You don't have a receipt, do you?" (4R.T. at 180-81) rather than asking to see a receipt. Then, although Koepnick responded that he had a receipt, he was nevertheless detained for shoplifting without further questioning on that subject. Koepnick submits the manner of his initial detention was thus improper for that reason.

Koepnick was then escorted to an upstairs security room where he was denied a drink of water and seated with no inquiry as to whether he had a receipt for the wrench (4R.T. at 180). When Koepnick entered the hallway to obtain a drink of water, he and Officer Campbell got into a pushing match which resulted in Koepnick falling or being thrown head first through the wall of the security room, causing him to incur neck and other injuries (4R.T. at 60-64). Koepnick was then handcuffed. However, had Koepnick been offered a drink of water and had the proper inquiries been made by Sears employees initially, his injuries arguably would not have occurred.

Koepnick submits these facts all raise factual issues as to whether the manner of his detention was reasonable. Based on these facts, a jury could reasonably have found that Sears security guards did not handle his detention in a reasonable manner.

II. THE TRIAL COURT PROPERLY DENIED SEARS' MOTION FOR JUDGMENT NOTWITHSTANDING THE VERDICT AS TO KOEPNICK'S PUNITIVE DAMAGES BASED ON HIS FALSE ARREST CLAIMS.

A. The Applicable Standards of Review.

The recent Arizona appellate decisions modifying the standard for determining whether there has been a *prima facie* showing permitting the assessment of punitive damages do not necessarily require that all prior jury verdicts awarding such damages be reversed. For example, *Filasky v. Preferred Risk Mutual Insurance Co.*, 152 Ariz. 591, 734 P.2d 76 (1987), instead recognizes that "a jury's decision to award punitive damages should be affirmed if any reasonable evidence exists to support it." *Gurule v. Illinois Mutual Life and Casualty Insurance Co.*, 152 Ariz. 600, 734 P.2d 85 (1987), also states that the appellate court must review the facts in a light most favorable to the party obtaining a punitive damage award and affirm the jury's verdict if a reasonable juror could conclude that the defendant either intended to violate his rights or consciously pursued a course of conduct knowing that it created a substantial risk of doing so. 734 P.2d at 88.

Of the various recent decisions, both *Hawkins v. Allstate Insurance Co.*, 152 Ariz. 490, 733 P.2d 1072 (1987), and this Court's Opinion in *Carter-Glogau Laboratories, Inc. v. Construction, Production & Maintenance Labors Local 383*, (1 CA-CIV 8107, 8128 filed October 30, 1986, *review denied*, May 12, 1987), have affirmed punitive damages awards where the evidence presented met the standards stated in *Linthicum v. Nationwide Life Insurance Co.*, 150 Ariz. 326, 723 P.2d 675 (1986). *Rawlings v. Apodaca*, 151 Ariz. 149, 726 P.2d 565 (1986), also remanded for further proceedings as to punitive damages where it was uncertain whether the trial judge had applied the appropriate standards.

According to *Gurule, supra,* the "evil mind" required for punitive damages may be satisfied by "defendant's conscious and deliberate disregard of the interests and rights of others." 152 Ariz. at 602, 734 P.2d at 87. It may also be established by defendant's expressed statements or inferred from his expressions, conduct or objectives. *Id*. If a defendant conducts himself in an outrageous or egregiously improper manner, the inference is permitted that he intended to injure or consciously disregarded the substantial risk that his conduct would cause significant harm. The "evil mind" may also be inferred if a defendant "deliberately continued his actions despite the inevitable or highly probable harm that would follow." *Id*.

B. Applying These Standards, the Evidence Demonstrated a *Prima Facie* Case for Punitive Damages with Respect to Koepnick's False Arrest Claim.

Numerous deficiencies in Sears' investigation support a jury's finding that its employees acted with conscious and deliberate disregard of Koepnick's rights and interests. The "bottom line" of Lessard's investigation at the time Koepnick left the Sears store was that he and Pollack "felt we had done a thorough enough investigation for us to ask [Koepnick] if he had a receipt for the wrench" (3R.T. at 35). Significantly, Lessard himself apparently did not then believe he had sufficient cause to detain Koepnick for shoplifting at that time without further questioning. Yet Lessard and Pollack accosted Koepnick in a hostile and threatening manner in a dark corner of the parking lot and accused him of not having a receipt, instead of asking in a more normal manner whether he had a receipt. Then, even though Koepnick told Lessard and Pollack in response to their accusations that he did have a receipt, he was ordered under arrest for shoplifting without further discussion or inquiry (4R.T. at 178-81). These facts clearly could support a reasonable conclusion that Sears employees had the required "evil mind" in making their initial decision to detain Koepnick without adequate investigation or proper inquiry concerning whether he in fact had the receipts they should be seeking.

. . . .

C. The Evidence Supporting Koepnick's Punitive Damages with Respect to His Trespass to Chattel Claim Was Sufficient to Submit That Issue to the Jury as Well.

. . . .

CONCLUSION

For all the foregoing reasons, the trial court properly denied Sears' motions for judgment notwithstanding the verdict as to Koepnick's claim for false arrest claim, for punitive damages with respect to the false arrest, and for punitive damages with respect to Koepnick's trespass to chattels claim. The trial court's rulings concerning the issues properly before this Court should therefore be affirmed.

DATED this _____ day of May, 1987.

Respectfully submitted,

THOMAS J. QUARELLI, ESQ.
WILLIAM J. MONAHAN, P.C.

By _____
William J. Monahan

and

PAUL G. ULRICH, P.C.

By _____
Paul G. Ulrich
Attorneys for Appellant
Cross-Appellee

Fred Cole
Roger W. Perry
Gust, Rosenfeld, Divelbess & Henderson
3300 Valley Bank Center
Phoenix, Arizona 85073

Attorneys for Defendant-Appellee/Cross-Appellant

IN THE COURT OF APPEALS
STATE OF ARIZONA
DIVISION ONE

MAX KOEPNICK, 　　　Plaintiff-Appellant 　　　Cross-Appellee, 　　v. SEARS, ROEBUCK & COMPANY, 　　　Defendant-Appellee 　　　Cross-Appellant.	1 CA-CIV 9147 MARICOPA County Superior Court No. C-502081

APPELLEE'S REPLY BRIEF ON CROSS-APPEAL

TABLE OF CONTENTS

TABLE OF AUTHORITIES

ARGUMENT

I. SEARS IS ENTITLED TO JUDGMENT NOTWITHSTANDING THE VERDICT ON THE FALSE ARREST CLAIM.

Koepnick fails to demonstrate any valid issue of fact that would preclude the granting of judgment in favor of Sears on the false arrest count. All four of the necessary elements for a privileged detention under A.R.S. § 13-1805 C are undisputedly established in the record. On the element of reasonable cause, the trial court, after hearing all the evidence, determined that reasonable cause existed for Koepnick's detention. This ruling was a proper exercise of the trial court's discretion and is fully justified by the evidence. There is no basis for this court to reverse the trial court's determination on this issue. To avoid duplication, Sears incorporates all its proper arguments on this issue by this reference.

The evidence also undisputedly establishes a proper purpose for Koepnick's detention pursuant to the statute. It is uncontroverted that Sears detained Koepnick to summon the Mesa police concerning the suspected shoplifting. Indeed, Koepnick never made any claim or offered any jury instruction with respect to some other purpose for his detention by Sears. For Koepnick to now make the bald, totally unsupported statement in his response brief that "He was not necessarily detained for that purpose" is ridiculous (Cross-appeal answering brief, p. 5). Koepnick does not even suggest any other purpose in support of this statement. As for the period of time after the police arrived, the evidence is also undisputed that Koepnick was legitimately in the Mesa police department's custody, not Sears. Probable cause existed for the police to detain Koepnick during this period, and Sears had no control over whether or how Koepnick was kept in detention by the police.

There is also no dispute concerning the reasonableness of the length of time Sears detained Koepnick. Koepnick concedes that the length of his detention in Sears' custody until the police arrived and investigated was reasonable (Cross-appeal answering brief, p. 6). As stated above, from that point on, Koepnick was in the Mesa police department's custody, not Sears. Koepnick was under arrest for his altercation with Officer Campbell. Prior to trial, the trial court ruled that probable cause existed for the Mesa police department's detention of Koepnick during that period for the alleged assault on Officer Campbell. (*See* Minute entry dated January 9, 1986.) Koepnick has never raised any issue or objection with respect to that ruling.

Although Koepnick repeatedly states that Steve Lessard "requested" his continued detention by the Mesa police department during this period, such statements have no support in the record. Koepnick fails even to cite to the record when making such assertions of "fact." (*See,* e.g., cross-appeal answering brief, p. 6.) The uncontroverted evidence is that Lessard simply told the police the information and knowledge he had in his possession (4R.T. at 105-06). This information included the fact that the bag Jeff Ward stated he had wrapped the wrench in before placing it in the larger shopping bag was missing (4R.T. at 104-05). Contrary to Koepnick's statements in his briefs, that bag was never accounted for in the security office (4R.T. at 104-05). It was the police officers who made the decision to search Koepnick's truck (6R.T. at 128). Lessard had no control over whether Koepnick was detained or released by the police during that period (8R.T. at 59-60).

Finally, the element of the reasonableness of the manner of Sears' detention of Koepnick is also undisputedly established by the record. Koepnick's arguments in trying to explain why Sears' detention of him should be viewed as unreasonable are nothing less than frivolous. Koepnick's first argument revolves around the fact that, according to Koepnick's testimony, Lessard approached him and said, "You don't have a receipt, do you?" rather than asking to see his receipt. Even accepting all of Koepnick's testimony as true, as we must on this appeal, there is still no evidence of any abusive conduct that would rise to the level of a tortiously unreasonable specific manner of detention. If the court were to accept Koepnick's argument, potential liability would exist any time a subject stopped pursuant to A.R.S. § 13-1805 did not like the manner in which he was addressed. It is inconceivable that the legislature intended such a result when referring to a "reasonable manner" of detention in A.R.S. § 13-1805 C. Much more substantial conduct is required for liability to exist for false arrest.

Koepnick further argues that the manner of his detention was unreasonable in that he should have been questioned by Sears. A.R.S. § 13-1805 C, however, indicates that store personnel are not required to question a subject; they can simply detain for the purpose of summoning a law enforcement officer to handle the investigation.

Finally, Koepnick stretches so far as to attempt to attribute the injuries he received in his altercation with Officer Campbell in the hallway to the fact that the Sears employees declined to give him a drink of water. Koepnick's need for such a nonsensical argument makes readily apparent the total lack of any factual basis for any claim that Sears detained Koepnick unreasonably. The undisputed facts show that Koepnick was simply stopped outside the store and then taken to the security office to await the arrival of the police. According to even Koepnick's testimony, he was not physically or verbally abused by the Sears employees. As such, there is no evidence that would warrant submitting this issue to the jury.

As all the elements for a privileged detention under A.R.S. § 13-1805 C are undisputedly established in the record, Sears is entitled to have judgment entered in its favor on the false arrest claim.

II. SEARS IS ENTITLED TO JUDGMENT NOTWITHSTANDING THE VERDICTS ON THE PUNITIVE DAMAGE CLAIMS.

As Koepnick acknowledges in citing *Filasky v. Preferred Risk Mutual Insurance Co.*, 152 Ariz. 591, 734 P.2d 76 (1987), and *Gurule v. Illinois Mutual Life and Casualty Co.*, 152 Ariz. 600, 734 P.2d 85 (1987) (en banc), a punitive damage award will only be sustained on appeal when there is reasonable evidence to support it. In discussing the nature of an act necessary to permit punitive damages, the Arizona Supreme Court observed that "[p]unishment is an appropriate objective in a civil case only if the defendant's conduct or motive involves 'some element of outrage similar to that usually found in a crime.' " *Gurule,* 734 P.2d at 86 (quoting *Rawlings v. Apodaca,* 151 Ariz. 149, 162, 726 P.2d 565, 578 (1986)). Where a trial court submits the issue of punitive damages to the jury on slight and inconclusive evidence of such conduct, an appellate court may correct the error. *Filasky,* 734 P.2d at 84. In both *Filasky* and *Gurule,* the Supreme Court found that the evidence did not measure up to the requisite standard and reversed the awards of punitive damages. The same conclusion should be reached in this appeal.

A. The False Arrest Claim.

Koepnick attempts to support the punitive damage award on the false arrest claim based on alleged "deficiencies" in the initial investigation and Lessard's alleged "request" that the Mesa police officers continue to detain Koepnick while his truck was searched. Both of these arguments ignore the uncontroverted facts in the record and fail to demonstrate a level of conduct sufficient to justify an award of punitive damages. First, Koepnick's assertion that the investigation by Lessard was inadequate and unreasonable is belied by the trial court's ultimate determination that reasonable cause existed for Sears' detention of Koepnick. Inherent in the trial court's ruling that reasonable cause existed for Koepnick's detention is the determination that the pre-stop investigation conducted by Lessard was reasonable. If the facts and investigation relied on by Sears were unreasonable, reasonable cause could not exist for the detention. It would be completely illogical for the same evidence that the trial court found to establish reasonable cause for the detention to also be deemed sufficient to support an award of punitive damages for the same detention.

. . . .

B. The Trespass to Chattel Claim.

. . . .

CONCLUSION

The trial court properly granted Sears' judgment notwithstanding the verdict on the claim of trespass to chattel. The trial court erred, however, in not doing the same on the claim of false arrest. There are no issues of fact present to justify submitting this claim to the jury. This court should therefore reverse the trial court's ruling that denied Sears' motion for judgment N.O.V. on this count.

Furthermore, there was no evidence to justify the submission of the claims for punitive damages on either of the two counts submitted to the jury. Thus, regardless of the ultimate decisions on the trespass to chattel and false arrest counts, Sears is entitled to have the trial court instructed to grant it judgment N.O.V. on the punitive damage claims.

Respectfully submitted this 8th day of June, 1987.

GUST, ROSENFELD, DIVELBESS & HENDERSON

_____

By
Fred Cole
Roger W. Perry
Attorneys for Defendant-Appellee/Cross-Appellant

Part IX

Writing to Parties: Contracts

and Correspondence

Parts V through VIII examined advocacy to a court and written communication between members of a law firm. As a practicing attorney, however, you will communicate not only with judges and other attorneys but also with your clients and other parties.

For example, you may draft a written contract that the parties adopt as the final and complete expression of their negotiated agreement. If your client later complains that the other party has breached the contract, you may draft an "advice letter" to your client, advising her of her legal rights and recommending certain action. Depending on your client's assessment of her options, you might then send a "demand letter" to the opposing party, demanding that he take certain action to satisfy your client's claims.

Part IX examines contracts and letters as examples of drafting directed to parties. It does not proceed on the premise that your immediate audience will invariably be the parties themselves. On the contrary, if you know that the opposing party is represented by counsel, you will ordinarily address your contract proposal or your demand letter to the opposing counsel. Similarly, if you or your law firm is the outside counsel for a corporation, you may address your advice letter to the corporation's in-house counsel. Nonetheless, more so than with office memoranda and briefs, contracts and letters are directed ultimately to the parties themselves.

Contracts and letters may be useful at various stages of litigation. For example, a contract may precede a dispute, or it may express the parties' agreement to settle a dispute that has already proceeded through pretrial, trial, or even appellate litigation. Similarly, although you will often draft advice and demand letters at the earliest stages of litigation, you may use them at any stage of the litigation that raises new questions or that creates a new opportunity to state your demands.

Chapter 23

Contracts

I. BASIC APPROACHES

With some limitations, parties can privately shape their legal rights and obligations by exchanging enforceable promises in a contract. Each party's promises impose contractual duties on that party and create contractual rights in the other.

The authors of one contracts casebook believe that the contractual promise is the greatest human invention, even greater than the wheel, the lever, and the pulley:

> [F]or it is the promise that breaks the ultimate physical restraint. It permits us to live a bit of the future today. When two or more employ the tool of promise in concert, they create a unique social engine—the *bargain*.[1]

Although this claim may provoke some debate about the relative merits of the promise and the pulley, none will dispute that enforceable contracts are indispensable to modern commerce.

---

1. Daniel W. Fessler & Pierre R. Loiseaux, CONTRACTS, MORALITY, ECONOMICS AND THE MARKETPLACE (CASES AND MATERIALS) 1 (1982).

As with pleadings, you can readily find forms for contracts in a formbook or in a dusty file cabinet of a law office. However, many such forms are as antiquated as the parody of a contract presented in Exercise 13-1 near the beginning of Chapter 13. You will produce a much better contract if you throw away the outdated forms, understand the purposes of each section of a contract, and express the agreement of the parties in plain, simple, clear English.

On the other hand, you need not reinvent the wheel with every contract. Some law firms produce high-quality form contracts for common transactions that require similar provisions. For example, some firms have created and maintain a series of provisions for real estate contracts on computer files. An attorney assigned to a real estate transaction can (1) leaf through a hard copy of the available provisions, (2) select the paragraphs that are best suited to the current transaction, (3) use a word processor to create a document with the selected paragraphs, and (4) tailor the document to the particular facts and requirements of the current transaction. Such a system can be highly successful if its users ensure that the forms are well written and if they avoid complacency in tailoring the forms to particular transactions.

For contracts that do not lend themselves to a computerized form system, you should feel comfortable drafting "from scratch" without reliance on an antiquated form. You can draft with confidence if you understand the fundamental components of a contract.

II. FUNDAMENTAL COMPONENTS

A. General Format

A written contract should always contain the following provisions:

1. an introduction identifying the parties to the transaction,
2. a section describing the rights and obligations of the parties, and
3. signature lines showing the parties' agreement to the terms of the contract.

A contract may also include:

1. a statement of "recitals," which describes the background of the transaction and the parties' reasons for entering into the contract,
2. a glossary of defined terms, or
3. a section of miscellaneous provisions addressing such topics as termination or modification of the contract, the relationship of the contract to other transactions, or choice of law or forum in the event of a dispute.

B. Introduction to the Contract

In the first lines after the title of a contract, you should identify the parties as simply and clearly as possible. If more than two parties join in the transaction, or if at least one of the parties is a complex entity, you should set the parties' names apart from each other on the page.

For example, you can start with a descriptive section heading and use paragraphing to separate the parties' names:

I. PARTIES

The parties to this contract for the purchase and sale of sand are:

1. SOONER SAND CO., a general partnership consisting of Harley T. Price and W. M. McMichael, general partners, and

2. BASSI DISTRIBUTING CO., a joint venture of Bassi Trucking Co. and Hardcore Rock & Gravel, Inc.

If you use this format for the introduction, you can refer to the parties throughout the contract by the formal names of their business entities: SOONER SAND CO. and BASSI DISTRIBUTING CO. Alternatively, you can assign descriptive labels to the parties, such as Seller and Buyer:

---

1. Sooner Sand Co. ("Seller"), a general . . . .

2. Bassi Distributing Co. ("Buyer"), a joint . . . .

Many drafters also like to assign a label to the contract itself and to include the date of the agreement in the introductory sentence:

This contract for the purchase and sale of sand (the "Agreement") is entered into on May 1, 2002, by the following parties:

C. Recitals

Although not essential to an enforceable contract, a statement of the factual background of the transaction can help a neutral party interpret the contract if the parties dispute its meaning. Such recitals can even help establish consideration for the contract by showing the parties' reciprocal inducements or by providing a basis for implying obligations. For example, in the celebrated contracts case *Wood v. Lucy, Lady Duff-Gordon*,[2] Justice Cardozo of the New York Court of Appeals relied partly on the recitals of a written contract to imply an obligation by an exclusive agent to use reasonable efforts, thus satisfying the consideration requirement.

Recitals in an outdated contract are easy enough to spot. Each recital of a background fact appears in a clause beginning with the word "Whereas"

---

2. 118 N.E. 214 (N.Y. 1917).

and is strung together with other recitals in a single, unmanageably long run-on sentence. To provide better guidance to your reader, you should (1) introduce the recitals with a section heading, such as "Recitals" or "Background" and (2) state your recitals in conventional sentences within numbered paragraphs:

II. RECITALS

1. Seller is engaged in the business of selling and shipping sand from Phoenix to various customers in the State of Arizona but has not developed markets outside of Arizona. Seller desires to supply sand wholesale to a distributor with customers outside the state.
2. Buyer has an established business . . . .

When used in a traditional manner, recitals state only the background of the transaction and the motivations of the parties, not the actual obligations that the parties have assumed by their agreement and have stated with special precision in a different section of the written contract. Drafters of some contracts, however, have expressly incorporated their "Recitals" section into their statement of mutual rights and obligations, either by reference or by making it a subsection of a portion of the contract devoted to mutual promises. In doing so, the drafter hopes to legally bind the parties to the recitals, making the recitals the equivalent of warranties of the stated facts.

D. Statement of Reciprocal Promises

The heart of any contract is the parties' statement of their reciprocal promises. Those promises define the parties' mutual rights and obligations, which form the consideration for the agreement.

1. INTRODUCTORY CLAUSE; RECITAL OF CONSIDERATION

Perhaps in an excess of caution, many drafters still begin their statements of reciprocal promises with outdated recitals of consideration such as the following:

NOW, THEREFORE, in consideration of the mutual covenants herein contained, and other good and valuable consideration the receipt of which is hereby acknowledged, the parties hereby agree . . . .

Aside from displaying an antiquated writing style, such passages fail to establish consideration in many jurisdictions. In many states, expressing a promise in a signed writing raises a presumption of consideration,[3] but a

---

3. *See* E. Allan Farnsworth, William F. Young & Carol Sanger, Cases and Materials on Contracts 114 (6th ed. 2001) (citing to Cal. Civ. Code § 1614 (West 2001) as typical statute).

recital of consideration has no additional legal effect.[4] In most transactions, moreover, the reference to "the receipt" of "other . . . consideration" is simply false. Instead, the consideration in a typical contract consists of the parties' mutual promises, exchanged for one another with reciprocal induce- ment, in what is sometimes called a "bargained-for exchange." Rather than pompously recite the existence of consideration, you should simply state the mutual promises under a descriptive section heading and a simple introduc- tory clause that refers to the promises as "mutual," "reciprocal," or other- wise part of a "bargained-for exchange":

III. MUTUAL RIGHTS AND OBLIGATIONS

Seller and Buyer agree to the following exchange of reciprocal promises:

1. *Supply.* For a period of five years from the date of formation of this contract, Seller will supply Buyer with all the sand that Buyer requires . . . .

2. *Delivery.* . . .

3. *Quality.* . . .

4. *Price.* For each ton of sand delivered, Buyer will pay Seller a sum equal to. . . .

Some drafters are tempted to begin each statement of an obligation with a phrase such as "Seller promises to supply" or "Seller agrees to supply." The reference to "promises" or "agrees," however, is unnecessary. If you begin your section with an appropriate heading, such as "Mutual Rights and Obligations" or "Mutual Promises," and if you follow immediately with an umbrella statement such as "Seller and Buyer agree to the following bargained-for exchange:," you need not repeatedly invoke the word "agree" in each statement of a promise. Moreover, to state a promise, you need not use the word "promise." If preceded by the appropriate section heading and umbrella statement, words such as "will" and "must" in the statements of obligation will appropriately convey a party's intent to commit herself to a future performance.

Some may object that the word "will" does not adequately express an obligation but instead expresses only a prediction about a person's actions or a description of someone's intentions to perform an action. That could be true in the context of a factual description in the recitals of a contract or in a statement of facts in a brief or memorandum. For example, the word "will" is not reassuring if used in a memorandum's statement of fact to assert as a factual matter that "the Bank will approve the loan application in its present form." Is the writer simply expressing his confidence or predic- tion that the loan application is so attractive that the bank will not reject it? In such a context, the writer more precisely states his meaning by writing "the Bank is obligated under the K.Y. Construction Agreement to approve the loan application in its present form," or "the chief loan officer has stated in a recent letter that the Bank will approve the loan application," if the facts support either assertion. Nonetheless, the word "will" is perfectly

---

4. *See* John D. Calamari & Joseph M. Perillo, The Law of Contracts § 4.6 at 177 n.3 & accompanying text (4th ed. 1998).

sufficient to state the Bank's obligation in the K.Y. Construction Agreement, if coupled with headings or umbrella statements that convey the Bank's promises to take certain actions:

IV. MUTUAL RIGHTS AND OBLIGATIONS

The parties agree to the following exchange of mutual promises:

1. Bank will approve a construction loan application submitted by Contractor, if the application satisfies the following requirements: . . . .

---

2. PRECISION IN DRAFTING

a. Simplicity; Terms of Art

The terms of the exchange are a matter of negotiation between the parties. If you represent your client in the negotiations, you can participate in shaping the substance of the bargain. As part of that process, you may draft proposed contract provisions to serve as offers or counteroffers to the other party. In other cases, your client may ask you to prepare a formal written document expressing a bargain that the parties have previously negotiated. In either case, one of your primary tasks as drafter of the final document is to express the parties' negotiated rights and obligations as precisely as possible to reduce the risk of misunderstanding and costly disputes during performance of the contract.

To draft precisely, you should take advantage of helpful terms of art but avoid unnecessary jargon. For example, the provisions below refer to the buyer's "requirements," a legal term of art that has special meaning and legal consequences under the Uniform Commercial Code.[5] Otherwise, however, the provisions contain plain, simple English:

---

1. *Supply.* For a period of five years from the date of formation of this contract, Seller will supply Buyer with all the sand that Buyer requires for Buyer's business of selling and shipping sand to customers outside the State of Arizona.

2. *Delivery.* Buyer may order sand as Buyer's requirements arise by sending a written purchase order to Seller. . . .

Some legal terms are not necessarily terms of art but may be generally helpful and inoffensive. In the following passage, for example, the seller makes a special kind of promise by "warranting" the quality of the goods:

---

3. *Quality.* Seller warrants that the quality of the sand that is delivered to Buyer will be at least equal to that of sand of corresponding grades sold by other sand companies in the City of Phoenix, Arizona.

---

5. U.C.C. § 2-306(1) (2000).

The word "warrants" in this passage is not a necessary term of art under the Uniform Commercial Code. The seller would assume the same legal obligation by simply promising that

---

Seller will deliver to Buyer sand of a quality that is at least equal . . . .[6]

Nonetheless, drafters typically and reasonably use the term "warrants" or "warranty" to draw attention to the special nature of a promise that goods or services will meet certain standards.

Similarly, many drafters use special phrases to draw attention to statements of "conditions," which qualify or limit contractual duties. In a standard insurance contract, for example, the insured will assume an absolute obligation to pay premiums to the insurer, but the insurer will pay money to the insured only if the insured suffers a loss of the type covered by the insurance contract. You could introduce the insurer's conditional promise with the simple word "if":

If the insured suffers a covered loss as defined in section VI above, the insurer will reimburse the insured for . . . .

Many insurers, however, like to emphasize the conditional nature of their promises with special phrases, such as "on the condition that" or "in the event that":

In the event that the insured suffers a covered loss as defined in section V above, the insurer . . . .

---

b. Deliberate Imprecision

Occasionally, precision is neither feasible nor desirable. In some cases, for example, the parties may have failed to reach precise agreement on some difficult issue, even though they are ready to go forward with their general transaction. If so, you may be forced to express their imperfect agreement on the difficult issue in terms that are sufficiently imprecise to encompass the range of interpretations that describe their divergent positions.

For example, the buyer of factory equipment may demand during negotiations that the seller agree to repair or replace defective parts within 10 days after receiving notice of the defect. The seller might counteroffer to repair or replace defective parts within 45 days after receiving notice of the defect. If the parties cannot agree on a time period measured by a specific number of days, they might instead agree on the vague language "within a reasonable time in light of all the circumstances," realizing that they might not share the same interpretation of that language in particular applications.

Language such as this may save the deal if negotiations are stalled on

---

6. *See* U.C.C. § 2-313(1)(a), (2) (2000).

the sticky point. Moreover, if performance of the contract proceeds smoothly, the parties may never test their divergent interpretations of the language. On the other hand, if adverse circumstances place a strain on performance, the lack of perfect agreement on the precise meaning of the provision may erupt into a serious dispute. Thus, during the negotiation of such a deal, you must help your client weigh the benefits of reaching general agreement against the risks of subsequent disputes over the meaning of vague language.

3. MERGER CLAUSES AND PAROL EVIDENCE

As an example of a typical miscellaneous provision, a "merger clause" states that the written contract is the exclusive statement of the parties' agreement. If the other party subsequently asserts that the total agreement includes rights and obligations not expressed in the written contract, you can refer to the merger clause and seek to exclude evidence of the alleged unwritten obligations under the "parol evidence rule."

A typical merger clause refers only generally to the subject matter of the agreement:

XXV. *Prior Agreements Superseded*—This written contract constitutes the parties' complete and exclusive statement of their agreement on the subject matter covered by this contract, and it supersedes all previous agreements, promises, or representations regarding that subject matter.

Unfortunately, such a clause does not eliminate the risk of litigation of a common question under the parol evidence rule: Does an alleged additional agreement address topics within the subject matter of the main written contract so that the main contract supersedes it, or does the additional agreement address unrelated topics so that it can stand separately as an independent, enforceable contract?[7]

For example, suppose that on July 1 the parties signed a written contract for the lease of empty restaurant space. The lessee later asserted that the lessor also orally agreed on June 28 to sell dining tables and chairs to the lessee at the spectaculary low price of $450. The lessor denies the oral agreement. He also points to the merger clause and argues that, assuming he did tentatively agree on June 28 to sell the dining furniture, such an agreement was simply part of continuing negotiations that the parties abandoned and superseded in their July 1 agreement.

However, to successfully invoke the merger clause to exclude evidence of the oral agreement, the lessor must demonstrate that the alleged agreement to sell dining furniture falls within the subject matter of the July 1 contract; otherwise, the alleged June 28 agreement can stand outside the field occupied exclusively by the July 1 contract. Unfortunately, the merger clause cannot help the lessor much because it fails to define the subject matter of the contract.

If you intend a written contract to broadly supersede prior agreements

---

7. *See, e.g.,* Gianni v. R. Russell & Co., Inc., 126 A. 791 (Pa. 1924).

or promises on related transactions, you must describe the subject matter of your contract expansively so that the merger clause can have the intended effect. If you anticipate particular problems stemming from failed negotiations on collateral matters, you can address those matters explicitly:

XXV. *Prior Agreements Superseded*—This written contract constitutes the parties' complete and exclusive statement of their agreement on all matters relating to the lease of the Scottsdale premises, the operation of a restaurant on those premises, and the furnishings and equipment needed for the operation. This contract supersedes all previous or contemporaneous agreements, promises, or representations regarding that subject matter.

This merger clause expresses the parties' intent to abandon any prior agreement for the sale of restaurant furnishings or equipment and to replace it with the terms of the lease agreement.

E. Signature Lines

You may end your contract with any reasonable means of presenting the parties' signatures as evidence of their agreement to the terms of the contract. You do not need to invoke formalistic jargon such as:

In witness whereof, the said parties have hereunto set their hands and seals the day and year first above written.

Instead, you may simply precede the signature lines with the single word "Signed." At most, you might introduce the signatures with a clause such as "The undersigned parties agree to these terms."

If you have not already dated the contract at the beginning, you can include a space for the date next to each party's signature. The latest date on a signature line will correspond to one party's acceptance of the other party's offer and will mark the date of contract formation.

III. SUMMARY

To draft a simple contract, you should

1. identify the parties in an introductory provision,
2. recite the background facts, if helpful,
3. state the reciprocal promises of the parties as precisely as possible, and
4. provide signature lines as a means for the parties to express their assent to the terms of the contract.

Exercise 23-1

1. SAMPLE REQUIREMENTS CONTRACT

Study the following contract. Compare it with the antiquated version presented in Exercise 13-1, near the beginning of Chapter 13, and with your revision of that contract.

REQUIREMENTS CONTRACT

I. PARTIES

The parties to this contract for the purchase and sale of sand are:

1. Sooner Sand Co. ("Seller"), a general partnership consisting of the general partners Harley T. Price and W. M. McMichael, and

2. Bassi Distributing Co. ("Buyer"), a joint venture of Bassi Trucking Co. and Hardcore Rock & Gravel, Inc.

II. RECITALS

1. Seller is engaged in the business of selling and shipping sand from Phoenix to various customers in the State of Arizona but has not developed markets outside of Arizona. Seller desires to supply sand wholesale to a distributor with customers outside the state.

2. Buyer has an established business in Phoenix selling and shipping sand to various customers in several states outside Arizona, including California, Nevada, Utah, and Colorado. Buyer desires a stable source of supply of sand for that business.

III. MUTUAL RIGHTS AND OBLIGATIONS

Seller and Buyer agree to the following bargained-for exchange:

1. *Supply.* For a period of five years from the date of formation of this contract, Seller will supply Buyer with all the sand that Buyer requires for Buyer's business of selling and shipping sand to customers outside the State of Arizona.

2. *Delivery.* Buyer will order sand as Buyer's requirements arise by sending a written purchase order to Seller. On receipt of such a purchase order, Seller will deliver the ordered sand within ten days to Buyer's facility at 1531 Range Road in Glendale, Arizona.

3. *Quality.* Seller warrants that the quality of the sand that is delivered to Buyer will be at least equal to that of sand of corresponding grades sold by other sand companies in the City of Phoenix, Arizona.

4. *Price.* For each ton of sand delivered, Buyer will pay Seller a sum

equal to sixty percent (60%) of the market price per ton of concrete in the City of Phoenix at the time of Seller's delivery to Buyer.

5. *Term of Payment.* Seller may give an invoice to Buyer for sand on or after Seller delivers the sand to Buyer. Buyer will pay the full amount of such an invoice within thirty (30) days of its receipt of the invoice.

Signed:

_____   _____
SELLER—Authorized Agent for Sooner Sand Co.   Date

_____   _____
BUYER—Authorized Agent for Bassi Distributing Co.   Date

2. FORMAT FOR MORE COMPLEX AGREEMENT

a. Compare the following outline of a sample contract with the sample contract in Problem 1 above. The sample below displays an alternative introductory section, and it contemplates more complex provisions that must be subdivided into more numerous subsections.

b. In section 4.2 of the contract, draft a merger clause that identifies your document as the complete and exclusive statement of the parties' agreement. In particular, be certain to supersede prior failed negotiations in which Seller proposed to lease trucks to Buyer for the transportation of the sand to other states.

REQUIREMENTS CONTRACT

This contract for the purchase and sale of sand (the Agreement) is entered into on _____ by the following parties:

1. Seller—Sooner Sand Co., a general partnership consisting of Harley T. Price and W. M. McMichael, general partners, and

2. Buyer—Bassi Distributing Co., a joint venture of Bassi Trucking Co. and Hardcore Rock & Gravel, Inc.

RECITALS

1. Seller is engaged . . . .
2. Buyer has an established . . . .

MUTUAL RIGHTS AND OBLIGATIONS

Seller and Buyer agree to the following bargained-for exchange:

ARTICLE I
Definitions

1.1 *Grades of sand—* . . . .
1.2 *Market price—* . . . .

ARTICLE II
Supply of Sand

2.1 *Quantity—* . . . .
2.2 *Quality—* . . . .
2.3 *Delivery—* . . . .

ARTICLE III
Payment

3.1 *Price—* . . . .
3.2 *Terms of Payment—* . . . .

ARTICLE IV
Miscellaneous Provisions

4.1 *No Oral Modification—* . . . .
4.2 *Prior Negotiations Superseded—* . . . .
4.3 *Mandatory Arbitration of Disputes—* . . . .

SIGNED

_____

_____

Chapter 24

Advice Letters

As counselor and advocate, you will draft many kinds of letters to your client or to others on your client's behalf. Two of the most important are advice letters and demand letters. These letters are closely related to two kinds of documents examined in previous chapters: office memoranda and briefs. Like an office memorandum, an advice letter communicates a balanced legal analysis of a dispute or proposed action. In contrast, like a brief, a demand letter advocates a position, and it usually requests the addressee to take specific action. This chapter examines advice letters; Chapter 25 examines demand letters.[1]

I. ADVICE LETTERS DISTINGUISHED FROM OPINION LETTERS

Many attorneys and commentators use the term "opinion letter" to refer to any letter addressed to a client that offers a legal analysis, opinion, or

---

1. Many of the ideas in Chapters 24 and 25 are taken with permission from lecture materials prepared by Frank M. Placenti and Mark Hileman, shortly before submission of the first edition of this book in 1989, when they worked for the Phoenix law firm Streich, Lang, Weeks & Cardon, P.A., which has since merged with the law firm of Quarles & Brady.

recommendation. Within this general class of letters, however, are two important subcategories, each of which warrants a narrowly descriptive label. The term "opinion letter" best describes only a small subcategory of letters in which you will provide your clients formal opinions on certain kinds of legal questions. The term "advice letter" accurately describes the far more common kind of letter in which you will more generally analyze a legal problem and advise your client about the relative merits of alternative courses of action.

More specifically, an opinion letter is a highly specialized and formal document that expresses your opinion or that of your law firm that a specified act is legally valid. For example, you might issue to a corporate client your formal opinion that the corporation has validly issued certain stock under applicable laws and under the articles and bylaws of the corporation. Because the client will significantly rely on such an opinion, the standards for an opinion letter are high, and its format is fairly rigid.

In contrast, in an advice letter, you will communicate your analysis of a legal problem to a client in much the same way that you would use an office memorandum to communicate the analysis to a supervising attorney. Even if you cannot definitively resolve the legal issues in the analysis, you can evaluate the relative merits of the parties' claims and defenses and estimate the probability of success on the merits. You can thus provide your client with valuable advice short of giving a definite opinion of the legality of certain actions.

In many law firms, only designated attorneys are authorized to issue formal opinion letters on behalf of the firm. Moreover, those attorneys tend to follow carefully developed forms when drafting their opinion letters, leaving little room for flexibility in format or creativity in analysis. Further examination of opinion letters is beyond the scope of this book. Instead, this chapter will explore the more common advice letter.

II. PURPOSE, AUDIENCE, AND WRITING STYLE

The writing style that you adopt for a document is partly a function of your intended audience and the purpose of your document. When you draft an office memorandum, you can easily identify your audience and purpose: You will communicate a balanced legal analysis to an experienced attorney. When you draft an advice letter, however, your audience and purpose may be less clear.

For example, the legal experience and general sophistication of your audience may vary greatly from one letter to the next. One client may be new to his business, have no legal training, and have learned English only after recently arriving from a foreign country. Another client may be a sophisticated, experienced businessperson with at least a rudimentary knowledge of the laws that affect her business. Still another client may be a corporation with an in-house counsel to whom you will direct your advice letter. Obviously, you should adapt your writing style to suit the experience and legal training of your audience. In a letter to the legally inexperienced client described above, you should take particular care to use plain, simple English and to avoid or explain even rudimentary legal terms. In letters to other, more experienced and legally knowledgeable clients, you can safely use more sophisticated language and legal terminology. In each case, however, your goal is the same: to communicate, not to impress.

In some cases, your client may wish to share your advice letter with customers, partners, or other attorneys. If so, you should draft the letter with the needs of the secondary audience in mind. For example, if your law firm's client is a corporate manager, she may intend to discuss your advice letter with the corporation's separate, in-house counsel. If so, you may want to provide a full explanation of your underlying legal analysis or even attach a copy of the formal office memorandum on which the advice letter is based.

III. FORMAT

You should flexibly adopt any format that suits your audience and the purpose of your advice letter. As a starting point, you can follow the basic elements of a reasonable format for an office memorandum:

Issues
Brief Answers
Facts
Discussion
Conclusion

With this format, your advice letter would

1. restate the questions that your client posed to you,
2. briefly summarize your conclusions,
3. state the facts on which your analysis is based,
4. summarize your analysis of the law and the facts, and
5. state your conclusions and your strategic recommendations.

If your advice letter is simple and brief, you need not use formal section headings to display the transitions between elements of your format. Instead, you can simply use sensible paragraphing to lead the reader from one element to the next.

On the other hand, if your letter is long and complex, you should use section headings, just as you would in an office memorandum or a brief. You need not use precisely the same format headings as you would for an office memorandum. One attorney used the following primary headings in an advice letter to introduce the issues, brief answers, facts, discussion, and conclusion:

Issues Addressed
Executive Summary of Conclusions
Background
Analysis (divided into subsections)
Recommendations

IV. INTRODUCTION AND STATEMENT OF ISSUES

Immediately after the address and before the salutation of your advice letter, you should concisely state the general subject matter of the letter:

Clay Franks
Vice-President, Construction
GRT Developers
1212 Central Ave, Suite 2201
Boomtown, Calzona 81717

RE: TRI Corp.'s possible breach of contract on the Westcourt project.

Dear Mr. Franks,

Then, in the first paragraph after the salutation, you should refer to your client's inquiry on this subject matter and state the issues that your letter addresses.

In some cases, your client will pose a general question that asks for strategic advice rather than legal conclusions: "Should we fire TRI and sue it for breach of contract?" If so, you may want to inform your client of the legal issues on which your strategic advice will depend:

Dear Mr. Franks,

You have asked us to advise you whether you should fire TRI from the Westcourt project and sue it for breach of contract. In formulating our advice on this matter, we have analyzed the following questions:

(1) Did TRI breach the construction contract by using Cohoes pipe rather than the Reading pipe called for in the architect's plans?

(2) If so, was TRI's breach "material," thus permitting you to cancel the construction contract and fire TRI from the project?

(3) If TRI has breached the contract, to what remedies is GRT entitled?

If you decide to introduce the primary parts of your letter with formal section headings, you could begin with "Issues":

Dear Mr. Franks,

You have asked us to advise you whether you should fire TRI from the Westcourt project and sue it for breach of contract.

I. Issues

In formulating our advice on this matter, we have analyzed the following questions:

A. Did TRI breach the construction contract by using Cohoes pipe rather than the Reading pipe called for in the architect's plans?

B. If so, was TRI's breach "material," thus . . . .

C. If TRI has breached . . . .

V. BRIEF ANSWERS

Some attorneys will discourage you from summarizing your conclusions in brief answers near the beginning of your advice letter. They fear that your client will fail to appreciate or will even misinterpret your conclusions if he has not read your full analysis first. Like a supervising attorney reading an office memorandum, however, a client reading an advice letter is anxious to reach the bottom line. You should not withhold it from him out of some misplaced concern that he is not ready to face it. Moreover, mindful that he has paid for the entire letter, the client is nearly certain to read beyond the brief answers and to appreciate your full analysis. Thus, unless the letter is very short, or unless exceptional circumstances compel you to lay unusual groundwork before revealing an unfavorable conclusion,[2] you should satisfy your client's curiosity early in the letter.

If you use a simple format without section headings, you may briefly summarize your conclusions in a sentence or two immediately following your statement of the issues in the opening paragraph:

Dear Ms. Price,

You have asked us whether you would be liable for damages if you discharged your head chef in retaliation for his testifying against you in a hearing of the state Food and Beverage Commission. As discussed more fully below, we conclude that such a discharge would not constitute a breach of your employment contract, but it would render you liable under the state tort law of "wrongful discharge."

In a more complex letter, you could state your brief answers under some appropriate heading, such as "Brief Answers" or "Summary of Conclusions":

2. *See* Henry Weihofen, Legal Writing Style 178, 199 (2d ed. 1980).

Dear Mr. Franks,

You have asked us to advise you whether you should fire TRI from the Westcourt project and sue it for breach of contract.

I. Issues

In formulating our advice on this matter, we have analyzed the following questions:

A. Did TRI breach the construction contract by using Cohoes pipe rather than the Reading pipe called for in the architect's plans?

B. If so, was TRI's breach "material," thus permitting you to cancel the construction contract and fire TRI from the project?

C. If TRI has breached the contract, to what remedies is GRT entitled?

II. Summary of Conclusions

A. TRI breached the construction contract, because the architect's plans clearly call for Reading pipe and do not permit substitutes.

B. TRI's breach almost certainly is not material, because Cohoes pipe is nearly identical to Reading pipe in all important specifications. Therefore, you cannot cancel the contract.

C. GRT is entitled to the difference between the value of the Reading pipe and that of the Cohoes pipe, a difference that may be insubstantial.

In addition to providing these answers to the specific legal issues that you have formulated, you might add a sentence to your overview paragraph that summarizes your response to the client's general strategic question:

Dear Mr. Franks,

You have asked us to advise you whether you should fire TRI from the Westcourt project and sue it for breach of contract. In this letter, we summarize our legal analysis and advise you not to fire TRI or withhold its payments.

VI. FACTS

In every advice letter, you should state the facts on which your analysis is based. By making a record of the factual premises of your analysis, you can protect yourself against criticism or liability if subsequently discovered facts render your legal analysis obsolete. Indeed, if your client has supplied you with the facts, you may want to disclaim responsibility for any fact investigation:

III. Facts

The advice in this letter is premised on the following facts, which you have supplied and which we have not yet independently investigated. If the following facts prove to be incomplete or incorrect, you should not rely on the advice in this letter without first consulting us.

VII. LEGAL ANALYSIS

In the body of your letter, you should reach a conclusion on each issue by applying the relevant law to the facts. In a letter to a corporate client's in-house counsel or to a sophisticated client who has some legal knowledge, you can develop your legal analysis and cite to authority in much the same way that you would in an office memorandum. Other clients, however, will have little use for your in-depth analysis of authority. They would rather read a simplified summary of your legal analysis, and they are willing to assume that your underlying research and analysis has been thorough.

Thus, even if you have more fully expressed your analysis in another document, you may want to simplify the discussion in your advice letter. For example, as an initial reaction to a client's inquiry, you often will draft a full office memorandum addressed to a supervising attorney. The memorandum will then serve as a basis for formulating advice to the client. In the advice letter, however, you need not analyze the legal authority with the same depth and formality that you found useful in the memorandum. Instead, you can more simply and briefly convey your analysis of each issue by (1) abstractly summarizing the law with little or no citation to authority, (2) identifying the relevant facts, and (3) stating your conclusion:

> Under state tort law, you are liable for damages if you discharge an employee for a reason that violates public policy. Legislation of this state establishes public policies of maintaining health standards in restaurants and encouraging witnesses to testify fully and truthfully at state administrative hearings. Therefore, if you discharge Chef Boyardi in retaliation for his testifying about violations of hygiene standards in your restaurant, you will be liable for violation of public policy.

In some cases, you can even leave the legal rule implicit by simply stating a conclusion, after identifying the facts on which it is based:

> Your contract with Chef Boyardi does not commit the parties to a definite term of employment, and it does not restrict your right to terminate the contract. Therefore, under state contract law, you can discharge Chef Boyardi at any time and for any reason without breaching the contract.

If your client has some legal training or expects to share your letter with another attorney, you may want to analyze authority to an extent that approaches the depth of analysis in your office memorandum. Alternatively, you can summarize your analysis in the letter and simply attach the office memorandum on which the advice in your letter is based. In this way, the client can rely primarily on the more accessible information in the letter, but he also has access to your more thorough and formal memorandum if the need for it arises.

VIII. CONCLUSION; STRATEGIC RECOMMENDATIONS

In a final paragraph or section of your advice letter, you should summarize your subsidiary conclusions and offer your ultimate advice. If your client's legal rights and obligations are unclear, do not hesitate to convey the uncertainty with words and phrases that permit you to hedge. Even so, you should reach a conclusion, even if only a qualified one:

> **Although the question is a close one, TRI's breach probably is not material. . . .**

Your ultimate advice likely will be strategic, such as a recommendation to file a lawsuit, communicate a settlement offer, or refrain from discharging an employee. If the ultimate decision for the client is essentially a business decision, such as whether to purchase property for development, you should outline the legal consequences of the purchase but leave the actual business decision to the client. On the other hand, if the ultimate decision is more clearly tied to the legal merits of a claim or defense, such as whether to settle a legal dispute, you can more strongly recommend a particular course of action.

Nonetheless, in all cases, you should invite the client to make the final decision. For example, when advising a client to settle, you should recommend a range of settlement offers within which your client can exercise some judgment to choose a particular position or to reject settlement altogether.

IX. SUMMARY

In an advice letter, you should

1. use plain English whenever possible,
2. adapt your format and depth of legal analysis to your audience and your purpose,

3. restate the questions that your client has posed to you and identify the legal issues that they encompass,

4. briefly answer the issues,

5. state the facts on which your analysis and advice are premised,

6. discuss the law and apply the law to the facts to reach a conclusion for each issue, and

7. summarize your subsidiary conclusions and state your advice.

Exercise 24-1

1. ADVICE LETTER WITHOUT SECTION HEADINGS

The following advice letter is addressed to a restaurant owner with no legal training. The author has used only paragraphing to signal the transition from one element of the letter to the next, and he has not cited to authority.

a. Identify the purpose or purposes of each paragraph in the letter.

b. Research the problem and rewrite the letter so that it conveys additional information to a client with legal training. Specifically, cite to authority and briefly analyze the authority. If appropriate, divide the expanded letter into sections with section headings.

August 1, 2002

Leona Price
Hep Crepe Restaurant
123 Washington St.
Spinach Village, New Maine 10307

Dear Ms. Price,

You have asked us whether you would be liable for damages if you discharged your head chef in retaliation for his testifying against you in a hearing of the state Food and Beverage Commission. As discussed more fully below, we conclude that such a discharge would not constitute a breach of your employment contract, but it would render you liable under the state tort law of "wrongful discharge."

Our analysis is premised on the following facts, as you have supplied them. The state Food and Beverage Commission has recently held hearings on violations of state health and hygiene regulations at various restaurants within the Village. The Commission requested your head chef, Anthony Boyardi, to testify at the hearings. Under examination by Commissioners, Chef Boyardi testified that employees have failed to control rat and insect infestations at Hep Crepe, resulting in continuing violations of state regulations. Because you view Chef Boyardi's act of testifying as disloyal conduct, you wish to fire him.

Your contract with Chef Boyardi does not commit the parties to a definite term of employment, and it does not restrict your right to terminate the contract. Therefore, under state contract law, you can discharge Chef Boyardi at any time and for any reason without breaching the contract.

Under state tort law, however, you will be liable for damages if you discharge an employee for a reason that violates public policy, regardless of whether the discharge would constitute a breach of contract. Legislation of this state establishes public policies of maintaining health standards in restaurants and encouraging witnesses to testify fully and truthfully at state administrative hearings. Therefore, if you discharge Chef Boyardi in retaliation for testifying at the administrative hearings, you will be liable for violation of public policy. Your liability may extend to damages designed to compensate Chef Boyardi for his losses and to additional damages designed to punish you for your intentional misconduct.

In conclusion, if you discharge Chef Boyardi in retaliation for his testimony, he will have a valid claim against you for damages. We advise you not to discharge him unless you are prepared to justify the discharge on other grounds.

If you have any questions on this matter, please call me at (898) 123-4567.

Sincerely,

_____

Robert Linzer
for Avila and Celaya, P.C.
222 N. 3d St.
Spinach Village, New Maine 10307

2. ADVICE LETTER WITH SECTION HEADINGS

a. Compare the following letter with the one above. Describe each way in which the letters differ in style and format.

b. Assume in the letter below that your client, Clay Franks, is an Anglo-American with racist tendencies and that the opposing party's representative, Cal Dunlap, is African American. Do those facts affect your analysis of the problem? Does the letter below adequately address the problems potentially caused by your client's racism without unduly offending him? Should you be worried about offending him?

c. The letter below is addressed to a client who has at least a basic knowledge of the law relating to performance and breach of construction contracts. Rewrite the letter so that it is appropriate for a client who has no legal training or knowledge. Specifically, summarize your analysis without citing to specific authority. If appropriate, eliminate the section headings and guide your reader through the simpler letter with good paragraphing and transition sentences.

Marcia Todd
Todd, Brown & King
1212 Central Ave., Suite 401
Boomtown, Calzona 81717
July 5, 2002

Clay Franks
Vice-President, Construction
GRT Developers
1212 Central Ave, Suite 2201
Boomtown, Calzona 81717

RE: TRI Corp.'s possible breach of contract on the Westcourt project.

Dear Mr. Franks,

You have asked us to advise you whether you should fire TRI from the Westcourt project and sue it for breach of contract. In this letter, we summarize our legal analysis and advise you not to fire TRI or withhold its payments.

I. ISSUES

In formulating our advice on this matter, we have analyzed the following questions:

A. Did TRI breach the construction contract by using Cohoes pipe rather than the Reading pipe called for in the architect's plans?

B. If so, was TRI's breach "material," thus permitting you to cancel the construction contract and fire TRI from the project?

C. If TRI has breached the contract, to what remedies is GRT entitled?

II. SUMMARY OF CONCLUSIONS

A. TRI breached the construction contract, because the architect's plans clearly call for Reading pipe and do not permit substitutes.

B. TRI's breach almost certainly is not material, because Cohoes pipe is nearly identical to Reading pipe in all important specifications. Therefore, you cannot cancel the contract.

C. GRT is entitled to the difference between the value of the Reading pipe and that of the Cohoes pipe, a difference that may be insubstantial.

III. FACTS

The advice in this letter is premised on the following facts, which you have supplied. We have not yet independently investigated the facts. If the following facts prove to be incomplete or incorrect, you should not rely on the advice in this letter without first consulting us.

GRT Developers is constructing a shopping center at the southwest corner of 27th Ave. and Marconi Way in Boomtown. As Vice-President of the Construction Division, you have hired TRI to install the plumbing system. GRT's contract with TRI incorporates the architect's plans, which you first transmitted to TRI in a letter soliciting its bid on the project. Those plans clearly call for the plumbing subcontractor to use Reading brand pipe for all plumbing: "All pipes in the plumbing system must be Reading pipe, in the sizes and grades specified in these plans, and no other brand pipe."

From the beginning, you have had difficulty working with TRI's foreman, Cal Dunlap. When TRI had completed about half the plumbing on the project, you discovered that TRI had installed Cohoes brand pipe rather than Reading pipe. In a heated conversation with Dunlap, you demanded that TRI remove the Cohoes pipe, install Reading pipe, and compensate GRT for the resulting delay in construction. Dunlap agreed to install Reading pipe in the remainder of the plumbing, but he refused to replace the previously installed pipe. You now want to know whether you can fire TRI if Dunlap does not meet your demands.

Your own engineers have concluded that Cohoes pipe is equal to Reading pipe in durability and other relevant specifications. You do not know why the architect required Reading pipe, but you know that his brother-in-law is a sales manager for Reading Manufacturing Co.

IV. ANALYSIS

If TRI has breached the construction contract, GRT may sue it for all foreseeable damages caused by the breach, provided that GRT can prove the damages with reasonable certainty. *See Johnson v. Coombs Constr. Co.*, 345 Calz. 2d 331, 334 (1979). However, you may not fire TRI from the project unless TRI's breach is so substantial that a court would characterize it as "material," rather than "minor." *Lehman Brothers, Inc. v. Steenhook Enters.*, 401 Calz. 2d 112, 115 (1985). If a breach is only minor, you may not terminate the contract; instead, you must permit TRI to complete its performance, while reserving GRT's claim for damages resulting from its minor breach. *See id.* If you terminate the construction contract for only a minor breach, GRT will itself be guilty of the first material breach and will be liable to TRI for damages. *See id.*

A. Breach of Contract

The construction contract plainly requires TRI to use Reading pipe and no other. TRI has admitted that it used Cohoes pipe in approximately half of the plumbing. Therefore, TRI has breached the contract, and it is liable to GRT for foreseeable damages that GRT can prove with reasonable certainty.

B. Materiality of Breach

TRI's breach is material if it is so substantial that it either (1) robs GRT of the primary benefit that it expected from the contract, or (2) demonstrates that TRI is not competent to perform the work and therefore should not be allowed to continue. *See id*. at 116. Stated conversely, the breach is minor if TRI is competent to complete the contract and GRT can be fully compensated for its losses by an award of money damages that is small in proportion to the value of the entire contract. *See id*.

In this case, TRI's breach probably is not material under either branch of the test of materiality. First, GRT's primary benefit from the plumbing contract presumably is high-quality durable plumbing. Cohoes pipe is equal to Reading pipe in durability and other relevant specifications. The architect apparently required Reading pipe for personal reasons and not because it is superior to Cohoes pipe. Therefore, unless GRT has some special need for Reading pipe, it will get its primary benefit from the contract even though half of the plumbing consists of Cohoes pipe.

Second, although TRI's use of Cohoes pipe shows that Dunlap departed from the architect's plans, we have no evidence that he has failed to follow more important specifications of the plans or that his crews have performed poorly in the actual installation. Dunlap probably knows that Cohoes pipe is equal to Reading pipe, and he may have decided not to take that architect's requirement seriously. Therefore, the events do not suggest that TRI is incompetent to perform Dunlap's promise to complete the installation of plumbing with Reading pipe.

In summary, a court likely would infer that your unhappiness with TRI stems more from your personal dislike for Dunlap than from problems caused by TRI's use of Cohoes pipe. Therefore, a court almost certainly will find that TRI's breach is not material.

C. Remedies

Assuming TRI's breach was only minor, you have no right to fire TRI from the project. Instead, you must permit TRI to complete its performance, and you may demand that it compensate GRT for any damages that result from its minor breach. If you are reasonably certain about the breach and the extent of damages, you may collect the damages yourself by withholding an appropriate amount of payments that GRT otherwise would owe to TRI. *See Johnson,* 345 Calz. 2d at 335. On the other hand, if you wrongfully withhold a substantial portion of TRI's payments above any amount that it owes GRT for breach, GRT may itself be liable for breach. *See id*.

Unfortunately, without further evidence that the choice between Reading pipe and Cohoes pipe will affect the value of your project in any way, you will have difficulty proving any damages. Therefore, we advise you not to withhold any payments owed to TRI.

V. CONCLUSION

Although TRI has breached its contract with GRT, the breach almost certainly is not material, and it may not have caused any damages. In these circumstances, if you fire TRI from the project, GRT will be liable to TRI for breach of contract. Indeed, even withholding TRI's payments to cover damages caused by its breach is risky, because we have difficulty identifying any such damages.

We recommend that you cooperate with Dunlap to ensure the best possible performance of TRI's remaining duties under the contract. In the meantime, you may want GRT's engineers to determine what damages, if any, the installation of Cohoes pipe has caused. If you find any damages, we will be happy to advise you about the best possible means of demanding compensation from TRI.

Please do not hesitate to call me if you have any questions about this matter. My direct line is (111) 232-3232.

Sincerely,

_____

Marcia Todd
for Todd, Brown & King

Chapter 25

Demand Letters

I. PURPOSES OF A DEMAND LETTER

With a demand letter, you may seek to achieve one or more of three goals. First, you may seek to persuade another party to take or cease some action. For example, you may send a demand letter to your client's tenant in an office building, demanding that it stop entering into unauthorized subleases and that it pay past rent due.

Second, you may seek to revoke a waiver of rights to permit your client to assert those rights in the future. For example, even though your client's lease agreement clearly requires payment of rent on the first of each month, your client may have implicitly waived his right to demand timely payment by frequently accepting late rent payments over the previous year without complaint. If so, you can help your client reassert his rights by sending a demand letter that (1) revokes any implied consent, (2) demands prompt payment of rent strictly according to the contract for the remainder of the lease, and (3) warns of your client's resolve to pursue legal remedies for future breaches of the lease.

Third, you may seek to obtain information or concessions from the opposing party to help your client assert rights in the future. In such a letter, you do not really expect the opposing party to accede to your client's demand; rather, you hope to provoke a reaction that you can use to your client's advantage. For example, suppose that your client orally agreed to purchase goods from a supplier for a total price of $10,000, but the supplier has balked at performing. You know that your client will have trouble enforcing the oral agreement, because the Uniform Commercial Code generally requires such agreements to be evidenced in a writing signed by the party against whom enforcement is sought.[1] You might nonetheless send a letter to the supplier setting forth the terms of the oral agreement and demanding performance pursuant to those terms. In so doing, you may hold out little hope that the supplier will immediately perform as promised; instead, you hope that the supplier will either (1) respond by repeating its decision not to perform but admitting that it entered into the oral agreement or (2) fail to respond within ten days of receiving the letter, thus implicitly adopting your letter's description of the agreement.[2] Either reaction to the demand letter will satisfy the Uniform Commercial Code's requirement that the oral agreement be evidenced by a signed writing, thus enabling your client to assert a contract claim.[3]

II. AUDIENCE, TONE, AND WRITING STYLE

The audience for your demand letter is the opposing party, her attorney, or both. Because your purpose is to persuade the other party to take or cease some action or to otherwise modify his relationship to your client, you will advocate your client's position in a demand letter in much the same way that you would advocate her position in a brief to a court. Indeed, you will often adopt an even stronger tone of advocacy in a demand letter than in a brief, because a self-interested adversary may be more difficult to persuade than a disinterested judge.

Of course, you should adopt a tone that will most likely achieve your goals. Your task is complicated, however, by the multiplicity of audiences and goals. For example, although your primary audience is the opposing party, his attorney, or both, your own client is an important secondary audience. Even if you think that a conciliatory tone will achieve the best results with the opposing party, your client may make it clear that she has hired you to take the strongest possible stance and to intimidate the opposing party. On the other hand, the community as a whole is a possible tertiary audience, because the opposing party may seek to gain public support by airing the dispute in the news media. If a particularly strident passage in your demand letter is published in the news media, adverse public reaction may hinder your client's ability or willingness to assert her claims. Thus, you should adopt a tone that is firm and precise, but not nasty.

1. *See* U.C.C. § 2-201(1) (2000).
2. *See* U.C.C. § 2-201(2) (2000).
3. *See* U.C.C. § 2-201(1), (2) (2000).

Aside from tone, your style should be straightforward, businesslike, and professional. As is true in a brief, the most persuasive style in a demand letter is one that the reader does not notice, one that focuses the reader's attention on your demands, justifications, and threats. Thus, you should write in plain English and avoid legal jargon or florid, distracting prose.

III. FORMAT

You may flexibly adopt any reasonable format that will achieve the goals of your demand letter. At a minimum, your demand letter should include

1. an introductory sentence or overview paragraph,
2. a statement of the legal and factual support for your demands, and
3. a specific statement of the demands and the consequences of the opposing party's failure to satisfy the demands.

You need not divide a simple demand letter into sections; good paragraphing will suffice. If you divide a long or complex demand letter into sections, you should use whatever section headings suit the purposes of your letter.

IV. OVERVIEW

Immediately below the address and before the salutation of your demand letter, you should identify the general subject matter of the letter:

Arnold G. Hooper
Hooper Hardware
4094 East Laurel Lane
Fairbanks, New Maine 10713

RE: Eastern Savings and Loan Association Business Loan No. 082168

Dear Mr. Hooper,

In the first paragraph of your demand letter, you should provide any introductory information necessary to orient your reader. If this is your initial correspondence to the addressee, your opening paragraph should identify your representative capacity. Beyond that, the opening paragraph can provide such information as a general description of the relationships of the parties and an overview of your client's demands.

For example, the following unusually direct opening sentence states the author's representative capacity and captures the reader's attention with a threat:

RE: Eastern Savings and Loan Association Business Loan No. 082168

Dear Mr. Hooper,

Our client, Eastern Savings and Loan Association, has directed us to prepare to foreclose your interest in the business loan identified above. . . .

In contrast, the following opening paragraph in a settlement proposal develops the background and purpose of the letter more deliberately, and it introduces the demand for payment in a more conciliatory fashion:

RE: *Araiza v. Udave*

Mr. Phillips,

I met last Wednesday night with my clients, the plaintiffs in the suit against Max and Josephine Udave. All the plaintiffs are keen to press their claims. Nonetheless, they have agreed to make the following settlement offer: They will withdraw their suit if Max and Josephine Udave pay them a total of $10,000, conditioned on actual payment by noon on June 30, 2002. In light of my following evaluation of the case, I think you will find this offer to be quite reasonable.

V. FACTUAL AND LEGAL BASIS FOR THE DEMANDS

A. Stating Your Legal Premises

Your explanation of the factual and legal justification for your client's demands may take many forms. In a routine collection letter, you can simply state the amount that is past due under an identified loan agreement or installment contract. In such a demand letter, the opposing party ordinarily will not dispute the general enforceability of such contracts, and you need not discuss the legal principles that make contractual obligations enforceable:

You are now delinquent in the installments due for the months of January and February 2002. The total amount that you must pay Eastern Savings to bring your loan payments current, including penalties for late payment, is

$2,075. Also, your next payment of $1,000 will be due on March 1, 2002. Therefore, as of March 1, the amount necessary to bring your loan payments current will be $3,075.

In other cases, the fact or amount of the opposing party's liability may be more doubtful, prompting you to more thoroughly explain the legal basis for your client's demands. Such an explanation may look very much like the legal analysis and application to facts in a brief. For example, the following passage justifies a demand for consequential damages stemming from a breach of contract:

In addition, the plaintiffs will be entitled to foreseeable consequential damages stemming from the breach. *See Southern Ariz. Sch. for Boys, Inc. v. Chery,* 119 Ariz. 277, 280, 580 P.2d 738, 741 (1978). Those will include the plaintiffs' expenditures on specialized accessories that were suitable only for the wedding and that some plaintiffs were unable to use. *See A.R.A. Mfg. Co. v. Pierce,* 86 Ariz. 136, 341 P.2d 928, 932 (1959) (victim of breach entitled to award of damages for wasted promotional expenditures). Those members of the wedding party who could not fully participate in the wedding, the sole event for which the specialized gowns were ordered, can also recover damages for that lost opportunity. *See, e.g., Mieske v. Bartell Drug Co.,* 593 P.2d 1308 (Wash. 1979) (in UCC case, upholding award of $7,500 for emotional value associated with contracting parties' loss of home movies of significant events). Indeed, the opportunity to participate in the wedding formed the basis for the contracts for the gowns.

All of these losses are itemized in Count I of the complaint. They total approximately $20,000. Because the plaintiffs will certainly prove a breach of contract and will establish at least some of their alleged damages, they will also be entitled to an award of attorney's fees, which could add thousands more to the total recovery.

B. Audience

The appropriate level of formality of your legal analysis will depend on the sophistication of your audience. If you address your demand letter to the opposing party's attorney, or if you are certain that the opposing party will consult an attorney, you can reasonably cite to legal authority, as in the immediately preceding example. On the other hand, if the opposing party does not have legal training, and if you can appropriately address your letter directly to that party, then you should express your arguments in terms that the party can understand. If you try to intimidate the opposing party with formal citations to authority, you might simply confuse or antagonize rather than persuade.

For example, the following excerpt of a demand letter to an insurance company's subrogation analyst assumes that the analyst has a sophisticated knowledge of business practices but has no formal legal training. The excerpt refers to three legal concepts: waiver, offer, and the "mailbox rule" governing the timing of acceptance. The author of the letter has tried to use these concepts in a persuasive manner without diverting the reader's attention to distracting citations:

Even if Mr. Upton's premium had arrived after expiration of the grace period, his rights were preserved in the conversation between him and Diane Campbell, assistant to Dee Boston, on March 12. In that conversation, Ms. Campbell notified Mr. Upton that his claim would be covered but that she would delay processing his claim until he paid his late premium. Mr. Upton stated over the phone that he would mail his premium. In effect, Ms. Campbell waived any condition to coverage that would require Mr. Upton to deliver the premium to her within the grace period. She thus made the date of her receipt of the premium relevant only to the matter of processing his claim. At worst, Ms. Campbell may have communicated a new offer of coverage that invited Mr. Upton's return promise to pay the premium. If so, Mr. Upton accepted the offer either over the phone or under the "mailbox rule" when he placed his premium in the mailbox.

C. Avoiding Concessions, Admissions, and Waiver

A demand letter is not the proper place to make concessions or admissions that may come back to haunt you later. Therefore, if you choose to adopt a conciliatory tone, do so in a way that does not preclude you from taking a stronger position in the future. For example, suppose that your client demands compensation on the basis of a strong contract claim and a weak tort claim. To maintain credibility and to avoid antagonizing the opposing party, you might invoke only the contract claim to justify your client's demands in a demand letter. If so, you should remain silent about the weaker tort claim or refer to it only vaguely. If you affirmatively concede the weakness of that claim in writing, you may hinder your ability to pursue it later if newly discovered facts enhance its potential merit.

You should also avoid ambiguous conciliatory language that might grant unintended rights to the opposing party. For example, in a letter demanding payment of amounts past due on a loan agreement, you should exercise caution before inviting the opposing party to apply to your client for an extension of the loan. If you state the invitation in a way that raises reasonable expectations in the opposing party of receiving the extension, you may obligate your client to grant such an extension in some circumstances.

VI. DEMANDS AND THREATS

You should not send a demand letter unless your client has a well-defined goal that you can formulate into a straightforward demand to the opposing party. Moreover, to maximize the chances of achieving that goal, you must provide the opposing party with an incentive to satisfy your client's demand. If the opposing party is fair-minded and your demand is just, your persuasive presentation of the legal and factual bases for the demand may help induce him to accede to the demand. In most cases, however, you can provide the greatest incentive to the opposing party by threatening to take actions that would be more costly for the opposing party than satisfying the demand.

Thus, you must clearly state both your client's demand and the actions your client will take if the opposing party rejects the demand. To ensure prompt action, you should set a specific date by which the opposing party must satisfy your client's demand or suffer the adverse consequences of the threatened action.

If the relief to which your client is entitled is uncertain, your objective may simply be to initiate settlement negotiations. More specifically, you may desire to induce your opponent to advance the first settlement offer, which might reveal something about her evaluation of the case or her client's interests. If so, your demand letter might state the maximum possible liability and threaten formal action unless the opposing party takes action to reach a settlement.

In other cases, your client may seek payment of a certain sum of money. For example, if your client is demanding the payment of amounts past due on a loan or an installment contract, you should

1. state the precise payment that your client demands;
2. set a date by which the opposing party must deliver the payment to a particular address;
3. depending on the circumstances, threaten to foreclose on secured property, to sue on the contract, or to take other appropriate legal action if the demand is not satisfied; and
4. take care to satisfy any statutory or common law duties that apply to your transaction. For example, some attorneys or law firms may qualify as debt collectors subject to the provisions of the federal Fair Debt Collection Practices Act,[4] which will require some kinds of demand letters to disclose certain information and to refrain from making certain kinds of threats,[5] as illustrated in the final paragraph of the illustration immediately below.

The following excerpt from a loan collection letter illustrates the clarity, specificity, and directness for which you should strive:

. . . Therefore, as of March 1, the amount necessary to bring your loan payments current will be $3,075.

If you desire to avoid legal proceedings, you must submit $3,075 on or before March 5, 2002, in cash, cashier's check, or certified funds made payable

---

4. 15 U.S.C. §§ 1692-1692o (1994).
5. For a helpful discussion of the Act's requirements, see Scott J. Burnham, *What Attorneys Should Know About the Fair Debt Collection Practices Act, or, the 2 Do's and the 200 Don'ts of Debt Collection*, 59 Mont. L. Rev. 179 (2000).

to Eastern Savings and Loan Association. You must mail or deliver the payment directly to:

> Eastern Savings and Loan Association
> Suite 11000, Financial Plaza
> 1901 South Alma School Road
> Fairbanks, New Maine 10701
> Attention: Kathy Growl

Take notice that time is of the essence. . . .

If Eastern Savings has not received the above amount on or before March 5, 2002, it will accelerate the principal balance of the loan and will immediately commence foreclosure proceedings. These proceedings could result in a sale of the property securing the loan.

. . . Unless you notify this office within 30 days after receiving this notice that you dispute the validity of any portion of this debt, this office will assume that this debt is valid. If you dispute the debt in a written notification sent to this office within 30 days from receiving this notice, this office will obtain verification of the debt or obtain a copy of a judgment and mail you a copy of the judgment or verification. If you submit a request to this office in writing within 30 days after receiving this notice, this office will provide you with the name and address of the original creditor, if different from the current creditor.[6]

To avoid any dispute about the opposing party's receipt of your demand letter, you should always send the demand letter by registered mail. Finally, to preserve your credibility in future correspondence, you must confirm that your client is willing and able to back up its threats with action.

VII. SUMMARY

In a demand letter, you should

1. use plain English whenever possible,
2. adapt your format and depth of legal analysis to your audience and your purpose,
3. use an introductory sentence or paragraph to identify your representative capacity, provide an overview of the purpose of your letter, or orient the reader in some other fashion,
4. state the legal and factual bases for your demand,
5. state your demands, including the time and place for satisfaction of the demands, and threaten to take action if the demands are not met, and
6. stay abreast of common law and statutory regulation of demands in your transaction, and comply with the law in your communications.

6. With minor changes, this paragraph quotes from one recommended by author Scott Burnham as offering language that would satisfy some disclosure requirements of the Fair Debt Collection Practices Act. *Id.* at 190.

Exercise 25-1

1. COLLECTION LETTER

Study the following collection letter and explain the purpose or purposes of each paragraph.

Scott L. Short
Stanley, Leeds & Cardon
100 W. Central Ave., Suite 2100
Fairbanks, New Maine 10701
February 16, 2002

CERTIFIED MAIL
RETURN RECEIPT REQUESTED

Arnold G. Hooper
Hooper Hardware
4094 East Laurel Lane
Fairbanks, New Maine 10713

RE: Eastern Savings and Loan Association Business Loan No. 082168

Dear Mr. Hooper,

Our client, Eastern Savings and Loan Association, has directed us to prepare to foreclose your interest in the business loan identified above. You are now delinquent in the installments due for the months of January and February 2002. The total amount that you must pay Eastern Savings to bring your loan payments current, including penalties for late payment, is $2,075. Also, your next payment of $1,000 will be due on March 1, 2002. Therefore, as of March 1, the amount necessary to bring your loan payments current will be $3,075.

If you desire to avoid legal proceedings, you must submit $3,075 on or before March 5, 2002, in cash, cashier's check, or certified funds made payable to Eastern Savings and Loan Association. You must mail or deliver the payment directly to:

Eastern Savings and Loan Association
Suite 11000, Financial Plaza
1901 South Alma School Road
Fairbanks, New Maine 10701
Attention: Kathy Growl

Take notice that time is of the essence on this matter. Eastern Savings will strictly adhere to the above deadline and future due dates despite any past acceptance of late or partial installment payments, any prior reinstatement, any prior negotiations, or any other actual or implied forbearance of any nature by Eastern Savings.

If Eastern Savings has not received the above amount on or before March 5, 2002, it will accelerate the principal balance of the loan and will immediately commence foreclosure proceedings. These proceedings could result in a sale of the property securing the loan.

Pursuant to the terms of the deed of trust, you have the right to challenge any such acceleration or to assert the absence of a default or any other defense in court. However, unless you notify this office within 30 days after receiving this notice that you dispute the validity of any portion of this debt, this office will assume that this debt is valid. If you dispute the debt in a written notification sent to this office within 30 days from receiving this notice, this office will obtain verification of the debt or obtain a copy of a judgment and mail you a copy of the judgment or verification. If you submit a request to this office in writing within 30 days after receiving this notice, this office will provide you with the name and address of the original creditor, if different from the current creditor.

Sincerely,

_____

Scott L. Short
Stanley, Leeds & Cardon

2. THE BAD EXAMPLE

Study the following collection letter and explain why it is less effective than the letter in Problem 1 above. Identify and describe each defect.

Green and Gain
120 West Washington
Phoenix, AZ 85003
April 1, 2002

Mr. and Mrs. Joe Smith
5555 North 55th Street
Phoenix, AZ 85055

RE: Delinquent Loan #9-1403726-841

Dear Borrower:

We are counsel of record for the Bank of Phoenix (hereinafter referred to as the Bank). Our client has informed us that you are behind in your home loan payments, and has asked that we write you on its behalf to request that you take some action to bring your loans current. We understand that you presently are approximately $2,500.00 behind in your payments.

Over the past several months, the few loan payments you have actually made have been consistently late. While the Bank was happy to take whatever it could get from you, it would prefer that you try to make payments on time. If you are having difficulty making your payments, the Bank would be happy to consider and, if reasonable, would agree to an extension of your loan, a modification of its terms, or a second loan to see you through whatever difficulties you may be experiencing. If you desire to pursue this offer, please call your loan officer or some other authorized representative of the Bank.

Please be advised, however, that the Bank has no intention of waiting forever for you to make good on your commitments. Frankly, in our experience the Bank has very little patience with deadbeat borrowers such as you appear to be. The Bank has ruined the credit of thousands of borrowers who, like you, did not take their obligations seriously. Hundreds more have been forced into bankruptcy. Moreover, the Bank is a large, powerful institution which can afford to hire big law firms such as this one, against which the average debtor has little chance of prevailing.

We spoke to your attorney about this matter over the phone this morning but found him to be uncooperative. We sincerely hope that you adopt a more constructive attitude and pay up.

The Bank therefore suggests that you make arrangements to bring the aforementioned loan current by paying the amount hereinbefore stated or making such other arrangements as you and said Bank may subsequently agree upon.

Sincerely,

_____

Bob Jenkins
Green & Gain

3. SETTLEMENT LETTER

a. The settlement letter below was written several months after suit was filed and shortly before a scheduled arbitration hearing. Explain the purpose or purposes of each paragraph. Precisely what does the letter demand? What action does the author of the letter threaten to take if the demand is not met?

b. The letter below is addressed to the opposing party's attorney in response to preliminary settlement discussions. Rewrite the letter so that it is appropriate for an unrepresented opposing party who has no legal training or knowledge. Summarize your analysis without citing to specific authority.

Charles Rehnquist, Esq.
333 S. Central Ave.
Phoenix, Arizona 85001
(602) 849-0101
June 1, 2002

Robert M. Phillips, Esq.
Kim, Phillips, Burley & Stewart
3301 E. Bethany Home Road, Suite B-111
Phoenix, Arizona 85012

RE: *Araiza v. Udave*

Mr. Phillips,

I met last Wednesday night with my clients, the plaintiffs in the suit against Max and Josephine Udave. All the plaintiffs are anxious to press their claims. Nonetheless, they have agreed to make the following settlement offer: They will withdraw their suit if Max and Josephine Udave pay them a total of $10,000, conditioned upon payment by noon on June 30, 2002. In light of my following evaluation of the case, I think you will find this offer to be quite reasonable.

I have no doubts about our ability to prove the claim for breach of contract. Indeed, your early correspondence and the defendants' answers to the complaint and interrogatories admit that Josephine failed to perform as promised. Even if she had acted in good faith and with best efforts, that would be no excuse for breach of the contract. Therefore, the defendants have essentially admitted to their breach of contract. The direct loss in value is easily computed: the difference between the value of each gown as promised ($900 each by your own correspondence) minus the value of the dress as delivered (we can prove that some are total losses).

In addition, the plaintiffs will be entitled to foreseeable consequential damages stemming from the breach. *See Southern Ariz. Sch. for Boys, Inc. v. Chery,* 119 Ariz. 277, 280, 580 P.2d 738, 741 (1978). Those will include the plaintiffs' expenditures on specialized accessories that were suitable only for the wedding and that some plaintiffs were unable to use. *See A.R.A. Mfg. Co. v. Pierce,* 86 Ariz. 136, 142, 341 P.2d 928, 932 (1959) (victim of breach entitled to award of damages for wasted promotional expenditures). Those members of the wedding party who could not fully participate in the wedding, the sole event for which the specialized gowns were ordered, can also recover damages for that lost opportunity. *See, e.g., Mieske v. Bartell Drug Co.,* 593 P.2d 1308 (Wash. 1979) (in UCC case, upholding award of $7,500 for emotional value associated with contracting parties' loss of home movies of significant events). Indeed, the opportunity to participate in the wedding formed the basis for the contracts for the gowns.

All of these losses are itemized in Count I of the complaint. They total approximately $20,000. Because the plaintiffs will certainly prove a breach of contract and will establish at least some of their alleged damages, they will also be entitled to an award of attorney's fees, which could add thousands more to the total recovery.

Josephine's own theory of the case is that she breached the contract because she lost the ruffles. Coupled with her failure to warn the plaintiffs to obtain gowns from an alternative source, those facts should easily support the negligence claim in Count II. That claim provides even stronger support than Count I for an award of general compensatory damages, including damages for emotional distress.

Also solid are the claims for promissory fraud and consumer fraud in Counts III and VI. The consumer fraud statute prohibits use of deception, fraud, false promises, or suppression of material fact with intent that others rely, in connection with the sale of any merchandise. A.R.S. § 44-1522. "Merchandise" includes services. A.R.S. § 44-1521(5). Like the common law tort of promissory fraud, a claim under the consumer fraud statute will support an award of punitive damages. *See Schmidt v. American Leasco*, 139 Ariz. 509, 512, 679 P.2d 532, 535 (Ct. App. 1983). We should have little trouble proving a claim under either theory: The plaintiffs will offer abundant and vivid testimony describing the way in which Max and Josephine deliberately misrepresented that many of the gowns would be ready on time, thus inducing many of the plaintiffs to wait until the last minute and beyond, when in fact Max and Josephine knew that the gowns could not possibly be completed on time. In light of the "evil minds" associated with such actions, these claims potentially could add thousands of dollars in punitive damages to the compensatory damages detailed in Count I.

In sum, the plaintiffs are angry and confident. They are anxious to go to an arbitration hearing, and they are ready to enforce their judgment by attaching the Udaves' property. Indeed, I experienced some difficulty getting them to agree to propose this settlement offer. I can assure you that it is not a bargaining posture; it represents their current bottom line, before they have incurred significant legal fees. Despite their passionate views on this matter, however, they have compromised their full claims substantially. The $10,000 figure represents 50% of the compensatory damages for Count I, without costs or attorney's fees, and without any punitive damages.

This offer remains open until noon, June 15. Please call or write to me before then if your clients wish to settle.

Sincerely,

_____

Charles Rehnquist, Esq.

4. RESPONSE TO DEMAND LETTER: DEMAND FOR WITHDRAWAL OF CLAIM

The following letter responds to a demand letter from an attorney for Framer Insurance Co. addressed to Michael Upton. Mr. Upton caused an automobile accident, resulting in injuries to Eileen Bradley, who was insured by Framer. Framer paid Ms. Bradley's claim for $10,000 in losses and medical expenses arising out of the accident. Framer then demanded that Mr. Upton reimburse Framer for Framer's payment to Ms. Bradley. Mr. Upton, however, claimed that he had liability insurance from Framer and that Framer thus was obligated to assume the cost of his liability to Ms. Bradley. The primary matter of dispute between Framer and Mr. Upton was whether Mr. Upton had validly renewed his insurance contract with Framer despite Framer's assertion that it received his late premium payment only after expiration of the policy's grace period.

    a. Although it responds to a demand letter, the letter below is itself a demand letter, albeit a subtle one. What does it demand? What action does it implicitly threaten if the demand is not met? Should the author have stated the demand and threat more strongly?

    b. Who is the audience for this letter? Assuming that Marilyn Branscomb is not a lawyer, would she likely consult with Framer's attorney, Jon Drake, before deciding whether to drop Framer's claim against Mr. Upton? If so, should the author have advanced a more formal legal analysis with citation to authority?

                                                  Charles Rehnquist, Esq.
        333 S. Central Ave.
        Phoenix, Arizona 85001
        (602) 849-0101
        January 27, 2002

Marilyn Branscomb
Subrogation Analyst for Framer Insurance
P.O. Box 3108
Mesa, Calzona 89211

Policy No. 881347 94

Dear Ms. Branscomb,

    I represent Michael Upton in his claim for coverage under the above policy. I write in response to Jon C. Drake's letter dated January 7 to Michael Upton, in which Mr. Drake requests Mr. Upton to indemnify Framer for Framer's payment of claims to Eileen Bradley. I address this letter to you because Mr. Drake directed Mr. Upton to contact you.

I'm sure that everyone hopes to resolve this matter before either party must incur the enormous legal expenses associated with litigation.

Mr. Upton is unwilling to pay the claim because he claims liability coverage under his policy and thus expects Framer to satisfy Ms. Bradley's claims. Mr. Upton recognizes that his insurance policy requires actual receipt of a late premium before expiration of the grace period. Even so, Mr. Upton is certain that the post office in fact delivered his premium within the three days remaining in the grace period, and he doubts Framer's claim that it received the premium a full week after it was posted five miles away. A jury would have the same doubts. Once Mr. Upton proves to a jury with his testimony and that of a witness that he posted the letter three days before expiration of the grace period, the jury will not likely believe that the letter took longer than the standard one to three days for delivery.

Mr. Upton is confident of his ability to prove his version of events before a jury, particularly in light of his previously communicated willingness to submit to a lie detector test. Of course, if litigation or other inquiry reveals that anyone within the Framer organization sought in bad faith to deny Mr. Upton coverage by covering up the facts, the resulting issues would transcend the relatively small dispute now before us. Thus, you should consider the possibility of a counterclaim to any claim that Framer might consider pursuing against Mr. Upton.

In sum, Mr. Upton is prepared to prove that he owes Framer nothing because Framer had a contractual duty to provide him insurance coverage for his liability to Ms. Bradley stemming from the March 12 accident. If Framer drops its claim, Mr. Upton will be happy to cease any further inquiry into possible claims he might have against Framer based on bad faith or other misconduct that Framer may have engaged in.

Sincerely,

Charles Rehnquist, Esq.

cc: Jon C. Drake

Appendices

In a legal method and writing course, you can best master a challenging writing assignment by preparing for and accomplishing your task in at least three separate steps. First, you should acquire information about the topic of your assignment by reading assigned portions of a descriptive text, such as the main text of LEGAL METHOD AND WRITING, and by attending classes in which an instructor lectures and leads class discussion. Second, you must become an active participant in the educational process by analyzing assigned problems and preparing legal documents, such as case briefs, office memoranda, and briefs. Third, you should welcome constructive criticism from instructors or peers, and you should thoughtfully react to their editorial comments by deciding which have merit and by revising your draft accordingly.

Along with the exercises in the main text, the Appendices provide you with the problems and other materials you need for the second step of the educational process—your active participation in research, analysis, and writing. The exercises in the main text are suitable for class discussion or for in-class writing exercises. They include policy questions, invitations to critique sample documents, an essay examination, and composition problems.

The Appendices include "problems" that are similar to the "exercises" in the main text: They provide further opportunities to think about and discuss fundamental questions of legal method and writing. Although an instructor could make these problems the subjects of formal writing assignments, they are primarily designed for individual review or for class discussion.

The "assignments" in the Appendices, on the other hand, are take-home assignments requiring formal written documents. They ask you to analyze a problem and draft a document such as an office memorandum or a pretrial brief. Many of the assignments requiring formal documents provide all necessary materials and require no supplementary research. Others, particularly the more complex ones, provide you with little or no authority and require you to perform all necessary research in the library.

The assignments that require research will inspire different analyses depending on when you perform them and what authorities have been issued at that time. For example, statutes or judicial decisions issued after the publication of this book might radically alter the nature of the issues originally intended to be raised. Similarly, one of the office memorandum assignments is set in the state in which your law school is located. Because your analysis of the problem in that assignment will depend on the law of your particular state, the assignment may be more interesting in some law schools than in others. For all these reasons, your instructor may perform some "fine tuning" of some of the assignments by modifying the facts or otherwise adjusting the problems to avoid unintended difficulties raised by intervening laws or the laws of a particular state.

Appendix I

Problem 1. Sources and Limits of
Lawmaking Powers

Examine each government action described in the sections below. Which represents a legitimate exercise of legislative, judicial, or executive authority?

a. The Flag-Bashing Bill
The First Amendment to the United States Constitution provides in part that "Congress shall make no law . . . abridging the freedom of speech, or of the press." Shortly before July 4, however, Congress sought to override the First Amendment by restricting speech critical of the American flag. Offended by a wave of public criticism of the American flag and the values for which it stands, Congress enacted the "Flag-Bashing Bill," which the President signed into law. Section 1 of that statute makes it an "unlawful publication practice for any person to publish any oral or written statement

525

critical of the flag of the United States of America." Section 2 provides for fines of up to $5,000 for each violation of the statute.

Section 3 of the statute created the Flag Protection Commission (FPC), a federal agency, and granted it powers to investigate violations of the statute, to hold hearings on alleged violations, to impose fines for violations, and to issue rules and regulations to aid in its investigative and enforcement activities. Section 4 of the statute grants jurisdiction to the United States Courts of Appeals to review the FPC's actions, subject to further appeal to the United States Supreme Court.

b. The FPC Flexes Its Muscle

As the chief officer of the executive branch of the United States government, the President appointed several staunch flag enthusiasts to the FPC. Without delay, the FPC issued rules and regulations that, among other things, (1) describe procedures for FPC hearings, (2) authorize FPC hearing officers to impose fines of $1,000 to $10,000 for various kinds of violations of the Flag-Bashing Bill, and (3) define the statutory phrase "unlawful publication practice" to include any public criticism of the flag or the President's wardrobe.

c. Judicial Review

In the FPC's first major hearing, an FPC hearing officer found that a Washington, D.C., newspaper publisher had violated the Flag-Bashing Bill by publishing a critical commentary entitled "The Stars and Stripes—Do the Colors Clash?" The hearing officer fined the publisher $2,000. The publisher appealed to the United States Court of Appeals for the District of Columbia Circuit.

On appeal, the court of appeals overturned the hearing officer's decision. Contrary to the plain language, legislative history, and clear purpose of the Flag-Bashing Bill, the court found that the bill prohibited only oral criticism of the President's foreign trade policies.

The FPC appealed to the United States Supreme Court. The Supreme Court upheld the court of appeals' overturning of the hearing officer's decision, but on different grounds. The Supreme Court concluded that (1) the FPC had validly issued the rules and regulations on which the hearing officer had relied in this case, and (2) the hearing officer's findings and imposition of a fine were consistent with a proper interpretation of the Flag-Bashing Bill. However, the Supreme Court held that the statute was unenforceable because it violated the First Amendment to the United States Constitution.

Problem 2. Developing the Common Law and Interpreting Statutes That Modify the Common Law

In each of the sections below, fully explain the reasons for your conclusions. Express each step of your analysis.

a. Survival of the Fittest and the Common Law

If you have not already done so, perform Exercise 1-1 at the end of Chapter 1 in the main text. If you have already performed that exercise, review that exercise and your response to it.

b. The Justification of Self-Preservation

Assume that your court responded to *State v. Blight* by adopting the following common law rule and by remanding to the trial court for a new trial with jury instructions consistent with the new rule:

> A defendant is justified in killing another human being if the defendant is reasonably certain at the time of the killing that the killing is necessary to preserve his own life and that failure to kill the other will result in the death of both.

Do you support the rule? Apply this rule to the facts of *State v. Blight*. Should the jury acquit if instructed to apply this rule? Explain your answer in detail.

c. Mercy Killing and the Criminal Code

One hundred years after *State v. Blight,* your state has largely replaced the common law crimes with a comprehensive criminal code: a collection of statutes that defines criminal conduct and penalties, incorporating some common law principles and modifying or rejecting others. Section 101 of the criminal code defines the crime of murder as "the killing of another human being without justification." Section 101.A provides that "premeditated murder" constitutes first-degree murder, which carries a maximum penalty of life in prison. Section 101.G, enacted just last year, provides that "a desire to ease the suffering of a terminally ill person is not justification for ending the person's life prematurely." A state legislative committee report explained the purpose of the bill that later was codified as section 101.G:

> This bill makes it clear that euthanasia, popularly known as "mercy-killing," is not "justified" under § 101 of our criminal code and therefore is not excluded from our definition of murder. With this bill, the state declares its policies to promote the use of life-sustaining measures and to preserve the life of even a terminally ill patient for as long as possible, in the hope that a cure for the illness may be found before the patient dies. The physical and emotional suffering of terminally ill patients should be relieved through counseling and the prescription of pain-relieving drugs rather than the termination of life-sustaining medical equipment or treatment. Thus, even well-meaning friends or relatives who "pull the plug" on a terminally ill patient may be charged under our murder statute.

(1) *Blight* Revisited

Review Sections a and b above. If facts identical to those of *State v. Blight* were presented to a jury today, should the jury convict the defendant of first-degree murder under the criminal code? How should the trial judge instruct the jury? If the state appellate courts have not yet interpreted section 101's reference to "justification," should the trial judge attempt to define that term for the jury? On what would it base its definition? Suppose that Blight has argued that the trial judge should not instruct the jury according to section 101.G, on the ground that section 101.G does not apply to his case. How should the trial court rule and why?

(2) The Pact

Emma Padilla was losing her battle against cancer. Although she continued to receive chemotherapy, it made her quite ill and offered her almost no hope of remission. Preferring to live her final days in familiar surroundings, she arranged for full-time nursing care in her home. She often spoke to her nurses about her desire to die and about her wish that no one prolong her life with heroic lifesaving measures.

One evening, Padilla suffered a seizure; her heart stopped beating, and she ceased breathing. Her night nurse, Jim Murrow, rushed to Padilla's side to administer cardiopulmonary resuscitation and to hook up a portable respirator and other lifesaving equipment. He stopped short, however, remembering Padilla's wish to die naturally. Murrow allowed Padilla to die, notified the hospital that had been treating Padilla with chemotherapy, and admitted to several colleagues that he had honored Padilla's wishes that he refrain from prolonging her life.

Is Murrow guilty of murder under sections 101 and 101.G of the criminal code? Fully analyze the law and the facts, taking care to advance arguments for both the defense and the prosecution.

Appendix II

Problem 1. Analogy, Distinction, and Precedent

Read the materials for Office Memorandum Assignment 1 in Appendix IV. The only two Arizona cases provided in the materials, *Henderson* and *Fogleman,* deny any award of damages for emotional distress. The only case in your materials that approves of such an award for breach of contract is *Browning,* an early decision from another jurisdiction. Fully explain how you could distinguish the facts of *Henderson* and *Fogleman* from Araiza's case, and explain how you could analogize the facts of her case to those of *Browning.* Further explain how dicta in *Henderson* and *Fogleman* support an analogy to *Browning.*

Problem 2. Legal Policy and Application to Facts

Cheryl Watkins, an expert pilot, retained Flight Ready, a private aircraft service, to maintain her single-engine private plane based at Palm City

529

Airport in Calzona. While flying from Palm City to a nearby town on a business trip, Watkins noticed that the passenger door of the cabin had sprung partially open. She knew that the partially open door would reduce the stability of the aircraft under certain conditions and that flying for more than a few minutes with the door open would be distracting, if not hazardous. She rejected the idea of making an emergency landing on the busy highway below or on the desert dotted with massive saguaro cacti. Instead, Watkins leaned across the passenger's seat to close the passenger door, even though her instructor had twice warned her never to do so. As Cheryl reached for the passenger door, the plane abruptly rolled to the right and spiraled into a sharp dive. Watkins was not in position to take control of the aircraft, and it crashed into the desert seconds later, killing Watkins instantly. A tape recorder found in the wreckage had recorded Watkins's comments during the emergency, allowing investigators to reconstruct the events.

In a wrongful death action brought by Watkins's survivors in Calzona, the jury answered several specific questions called "special interrogatories," submitted to it by the court. Specifically, the jury found that personnel for Flight Ready had negligently repaired a latch on the passenger door of Watkins's aircraft, which door had previously stuck in the closed position. The negligent repair caused the door to spring open during the flight. The jury also found that the partially open door had reduced the stability of the aircraft, causing it to roll and dive when Watkins shifted her position in the aircraft. Finally, the jury found that had Watkins remained in the pilot's seat, she likely could have maintained control of the plane and either reached her destination without mishap or survived an emergency landing on the desert. Following an instruction based on the doctrine of "contributory negligence," the jury denied Watkins's survivors any recovery.

Under the traditional common law doctrine of contributory negligence, a victim of a tort is precluded from recovering damages from the tortfeasor if the victim negligently contributed to her own injuries. At the time of trial, Calzona courts still applied the doctrine of contributory negligence as a defense in a tort action brought either by the victim or by her survivors. Accordingly, the trial court had rejected a jury instruction proposed by counsel for the plaintiffs that would have permitted the jury to apply the doctrine of "pure comparative negligence." Under the proposed instruction, Watkins's own negligence would not preclude the plaintiffs from all recovery; instead, their recovery would simply be diminished in proportion to which Watkins's own negligence contributed to her death.

In class discussion or a written essay, respond to the following questions:

a. In the process of developing its common law, should the Calzona Supreme Court abandon its contributory negligence doctrine by adopting a pure comparative negligence scheme? Discuss the policy arguments supporting both sides of this issue.

b. As a legislator, would you support proposed legislation that would create a modified comparative fault system in which a plaintiff would receive the benefits of comparative negligence if she is no more than 50 percent at fault but would recover nothing if she is more than 50 percent at fault? State your reasons for your support or opposition.

c. How would either a pure or a modified comparative negligence standard likely apply to the facts on remand?

Problem 3. Legal Policy—Economic Analysis

Read the following problem and use it to construct an economic rationale for a general rule disallowing punitive damages for even intentional breaches of commercial contracts. If a policy supports application of a general rule in most cases, should courts apply the rule without exception to promote certainty in the law, or should they recognize exceptions to the general rule to reach a fair result in exceptional cases? Consider the ethical problems, if any, of advising a client to intentionally breach a clearly binding contract.

Problem

Uptown, Inc., is a chain of department stores. It owns the Uptown Mega Mall, a sprawling shopping mall in Bonneville. An Uptown department store is the anchor store at the shopping mall, attracting shoppers to dozens of other retail outlets at the mall. The mall employs 400 Bonneville residents. Brisk business at the Uptown Mega Mall put pressure on the store's ground-level parking lot during peak hours. In January, the Board of Directors of Uptown committed funds to construct a three-level underground parking facility at the Bonneville store. On January 25, Uptown contracted with the largest excavator in Bonneville, Pierce Excavation Co., to excavate the site for the new parking facility. In the written contract, Pierce Excavation Co. promised to begin excavation on July 1 and to complete the work by August 15, and Uptown promised to pay Pierce Excavation Co. $100,000. John Pierce, owner of Pierce Excavation Co., estimated that he would earn about $15,000 profit from the project and that it would use about half the capacity of his firm; he did not have any other offers for work beyond the last week of May.

On June 10, the City Council of Bonneville unexpectedly broke a year-long deadlock and approved the plans of a developer, Lynn Mullins, to construct an enormous and lavish convention center near the Bonneville airport. Once completed, the convention center will employ 800 Bonneville residents and contribute millions of dollars annually to the Bonneville economy. Pierce Construction Co. is the only excavator in Bonneville with sufficient equipment to efficiently excavate the convention center site. Anxious to begin construction of the long-delayed project, Mullins offered to pay Pierce Construction Co. $240,000 to perform excavation and other earth moving at the convention center site if Pierce agreed to begin work immediately and complete work sometime in August. Pierce estimated that he would earn $60,000 profit from the project and that it would employ the full capacity of his firm for approximately eight weeks beginning in mid-June.

On June 11, John Pierce met with officers of Uptown and discussed the possibility of modifying their contract to postpone beginning excavation until mid-August. The Uptown officers refused to modify the contract; a six-week delay in excavation would extend the construction period into the holiday shopping season, disrupting even the existing ground-level parking. Another Bonneville excavator was available to perform the Uptown work in July, either as an independent contractor or as a subcontractor to Pierce Construction Co. However, in light of market conditions caused by the approval of the convention center plans, the substitute excavator insisted on a price of $120,000 for the Uptown project. Moreover, even if the substitute excavator acted nominally as Pierce's subcontractor, Pierce would not have the capacity during the month of July to supervise the Uptown project full time. Uptown had hired Pierce Construction Co. partly for its reputation for high-quality work, and it was reluctant to replace it with a substitute, which might increase final construction costs with imperfect excavation. Uptown credibly represented that it would suffer $30,000 in damages if it were forced to hire a substitute excavator or delay excavation until mid-August.

On June 12, John Pierce met with his attorney, Patricia Ruiz, to discuss his options. Ruiz advised Pierce to repudiate the Uptown contract, accept Mullins's offer, and pay the consequences of his breach of the Uptown contract. Ruiz knew that Pierce would not be liable for punitive damages, and she was confident that she could negotiate a reasonable settlement of Uptown's claim. What terms should Pierce authorize Ruiz to accept in settlement negotiations?

Appendix III

Assignment 1. Case Briefs with Syntheses

Exercise 7-1(1, 2) in Chapter 7 of the main text includes excerpts and a sample case brief of *White v. Benkowski*. Review those materials now.

a. The Tort

Read the following excerpt from the appellate opinion in *McKibben v. Mohawk Oil Co., Ltd.*, and prepare a case brief for a contracts class that includes a synthesis of this case with *White v. Benkowski*.

McKIBBEN v. MOHAWK OIL COMPANY, LTD.
Supreme Court of Alaska
667 P.2d 1223 (Alaska 1983)

BURKE, Chief Justice.
Plaintiffs Harley McKibben, Adolph Vetter, and Roudolph Vetter are

533

the owners of the Christina mining claim located near Fairbanks. On December 2, 1977, plaintiffs entered into a mining lease agreement with Joseph Taylor and Paul Rice, giving Taylor and Rice the right to mine the land in a workmanlike manner until March 15, 1978. The lease also provided that the plaintiffs would receive forty-five percent of the value of all ores and minerals mined and extracted from the claims after deducting smelting and refining costs. Taylor and Rice would bear the entire costs of mining and milling the ore.

Taylor and Rice assigned their interest in the lease to Tri-Con Mining, Inc. [Tri-Con] with plaintiffs' consent. Plaintiffs and Tri-Con entered into an addendum of the lease, which provided that whenever the lessee's ore shipments had a specified low assayed value, plaintiffs' royalty interest would be reduced to ten percent. Soon after Tri-Con began mining the Christina claim, Tri-Con entered into a joint venture with Mohawk Oil and Gas, Inc. [Mohawk Inc.], a wholly owned subsidiary of Mohawk Oil Company, Ltd. [Mohawk Ltd.]. With only two weeks remaining in the term of the lease, Tri-Con and Mohawk Inc. engaged in a bulk mining program during which some 12,000 to 15,000 tons of ore were mined from the property and shipped to the nearby Fox Mill. Tri-Con and Mohawk Inc. processed and milled approximately 6,000 tons of the stockpiled ore. The percentage recovery of precious metals from the ore was extremely low. . . .

On March 21, 1980, plaintiffs filed a complaint against Tri-Con, Mohawk Ltd., and Mohawk Inc. First and second amended complaints were filed on September 18, 1980. As amended, the complaint alleges that defendants breached the lease; committed waste and conversion; engaged in unworkmanlike mining; and intentionally diluted the ore. Plaintiffs also requested punitive damages for the "purposeful and outrageous conduct" committed by defendants.

Defendants subsequently moved for partial summary judgment to dismiss plaintiffs' claims for intentional dilution, unworkmanlike mining, punitive damages, and waste. . . . [T]he superior court . . . denied defendants' motion to dismiss plaintiffs' claims for waste, intentional dilution, and unworkmanlike mining, but dismissed plaintiffs' punitive damages claim.

. . . .

VII. PUNITIVE DAMAGES

In their complaint, plaintiffs requested punitive damages for the defendants' purposeful and outrageous conduct, which apparently consisted of intentionally diluting the ore. Defendants moved for summary judgment on the punitive damages claim on the ground that punitive damages are not available in Alaska for a breach of contract. The motion was granted by the superior court.

In *Lull v. Wick Construction Co.*, 614 P.2d 321, 325-26 (Alaska 1980), we stated that it was an open question whether punitive damages may be awarded in a contract action, and noted that some states permit punitive damages when the breach is maliciously or grossly reckless or when the conduct associated with the breach also constitutes an independent tort. We refused to decide the issue in *Lull* because the breach in that case was neither malicious nor tortious in character. *Lull*, 614 P.2d at 326. However, in the case at bar, plaintiffs' claim that defendants intentionally diluted the ore is clearly tortious in character, since the alleged act is the basis of plaintiffs' claim for conversion. . . . Thus, the issue is now squarely before us.

According to the Restatement, punitive damages are recoverable for a breach of contract if the conduct constituting the breach is also a tort for which punitive damages are recoverable. *See* Restatement (Second) of Contracts § 355 (1981). We now adopt this view[1] because it furthers our policy of allowing punitive damages for certain tortious acts. *See Bridges v. Alaska Housing Authority*, 375 P.2d 696, 702 (Alaska 1962). Since defendants' alleged conduct also constituted a tort for which punitive damages might have been recoverable, the superior court erred in dismissing plaintiffs' punitive damages claim.

Accordingly, the judgment below is affirmed in part, reserved in part, and remanded for proceedings consistent with this opinion.

b. Statutory State of Mind

Read the following excerpt from the appellate opinion in *Davies v. Bradley*. Prepare a case brief for a contracts class that includes a synthesis of this case with both *White v. Benkowski* and *McKibben v. Mohawk Oil Co.*

DAVIES v. BRADLEY
Colorado Court of Appeals
676 P.2d 1242 (Colo. Ct. App. 1983)

KELLY, Judge.

This case involves the sale of a house built and sold by defendants Bobby and Mary Lee Bradley to the plaintiffs, James and Judith Davies. Citing the existence of 11 defects, including the failure to obtain a certificate of occupancy, all in violation of the county building code, the trial court found that the house was unsuitable for habitation and ruled that the Bradleys had breached the implied warranty of habitability.

. . . We affirm.

The Bradleys worked full time on the construction of the house for almost a year. It was the third house which they had built and lived in, and subsequently sold. When the house was put on the market, it appeared to be complete with the exception of a partially completed deck on the exterior of the house. The Bradleys obtained a building permit prior to construction of the house, but did not obtain a certificate of occupancy. The Bradleys performed substantially all the work on the residence themselves.

The plaintiffs submitted an offer to purchase the house which was accepted by the Bradleys, who added a clause to the standard form contract stating that "the buyers agree to accept said property as-is with the exception of the deck which will be completed by (illegible) 1978." The plaintiffs

---

1. We do not now reach the issue of whether punitive damages are recoverable for a breach of contract, if the conduct constituting the breach is malicious but not tortious in character.

agreed to the inclusion of this clause. The trial court found that the purpose of this clause was to relieve the Bradleys of the obligation of performing further work on the house except as specified in the contract. The court further found that the parties did not intend for the clause to waive or limit any implied or express warranties of workmanlike construction or habitability.

After closing, the plaintiffs took possession of the house and discovered it to be in violation of the Uniform Building Code of Pitkin County. An inspection revealed 11 distinct defects in quality and workmanship rendering the house unsuitable for habitation. The trial court found that the plaintiffs had no knowledge of the defects at the time of the closing, and that the Bradleys knew or should have known of their obligation to obtain periodic building inspections and a certificate of occupancy under the Uniform Building Code.

The trial court held that the Bradleys' failure to disclose that no such inspections or certificate had been obtained was done willfully and with a wanton and reckless disregard for the rights and interests of the plaintiffs. Therefore, the court awarded the plaintiffs the actual costs of making the house habitable and bringing it into compliance with the county's building code, and exemplary damages in an amount equal to the legal fees incurred by the plaintiffs because of the Bradleys' willful and wanton failure to disclose. . . .

IV

The Bradleys argue that the trial court erred in awarding exemplary damages. . . . We disagree.

Exemplary damages are not ordinarily a proper remedy in breach of contract cases. *Williams v. Speedster, Inc.*, 175 Colo. 73, 485 P.2d 728 (1971); *Sams v. Curfman*, 111 Colo. 124, 137 P.2d 1017 (1943). This is because the allegations in an action for breach of contract do not ordinarily bring the case within the confines of the statute. *See* § 13-21-102, C.R.S. 1973.[2] Where, however, as here, the facts alleged and proved establish willful and wanton conduct and reckless disregard for the rights of the plaintiff, the maleficent intent on which exemplary damage awards in tort are based is present, and exemplary damages may be awarded though the action sounds in contract. The punitive and deterrent purposes of the statute authorizing exemplary damages in civil cases are thereby effected. . . .

The judgment is affirmed.

Smith and Van Cise, JJ., concur.

Assignment 2. Course Outline

Imagine that you have studied the doctrine of quasi-contract in your contracts class and that you are ready to summarize your case briefs and to

---

2. Author's Note: At the time of the court of appeals' decision in Davies v. Bradley, § 13-21-102 provided:

Exemplary damages. In all civil actions in which damages are assessed by a jury for a wrong done to the person, or to personal or real property, and the injury express your understanding of the subject in outline form. Further imagine that the notes reproduced below represent your briefs of principal and note cases on the topic. To prepare your outline, classify the holdings of the cases according to topic and subtopic, synthesize the holdings to arrive at an understanding of general legal rules, and develop a logical organization of the rules or problem areas. Then, summarize your ideas about them in outline form, using summaries of your case briefs as illustrations of legal rules.

Boswell v. Weldon (Texarkana S. Ct. 1958), CB 201.

Issues and Holdings:

I. Did a bank employee enrich an accident victim by rendering nonprofessional but competent first aid that nonetheless failed to save the victim's life? Yes.

II. Was the enrichment unjust even though the bank employee did not expect compensation at the time that he rendered aid? No; judgment for Defendant Estate affirmed.

Facts:

Bank robbers shot and critically wounded Boswell, a security guard. Weldon, a bank loan officer, attempted to stop the guard's bleeding and to revive him with CPR. The loan officer had no medical training other than a single CPR class sponsored by the bank for all employees. He had never charged for first-aid services and had never expected to. Although he rendered competent first aid, the guard died of his wounds before an ambulance could arrive.

Procedural History:

The loan officer sued the guard's estate for compensation for the emergency first-aid services. The trial court granted the estate's motion for summary judgment on the grounds that (1) the loan officer provided no benefit to the security guard, and (2) any benefit provided by the loan officer to the guard did not unjustly enrich the guard. The loan officer appealed, and the state's only appellate court affirms.

Reasoning on Each Issue:

I. Quasi-contract permits recovery on proof of unjust enrichment. Summary judgment cannot be based on lack of enrichment, because the record raises a genuine fact dispute about whether the loan officer transferred an actual benefit with measurable value to the guard. Even though the guard

complained of is attended by circumstances of fraud, malice or insult, or a wanton and reckless disregard of the injured party's rights and feelings, the jury, in addition to the actual damages sustained by such party, may award him reasonable exemplary damages.

died, a jury could find that he received services with a market value that increased his chances of surviving.

II. On the undisputed facts, the loan officer could not reasonably have expected compensation at the time he rendered the emergency services. He is presumed to have rendered them gratuitously, and no facts rebut that presumption. Therefore, as a matter of law, it was not unjust for the guard and his estate to retain the benefit of the loan officer's services without compensating the loan officer.

Evaluation:

I find it odd to recognize enrichment in a person who dies soon after services are rendered. However, I agree with the ultimate disposition—it is reasonable to presume that emergency services would be rendered without expectation of compensation in a case such as this.

Cutter v. Noble (Texarkana S. Ct. 1982), CB 205.

Issues and Holdings:

I. Was it unjust for the victim of an auto accident to retain emergency lifesaving medical services from a physician without compensating the physician? Yes.

II. Did the trial court correctly instruct the jury that it must award compensation based on the results of the emergency services, as valued by someone in the position of the recipient? No.

Facts:

The victim of an automobile accident lay in the street near the office of a physician who engaged in the general practice of medicine. Alerted by a witness to the accident, the physician ran to the accident site with medical instruments, and she stabilized the unconscious victim until an ambulance could transport the victim to a hospital. The victim fully recovered. He almost certainly would have died had not the physician rendered emergency aid before arrival of the ambulance. The physician sent a bill of $300 to the victim, which the victim refused to pay.

Procedural History:

The physician sued the victim on the theory of quasi-contract. After a trial before a jury, the victim moved for a directed verdict on the ground that no reasonable juror could find that the enrichment was unjust. The trial court denied the motion and instructed the jury that, if it found unjust enrichment, it could award the physician the full value of the benefit received by the victim. The jury awarded the physician $500,000. The victim appealed, and the appellate court reverses.

Reasoning on Each Issue:

I. Because the physician ordinarily charged for such services, and because the services she rendered were nontrivial, a reasonable jury could find that the physician reasonably expected compensation when she rendered the services. Therefore, the question whether the enrichment was unjust was properly before the jury.

II. Full restitution of the benefit received by the victim would be disproportionately high if measured by the value of the life saved. To put practical limits on such awards more consistent with the quasi-contractual basis for relief, the trial court should have specifically instructed the jury that the benefit in such a case is measured by the general market price of the medical services rendered, or by some other measure that incorporates the physician's costs plus reasonable profit.

Evaluation:

I agree with the results on both issues, but some of the language of the second holding is analytically unsatisfying. If measured by the physician's costs, the interest protected is more like reliance than restitution.

Valenzuela v. Rose (Calzona S. Ct. 1942), CB 209.

Issue and Holdings:

When a house painter enriched a homeowner by painting the owner's newly constructed house pursuant to a contract between the painter and the general contractor, was it unjust for the owner to retain the benefits of the paint job without compensating the painter for it? No.

Facts:

The owner, Rose, hired a general contractor to build a custom home, but the owner omitted painting from the tasks covered by their contract because a friend of the owner, Tierney, had separately agreed to paint the interior and exterior at a bargain price. The general contractor months later mistakenly hired Valenzuela to paint the interior and exterior of the owner's new house. When Valenzuela completed the painting according to his contract with the general contractor, the owner reminded the general contractor that painting was omitted from their contract, and the owner refused to pay either the general contractor or Valenzuela for the painting. In turn, the general contractor refused to pay Valenzuela for the work.

Procedural History:

Valenzuela sued the owner in quasi-contract for the reasonable value of the paint job. On the owner's challenge to the sufficiency of the complaint, the trial court dismissed the action. Valenzuela appealed, and the intermediate court of appeals affirmed. Here, the Supreme Court also affirms.

Reasoning:

In contracting with Valenzuela, the general contractor acted independently and not as the agent of the owner. At the time of painting, the painter expected compensation from the general contractor, not from the owner. The court sympathizes with the painter's fear that local contractors would exclude the painter from bid lists if he sued the general contractor. Nonetheless, the painter's proper remedy is against the general contractor for breach of their contract. Given the posture of the case, it was not unjust for the owner to retain the benefit of the painting without paying the painter for it.

Evaluation:

It seems unfair that the owner is permitted to enjoy this windfall; perhaps the owner ought to pay the painter the same bargain rate that the owner's friend had agreed to charge, even if that would be less than the normal market rate. Also, I wonder whether the general contractor could recover against the owner if the general contractor were liable to the painter. If so, why not permit the painter to sue the owner directly and bypass the general contractor?

Note Cases, CB 213-214:

1. *Cirankowitz v. Pastorini* (New Maine Ct. App. 1957). On facts similar to those of *Valenzuela v. Rose*, the court permitted a carpenter's suit against the owner, because the general contractor with whom the carpenter contracted had declared bankruptcy by the time of suit.

2. *Firello v. Combs* (W. Dakansas Ct. App. 1975). While the owner of a new structure solicited bids directly from painters, an unemployed painter painted the exterior of the structure without the prior knowledge of the owner and demanded that the owner pay him the amount of the lowest bid that the owner received from other painters for the job. Although the paint job was exactly as the owner specified in the job solicitation, the owner refused to pay. The court affirmed dismissal of the painter's action against the owner, ruling that the owner was not unjustly enriched.

3. *Spencer's Distributing Co. v. Hometown Appliances* (New Maine S. Ct. 1981). A distributor sent ten microwave ovens to a retailer that had not ordered the ovens. The court held that the retailer was unjustly enriched, because the distributor had sent the microwave ovens under a reasonable mistake to which the retailer had contributed. The distributor was entitled to restitution of the value of the benefit bestowed upon the retailer measured by the wholesale price at which the retailer normally could buy such ovens rather than by the retail price at which it sold them to the public or the relatively high wholesale price that the distributor usually offered to retailers.

Appendix IV

Office Memoranda:
Assignments for Part V
of the Main Text

The five assignments below vary in their complexity and in the extent to which they require research in your law library. Each of the first two assignments presents a single issue for analysis. Assignment 3 is identical to Assignment 2 except that it adds a second issue for analysis. Assignments 4 and 5 present one or more issues for analysis, some of which may break into subissues. To some extent, precisely which and how many issues you discuss in Assignments 4 and 5 is a matter of judgment.

The first three assignments are "closed universe" problems: All the necessary authority is provided at the end of each assignment. In contrast, Assignments 4 and 5 are "open library" problems: You must conduct your own research in the law library to find authorities that will help you analyze the problems. Of course, your instructor can modify these problems by (1) asking you to conduct research to supplement the materials provided to you in Assignment 1, 2, or 3, or (2) providing you with some or all of the authorities that you will need for Assignment 4 or 5.

Even if you are restricted to the authorities supplied in an assignment

541

below, you will notice that some of the judicial opinions set forth at the
end of an assignment cite to other decisions. In your memorandum, you
may refer to such cited decisions, but only to the extent appropriate in light
of your limited knowledge of the content of those cited decisions. For
example, *Consolidated Edison,* the second judicial opinion set forth at the
end of Assignment 2, cites to *Ben Construction Corp. v. Ventre* for the
proposition that New York courts look to "the main objective sought to be
accomplished by the contracting parties." In discussing *Consolidated Edison*
in your memorandum, you may want to, though you need not, cite to *Ben
Construction Corp.* as further support for the point made in *Consolidated
Edison* or perhaps as the original source of language that you quote from
Consolidated Edison. However, you should not rely more heavily on *Ben
Construction Corp.,* because you do not have the benefit of the full text of
that decision in your materials.

The page numbers within the opinions in the original reporters appear
in brackets in the reproductions of the opinions at the end of Assignments
1 and 2. Some of the opinions cite to other authorities in a form other than
the citation form recommended in Chapter 14 of this book. When you cite
to any authority, adopt the citation form recommended in Chapter 14 or
recommended by your instructor, rather than other forms reflected in some
of the opinions.

Finally, the assignments are set in different jurisdictions. Assignments 1
and 5 are set in actual states, including the state of residence of your law
school. In those assignments, you can use both mandatory case law from
the forum state and persuasive case law from other states. Assignments 2,
3, and 4 are set in the fictitious states of Calzona and New Maine. In those
assignments, the forum state has some relevant statutes but no helpful case
law; all case law, therefore, is from other states and is persuasive only.

Assignment 1. Office Memorandum
Single Issue
Jurisdiction: Arizona
Closed Universe

You are an associate in a firm that represents 15 young women and their
mothers who complain that a seamstress intentionally breached a contract
to provide gowns for their use in a Quinceanera ceremony in Phoenix,
Arizona. As part of its professional responsibility to provide free legal services,
your firm agrees to represent them without charge.

A Quinceanera ceremony is a traditional "coming out" party for a
woman on her fifteenth birthday. It is celebrated in many Hispanic communi-
ties throughout the world. The celebration consists of a Catholic mass,
followed by a formal reception that includes a dinner and dance. The cele-
brant, known as the "Quinceanera," traditionally wears a gown that is nearly
as formal and ornate as a wedding gown. She is attended by relatives, by
godmothers and godfathers, and by 14 maids of honor. The maids of honor
are typically peers and close friends of the Quinceanera. The maids tradition-

ally wear fancy gowns that match each other either in color or in pattern. Along with their male attendants, they participate in both the mass and the reception.

Your primary client, Trina Araiza, turned 15 last July 10. She and her 14 chosen maids of honor hired Ramona Udave to sew gowns of a particular pattern for the Quinceanera celebration. Trina's mother, Cristina, negotiated the contract with Udave. Because the Quinceanera and her maids of honor were minors, their parents cosigned the contract to ensure enforceability. On March 15, the Quinceanera participants provided Udave with material for the gowns and met with Udave so that she could take measurements. On May 5, Udave met with each participant for final fittings. At that meeting, each gown was only partially sewn, was partially held together with pins, and was not wearable.

Throughout May and June, Udave repeatedly assured all the participants that she was making normal progress on the gowns and that the gowns would be ready on time. In early July, Udave represented that she was putting the finishing touches on the gowns and that they would all be ready by the morning of the Quinceanera. Although some of the participants were anxious to see the gowns, Udave said that she never let her clients see her work until the last stitch was in place.

On the morning of the Quinceanera celebration, the participants arrived at Udave's shop to pick up their gowns. Udave repeatedly assured each of them that her gown was minutes away from completion and that each one should wait for the gown in the front room of Udave's shop. Udave kept the participants waiting for varying periods of time, some beyond 1:00 P.M., the time for commencement of the mass. Araiza herself received her gown at 12:30. At that time, she was nearly ill with anxiety. She dressed quickly and arrived at the site of the mass by 1:10 P.M. Her maids of honor, however, were still waiting for their gowns and therefore could not yet participate in the formal procession that begins the mass. By 1:30 P.M. five of the maids of honor had arrived with their gowns. Although the gowns were unfinished and looked terrible, Araiza and her five maids of honor walked in the processional and began the mass. Araiza was emotionally distraught during the mass, partly because of the absence of two maids of honor who were designated to recite prayers with her; those maids of honor were still waiting at Udave's tailoring shop on Udave's representations that their gowns were nearly complete.

In fact, the remaining gowns were in the same condition as they had been during the March fitting, and Udave never completed them. Although Udave continued to represent that the gowns were nearly completed, the remaining Quinceanera participants left her shop shortly after the mass and attended the reception in casual or semi-formal clothes. Although they participated in the traditional reception procession and waltz, they felt humiliated because of their inappropriate attire.

Araiza and the maids of honor suffered embarrassment and other forms of emotional distress as a result of Udave's actions. Based on information they acquired after the Quinceanera ceremony, they are convinced that Udave intentionally ruined the Quinceanera because of her friendship with a bitter rival of the Araiza family.

Your supervising attorney, Daniel Adams, intends to explore various potential claims, including breach of contract, fraud, and negligence. He wants you to assume that he can establish only the contract claim, and he wants you to analyze the question whether the Quinceanera and her maids of honor can recover damages for emotional distress on their claims for breach of their collective contract with Udave. He knows that they can recover damages for other kinds of losses stemming from the breach, but he thinks that the damages for emotional distress may be problematic.

Using only the following research materials, prepare an office memorandum, five to seven pages in length, discussing this question. In reciting the facts of this dispute, summarize only the facts material to your analysis. You may assume that the Quinceanera and her maids of honor are parties to an enforceable contract and that any dispute regarding the contract will be governed by Arizona law. Because Mr. Adams intends to use your memorandum to help him prepare a brief that he will submit to an Arizona tribunal, he wants you to use parallel citations when citing to either of the two Arizona decisions. To help you find your way through those decisions, internal page numbers for the official Arizona Reports are noted in bold in brackets, and internal page numbers for the Pacific Reporter are noted in italics in brackets. When citing to the Alabama decision, you may cite only to the regional reporter.

Research Materials

CONTRACTS
E. Allan Farnsworth
(3d ed. 1999)
(p. 840, footnotes omitted)

§ 12.17   Other Limitations, Including Emotional Disturbance . . .

A limitation more firmly rooted in tradition is that generally denying recovery for emotional disturbance, or "mental distress," resulting from breach of contract, even if the limitations of unforeseeability and uncertainty can be overcome. . . . Whatever the basis of the limitation, courts have not applied it inflexibly. Some courts have looked to the nature of the contract and made exceptions where breach was particularly likely to result in serious emotional disturbance. . . .

FARMERS INSURANCE EXCHANGE v. HENDERSON
82 Ariz. 335, 313 P.2d 404 (1957)
(Arizona Supreme Court)

[**pg. 337**, *pg. 405*] WINDES, Justice.

The appellant, Farmers Insurance Exchange, issued to appellee, George Henderson, a public liability insurance policy insuring him against claims for death or bodily injury and property damage resulting from the operation of Henderson's car. The limit of the policy for death or bodily injury was $5,000 for one person and $10,000 for one accident and $5,000 for property damage. There was a collision between the Henderson car when operated by his employee, one Whitehead, and an automobile operated by Charles Breesman. Three actions were filed for damages resulting from the accident. One action was by . . . Breesman against Henderson and Whitehead. This . . . action was tried in the superior court. The present case is a suit by Henderson against the company for damages claimed to have resulted from the failure to settle the Breesman claim for an amount within its policy limits when opportunity was presented for such settlement. This failure caused Henderson and his wife to lose their business, because they were forced to sell the business to pay for liability in excess of their liability insurance limits. A jury trial resulted in a verdict and judgment against the company in the sum of $45,000. The company appeals. The appellant will be referred to as the company and individuals by name.

The principal questions presented for solution are the extent of the obligations of the insurer to the insured to settle within the policy limits a claim against the insured and, if liability is established, the correct measure of the insured's damages.

. . . .

[**pg. 342,** *pg. 408*] On the question of damages Henderson submitted and the court gave instructions that if the jury found the company breached its contract, it could assess damages for the following items: loss of the property as a going business and interest from time of loss, humiliation, pain and suffering, attorney fees incurred by Henderson, loss of earnings, expenses of seeking employment [*pg. 409*] including traveling expenses to that end, and his loss of business reputation and credit. Over the company's objection evidence on these items was admitted. Except as to the value of the business as a going concern and interest thereon from the time of its sale, the court erred in the admission of evidence and giving instructions on the foregoing items of damages.

The wrong involved is causing the destruction or conversion of insured's business property in satisfaction of the [**pg. 343**] company's obligation. The court correctly instructed that as a general rule the damages for the loss or destruction or conversion of a going business is its value at the time and place of destruction with interest. This is in accord with the pronouncements of this court. Jones v. Stanley, 27 Ariz. 381, 233 P. 598. The humiliation, mental pain, suffering and anguish incurred by the Hendersons was the direct result of the pecuniary loss suffered. If it is to be considered a breach of contract, to recover for these items the contract must be of such a nature that its breach would cause mental suffering for reasons other than the pecuniary loss. Restatement of Law, Contracts, section 341. . . .

[**pg. 344,** *pg. 409*] The judgment is reversed with instructions for a new trial on the entire case as to all issues.

FOGLEMAN v. PERUVIAN ASSOCIATES
127 Ariz. 504, 622 P.2d 63 (Ct. App. 1980)

[**pg. 505,** *pg. 64*] HATHAWAY, Chief Judge.
In August of 1973, appellants were residents of Tucson, Arizona, and

Mr. Fogleman was employed as a welder at a copper mine near Tucson. Appellees offered him employment at a mine operated by appellees at Quajone, Peru, and he accepted. The contract of employment was dated September 24, 1973, and was for a two-year period, employing Mr. Fogleman as welding supervisor at $1,700 per month plus housing allowance and other benefits.

Appellees terminated Fogleman's employment on March 8, 1974. Appellants brought this action alleging wrongful termination of the employment contract and seeking damages. After trial to the court, without a jury, judgment was entered in favor of appellants in the amount of $14,989.33, plus costs, together with interest commencing on the date of judgment. The trial court entered findings of fact and conclusions of law.

On appeal, appellants contend that they were entitled to an award of consequential general damages. . . .

[**pg. 506,** *pg. 65*] Appellants first contend that the trial court erred in not awarding consequential general damages because the evidence and findings support such an award. Specifically, the court found that appellees could terminate appellants' employment contract only for cause and that they did not have cause. This breach caused appellants economic loss of $14,989.33. In finding of fact number 10, the court found:

> 10. The wrongful conduct of the Defendants S.P.C.C., Fluor Utah and Peruvian Associates also caused Plaintiffs to suffer general damages, including emotional distress, anxiety, embarrassment, humiliation and other items listed on page 14 of Plaintiffs' Post-Trial Memorandum.

The court refused to award consequential damages, perceiving the rule to be that such damages are not allowed in a breach of contract action, and so stated in conclusion of law number 15.

Appellants argue that consequential damages are allowable in a breach of contract action and that appellees' wrongful conduct was both a breach of contract and a tort, therefore such damages were allowable. The trial court's first finding of fact stated that the action was for breach of contract. . . . We do not have before us an appeal from a tort action, and appellants' citations for the proposition that damages for mental anguish are allowable in actions which sound both in contract and in tort, are not applicable. The appropriate measure of damages for an employee who has been wrongfully discharged is the unpaid balance of the salary less the sums earned during the remainder of the contract period. . . .

In *Browning v. Fies,* 4 Ala. App. 580, 58 So. 931 (1912), cited by appellants, a special situation was presented where the plaintiff had hired a carriage to transport him to church for his wedding. The defendant was aware of the reasons and the time frame for performance and that the failure of performance would, under the circumstances, expose plaintiff to particular consequences, alluded to by the court and for which the plaintiff was allowed damages. This case is inapplicable to the facts herein. . . .

[**pg. 507,** *pg. 66*] Affirmed as modified.

BROWNING v. FIES
58 So. 931 (Ala. Ct. App. 1912)

[**pg. 932**] Appeal from City Court of Birmingham; Chas. A. Senn, Judge.

PELHAM, J. This is a suit for damages for the breach of a contract entered into between the appellant, who was the plaintiff below, and the appellees. Under the terms of the contract, the defendants, for the consideration of $5 paid to them by the plaintiff, agreed to furnish a carriage and team for the special purpose of carrying the plaintiff, his friends, and relatives from the home of the plaintiff near Rising Station to a church in Birmingham, Ala., a distance of about three miles, at which church the plaintiff on this particular occasion was to be married. The damages claimed and sought to be recovered were for the actual financial loss arising out of a breach of the contract, and damages for mental suffering, physical pain, humiliation, mortification, etc.

[The defendants] filed two motions to strike from each count of the complaint as amended the averments as to the plaintiff's having suffered great mental anguish, humiliation, distress, etc., on the ground that such allegations did not set up matters constituting proper elements for the recovery of damages. The defendants also separately moved to strike from each count of the complaint any claims for damages based on delay in reaching the place appointed for the marriage ceremony, for being compelled to ride to the church in a public street car, and for physical and mental pain and suffering, for humiliation, etc., etc., in consequence thereof, on the grounds that such damages were speculative, too remote, and not recoverable in an action of this nature. The court granted the defendants' motion to strike from the complaint these elements as claims of damage as to each count, and the plaintiff reserved exceptions to the court's ruling. On the pleadings as thus framed, the issues were tried before a jury. . . .

The evidence without conflict showed that the plaintiff, on the day of the evening upon which he was to be married, went to the defendants' place of business in Birmingham, Ala., and entered into a contract with the defendants, who were engaged in conducting a public livery business, to furnish the plaintiff, for the use of himself, friends, and family, a carriage and team which was to be sent to the plaintiff's residence at or near Rising Station at 7:30 o'clock P.M. on that day to carry plaintiff and his wedding party to the church in Birmingham, three miles distant, where the plaintiff was to be married at 8 o'clock on that evening. The defendants made a charge of $5 for this specified use of the carriage and team, which amount was paid to the defendants by the plaintiff, who at the time of making the contract informed the defendants of the purpose [**pg. 933**] for which the same was to be used and the hour appointed for the ceremony, and the defendants agreed and contracted to furnish the carriage and team to be used by the plaintiff for this specific purpose. It was also shown without conflict in the evidence that the defendants made default and breached the contract and failed to send the carriage at the time and place as they contracted to do, and no excuse whatever was offered upon the part of the defendants for having failed to perform the contract. The plaintiff, on account of the defendants' breach of the contract, was compelled, in order to reach the church where his prospective bride and friends were awaiting his coming, to resort to a public street car in which plaintiff and his family and friends, at the expenditure of 30 cents for street car fare, attended the wedding appareled in "dress" or "evening" clothes. The plaintiff and the lady members of his family, unsuitably attired for riding in a street car and for walking along the public streets, had to walk for several squares from the place necessary to leave the car line in going to the church, and the wedding ceremony was delayed for 45 or 50 minutes on account of the failure of the plaintiff to reach the church on time. During this period of delay, the bride, family, minister, and friends in attendance at the church were kept waiting upon the delayed arrival of the prospective groom.

On the trial the plaintiff offered in varying forms questions to elicit evidence going to show that he suffered mental and physical pain, mortification, and humiliation, but on objection of the defendants he was not allowed to make such proof or to show any elements of damage of this nature. At the instance of the defendants, the court gave the following charge in writing to the jury: "If the jury believe the evidence, they can only find a verdict for the plaintiff for $5.30 with interest thereon from the 26th day of April, 1906." The plaintiff requested charges in writing, which were refused by the court, to the effect that the plaintiff was entitled to recover for any mental suffering and physical pain caused as a proximate consequence of the defendants' breach of the contract. The jury returned a verdict for plaintiff for $6.55, and, from the judgment entered on this verdict, the plaintiff prosecutes this appeal.

The main contention of appellant is that the court was in error in its ruling on the pleading and on the evidence, and its rulings on the charges in refusing to allow mental suffering and physical pain as an element of recoverable damages for breach of the contract.

The plaintiff's special or ulterior purpose in making the contract was disclosed at the time it was entered into and thereby became incorporated into it and thus afforded a substantial basis for the assessment of special damages. The special circumstances having been known and assented to by each of the contracting parties, each is deemed to have contracted with reference to them, and the party who breaches the contract may be justly held to make good to the other whatever damages, general or special, he has sustained which are the reasonable and natural consequences of the breach under the known circumstances with reference to which the parties acted in making the contract.

When a contract is entered into under special circumstances within the knowledge of both parties, the natural and proximate consequences of a breach of which will entail special damages upon the party not in default, the larger amount of damages may be recovered as having been in the contemplation of both parties. [citation omitted] This was also the English rule and the rule at common law. Damages recoverable for the breach of a contract are measured, not only by the actual loss sustained that naturally results as the ordinary consequence of the breach, but extend to consequences which may, under the circumstances of entering into the contract, be presumed to have been in the contemplation of both parties as the probable result of a breach. [citation omitted] And, if the special circumstances are communicated, they become an element of the contract. [citation omitted]

But are damages for mental suffering an element of the special damages recoverable? "Injury to the feelings—mental harassment—is an element of actual damages. 'Wounding a man's feelings is as much an element of actual damages as breaking his limb.' *Head v. Georgia Pac.*, 79 Ga. 358 [7 S.E. 217, 11 Am. St. Rep. 434]." *Birmingham Water Wks. Co. v. Martini*, 2 Ala. App. 652, 56 So. 833.

The right to recover special damages for mental anguish growing out of a breach of contract to send and deliver a telegram, as said in the recent case of *W. U. Tel. Co. v. Cleveland*, 169 Ala. 131, 135, 53 So. 80, 82, "has been settled in this court," citing the cases sustaining this proposition.

If damages for mental suffering are actual damages and recoverable as compensatory damages when proximately resulting from a breach of the contract, because of the nature of a telegram and the relationship disclosed bringing this consequence of the breach within the contemplation of the parties, as was held in *W. U. Tel. Co. v. Haley*, 143 Ala. 586, 39 So. 386, we cannot perceive under what rule or by what sound reason such *actual* damages can be excluded as a proper measure of recovery in connection with the pecuniary loss sustained in any case where they flow naturally and as a direct consequence from the infraction [**pg. 934**] of a contract entered into under special circumstances known to both parties, and with reference to which they contracted. . . .

This court has also held [citation omitted] that, for a breach of contract for transportation, a woman may recover for mental distress and worry due to having been prevented and delayed in securing stateroom accommodations while on her bridal trip.

In this particular case, considering the subject matter of the contract, the special purpose and exceptional use to which plaintiff intended to put the carriage, which was communicated and well known to the defendants, and with reference to which they contracted, it would seem that it was in the reasonable contemplation of the parties when the contract was entered into under the special known circumstances, that the immediate effect and proximate result ensuing from a breach of the contract by the defendants would cause the plaintiff inconvenience, annoyance, mental harassment, or distress, and make him to suffer physical delay with the attendant discomfort, as well as mental pain in consequence thereof. Certainly it is but common knowledge that some distress of mind must be the natural and proximate consequence of being delayed and not having proper conveyance to meet an appointment of such delicate nature.

The plaintiff by proper averments claimed damages in different counts of the complaint for physical discomfort in consequence of being delayed and not having proper conveyance to meet the special and particular appointment (undoubtedly of great moment to him), and for mental distress attendant upon and suffered in consequence of these physical inconveniences, delay, etc. The court was in error in not submitting these questions to the jury as a proper element of recoverable damages, and in limiting the recovery to the actual financial loss sustained.

A detailed discussion of the various assignments of error is unnecessary. The main proposition involved in each of all of them goes to the question we have considered and determined in what has been said.

Reversed and remanded.

Assignment 2.   Office Memorandum
Single Issue
Jurisdiction: Fictitious State of New Maine
Closed Universe

You work as a law clerk for attorney Susan Corleone. This morning she called you into her office and initiated the following conversation with you:

Corleone: I just finished an interview with Bob Carson, a new client. He spent ten years working as a plumbing subcontractor on construction sites. Now he owns and manages Carson Plumbing Supply, and he sells and installs pipe and plumbing fixtures in Sweetwater, New Maine, and surrounding areas.

Law Clerk: What's Mr. Carson's problem?

Corleone: John King, owner of King Enterprises, Inc., is suing him for breach of a written contract. Here's a copy of the contract. King is the owner of an office building currently under construction in Sweetwater; King alleges that Carson breached a contract to supply and install the plumbing in the new building.

Law Clerk: Did Carson try to perform at all?

Corleone: No. He took on a different job instead. He says that he revoked his bid over the telephone August 11, ten days after he submitted it and five days before King tried to accept; in other words, Carson asserts that he never formed a contract with King in the first place. It looks like Carson clearly notified King of his intent to revoke the bid before King accepted it. Unfortunately for Carson, the bid form supplied by King included a promise by Carson to hold the bid open for 30 days; Carson used and signed that form, and King accepted Carson's bid within 30 days.

Law Clerk: Did King give any consideration for Carson's promise to hold his bid open and irrevocable for 30 days?

Corleone: I don't see any. And he apparently didn't rely on the promise either.

Law Clerk: Doesn't that end the inquiry? Carson's promise to hold his bid open was gratuitous and unenforceable; therefore, Carson validly revoked his bid before King accepted it.

Corleone: That's good analysis under common law, but the Uniform Commercial Code provides that, in some circumstances, "firm offers" like the one that Carson gave are irrevocable even though the offeree gave no consideration for the offeror's promise to hold the offer open.

Law Clerk: Does the UCC apply to this case?

Corleone: That's what I want you to tell me. Give me your analysis and conclusions in memorandum form. New Maine has adopted the UCC as part of the New Maine Commercial Code, but no New Maine court decisions have addressed the issue in this case. You'll have to rely on the UCC provisions and on interpretive case law from other jurisdictions.

Law Clerk: Do you want me to discuss the question whether the parties successfully formed a contract under either the UCC or the common law?

Corleone: Not at this point. Just address the question of choice of law; tell me whether the UCC or the common law will apply to the dispute.

Law Clerk: Did Carson tell you anything about the negotiations leading up to the bidding?

Corleone: Yes. King especially wanted Carson to do the job because Carson is the exclusive distributor of patented pipe fittings designed by Carson himself. Carson's pipe fittings reduce the difficulty and expense of installation. King had originally asked Carson to submit only a bid for the parts; it had planned to hire another subcontractor to install them. However, Carson insisted that he install any parts that he sold.

Law Clerk: Why is that? Does Carson make most of his profit on the installation?

Corleone: I don't know what his profit margins are. I do know that Carson quoted prices over the phone to King of $36,000 for all the parts and $38,000 for installation. However, the bid form simply calls for a total price, which Carson filled in for $74,000. When Carson refused to perform, King had to use another supplier and installer at a higher cost. Here's a copy of their contract, which incorporates the architect's plans. The architect's plans are in the conference room, but I can tell you that they explicitly call for the plumber to supply designated sizes of Carson's special pipes and fittings, so you can assume that the contract calls not only for installation but also for a sale of goods that would be identified to the contract while still movable.

AGREEMENT FOR SUPPLY AND INSTALLATION OF PLUMBING

I
PARTIES

The parties to this agreement are:

King Enterprises, Inc. (OWNER), and
Bob Carson, d.b.a. Carson Plumbing Supply (CONTRACTOR).

II
MUTUAL RIGHTS AND OBLIGATION

OWNER and CONTRACTOR agree to the following bargained-for exchange:

1. . . .

2. . . .

3. CONTRACTOR will supply and install pipe and plumbing fixtures in accordance with the specifications in the architect's plans (attached and incorporated). All fixtures so installed will be incorporated into OWNER's building and will become the sole property of OWNER.

4. Within 30 days of the architect's certifying satisfactory installation of the plumbing, OWNER will pay CONTRACTOR the total sum of __*$74,000*__ .

5. . . .

6. . . .

7. The parties understand that CONTRACTOR will use this document as a bid form to make an offer to OWNER. This document becomes a contract when OWNER accepts CONTRACTOR's bid by notifying CONTRACTOR orally or in writing of OWNER's decision to use CONTRACTOR's services.

Signatures: *By signing this document immediately below, CONTRACTOR promises to hold its offer open and irrevocable for 30 days from the date of CONTRACTOR's signature below.*

Bob Carson _____   *August 1, 200*x[1] _____
Offered by CONTRACTOR   Date

John King _____   *August 16, 200*x _____
Accepted by OWNER   Date

Research Materials

NEW MAINE COMMERCIAL CODE
(N.M.C.C.) (2000)
(Enacting the Uniform Commercial Code)

ARTICLE 2. SALES

N.M.C.C. § 2-102. Scope: . . .

Unless the context otherwise requires, this article applies to transactions in goods; . . . .

N.M.C.C. § 2-105. Definitions: . . .

A. "Goods" means all things (including specially manufactured goods) which are movable at the time of identification to the contract for sale other than the money in which the price is to be paid, investment securities (article 8) and things in action. "Goods" also includes the unborn young animals and growing crops and other identified things attached to realty as described in the section on goods to be severed from realty (§ 2-307).

_____

1. In place of "200x" after each signature, write in the year of the August immediately preceding your work on this assignment.

COAKLEY & WILLIAMS INC. v. SHATTERPROOF
GLASS CORPORATION
706 F.2d 456 (4th Cir. 1983)
[footnotes omitted]

[**Pg. 457**] Before HALL, MURNAGHAN and SPROUSE, Circuit Judges:
MURNAGHAN, Circuit Judge:

On appeal from a dismissal under 12(b)(6) the accepted rule is "that a complaint should not be dismissed for failure to state a claim unless it appears beyond doubt that the plaintiff can prove no set of facts in support of his claim which would entitle him to relief." . . . Liberal construction in favor of the plaintiff is mandated. . . . We state as "facts" the allegations and inferences most favorable to the plaintiff. . . .

Washington Plate Glass Company had a contract to "furnish and install aluminum and glass curtain wall and store front work" on a building located in Lanham, Maryland being built by Coakley & Williams, Inc., the plaintiff. To accomplish its contractual undertaking, Washington purchased the glass spandrel required from the defendant, Shatterproof Glass Corp. Still other materials needed for the project, predominantly aluminum, it appears were acquired in part at least elsewhere.

The contract price under the Coakley and Washington agreement amounted to $262,500, subsequently increased by amendment to $271,350. The glass purchased by Washington from Shatterproof cost $87,715.00, [**pg. 458**] with the proviso that units were "to be properly marked for field installation."

The work progressed and the contract for the aluminum and glass curtain wall and storefront work was completed in March of 1974. Discoloration of the glass ensued, and Coakley complained. To remedy the situation, Washington agreed to replace the glass at no cost to Coakley, and did in fact replace a substantial portion of the glass. Shatterproof supplied the replacement glass and reimbursed Washington for the cost of re-installation, accomplished in April of 1977.

By December of 1977, the glass had again discolored, and complaints began to flow from Coakley to Washington and Shatterproof in or about December 1978. Shatterproof declined to replace a second time. On January 14, 1981, Coakley filed suit against Shatterproof in the Circuit Court for Montgomery County, Maryland alleging breach of implied warranties of merchantability and fitness for a particular purpose. Reliance was placed on certain provisions of the Maryland Uniform Commercial Code, Annotated Code of Maryland, § 1-101 et seq. Removal to the United States District Court for the District of Maryland followed, and Shatterproof sought dismissal under Fed. R. Civ. P. 12(b)(6).

A hearing on the 12(b)(6) motion followed at which Shatterproof contended (1) that the U.C.C. was inapplicable, (2) that lack of privity was fatal to the claim, and (3) that the statute of limitations had run prior to commencement of the action. We now have the case before us on appeal from an order granting the 12(b)(6) motion and dismissing the case solely on the grounds that the U.C.C. was not applicable.

Whether the U.C.C. applies turns on a question as to whether the contract between Washington and Coakley involved principally a sale of goods, on the one hand, or a provision of services, on the other. U.C.C. § 2-314 creates an implied warranty "that the *goods* shall be merchantable" to be "implied in a contract for their sale." Section 2-315 establishes an implied warranty "that the *goods* shall be fit" for a [**pg. 459**] particular purpose, "[w]here the seller at the time of contracting has reason to know [the] particular purpose." (Emphasis added.)

Consequently, unless there has been a buyer of goods, the U.C.C. warranties of merchantability and of fitness for a particular use do not apply. Furthermore, unless there has been a buyer of goods, the elimination of a requirement of privity would not have been achieved. Accordingly, both questions (1) as to the availability of the warranties and (2) as to the amenability of Shatterproof, who was not in privity with Coakley, to suit by Coakley, come down to whether the transactions between Washington and Coakley were a sale of goods or the provision of services.

To resolve that question, we must address ourselves to a welter of cases reaching varying results depending on the considerations deemed to predominate in each particular case. It should not pass unnoticed that all were decided at summary judgment [**pg. 460**] or beyond. No case involving the issue appears to have been disposed of at the rule 12(b)(6) or demurrer stage. They emphasize, in particular, three aspects which may, or may not, constitute indicia of the nature of the contract: (1) the language of the contract, (2) the nature of the business of the supplier, and (3) the intrinsic worth of the materials involved.

A distillation of the cases outlined in the foregoing notes 11-14 [omitted by editor] produces an inescapable conclusion that, on the facts in their present pro-plaintiff posture, a reasonable viewing of them would permit a factfinder to conclude that the contract between Washington and Coakley predominantly concerned a sale of goods, and consequently was governed by the U.C.C. A Rule [**pg. 461**] 12(b)(6) motion simply cannot serve to dispose of the case.

As to the first of the emphasized aspects, the contract between Washington and Coakley speaks in terms of furnishing and installing a wall and performing storefront work. Clearly, at the very outset of performance Washington had the responsibility to bring to the affected premises the materials which ultimately would form the glass curtain wall and storefront. The U.C.C. in § 2-105 defines "goods" as "*all* things (including specially manufactured goods) which are movable at the time of identification to the contract for sale other than the money in which the price is to be paid, investment securities (Title 8) and things in action." (Emphasis added.) That at least creates an uncertainty to be resolved only by a full factual presentation to determine whether the nature of the Washington business was predominantly the provision of goods or the furnishing of services. The fact that Coakley was a building contractor specializing in construction is not sufficient to provide a completely definitive answer. While often, and perhaps customarily, a contractor is engaged in the provision of services, the scope of a contractor's work is not necessarily monolithic and, in the present circumstances, it becomes a question of unresolved fact whether Coakley, for the purposes of the single relationship to which we are restricted, was a buyer of goods.

In this connection, it is not irrelevant that Coakley has alleged that the purchases by Washington from Shatterproof included anchor clips and field fasteners. At the early stage at which we find ourselves, the allegation requires us to indulge the inference urged by counsel for Coakley that putting the glass in place was a simple snap-on process requiring little expenditure of time or labor. One can readily imagine, without the advantage of specificity deriving from a full trial on the merits, that the contract largely contemplated the provision of precast panels as goods, without the installation being nearly so extensive or significant as the supplying of the glass itself.

The fact that the contract does not follow a standard, routine or regularized form, coupled with the plaintiff's contention that standard form contracts are virtually universal for construction (i.e., generally, service) contracts, operates to leave open the possibility of a finding that the contract is more one for goods than would be the customary construction contract.

Turning to the second point, the nature of Washington's business, the fact that Washington was a dealer and not a manufacturer does not have any particularly dispositive significance. Many retailers of goods function in the role of middleman. Shatterproof sold Washington materials in a transaction which unquestionably, on the sparse record before us at the preliminary stage at which we find ourselves, was a sale of goods, and the question comes down essentially to whether those materials or the services which Washington also provided under its contract with Coakley predominated. Without full consideration of as yet unascertained facts that question is simply not ripe for resolution. It is one of fact, not law; at least it is at this early stage.

Third, the complaint affords no realistic, and certainly no dispositive, information as to the value of the spandrels et al. in case of breakup into the component parts of the glass curtain wall and storefront work. That can only be determined by further development of the record, and is, in all events, but one of several factors which must be evaluated in conjunction with all the others in resolving the ultimate factual issue: Did Washington and Coakley deal primarily with goods or services?

Accordingly, Coakley has alleged enough to survive a motion to dismiss under Fed. R. Civ. P. 12(b)(6). [pg. 462] Nor, at the other extreme, has it alleged too much, permitting sure ascertainment that services, not goods, were the gravamen of the transaction. Coakley should, therefore, be permitted to show, unless the statute of limitations bars recovery, that it was a buyer of goods and, therefore, entitled to proceed under the U.C.C. provisions. . . .

[pg. 463] Accordingly, the judgment is reversed and the case remanded for further proceedings not inconsistent with this opinion.

Reversed and remanded.

CONSOLIDATED EDISON COMPANY OF NEW YORK, INC. v. WESTINGHOUSE ELECTRIC CORPORATION
567 F. Supp. 358 (S.D.N.Y. 1983)

[pg. 360] LASKER, District Judge.
On December 3, 1971, Westinghouse Electric Corporation ("Westing-

house") entered into an agreement (the "Agreement") with Consolidated Edison Company of New York, Inc. ("Con Ed"), calling for Westinghouse to "furnish and construct a complete and operable nuclear power plant (excluding, however, the nuclear fuel assemblies) built to Westinghouse commercial utility standards and specifications. . . ." (Agreement, Article I) (Def. Ex. A). The facility, since built, is known as the Indian Point Power Plant Unit Number 2 (IP 2 Plant) and is located in Buchanan, New York.

Con Ed's complaint alleges that, following completion of the plant, and beginning in 1975, defects began to appear in various components of the plant that, *inter alia,* have required extensive monitoring, repairs and modifications, have impeded Con Ed's ability to obtain maximum output from the IP 2 Plant, and may in the future require a complete shutdown of the plant for the replacement of defective equipment. The complaint divides the defects into three groups: (1) denting, corrosion and cracking of the tubes and tube support plates contained in the plant's steam generators; (2) cracks in certain turbine rotating components known as discs; and (3) defects in "other equipment," including low pressure turbine blades, the high pressure turbine casing joint, condenser tubes, cross-under piping, and circulating water pumps.

The complaint alleges seven causes of action. The first through sixth allege breach of express warranty and implied warranties of merchantability and fitness for intended purpose (first, second and third causes of action), breach of contract (fourth cause of action), negligence (fifth cause of action), and strict products liability (sixth cause of action). . . .

Westinghouse moves to dismiss various causes of action pursuant to Fed. R. Civ. P. 12(b)(6). It argues that (1) all seven causes of action are barred in whole or in substantial part by the applicable New York statutes of limitation,
. . . .

[pg. 361]

I. APPLICABLE STATUTE OF LIMITATIONS—COUNTS ONE THROUGH FOUR (WARRANTY AND CONTRACT CLAIMS)

. . . Under New York law, a four-year statute of limitations applies to causes of action based on contracts for the sale of goods, which are governed by the New York Uniform Commercial Code ("N.Y.U.C.C."), while a six-year statute of limitations applies to causes of action based on service or construction contracts, which are governed by the common law. *See* N.Y.U.C.C. § 2-725; New York Civil Practice Law & Rules ("C.P.L.R.") § 213(2). Thus, although Con Ed's contract claims with respect to the steam generators are timely under either measure, the timeliness of its contract claims with respect to the steam turbines and other equipment depends upon whether the IP 2 Agreement is "in essence" a contract for the sale of goods under the N.Y.U.C.C., or whether instead it is a service contract—a "work, labor and materials contract." *Schenectady Steel Co., Inc. v. Bruno Trimpoli General Construction Co.,* 43 A.D.2d 234, 237, 350 N.Y.S.2d 920, 923 (3rd Dep't), *aff'd on other grounds,* 34 N.Y.2d 939, 359 N.Y.S.2d 560, 316 N.E.2d 875 (1974). In deciding whether a contract is one for the sale of goods or for the rendition of services, New York courts look to "the main objective sought to be accomplished by the contracting parties," *Ben Construction Corp. v. Ventre,* 23 A.D.2d 44, 45, 257 N.Y.S.2d 988, 989 (4th Dep't 1965).

Westinghouse argues, in favor of the applicability of the N.Y.U.C.C., that the primary object of the agreement was the purchase by Con Ed of Westinghouse-manufactured and designed component parts—the steam generators, turbines, and other components of the IP 2 Plant. . . .

In answer Con Ed points out that the IP 2 Agreement is a contract not simply for the sale of specific items of power plant equipment, but for the construction of a complete nuclear power plant. The Agreement, [**pg. 362**] Con Ed argues, not only required Westinghouse to provide all architectural and engineering services necessary to the construction of the plant, along with the labor required for its construction, but also provided that Westinghouse would take all necessary steps to assure that the plant would be granted an operating license under the requirements established by the United States Atomic Energy Commission. Con Ed contends that the scope of Westinghouse's responsibilities under the Agreement, which continued throughout several years of design, construction, testing and licensing, differentiates the Agreement from typical "goods" contracts involving the one-time installation of a specific item of equipment. Con Ed also argues that, because "goods" by definition must be "movable at the time of identification to the contract for sale," see N.Y.U.C.C. § 2-105(1), a contract for the furnishing and construction of a nuclear power plant cannot be considered a contract for the sale of goods. Finally, although Con Ed asserts that the IP 2 Agreement is in essence a service contract as a matter of law, it contends, in the alternative, that at most Westinghouse has raised a question of fact as to the nature of the contract that cannot be resolved on the basis of the pleadings.

The New York cases exploring the distinction between sales and services contracts provide no clear answer to the proper classification of the IP 2 Agreement. In several instances New York courts have held that contracts as to which "service predominates and the transfer of title to personal property is an incidental feature of the transaction" are outside the scope of the U.C.C. *Schenectady Steel, supra,* 43 A.D.2d at 237, 350 N.Y.S.2d at 922 (contract to furnish and erect the structural steel for a bridge), ... In the present case, however, on the record as it stands, neither the goods nor the services aspect of the Agreement can reasonably be characterized as "incidental." Just as Con Ed plainly could not have considered the power generating equipment to be an incidental feature of its contract with Westinghouse, so also the architectural, engineering and testing services provided by Westinghouse, and the labor necessary to carry them out were crucial to the Agreement's objective.

Moreover, contrary to Westinghouse's rationale, the applicable law cannot be determined simply by looking to the matters about which Con Ed is seeking relief—primarily, defects in various items of equipment supplied by Westinghouse. The New York courts appear to have rejected an approach of applying sales law to the sales aspect of a transaction which combines both sales and service features, requiring instead that the applicable law be determined by looking to the essential nature of the underlying contract. *Compare Schenectady Steel, supra,* 43 A.D.2d at 238, 350 N.Y.S.2d at 924 (concurring opinion of Greenblott, J.) *with Milau Associates, supra,* 42 N.Y.2d at 485, 398 N.Y.S.2d at 884, 368 N.E.2d at 1249. Where, as here, the question is closely balanced, factual development is necessary before the issue is resolved. [citations omitted] The pleadings do not reveal the allocation of contract price as between construction and equipment costs, the precise nature and scope of the services undertaken by Westinghouse, or other matters that may contribute to a proper resolution of the question. It may be, as Westinghouse argues, that the "essential" nature of the contract will not be significantly clearer [**pg. 362**] following development of the record, but the accuracy of this prediction cannot be determined in advance of obtaining the facts. . . .

[**pg. 369**] . . . [T]he motion to dismiss is denied without prejudice. It is so ordered.

OSTERHOLT v. ST. CHARLES DRILLING COMPANY, INC.
500 F. Supp. 529 (E.D. Mo. 1980)

[**pg. 530**] *Memorandum*
FILIPPINE, District Judge.

This matter is before the Court for a decision on the merits, after a trial to the Court, of plaintiff's two-count complaint. Count I of the complaint alleges a breach of contract; Count II alleges misrepresentation. After consideration of the testimony of the witnesses, the exhibits, and the stipulations of the parties, the Court makes the following findings of fact and conclusions of law.

FINDINGS OF FACT

Plaintiff is a resident of the City of Collinsville, Illinois, and a citizen of the State of Illinois. Defendant Osage Homestead, Inc., d/b/a St. Charles Drilling Co., Inc., is a Missouri corporation with its principal place of business in St. Charles County, Missouri.

In November, 1974, plaintiff contacted the defendant to inquire about the possibility of defendant installing a well and water system on plaintiff's property in Illinois. Plaintiff's property consists in twenty acres located on Kosten Hill Road in Collinsville, Illinois, east of Illinois Highway 157. . . .

[**pg. 531**] . . . On July 11, 1975, plaintiff and Bob Torrance [defendant's salesman] executed an agreement for the installation by defendant of the well and water system. The agreement, plaintiff's Exhibit 9, was signed on plaintiff's Illinois property.

The agreement itself contained no description of the items which were to be included in the water system. It did show a maximum total price of $4,620.00 for the well and water system. Among the general terms and conditions contained in the agreement were a one-year guarantee on labor and parts, and the statement "[n]o agreements, expressed or implied, other than stated herein shall be considered as part of this contract." Next to the quoted statement was written "See Supplement Letter 7-11-75."

In the "Supplement Letter," dated July 11, 1975, plaintiff specified certain items which he wanted to be certain were part of the agreement; he would have allowed no work to be done by defendant on his property had the defendant not agreed to the terms in the "Supplement Letter." Defendant sent a letter to plaintiff, dated July 18, 1975, in which it confirmed the terms of the plaintiff's supplement letter; but defendant added a qualification. Part of defendant's letter to plaintiff, plaintiff's Exhibit 12, reads as follows: "1 1/4 pipe is large enough to supply 12 homes at 12 GPM each, total 144 GPM (30 # to 50 # pressure at houses); *with proper sized pump and accumulator system*." (Emphasis added.) The underlined words or their equivalent were not contained in plaintiff's supplement letter. Defendant's letter also confirmed plaintiff's understanding that the "[w]ater line [was] to be buried 36 inches deep." . . .

Plaintiff was ultimately billed for $4,778.39; the billing included certain authorized extra items. Plaintiff has paid the defendant the full amount billed. . . .

[**pg. 532**] The system did not function perfectly from the date of its installment, and defendant made numerous service calls to plaintiff's property in an attempt to correct the problems. Defendant has replaced the pressure controls at the squat tank four times. The squat tank operates at a significantly higher pressure than its rating.

The pump in the well short-cycled from the day of installation, but it has not been replaced. The shortcycling has since been rectified by plaintiff's installation of a time-delay, but this is only a temporary solution. . . .

CONCLUSIONS OF LAW

. . . [**pg. 533**] The parties have not addressed the possibility that the Uniform Commercial Code, as adopted by Illinois, governs this case. The Court has given strong consideration to that possibility, but has concluded that the contract at issue was primarily a service contract, with a sale of goods incidental thereto, rather than vice versa. *See generally* 1 Anderson, Uniform Commercial Code §§ 2-102:5 and 2-102:6 (1970 and Supp. 1979). At least one Illinois appellate court has adopted a "predominate factor in the contract" test, developed in *Bonebrake v. Cox,* 499 F.2d 951 (8th Cir. 1974), to determine the applicability of the U.C.C. *Executive Centers of America Inc. v. Bandon,* 62 Ill. App. 3d 738, 19 Ill. Dec. 700, 703, 379 N.E.2d 364, 367 (1978). . . .

This Court finds that the transaction between the parties in the instant case falls on the "service" side of the *Bonebrake* test, for two reasons: With two exceptions discussed below, the parties had no agreement specifying the various component parts of the "water system" which were to be installed. The defendant was not bound to use specified items of "goods" in the water system. Neither party has suggested that the estimate sheet (plaintiff's Exhibit 8) prepared by defendant the day before the contract was signed, was a part of the parties' contract. Essentially, defendant undertook to install a "water system" of indefinite description but with a certain warranted capacity, rather than to install a detailed list of specific "goods." Therefore, not only was the contract essentially for defendant's services, but the component parts did not become identified to the contract until they were actually installed on plaintiff's property, and thus it is doubtful that they fell within the definition of "goods" contained in Ill. Rev. Stat., ch. 26, para. 2-105.

Secondly, the language of the instant contract is unmistakably that of service rather than of sale. Defendant is identified as the "contractor," and the contract acknowledges "an express mechanics lien . . . to secure the amount of contract or repairs." Plaintiff's Exhibit 9, General Terms & Conditions no. 9.

Thus, the Court concludes that the U.C.C. does not, strictly speaking, govern this case. . . .

Assignment 3. Office Memorandum
          Two Issues
          Jurisdiction: Fictitious State of New
          Maine
          Closed Universe

Assume that you have had the conversation with your supervising attorney, Susan Corleone, that is set forth in Assignment 2 above. Assume further that Corleone approached you in your office a few hours later with the following additional assignment:

Corleone: I would like you to address a second issue in your memorandum in the *Carson* case. After discussing whether the UCC or common law applies to this dispute, and regardless what conclusion you reach on that issue, I would like you to then assume that the UCC applies and to discuss whether the parties formed a contract under the UCC. Specifically, you can assume that Carson's bid was a valid offer, that Carson expressed his intent to revoke that offer ten days later, and that King expressed his intent to accept the bid five days after that. I want to know whether Carson's offer was irrevocable under the UCC.

Law Clerk: Are we certain that King gave no consideration for Carson's promise not to revoke the bid for 30 days?

Corleone: Yes. At least, I want you to assume for purposes of this memo that King cannot prove that he gave consideration for the promise or that he relied on it.

In addition to the statutory materials provided in Assignment 2, you may use the following provision of the New Maine Commercial Code (2000) (New Maine's version of the UCC):

N.M.C.C. § 2-205. Firm Offers
    An offer by a merchant to buy or sell goods in a signed writing which by its terms gives assurance that it will be held open is not revocable, for lack of consideration, during the time stated or if no time is stated for a reasonable time, but in no event may such period of irrevocability exceed

three months; but any such term of assurance on a form supplied by the offeree must be separately signed by the offeror.

You have found no case law, in New Maine or any other jurisdiction, that interprets the relevant language of section 2-205. You may assume that Carson is a merchant of plumbing supplies for purposes of the statute. On other matters of statutory interpretation, advance your own interpretation of the relevant language based on your understanding of (1) the ordinary meaning of the statutory language and (2) the apparent purpose of the provisions. For general background information on option contracts and the enforceability of a promise not to revoke an offer, you may consult the following excerpt from a secondary source:

CONTRACTS
E. Allan Farnsworth
(3d ed. 1999)
(pp. 180-81, 183-84; footnotes omitted)

[p. 180] § 3.23 Irrevocable Offers. An offeree may need time to decide whether to accept the offer and, during that time, may need to spend money and effort. Even if the offeror is willing to assure the offeree that the offer will be held open for that time, the traditional common law rules make it difficult to protect the offeree against the offeror's power of revocation. Not only does the common law posit that offers are generally revocable, but the offeror's mere promise not to revoke the offer—or its mere statement that the offer is not revocable—has traditionally been regarded as unenforceable unless under seal or supported by consideration. **[p. 181]** The doctrine of consideration, combined with the principle of free revocability, makes it impossible for the offeror to give the offeree the desired protection merely by saying so. The result has been increasingly subjected to criticism, especially where irrevocability does not expose the offeror to a substantial risk of speculation by the offeree. . . .

An irrevocable offer is sometimes called an *option*. . . . An option is itself a contract, sometimes called an *option contract* to distinguish it from the main contract to be formed on acceptance of the offer.

Before the abolition of the seal, the offeror could make an option by promising under seal not to revoke the offer. Now that the seal has been generally abolished, the offeror can still make an option if its promise not to revoke is supported by consideration. The consideration may consist of either a promise or a performance. Often it consists of a sum of money that is small in relation to the opportunity that speculation affords the offeree and the risk that speculation imposes on the offeror. . . .

. . . .

[p. 183] UCC § 2-205 goes further in providing for *firm offers*, as the Code chooses to call irrevocable offers. The offer need only be "in a signed writing which by its terms gives assurance that it will be held open." It is then irrevocable "during the time stated or if no time is stated for a reasonable time." In keeping with the policy of shielding the offeror from excessive risk of speculation, the period of irrevocability may not exceed three months. In order to prevent imposition on consumers, only a merchant can make a firm offer. Even a merchant must separately sign the firm offer clause if [**p. 184**] it is on a form supplied by the other party. These Code provisions are, of course, limited to the sale of goods.

Assignment 4. Office Memorandum
One or More Issues
Jurisdiction: Fictitious State of Calzona
Open Library

The following problem is set in the fictitious state of Calzona. Study the problem, research and analyze it using resources available in your library, and draft an office memorandum to your supervising attorney. In this problem, fill in "200Y" with the year of the summer immediately preceding your work on this assignment, and fill in "200X" with the year previous to "200Y."

You are an associate in Simpson, Sanchez, and Summers, a law firm in Lennox, Calzona. Last week, firm partner Mark Simpson asked you to (1) interview a potential new client, George Bryant, who complains that his employer unlawfully fired him, and (2) draft an office memorandum to help Simpson determine whether the firm should take Bryant's case. You arranged to meet Bryant in your office, and you instructed him to bring any employment documents that he has. Following are excerpts of your interview with Bryant.

Associate: I understand that you have a grievance against your former employer.

Bryant: Yes. I worked as a waiter at Chez Marie for more than a year, from September 200X through August 8, 200Y. That's when the maître d' fired me—at the end of the dinner shift.

Associate: Did he give you any reason for firing you?

Bryant: You bet, and one of the other waiters heard the whole thing. He said right to my face that he wouldn't have a gay waiter on his staff. When I protested that my sexual orientation had nothing to do with my job, he got pretty ugly—he said I probably had AIDS and might give it to the customers. In case you're wondering—Yes, I am gay; no, I don't have the H.I.V. virus; and even Mario will admit that I'm the best waiter in the state.

Associate: Who's Mario? Is he the one who fired you?

Bryant: Yes, Mario Prieto. He is the maître d' at Chez Marie. Marie Jardon owns the restaurant, and she supervises the kitchen, but she delegates to Mario all the hiring, firing, assignment, and supervision of the waiters and other table staff. Oh, he's smooth with the customers, all right; he's been a popular institution at Chez Marie for six years. But to his employees, he's arrogant, demanding, and arbitrary.

Associate: Did Mario know that you were gay when he hired you?

Bryant: No, why would he? That's one question the application form doesn't ask, and I don't advertise it to the customers or other employees at the restaurant. You see, I've lived with the same man, Larry, for more than a year, and he used to come to the restaurant near closing time every now and then to have coffee and dessert and to go on the town with me when I got off work. A couple of weeks ago Mario asked some of my closer friends on the staff about Larry, and he discovered our relationship.

Associate: I see that you have brought some documents with you. What are they?

Bryant: This is a copy of my employment application; I think they give a photocopy to all the employees to remind them of the clause at the bottom that shows that Mario has complete control over their lives.

Associate: Yes, that shows that you were hired as an "at-will" employee. That gives Mario a lot of discretion.

Bryant: Does that mean that he can fire me because of my sexual orientation?

Associate: Well, that's a question I'll have to research. In the meantime, are you certain he fired you because of your sexual orientation? Is it possible that you simply didn't meet his exacting standards in your work?

Bryant: Oh no, my performance as a waiter was impeccable. Quite simply, I'm the best. A distinguished restaurant like Chez Marie requires waiters with the charm of a diplomat, the grace of a ballet dancer, and the timing of a stand-up comic; add to those qualities a pleasing voice, a computer-like memory, and the proper balance between confidence and humility, and you have the package that I've perfected during my years in the profession. Mario never complained about my work; instead, he put me on the best weekend shifts because of my popularity with important customers. His discovery of my sexual orientation is the only possible explanation for his change in attitude.

Associate: Has this whole affair upset you emotionally in any serious way? Has it made you nervous? Have you suffered insomnia, headaches, anything like that?

Bryant: No, not at all. I got another job right away. And I learned to accept my sexuality a long time ago; I've learned to roll with the punches when guys like Mario treat me like some kind of freak. Why do you ask that?

Associate: I'm just trying to identify potential claims. Where are you working now?

Bryant: L'Orangerie. As soon as word got around that I was fired, I got offers from three top restaurants to start working immediately. They didn't even care that I was fired; they know my reputation for excellence, and they know Mario's reputation for impulsive and arbitrary action. I took a waiter's position with L'Orangerie; it's not a headwaiter's position, but it's a job.

Associate: So, what are you seeking from our law firm?

Bryant: To get even with Mario. I want to see him squirm a little. But that's not all; it's the principle of the thing. I don't think that I should be pushed around because of my sexual orientation; I want to show everyone that gays have a right to employment just like everyone else. Besides that, you've got to understand: Chez Marie is one of the top 20 restaurants in the country, and it's in a class all by itself in Lennox. No other restaurant in the state can come close to matching the pay and prestige enjoyed by Chez Marie's staff. And its clientele is the wealthiest and most sophisticated that the Valley can offer. In my year at Chez Marie I earned a base salary of $45,000 and tips of $25,000; even at L'Orangerie I'll pull in only about $50,000 per year in salary and tips combined, and the prestige is much lower. I've saved up quite a bit of money, and I'm willing to pay you your normal fees to see this through.

Associate: Okay. Thank you for visiting with me today. I'll get back to you as soon as the firm decides whether to take your case.

After taking the case and interviewing one of the other waiters at Chez Marie over the telephone, you are convinced that Bryant's version of the facts is generally accurate and that Mario at all times acted with full authority on behalf of Marie, Bryant's ultimate employer.

Your preliminary research shows that the City of Lennox has adopted an antidiscrimination ordinance:

> It is contrary to the policy of the City and unlawful to discriminate against any person because of sex, age, physical disability, marital status, sexual orientation, race, color, creed, national origin, or ancestry in places of public accommodation, in employment, or in housing.

Lennox, Calz. City Code ch. 18, art. I, § 7(a) (2000). The ordinance provides for a $500 fine, payable to the City for violation of the ordinance. *Id.* at § 7(b). In 2002, the legislature repealed a state statute making it a misdemeanor to engage in certain kinds of sexual conduct between members of the same sex. Calz. Rev. Stat. § 13-1411 (repealed 2002). A section of comprehensive state legislation guaranteeing equal opportunity in employment, Calz. Rev. Stat. § 22-3202 (1999), is identical to § 703(a) of Title VII of the 1964 Civil Rights Act, 42 U.S.C. § 2000e-2(a) (1994).

Bryant's application form is reproduced below and on the next page.

APPLICATION FOR EMPLOYMENT

Bryant, M. George	*658-80-2240*
Name: Last, Middle Initial, First	**Social Security Account #**

721 E. Culver St., Apt. #23
Address

Lennox	*86209*	*(393)253-7821*
City	**Zip Code**	**Phone Number**

Waiter, headwaiter, maître d'
Positions for which you are applying

Experience—Describe all prior employment in the restaurant industry. Identify the employer, the employer's location, and your position with the employer.

> *Waiter at La Chaumiere, Scottsdale, Calzona, Sept. 1997–*
> *present*
> *Waiter at Narsi's, Berkeley, CA, Sept. 1995–August 1997*
> *Waiter at various casual restaurants 1981–95.*

To the best of my knowledge, all of the above information is accurate. I understand that this application constitutes an offer to work in any of the positions listed above at the standard salary for that position at the time of hire plus gratuities. I also understand that, if the employer accepts this offer by approving the application, the resulting employment contract is one for indefinite duration and may be terminated at the will of the employer.

George Bryant   *Sept. 10, 200x*

Applicant's signature   Date

FOR OFFICE USE ONLY

Mario Prieto   *9-16-200x*

Application approved by   Date of hire

Chez Marie, 112 W. Camelback, Lennox, Calzona 85272

Assignment 5. Office Memorandum
Multiple Issues
Jurisdiction: State in which your law school
is located, or as dictated by your instructor
Open Library

You are an associate with the law firm of Roberts and Cray. Partner Susan Cray asks you to prepare an office memorandum analyzing the claims of Charlotte Rembar, a potential client. The following is a transcript of your interview with Rembar. Fill in "200z" with the current year, "200y" with the year before the current year, and "200x" with the year before "200y."

Associate: I understand that you have a problem with your employer.
Rembar: My ex-employer—he fired me November 200y; that's my
        problem.
Associate: Did he tell you why he fired you?

Rembar: It was pretty obvious—he cut me off because I wouldn't go to bed with him.

Associate: Start from the beginning. Tell me about your job and your employer.

Rembar: I worked for Alexander Hart. He owns Comcon, a local computer consulting firm; they help businesses determine the best computer system for their needs, and they create custom computer programs for them. Alex is a real genius, and he hires the best consultants to work for them, so his business is booming. I started working there January 1, 200y.

Associate: What was your position with the firm?

Rembar: I was one of his consultants; I designed computer systems and developed programs. I graduated from Stanford with honors in May 200x with a degree in computer programming; this was my first decent job in the computer industry.

Associate: How many of you work at the firm?

Rembar: Alex works in the field himself as a consultant, and he had six of us working also as consultants. Other than that, he's got a secretary and a part-time accountant.

Associate: Is that his full work force? Has it ever been bigger?

Rembar: As far as I know, that work force represented substantial expansion for him from previous years; his firm has never been bigger.

Associate: Tell me about your termination.

Rembar: Well, Alex had an eye for me since the day he hired me. He was always flirting and asking me out on dates. I always thought of some polite excuse not to go out with him; I didn't want to offend him, but I don't like him that much, and I didn't think it would be good for our working relationship to get involved in dating. It started getting worse last fall, and near the end of October, 200y, he called me into his office at the end of the day and flatly propositioned me. I refused, and he fired me.

Associate: Precisely what did he say, and how did you respond?

Rembar: First he asked me how I liked my job and my pay; I said I liked it fine. Then he said that he was in love with me and that he wanted me to go home with him that night and sleep with him and that I wouldn't regret it if I did. I didn't know what to say—I was so shocked. I think I just stood there with a stupid expression on my face for a few seconds; then I told him I had to go to a Halloween party, and I ran out of his office.

Associate: Did he fire you then?

Rembar: Not at that meeting. I was so distressed, I could hardly eat or sleep the whole weekend. I was worried about how we were going to maintain a decent working relationship if he was infatuated with me. I decided to talk to him about it the next morning, but I never got a chance. When I arrived at work, Alex called me into his office and told me that he didn't need my services any longer and that I had one week to clean out my office. I was literally speechless. I just walked out to my car and cried and cursed him. I got my last paycheck a week later.

Associate: Were you upset for a long time?

Rembar: Oh yes. I had trouble sleeping for a month. I was so nervous and depressed that I couldn't attend normal social functions. And I felt guilty—and stupid. I thought that I could have avoided all this if I had been more assertive in the beginning and told Alex more clearly that I wasn't interested. I started seeing a doctor and a counselor so that I could cope with it. I guess you've probably handled bigger problems than this, but I felt like my world was coming apart. This was my dream job—I was making $5,000 a month doing work that I love. When Alex fired me, I didn't know how I would ever explain it to other employers in job interviews. Luckily, I told the truth to the Personnel Manager at IBM, and she believed me. I started working there at the same salary in early January, 200z.

Associate: How was your performance at Comcon?

Rembar: Great. I was the newest consultant, but I was better than two or three of the more experienced ones.

Associate: Did Alex ever praise your work, either orally or in writing?

Rembar: Sure. In my first month, he said I was learning fast. And in August, he complimented me on a particularly good job I did with one account. But he never put anything like that in writing.

Associate: Did he ever complain about your work, either orally or in writing?

Rembar: Never.

Associate: Do you want your job back at Comcon?

Rembar: No. I'm happy at IBM, and I don't want to ever work for that worm again. But I went through a lot of pain, and I think he owes me something for it.

Associate: Did you have a written contract of employment with Comcon?

Rembar: No, we just orally agreed that I would provide the consulting services for a starting salary of $60,000 a year. But he gave me a little policy manual to look at when I interviewed for the job. I've got a copy of it right here.

Associate: Did he say anything when he gave it to you?

Rembar: Yeah, he said that he believed in treating his consultants like professionals and that he could offer me better benefits and working conditions than I would get at the bigger firms. He encouraged me to read the policy manual to confirm that. He obviously wanted to give the appearance of a class operation so that he could attract the best consultants; he made a lot of money off of us.

Associate: I think that's all I need. I don't have authority to take your case; I'll have to report to the partners and get a decision from them. I'll get back to you by the end of the month. If we don't take the case, I'll help steer you toward some other attorneys who may be interested. In the meantime, read this explanation of our fee system and call me if you have any questions.

POLICY MANUAL
for Employees of Comcon

I. INTRODUCTION

The success of Comcon lies in its ability to recruit and retain the best employees available nationally. To promote a stable and productive work force, Comcon endeavors to provide attractive terms and conditions of employment, as reflected in the following policies.

II. SALARY

. . . .

III. HOLIDAYS, VACATIONS, SICK LEAVE

. . . .

IV. TERMINATION

A. *Probationary Employment*

Each employee will work on probationary status during his or her first 60 days of employment. During this probationary period, Comcon reserves the right to terminate the employee for any reason, or for no reason at all.

B. *Nonprobationary Employment*

Comcon reserves the right to terminate the employment of any employee who is not performing satisfactorily.

. . . .

Appendix V

Problem 1. Conventions of Punctuation: Policy and Style

Described below are several conventions for use of commas, semicolons, and colons.[1] For each convention of usage,

1. describe the policies of composition that support the rule; alternatively, critique the rule or otherwise comment on it;
2. explain what practical problems may arise if the rule is ignored;
3. determine whether the rule should be viewed as sufficiently flexible to permit exceptions when adherence to the rule is not necessary to satisfy important policies or to avoid significant problems; and
4. consider alternatives to the approach described in the rule.

If helpful, illustrate your points with examples.

---

1. For further examples, *see* William Strunk, Jr., and E. B. White, THE ELEMENTS OF STYLE 1-9 (4th ed. 2000).

a. Independent Clauses

An independent clause is a clause with a subject and verb, structured so that it could stand alone as a complete sentence. You should separate independent clauses either with a period, thus creating two sentences, or with the following punctuation:

(1) In the absence of a conjunction, use a semicolon, not a comma:

The roughest American team sport is football; basketball and baseball are comparatively gentle.

(2) Use a comma if the second independent clause begins with a coordinating conjunction, such as *and, but, yet, for, so, or, nor:*

For two weeks after the earthquake, the tap water in Sarah's house was contaminated, **but** potable water was available in plastic containers at a nearby Red Cross outpost.

(3) Use a semicolon if the second independent clause begins with a conjunctive adverb, sometimes called an adverbial connective, such as *therefore, however, moreover, consequently, accordingly, nevertheless, thus.* Follow the connective with a comma:

Basketball is not intended to be a contact sport; **nonetheless,** basketball players often deliver crushing blows to one another without incurring penalties.

For two weeks after the earthquake, the tap water in Sarah's house was contaminated; **however,** potable water was available in plastic containers at a nearby Red Cross outpost.

(4) Multiple verbs of the same subject do not create independent clauses and therefore should not be separated with a comma:

Joanie dribbled the ball past a defender and drove to the basket.

b. Lists or Illuminations

After an independent clause, use a colon to introduce a list or illumination of the first clause:

A claim under the due process clause requires proof of three elements: a protectable interest, deprivation of the interest by a state official, and the state's failure to afford procedural protections appropriate in the circumstances.

When the clause following the colon is independent, you may exercise discretion to begin it with a capital letter:

Judge Crowder looked forward to oral argument: He learned much from well-prepared advocates, and he took a perverse pleasure in grilling those who were ill-prepared.

---

c. Parenthetic Words, Phrases, or Clauses

Use a comma or commas to set off parenthetic words or phrases and nonrestrictive clauses:

One disgruntled patron in the back row, **however,** complained bitterly about the acoustics of the concert hall.

Carlos Nakai, **the flutist and leader of the band,** had composed the finale while visiting the Yucatan peninsula.

The audience stood and cheered for Carlos Nakai, **who had composed the finale while visiting the Yucatan peninsula.**

The court held that, **in light of the predominance of service activities,** Article 2 of the UCC did not apply to the transaction.

Problem 2. Prehistoric Prohibitions

The following questionable clichés of composition are outdated; indeed, some never rose to the level of an accepted rule. Nonetheless, they still have currency among some editors. If you accept any of these "rules," justify it according to the directions in Problem 1 above. If you reject a rule or would limit it significantly, explain the reasons for your more flexible approach.

1. Never start a sentence with "because," "however," "and," or "but."
2. Never split an infinitive, as in "to severely limit his use of water."
3. Do not insert a comma between the last two elements of a series of three or more elements joined by a conjunction, as in "red, white, and blue."

Appendix VI

Pleadings and Briefs: Assignments for Parts VI-VIII of the Main Text

Assignment 1. Format—Trial Brief

Review Office Memorandum Assignment 1 in Appendix IV. Assume that (1) you have filed a complaint on behalf of the plaintiffs against Ramona Udave, and (2) the trial court has assigned the case to mandatory arbitration because of the relatively low amount in controversy.

The arbitrator has set the case for a hearing, but she is concerned about your claim for damages for emotional distress based on breach of contract. She has asked you to write a trial brief explaining why the plaintiffs would be entitled to such relief under the facts that you intend to prove at the hearing. She has specifically asked both parties to limit their briefs to that issue.

Without referring to a sample trial brief, draft the document requested by the arbitrator, and argue your clients' case persuasively. You are limited to the authorities reproduced in the office memorandum assignment. You may begin with the caption on the next page; otherwise, use any reasonable format that satisfies the purpose of the document and the needs of your audience. Although you may never have seen a trial brief before, have confidence in your common sense.

Your Name
Your Address

ARIZONA SUPERIOR COURT
MARICOPA COUNTY

Trina ARAIZA, et al., Plaintiffs, v. Ramona UDAVE, Defendant.	No. CIV-9X-1279 OPENING TRIAL BRIEF Before Elena Long, Arbitrator

Assignment 2. Revision of Sample Complaint

Critically evaluate the following sample complaint for substance and style.

a. Specificity of Allegations

Identify the fact allegations that are especially detailed and redraft them to achieve greater generality. What are the advantages and disadvantages of each version?

b. Simplicity

Discard clichés or jargon in the sample complaint and replace them with simple, plain English.

c. Request for Relief

Each count in the sample complaint includes a request for punitive damages, as well as compensatory damages. Would a court be likely to instruct a jury that it could award punitive damages on the first count, for breach of contract? What tort, if any, does the second count allege?

IN THE SUPERIOR COURT OF
THE STATE OF ARIZONA
IN AND FOR THE COUNTY OF MARICOPA[1]

Georgia Anne TUCKER, Plaintiff,	No. _____
v.	C O M P L A I N T
Harry Joe CLYDE, Defendant.	(Breach of Promise; Tort, Non Motor Vehicle)

Plaintiff alleges:

I

This is an action for money damages exceeding $1,000.

II

Plaintiff is a resident of Cushing, Oklahoma. Defendant is a resident of Morris, Oklahoma. Defendant has caused an act to occur in Maricopa County, Arizona, out of which this cause of action arises.

COUNT ONE
(*Breach of Promise*)

III

At all relevant times, both Plaintiff and Defendant were over the age of 18 years, and in all respects capable of entering into a marriage contract.

IV

Plaintiff and Defendant were introduced and became acquainted with each other in September 1983. On or about December 8, 1983, Defendant proposed marriage to Plaintiff, and Plaintiff accepted. On January 17, 1984, the proposal and acceptance of marriage were reaffirmed when Defendant purchased a diamond engagement ring for Plaintiff.

V

Plaintiff and Defendant discussed their marriage agreement from time to time and on a great many occasions too numerous to mention herein.

1. A few years after the filing of this complaint, local court rules were amended to require identification of the authoring attorney at the beginning of the pleading as well as at the end.

In the course of these discussions, Plaintiff and Defendant confirmed plans to be married in Hawaii on March 10, 1984.

VI

In January and February of 1984, Plaintiff and Defendant came to Phoenix, Arizona, for the purpose of locating and purchasing a home for their future marital residence. Defendant purchased a house located at 6052 East Cortez Drive, Scottsdale, Arizona. In addition, in preparation for the marriage, Defendant opened bank accounts, charge accounts, and utility service accounts in the names of Harry Joe Clyde and Georgia Anne Clyde.

VII

At the insistence of Defendant and in reliance on the agreement to marry, Plaintiff gave up a profitable business as a hair stylist in Cushing, Oklahoma; borrowed and spent the sum of $12,000.00 to refurbish her residence in order to facilitate its sale; listed her residence for sale with a real estate agency; leased her residence to Defendant's son; withdrew her children from school; and moved her household possessions and her children from Cushing, Oklahoma, to Scottsdale, Arizona, at great expense and inconvenience.

VIII

On March 1, 1984, after having moved to Scottsdale, Arizona, Defendant presented to Plaintiff a prenuptial agreement that, among other things, listed the State of Arizona as the domicile of the parties and that provided for execution of the agreement in Maricopa County, Arizona. Plaintiff refused to sign the prenuptial agreement as written; however, despite Plaintiff's refusal to sign the prenuptial agreement, Defendant again renewed his promise to marry Plaintiff.

IX

On March 8, 1984, Defendant, Plaintiff, and three of Plaintiff's four children flew to Hawaii for the purpose of consummating the marriage, which was scheduled for March 10, 1984.

X

At approximately 8:00 A.M. on the morning of March 9, 1984, Defendant informed Plaintiff that he would not go through with the wedding. Since that date, Defendant has refused to carry out his promise to marry Plaintiff.

XI

On March 9, 1984, Defendant, Plaintiff, and Plaintiff's three children returned to Scottsdale, Arizona, where Defendant left Plaintiff and her three children in the house that was to have been the marital residence. On March 22, 1984, Defendant demanded that Plaintiff and her three children vacate the Scottsdale residence; for lack of other accommodations, Plaintiff was forced to return to Cushing, Oklahoma.

XII

By reason of Defendant's breach of promise to marry, Plaintiff has been deprived of Defendant's support and care for herself and her children, and of the commensurate standard of living that she would have enjoyed had the marriage been consummated. In addition to the foregoing, Plaintiff has suffered, and will continue to suffer, the following damages: a loss of past and future income as the result of Defendant's insistence that she give up her business; economic loss as the result of monies expended for refurbishing her residence in preparation for sale; economic loss resulting from the move from Cushing, Oklahoma, to Scottsdale, Arizona, and from Scottsdale, Arizona, back to Cushing, Oklahoma; and mental pain and anguish, wounded pride, mortification, humiliation, shame, and disgrace, which has directly impaired Plaintiff's health.

XIII

Defendant's actions in breaching his promise to marry were intentional or taken with reckless disregard for the rights of Plaintiff.

Plaintiff therefore requests judgment as follows:

1. past and future lost income in an amount to be determined at trial;
2. out-of-pocket expenses in an amount to be determined at trial, but not less than $2,000;
3. mental pain and anguish in an amount to be determined at trial, but not less than $10,000;
4. other compensatory damages in an amount to be determined at trial;
5. reasonable attorney's fees;
6. punitive damages in an amount to be determined at trial; and
7. such other and further relief as the Court deems just and proper.

COUNT TWO
(*Tort*)

XIV

Plaintiff realleges and incorporates into this count paragraphs I through XIII.

XV

Defendant stated to friends, relatives, and acquaintances of Plaintiff that Plaintiff and Defendant were engaged, that Plaintiff and Defendant were moving to Scottsdale, Arizona, and that Plaintiff and Defendant would be married on March 10, 1984.

XVI

After Defendant informed Plaintiff that he would not go through with the marriage, Defendant promised Plaintiff that he would provide her with the financial means to relocate wherever she desired so that she would not have to return to Cushing, Oklahoma, where she would experience the humiliation, shame, disgrace, pain, and anguish of explaining Defendant's failure to fulfill his marriage promise.

XVII

Defendant, after making the above-described promise to Plaintiff, forced Plaintiff to move out of the residence located in Scottsdale, Arizona, and refused to provide any financial assistance except transportation expenses to Cushing, Oklahoma.

XVIII

Defendant's actions in providing only transportation expenses for Plaintiff's return to Cushing, Oklahoma, were extreme and outrageous, were intentional, and were done with full knowledge of the emotional consequences to Plaintiff.

XIX

Plaintiff has suffered grievous mental pain, anguish, mortification, humiliation, shame, and disgrace; Plaintiff's mental and physical health has been impaired.

Plaintiff therefore prays for judgment as follows:

1. compensatory damages in an amount to be determined at trial, but not less than $12,000;
2. punitive damages in an amount to be determined at trial; and
3. such other and further relief as the Court deems just and proper in the premises.

Dated May 21, 1984   TICKER, STRANGER & NEAR

By _____
James R. Near
Joseph A. Hammer
900 East Camelback Road
Suite 1010
Scottsdale, AZ 85281
Attorneys for Plaintiff

Assignment 3. Drafting an Answer

Review the sample complaint in Assignment 2 above or the revised version prepared by you or by a classmate. The defendant, Harry Joe Clyde, is prepared to prove that Georgia Anne Tucker repudiated the marriage agreement when she refused to sign a written prenuptial agreement, that he never renewed his promise after Tucker's repudiation, that Tucker called off the wedding, and that he suffered severe disappointment as a result. Draft an answer on behalf of Clyde.

Assignment 4. Drafting a Complaint

Review Office Memorandum Assignment 5 at the end of Appendix IV. Based on the analysis in your office memorandum, determine what claims you could allege in good faith, and draft a complaint for an action in state court on behalf of Charlotte Rembar.

Assignment 5. Opposition to Motion for Summary Judgment

Review (1) Office Memorandum Assignment 5 in Appendix IV, (2) Assignment 4 above, and (3) the sample motion for summary judgment at the end of Chapter 19 of the main text. Prepare materials opposing Hart's motion for summary judgment, or opposing a similar motion on Hart's behalf supplied by your instructor.

In preparing your opposition, you may assume the following developments:

a. Your firm filed a complaint alleging four claims for relief: (1) breach of a promise of job security, (2) violation of the Arizona Civil Rights Act, (3) wrongful discharge in violation of public policy, and (4) infliction of emotional distress. In his answer, Hart denied that Rembar's contract contained any provisions for job security and denied the allegations of sexual harassment. He alleged that he discharged Rembar for poor performance.

b. Rembar stands by the information she provided in the initial interview, and she is willing to swear to it in an affidavit. Your independent fact investigation has revealed some corroborating evidence from Leslie West, Alex Hart's secretary during Charlotte Rembar's tenure at Comcon. In a recent interview, West revealed that she and Rembar developed a close friendship and that she was distressed to learn of Rembar's discharge. After Rembar filed suit, Hart became irritable and unpleasant to work for; West voluntarily quit her job two weeks ago and immediately offered to support Rembar with trial testimony and statements in an affidavit. The following is an excerpt from your interview of West:

West: That was near Halloween last fall. I saw Charlotte run out of the office in tears just before quitting time. The following workday, in the afternoon, Mr. Hart told me to process the paperwork to terminate Charlotte's payroll at the end of the week. When I said that I had thought Charlotte was one of his best consultants, he said "Her consulting isn't my problem—it's her stuck-up attitude." I asked him what I should put down on the paperwork as the reason for her termination, and he said something like, "I don't care what you put—just say that she has a negative attitude."

Through discovery requests, you have obtained copies of the contents of Rembar's employment file at Comcon. The file includes only a few insignificant notes and the two Payroll Action forms attached to Hart's motion for summary judgment.

Assignment 6. Motion to Exclude Evidence

Review Office Memorandum Assignment 5 in Appendix IV and Assignments 4 and 5 above. Assume that you have successfully opposed Hart's motion for summary judgment and that the trial judge has scheduled a pretrial conference.

You are concerned about some embarrassing evidence that Hart has obtained through the discovery process. While a freshman at Stanford University, Rembar posed nude for a two-page spread in *Hustle and Bustle*, an adult magazine; some of the poses would strike the average juror as lewd and tasteless. Rembar explained that she posed for the pictures on a dare and that she didn't realize until later how lewd and revealing they would be. She regrets her decision to pose, and she insists that the pictures do not reflect her current personality or style of relating to friends or colleagues.

Hart probably learned of the magazine spread through one of Rembar's freshman college classmates or instructors. In a discovery request, Hart requested confirmation of the event, along with a copy of the out-of-print magazine. Pursuant to your state's counterpart to Federal Rule of Civil Procedure 26(c), you objected to the request on the ground that the information requested would be inadmissible at trial and that its production would result in annoyance, embarrassment, and oppression. The trial judge, however, compelled discovery on the ground that the information sought, whether or not admissible itself, might lead to the discovery of evidence relating to a claim or defense. *See* Fed. R. Civ. P. 26(b)(1); *Kidwiler v. Progressive Paloverde Ins. Co.*, 192 F.R.D. 193, 199 (N.D.W. Va. 2000).

You now seek an advance ruling barring any reference to the magazine spread at trial. Draft a motion to exclude the evidence before trial.

INDEX